IFIP Advances in Information and Communication Technology 338

IFIP – The International Federation for Information Processing

IFIP was founded in 1960 under the auspices of UNESCO, following the First World Computer Congress held in Paris the previous year. An umbrella organization for societies working in information processing, IFIP's aim is two-fold: to support information processing within its member countries and to encourage technology transfer to developing nations. As its mission statement clearly states,

> IFIP's mission is to be the leading, truly international, apolitical organization which encourages and assists in the development, exploitation and application of information technology for the benefit of all people.

IFIP is a non-profitmaking organization, run almost solely by 2500 volunteers. It operates through a number of technical committees, which organize events and publications. IFIP's events range from an international congress to local seminars, but the most important are:

- The IFIP World Computer Congress, held every second year;
- Open conferences;
- Working conferences.

The flagship event is the IFIP World Computer Congress, at which both invited and contributed papers are presented. Contributed papers are rigorously refereed and the rejection rate is high.

As with the Congress, participation in the open conferences is open to all and papers may be invited or submitted. Again, submitted papers are stringently refereed.

The working conferences are structured differently. They are usually run by a working group and attendance is small and by invitation only. Their purpose is to create an atmosphere conducive to innovation and development. Refereeing is less rigorous and papers are subjected to extensive group discussion.

Publications arising from IFIP events vary. The papers presented at the IFIP World Computer Congress and at open conferences are published as conference proceedings, while the results of the working conferences are often published as collections of selected and edited papers.

Any national society whose primary activity is in information may apply to become a full member of IFIP, although full membership is restricted to one society per country. Full members are entitled to vote at the annual General Assembly, National societies preferring a less committed involvement may apply for associate or corresponding membership. Associate members enjoy the same benefits as full members, but without voting rights. Corresponding members are not represented in IFIP bodies. Affiliated membership is open to non-national societies, and individual and honorary membership schemes are also offered.

Bruno Vallespir   Thècle Alix (Eds.)

Advances in Production Management Systems

New Challenges, New Approaches

IFIP WG 5.7 International Conference, APMS 2009
Bordeaux, France, September 21-23, 2009
Revised Selected Papers

 Springer

Volume Editors

Bruno Vallespir
Thècle Alix
University of Bordeaux
Laboratory IMS-CNRS
351 Cours de la Libération, 33405 Talence Cedex, France
E-mail: {bruno.vallespir, thecle.alix}@ims-bordeaux.fr

CR Subject Classification (1998): H.4, C.2, D.2, C.2.4, J.1, K.4.3

ISSN   1868-4238
ISBN-10   3-642-42364-7 Springer Berlin Heidelberg New York
ISBN-13   978-3-642-42364-2 Springer Berlin Heidelberg New York

springer.com

© IFIP International Federation for Information Processing 2010
Softcover re-print of the Hardcover 1st edition 2010

Typesetting: Camera-ready by author, data conversion by Scientific Publishing Services, Chennai, India
Printed on acid-free paper   219/3180

Preface

The present economic and social environment has given rise to new situations within which companies must operate. As a first example, the globalization of the economy and the need for performance has led companies to outsource and then to operate inside networks of enterprises such as supply chains or virtual enterprises. A second instance is related to environmental issues. The statement about the impact of industrial activities on the environment has led companies to revise processes, to save energy, to optimize transportation.... A last example relates to knowledge. Knowledge is considered today to be one of the main assets of a company. How to capitalize, to manage, to reuse it for the benefit of the company is an important current issue.

The three examples above have no direct links. However, each of them constitutes a challenge that companies have to face today. This book brings together the opinions of several leading researchers from all around the world. Together they try to develop new approaches and find answers to those challenges. Through the individual chapters of this book, the authors present their understanding of the different challenges, the concepts on which they are working, the approaches they are developing and the tools they propose.

The book is composed of six parts; each one focuses on a specific theme and is subdivided into subtopics.

- Production systems
    - Production processes
    - Production management
    - Production systems design
    - Lean management
    - Maintenance, inspection and monitoring
    - Risks and uncertainty
    - Sustainability
- Supply chains
    - Supply chains operation management
    - Production networks
    - Cooperative supply chains: models and challenges
    - Relationships with suppliers
    - Relationships with customers
    - New practices in transportation and logistic organisations
- Interoperable and distributed systems
    - Interoperable and agile production systems
    - Agent modelling, distributed simulation and control frameworks for production management systems

- Strategy and innovation
  - Change, strategy and innovation
  - Projects and life cycle
  - Knowledge management
  - Information and Communication Technologies
  - Co-evolution of product design and supply chain considering change management strategies
- Performances
  - Performance measurement and costing
  - Quality
  - From single to networked enterprises performance measurement and management
- Service
  - Services
  - Business process and performance management of product-service systems

Each paper in the book has been peer reviewed and presented by one of its co-authors at the Advanced Production Management Systems Conference – APMS 2009 – which was held in Bordeaux, France, September 21–23, 2009. The conference was supported by the Working Group #7 of the Technical Committee #5 of the International Federation for Information Processing called *Integration in Production Management* and was hosted by the IMS laboratory of the University of Bordeaux.

As the book editors, we would like to thank all the contributors for the high-standard preparation and presentation of their papers.

We would like to thank as well the members of the International Programme Committee for their work in reviewing and selecting the papers.

August 2010

Bruno Vallespir
Thècle Alix

Organization

Programme Committee

Erry Y.T. Adesta, Malaysia
Thècle Alix, France
Bjørn Andersen, Norway
Eiji Arai, Japan
Frédérique Biennier, France
Umit S. Bititci, UK
Abdelaziz Bouras, France
Mike Bourne, UK
Jean-Paul Bourrières, France
Jim Browne, Ireland
Luis Manuel Camarinha-Matos, Portugal
Stephen Childe, UK
Shengchun Deng, China
Alexandre Dolgui, France
Guy Doumeingts, France
Heidi Carin Dreyer, Norway
Yves Ducq, France
Rémy Dupas, France
Eero Eloranta, Finland
Peter Falster, Denmark
Jan Frick, Norway
Susumu Fuji, Japan
Masahiko Fuyuki, Japan
Marco Garetti, Italy
Bernard Grabot, France
Thomas R. Gulledge, Jr., USA
Gideon Halevi, Israel
Bernd Hamacher, Germany
Hans-Henrik Hvolby, Denmark
Ichiro Inoue, Japan
Christopher Irgens, UK
Hari Jagdev, UK
John Johansen, Denmark
Toshiya Kaihara, Japan

Dimitris Kiritsis, Switzerland
Tomasz Koch, Poland
Ashok K. Kochhar, UK
Andrew Kusiak, USA
Lenka Landryova, Czech Republic
Jan-Peter Lechner, Germany
Vidosav Majstorovic, Serbia
Kai Mertins, Germany
Masaru Nakano, Japan
Jinwoo Park, S.Korea
Henk-Jan Pels, The Netherlands
Fredrik Persson, Sweden
Alberto Portioli Staudacher, Italy
Jens O. Riis, Denmark
Asbjörn Rolstadås, Norway
J.E. Rooda, The Netherlands
Krzysztof Santarek, Poland
Paul Schoensleben, Switzerland
Riitta Smeds, Finland
Kathryn E. Stecke, USA
Volker Stich, Germany
Richard Lee Storch, USA
Jan Ola Strandhagen, Norway
Stanislaw Strzelczak, Poland
Marco Taisch, Italy
Ilias Tatsiopoulos, Greece
Sergio Terzi, Italy
Klaus-Dieter Thoben, Germany
Jacques H. Trienekens, The Netherlands
Mario Tucci, Italy
Shigeki Umeda, Japan
Bruno Vallespir, France
Agostino Villa, Italy
Gert Zülch, Germany

Table of Contents

Part I: Production Systems

Production Processes

Production Management

Production Systems Design

Sustainability

Part II: Supply Chains

Supply Chains Operation Management

Production Networks

Cooperative Supply Chains: Models and Challenges

Relationships with Suppliers

Relationships with Customers

New Practices in Transportation and Logistic Organisations

Part III: Interoperable and Distributed Systems

Interoperable and Agile Production Systems

Agent Modelling, Distributed Simulation and Control Frameworks for Production Management Systems

Part IV: Strategy and Innovation

Change, Strategy and Innovation

Projects and Life Cycle

Knowledge Management

Information and Communication Technologies

Part VI: Service

Services

Business Process and Performance Management of Product-Service Systems

Part I

Production Systems

Integration of Supplier and Customer's Production Processes

Marek Eisler[1] and Remigiusz Horbal[2]

[1] Institute of Mechanical Engineering and Automation
Wroclaw University of Technology
ul. Lukasiewicza 5
50-371 Wroclaw, Poland
marek.eisler@pwr.wroc.pl
[2] Lean Enterprise Institute Poland
ul. Muchoborska 18
54-424 Wroclaw, Poland
info@lean.org.pl

Abstract. This paper is based on the findings from the project funded by the Ministry of Science and Higher Education of Poland. It presents the application of value stream mapping in supply chains and some inadequacy of this method for supply chain integration. Based on the findings, a new Supplier Customer Production process Integration SCPI methodology is proposed. The paper presents problems with integration of companies within the lean supply chain. Usually separate actions are undertaken by the companies within the same supply chain to implement lean management philosophy for production systems and external logistics processes. These isolated activities may lead to pushing inventories from one supply chain partner to another instead of reducing them. To reduce inventories along the supply chain the new approach of production and logistics process improvement needs to be applied. The new concept must take into consideration influence of local improvements in one plant on other cooperating enterprises as well as on the logistics system between them.

Keywords: supply chain integration, Extended Value Stream.

1 Introduction

Lean Manufacturing idea is well known around the world for more than two decades. Organisations in almost every country strive to use several lean tools and techniques in order to become more competitive. Many of them achieved encouraging results by improving processes and consequently competitiveness. However, authors of some publications [1], [2] claim that now and in upcoming future the competitiveness of the organisations will depend on the efficiency of the whole supply chains rather than on improved efficiency of its individual links. This means that all parties involved in a supply chain should improve theirs processes in "synchronised" way and understand that they form a system and improvement on single element of the system does not necessary result in improving the whole. This phenomenon can be observed for

B. Vallespir and T. Alix (Eds.): APMS 2009, IFIP AICT 338, pp. 3–10, 2010.
© IFIP International Federation for Information Processing 2010

example in area of inventory management in customer and supplier plants. In some cases reduction of inventories at customer side may cause increasing inventories at supplier side [3, pp. 61-62], [4]. The inventories are pushed to suppliers rather than reduced. Therefore to reach the lowest possible level of inventories in supply chain, improvement efforts must be coordinated. Coordination of those efforts has been a popular research topic for last several years [5, pp. 12]. There are still few important issues that seem not to be resolved, such as different objectives defined by cooperating companies, excessive inventory levels or slow response to changes in customer demand [6, pp. 4-5].

The objective of the research undertaken by the authors was to propose a method to analyse and improve a selected portion of supply chains in cooperative way by customers and suppliers. Researches conducted in industry are described in section 2 of this paper. Proposed Supplier Customer Production process Integration SCPI methodology is presented in section 3. The last section 4 encompasses the conclusions.

2 Data Collection and Analysis for a Customer-Supplier Pair

The scope of research was limited to the pairs of cooperating companies and logistics processes between them. For data gathering and analysis researchers used Extended Value Stream Mapping method proposed by Womack and Jones in 2002 [7]. Because the supply chains are usually complex networks of organisations the research were focused on supplier – customer pairs. A pair encompasses two cooperating, manufacturing companies: a customer making products and a supplier providing components or materials for these products. Two pairs were considered in the analysis phase. Pair 1 is a part of supply chain providing home appliances. In this pair the customer company assembles finished goods and supplier company provides foamed polystyrene parts used for packaging. The second supplier – customer pair (Pair 2) belongs to the supply chain providing industrial valves. The customer company in Pair 2 is a manufacturer of industrial valves and the supplier company provides machined steel components. Conducted research encompassed a deep analysis of inventory levels in the two pairs as well as an analysis of how production processes and logistics process impacts these inventories. Summary of the most essential data is presented in Table 1.

Table 1. Summary of essential data for the analysed pairs

Analysed pair	Supplier's finished goods inventory	Transportation frequency	Transportation time	Customer's component inventory
Pair 1	14,2 days	3 x week	0,1 day	10,4 days
Pair 2	8,3 days	1 x week	0,1 day	9 days

It can be noticed that inventory levels converted to days of consumption of final customer (in both cases the final customers are retailers) are too high, especially when transportation frequency and time is considered. In case of Pair 1 components are delivered to the customer every 2-3 days, however the customer holds 10,4 days of inventory for those components. Also at supplier's facility in Pair 1 ready to deliver components are at high level (14,2 days). Similar situation can be noticed for Pair 2. Even though the stock levels are lower, the level of components in customer facility seems to be too high (9 days) in comparison to transportation frequency (once a week = every 5 days). Such situation in both cases could be due to the fluctuations in transportation process caused by delays or incomplete deliveries as well as by changes in demand. Supplier and customer may strive to protect themselves against demand changes by increasing the level of inventories. However, the other reason of high inventories is unsynchronized production processes of supplier and customer and transportation process between them. This issue will be described in section 2.1 of this paper.

2.1 Production and Transportation Processes Synchronization and Improvement Objectives in EVSM Method

According to Womack and Jones "production at every stage should run on average the same rate, as adjusted for available amount of production time at each step. "[7, pp. 44] They also claim that each facility in the stream should not follow the rate of end facility. Each facility should produce each morning a leveled mix of what the next downstream facility requires for delivery in the afternoon or next morning. However, in many cases this idea is the ultimate goal company should strive to reach, but it is hardly achievable due to changeover times, breakdowns or rejects in production. Those problems force companies to produce in advance and built so called safety stocks. The authors of EVSM method propose [7, p. 45]:

- to reduce the noise in sending demand through the stream,
- to increase delivery frequency,
- to decreasing batch sizes,
- to level demand,
- or to improve capability.

This may lead to solely improving each production and logistics process in the stream as EVSM method does not give clear direction to what extent improvement at each production facility should be done. Also there are no tools proposed to identify the relations between improvements at particular supply chain link and other links.

3 The Supplier-Customer Production Process Integration Methodology

Due to lack of clear methodology that would allow implementing improvements in cooperating companies beneficial for the whole supply chain rather than for a solely link, authors of this article proposed the Supplier-Customer Production Process Integration (SCPI) methodology. The SCPI methodology complements EVSM method with clear guidelines for managers. The goal of the methodology is to analyse production processes of cooperating companies and transportation process between them in order to lower inventories level without harm to components availability. The methodology is based on EPEI index (EPEI is the acronym of Every Part Every Interval). EPEI indicates the period in which different part numbers are produced in a production process or shipped from one plant to another [8, pp.19]. The new definitions for several types of EPEI were proposed to describe flexibility of supply chain links. Introduced definitions are presented in Table 2. Fig 1 depicts referring supply chain link for each of introduced EPEI indices.

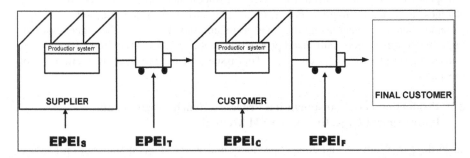

Fig. 1. Referring supply chain links for introduced definitions of different types of EPEI indices

Table 2. EPEI definitions used in SCPI methodology

Introduced index	Definition	Referring supply chain link (see also in Fig. 1)
$EPEI_F$	The period of deliveries from the customer to the final customer	Final customer of supplier – customer pair
$EPEI_C$	EPEI index of customer's production system	Customer in supplier – customer pair
$EPEI_T$	The period of deliveries from supplier to customer	Transportation process between supplier and customer
$EPEI_S$	EPEI index of supplier's production system	Supplier in supplier – customer pair

As mentioned above the goal of SCPI methodology is to reduce inventory levels in supply chain. Three locations of inventories in supply chain were analysed:

- components in supplier plant – finished goods from stand point of supplier that are components from customer's point of view,
- components in customer plant, that are used to assemble products (final finished goods),
- final finished goods in customer plant.

In order to allow managers of cooperating companies understand how changes in production or transportation system impacts inventory levels, authors proposed the new method of calculating required stock levels at customer and supplier company. The method combines introduced EPEI indices with a concept of standard inventory. Standard inventory encompasses three elements of inventories: cycle stock, buffer stock and safety stock [9]. Each element of standard inventory is defined in Table 2. Based on the proposed equations for standard inventories (see table 5) it can be noticed that standard inventories are in most cases proportional to different EPEI indices. Table 3 presents which EPEI index influence which inventories within supplier-customer pair.

Table 3. Influence of EPEI indices on standard inventory

Location of standard inventory	EPEI index deciding about required standard inventory level	
components in supplier plant	$EPEI_S$	
components in customer plant	If $EPEI_T \geq EPEI_C$	If $EPEI_T < EPEI_C$
	$EPEI_T$	$EPEI_C$
final finished goods in customer plant	If $EPEI_C \geq EPEI_F$	If $EPEI_C < EPEI_F$
	$EPEI_C$	$EPEI_F$

If assumed that neither customer nor supplier from analysed pair have influence on $EPEI_F$ index (time interval for deliveries from customer to final customer), d (demand of final customer) and SF_1, SF_2, SF_3 are constant, the lowest level of final finished goods in customer plant is reached when $EPEI_C = 0$. However, this is true only when $EPEI_C \geq EPEI_F$. If $EPEI_C < EPEI_F$, customer of analysed pair has bigger flexibility than final customer requires. In such situation $EPEI_C$ index has no influence on standard inventory level. Thus, the lowest standard inventory level for final finished goods hold at customer is achieved when $EPEI_C = EPEI_F$. Similarly, standard inventory levels for components at customer and for finished goods at supplier could be considered. In case of components held at customer either $EPEI_T$ or $EPEI_C$ influence standard inventory level. If $EPEI_T \geq EPEI_C$ standard inventory level will be as low as low is $EPEI_T$ index. If $EPEI_T$ is reduced till level of $EPEI_C$ ($EPEI_T = EPEI_C$), standard inventory level of components in customer plant will depend on $EPEI_C$. If taking into consideration reduction of $EPEI_C$ index in order to lower final finished goods standard inventory level, the lowest level of standard inventory components in customer plant will be achieved when $EPEI_T = EPEI_C = EPEI_F$. If standard inventory level for components held at supplier are considered in similar way it could be argued that inventories held in three locations (final finished goods, components and supplier's finished goods) are at the lowest level without harm to theirs availability when: **$EPEI_S = EPEI_T = EPEI_C = EPEI_F$.** If this is achieved, production processes of supplier and customer as well as transportation process will be synchronized. Authors of this article claim that EPEI indices related to production systems of customer and supplier as well as $EPEI_T$ could be reduced by implementation of improvements using SMED, milk run deliveries and other methods described in section 3.1. However, the cost of those improvements in many cases is not negligible. Therefore, managers of cooperating companies should strive for synchronizations in small steps. Implementing improvements in this way at each supply chain link will be better

Table 4. Definitions of different standard inventory elements for different locations

Standard inventory element	Locations of standard inventory		
	Components in supplier plant	Components in customer plant	Final finished goods in customer plant
Cycle Stock (CS)	Allows to provide required components for customer between replenishments from supplier production system	Allows customer production system to produce between deliveries from supplier	Allows customer to provide final finished goods between replenishments from customer production system
Buffer Stock (BS)	Protects customer from shortages of components when demand is bigger than average	Protects customer from shortages of components when demand is bigger than average	Protects final customer from shortages of final finished goods when demand is bigger than average
Safety Stock (SS)	Protects customer from shortages of components when supplier production system breaks down	Protects customer from shortages of components when delivery is delayed or incomplete	Protects final customer from shortages of final finished goods when customer production system breaks down

Table 5. Standard inventory equations for each standard inventory element in three analysed locations

Standard inventory element	Locations of standard inventory				
	Components in supplier plant	Components in customer plant		Final finished goods in customer plant	
		If $EPEI_T \geq EPEI_C$	If $EPEI_T < EPEI_C$	If $EPEI_C \geq EPEI_F$	If $EPEI_C < EPEI_F$
Cycle Stock (CS)	$CS_{Sup} = EPEI_S$ [days] x d [pcs./day]	$CS_{Cus} = EPEI_T$ [days] x d [pcs./day]	$CS_{Cus} = EPEI_C$ [days] x d [pcs./day]	$CS_{FG} = EPEI_C$ [days] x d [pcs./day]	$CS_{FG} = EPEI_F$ [days] x d [pcs./day]
Buffer Stock (BS)	BS_{Sup} = Variation* from average demand in intervals of $EPEI_S$	BS_{Cus} = Variation* from average demand in intervals of $EPEI_T$	BS_{Cus} = Variation* from average demand in intervals of $EPEI_C$	BS_{FG} = Variation* from average demand in intervals of $EPEI_C$	BS_{FG} = Variation* from average demand in intervals of $EPEI_F$
Safety Stock (SS)	$SS_{Sup} = (CS_{Sup} + BS_{Sup}) \times SF_1$	$BS_{Sup} = (CS_{Cus} + BS_{Cus}) \times SF_2$	$BS_{Sup} = (CS_{Cus} + BS_{Cus}) \times SF_2$	$SS_{FG} = (CS_{FG} + BS_{FG}) \times SF_3$	$SS_{FG} = (CS_{FG} + BS_{FG}) \times SF_3$

d – average demand; SF_1 – safety factor for customer's production system; SF_2 – safety factor for transportation process; SF_3 – safety factor for supplier's production system; Variation* – maximal variation the company decided to accept, expressed in pieces coordinated; also involved parties will be able to understand impact of local improvements on supply chain. In section 3.1 some practical solutions to lower EPEI indices are presented.

3.1 How to Reduce EPEI Indices

Cost of EPEI reduction in production processes as well as in transportation processes in not negligible. However there are existing and well known solutions that allows reducing EPEI indices. In area of production systems, reduction of EPEI index might be in some cases brought down to reduction of changeover times by applying SMED (Single Minute Exchange of Die) method [10]. Also decreasing number of defective products with Quality Management tools will result in EPEI indices reduction as time required for production of bad quality products increases EPEI in production system [11]. In production processes with well applied idea of continuous flow, EPEI reduction might be brought down to improvement of internal logistics process by applying kanban system and internal milk routes for frequent deliveries of components [9]. The same idea of milk runs could be also considered for reduction of $EPEI_T$ index [7], [12], [13].

4 Conclusions

Supply chain integration is one of the most important area for improving competitiveness of companies nowadays. Researches carried out by the authors of this article indicated that inventory levels in analysed supply chains are too high. Authors argued that this is due to lack of supplier – customer production and logistics systems' synchronization. Existing EVSM method allows mangers of cooperating companies to becom aware about too high levels of inventories but does not give clear methodology to reduce inventories in the whole supply chain. Without clear methodology for inventory reduction in supply chain, managers may implement improvements in their own companies that may cause worsening performance of other parties within the same supply chain. Therefore the SCPI methodology was proposed, which complements EVSM method with clear guidelines to follow for managers of all interested parties. The SCPI methodology is based on EPEI indices. Authors of the article argue that inventory levels are the lowest within supplier-customer pair when all EPEI indices are equal to EPEI index of final customer that describes its flexibility ($EPEI_F$) . Proposed methodology allows managers of cooperating companies to implement improvements in theirs own companies and being aware of their impact on the whole analysed supply chain.

References

1. Goldsby, T., Martichenko, R.: Lean six sigma logistics. In: Strategic Development to Operational Success, pp. 9–10. J. Ross Publishing, Boca Raton (2005)
2. Lacioni, R.A.: New Developments in Supply Chain Management for the Millennium. Industrial Marketing Management 29, 1–6 (2000)
3. Holweg, M., Frits, K.P.: The Second Century. In: Reconnecting Customer and Value Chain through Build – to – Order. The MIT Press, Cambridge (2004)

4. Szajter, P.: Jak zredukować zapasy materiałów przy dwukrotnym wzroście produkcji? In: 9th International Lean Manufacturing Conference, Wrocław (2009) (in Polish, not Publicized)
5. Ballou, R.H., Gilbert, S.M., Mukherjee, A.: New Managerial Challenges from Supply Chain Opportunities. Industrial Marketing Management 29, 7–18 (2000)
6. Walters, D.: Trends in the supply chain. In: Walters, D. (ed.) Global Logistics. New Directions in Supply Chain Management. MPG Books Ltd., Bodmin (2007)
7. Womack, J.P., Jones, D.T.: Seeing the Whole: Mapping the Extended Value Stream. Lean Enterprise Institute, Brookline (2002)
8. Lexicon, L.: A graphical glossary for Lean Thinkers, Version 4.0. The Lean Enterprise Institute, Cambridge (2008)
9. Harris, R., Harris, C., Wilson, E.: Making Materials Flow: A Lean Material-Handling Guide for Operations, Production-Control, and Engineering Professionals. The Lean Enterprise Institute, Brookline (2003)
10. Shingo, S.: Quick Changeover for Operators: The SMED System. Productivity Press, New York (1996)
11. Duggan, K.J.: Creating Mixed Model Value Streams. In: Practical Lean Techniques for Building to Demand. Productivity Press, New York (2002)
12. Baudin, M.: Lean Logistics. In: The Nuts and Bolts of Delivering Materials and Goods. Productivity Press, Nowy York (2004)
13. Eisler, M., Horbal, R., Koch, T.: Cooperation of Lean Enterprises – Techniques used for Lean Supply Chain. In: International IFIP TC 5, WG 5.7 Conference on Advances in Production Management Systems, Linkoping, Sweden, pp. 363–370 (2007)

Methodology of Designing Disassembly and Reassembly Processes Using Lean Thinking Approach

Tomasz Kanikuła and Tomasz Koch

Centre for Advanced Manufacturing Technologies (CAMT),
Institute of Production Engineering and Automation,
Wroclaw University of Technology, Poland
www.itma.pwr.wroc.pl

Abstract. In this paper a conception of using Lean Manufacturing methodology in disassembly and reassembly processes (Remanufacturing) is presented. Nine scenarios of material and information flows in Remanufacturing processes were developed in order to cover most of possible real situations.

Keywords: Remanufacturing, Lean Manufacturing, Pull System, Lean Remanufacturing.

1 Introduction

This paper presents some results of the research project funded by Polish Ministry of Research and Higher Education (4 T07D 004 29). Aim of this research project is to prepare transparent and adaptable methodology of designing disassembly and reassembly processes using Lean Thinking approach. The project required a review on current best industrial practices in managing and organization of remanufacturing processes. At the beginning literature review of current state of the art in Remanufacturing was carried out. The objective of the next step was to examine which Lean tools and methods could be applied in Remanufacturing system design and therefore could be incorporated into Lean Remanufacturing methodology. Simultaneously data were collected from industry to understand how disassembly and reassembly are organized in various industries. Several Remanufacturing companies were visited in order to carry out observations of current practices and to carry out interviews by using special questionnaire. The next step was to develop generic Lean Remanufacturing methodology in collaboration with one of remanufacturing companies from automotive sector. This way practical point of view for the research work was ensured and each element of elaborated methodology could be at least conceptual tested.

1.1 Remanufacturing

Remanufacturing is an industrial process where used products are restored to useful life. Remanufacturing consist of disassembling (sometimes with first inspection), cleaning, inspection, repairing (with inspection of 100% parts), replacing and reassembling (with final tests) the components of part or product in order to return it to

B. Vallespir and T. Alix (Eds.): APMS 2009, IFIP AICT 338, pp. 11–18, 2010.

like-new condition. In some Remanufacturing processes there are operations that are not needed in other. Examples are: galvanization, additional inspection and tests.

Remanufacturing is often confused with repair or overhaul, but it has to be underline that remanufacturing is different than refurbishing, overhaul or repair. Remanufacturing can also offer additional economic and environmental benefits because it recaptures approximately 85% [3] of the labour and energy that comprise the "value added" content.

2 Lean Remanufacturing - Methodology

The aim of applying lean into remanufacturing processes is to increase efficiency of remanufacturing businesses. Therefore several research studies on this topic have been already undertaken in recent years [6,7,8]. Those studies identify problems of Lean implementations trials in Remanufacturing e.g.:

- not every remanufacturing operation is needed in each remanufacturing process,
- difficulties in definition of takt time for remanufacturing systems (not always consumer demand is known)
- cycle times varies and it depends on quality or repeatability of incoming products,
- quantity of disassembled parts varies and it also depends on quality or repeatability of incoming products,
- diversity in range of products,
- possible huge amount of core (used products) inventory waiting for disassembly,
- sometimes no high-runners.

In order to respond to those problems a new Lean Remanufacturing methodology is proposed, and will be described in further parts of this paper.

2.1 Research Limitations

Several boundary conditions for developed methodology was defined like:

- full availability of cores
- technology of disassembly is known
- technology of reassembly is known
- rate of using new parts is known
- methods of supplying new parts are the same in each nine scenarios.

For future research all of nine scenarios of material and information flows developed within Lean Remanufacturing methodology should be analyzed and tested in real industrial environment in order of further improvement and fine tuning.

2.2 Lean Remanufacturing – Where to Start?

Remanufacturing is a specific environment, where the range of products is usually very wide. The first thing that have to be done is to chose pilot area to implement Lean conception. The tool that could be used to chose the best product family to start from is Glenday Sieve [4]. This tool separates products (SKU's) into four groups based on sales volume (or value if this is more appropriate). Typical result is presented in Table 1 [4].

Table 1. Glenday Sieve

% Cumulative Sales	% Product Range
50%	6%
95%	50%
99%	70%
1%	30%

The first steps in the proposed methodology is to use Glenday Sieve to separate 6% of product range that are responsible for 50% of the sales volume. These products families will be the pilot area to start implementing Lean. Second step will be to chose one of nine scenarios suggested. To be able to do this, it is recommended to use table 2.

Table 2. Matching scenario with current Remanufacturing condition

Features of Remanufacturing:	Scenarios								
	1	2	3	4	5	6	7	8	9
Instability of repair cycle time	●	●				●		●	●
Instability of disassembly cycle time		●	●		●	●	●	●	●
Unstable recovery percentage at repair	●	●				●		●	●
Unstable recovery percentage at disassemble		●	●		●	●	●	●	●
Not enough place for core (used products)							●	●	●
Disassembled parts inventory recommended		●	●		●	●			
Repaired parts inventory recommended	●	●				●		●	●
Finished products inventory recommended				●	●	●			
No need to control disassembly process							●	●	●
Repair is expensive and time consuming			●	●	●		●		
Disassemble is expensive and time consuming	●			●					
High cost of finished products inventory	●	●	●				●	●	●
Different cycle time in each process		●				●		●	●

In the table 2, the most important features of Remanufacturing process were listed. These should be carefully analyzed to chose the most appropriate scenario. Black points indicate the most adequate scenario that could be applied to particular feature (problem). It should be noticed that some of Remanufacturing problems could be solved by more than one scenario.

2.3 Nine Scenarios

During this project several alternative solutions were identified and described to enable using Lean approach in such specific area like Remanufacturing. Techniques and methods such as One Piece Flow, Pull System, Visual Control, Kanban System, SMED, TPM, Kaizen, Glenday Sieve, Value Stream Mapping, PFEP were examined. Nine scenarios (graphics symbols based on "Learning to See" [5]) that make use of some of those methods in Remanufacturing were developed in order to cover most of possible real situations.

Scenario 1 – Supermarket of repaired parts
Each core that is delivered to Remanufacturing company should be stored in core
warehouse, waiting for signal to be disassembled. Customer orders should be collected at reassembly. Based on them, proper parts have to be picked up from supermarket, reassembled (with new parts also) and shipped to customer according to FIFO
rule. Replenishment pull signal (kanban) is sent from supermarket to disassembly to
inform: what, when, and where needs to be disassembled (Fig. 1).

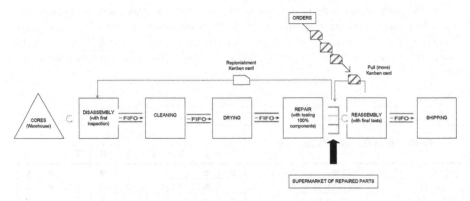

Fig. 1. Scenario 1 with Supermarket of repaired parts

Scenario 2 – Two supermarkets for disassembled and repaired parts
Each core that is delivered to Remanufacturing company should be stored in core
warehouse, waiting for a signal to be disassembled. Customer orders should be collected at reassembly. Based on them, proper parts have to be picked up from supermarket of repaired parts, reassembled (together with new parts) and shipped to
customer according to FIFO rule. First, pull system (1) sends an information (kanban)
to repair: what, when, and where has to be replenished in supermarket of repaired
parts (Fig. 2). Repair process takes the parts from supermarket of disassembled parts.
Second, pull system (2) sends information signal to disassembly: what, when, and
where needs to be replenished in supermarket of disassembled parts.

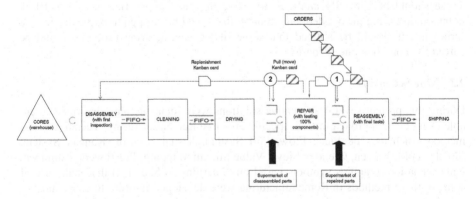

Fig. 2. Scenario 2 with two supermarkets for disassembled and repaired parts

Scenario 3 – Supermarket of disassembled parts

Each core that is delivered to Remanufacturing company should be stored in core warehouse, waiting for signal to be disassembled. Customer orders should be collected at reassembly. Based on them, proper parts have to be picked up from supermarket, repaired, reassembled (together with new parts) and shipped to customer according to FIFO rule (Fig. 3). Pull system sends an information (kanban) to disassembly: what, when, and where needs to be replenished.

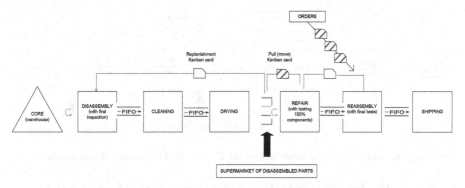

Fig. 3. Scenario 3 with Supermarket of disassembled parts

Scenario 4 – Supermarket of finished products

Each core that is delivered to Remanufacturing company should be stored in core warehouse, waiting for signal to be disassembled. Customer orders should be collected at shipping. Based on them, proper products have to be picked up from supermarket and sent to customer. Pull system sends an information (kanban) to disassembly: what, when, and where needs to be replenished (Fig. 4).

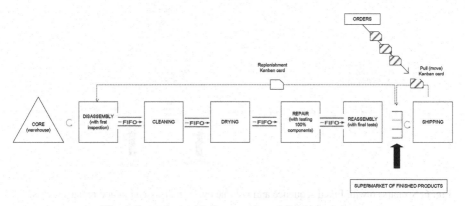

Fig. 4. Scenario 4 with Supermarket of finished products

Scenario 5 – Two supermarkets for disassembled parts and finished products

Each core that is delivered to Remanufacturing company should be stored in core warehouse, waiting for a signal to be disassembled. Customer orders should be collected at shipping. Based on them, proper parts have to be picked up from finished products supermarket and sent to customer. First, pull system (1) sends an information (kanban) to repair: what, when, and where needs to be repaired in order to replenish finished parts supermarket (Fig. 5). Repair process takes parts from supermarket of disassembled parts. Second, pull system (2) sends information to disassembly: what, when, and where needs to be replenished in supermarket of disassembled parts.

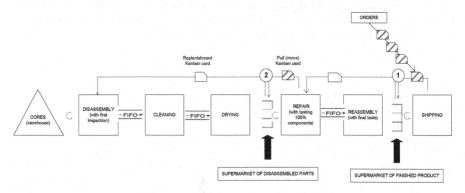

Fig. 5. Scenario 5 with two supermarkets for disassembled parts and finished products

Scenario 6 – Fixed sequence and volume cycle in disassembly and repair processes

For 6% of product range both, the sequence and volumes in the cycle, should be fixed. What to do next in disassembly and repair processes should be determined by the cycle. The aim of this fixed cycle is to create economies of repetition that generate several benefits [4]. Both "buffer tanks" with control limits (Fig. 6) absorb the variability between demand and supply e.g. between repair and disassembly. If the level of parts is between control limits the plan is still fixed. Reassemble process should collect orders, based on them, assemble products (together with new parts) and ship them to customers.

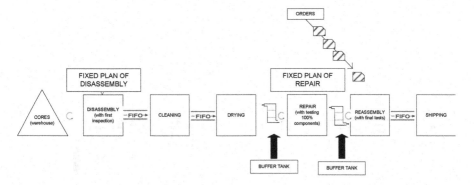

Fig. 6. Scenario 6 with Fixed sequence and volume cycle in disassembly and repair processes

Scenario 7 – Warehouse of Disassembled Parts & sequential pull system from repair to shipping

Each core that is delivered to Remanufacturing company has to be disassembled immediately on arrival. When order appears in reassembly process, required parts are picked up from warehouse of disassembled parts. Next step is to repair, reassemble (together with new parts) and ship according to FIFO rule (Fig. 7).

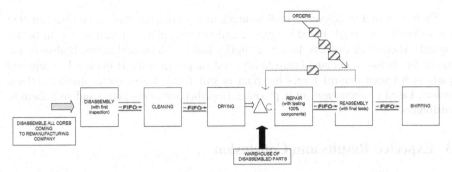

Fig. 7. Scenario 7 with Warehouse of disassembled parts & sequential pull system from repair to shipping

Scenario 8 – Warehouse of disassembled parts & Supermarket of repaired parts

Each core that is delivered to Remanufacturing company has to be disassembled immediately on arrival. When order appears in reassembly process, required parts are picked up from Supermarket of repaired parts, reassembled (together with new parts) and shipped to customer according to FIFO rule (Fig. 8). Parts, that are taken from Supermarket have to be replenished by repair process.

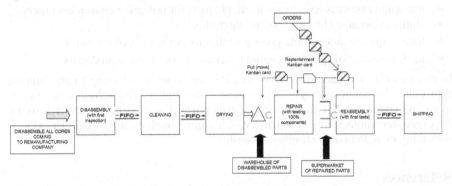

Fig. 8. Scenario 8 with Warehouse of disassembled parts & Supermarket of repaired parts

Scenario 9 – Warehouse of disassembled parts & Fixed sequence and volume in repair process

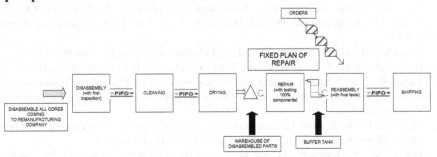

Fig. 9. Scenario 9 with Warehouse of disassembled parts & Fixed sequence and volume in repair process

Each core that is delivered to Remanufacturing company has to be disassembled immediately on arrival. Fixed (sequence and volume) plan of repairing has to be designed. After repair process there is a "buffer tank" with control limits. It absorbs the variability between demand (reassembly) and supply (repair). If the level of repaired parts is between control limits the plan is still fixed. Reassemble process collects orders, based on them, assemble products (together with new parts) and ship them to customers.

3 Expected Results and Conclusion

Desired result of implementing Lean Remanufacturing methodology:

- improvement of consumer service (reduced number of complains),
- improvement of Lead Time (time between order and shipping to customer),
- decrease of finished products stock,
- decrease of value of new parts in remanufactured products,
- decrease in number of cores that have to be disassembled to remanufacture ordered number of products,
- reduced space needed for cores,
- reassembly process has always available parts for preparing consumers orders,
- ability to manage changing orders, flexibility.
- fixed sequence and volume gives potential for economies of repetition,
- no delays in repair process caused by awaiting for disassembled parts.

In this paper a vital part of new and original methodology of using Lean Thinking approach in Remanufacturing was presented. Several alternative solutions were identified and described. The methodology development intention was to make it useful for every Remanufacturing company, which aim of implementing Lean Thinking is something more than only eliminating waste.

References

1. Smalley, A.: Creating Level Pull, pp. 13–69. The Lean Enterprise Institute, Brookline (2004)
2. Womack, J., Jones, D.T.: Lean Thinking. Simon & Schuster, New York (1996)
3. Nasr, N.Z.: Remanufacturing from Technology to Applications. In: Proceedings Global Conference on Sustainable Product Development and Life Cycle Engineering, Berlin (2004)
4. Glenday, I.: Breaking through to flow. Lean Enterprise Academy, Ross-on-Wye (2007)
5. Rother, M., Shook, J.: Learning to See. The Lean Enterprise Institute, Brookline (1998)
6. Kagan, R.: Lean Solutions for Remanufacturing Systems? In: Proceedings Polish-German Workshop on Lean Remanufacturing, Oficyna Wydawnicza Politechniki Wrocławskiej, Wrocław (2006)
7. Mähl, M., Östlin, J.: Lean Remanufacturing – Material Flow at Volvo Parts Flen. Master Thesis, Department of Business Studies, Upsala University (2006)
8. Dunkel, M.: Methodenentwicklung für Lean Remanufacturing. Shaker Verlag, Aachen (2008)

Evaluating Energy Efficiency Improvements in Manufacturing Processes

Katharina Bunse, Julia Sachs, and Matthias Vodicka

ETH Zurich, BWI Center for Enterprise Sciences, 8092 Zurich, Switzerland
kbunse@ethz.ch, sachsj@student.ethz.ch, mvodicka@ethz.ch

Abstract. Global warming, rising energy prices and increasing awareness of "green" customers have brought energy efficient manufacturing on top of the agenda of governments as well as of industrial companies. The industrial sector still accounts for about 33% of the final energy consumption. This paper will contribute to a more energy efficient manufacturing by demonstrating how energy efficiency can be integrated into different levels of decision-making in companies. The paper will present methods for measuring and evaluating energy efficiency improvements in manufacturing processes. Different Key Performance Indicators (KPI) will be considered and economic evaluation methods will be outlined. Moreover, an example of the integration of energy efficiency aspects into the Balanced Scorecard (BSC) will show how energy efficiency improvements in the manufacturing process can be facilitated by influencing the tactical and operational level of decision making.

Keywords: Energy Efficiency, Manufacturing Processes, Decision-Making, Economic Evaluation, Key Performance Indicator, Balanced Scorecard.

1 Introduction

Climate change due to greenhouse gas emissions, unsecured energy supply and rising energy prices are subjects which are becoming more and more important in today's society. Although renewable energy technologies can be the long-term solution, more efficient energy use is predestinated to make the highest and most economic contribution to the solution of these problems in the short term [1]. Moreover, the reduction of CO_2 emissions and the protection of resources and materials are some further benefits accompanied by energy efficiency.

With its 33% of the final energy consumption the manufacturing industry is the main consumer of energy (see Fig. 1). Although there is a continuous progress in the industrial sector in the last decades, economically beneficial energy efficiency improvement potential is by far not exhausted [2]. According to the EC's Green Paper on Energy Efficiency, at least 20 percent of its current energy consumption could be saved EU-wide [3]. Companies that improve their energy efficiency and therefore also their carbon footprint are well positioned to face future challenges and costs, resulting e.g. from future CO_2-regulations.

B. Vallespir and T. Alix (Eds.): APMS 2009, IFIP AICT 338, pp. 19–26, 2010.
© IFIP International Federation for Information Processing 2010

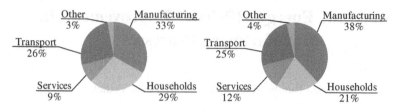

Fig. 1. Shares of global final energy consumption and CO_2 emissions by sector, 2005 [4]

Further, "green" becomes more important to the customer, which has an impact on developments in the whole supply chain and, therefore, can be a significant driver of competitiveness. "Energy efficiency improvement is a fundamental, yet significant, way of addressing both energy security and environmental concerns" [5].

1.1 Objective of the Paper

In order to achieve energy efficiency improvements in manufacturing, the benefits and cost savings have to be measured. Therefore, at first adequate KPIs and an economic evaluation method including energy efficiency aspects have to be chosen, e.g. in case of replacing equipment. Only with a solid validation by such evaluations, energy efficiency decisions can be supported and good results ensured.

The aim of this paper is to demonstrate how energy efficiency can be integrated into company activities by combining theoretical methods with practical experience. This paper presents a method to quantify the value generated by energy efficiency improvements from the perspective of manufacturing companies. This method combines several concepts from financial and supply chain management and integrates recently developed frameworks to provide the required transparency.

1.2 Methodology and Data

This paper bases on a literature research as well as on interviews and workshops with representatives of companies from the mechanical engineering and process industry. In order to assure a structured research process the approach of "Systems Engineering" [6] is applied guided by the principles of case study research. The existing approaches for evaluating energy efficiency improvements are analyzed and a proposal for a new approach to integrate energy efficiency into companies' decision making process is outlined. The concept still has to be tested and validated with industrial partners.

This research is based on the results of the project IMS2020, which has the objective to support future manufacturing environment by building a roadmap. The roadmap highlights the main milestones for future research activities needed to achieve a desired vision for manufacturing systems. IMS2020 is embedded in the global activities of the Intelligent Manufacturing Systems (IMS) initiative. IMS is a platform for global collaborative research and experience exchange.

IMS2020 focuses on five research areas, the so called Key Area Topics (KAT), namely Sustainable Manufacturing, Energy Efficient Manufacturing, Key Technologies, Standards, and Education. This paper is based on results from the area of Energy Efficient Manufacturing (EEM).

2 Evaluation of Energy Efficiency for Manufacturing Decisions

For the evaluation of energy efficiency improvements in manufacturing environments, firstly the term energy efficiency is defined. Secondly, different methods for measuring energy efficiency are presented and finally an overview on economic evaluation approaches for energy efficiency projects is presented.

2.1 Energy Efficiency

Energy efficiency has become a central focus of energy policies as well as for industrial companies; however, little attention has been given to defining and measuring it [7]. "When energy efficiency improvements are discussed for the industrial sector, quite often very different concepts are used for defining energy efficiency, which convey different messages that can even be contradicting" [2].

In the context of this paper energy efficiency is understood as reducing the energy consumption while performing the same task. This is achieved by eliminating energy waste [1]. Better energy efficiency can be accomplished by e.g. more efficient technology, better energy management, and better operational practices.

2.2 Measurement of Energy Efficiency

Companies usually accomplish changes in the operational business only if they gain a verifiable benefit. To detect such advancement in the area of energy efficiency these benefits have to be measurable. Hence, indicators are needed.

The development and application of energy efficiency indicators depend on the purpose they are applied for. Usually such indicators are ratios describing the coherence between an activity and the required energy. In the industrial sector such activity - as the production of a product - can be described in either economic or physical terms. As a result, indicators measuring the energy efficiency can be economic or physical indicators. Two typical indicators are the energy intensity and the Specific Energy Consumption (SEC). Energy intensity is called an economic indicator because its denominator is measured in economic terms like GDP. In comparison, the SEC with its denominator in units as tonne or product is a physical indicator. For both indicators the numerator measures energy use, which can be measured in various ways, e.g. demand for primary energy carriers, net available energy or purchased energy [8]. Economic indicators are useful at an aggregated level, for e.g. comparing different sectors, but to get insight into particular manufacturing processes, physical indicators are more illuminating [8].

Increasing energy efficiency is reflected in decreasing energy intensity and decreasing SEC. Due to the amount of different industrial processes and their complexity, there exists a multitude of structural and explanatory indicators designed for the various manufacturing sectors as in the pulp and paper, cement, and iron and steel industry [9]. Special care has to be taken when comparing energy efficiency indicators internationally because the results of such an analysis can vary strongly based on different energy consumption measurements, aggregate levels, boundary definitions, and activity measurements of heterogeneous products. "Depending on the goal of the analysis, it may also be required to convert net available energy consumption to primary energy or even CO_2-emissions" [8].

In conclusion, there is no singular energy efficiency indicator that can be applied in every situation, but the appropriate indicators have to be defined depending on the decision to make or decision tool to be applied. Table 1 presents an overview about different energy efficiency indicators, their application and their formula or unit.

Table 1. Selection of Energy Efficiency Indicators

Reference	Indicator	Indicator type	Application	Formula/Unit
[8]	Energy Intensity	economic	aggregated level	
	Specific Energy Consumption	physical	disaggregated level	GJ per t
[9]	Energy Intensity			energy use/unit of industrial output
	Energy Use per Unit of Value Added	economic	aggregated level	
	Specific Energy Consumption	physical	comparison	energy use/tonne of product (material)
[10]	Energy Intensity	macroeconomic	aggregated level	energy consumption/monetary variables
	Degree of Efficiency	engineering view		net energy/used primary energy
	Final Energy Efficiency			energy savings by the same benefits
[11]	Energy Intensity	economic		energy/output like energy/tonne
[12]	Ratio of Energy Consumption	macroeconomic		
	Value Added	macroeconomic		
	Specific Energy Consumption		process level	energy use/physical unit of production
	Thermal Energy Efficiency of Equipment		for single equipment	energy value available for process/input energy value
[13]	Energy Consumption Intensity		broader than the thermal one: companies etc.	energy consumption/physical output value
	Absolute Amount of Energy Consumption		attended by indication of production volumes	energy value
	Diffusion Rates of Equipment		rate of deployment	
	Energy (costs)/GDP	macroeconomic		
[14]	Specific Energy Consumption	technical	for homogeneous products like cement etc.	final energy consumption/amount
	Energy Intensity			final energy consumption/real variables

2.3 Economic Evaluation of Energy Efficiency Improvements

The key criteria for the decision making process for energy efficiency improvements is the economic evaluation. "The objective of an economic analysis is to provide the information needed to make a judgment or a decision. The most complete analysis of an investment in a technology or a project requires the analysis of each year of the lifetime of the investment, taking into account relevant direct costs, indirect and overhead costs, taxes, and returns on investment, plus any externalities, such as environmental impacts, that are relevant to the decision to be made" [15]. Different economic measures and analytical techniques can be consulted for evaluating energy efficiency improvements.

For profitability calculations there are three common methods: the net present value method (NPV), the method of annualized value and the method of internal rate of return [16]. In addition to these three methods many companies also calculate the payback period. The simple payback period is commonly used and recommended for risk assessment. The risk of an investment is higher, if the payback period is longer, because the capital is tied for a longer time period. More specific economic measures for evaluating energy efficiency investments can be found in Short et al. (2005) [15].

In order to support energy efficiency investments it can be advisable to consider also productivity benefits that are associated with energy efficiency improvements in the economic evaluation [17]. These non-energy benefits could be for example lower maintenance costs, increased production yield, safer working conditions and many others. Some authors argue that additional productivity benefits should be included, for example in modeling parameters in an economic assessment of the potential of energy efficiency improvements [18]. Nevertheless it is not always straight forward to identify and quantify these benefits in monetary terms.

For energy efficiency investments there are normally no real future cash inflows to be considered for the economic evaluation. The costs for the investment, namely capital invested, and additional fixed and variable costs (e.g. cost for personnel, administration, insurance and taxes), have to be compared to the cost that can be avoided by implementing the improvement measure – these are mainly energy cost, but could also be other avoidable fixed or variable costs (especially when including other non-energy productivity benefits). On the other side, in the context of energy efficiency taxes play a specific role. For example, energy tax credits for energy efficient technologies can enhance after-tax cash flow and promote the investment.

3 Integration of Energy Efficiency in Manufacturing Decisions

In order to integrate energy efficiency aspects into the decision making of manufacturing companies, appropriate approaches for measuring energy efficiency and evaluating energy efficiency investments have to be applied. To structure the decision making process of a company we propose to look at three different levels of management and to enhance commonly known management tools by integrating energy efficiency indicators and measures. An example is given how to integrate energy efficiency aspects into the Balanced Scorecard (BSC).

3.1 Levels of Decision-Making in Manufacturing Companies

In management science, three levels of decision-making are generally distinguished: the strategic level, the tactical level, and the operational level. They are in hierarchical order and, therefore, reducing complexity of companies' activities [19].

An important characteristic of the *strategic level* is its long-term nature and its consideration of business areas instead of single products [20]. At this level decisions are made, on which markets with what kind of products the company wants to operate and how the resources basically will be used [21].

The *tactical level* serves the efficient and effective realization of the goals, which were determined before at the strategic level. At this level the layout and the capacities of the manufacturing process have to be planned. Task to be executed on this level comprise investment planning, equipment acquisition, and their maintenance, as well as the design of products and the preparation of their production. By the completion of these tactical tasks a basis for the operational level is provided.

With the *operational level* the third stage of the hierarchic planning system is described. The operational planning translates the targets defined in previous levels into precise activities. Decisions influence the kind and amount of the products, which have to be manufactured, and the production itself has to be organized and accomplished [21]. For the operational level disaggregated targets have to be defined in order to prove and measure the achievements.

3.2 The Balanced Scorecard as an Example for Integrating Energy Efficiency

In the following we would like to propose an approach to integrate energy efficiency on the strategic level using the BSC. Because the BSC links strategic goals to operational measures, changes in the direction of energy efficiency reach out to all levels of the decision making process (see Fig. 2).

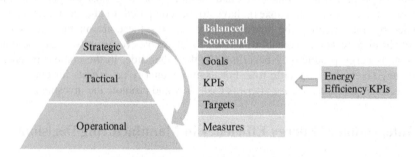

Fig. 2. The Balanced Scorecard and the different levels of companies' decision making

On the strategic level various tools exist which can assist mangers in decision-making. As an example the widely-known and -used "Balanced Scorecard" is chosen to show how energy efficiency can be included into management tools. Referring to an already existing variation of the BSC, the Sustainability Balanced Scorecard (SBSC) [22], there are three possibilities to integrate energy efficiency into the traditional BSC:

In the first option, new aspects of energy efficiency can be integrated into one, several, or all of the four existing perspectives. Therefore energy efficiency goals have to be defined and linked to each other by cause and effect relationships. Afterwards appropriate indicators and measures have to be defined.

As second option an additional fifth perspective as "energy efficiency" can be added to the existing four perspectives. This extension is adequate if energy efficiency represents an important success factor for the business model of a company. Energy efficiency can serve as competitive factor, if customers ask not only for efficient products but also for efficient production processes.

Additionally, a specific energy efficiency scorecard can be formulated. But this variation is not independent but rather just an extension to one of the earlier described options. The energy efficiency goals, indicators, and measures are transferred and detailed into a separate scorecard. The type of integration depends on the importance a decision-maker is paying to energy efficiency.

Although the BSC is a tool of the strategic level it has consequences on all three levels. By the application of the BSC a strategy is developed out of the company's mission and vision. Consequently, through gradual specification of strategic goals measures and actions are deduced. Thus, an operationalization of the company's vision and strategy is gained. Moreover, indicators are determined. These indicators that are collected at the operational level are available for upper levels to control the achievement of the strategic goals of the BSC. A possible strategic goal like "saving 10% energy during the next year" could be detailed on the tactical level by building up a new more efficient production line or modifying the capability utilization. The corresponding Energy KPI could be the SEC. This could imply on the operational level that if a company has different machines varying in their efficiency, the more efficient machine should be scheduled first and the remaining capacities needed should be assigned to the less efficient machine. Hence, energy efficiency indicators are transferred into measures and actions.

4 Conclusion and Outlook

This paper is based on first results from the project IMS2020 in the area of energy efficient manufacturing. It defines a structured concept how to measure energy efficiency improvements and how energy efficiency aspects can be included in companies' decision making. Moreover, an approach to use the balanced scorecard to integrate energy efficiency on the strategic level of a company, with impacts on the tactical and operational level is presented.

There are many technologies available, which can contribute to the objective of reduction of energy consumption in manufacturing. A detailed knowledge and analysis of the production processes is a prerequisite to find energy saving potentials in manufacturing industries. The objective is to overcome existing process limitations by developing new production processes integrating innovative energy efficient technologies, e.g. the utilization of waste heat.

In the project IMS2020 different research topics that address research needs on all three levels of decision making are developed. On the operational level, for example, an effective measurement system for energy use has to be developed (including sensors and visual systems for in-process measurements and Energy KPIs), followed by energy control concepts, which facilitate the evaluation, control and improvement of energy efficiency in production.

The analysis is restricted to an outline of a concept for evaluating energy efficiency improvements in the environment of the mechanical engineering and the process industry. The results could be transferred to other industries as well. The proposed integration of energy efficiency on all levels of decision making has to be validated in an implementation phase. Further research can enhance the presented concept by detailing the economic evaluation of energy efficiency improvements in the production process and to develop a method to quantify non-energy benefits gained from energy efficiency improvements. This paper provides the basis for measuring, evaluating and improving energy efficiency in manufacturing processes, which is crucial for companies to meet the challenges imposed by environmental regulations, scarce resources and a rising oil price.

References

1. Environmental and Energy Study Institute (EESI), http://www.eesi.org
2. Eichhammer, W.: Industrial Energy Efficiency. In: Cleveland, C.J. (ed.) Encyclopedia of Energy, vol. 3, pp. 383–393. Elsevier, New York (2004)
3. European Commission (EC): Green Paper, A European Strategy for Sustainable, Competitive and Secure Energy (2006), http://ec.europa.eu
4. International Energy Agency (IEA): Worldwide Trends in Energy Use and Efficiency, Key Insights from IEA Indicator Analysis (2008), http://www.iea.org
5. International Energy Agency (IEA): Assessing measures of energy efficiency performance and their application in industry (2008), http://www.iea.org
6. Haberfellner, R., Daenzer, W.F.: Systems Engineering: Methodik und Praxis (11. durchgesehene Auflage). Verlag Industrielle Organisation, Zürich (2002)
7. Patterson, M.G.: What is Energy Efficiency? Energ. Policy 24(5), 377–390 (1996)
8. Phylipsen, G.J.M., Blok, K., Worrell, E.: International Comparisons of Energy Efficiency-Methodologies for the Manufacturing Industry. Energ. Policy 25(7-9), 715–725 (1997)
9. International Energy Agency (IEA): Tracking Industrial, Energy Efficiency and CO2 Emissions (2007), http://www.iea.org
10. Irrek, W., Thomas, S.: Definition Energieeffizienz. Wuppertal Institut für Klima, Umwelt, Energie GmbH (2008), http://www.wupperinst.org
11. Love, R., Cleland, D.: Tools for Energy Efficiency in Industrial Processes. In: Proceedings of the 2nd International Conference on Sustainability Engineering and Science, Auckland, NZ (2007)
12. Farlat, J., Blok, K., Schipper, L.: Energy Efficiency Developments in the Pulp and Paper Industry. Elsevier Science Ltd., Great Britain (1997)
13. International Energy Agency (IEA): Assessing Measures of energy efficiency performance and their application in industry (2008), http://www.iea.org
14. Diekmann, J., Eichhammer, W., Neubert, A., Rieke, H., Schlomann, B., Ziesing, H.-J.: Energie-Effizienz-Indikatoren. Physica-Verlag, Heidelberg (1999)
15. Short, W., Packey, D.J., Holt, T.: A Manual for the Economic Evaluation of Energy Efficiency and Renewable Energy Technologies. National Renewable Energy Laboratory, U.S, Department of Energy, University Press of the Pacific, Honolulu, Hawaii (2005)
16. Schmidt, R., Terberger, E.: Grundzüge der Investitions- uns Finanzierungstheorie. 3. Auflage. Gabler, Wiesbaden (1996)
17. Boyd, G.A., Pang, J.X.: Estimating the Linkage between Energy Efficiency and Productivity. Energ. Policy 28, 289–296 (2000)
18. Worrell, E., Laitner, J.A., Ruth, M., Finman, H.: Productivity Benefits of Industrial Energy Efficiency Measures. Energy 28, 1081–1098 (2003)
19. Kistner, K.-P., Steven, M.: Produktionsplanung. Physica, Heidelberg (2001)
20. Voigt, K.-I.: Industrielles Management. Springer, Berlin (2008)
21. Hansmann, K.-W.: Industrielles Management. Oldenbourg, München (2006)
22. Figge, F., Hahn, T., Schaltegger, S., Wagner, M.: The Sustainability Balanced Scorecard – Linking Sustainability Management to Business Strategy. Business Strategy and the Environment 11, 269–284 (2002)

Integrated Micro Process Chains

Bernd Scholz-Reiter, Nele Brenner, and Alice Kirchheim

BIBA - Bremer Institut für Produktion und Logistik GmbH at the University of Bremen,
Hochschulring 20, 28359 Bremen, Germany
{bsr,bre,kch}@biba.uni-bremen.de

Abstract. High quality mechanical manufacturing of small components and subassemblies having geometric features in the micrometer range requires controlled and coordinated processes. Considering full automation of the production process as essential, not only manufacturing processes have to be optimized but also handling and quality assurance operations take an integral part of the production process. We outline requirements for handling and test operations in micro production and introduce a concept of an integrated micro process chain which meets the conditions and challenges in micro production process planning.

Keywords: micro manufacturing, production planning, artificial neural network, quality, handling.

1 Introduction

Micro systems technology is one of the most important cross-sectional technologies and the trend of miniaturization will outlast the next decades [1]. In comparison to chip manufacturing, micro production with mechanical manufacturing methods is not yet widely advanced. Manufacturing technologies and the development of concepts supporting the industrial production of micro components is still an active field of research. The Collaborative Research Center (CRC) 747, an interdisciplinary research project involving eight institutes of the University of Bremen, is focused on micro cold forming. Processes are developed for mechanically manufactured components and subassemblies, made from parts smaller than 1 mm in at least two dimensions, but having geometric features at the micro scale.

In the present state of research, the percentage of manually effected operations is still very high. This concerns handling operations like positioning and transport of micro parts. In order to reach production rates of up to 200 parts per minute with a throughput of several hundred to hundred-thousand parts per series, micro processes have to be automated. Quality control and handling operations are an integral part of the production process and have to be adapted to the speed and tolerances of the manufacturing process. In a field where accuracy deviations of one micrometer can have disastrous effects, an automated process chain is not realizable without controlled and monitored processes. Besides the improvement of the manufacturing methods themselves, which is not topic of this paper, the development of supporting systems like handling and measurement technologies as well as concepts for process planning and process-oriented quality assurance are the challenges faced by research in micro production.

B. Vallespir and T. Alix (Eds.): APMS 2009, IFIP AICT 338, pp. 27–32, 2010.

2 Characteristics of Micro Production

Downscaling macro processes to micro scale works out up to a certain extent. The occurring *size effects* [2] describe several phenomena, which have physical and structural sources. In addition to the technical effects, production and logistics related effects like the possible use of smaller machines lead to new possibilities and challenges in production planning. Due to the lack of stable processes and standardized interfaces as well as suitable handling and measurement methods in the micro scale, production process planning is joined with and has to be integrated in the product development process. The following characteristics describe relevant conditions in micro production processes:

- High production volumes and high accuracy require an automated process chain,
- the parameters influencing the quality are increasing,
- due to highly sensitive processes, the quality of the product can vary widely,
- measurement and handling techniques have to be adapted for micro parts and processes (e.g. high production rates, high accuracies, suitable for clean-room)

In the following chapters the specific conditions of the areas, handling and material flow as well as quality control, are discussed in more detail.

3 Handling and Material Flow in Micro Production

Due to the increased surface-to-volume ratio of micro parts, their gravitational force is lower than the adhesion forces. Therefore, controlled picking and highly accurate placing of micro parts is a great challenge. Several research groups have developed handling devices; examples are given for micro-grippers [4], assembly [5], and transportation [6]. As described in [7], micro grippers should be designed in a way to fulfill the following requirements.

- Cost efficient and fast set up
- Small size, compact design and low weight
- Suitable for clean-rooms
- Ability to measure and control grip force in order to avoid destruction of fragile parts
- Integration of sensors to control and enable precise picking and placing
- Flexibility regarding object size and geometry able to be gripped
- Standardized interface (mechanical, electrical)

As the micro parts are very sensitive to electrical and mechanical forces as well as contamination, contactless handling is advantageous. Furthermore, the alignment and orientation of micro parts is difficult once they are disarranged. Therefore, the aim is to keep the parts in a defined orientation throughout the production process. This means, that the subassemblies and components are either produced in a larger composite and separated as late as possible or are placed in a component carrier right after processing. In both ways, they can be handled like macro parts with standard conveyer machinery.

4 Quality Management in Micro Production

Quality management systems are generally based on the ISO 9000 [3]. In this paper, we concentrate on micro part control and the consequences for quality assurance. Quality assurance describes processes and procedures as well as measurement technologies in order to attain quality objectives. The material and information flow define the requirements for quality assurance. Figure 1 gives an overview of a process-based quality management system.

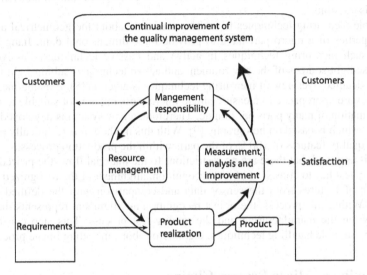

Fig. 1. Process-based quality management system [3]

It is a challenge to develop a quality management system for micro production as processes cannot be controlled sufficiently. Referring to ISO 9000 the development of a quality management system consists of the following steps [3]:

1. Determining the needs and expectations of customers and other interested parties
2. Establishing the quality policy and quality objectives of the organization
3. Determining the processes and responsibilities necessary to attain the quality objectives
4. Establishing methods to measure the effectiveness and efficiency of each process
5. Applying these measures to determine the effectiveness and efficiency of each process
6. Determining means of preventing nonconformities and eliminating their causes
7. Establishing and applying a process for continual improvement of the quality management system

As it is impossible to handle and test micro parts manually, it is necessary to focus research activities on measurement and test engineering: Features for a quality test have to be defined, an appropriate measuring technique has to be chosen and an automated method for quality tests has to be developed.

The objectives of a quality test consist of comparing features from a produced part with the optimal values taken from a design drawing or reference values. Features might be geometrical properties, surface properties or material properties. Afterwards a statement is made from the results of the quality test. This could be a decision about a violation of any chosen property or a detailed description of the violated quality property. Within the CRC quality properties are restricted to geometrical and surface properties and each violated feature is described in detail such that an analysis of the process is possible.

Possible measuring techniques to make a statement about the geometrical and surface properties of a micro part have to provide three-dimensional data. Jiang [8] has divided such measuring techniques in active and passive techniques. Passive techniques use light sources of the environment and active techniques submit light into the scene. A detailed overview of measuring techniques is given in [8]. Existing measuring techniques are appropriate to measure single micro parts but are not suitable to acquire 3D-information of many parts per minute. Therefore, a new system is developed within the CRC, which is based on holography [9]. With this method, it is technically possible to detect quality features of 100 % of the parts within the production process.

As it is assumed that there are no restrictions to the material flow, the procedure for the quality test has to consist of object recognition, alignment of the recognized object, extraction of features from the sensor data and comparison with the defined quality features. Within this process, the object recognition an alignment represents the interface between the manufacturing and the quality test process. This step can be performed by suitable handling techniques, e.g. micro robots, including image processing.

5 Planning of Micro Process Chains

A manufacturing process chain describes the chronological and logical order of all operations necessary to produce the component or subassembly. Due to the complexity of planning constraints and the absence of standardized technology and interfaces in micro production, handling and test operations have to be taken into account at an early state of the production planning process in order to avoid later cost and time efficient adjustments. This means, that production technology, test and handling techniques should be developed simultaneously. Thus, possible adaption problems between production technology and handling operations including discrepancies in handling time can be detected early and bottlenecks can be found. Taking this into account, an *integrated micro process chain* (Fig. 2) is suggested to provide a basis for production planning in micro cold forming. It illustrates the interaction between manufacturing technology, handling and transportation and quality management. The idea of the integration of these main fields of a production process bases on the experiences gained in the CRC 747, an interdisciplinary research project. Processes in all three areas are in state of development and strongly depend on each other. Taking into account the fragileness of the micro parts, their relatively high adhesion forces and sensitivity to environmental parameters like temperature or dust, handling devices have to pick up parts directly from the machine tools. In general, standardized handling techniques cannot be used for these tasks.

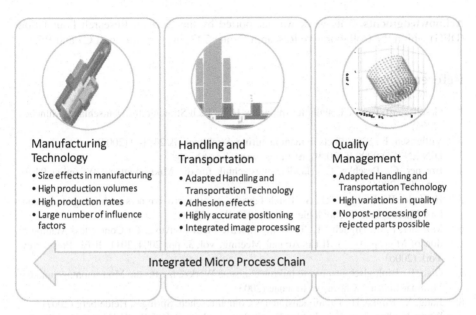

Fig. 2. Micro process chain integrating micro specific planning requirements in manufacturing technology, handling and transportation, and quality management

The planning of processes in micro cold forming requires a plan of material flow including details like the orientation of the part, whether or not the parts are transported individually or in a component carrier, or the production velocity. With simultaneous consideration of all theses parameters and the quality requirements and geometric features of the product, a suitable measurement technology has to be chosen, respectively developed. Project reality has shown, that even the (from a macro production point of view) obvious correlations and planning steps are not self-evident in micro production. Therefore, the focus of development cannot be restrained to manufacturing technology but must also be pointed to the interaction between machines, handling devices and measurement instruments.

6 Summary

We outlined the challenges in micro production with emphasis on handling and quality test operations. Due to high accuracy and a strong dependency between quality, handling and manufacturing in micro production processes, these three fields should be considered while planning and modeling micro processes. The proposed concept of the integrated view of micro process chain provides a framework for the generation of a planning tool kit for production planning with respect to specific characteristics in micro production. A modeling method which takes into account the correlations between the different parameters of all three areas will be the objective of further research.

Acknowledgments. This work was supported by the German Research Foundation (DFG) within the Collaborative Research Center 747, in cooperation of C4 and B5.

References

1. Gesellschaft, F.: Die Fraunhofer Initiative: High-Tech Strategie für Deutschland. München (2006)
2. Vollertsen, F.: Size effects in manufacturing. Strahltechnik 24, 1–9 (2003)
3. DIN EN ISO 9000 ff (2009), http://www.beuth.de
4. Brecher, C., Peschke, C.: Handhabungstechnik für die Mikromontage. Wt online 94(9), 395–397 (2004)
5. Hoxhold, B., Büttgenbach, S.: Batch fabrication of micro grippers with integrated actuators. Microsystem Technologies 14(12), 917–924 (2008)
6. Moesner, F.M., Higuchi, T.: Traveling Electric Field Conveyer for Contactless Manipulation of Microparts. In: IEEE Annual Meeting, vol. 3, pp. 2004–2011. IEEE Press, New York (2006)
7. Qiao, F.: Biologisch inspirierte mikrotechnische Werkzeuge für die Mikromontage und die Minimal-Invasive Chirurgie. Ilmenau (2003)
8. Jiang, X., Bunke, H.: Dreidimensionales Computersehen. Springer, Heidelberg (2007)
9. Wang, N., Kopylow, C.v., Lübke, K., Goch, G., Scholz-Reiter, B., Kirchheim, A., Albertin, E.: Schnelle Qualitätsprüfung mikroumgeformter Bauteile. Industrie-Management 25(1), 62–65 (2009)

Improvement Tools for NEH Based Heuristics on Permutation and Blocking Flow Shop Scheduling Problems

Ramon Companys[*], Imma Ribas, and Manel Mateo

Dpto. de Organización de Empresas, Escuela Técnica Superior de Ingeniería Industrial de Barcelona, Universidad Politécnica de Cataluña, Av. Diagonal 647, 08028 Barcelona
{ramon.companys,imma.ribas,manel.mateo}@upc.edu

Abstract. In this paper, two tools to improve the performance of the NEH-based heuristics for the flow shop problem with and without buffer constraints are proposed. The first tool is the use of the reversibility property of the problems considered and the second one is a new tie-breaking strategy to be use in the insertion phase of the NEH heuristic. In addition, we have analyzed the behavior of five initial solution procedures for both problems. The analysis of results confirms the effectiveness of the measures proposed and allows us to recommend the best ordering procedure for each one of the problems.

Keywords: Scheduling, heuristic algorithms, permutation flow shop, blocking flow shop.

1 Introduction

This work deals with the permutation flow shop scheduling problem with and without storage space between stages. If there is enough storage space between successive machines, when a job finishes its operation can leave the machine. But, if there is no storage space between stages, intermediate queues of jobs waiting in the system for their next operation are not allowed. If operation on machine j for a job i is finished and the next machine, $j+1$, is still busy on the previous job, the completed job i has to be blocked into machine j. For simplicity purposes we shall refer to these problems as PFSP (permutation) and BFSP (blocking), respectively.

The most common criterion, here considered, is the minimization of the makespan or maximum completion time. Using the proposed notation by Graham et al. [1], these two problems are denoted by $Fm \mid prmu \mid C_{max}$ and $Fm \mid block \mid C_{max}$.

The PFSP has become one of the most intensively investigated topics in scheduling since the publication of the paper of Johnson [2]. For $m \geq 3$ the problem is shown to be strongly NP-hard [3]. Nawaz et al. [4] proposed a NEH heuristic which is considered one of the best heuristics for the PFSP. The NEH procedure can be divided into two steps: (1) the generation of an initial order for the jobs applying the Largest Processing Time (LPT) rule and (2) the iterative insertion of jobs, in a partial sequence, in accordance with the initial order obtained in the first step. Given its efficiency, this procedure has been widely

---

[*] Corresponding author.

B. Vallespir and T. Alix (Eds.): APMS 2009, IFIP AICT 338, pp. 33–40, 2010.

studied and different variants of it have been proposed in the literature. Nagano and Moccellin [5] proposed a different initial ordering; Framinan et al. [6] examined 176 rules used to obtain the initial sequence and showed that the ordering proposed initially in the NEH heuristic is the one which obtains the best results when the objective is to minimize the makespan. However among these rules, the Nagano and Moccelin's [5], the trapezium [7], the Pour's [8] and the *Profile Fitting* procedures are not included.

Considering now the BFSP, Reddi and Ramamoorthy [9] showed that exist a polynomial algorithm for $F2 \mid block \mid C_{max}$, which gives an exact solution. Hall and Sriskandarajah [10] showed, using a result from Papadimitriou and Kanellakis [11], that $Fm \mid block \mid C_{max}$ problem for $m \geq 3$ machines is strongly NP-hard.

In this paper we propose two tools to improve the performance of the NEH-based heuristics: the use of the reversibility property of problems considered and a new tie-breaking strategy to be used in the step 2. The computational results show the effectiveness of these tools. In addition, we have compared the performance of four initial sequencing procedures with the NEH's sequencing rule (LPT).

2   Problem Statement

At instant zero there are n jobs which must be processed, in the same order, in m machines. Each job goes from machine 1 to machine m. The process time for each operation is $p_{j,i}$, being $p_{j,i} > 0$, where $j \in \{1,2,...,m\}$ indicates the machine and $i \in \{1,2,...,n\}$ the job. The setup times are included in the processing time. The objective function considered is the minimization of the makespan, which is equivalent to maximizing the use of the machines.

Given a permutation, P, of the n jobs, [k] indicates the job in position k in the sequence. Given a feasible schedule associated to a permutation, $e_{j,k}$ is defined as the initial instant in which the job that occupies position k starts to be processed in the machine j and $f_{j,k}$ is defined as the instant when the job that occupies position k in machine j is finished. The PFSP can be expressed with the following formulation:

$$e_{j,k} + p_{j,[k]} \leq f_{j,k} \qquad j=1,2,...,m \qquad k=1,2,...,n \qquad (1)$$

$$e_{j,k} \geq f_{j,k-1} \qquad j=1,2,...,m \qquad k=1,2,...,n \qquad (2)$$

$$e_{j,k} \geq f_{j-1,k} \qquad j=1,2,...,m \qquad k=1,2,...,n \qquad (3)$$

$$C_{max} = f_{m,n} \qquad (4)$$

being, $f_{j,0} = 0 \quad \forall j$, $f_{0,k} = 0 \quad \forall k$, the initial conditions.

The program is semi-active if the equation (1) is written as $e_{j,k} + p_{j,[k]} = f_{j,k}$ and the equations (2) and (3) are summarized as $e_{jk} = \max\{f_{j,k-1}; f_{j-1,k}\}$.

As it is said, when there is no storage space between stages, BFSP case, if a job i finishes its operation on machine j and the next machine, $j+1$, is still processing the previous job, the completed job i has to remain in machine j until machine j+1 is free. This condition requires an additional equation (5) in the formulation of the problem.

$$f_{j,k} \geq f_{j+1,k-1} \qquad\qquad j=1,2,...,m \qquad k=1,2,...,n \qquad\qquad (5)$$

The initial condition $f_{m+1,k} = 0$ $k=1,2,...,n$ must be added.

The schedule obtained is semi-active if equation (1) and (5) is summarized as (5'):

$$f_{j,k} = \min\{r_{j,k} + p_{j,[k]}, f_{j+1,k-1}\} \; . \qquad\qquad (6')$$

Consequently, the Fm | prmu | C_{max} problem can be seen as a relaxation of the Fm | block | C_{max} problem.

Both problems, Fm | prmu | C_{max} and Fm | block | C_{max}, are reversible. Given an instance I, which can be called direct instance, with processing times $p_{j,i}$, one can determine another instance I', which can be called inverse instance, with processing times $p'_{j,i}$ calculated as (6) :

$$p'_{j,i} = p_{m-j+1,i} \qquad j = 1, 2, ..., m \qquad i = 1, 2, ..., n \qquad\qquad (7)$$

For a permutation P, the value C_{max} in I is the same as the one given in I' for the inverse permutation P'. So, the minimum of maximum completion time is the same for I and I', and the permutations associated to both instances are inverse one each other. Therefore, it does not matter to solve I or to solve I'.

3 Heuristics

As it is mentioned above, the NEH heuristic is considered one of the best heuristic for the PFSP and it has also a good performance for the BFSP [12]. It consists of two steps:

Step 1: ordering jobs according the LPT rule.

Step 2: in accordance with the order established in step 1, take the first two jobs and schedule them in such a way that they minimize the partial makespan, considering an instance with only two jobs. Then for $k=3$ up to n, insert the k-th job into one of the possible k positions of the partial sequence. The objective is to minimize the C_{max} with k jobs.

For step 1, we have considered four initial sequencing procedures, from the literature: the proposed by Nagano and Moccellin's [5], (NM), the *Trapezium* [7] (TR), the proposed by Pour [8] (PO) and the *Profile Fitting* [13] (PF). The three first procedures were designed for the PFSP, whereas the last one was specially designed for the BFSP.

For step 2, we propose a new tie breaking method when two different positions give the same makespan. This method consists in calculating the total idle time (IT) for each position as (7):

$$\sum_{j=1}^{m} IT(j) = \sum_{j=1}^{m}\left(f_{j,n} - e_{j,1} - \sum_{i=1}^{n} p_{j,i} \right) \qquad\qquad (8)$$

If there is a tie between two positions the job is inserted in the position with lower total idle time. If there is still a tie, the procedure defined in [14] for NEHKK1 is used.

Finally, as a second way to improve the solutions, we apply the procedures on the direct and inverse instance retaining the best of both solutions.

4 Computational Experience

The objective of the computational experience is to analyze the effectiveness of the proposed tools and to compare the performance of the sequencing procedures considered in step 1 to find the best procedure for each problem. We shall refer as NME2 to the variant of the proposed algorithm with NM rule [5] in step 1, as TRE2 to the variant with TR rule [7], as POE2 to the one with the PO procedure [8] and, finally, as PLE2 to the variant with PF rule [13]. As in PF rule, there is no efficient criterion for determining which job is the most suitable for the first position; therefore, we have chosen the job with the largest processing time (named as PL).

The test has been done running the algorithms on two different problem sets: the Taillard's benchmarks (1993) and nine generated sets of a thousand instances, with 3, 4 and 5 machines and 13, 14 and 15 jobs. For these instances, namely LOI instances, the optimal solutions, for the $Fm \mid prmu \mid C_{max}$ and for the $Fm \mid block \mid C_{max}$ problem, were obtained by the LOMPEN algorithm [15]. The experiments were carried out on an Intel Core 2 Duo E8400 CPU, 3GHz and 2GB of RAM memory.

To analyze the experimental results we have used the index I_{hi} calculated as (9):

$$I_{hi} = \frac{Heur_{hi} - Best_i}{Best_i} x100. \tag{9}$$

Where $Heur_{hi}$ is the average of the makespan values obtained by the heuristic h. and $Best_i$ is optimum or the lowest makespan known for instance i.

4.1 The Fm|prmu|C_{max} Problem

The Taillard instances are arranged on 12 sets of ten instances each, the sets differs by the values of the couple (n, m). Optimal or best known solutions are found in http://ina2.eivd.ch/collaborateurs/etd/problemes.dir/ordonnancement.dir/flowshop.dir/best_lb_up.txt.

Table 1. Average of I_{hi}, on Taillard instances, for $Fm \mid prmu \mid C_{max}$ for each tie breaking method

	NEH0	NEH1	NEH_KK1	NEH_IT
20x5	3.3	2.69	2.73	**2.52**
20x10	4.6	4.35	**4.31**	4.32
20x20	3.73	3.68	**3.41**	3.54
50x5	0.73	0.87	**0.59**	0.6
50x10	5.07	5.08	4.87	**4.83**
50x20	6.66	6.51	6.42	**5.77**
100x5	0.53	0.48	0.4	**0.35**
100x10	2.21	2.1	**1.77**	2.08
100x20	5.34	**5.28**	**5.28**	5.43
200x10	1.26	1.19	1.16	**1.02**
200x20	4.42	4.42	4.25	**4.19**
500x20	2.06	1.98	2.03	**1.96**
All	3.33	3.22	3.1	**3.05**

First, to analyze the effectiveness of the tie breaking method proposed, we have compared the average values of index I_{hi} for the original NEH procedure (denoted as NHE0), the two tie breaking methods proposed in Kalcynski and Kamburowski [14] (denoted as NEH1and NEH_KK1) and the tie breaking here proposed (denoted as NEH_IT). The values corresponding to each version of the NEH procedure are shown in Table 1. To carry out this comparison we have applied the procedures only on the direct instances.

As it can be seen in Table 1, the minimum overall average value of index I_{hi} is obtained when our tie breaking method is applied. Therefore, we can conclude that it is an effective tool to improve the performance of the NEH heuristic.

Table 2. Average of I_{hi}, for Taillard instances for Fm | prmu | C_{max} problem

n x m	NEH	NEH2	NME	NME2	TRE	TRE2	POE	POE2	PLE	PLE2
20x5	2.69	2.32	2.58	2.29	2.71	1.77	3.51	2.40	2.82	2.14
20x10	4.42	3.80	4.20	3.05	6.18	4.29	4.99	4.39	5.31	4.22
20x20	3.71	3.43	4.23	3.62	5.01	4.44	5.12	4.09	4.01	3.57
50x5	0.57	0.56	0.92	0.67	1.04	0.64	1.06	0.79	0.96	0.55
50x10	5.05	4.34	4.91	4.72	6.01	5.53	5.96	5.24	5.00	4.44
50x20	5.78	5.76	5.82	5.60	8.05	7.14	6.93	6.71	6.68	6.15
100x5	0.36	0.35	0.45	0.35	0.67	0.39	0.66	0.44	0.52	0.38
100x10	2.06	1.65	2.18	1.71	3.17	2.46	2.76	2.44	2.26	1.88
100x20	5.43	5.00	5.47	5.03	6.68	6.39	6.43	6.07	5.24	4.84
200x10	1.07	0.97	1.12	0.96	1.42	1.13	1.57	1.18	1.12	0.96
200x20	4.11	3.96	4.19	3.94	5.34	4.98	4.94	4.81	4.29	4.16
500x20	2.02	1.80	1.91	1.82	3.17	2.85	2.75	2.70	2.21	1.96
All	3.11	2.83	3.16	2.81	4.12	3.50	3.89	3.44	3.37	2.94

Next, to compare the improvement obtained when the reversibility property is used we have reported (Table 2) the average values of I_{hi} for each set of Taillard instances and procedure. Number 2 is omitted from the name of variants when procedures are applied only on the direct instance. It can be observed that the performance increases, between 10 and 20%, when the procedures are applied on the direct and inverse instances retaining the best of both solutions

Table 3. Average CPU time, in seconds, required by each variant on each instance

n x m	NEH2	NME2	TRE2	POE2	PLE2
20x5	0.02	0.01	0.01	0.07	0.02
20x10	0.03	0.02	0.03	0.13	0.02
20x20	0.06	0.04	0.06	0.23	0.04
50x5	0.13	0.13	0.25	1.21	0.27
50x10	0.25	0.26	0.25	1.51	0.26
50x20	0.50	0.52	0.81	3.44	0,494
100x5	1.01	1.03	1.00	13.95	1.08
100x10	2.00	2.03	2.91	20.60	2.44
100x20	3.94	4.04	4.84	32.21	4.12
200x10	16.01	15.99	16.01	283.57	19.17
200x20	31.47	33.33	31.44	437.35	38.03
500x20	500.95	491.01	493.04	15147.06	588.98

Regarding the performance of the proposed variants, we can say, according to the overall average value of index I_{hi} (Table 2), that NME2 is slightly better than NEH2. It is worth noting that PLE2, with an initial procedure designed for the blocking problem, has better results than TRE2 and POE2.

To analyze the efficiency of these procedures, we have reported in Table 3, the CPU time required by each. It can be observed that all variants require a similar time except POE 2 which requires much more time.

The results obtained for the second set of problems, LOI instances, confirm the little advantage of NME2. Table 4 show the average value of I_{hi} for each set of instances and procedure. In all cases, the CPU time required to solve each instance is lower than 0.014 seconds.

Table 4. Average values of I_{hi} for each set of LOI instances and each heuristic

nxm	NEH2	NME2	TRE2	POE2	PLE2
13×3	0.24	0.17	0.27	0.26	0.23
13×4	0.88	0.76	0.86	0.88	0.82
13×5	1.59	1.52	1.59	1.60	1.41
14×3	0.24	0.18	0.27	0.32	0.21
14×4	0.79	0.70	0.85	0.91	0.71
14×5	1.59	1.46	1.69	1.71	1.43
15×3	0.17	0.13	0.24	0.23	0.18
15×4	0.75	0.65	0.84	0.84	0.67
15×5	1.49	1.44	1.65	1.68	1.47
All	0.86	0.78	0.92	0.94	0.79

4.2 The Fm|block|C_{max} Problem

First, we analyze the improvement obtained by applying the procedures on the direct and inverse instance obtaining the best of both solutions. For the BFSP problem, the best known solutions are found in Companys [16]. The average values of index I_{hi} by set and procedure are shown in Table 5. It can be seen that the improvement reached with the reversibility property tool is between 4 and 12%, less than for the permutation problem but significant.

Table 5. Average values of I_{hi} for Taillard instances for Fm│block│C_{max} problem

nxm	NEH	NEH2	NME	NME2	TRE	TRE2	POE	POE2	PLE	PLE2
20x5	5.09	4.94	6.32	4.85	7.02	5.05	5.95	5.20	5.27	4.57
20x10	5.45	5.23	5.83	4.27	5.75	5.05	6.24	4.76	4.68	4.16
20x20	3.39	3.37	4.03	2.80	4.11	3.66	4.25	3.70	4.02	3.12
50x5	8.76	8.42	8.43	7.81	9.30	8.32	7.68	7.27	8.62	8.02
50x10	7.96	7.15	8.11	7.64	7.43	6.91	7.25	6.23	7.14	6.75
50x20	7.10	6.87	6.69	6.26	5.97	5.34	5.55	4.85	5.17	5.03
100x5	7.52	7.25	7.92	7.63	8.33	8.01	7.17	6.73	7.63	7.19
100x10	6.81	6.72	6.70	6.27	6.38	6.07	6.16	5.62	6.69	6.58
100x20	5.55	5.30	5.70	5.18	5.42	4.70	4.54	4.41	4.75	4.48
200x10	6.95	6.74	6.80	6.59	6.82	6.54	6.43	5.93	6.73	6.48
200x20	4.36	4.12	4.49	4.28	3.74	3.47	3.54	3.20	3.82	3.70
500x20	3.62	3.46	3.58	3.41	2.90	2.83	2.87	2.69	3.25	3.04
All	6.05	5.80	6.22	5.58	6.10	5.50	5.63	5.05	5.65	5.26

Regarding the performance of the variants, we can see that POE2 has the lowest overall average value of index I_{hi} followed by PLE2. But, POE2 requires much more time than the others, as can be seen in Table 6. Therefore it is more recommendable PLE2 than POE2.

Table 6. Average CPU times, in second, required by each variant on each instance

nxm	NEH2	NME2	TRE2	POE2	PLE2
20x5	0.02	0.02	0.02	0.04	0.02
20x10	0.03	0.03	0.04	0.16	0.03
20x20	0.09	0.10	0.09	0.30	0.07
50x5	0.18	0.36	0.35	1.99	0.37
50x10	0.70	0.73	0.70	2.69	0.45
50x20	1.38	1.43	1.40	4.05	0.89
100x5	2.35	2.36	2.36	15.02	1.74
100x10	3.77	3.80	3.76	22.62	3.46
100x20	6.56	6.67	6.60	36.34	6.90
200x10	26.95	23.95	23.03	300.99	27.73
200x20	45.46	46.03	46.44	472.30	54.49
500x20	839.49	863.26	714.87	18713.45	841.75

The overall average of index I_{hi} obtained in the second test (Table 7), with the LOI instances, confirm this little advantage of POE2. But, due to the large CPU time required we recommend PLE2 to be used for the BFSP.

Table 7. Average values of I_{hi} for each set of LOI instances and each heuristic

nxm	NEH2	NME2	TRE2	POE2	PLE2
All	3.98	3.61	3.76	3.44	3.50

5 Conclusions

The computational experience shows the effectiveness of the tie breaking procedure and the use of the reversibility property as a way to improve the performance of the NEH-based heuristic. Regarding the performance of the variants implemented, we have seen that the behaviour of the algorithms on the permutation and the blocking cases are different. For $Fm \mid prmu \mid C_{max}$ problem, NME2 and NEH2 are the best procedures are. However, for $Fm \mid block \mid C_{max}$ problem, the best ones are POE2 and PLE2, but due to the CPU time necessary by POE2, PLE2 is more recommendable.

References

1. Graham, R.L., Lawler, E.L., Lenstra, J.K., Rinnooy Kan, A.H.G.: Optimization and approximation in deterministic sequencing and scheduling: A survey. In: Annals of Discrete Mathematics, pp. 5287–5326 (1979)

2. Johnson, S.M.: Optimal two- and three-stage production schedules with set up times included. Naval Research Logistics Quarterly 1, 61–68 (1954)
3. Garey, M.R., Johnson, D.S.: Computers and intractability: A guide to the theory of NP-Completness. Freeman, San Francisco (1979)
4. Nawaz, M., Enscore Jr., E.E., Ham, I.: A heuristic algorithm for the m-machine, n-job flow-shop sequencing problem. Omega 11, 91–95 (1983)
5. Nagano, M.S., Moccellin, J.V.: A high quality constructive heuristic for flow shop sequencing. Journal of the Operational Research Society 53, 1374–1379 (2002)
6. Framinan, J.M., Leisten, R., Ramamoorthy, B.: Different initial sequences for the heuristic of Nawaz, Enscore and Ham to minimize makespan, idletime or flowtime in the static permutation flowshop sequencing problem. International Journal of Production Research 41, 121–148 (2003)
7. Companys, R.: Métodos heurísticos en la resolución del problema del taller mecánico. Estudios Empresariales 5, 7–18 (1966)
8. Pour, H.D.: A new heuristic for the n-job, m-machine flow shop problem. Production Planning & Control 12, 648–653 (2001)
9. Reddi, S.S., Ramamoorthy, B.: On the flow-shop sequencing problem with no wait in process. Opers Res. Q. 23, 323–331 (1972)
10. Hall, N.G., Sriskandarajah, C.: A survey of machine scheduling problems with blocking and no wait in process. Operations Research 44, 510–525 (1996)
11. Papadimitriou, C.H., Kanellakis, P.C.: Flowshop scheduling with limited temporary storage. Journal of the ACM 27, 533–549 (1980)
12. Leisten, R.: Flowshop sequencing problems with limited buffer storage. Int. J. Prod. Res. 28, 2085–2100 (1990)
13. McCormick, S.T., Pinedo, M.L., Shenker, S., Wolf, B.: Sequencing in an Assembly Line with Blocking to Minimize Cycle Time. Operations Research 37, 925–936 (1989)
14. Kalczynski, P.J., Kamburowski, J.: An improved NEH heuristic to minimize makespan in permutation flow shops. Computers & Operations Research 9, 3001–3008 (2008)
15. Companys, R., Mateo, M.: Different behaviour of a double branch-and-bound algorithm on $Fm|prmu|C_{max}$ and $Fm|block|C_{max}$ problems. Computers & Operations Research 34, 938–953 (2007)
16. Companys, R.: Note on the blocking flowshop problem. Working paper (2009), http://upcommons.upc.edu/e-prints/handle/2117/420

A Basic Study
on the Installation of Distributed Autonomous
Production Scheduling System
in Ubiquitous Environment

Susumu Fujii, Tomomitsu Motohashi,
Takashi Irohara, and Yuichiro Miyamoto

Dept. of Information and Communication Sciences, Sophia University,
7-1, Kioi-cho, Chiyoda, Tokyo 102-8554 Japan
{susumu-f,tomomi-m,irohara,miyamoto}@sophia.ac.jp

Abstract. This paper considers an auction-based scheduling system in a job shop equipped with ubiquitous network environment to cope with dynamically changing market demands. Under such environment all machines and jobs are assumed to have computing and communication devices and can serve as intelligent agents. The functions for an auctioneer and for a participant are investigated to install the scheduling system as a distributed multi-agent system. The systems sending and receiving messages for the auction form a distributed system on a network, enabling an autonomous scheduling.

Keywords: Job shop scheduling, Two-way auction, Multi agent, Ubiquitous Network.

1 Introduction

Recent advances in the information and computer technology (ICT) are realizing a ubiquitous network environment in the factories. Dynamically changing market demands strongly require quick and timely responses of the manufacturing industries and force to fully utilize all assets in the factories by effectively and efficiently controlling and managing them with the aides of advanced ICT.

In the present advanced factories, most of the machine tools are devised with computers connected to information networks, enabling the real time data gathering and order dispatching. In the previous study [1], auction-based scheduling procedures, named one-way and two-way auctions, are proposed for a job shop equipped with the ubiquitous computing and communication environment. In this study, the software architecture to realize the proposed auction based scheduling procedure is investigated considering machine tools and work pieces, jobs hereafter, as intelligent agents playing roles of an auctioneer and participants in the auction.

A job shop model and the auction methods considered in this study are firstly outlined. The software architecture is then described as the functions for the auctioneer and the participant.

B. Vallespir and T. Alix (Eds.): APMS 2009, IFIP AICT 338, pp. 41–48, 2010.

2 Manufacturing Systems and Auction Methods

In this chapter, a job shop model considered in this study is firstly described and then the basic auction procedure and a two way auction procedure are illustrated.

2.1 Objective Model of Manufacturing System

This study considers a manufacturing system or a shop floor as an objective model, which consists of m automated machine tools connected to an information network. The system accepts n different kinds of products, each of which can be processed by one or more machines specified in advance. Machines are categorized into k types corresponding to the processing capability of jobs. Each job carries the information, such as the kind of product, the processing time and the due date. The processing time of a same kind of products may vary depending on the machine type. The setup times from one product kind to the other are given for each type of machines.

Arrived jobs will de assigned to machines which can process each job by a predetermined scheduling procedure if one or more machines are empty. If all machines which can process the jobs in the queue are busy, arrived jobs will line up in the queue waiting for the assignment. In this study, each job is assumed to have an intelligent devise which enables to process and store the information required for the execution of the scheduling procedure and to communicate with all machines independently. In practice, such functions will be replaced by a computer facilitated at storages holding the queue such as warehouses, pallet pools and so on.

2.2 Auction-Based Scheduling Procedure

In this study, jobs at the shop floor are assumed to be scheduled dynamically by a real time scheduling method to be proposed. The procedure is based on the auction between machines and jobs. In the auction-based scheduling procedures reported in [2,3,4], the bid value is evaluated as a weighted sum of some measures, such as processing time, due date, slack time and so on, and the new bid value raised for the new round is obtained by changing the weight to each measure in a predetermined manner. The auction procedure proposed in our previous study [1] adopts a bidding strategy to change the measure to be used as a bid value, bid criterion hereafter, from one round to the other as outlined below. The basic procedure is further modified to a scheduling procedure at the shop floor as one way auction procedures for the machine selection and the job selection as described later.

[Basic Auction Procedure]

<Step 1> The auctioneer broadcasts the information of the commodity to the participants. For the first round the first bid criterion is applied in the application order of bid criteria and the all participants are the bidders. After the second round, the bid criterion is selected from the application order list and the participants are the survived bidders in the preceding round except otherwise specified.

<Step 2> Each participant determines the bid value for the bid criterion indicated by the auctioneer and reports it to the auctioneer.

<Step 3> The auctioneer selects the best bid value. Go to Step 5 if the best value is reported by only one bidder, otherwise go to Step 4.

<Step 4> The auctioneer changes the bid criterion to the next one in the application order list if the criterion is not the last one in the list and go to Step 1. If the bid criterion is the last one, the auctioneer selects one winner randomly from the survived bidders reporting the best value and go to Step 5.

<Step 5> The commodity is awarded to the winner and the auction is terminated.

One Way Auction for Machine Selection. When a job arrives at the shop, an auction to select a machine to process the job will be initiated. The auctioneer and the commodity is the job itself. Machines, idle or free machines in most of the cases, are the participants. If all free or idle machines can not process the job, the auction will be terminated and the job will line up in the job queue.

One Way Auction for Job Selection. When a machine completes the processing of a job and becomes idle, an auction to select a job to process will be initiated. The auctioneer and the commodity is the machine and all jobs in the queue are the participants. If there is no job to process, the machine will line up in the idling machine queue.

2.3 Bid Criteria

As bid criteria in the auction, measures or rules used in the ordinary dispatching procedures are acceptable. In this study, FCFS (First Come First Service), EDD (Earliest Due Date), MS (Minimum Slack), SPT (Shortest Processing time), SST (Shortest Setup Time), Availability (Idling or Busy) and Capability (Processable or Not Processable) are considered as bid criteria.

These criteria are applied one after another in the predetermined order in the auction. Availability and Capability are firstly applied in the machine selection to select machines which are idling and can process the job, but only Capability is applied in the job selection since the auctioneer is an idling machine. The application orders of these criteria in the auction significantly affect the system performance as discussed in [1].

2.4 Two Way Auction-Based Scheduling

To avoid the dominant effect of the bid criterion applied after the default criteria on the scheduling performance in a heavily loaded shop floor, a two way auction procedure for the job selection auction is proposed in [1] as described in the following.

[Two Way Auction for Job Selection]
<Step1> When a machine M_i completes a job processing and becomes free, or returned from Step 3, M_i initiates a one way auction for the job selection as the auctioneer. If no job is selected, the auction is terminated and M_i lines up in the idling machine queue. If a job J_k is selected by the auction, go to Step 2.

<Step2> J_k initiates a one way auction for the machine selection as the auctioneer. In this auction all machines assume to process J_k after completing all jobs already loaded on them. If the selected machine M_j is the initiating machine M_i, J_k is assigned to M_i, and the auction is terminated. Otherwise go to Step 3.

<Step3> J_k is temporarily assigned to M_j loading at the end of its loaded jobs. J_k is also temporarily deleted from the job queue. If the job queue becomes empty, go to Step 4. Otherwise go to Step 1 for the secondary auction.

<Step4> The temporarily assigned jobs during the auction are released to the job queue and M_i again initiates a one way auction for the job selection and the selected job is assigned to it. The bid criteria applied may differ from those in Step 1. Then the auction is terminated.

3 Software Architecture of Auction System

An auction based scheduling procedure is proposed in the above to cope with dynamically changing manufacturing circumstances utilizing the recent advanced ubiquitous network environment. Machine tools, jobs and other facilities at the shop floor are assumed to be equipped with computing and communicating devices and autonomously develop appropriate schedules communicating each other through the network. In this chapter the software system installed on each machine or job is considered as an intelligent agent and the necessary functions and the architecture of each agent are investigated to realize such environment.

3.1 Basic Functions of Agent

The NC controller of CNC machines is equipped with the basic functions as an intelligent agent. The communication function checks messages on the network and if a message is addressed to the machine it will be analyzed to identify the proper activities to perform, such as handling the pallet, processing a work piece, updating track records in the data base and so on. After finishing such activity, a proper message may be sent to an addressee when necessary.

In this study, all agents in the job shop are assumed to have the communication function, i.e., receiving, sending and analyzing messages, the execution function of the activity and the data bases necessary for the operations. Each agent staying in the shop is assigned an agent specific local IP and a common multicast IP assigned to the shop. Local IP and multicast IP are assigned to jobs when they arrive at the shop.

3.2 Machine Agent and Job Agent

In Fig. 1, functions for a machine agent are shown with their relation. As described in the previous session, F1, F2, F3, F7-F10 in Fig. 1 are the basic functions of a machine agent. Three data bases necessary for the real operations of NC machine are A. Operational record DB, B. Job processing DB and C. Tooling DB.

Auctioneer and participant functions, F5 and F6, are to be installed for the auction based scheduling procedure and the simulation function, F4, is necessary to obtain a schedule for certain time period, e.g., one hour, one shift, one day and so on. A

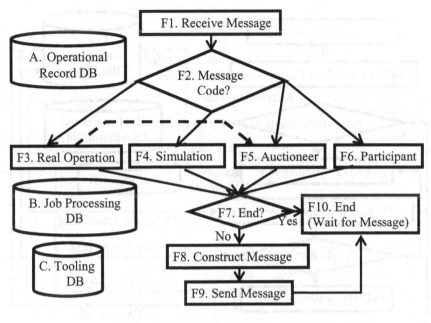

Fig. 1. Architecture of machine agent

received message in F1 is firstly distinguished whether it is addressed to the machine or not. If it is not, the next function is to wait for a next message in F10. In F2, a proper function, F3, F4, F5 or F6, is identified by analyzing the message code.

The real operation function in F3 is the one in the basic function, but is modified to initiate an auction procedure for the job selection to request a job to process as shown by dotted line when the machine completes the processing of a job and becomes empty. Data bases are referred by F5 and F6 while the auction procedure is in progress. In the simulation, duplicated data bases at the starting time of simulation are generated to serve as those for simulation.

The real job agent has similar functions as those of a machine agent, where the real operation is to report its arrival to the shop and to register processing data including due date to the data base in the shop or in a warehouse accepting incoming jobs. A job agent arriving at the shop initiates an auction for the machine selection and provides a job data base instead of three data bases in Fig. 1 to store its processing data, the arrival time, the due date and other status data required for the auction procedure.

3.3 Functions for Auctioneer and for Participant

As described in Chapter 2, auctions, one-way and two-way, are initiated by a job for the machine selection and a machine for the job selection. Since the detail procedures of auction for the auctioneer and the participants depend on the type of auction and the main or secondary auction in the two-way auction, the configuration of the functions for the auctioneer and participant will be partially different accordingly. This section describes the functions only in the main auction, of which configurations for an auctioneer and a participant are shown in Figs. 2 and 3, respectively.

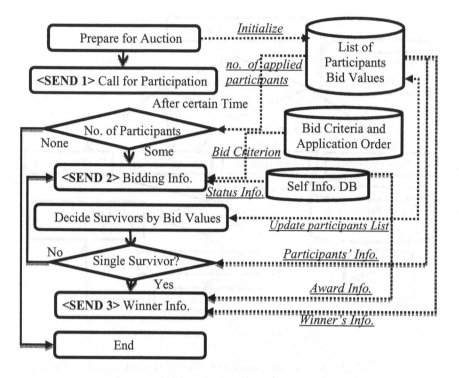

Fig. 2(a). Sending system of messages for the auctioneer

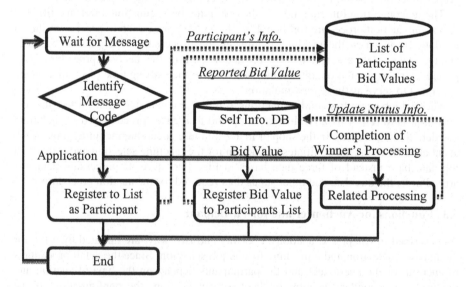

Fig. 2(b). Receiving System of messages for the auctioneer

Figures 2(a) and 2(b) show the sending and the receiving systems of messages. When an auction is initiated, the auctioneer calls for participation for the auction. The calling message with the machine capability for the job selection and with the kind of job for the machine selection, is broadcasted to all members in the shop (A-SEND 1). The message is received by a participants system in Fig. 3. The message is identified by the message code and decision is made whether to apply or not by referring the commodity information to its status and capability in the self information data base. The application message is sent to the auctioneer's local IP by PtoP manner (P-SEND 1). The communication could be made by broadcasting, but PtoP is adopted to ensure the reliable communication. All applications for the participation are received by the receiving system in Fig. 2(b) and their local IPs are registered to the participants list.

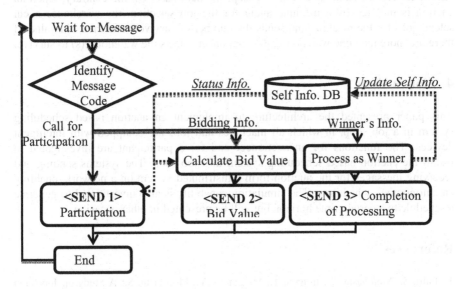

Fig. 3. Receiving and sending system for the participant

After waiting for predetermined time, which is sufficient to receive messages from all members in the shop, the sending system for the auctioneer counts the number of participants to the auction. If there is no participant, the auction is terminated after putting the auctioneer in the queue of empty machines or unprocessed jobs. If there are some, the bid criterion for the first auction is sent to each participant (A-SEND 2). The message received by the participant's system in Fig. 3 is identified as the one to calculate the bid value. The bid value is sent to the auctioneer (P-SEND 2).

The sending system of the auctioneer evaluates the bid values and selects the survivors after confirming all participants reported their values. If only one survived, the participant is the winner and the message of the winner is sent to all participants (A-SEND 3). By this message all participants recognize the auction is terminated. If the survivors are more than one, the bid criterion for the next round is sent to them (A-SEND 2). Participants who failed to survive are also notified their failure.

Participants receiving the new bid criterion calculate the bid value and send back to the auctioneer (P-SEND 2). The procedure will be repeated until a winner is decided or all criteria are exhausted. If the latter occurs, the winner is selected randomly. The winner processes the transaction as a winner and sends the completion message of the processing to confirm (P-SEND 3).

In the above, each job is assumed to be an independent agent. In practice, however, jobs are stored in some storage areas, such as warehouses, pallet pool and so on. To cope with such situation, it is more practical to consider a storage of jobs as an intelligent agent, say a warehouse agent. When a job arrives at the warehouse, the warehouse agent registers the job information and initiates an auction for the machine selection for the job. The configuration of the sending and receiving system of the auctioneer are the same as in Fig. 2 except the data base. On the contrary, when an auction is initiated by a machine agent for the job selection, the warehouse agent selects jobs for the machine and sends the number of survivors and their bid value. If there are more than one warehouse, the auctioneer selects the warehouse(s) to survive.

4 Conclusions

This paper presented the architecture to implement an auction based scheduling system in a job shop, in which all machines and jobs are equipped with intelligent devices. The functions for an auctioneer and for a participant are investigated to install the auction based scheduling system in a job shop. The systems sending and receiving messages for the auction form a distributed system on a network, enabling an autonomous scheduling. The simulation capability is also investigated to generate a schedule to a certain time horizon but will be presented in other occasion.

References

1. Fujii, S., Motohashi, T., Irohara, T., Miyamoto, Y., Moriguchi, S.: A Study on Job Shop Scheduling based on Two-Way Auction in Ubiquitous Environment. In: APMS 2008 (2008)
2. Saygin, C., Siwamogsatham, T.: Auction-based distributed scheduling and control scheme for flexible manufacturing systems. International Journal of Production Research 42(3), 547–572 (2004)
3. Srivinas, Tiwari, M.K., Allada, V.: Solving the machine-loading problem in a flexible manufacturing system using a combinational auction-based approach. International Journal of Production Research 42(9), 1879–1983 (2004)
4. Kumar, V., Kumar, S., Tiwari, M.K., Chan, F.T.S.: Auction-based approach to resolve the scheduling problem in the steel making process. International Journal of Production Research 44(8), 1503–1522 (2006)

Experimental Evaluation of Inventory-Based Discrete-Updating Market Maker for Intra-firm Prediction Market System Using VIPS

Hajime Mizuyama, Morio Ueda, Katsunobu Asada, and Yu Tagaya

Department of Mechanical Engineering and Science,
Kyoto University, Kyoto 606-8501, Japan
mizu@me.kyoto-u.ac.jp

Abstract. This paper develops an intra-firm prediction market system as a collective-knowledge-based forecasting tool for a company and evaluates its performance through laboratory experiments. The system uses the variable-interval prediction security (VIPS) as the prediction security to be traded in the market and is controlled by an original computerized market maker suitable for the security type. The market maker evaluates each unit of VIPS with a Gaussian price distribution and updates the distribution intermittently through an inventory-based updating logic according to the transactions in the market. Laboratory experiments are conducted with a virtual demand forecasting problem to study whether the system functions properly as a subjective forecasting tool. The experiments confirm that the system is capable of penalizing arbitrage actions and hence its performance is fairly stable. Further, the output price distribution can serve as an approximate forecast distribution.

Keywords: Collective knowledge, prediction markets, demand forecasting, information aggregation.

1 Introduction

To obtain an adequate demand forecast for a product in a future time period in the rapidly changing market environment, it is often insufficient or inappropriate to rely only on the information extracted from its historical sales data through a statistical method. Similar difficulties have also been encountered in other forecasting problems in a company, in recent years. Under the circumstances, one of the potentially valuable approaches to tackle the difficulties is to utilize the flexible forecasting capability of human agents, and which can be readily accomplished through a prediction market. The prediction market is a virtual futures market of a prediction security whose worth depends on the unknown realized value of a random variable of interest, and thus the market price of the security provides a dynamic forecast on the random variable reflecting the dispersed knowledge of the participants [1], [2], [3], [4]. Early industrial applications include [5], [6] and [7].

The prediction market is rapidly becoming popular, and now many companies are interested in testing it as an intra-firm forecasting tool. However, most applications

B. Vallespir and T. Alix (Eds.): APMS 2009, IFIP AICT 338, pp. 49–56, 2010.

reported up to now are either for obtaining only a point estimate of a certain variable with the vote-share-type prediction security or for achieving subjective probabilities of the occurrence of several mutually exclusive events with the winner-takes-all-type prediction security. Whereas, most forecasting problems in a company are those require a forecast distribution of a variable of interest. Thus, the authors have introduced a new type of prediction security called the variable-interval prediction security (VIPS) and an intra-firm prediction market system with a computerized market maker suitable for the security type [8].

An arbitral prediction interval regarding the variable of interest can be specified to VIPS, and each unit of which will pay off a prescribed amount of money, when the market is closed, if and only if the realized value of the variable is actually contained in the interval. During the market is open, the computerized market maker accepts every offer of buying or selling VIPS given by a participant at a price calculated according to a Gaussian price distribution. It is also required of the market maker to update the price distribution itself so that it can be regarded as a latest collective forecast of the participants. It is found that a simple weighted average updating logic is vulnerable to arbitrage actions [9]. Hence, the inventory-based updating logic and the book value constraint are further introduced in order to fix the vulnerability [10].

This paper is aimed at implementing the refined market maker into a pilot prediction market system and conducting laboratory experiments on the system to confirm that it can actually diminish the arbitrage actions and will function properly as a subjective forecasting tool in the real world. The remainder of the paper first presents the outline of the developed system, then discusses the experimental design, the experimental results and their implications, and finally concludes the paper.

2   Intra-firm Prediction Market System

2.1   Outline of Pilot Market System

The market system is aimed at providing a company with a continuous forecast distribution of, for example, the demand quantity x of a certain product in a predetermined time period in the future. The system is supposed to be run for a certain time period with not so many participants who are potentially knowledgeable about the variable of interest x, for example, the salespeople of the company. The system provides a marketplace where the participants can buy and sell VIPS concerning x. The transactions are play-money-based and all with the market maker of the system. The play money used is referred to as the prediction dollars (P\$).

Each unit of VIPS pays off a fixed amount of prediction dollars after the market is closed, if and only if the realized value of x is contained in the specified prediction interval. Each participant k $(= 1, 2, ..., K)$ is given a certain amount of prediction dollars as the initial endowment and is properly motivated to invest it on VIPS so as to increase her/his posterior wealth. In the following laboratory experiments, the initial endowment is 10000 (P\$) and the unitary payoff is 100 (P\$).

Each participant k can hold plural units of VIPS but their prediction intervals must be identical. Thus, her/his VIPS holding position can be represented by (a_k, b_k, v_k), where $[a_k, b_k]$ represents the prediction interval and v_k denotes how many units.

Further, the amount of prediction dollars at hand is denoted by u_k. Each participant k can buy some additional VIPS from or sell some of the owned VIPS to the market maker easily by changing the position parameters (a_k, b_k, v_k), as far as u_k does not become negative. In the following laboratory experiments, the values of (a_k, b_k, v_k) are bound to [0, 5000].

The market maker of the system has a Gaussian price density $N(\mu_g, \sigma_g^2)$, whose integral from a_k to b_k times 100 determines the unitary price of VIPS with interval [a_k, b_k]. The price distribution is updated by the market maker intermittently every time an offer of buying or selling VIPS given by a participant has been processed.

2.2 System Architecture and Its Implementation

Simple client-server architecture is used for the pilot market system. The server part is built on a commercial database software and the client part is installed in PCs that are connected to the server machine through LAN. Hence, the entire system can be easily implemented in a typical intranet environment. The server part stores all the necessary information mainly in the asset profile table, the transaction history table and the price history table. The asset profile table contains the current values of a_k, b_k, v_k, and u_k of each participant. Whereas the transaction history table is a stack of the records of these parameter values, etc. with a time stamp corresponding to every transaction. The price history table is a growing list of the values of μ_g and σ_g.

The client part for each participant is realized as a GUI-based system which communicates with the server part in the structured query language. It mainly provides three functions; current status visualization, position change simulation, and transaction realization. The current status visualization function first receives the current asset profile of the participant and the price history information from the server part. Then it visualizes the current shape of the price density distribution and her/his current VIPS holding position simultaneously on a same window, and displays the historical shapes of the price distribution under the window as a sequence of box and whisker plots. It also shows the contingent values of the posterior wealth as a bar chart. Further, by opening a separate window, she/he can consult a simple table showing the current VIPS holding positions of the other participants.

The position change simulation function allows the participant to perform simulations of changing her/his VIPS holding position on the GUI before actually changing it. The simulation can be easily done by dragging the square representing her/his VIPS holding position by a mouse in the main window. Then it shows the resultant contingent values of the posterior wealth after the position change as a separate bar chart. When the participant likes the resultant position, she/he can easily realize it by activating the transaction realization function with pushing a button. Then, the transaction realization function automatically updates the related values in the asset profile table, and adds a record of the updated position, the cost of the update, the parameter values of the corresponding price distribution, the time stamp, etc. to the transaction history table. It also updates the price distribution, and adds a record of the updated values of μ_g and σ_g to the price history table.

2.3 Possible Arbitrage Actions and Their Prevention

As described earlier, a simple weighted average price updating logic was found to be vulnerable to the following arbitrage actions [9]:

A. To escalate the price density around a certain prediction interval by buying many units of VIPS in the area, and then make a profit by soon selling the units at the boom price.

B. To lower the price density around a certain interval she/he actually wants by buying many units of VIPS away from the area, and then buy the interval she/he actually wants at the compressed price.

Thus, the pilot market system developed here diminishes the opportunities for these arbitrage actions by adopting an inventory-based updating logic called the LMSR-like and the book value constraint [10].

The LMSR-like updating logic first captures the inventory of VIPS owned by a participant k as:

$$s_k(x) = \begin{cases} v_k & (a_k \leq x \leq b_k) \\ 0 & \text{otherwise} \end{cases} \tag{1}$$

and the whole inventory of VIPS in the market as $S(x) = s_1(x) + s_2(x) + \cdots + s_K(x)$. It then determines the values of the mean and variance of the price distribution by those values of the distribution of $\exp\{S(x)/\eta\}$, where η is a parameter that controls the price updating sensitivity. This is called the LMSR-like because it can be regarded as a Gaussian approximation of the LMSR market maker proposed by [11].

Whereas the book value constraint works as follows. Each time a participant buys a set of VIPS, the price density at the moment is stored into the database as the book value information corresponding to the set. And when she/he offers to sell, at least a part of, the set later, the offer will be settled at the cheaper price between the corresponding book value and the current market value. When an offered position change has both a selling part and a buying part, the book value constraint has the market maker settle only the selling part first, and after updating the price density once, then settle the remaining buying part. The inventory-based updating logic has a preferable characteristic that when a participant sells a set of VIPS that she/he has just bought, the price distribution goes back to the shape before she/he bought the set. Hence, when combined with the book value constraint, it can diminish the arbitrage opportunities A and B even under the discrete updating frequency.

3 Laboratory Experiments

3.1 Research Questions and Experimental Design

The laboratory experiments are conducted in two experimental sessions. Each session consists of six experimental terms. The number of participants is nine in session 1 and seven in session 2. The participants are graduate or undergraduate students in different departments of Kyoto University. In each term, a virtual sales history of a product from January to September ($d_1, d_2, ..., d_9$) is shown to the participants, and they are expected to speculate on the demand quantity $x = d_{12}$ to be realized in December. The virtual sales history data are generated by:

$$d_t = \beta_0 + \beta_1 \cdot (t - 6.5) + e \qquad\qquad e \sim N(0, 300^2) \qquad\qquad (2)$$

where the values of the parameters β_0 and β_1 are drawn from the uniform distributions [2250, 2750] and [-87.5, 100] respectively. This is formally a simple linear regression problem, but which is not revealed to the participants. In order to make the participants motivated towards the contest to maximize their posterior wealth, the participation fee to be actually paid to them for each term is set to be negatively proportional to the order of their posterior wealth.

The research questions considered in the experiments are whether the refined market maker successfully diminishes the arbitrage actions and whether the price distribution converges to an adequate forecast distribution. To answer the questions, the experimental design matrix shown in the left half of Table 1 is used. The sessions are treated as blocks, and each session is designed as a factorial design between two control factors Eta and Info. Eta represents the sensitivity parameter η of the market maker and has three levels 300, 500 and 700. Info controls how information arrives and has two levels S and D. When Info is S, all the corresponding sales history information is shown to the participants at the beginning of the term and the term is continued for five minutes. Whereas if it is D, only the sales history from January to March is shown to them at starting the term, and when three minutes elapses that from April to June and when six minutes passes the rest of the information are disclosed respectively. In this case, the term lasts nine minutes in total.

Table 1. Experimental design matrix and experimental results

Term	Session	Eta	Info	Pe	Dlt	μ_g	σ_g	Cm	Cs
1	1	300	S	2314	879	2374	321	0.07	0.37
2	1	500	S	2454	1096	2320	404	0.12	0.37
3	1	700	S	2120	1288	2278	671	0.12	0.52
4	1	300	D	2773	1091	2855	324	0.08	0.30
5	1	500	D	2432	1207	2659	611	0.19	0.51
6	1	700	D	2337	850	2474	629	0.16	0.74
7	2	300	S	2200	787	2143	337	0.07	0.43
8	2	500	S	2845	1116	2626	604	0.20	0.54
9	2	700	S	2163	1027	2367	835	0.20	0.81
10	2	300	D	2863	770	2488	227	0.49	0.30
11	2	500	D	2227	1067	2360	580	0.12	0.54
12	2	700	D	2099	621	2396	684	0.48	1.10

3.2 Experimental Results and Their Implications

In the right half of Table 1, together with the point estimate Pe and the half-width of the 95% confidence interval Dlt achieved by linear regression, the parameter values of the final price distribution are shown. Further, Cm and Cs in the table denote the following measures of the appropriateness of the obtained mean and standard deviation relative to the point estimate and confidence interval:

$$Cm = | \mu_g - Pe | / Dlt \tag{3}$$

$$Cs = \sigma_g / Dlt \tag{4}$$

where Cm is a smaller-the-better measure, and Cs should take a value around 0.5 since $\mu_g \pm 2\sigma_g$ covers approximately 95% of the distribution. Tables 2 and 3 show the results of analysis of variance applied to Cm and Cs respectively.

Table 2. ANOVA table of Cm

	Degrees of freedom	Sum of squares	Mean square	F value	P value
Eta	2	0.015	0.007	0.468	0.645
Info	1	0.045	0.045	2.825	0.137
Session	1	0.056	0.056	3.499	0.104
Residuals	7	0.112	0.016		

Table 3. ANOVA table of Cs

	Degrees of freedom	Sum of squares	Mean square	F value	P value
Eta	2	0.418	0.209	12.471	0.005
Info	1	0.017	0.017	0.996	0.352
Session	1	0.071	0.071	4.254	0.078
Residuals	7	0.117	0.017		

In most cases, the absolute bias of the obtained mean from the corresponding point estimate seems acceptable considering that the system is a subjective forecasting tool. It is also confirmed that any noticeably high biases, for example, those in terms 10 and 12, can be attributed to the superficial curvature trend in the corresponding virtual sales history. Since it is not announced that the data is created by a simple linear model, capturing the curvature trend is not problematic for a subjective forecasting tool. The average magnitude of the obtained standard deviation also seems adequate. Thus, the output price distribution can serve as an approximate forecast distribution.

Table 3 shows that the standard deviation is significantly affected by Eta. Therefore, in order to further refine the output forecast distribution, the value of η should be appropriately chosen from this aspect. In the current experimental setting, its desirable value seems to be around 500. How to fine-tune the sensitivity parameter in general setting is an important future research topic. It is also noted that the significance of the effect of Info is rejected on both Cm and Cs. This implies that the newly introduced book value constraint does not seriously decrease the sensitivity of the market system to dynamically arriving information.

Next, it is studied how the price distribution changes along the transactions. In most cases, the process followed a smooth convergence to a certain distribution. It is also observed that, when Info is D, the arrival of additional information can change

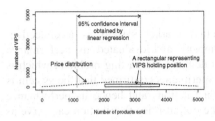

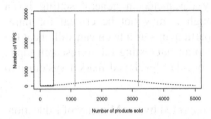

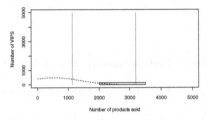

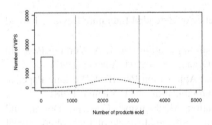

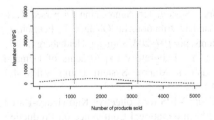

Fig. 1. How participant 5 changes his VIPS holding position in term 9; from the top figure to the bottom one

the target distribution and accelerate the convergence to it, but the partial process between information arrivals looks similar to the process formed when Info is S. Thus, in those cases, the system does not seem to suffer from the arbitrage actions and successfully captures the provided information rapidly at the beginning and then gradually.

However, there are two exceptional cases, terms 9 and 11. In these cases, the price distribution became quire instable in the middle of the process. Investigating the transaction history table reveals that, in these terms, a few participants tried to take the arbitrage actions. For example, Fig. 1 shows how participant 5 changed his VIPS holding position in term 9. It is obvious from this figure that his second and fourth transactions were intended to take the arbitrage actions A and/or B. It is also observed that, on the contrary to his intension, these actions have shrunken his asset, after all into a tiny rectangular shown in the bottom of Fig. 1.That is, in this case, and in the other similar cases as well, the troublesome efforts towards arbitrage have been successfully punished and will not be continued. It is also confirmed that the disturbing transaction gave the other participants a chance to buy VIPS in an appropriate area at a very cheap price. The chance was soon taken by a shrewd participant and thus the price distribution soon came back into an appropriate shape. This is why the troublesome efforts towards arbitrage did not give a serious damage to the final price distribution.

One potential problem revealed by the observation above is that more than two participants as a team can still cheat the system. Although this may not be critical in the case of intra-company usage of the system, how to tackle the problem is an interesting future research topic.

5 Conclusions

This paper developed an intra-firm prediction market system as a collective-knowledge-based forecasting tool for a company and evaluated its performance through laboratory experiments with a virtual demand forecasting problem, which is essentially a linear regression problem. The experiments confirmed that the system is capable of penalizing the troublesome arbitrage actions and hence its performance will be fairly stable. It is also observed that the output price distribution can serve as an approximate forecast distribution. In order to further refine the output forecast distribution, how to fine-tune the sensitivity parameter in general setting is an important future research topic. Further, though it may not be critical for intra-company usage of the system, more than two participants as a team can still cheat the system. Thus, how to tackle the problem is also an interesting future research topic. Finally, field experiments will be required to put the developed market system into practical use.

Acknowledgments. This research is partially supported by the Ministry of Education, Science, Sports and Culture, Grant-in-Aid for Scientific Research (B) 20310087.

References

1. Plott, C.R.: Markets as Information Gathering Tools. Southern Economic Journal 67, 1–15 (2000)
2. Pennock, D.M., Lawrence, S., Giles, C.L., Nielsen, F.A.: The Real Power of Artificial Markets. Science 291, 987–988 (2001)
3. Wolfers, J., Zitzewitz, E.: Prediction Markets. Journal of Economic Perspectives 18, 107–126 (2004)
4. Tziralis, G., Tatsiopoulos, I.: Prediction Markets: An Extended Literature Review. Journal of Prediction Markets 1, 75–91 (2007)
5. Ortner, G.: Forecasting Markets – An industrial Application Part I. A Working Paper in Dept. of Managerial Economics and Industrial Organization at TU Vienna (1997)
6. Ortner, G.: Forecasting Markets – An industrial Application Part II. A Working Paper in Dept. of Managerial Economics and Industrial Organization at TU Vienna (1998)
7. Chen, K., Plott, C.R.: Information Aggregation Mechanisms: Concept, Design and Implementation for a Sales Forecasting Problem. California Institute of Technology. Social Science Working Paper #1131 (2002)
8. Mizuyama, H., Kamada, E.: A Prediction Market System for Aggregating Dispersed Tacit Knowledge into a Continuous Forecasted Demand Distribution. In: Olhager, J., Persson, F. (eds.) Advances in Production Management Systems, pp. 197–204. Springer, Heidelberg (2007)
9. Ueda, M., Mizuyama, H., Asada, K., Tagaya, Y.: Laboratory Experiments of Demand Forecasting Process through Intra-Firm Prediction Market System Using VIPS. In: Proceedings of 9th APIEMS Conference (2008)
10. Mizuyama, H.: A Prediction Market System Using VIPS for Collective-Knowledge-Based Demand Forecasting. In: Proceedings of the 20th International Conference on Production Research (2009) (to appear)
11. Hanson, R.: Combinatorial Information Market Design. Information Systems Frontiers 5, 107–119 (2003)

Database Scheme Configuration for a Product Line of MPC-TOOLS

Benjamin Klöpper, Tobias Rust,
Bernhard Vedder, and Wilhelm Dangelmaier

Heinz Nixdorf Institute, University of Paderborn,
Fürstenallee 11, 33102 Paderborn, Germany
kloepper@hni.upb.de
http://www.hni.upb.de/cim

Abstract. Data model, planning restrictions, and objectives related to manufacturing planning and control (MPC) strongly depend on the given production process and workshop. In our opinion, these individual properties are the reason, why standard software fails to properly support decisions in MPC. In this paper, we introduce a platform, which enables a configuration process to create affordable individualized MPC software from existing software components.

1 Introduction

Manufacturing Planning and Control (MPC) is a critical task in many industries and it encompasses a large variety of decision problems [1]. MPC posses features which differ from other application areas of decision support and optimization. These special features are the reason for a large number of individual problem formulations and heuristics. The first essential feature of MPC is the high frequency of decision-making. Decisions about production quantities and the matching of quantities to the available production capacities are made, or at least revised, several times a week or sometimes even several times a day. The reason for this high frequency is the changing environment: incoming orders, unexpected scrap rates or machine breakdowns. The second feature is the lack of clearly defined objectives. From the view point of cost-effectiveness the overall purpose of MPC is to achieve a predetermined output performance at minimal costs [2]. Unfortunately, the exact determination of costs in a production environment is often not possible, because the costs either are not continuously documented or cannot be documented (e.g. the long-term costs of delayed delivers are hard to estimate). Thus, usually alternative objectives and constraints are used in MPC. As the alternative objectives bear conflicts, it is not possible to describe a common objective function for MPC problems [3]. On the other hand, experienced human planners are able to modify existing plans in such a way, that they comply with soft factors, which can hardly be included in an automated decision making process (e.g. in-plant work time agreements). For this purpose, MPC tools must

B. Vallespir and T. Alix (Eds.): APMS 2009, IFIP AICT 338, pp. 57–64, 2010.
© IFIP International Federation for Information Processing 2010

provide interactive interfaces [4]. Finally, every production system and process has some unique properties. These properties may result from organizational or technical issues. Examples are buffers for decoupling of productions stages (organizational), set-up times or mandatory productions sequences (technical). These individual properties have to be included in order to achieve feasible or even high quality decisions. This opinion is supported by the fact that materials management and production planning are among the most frequently customized modules of ERP systems. Olhager and Selldin [5] present a survey about Swedish manufacturing firms, where 60.7% of the material management and 69.2% of the production planning modules were modified during the implementation.

For these reasons, a custom-made MPC solution for every production system (plant or workshop) is required while there is also a need for intuitive graphical user interfaces and effective planning procedures. Thus, a desirable platform enables the required individuality and cost-effective development process at the same time. The reuse of software may offer a custom-made and affordable MPC software.

2 Software Reuse

"Software reuse is the process of creating software systems from existing software rather than building software systems from scratch." [6] The main motivations for software reuse are gains in productivity by avoidance of redevelopment as well as gains in quality by incorporating components, whose reliability has already been established [7]. Obviously, the modularization and formation of encapsulated software components is an important issue in software reuse. An important step towards this vision was object orientation. According to Nierstrasz et al. "objects provide a paradigm for decomposing large application into cooperating objects as well as a reuse paradigm to compose application from pre-packaged software components" [8]. Szyperski and Pfisters deliver a more accurate definition of a software component and an important differentiation against pure objects: "A software component is a unit of composition contractually specified interfaces and explicit context dependencies only. A software component can be deployed independently and is subject to composition by third parties" [9].

The paradigm of generative programming goes beyond the idea of component-based software. The idea is not to focus on single software systems, but to create families of software products, from which custom-made variants are generated [10]. The generative domain model is the basis of the concept. It consists of the problem space, configuration knowledge and the solution space. The problem space encompasses domain specific concepts and features, which are described in domain specific languages (DSL). A DSL provides comprehensible but formal methods to describe the customer's requirements regarding the software product. The solution space is the power set overall components of a software product family, from which an appropriate configuration is selected.

3   OOPUS WEB - A Development Platform for MPC

OOPUS WEB is a platform to efficiently create individualized planning and scheduling tools. It provides flexible and adaptable master data functions as well as smart planning interfaces, which enable maximal information transparency for dispatchers. OOPUS WEB is intended to provide components and tools for a MPC tool product line. The basic principle of OOPUS WEB is to decouple MPC algorithms and user interfaces from the data model of the platform. In this way, the large variety of planning algorithms and models is available and may be selected depending on the current application scenario. OOPUS WEB focuses on the area of serial production in line production fashion. This limitation enables the definition of a lean but extensible data model. This data model is the basis of the OOPUS WEB platform. The Model of Serial Manufacturing is described in detail in [11].

Figure 1 shows the task-structure of OOPUS WEB. The task structure is the fundamental architectural concept in OOPUS WEB. The overall task, the detailed planning and scheduling of a given production process is decomposed in several subtasks, each working on a section of the overall model. Such a section or sub model consists in partial subsets of production stages (multiple stage planning methods), a single production stage (single stage planning methods) or even a single line (single machine planning methods). Furthermore, the overall model is also divided into sub models regarding the granularity of planning periods. In that way, it is possible to perform a planning and scheduling on the level of months, weeks, days or shifts or to directly create a machine scheduling down to the minute. To solve a subtask, modules are combined and applied, which can be selected from a toolbox.

These modules are defined task oriented. Two different types of modules and components are distinguished in OOPUS WEB: user interfaces and algorithms. All modules and algorithms are only loosely coupled by the data they

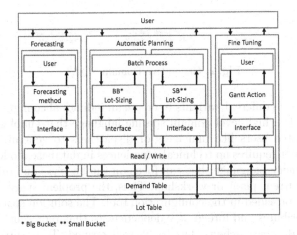

Fig. 1. OOPUS WEB Task Model

visualize and manipulate. Details about the OOPUS WEB task model and the semi-automated generation of the interface layer between modules and database models can be found in [12]. A detailed use case can be found in [13].

Finally, one important part of an OOPUS WEB product is left without tool support so far: the database. The database has to be modified for most companies and plants in order to meet their individual properties and requirements.

4 OOPUS Database Configurator

The OOPUS Database Configurator (ODC) is a tool to create individual database schemes for different applications from the OOPUS WEB family. The system enables the user to make several businesses, technical and organizational oriented decisions in order to generate a matching database model. The next section introduces the concept of ODC. Subsequently the prototype is presented.

4.1 Concept

The basic idea of generative programming is to automate the development of software products. The generative domain model is the basic element of generative programming. It consists of a problem space, a solution space and the configuration knowledge, which defines a mapping between the to spaces (shown in figure 2, for details cf. [10]).

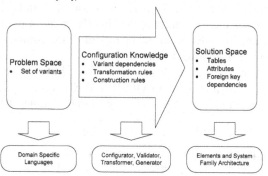

Fig. 2. Generative Domain Model

The user selects different variants to create an individual configuration. These variants provide a high-level domain specific language that enables business or technical oriented users like managers or dispatchers to generate a database scheme. The user requires no technical experiences in database modeling or SQL (Structured Query Language) but can focus on the business and organizational needs of the current plant or workshop. Thus, the problem space consists of a set of variants provided in the configuration tool. The solution space consists of the tables, attributes and foreign key dependencies that represent the database scheme. This database scheme has to be well formed. To ensure this, a validator checks the combination of selected. The required information about the

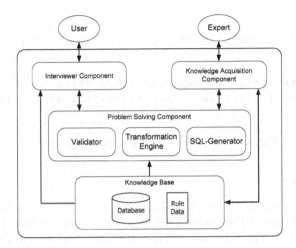

Fig. 3. Architecture of OOPUS Database Configurator

dependencies of the variants is stored in the knowledge space. Another important function of the configuration system is to map the users' point of view on a MPC system on a technical one. Thus, the configuration knowledge contains transformation rules and construction rules. A transformer converts the selected variants into a database model and the generator creates the resulting database scheme in SQL. The ODC follows the general architecture of expert systems introduced by Puppe [14]. It encompasses four basic components (Figure 3): the interviewer component, the problem solving component, the knowledge base, the knowledge acquisition component.

The validator checks the consistency of the selected configuration. Between variants, positive or negative conflicts can exist. A positive conflict arises, if a variant A requires another variant B that is not currently selected. A negative conflict denotes that a variant C must not be selected together with a variant D at the same time. If conflicts arise between two or more variants, they are directly reported to the interviewer component. The user is responsible to resolve them by changing the configuration. When the configuration is finished and no conflicts remain, the database scheme can be generated. This is done by the second component of the problem-solving component, the transformation engine. The transformation engine is the most complex element of the problem-solving component. It has to convert a given set of consistent variants into a set of database tables that define a specific and well-formed database scheme figure.

The knowledge applied in the transformation engine is represented in rules. To simplify the administration of the rules, a second DSL was developed. Compared to the business-oriented variants, this DSL is closer to technical problems. However, it enables the user to define rules in a natural language (cf. figure 4). The transformer generates a database scheme represented as Java objects. This is the input for the SQL-Generator that generates the database scheme in data definition language (DDL). The knowledge used in the problem solving components is stored in the knowledge base.

```
1      when
2        Variant "team-based processing time" is selected
3      then
4        Create table "team"
5        Create field "id_team" in table "times"
6        Create foreign key  from table "times" to table "team"
7      end
```

Fig. 4. Example rule from the knowledge base

4.2 Prototype

The core component of the application is the rules engine. In this case, the open-source software JBoss Rules Engine is used. It encompasses three basic elements (figure 5). The rule base contains the rules that are transformed by a compiler. The working memory contains the facts. The inference engine controls the application of the rules to the facts. To start the process, rule file and the DSL file are imported into the rule base. The DSL file contains the mapping information. Afterwards the application data (variants and table definitions) are loaded into the working memory. When firing the inference engine matches the facts against the rules. Depending on the selected variants, several elements like tables, attributes and key dependencies are activated. Therefore, every element has a flag that marks whether an element is active or not. Finally, the set of marked elements forms the resulting database definition. The prototype enables a user to select domain specific features of the desired product and visualizes possible conflicts. Figure 6 shows a screenshot from the prototype. The left hand side of the screenshot shows the selectable features in a hierarchical structure. The right hand side enables the user to select different product features. The red exclamation marks denotes a conflicts, which is explained by the message box. When the user resolved all conflicts, the rule engines uses the selected features as facts and generates the database definition.

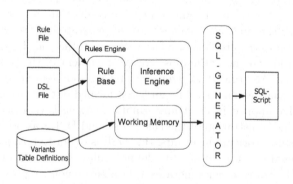

Fig. 5. Sketch of the Prototype

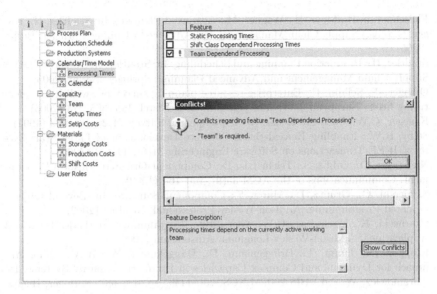

Fig. 6. Screenshot from the Prototype

5 Conclusion

Standard software applications provide unsatisfactory performance in many manufacturing planning and control use cases. The main reason for the poor performance is ignorance of individual properties of manufacturing environments. Only individual solutions can offer the performance required in today's competitive environment. Of course, individual solutions have the drawback of high investment costs. Thus, we introduced a platform, which enables the fast and lean development of custom-made MPC applications for serial manufacturing. The basic idea is the definition of a family of software products, where reusable components are combined in order to meet the requirements of a specific company or workshop. An important part of any MPC system is its database. To model a production system in an appropriate way, the database scheme is a crucial issue. Thus, in order to compose individual MPC solutions, a flexible database is essential. In this paper, we introduced a concept and a prototypical implementation of database-scheme configurator, which enables the definition of individual, well-defined database schemes by selecting the required business-related, technical, or organizational properties. Currently the OOPUS Database Configurator is used in two development projects at German automotive suppliers.

References

1. Tempelmeier, H., Kuhn, H.: Flexible Manufacturing Systems: Decision Support for Design and Operation. Wiley Interscience, San Francisco (1993)
2. Vollmann, T.E., Berry, W.L., Whybark, D.C., Roberts, R.J.: Manufacturing Planning and Control for Supply Chain Management. Taylor-Francis, New York (2005)

3. Fleischmann, B., Meyr, H., Wagner, M.: Advanced Planning. In: Stadtler, H., Kilger, C. (eds.) Supply Chain Management and Advanced Planning. Springer, Berlin (2005)
4. Stadtler, H.: Production Planning and Scheduling. In: Stadtler, H., Kilger, C. (eds.) Supply Chain Management and Advanced Planning. Springer, Berlin (2005)
5. Olhager, J., Selldin, E.: Enterprise resource planning survey of Swedish manufacturing firms. European Journal of Operational Research 146, 365–373 (2003)
6. Krueger, C.W.: Software Reuse. ACM Computing Survey 24(2), 131–183 (1992)
7. Selby, R.W.: Enabling Reused-Based Software Development of Large Scale Systems. IEEE Transactions on Software Engineering 31(6), 495–510 (2005)
8. Nierstrasz, O., Gibbs, S., Tsichritzis, D.: Component-Oriented Software Development. Communications of the ACM 35(9), 160–165 (1992)
9. Szyperski, C., Gruntz, D., Murer, S.: Component Software. In: Beyond Object-Oriented Programming. Addison-Wesley Professional, Reading (2002)
10. Czarnecki, K., Eisenecker, U.W.: Generative Programming: Methods, Tools and Applications. Addison-Wesley Longman, Amsterdam (2000)
11. Klöpper, B., Timm, T., Brüggemann, D., Dangelmaier, W.: A Modelling Approach for Dynamic and Complex Capacities in Production Control Systems. In: Abramowicz, W. (ed.) BIS 2007. LNCS, vol. 4439, pp. 626–637. Springer, Heidelberg (2007)
12. Klöpper, B., Rust, T., Timm, T., Dangelmaier, W.: A Customizing Platform for Individual Production Planning and Control Solutions. In: Proceedings of Wirtschaftsinformatik 2009, vol. 2, pp. 77–86 (2009)
13. Klöpper, B., Rust, T., Timm, T., Brüggemann, D., Dangelmaier, W.: OOPUS WEB: A MPC Customizing Platform with Ergonomic Planning Interfaces. In: Proceedings of the 1st International Conference on Business Innovation and Information Technology. Logos Verlag (2009)
14. Puppe, F.: Systematic Introduction to Expert Systems. Springer, Berlin (1993)

Balancing Mass Production Machining Lines with Genetic Algorithms

Olga Guschinskaya[1], Evgeny Gurevsky[1],
Anton Eremeev[2], and Alexandre Dolgui[1]

[1] École Nationale Supérieure des Mines de Saint-Étienne
158, cours Fauriel, 42023 Saint-Étienne Cédex 2, France
{guschinskaya,gurevsky,dolgui}@emse.fr
[2] Omsk Branch of Sobolev Institute of Mathematics SB RAS
Pevstsov St. 13, 644099 Omsk, Russia
eremeev@ofim.oscsbras.ru

Abstract. A balancing problem for serial machining lines with multi-spindle heads is studied. The objective is to assign a set of given machining operations to a number of machines while minimizing the line cost and respecting a number of given technological and economical constraints. To solve this problem, three different genetic algorithms are suggested and compared via a series of numerical tests. The results of computational experiments are presented and analyzed.

1 Introduction

Balancing serial machining lines with multi-spindle heads is a very hard combinatorial problem. It consists in assigning a set of given machining operations to a sequence of transfer machines. The number and the configuration of these machines are not known in advance and they must be defined by optimization procedure. In fact, each transfer machine can be equipped with a number of multi-spindle heads activated in sequence. The number and the order of activation of multi-spindle heads depend on the operations assigned to each spindle head. A set of operations assigned to the same spindle head is referred to as block. All operations within a block are executed simultaneously. The parallel execution of operations is possible due to the fact that multi-spindle heads carry several tools activated by the same driver. The assignment of an operation to a spindle head defines which tool must be fixed and in which position. Therefore, the final operations assignment defines the configuration of each spindle head and, as a consequence, each transfer machine. This assignment is subject to numerous technological constraints which must be respected for a feasible machining process. The design objective is to find a configuration of a line which satisfies all given technological and economical constraints and minimizes the line cost that depends directly on the number of used equipments.

Since the presented balancing problem is NP-hard, using optimization tools becomes indispensable for designers who seek for taking efficient decisions. The first mathematical model for this problem has been presented in [3] and referred

B. Vallespir and T. Alix (Eds.): APMS 2009, IFIP AICT 338, pp. 65–72, 2010.

to as the Transfer Line Balancing Problem (TLBP). Several exact and heuristic methods have been developed to solve TLBP, a quantitative comparison of the proposed solution methods has been presented in [8]. The numerical tests showed that solving exactly industrial instances of this problem is time consuming and inapplicable for end users who have to deal in practice with designing a number of lines at the same time. As a consequence, powerful metaheuristic approaches are clearly needed for effective solving real-size problem instances. In this paper, three different genetic approaches are suggested for getting relatively good solutions for real case problems.

2   Problem Statement

For a TLBP problem instance, the following input data is assumed to be given:

- N is the set of all operations involved in machining of a part;
- t_j is the processing time of operation j, $j \in N$;
- T_0 is the maximal admissible line cycle time;
- τ^S and τ^b are the auxiliary times needed for activation of a machine and a spindle head, respectively;
- C_1 and C_2 are the costs of one machine and one spindle head;
- m_0 is the maximal admissible number of machines;
- n_0 is the maximal number of spindle heads per machine.

The following constraints must be taken into account:

- *Precedence constraints* between the operations. These constraints define non-strict partial order relation over set of operations N. They are represented by a digraph $G = (N, D)$. An arc $(i, j) \in N^2$ belongs to set D if and only if the block with operation j cannot precede the block with operation i. If $(i, j) \in D$ then operations i and j can be performed simultaneously in a common block.
- *Inclusion constraints* defining the groups of operations that must be assigned to the same machine, because of a required machining tolerance. These constraints can be represented by a family I^m of subsets of N, such that all operations of the same subset $e \in I^m$ must be assigned to the same machine.
- *Exclusion constraints* defining the groups of operations that cannot be assigned to the same machine because of their technological incompatibility. These constraints are represented by a family E^m of subsets of N, such that all elements of the same subset $e \in E^m$ cannot be assigned to the same machine.
- *Cycle time constraint:* Let N_k be the set of operations of machine k, $k \in \{1, \ldots, m\}$, $m \le m_0$, m is the number of machines in a solution S. Let N_{kl} be the set of operations grouped into common block l, $l \in \{1, \ldots, n_k\}$, of machine k, $n_k \le n_0$, where n_k is the number of blocks of machine k in

solution S. Using these notations, the cycle line constraint can be introduced like follows:

$$\sum_{l=1}^{n_k} t^b(N_{kl}) + \tau^S \leq T_0, \quad k \in \{1, \ldots, m\},$$

where $t^b(N_{kl}) = \max\{t_j : j \in N_{kl}\} + \tau^b$ is the time of l-th block of k-th machine.

Therefore, a solution S of TLBP can be represented by a collection $S = \{\{N_{11}, \ldots, N_{1n_1}\}, \ldots, \{N_{m1}, \ldots, N_{mn_m}\}\}$, determining an assignment of $\mathbf{N}$ to machines and blocks. Solution S is feasible, if it satisfies all constraints described above. The studied problem consists in minimizing the investment costs which can be represented as follows:

$$C(S) = C_1 m + C_2 \sum_{k=1}^{m} n_k \rightarrow \min_{S \in \mathbf{S}},$$

where $\mathbf{S}$ is the set of all feasible solutions.

3   Genetic Algorithm: General Approach

A genetic algorithm (GA) is a metaheuristic which uses some mechanisms inspired by biological evolution: reproduction, mutation, crossover, and selection see e.g. [9,10]. Such an approach has been already successfully applied for solving different balancing problems, see for instance the review [11].

A genetic algorithm starts with an initial population which contains a number of individuals. In our implementation, each individual represents a feasible solution for the studied problem. These individuals are generated by using a heuristic. Each individual is characterized by the fitness function (the cost of the solution in our case) determining the chances of its survival.

The encodings of individuals are usually called genotypes. In this paper, three different techniques of encoding are presented and compared on a series of benchmark problems.

To model the evolution of a population, two parents (individuals) are chosen from the population and are used to create an offspring (new individual). In the presented implementation of the GAs, each parent is selected using the s-tournament method: s individuals are taken at random from the current population and the one with the best fitness is selected as a parent. Therefore, the population size N_{size_pop} remains constant during the execution of a GA.

New individuals are built by means of a reproduction operator that usually consists of crossover and mutation procedures. The crossover procedure produces an offspring from two parent individuals by combining and exchanging their elements. The mutation procedure adds small random changes to an individual. Finally, the obtained offspring replaces the worst individual in the current population, if the offspring has better value of the fitness function.

The algorithm is restarted with a new initial population every time the number of iterations during which the current solution has not been improved is equal to I_{non_imp}. This continues until the total execution time reaches the limit T_{max}. The best solution found over all runs is returned as the final output.

The aim of this paper is to find the most efficient genetic algorithm for balancing real-size machining lines with multi-spindle heads. To do it, three different GAs are presented and compared. The first one is based on MIP formulation of TLBP and, as a consequence, uses a binary-based encoding of individuals. This algorithm is described in Section 4. The second and the third genetic algorithms presented in Section 5 and 6, respectively, employ other mutation and crossover procedures and solution encodings based on using different heuristics. The performances of these algorithms are compared in Section 7 on a series of benchmark problems.

4   GA1: Binary-Based Encoding

The MIP model of TLBP proposed in [3] is employed by this algorithm. The individuals are coded using binary variables X_{jq}, $j \in \mathbf{N}$, $q \le n_0 m_0$: X_{jq} equals 1 if operation j is assigned to block q, 0 otherwise. These variables are used to describe the operations assignment to blocks in a feasible solution.

In this genetic algorithm, the initial population of individuals is obtained by heuristic suggested in [4]. Each individual is represented by a sequence of values of variables X_{jq}. A MIP-recombination operator is used to obtain an offspring from the selected parents. Firstly this operator fixes all Boolean variables equal to their values in parent p_1 and then it releases (with probability P_c) all Boolean variables having different values in p_1 and p_2 (analogue of crossover). Finally, it changes (with probability P_m) the values of randomly selected variables (analogue of mutation). The obtained MIP problem (with some fixed variables) is solved by a MIP solver.

In our implementation of GA1, ILOG CPLEX 9.0 is used to solve MIP problems. To avoid time-consuming computations, a limit time T_{rec} is fixed to the solver at each call. If the solver does not return a feasible solution to the subproblem, then the MIP-recombination outputs a genotype obtained by the standard mutation procedure.

The second and the third genetic algorithms (GA2 and GA3, respectively) use a non-binary based encoding of the individuals, like in [2]. This means that the way to obtain a feasible solution and not the solution itself is encoded. In the presented algorithms, two different heuristic methods are used for constructing feasible solutions from individuals. The two algorithms are based on using two different heuristics.

5   GA2: Encoding Based on GBL Heuristic

GA2 uses GBL (Greedy Blocks Loading) heuristic [6] for solution encoding. An individual consists of a sequence of parameters that are used by GBL heuristic for constructing a feasible solution. Here, a brief description of this heuristic is given, for more details see [6].

The solution construction starts with one machine with an empty block. Then, operations are assigned to the current machine by adding new blocks. When no more blocks can be created at the current machine, a new machine is created. This continues until all operations are assigned. To select an operation to be assigned to the current machine, list CL (Candidate List) is used. This list contains all operations that can be assigned in the current moment, i.e. for which precedence constraints are satisfied and there is no exclusion constraint with the operations assigned to the current block and machine. When CL is constructed, a greedy function is applied to each candidate operation and the operations are ranked according to their greedy function values. Well ranked candidate operations are placed into a restricted candidate list (RCL). Then, an element is randomly selected from RCL and added to the solution. Taking this into account, list CL is updated.

In GA2, instead of one determined greedy function, different criteria are employed for ranking operations in list CL. The following greedy functions can be used:

- Lower bound on the number of blocks required to assign all successors of operation i with condition that i will be assigned to the current block;
- Lower bound on the number of blocks required to assign immediate successors of operation i with condition that i will be assigned to the current block;
- Total number of all successors of operation i ;
- Total number of immediate successors of operation i ;
- Processing time of operation i.

Two possible techniques for constructing list RCL are also considered:

$$RCL = \{j \in CL : g(j) \geq g_{max} - \alpha(g_{max} - g_{min})\},$$

in order to select the operations with greater greedy values, and

$$RCL = \{j \in CL : g(j) \leq g_{min} - \alpha(g_{min} - g_{max})\},$$

to select the operations with smaller greedy values. Here g_{max} and g_{min} are respectively the minimum and the maximum of greedy function $g(j)$ over list CL. Parameter $\alpha \in [0,1]$ controls the trade-off between randomness and greediness in the construction process.

Therefore, each time list RCL is built, one of ten (2*5) criteria can be used. Taking into account the fact that each operation is to be chosen one time, an individual is represented by the number of genes equal to the number of operations. The value of each gene is the code of the criterion to be used for constructing list RCL. The first time, RCL is build using the criterion corresponding to the value of the first gene and so on. The initial population is created by attributing random values to genes.

The fitness value of an individual is measured by the cost of the corresponding solution obtained by GBL heuristic.

The crossover procedure is implemented as follows: each child's gene inherits the value of the corresponding gene either from parent p_1 (with probability P_c) or from parent p_2 (with probability $1 - P_c$). The mutation procedure selects at random two child's genes and increases (with probability P_m) or decreases (with probability $1 - P_m$) by one the integer value for any gene between these two positions.

A local search procedure presented in [6] is applied to the best individual in the current population. The used method is based on the decomposition and aggregate solving of sub-problems by a graph approach.

6   GA3: Encoding Based on FSIC Heuristic

This genetic algorithm (GA3) uses FSIC (*First Satisfy Inclusion Constraints*) heuristic for constructing feasible solutions from individuals. The last version of this heuristic and its parameters have been presented in [7]. Therefore, the encoding of individuals is based on the use of the parameters that the heuristic employs during the construction of a feasible solution for a TLBP problem.

In heuristic FSIC, as in heuristic GBL, the operations are assigned one by one and new blocks and machines are created when necessary. List CL is also used, but list RCL is not employed. As it was presented in [7], the selection of the operation to be assigned depends on 4 control parameters: $check\_time \in \{0,1\}$, $check\_blocks \in \{0,1,2\}$, $divide\_L_2 \in \{0,1\}$, $trials\_L_2 \in \{0,1\}$. Their values can be changed each time list CL is constructed. The results of test experiments presented in [7] have been used for selecting the ten most effective combinations of these parameters. A code was assigned to each of these ten combinations. These codes are used for individuals encoding in GA3. Taking into account the fact that each operation is to be chosen once, an individual is represented by the number of genes equal to the number of operations. The value of each gene is the code of a combination of the control parameters. The solution construction starts with the parameters corresponding to the value of the first gene. Then, each time list CL is rebuilt, the values of the control parameters are changed accordingly to the value of next gene. The fitness value of an individual is measured by the cost of the corresponding solution obtained by FSIC heuristic.

The initial population is generated randomly. The crossover and mutation procedures are the same as in GA2. As for GA2, a local search procedure presented in [6] is applied to the best individual in the current population.

7   Experimental Results

The purpose of this section is to compare the performances of three proposed genetic algorithms GA1, GA2, GA3 and the best heuristic method FSIC (the last version of this heuristic can be found in [7]). To do this, 2 series of randomly generated (S1-S2) and 2 series (SI1-SI2) of industrial instances have been used. All experiments were carried out on Pentium-IV (3 GHz, 1.5 RAM).

For series S1-S2, the following problem parameters are used: $C_1 = 10$, $C_2 = 2$, $T_0 = 100$, $\tau^b = \tau^S = 0$, $n_0 = 4$. Each series of S1-S2 contains 50 test problems. The number of operations and the order strength $(OS = \frac{2|D|}{|\mathbf{N}|(|\mathbf{N}|-1)})$ are as follows: $|\mathbf{N}| = 25$ and $OS = 0.5$ for Series S1, $|\mathbf{N}| = 50$ and $OS = 0.9$ for Series S2. The available time per test was limited by 90 sec for S1 and by 300 sec for S2.

The following notations are used for the presentation of the obtained results: NO is the number of instances where the optimal solutions were obtained; Δ_{max}, Δ_{av} are respectively the percentage of maximal and average deviation of a obtained solution from the optimal one for the same problem instance.

Table 1. Results for S1-S2

	S1				S2			
	GA1	GA2	GA3	FSIC	GA1	GA2	GA3	FSIC
NO	50	50	50	23	49	50	49	18
$\Delta_{max}, \%$	0	0	0	10.53	1.72	0	2.13	6.00
$\Delta_{av}, \%$	0	0	0	3.15	0.03	0	0.04	2.14

The results presented in Table 1 show that for Series S1-S2 the proposed genetic algorithms demonstrated rather similar performances. Algorithm GA2 found 100% of optimal solutions, GA1 and GA3 reached 99% of optimums while heuristic FSIC found only 41% of optimal solutions.

The both Series SI1-SI2 contain 20 industrial problems. The following parameters are the same for all these problem instances: $C_1 = 1$, $C_2 = 0.5$, $T_0 = 5.15$, $\tau^b = 0.2$, $\tau^S = 0.4$, $n_0 = 4$. The maximal, average and minimal numbers of operations are respectively 92, 72, 46 for the instances from Series SI1 and 127, 108, 87 for the instances from Series SI2. The maximal, average and minimal values of the order strength are respectively 0.53, 0.45, 0.39 for the instances from Series SI1 and 0.5, 0.43, 0.33 for the instances from Series SI2. The available solution time was limited by 720 sec for SI1 and 2400 sec for SI2.

Taking into account the fact that for these test series the optimal solutions are not known yet, the solutions obtained by GAs and FSIC are compared with the best known solutions. The following notations are used for the presentation of the obtained results: NB is the number of instances where the best known solution was obtained; Δ_{max}, Δ_{av}, Δ_{min} are the percentage of maximal, average and minimal deviation of a obtained solution from the best known one.

With respect to the results given in Table 2 GA2 provided in average a better solution than GA1, GA3 and FSIC. Algorithm GA2 found 38 best known solutions for 40 test problems while GA1, GA3 and FSIC obtained only 7, 3 and 1 ones, respectively. The average deviation of GA2 for series SI1-SI2 is equal to 0.51% while it is 2.79%, 4.32% and 18.92% for GA1, GA3 and FSIC, respectively. Therefore, it can be concluded that all suggested methods outperformed heuristic FSIC and algorithm GA2 performs in average better than other methods.

Table 2. Results for SI1-SI2

	SI1				SI2			
	GA1	GA2	GA3	FSIC	GA1	GA2	GA3	FSIC
NB	3	**20**	3	1	4	**18**	0	0
Δ_{max}, %	7.14	**0**	10	32	7.04	**0.09**	10.84	45.07
Δ_{av}, %	3.34	**0**	3.71	13.33	2.23	**1.01**	4.93	24.50
Δ_{min}, %	**0**	**0**	**0**	**0**	**0**	**0**	0.78	13.85

References

1. Baybars, I.: A survey of exact algorithms for the simple assembly line balancing. Management Science 32, 909–932 (1986)
2. Baykasoğlu, A., Özbakir, L.: Stochastic U-line balancing using genetic algorithms. The International Journal of Advanced Manufacturing Technology 32, 139–147 (2007)
3. Dolgui, A., Finel, B., Guschinsky, N.N., Levin, G.M., Vernadat, F.B.: MIP approach to balancing transfer lines with blocks of parallel operations. IIE Transactions 38, 869–882 (2006)
4. Dolgui, A., Guschinskaya, O., Eremeev, A.: MIP-based GRASP and genetic algorithm for balancing transfer lines. In: Maniezzo, V., Stützle, T., Voß, S. (eds.) Matheuristics, Annals of Information Systems, vol. 10, pp. 189–208. Springer US, Heidelberg (2010)
5. Ghosh, S., Gagnon, R.: A comprehensive literature review and analysis of the design, balancing and scheduling of assembly systems. International Journal of Production Research 27, 637–670 (1989)
6. Guschinskaya, O., Dolgui, A.: Équilibrage des lignes d'usinage à boîtiers multibroches avec la méthode GRASP. In: Actes de la 7ème Conférence Internationale de Modélisation et Simulation (MOSIM 2008), vol. 2, pp. 1121–1130 (2008)
7. Guschinskaya, O., Dolgui, A.: A transfer line balancing problem by heuristic methods: industrial case studies. Decision Making in Manufacturing and Services 2, 33–46 (2008)
8. Guschinskaya, O., Dolgui, A.: Comparison of exact and heuristic methods for a transfer line balancing problem. International Journal of Production Economics 120, 276–286 (2009)
9. Holland, J.H.: Adaptation in natural and artificial systems. University of Michigan Press (1975)
10. Reeves, C.R.: Feature article – genetic algorithms for the operations researcher. INFORMS Journal on Computing 9, 231–250 (1997)
11. Scholl, A., Becker, C.: State-of-the-art exact and heuristic solution procedures for the simple assembly line balancing. European Journal of Operational Research 168, 666–693 (2006)

A Top-Down Approach for an Automatic Precedence Graph Construction under the Influence of High Product Variety

Simon Altemeier, Daniel Brodkorb, and Wilhelm Dangelmaier

Heinz Nixdorf Institute, University of Paderborn,
Fürstenallee 11, 33102 Paderborn, Germany
{Simon.Altemeier,daniel.brodkorb,wilhelm.dangelmaier}@hni.upb.de
http://www.hni.upb.de/cim

Abstract. This paper describes a top-down method for an automatic precedence graph construction that can cope with high variant products. The concept generates a joint precedence graph including all variants of a product directly. The graph is automatically derived from the bill of materials and buildability rules as well as existing solutions for the assignment of tasks to workstations. The presented method is very error prone and can improve the practical applicability of many assembly line balancing problems, that could not be used in practice yet.

1 Introduction

Producing companies have to cope with an increasing product variety and frequently changing demands. Despite this development assembly lines are used to gain an efficient production process. The main focus in setting up and reconfigurating an assembly line is the assignment of tasks to workplaces. Sophisticated algorithms have been developed for this problem [1,2].

Almost all existing concepts assume that a precedence graph, describing the relations which tasks have to be done before others, exists. A manual definition of a precedence graph for products with high variety fails, due to the complexity. Some authors developed intelligent methods for an automatic assembly sequence generation [3,5,6,7,8,9,10,11]. Most methods proposed have in common that they start bottom up. Initially no relation exists and all tasks are independent. Restrictions between tasks are added successively. This proceeding is very error-prone as forgetting a relation can lead to an unfeasible setup solution, when the graph is used as an input in an assembly line balancing algorithm. Furthermore, none of the former approaches can handle a product portfolio without an explicit variant definition like it is predominant e.g. in the automobile industry. We propose a method that starts top-down with the existing feasible assignment and sequencing solution and uses automatic algorithms to break up restrictions successively. The algorithms use data that already exists in many producing companies. The first advantage of the top-down approach is the guarantee that in any stage of the precedence graph development, valid assignment solutions can be derived from the

B. Vallespir and T. Alix (Eds.): APMS 2009, IFIP AICT 338, pp. 73–80, 2010.

graph. There are no possibilities to change the order of tasks for assignment algorithms in the graph that could lead to unfeasible assignment solutions. Second, the approach can deal with a practical number of variants as the joint-precedence graph, consisting of all models produced in an assembly line, is created directly. Third, the method uses the existing product documentation.

2   Problem Statement

A precedence graph $G = (N, E, t)$ where N is the set of nodes, E the set of edges and t a weightingvector, can be used for different purposes. Within assembly line balancing problems, the precedence graph restricts the possible assignment solutions of tasks to workplaces. A mathematical formulation of a restriction in such a combinatorial problem, assuming an ascending numbering of the workstations, is given in equation 1, where a task a with a precedence relation to task b has to be assigned to an earlier workstation in the assembly line than task b. The set ST includes all workstations st and the binary variable $x_{a,st}$ describes the assignment of task $a \in N$ to station $st \in ST$.

$$\sum_{st=1}^{ST} x_{a,st} \cdot st \leq \sum_{st=1}^{ST} x_{b,st} \cdot st \quad \forall \quad a, b \in N \mid e_{a,b} \in E \qquad (1)$$

In the considered mixed model-case where different variants are produced in one assembly line, the precedence graph has to include the relations of all tasks from all products. The usual way to do this is generating a precedence graph for each of the variants and joining them ([12, p.228ff]). In a scenario with high product variety, e.g. in the automobile industry with a theoretical maximum of 10^{32} different variants [13, p.447], an approach is needed that generates the joint precedence graph directly.

2.1   Data-Basis

The concept is based on three types of input that are used by different algorithms. Even if one type of input is missing in an application of the concept, the other methods can still be processed as they are all independent from each other.

The **open variant bill of materials** fulfills the requirements for a product with high variety and thus is used in many manufacturing companies [14, p.266]. A typical implementation of this product documentation is done by so called codes and code-rules [15, p.1012ff]. Codes represent the product features a client can order, e.g. R1 for a standard radio and R2 for a Radio with GPS. A specific variant is described by a so called code bar, consisting of a combination of available codes. For the identification which parts are to be assembled in a certain variant, each part has its own code-rule assigned, that describes in which case it is needed. These code-rules are boolean expressions of propositional logic. An examplary code-rule which describes for a part that it is needed if engine M1 or M2 and the radio R2 but not the air conditioning K1 is selected could look like this: $(M1 \lor M2) \land R2 \land \neg K1$. The tasks in the assembly line are connected with the different parts in the BOM that are needed for an execution of the tasks. Thereby it is possible to identify the necessary tasks to produce a certain variant. Further details can be found in [16]. Based on the code-rules the product structure also includes information about dependencies between parts/processes that exclude each other in order to represent a specific product feature. In general any other product documentation type that fulfills this requirement can be used for the methods to be presented later on.

The **buildability rules** set defines which parts or part sets are compatible. Many producing companies use these rules for a reduction of the set of variants a client can order. For example it could be defined that the Radio with the GPS system is not offered with the smallest engine (i.e.: $M1 \rightarrow -R2$).

This concept is also used to model technically unavailable options as well as simple exclusive options like the engines, which can exist only once in each car.

The **assignment of tasks to different zones of the product** which could be the front, the back, the sides and the inside of e.g. a car or any other product is another input for the following methods. In the previously described open variant BOM, this assignment is already existing in the product documentation. The different zones should be selected in a way that it can be assured that tasks from different zones do not depend on each other and can be processed independently.

Over time **different assignment solutions** are generated, as a regular re-assignment of tasks to workplaces is necessary [17,23]. This is especially true if the product is available in many different variants and the demand for certain options changes over time. Apart from this assignment information, a sequencing solution of the tasks on every workplace is required.

3   Literature Review

The oldest way of building a precedence graph is to create it manually, relation by relation [18, p.243], [19,4]. This is done by asking the question:"Is there a precedence relation between process a and process b?". As the number of questions would be too high for a product with many tasks, [3] and [4] invented methods with more complicated but less questions. The drawback is that the questions are too complicated to answer even with products of low complexity, which leads to many errors [4], [5, p.310]. Many approaches ([7][8]) use geometrical data or CAD-Data ([5][6]) to do an automatic disassembly of a product in all possible sequences. Other concepts use self-defined data-structures which are only a preliminary step to get a precedence graph ([3,9,10]).

To sum up, many remarkable efforts have been made to generate precedence graphs. But, in practice, many of them generate problems. A manual definition of all relations for a product with thousands of parts is impossible and error-prone. CAD-Data based approaches need precise data. Approaches that need additional data-structures would even increase the complexity of the problem, as another data-basis must be maintained.

4   Concept

The main difference to existing approaches is that a top-down approach to the problem is suggested. Instead of starting with all tasks being independent from each other, we begin with an existing assignment sequencing solution, that gives us an initial joint precedence graph representing the whole product portfolio. This graph is generated by creating the precedence relations from each task i to its successor $i + 1$. Provided that the sequence of the workstations is known, the order of the tasks can be derived from the existing sequencing solutions on the workplaces. This initial graph is basically a linear list, without any degree of freedom. If it was used in an assembly line balancing process, only this assignment and sequencing solution would be feasible and the balancing method would be unable to change the given assignment. Starting from this situation three steps are processed to eliminate restrictions to identify other valid sequences of tasks:

1. Splitting the set of tasks into independent subsets
2. Identifying mutually exclusive tasks
3. Merging sequencing solutions from the past

4.1   Splitting into Independent Subgraphs

First the tasks are classified into different independent working-zones to build parallel subgraphs. If the open variant bill of materials is used, as described in 2.1, parts and thereby processes are already assigned to certain positions on the workpiece. Therefore, only a relation between positions and independent working-zones has to be defined. Introduced AND nodes are used to represent the parallelism of two subgraphs. This means that all branches in the AND-construct are independent and can be parallelized. After that, four steps to generate the constructs are undertaken. The main steps of the procedure are illustrated in figure 1.

1. Add all direct precedence relations between tasks belonging to the same working zone. These can be derived from the transitive paths.
2. Delete all precedence relations between tasks that belong to different independent working-zones.
3. Add AND-Open as new start node and AND-Close as new end node
4. Add precedence relations between the AND-Open and all first nodes in the different branches as well as relations between all last nodes in the branches to the AND-Close node.

4.2   Identify Mutually Exclusive Tasks

The following algorithm makes use of the fact that no precedence relations can exist between mutually exclusive tasks. E.g. only one engine can be built into a car. Accordingly, all precedence relations between two tasks that are necessary for two different types of engines can be eliminated.

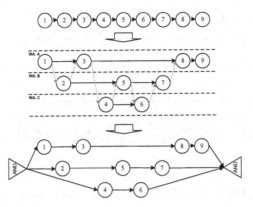

Fig. 1. Splitting of tasks into independent subgraphs

There are two options to identify mutually exclusive tasks. First, the code-rules of the parts, connected to processes, can be checked. Second buildability rules that define, which codes cannot be built together into one product can be analyzed.

The **code-rules** are transfered into the disjunctive normal form. Each conjunction in the first code-rule is checked against all conjunctions of the second code-rule. If a negation of a code c_i in the code-rule CR_i of part i is found in one of the codes c_j in the code-rule CR_j in part j, mutually exclusiveness between the parts i and j can be stated.

$$ME(i,j) = \begin{cases} 1 & if \quad c_i \neq \neg c_j \quad \forall \quad c_i \in CR_i, c_j \in CR_j \\ 0 & else \end{cases} \tag{2}$$

The **buildability rules** set defines directly which codes are mutually exclusive. Accordingly, two processes which need mutually exclusive parts are incompatible, cannot occur in one variant and all precedence relations between them can be eliminated.

As most processes are not dedicated to handle only one single part but sets of parts, the check for mutual exclusion of different processes has to be done matching all items of the sets of parts connected with the processes. In order to model the exclusion in the graph an XOR-construct with the nodes XOR-Open and XOR-Closed is introduced. Only one branch in these constructs can be needed for a single product. This means that the branches are mutually exclusive (see figure 2).

4.3 Merge Sequencing Solutions from the Past

As in modern assembly lines many different variants are produced and demand for variants changes over time, a regular reconfiguration of the assembly line and therefore reassignment of tasks is necessary. All of these assignment and sequencing solutions are valid in terms of their precedence relations. Otherwise

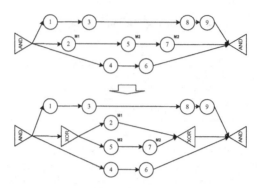

Fig. 2. Identifying mutually exclusive tasks

they could not have been implemented in the assembly line. These additional solutions can be used to identify further degrees of freedom in the precedence graph. For this purpose, the methods previously described are executed for the new assignment and sequencing solution that is to be analyzed. First, the resulting graphs are being united. Formally two graphs are united by unifying their nodes and their edges: $G_i \cup G_j = (N_i \cup N_j, E_i \cup E_j)$.

By this, cycles can come up, if $(n1, n2) \in E_i$ and $(n2, n1) \in E_j$. That means that both precedence relations can be omitted as both orders are possible for the involved tasks. Accordingly, cycles indicate degrees of freedom in united precedence graphs. These cycles can include more than two tasks and can even overlap. Therefore a matrix is built with an algorithm implementing a depth-first search through the precedence graph. The entries $p_{i,j}$ describe if a path between the two nodes i and j exists. A resulting relation in both directions means, that they are invalid and can be deleted.

$$p_{i,j} = \begin{cases} 0 & if \quad \exists \text{ path between } i \text{ and } j \\ 1 & else \end{cases} \tag{3}$$

An AND-construct is used, as shown in figure 3, for the separation of the processes.

This step is repeated with all assignment solutions available and at any time a new valid sequencing solution is found. Successively the precedence graph is improved like a knowledge base by the new sequencing and assignment solutions that are generated regularly in the reconfiguration process. Another benefit is that new tasks, just added to the assembly line are correctly integrated into the graph.

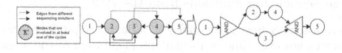

Fig. 3. Dissolving cycles

5 Results and Conclusion

The described concept was tested in a real-life scenario at a car manufacturer. An assignment and sequencing solution for an assembly line with 30 workstations and 578 tasks as well as four different assignment solutions from the past were used to generate a precedence graph automatically. For an additional manual editing process of the graph it is important that the complexity and therefore the number of tasks to be considered concurrently, is reduced. As the AND-branches, generated by step 1 of the algorithms, are independent from each other, the number of tasks to be looked at equals the number of tasks in the branches. The branch with the highest number of tasks contained only 28,4% of the total number of tasks. The nodes in one AND-construct, built by the splitting of tasks into different independent working-zones, are structured further by the second step, inducing an identification of mutually exclusive tasks. The resulting XOR-constructs reduce the number of tasks, that have to be kept in mind, even further. In the example the amount of tasks to be looked at per AND-branch were reduced additionally by 11% in average. In the example, the use of automatic assembly line balancing algorithms reduced the number of floater deployments necessary to produce the given car sequence by 10,3% in comparison with the manual assembly line configuration. Floaters are skilled workers which are reserved to support production if workstations reach their workload limits. The number of concurrent floater deployments, defining the necessary number of floaters to be hold ready, was reduced by 16,6%. It is thereby shown that enough degrees of freedom were identified in the graph for a successful application of automatic algorithms for a reconfiguration process.

To conclude, the presented method generates a precedence graph automatically by analyzing existing product documentation. It can be guaranteed that the precedence graph includes only really existing degrees of freedom. This assures that an assembly line balancing algorithm can generate only feasible solutions. It was shown that enough degrees of freedom were extracted to improve line balance. Still, precedence relations do exist in the graph that are not necessary, which restricts the solution space. In our further research we concentrate on a top-down approach for a manual analysis that eliminates more precedence relations and discovers even more degrees of freedom.

References

1. Boysen, N., Fliedner, M., Scholl, A.: Sequencing mixed-model assembly lines to minimize part inventory cost. OR Spectrum 192, 349–373 (2009)
2. Scholl, A., Becker, C.: State-of-the-art exact and heuristic solution procedures for simple assembly line balancing. Eur. Jour. of Operational Research 168, 666–693 (2006)
3. Bourjault, A.: Contribution a une Approch Methodology de L'assemblage Automatise: Elaboration Automatique des Sequences Operatoires. Universite de Franche-Comte (1984)
4. De Fazio, T.L., Whitney, D.E.: Simplified generation of all mechanical assembly sequences. IEEE Journal of Robotics and Automation RA-3(6), 640–658 (1987)

5. Wilson, R.H.: Minimizing user queries in interactive assembly planning. IEEE Transactions on Robotics and Automation 11, 308–312 (1995)
6. Jones, R.l.E., Wilson, R.H., Calton, T.L.: Constraintbased interactive assembly planning. In: Proc.: IEEE Int. Conf. on Robotics and Automation, vol. 1, pp. 913–920 (1997)
7. Kaufman, S.G., Wilson, R.H., Jones, R.E., Calton, T.L.: The archimedes 2 mechanical assembly planning system. In: Proc. IEEE Int. Conf. on Robotics and Automation, vol. 1, pp. 3361–3368 (1996)
8. Sanderson, A.C., Homem de Mello, L.S., Zhang, H.: Assembly sequence planning. AI Magazine 11, 62–81 (1990)
9. Santochi, M., Dini, G.: Computer-aided planning of assembly operations: the selection of assembly sequences. Robotics and Computer-Integrated Manufacturing 9, 439–446 (1992)
10. Yokota, Y., Rough, D.R.: Assembly/disassembly sequence planning. Assembly Automation 12, 31–38 (1992)
11. Cho, Y., Shin, C.K., Cho, H.S.: Automated inference on stable robotics assembly sequences based upon the evaluation of base assembly motion instability. Robotica 11, 351–362 (1993)
12. Domschke, W., Scholl, A., Vo, S.: Produktionsplanung. Springer, Heidelberg (1993)
13. Meyr, H.: Supply chain planning in the german automotive industry. OR Spectrum 26, 447–470 (2004)
14. Dangelmaier, W.: Produktion und Information-System und Modell. Springer, Heidelberg (2003)
15. Roeder, A.: A methodology for modeling inter-company supply chains and for evaluating a method of integrated product and process documentation. Eur. Jour. of Operational Research 169, 1010–1029 (2006)
16. Sinz, C.: Verifikation regelbasierter Konfigurationssysteme. Fak. fuer Informations- und Kognitionswissenschaften. Eberhard-Karls-Univ., Tuebingen (2003)
17. Boysen, N., Fliedner, M., Scholl, A.: Production planning of mixed-model assembly lines: Overview and extensions. Tech. rep., Friedrich-Schiller-University Jena (2007)
18. Chen, C.L.: Automatic assembly sequences generation by pattern-matching. Technical report, School of Engineering and Technology, Electrical Engineering and CAD/CAM Center, Purdue University (1989)
19. Jentsch, W., Kaden, F.: Automatic generation of assembly sequences. Artificial Intelligence and Information-Control Systems of Robots 1, 197–200 (1984)
20. Baldwin, D.F., Abell, T.E., Lui, M.-C., De Fazio, T.L., Whitney, D.E.: An integrated computer aid for generating and evaluating assembly sequences for mechanical products. IEEE Trans. Robot. and Automat. 7, 78–94 (1991)
21. Henrioud, J.M., Bourjault, A.: LEGA - A computer-aided generator of assembly plans. In: Computer-Aided Mechanical Assembly Planning, pp. 191–215. Kluwer Academic Publishers, Dordrecht (1991)
22. Dini, G., Santochi, M.: Automated sequencing and subassembly detection in assembly planning. Annals CIRP 41, 1–4 (1992)
23. Falkenauer, E.: Line balancing in the real world. In: Int. Conf. on Product Lifecycle Management (2005)

A Conceptual Model for Production Leveling (Heijunka) Implementation in Batch Production Systems

Luciano Fonseca de Araujo and Abelardo Alves de Queiroz

Federal University of Santa Catarina, Department of Manufacturing,
GETEQ Research Group, Caixa Postal 476, Campus Universitário, Trindade,
88040-900, Florianópolis, SC, Brazil
lfaraujo2005@gmail.com, abelardo@emc.ufsc.br

Abstract. This paper explains an implementation model for a new method for Production Leveling designed for batch production system. The main structure of this model is grounded on three constructs: traditional framework for Operations Planning, Lean Manufacturing concepts for Production Leveling and case study guidelines. By combining the first and second construct, a framework for Production Leveling has been developed for batch production systems. Then, case study guidelines were applied to define an appropriate implementation sequence that includes prioritizing criteria of products and level production plan for capacity analysis. This conceptual model was applied on a Brazilian subsidiary of a multinational company. Furthermore, results evidence performance improvement and hence were approved by both managers and Production personnel. Finally, based on research limitations, researchers and practitioners can confirm the general applicability of this method by applying it in companies that share similarities in terms of batch processing operations.

Keywords: Batch Production, Heijunka, Implementation Model, Production Leveling.

1 Introduction

Due intense competition, both traditional and emerging companies must improve existing methods for Operations Planning (OP). Indeed, Production Leveling improves operational efficiency in five objectives related to flexibility, speed, cost, quality and customers' service level [1], [6], [10].

Production Leveling combines two well known concepts of Lean Manufacturing: Kanban System and Heijunka. The former means pull signaling of production based on concept for supermarket replenishment to control work-in-process inventory. The latter means a smother pattern for daily production sequencing at assembling lines [8], [9], [10].

Even though such concepts are relevant on literature, one can argue about whether or not Lean Manufacturing concepts can be generally applicable [5]. Hence, three

B. Vallespir and T. Alix (Eds.): APMS 2009, IFIP AICT 338, pp. 81–88, 2010.

main gaps of literature review can also be used to support such statement. First of all, both conceptual models and problem solving [2] are focused on mixed model assembling lines. Secondly, it can be said that batch production is suitable to a wide variety of manufacturing processes, even in automotive supply chains [3]. Finally, regarding that Production Leveling is often described as simple models and concepts [9], [10], the control of batch processes is often referred by using a *triangle Kanban* for few product models [8], [10]. Indeed, this implies that batch production always comprises a minor part of a value stream. Based on those statements, one question arises above all others. The question is: What are the steps necessary to level out the production when batch processes represent a major part of a value stream? Thus, there was no method based on Production Leveling designed for batch production processes and its variations related to many industrial applications [1].

Based on those gaps found on literature, this paper aims to present an implementation model for Production Leveling designed for batch production systems. Additionally, this conceptual model was applied in a major qualitative research in early 2008 in a large multinational company, located on state of São Paulo, Brazil [1]. Thus, this paper is organized as follows. In section 2, a literature review of the main concepts is presented, including the structure of Production Leveling well its main activities. In section 3, research methodology is briefly explained. Section 4 presents an implementation model. This paper ends with conclusions in section 5. Furthermore, author state that this method is suitable with all manufacturing systems that share similarities within its processing operations [1]. Hence, this general applicability is briefly summarized by providing a classification of batch processing operations in Appendix A.

2 Literature Review

This section briefly presents the theoretical framework of the new method [1] which main structure was developed based on a previous literature review. This study was designed by combining the traditional framework for Operations Planning (OP) [9], [12] for make-to-stock positioning strategy and basic concepts of Lean Manufacturing [8], [10], [13].

2.1 Theoretical Framework for Production Leveling

The traditional approach for OP comprises three levels of decisions related to a planning horizon ahead of time: *Strategic* (long term), *Tactical* (medium term) and *Operational* (short term). Regarding that Lean Manufacturing practices differ from classical approach for OP in both Tactical and Operational Level [12], this method has developed by replacing classical activities of OP by Lean Manufacturing ones in such levels [1] as depicted in Fig. 1 as follows:

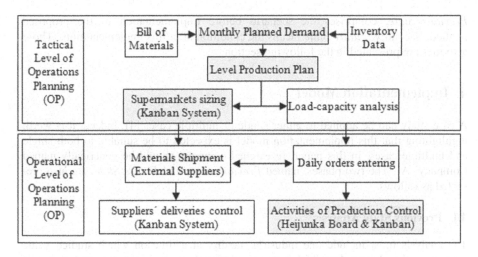

Fig. 1. Theoretical framework of Production Leveling and its main activities

Those activities highlighted at light gray boxes are shortly described as follows.

2.1.1 Tactical Level

The *Monthly Planned Demand* includes a decision based on inventory data, bill of materials and customers´ orders data. Hence, materials planners must define a planned volume (demand) for every product model for the following month. One of the key features of Production Leveling comprises the prioritization of product models due product variety. It usually suggests a make-to-stock production for both high and medium volume ('A' and 'B' items) whereas a make-to-order production for low volume ('C' items) [10]. Based on that decision, a *Level Production Plan* must be developed to generate a leveled production pattern [7]. It features information about production models, production batch size, set up time and a planning time horizon that can be fixed as six or more days [1], [7]. The 'required capacity', named as *production pitch* or *pitch,* is also calculated for every product model and comprises a total elapsed time necessary to produce an entire single batch for one given product model. Thus, it comprises an analysis of both required and available capacity of process. Finally, *Supermarket sizing* is a materials planning activity to quantify inventory storage points using the Kanban System.

2.1.2 Operational Level

Activities of Production Control feature shop-floor routines such as loading, sequencing, scheduling, dispatching and control. In a Lean Manufacturing environment, visual controls provide useful information about normal condition. These tools includes Kanban Board or Electronic Kanban as well Heijunka Board and Production Rate Control Board [1] for daily control of production completion.

3 Research Methodology

Based on objectives of this paper, the implementation model was grounded on guidelines for case studies [4]. Hence it was divided into two phases. The first one, named

Previous State, comprises the scenario before implementation of the proposed method. Secondly, *Future State* means the condition after this implementation. Those activities are presented in the following section.

4 Implementation Model

A case study can be applied to either single or multiple cases [4]. Indeed, it is worth highlighting that this implementation model is expected to be suitable to both single and multiple cases. In this paper, researched company should be generically named Company 'A'. The two phases, named *Previous State* and *Future State*, are also presented as follows.

4.1 Previous State Analysis

The analysis must include one industrial facility at a time on which studied value chain must be shortly described in terms of manufacturing processes and materials flow layout. Fig. 2 depicts the main activities of *Previous State* analysis:

Select case	Entering field	Enfolding literature	Case diagnosis	Reaching closure
Company 'A' Batch Production Flow Layout	History Performance OP practices	Qualitative assessment of original OP practices	Conclusions of Original State	Recommendations to Company 'A'

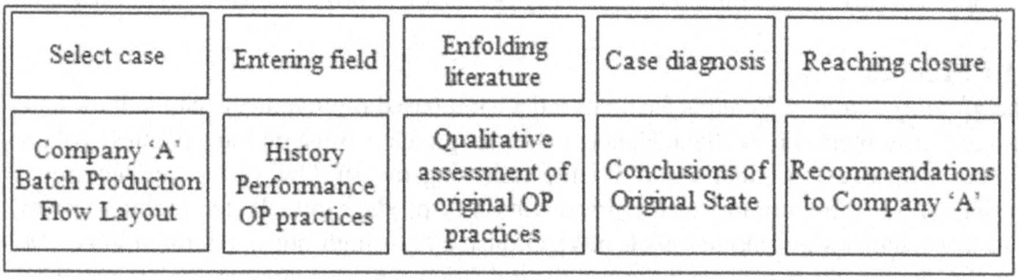

Fig. 2. First phase of the proposed methodology for *Previous State* analysis

If company and its processes features evidence that proposed method is suitable to *Previous State* scenario, then data must be collected in field including company history as well value stream performance and existing OP practices. After doing that, a qualitative assessment of such practices must be performed by comparing them with theoretical elements that composes Production Leveling. This activity comprises both principles and policies grounded on both Heijunka and Kanban Systems objectives and key features [1]. Hence, due paper limitation, a case study of this qualitative evaluation is going to be presented in details on a future research paper. After that assessment, researcher must conclude about *Previous State* and recommendations must be listed aiming to reach closure on the first phase.

4.2 Future State Analysis

Based on proposed approach [1], the second phase model begins with a training seminar, and a *Pilot Project Planning* structured on a *PDCA cycle* followed by a *Pilot Project Execution*. After that, performance indicators must be gathered and analyzed before and after the implementation. Furthermore, researcher must assess whether or not implemented practices adhere to Production Leveling principles and policies [1]. If so, based on facts and data, proposed method will be validated regarding research limitations. After that, the case study ends with conclusions and final recommendations. Those decisions are summarized in Fig. 3 as follows.

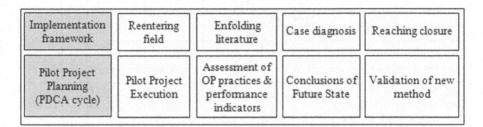

Fig. 3. Second phase of the proposed methodology for *Future State* analysis

4.2.1 Implementation Framework
Based on proposed model [1], the implementation framework highlighted on light gray box in Fig. 3 includes a *Pilot Project Planning* that starts with a *Level Production Plan*. Hence, such activity is described in Fig. 4 as follows:

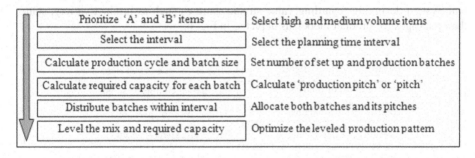

Fig. 4. Activities of the Level Production Plan designing

Fig. 4 shows the proposed method that includes the criterion for classification of products based on monthly demand, namely *ABC analysis*. After selecting prioritized items, researcher must to design a Level Production Plan for each machine that comprises the studied value stream. This plan can be alternatively designed by leveling the required capacity using the following information [1]: Set up or Changeover time, production batch size and production rate at the studied machine. Additionally, process stability and its related constraints must be listed for further analysis. The first decision is a calculation of production cycle within interval related to the theoretical number of monthly set up operations. Second decision comprises the required capacity (*production pitch* or *pitch*) for each product model related total processing time elapsed from setting up machine till processing an entire production batch. Finally, this plan comprises visual information as depicted on Fig. 5 [1].

Product Model	1	Pitch	2	Pitch	3	Pitch	4	Pitch	5	Pitch
A	250	213	250	213	250	213	250	213	250	213
B	220	190	220	190	220	190	220	190	220	190
C	210	183	210	183	210	183	210	183	210	183
D	256	217			256	217			256	217
E			250	213			250	213		
F	150	138			150	138			150	138
G			240	205						
H							180	160		
I	180	160							180	160
J					140	130				
Daily Required Capacity (min)		1,168		1,143		1,168		1,143		1,168
Total Available Time (min)		1,214		1,214		1,214		1,214		1,214
Daily Remaining Time (min)		46		71		46		71		46
Utilization of Capacity (%)		96%		94%		96%		94%		96%

Fig. 5. A Level Production Plan for one single machine featuring five days planning interval

Fig. 5 depicts a Level Production Plan with five days of planning interval. First left column has selected product models in machine whereas every day has production batches (columns labeled as numbers) and its related required capacity in minutes (columns labeled as 'Pitch'). After ending this activity, the next one comprises Kanban System designing regarding value stream features such as product variety, standard packages for product model, as depicted in Fig. 6.

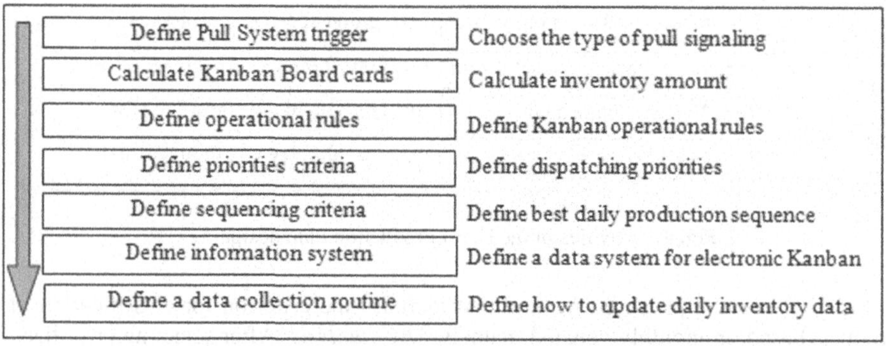

Define Pull System trigger	Choose the type of pull signaling
Calculate Kanban Board cards	Calculate inventory amount
Define operational rules	Define Kanban operational rules
Define priorities criteria	Define dispatching priorities
Define sequencing criteria	Define best daily production sequence
Define information system	Define a data system for electronic Kanban
Define a data collection routine	Define how to update daily inventory data

Fig. 6. Information flow applied to design a Kanban System

Finally, operational rules must be set to define how Production personnel must execute daily level scheduling and its five activities of production control by using visual controls such as Kanban Board and set of cards, Heijunka Board and Hourly Production Rate control. In some cases, due product variety, an electronic Kanban could be best suitable to control a Pull System. Finally, operational rules and its information flow are both depicted in Fig. 7.

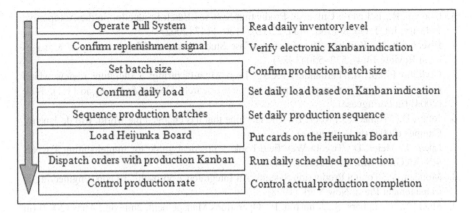

Operate Pull System	Read daily inventory level
Confirm replenishment signal	Verify electronic Kanban indication
Set batch size	Confirm production batch size
Confirm daily load	Set daily load based on Kanban indication
Sequence production batches	Set daily production sequence
Load Heijunka Board	Put cards on the Heijunka Board
Dispatch orders with production Kanban	Run daily scheduled production
Control production rate	Control actual production completion

Fig. 7. Operational rules for Activities of Production Control

5 Conclusions

This paper presented an implementation model grounded on Production Leveling designed to batch production. The methodological approach was designed by using a guideline for case study and comprises an *Previous State* and *Future State*. Both phases include an analysis of OP practices. The major contribution of this paper is to present a new and simple method Production Leveling that was empirically tested in early 2008 that helped to achieve satisfactory results. This method is grounded on Lean Manufacturing concepts with major changes at *Tactical* and *Operational* levels. By defining an alternate method for Level Production Plan, future papers will show results of an implementation and qualitative assessment of proposed method. To conclude, based on research limitations, researchers and practitioners can apply these concepts aiming to test its general applicability in different scenarios of batch production with product variety in make-to-stock positioning strategy.

Acknowledgements

We would like to thank Conselho Nacional de Desenvolvimento Científico e Tecnológico (CNPq) of Brazil for financial support. We would also like to thank the company where this research has been developed.

References

1. Araujo, L.F.: Method for application of Production Leveling in repetitive manufacturing systems with batch production (Master of Science Dissertation). Federal University of Santa Catarina. Department of Mechanical Engineering, p. 169 (2008) (in Portuguese)
2. Kotani, S., Ito, T., Ohno, K.: Sequencing Problem for a Mixed-Model Assembly Line In The Toyota Production System. Int. J. Prod. Res. 42(23), 4955–4974 (2004)

3. Cooney, R.: Is Lean a Universal Production System? Batch Production in the Automotive Industry. Int. J. Op. & Prod. Man. 22(10), 1130–1147 (2002)
4. Eisenhardt, K.: Building Theories from Case Study Research. The Academy of Management Review 14(4), 532–550 (1989)
5. Godinho Filho, M., Fernandes, F.C.F.: Lean Manufacturing: a literature review which classifies and analyses papers indicating new research. Gestão & Produção 11(1), 1–19 (2004) (in Portuguese)
6. Jones, D., Womack, J., Roos, D.: The machine that has changed the world. Rio de Janeiro, Campus (2004) (in Portuguese)
7. Liker, J., Meier, D.: Toyota Way field book: a practical guide for implementing Toyotás 4Ps. McGraw-Hill, New York (2007)
8. Monden, Y.: Toyota Production System: An Integrated Approach, 3rd edn. Engineering & Management Press, New York (1998)
9. Slack, N., Chambers, S., Johnston, R.: Operations Management, 2nd edn., Atlas (2002) (in Portuguese)
10. Smalley, A.: Creating Level Pull. Lean Enterprise Institute, São Paulo (2004) (in Portuguese)
11. Lee, H.L., Padmanabhan, V., Whang, S.: The bullwhip effect in supply chains. Sloan Management Review 38(3), 93–102 (1997)
12. Vollmann, T.E., Jacobs, F.R., Berry, W., Whybark, D.C.: Manufacturing planning and control systems for supply chain management, 5th edn. McGraw-Hill, New York (2006) (in Portuguese)
13. Shingo, S.: Toyota Production System: from the point of view of Production Engineering, Porto Alegre, Bookman (1996) (in Portuguese)

Appendix A: Classification of Batch Processing Operations

Proposed method can be generally applicable in batch process system whenever it shares the same kind of processing operations described as follows:

— Disjunctive type I – It converts a single piece of material into several parts, such as press stamping like processes by cutting up hot rolled steel coils to generate multiple purpose parts by varying materials, geometry and so forth.
— Disjunctive type II – It comprises some types of metallurgical processes that convert powder and pellets into a batch of parts such as extrusion and plastic injection molding.

The Moderating Role of JIT Links with Suppliers on the Relationship between Lean Manufacturing and Operational Performances

Pietro Romano[1], Pamela Danese[2], and Thomas Bortolotti[3],[*]

[1] Department of Electrical, Managerial and Mechanical Engineering, via delle Scienze 208,
33100 Udine, Italy
pietro.romano@uniud.it
[2] Department of Management and Engineering, Stradella S. Nicola 3, 36100 Vicenza, Italy
pamela.danese@unipd.it
[3] Department of Electrical, Managerial and Mechanical Engineering, via delle Scienze 208,
33100 Udine, Italy
thomas.bortolotti@unibg.it

Abstract. Lean manufacturing impacts several operational performances. The usefulness of JIT links with suppliers is also well known. However, literature lacks strong empirical evidences to exhibit the relationship between lean manufacturing, operational performances and JIT linkages with suppliers. This paper aims to investigate this relationship. A questionnaire-based international survey was used to obtain the main purpose of the research. Data from a sample of 200 companies were analyzed using a multiple regression methodology. The analysis demonstrates that JIT linkages with suppliers positively moderate the impact of lean manufacturing on punctuality, while the moderating effect is absent when considering efficiency and throughput time performance.

Keywords: Just-In-Time, Survey, Multiple regression analysis.

1 Introduction

Literature generally agrees that lean manufacturing impacts a number of operational performances: efficiency [1], [2] and [3], throughput time [3] and [4] and on time delivery [2] and [5]. JIT links with suppliers are also useful to improve operational performances listed above [1], [3], [6] and [7]. However, in literature we didn't find an empirical evidence to demonstrate whether companies implementing JIT links with suppliers and lean manufacturing practices show better operational performances than companies that don't implement JIT links with suppliers. In other words, this paper aims to investigate whether the relationship between lean manufacturing and operational performances – such as efficiency, throughput time and on time delivery – is positively moderated by the presence of JIT linkages with suppliers. A questionnaire-based survey was used to obtain the main purpose of the research. A total of 200 complete responses taken from the High Performance Manufacturing

---

[*] Corresponding author.

B. Vallespir and T. Alix (Eds.): APMS 2009, IFIP AICT 338, pp. 89–96, 2010.

research project dataset [8] and used to test and analyze three hypotheses included in the theoretical model: JIT linkages with suppliers positively moderate the relationship between lean manufacturing and efficiency (hypothesis H1), throughput time (hypothesis H2) and on time delivery (hypothesis H3).

2   Methods

2.1   Data Collection and Sample

The sampling universe is formed by manufacturing firms operating in machinery, electronic and transportation components sectors (SIC code: 35, 36 and 37). During the identification stage of the reference population, we selected for medium and large enterprises. Finally, we randomly selected, from this population, companies from different countries (i.e. Finland, US, Japan, Germany, Sweden, Korea, Italy, Australia and Spain). An international team of researchers collected data via questionnaires, that were administered by individual visits or sent by mail. The questionnaires were sent to different respondents within each company, such as production control managers, inventory managers, supervisors, and so on. Respondents gave answers on lean practices adopted (lean manufacturing and JIT links with suppliers) and operational performances obtained. A total of 266 responses were returned. We discarded 66 incomplete responses. Data analysis were based on a sample of 200 firms.

2.2   Research Variables and Measures

Two multi-item and three mono-item constructs were identified: lean manufacturing (LM), JIT links with suppliers (JITsup), efficiency (EFF), throughput time (TT), and on time delivery (OTD). As to the items composing LM and JITsup constructs, we asked respondents to indicate on a 7 point Likert scale to what extent each practice proposed was adopted in the company (1 means "not at all" and 7 "to a great extent"). As to the items composing the three mono-item constructs (EFF, TT and OTD), we asked respondents to provide their opinion about company's performances compared with its competitors on a 5 point Likert scale (1 is for "poor, low" and 5 is for "superior"). Table 1 reports the five constructs with their items, the results of factor analysis after Varimax rotation of factors and Cronbach's α. Convergent validity of the two multi-item constructs is demonstrated since factor loadings are all above 0.679 and only one component for each construct was identified with total variance explained above 52.18% [9]. Reliability was ensured by the high values of Cronbach's α, all above 0.70 [10]. Finally, scientific literature gave theoretical validity to the multi-item constructs:

(1) lean manufacturing: this is a six-item scale that measure the ability of a company to obtain a continuous production flow using appropriate tools and methods, such as 'cell' design (shop floor), SMED, and Heijunka. The cell provides remarkable benefits in terms of stream continuity, decrease of total lead time and stocks, flexibility performance and goods transfers [11]; SMED is a technique designed to improve dies and tools exchanges, minimizing set-up time, therefore maximizing machines capacity ratio [12]; Heijunka consists in a production balancing tool, related to production processes. It allows to balance production activities minimizing supply fluctuation [13].

(2) JIT links with suppliers: this is a three-item scale that measure the integration of JIT techniques and methods (kanban and pull systems) between the company and its suppliers. Kanban can be defined as a labels-based system, designed to mark and optimize materials and goods transfers along the production line and the supply network [14]; pull system implies that in a supply network nothing is produced upstream before a real request downstream [15].

Table 2 shows basic statistics for the five constructs.

Table 1. Validity test of measures

Factor	Item	Factor Loading	Variance explained	Cronbach α
Lean manufacturing (LM)	We have laid out the shop floor so that processes and machines are in close proximity to each other	0.689	52.18%	0.81
	The layout of our shop floor facilitates low inventories and fast throughput.	0.778		
	We are aggressively working to lower setup times in our plant	0.750		
	We have low setup times of equipment in our plant	0.715		
	Our workers are trained to reduce setup time	0.720		
	Our manufacturing capacity is balanced throughout the entire manufacturing process.	0.679		
JIT links with suppliers (JITsup)	Suppliers fill our kanban containers, rather than filling purchase orders.	0.879	67.65%	0.76
	Our suppliers deliver to us in kanban containers, without the use of separate packaging.	0.860		
	Our suppliers are linked with us by a pull system.	0.719		
Efficiency (EFF)	Unit cost of manufacturing	Mono-item mono-respondent		
Throughput time (TT)	Cycle time (from raw materials to delivery)	Mono-item mono-respondent		
On time delivery (OTD)	On time delivery performance	Mono-item mono-respondent		

Table 2. Constructs basic statistics

Variables	Mean	S.D.	Range
Lean manufacturing (LM)	4.90	0.70	2.83-6.50
JIT links with suppliers (JITsup)	3.61	1.01	1.44-6.44
Efficiency (EFF)	3.20	0.86	1.00-5.00
Throughput time (TT)	3.41	0.74	2.00-5.00
On time delivery performance (OTD)	3.79	0.87	1.00-5.00

3 Data Analysis

The research aims to investigate whether the relationship between lean manufacturing and operational performances is moderated by the presence of JIT linkages with suppliers. Moderated relationship is reflected in the concept of statistical interaction. The equation (1) describes the logic of moderated regression [16]:

$$y = \beta_0 + \beta_1 x + \beta_2 z + \beta_3 xz + \varepsilon \qquad (1)$$

where x is LM, the focal independent variable [17], z is JITsup and y, the dependent variable, is any of operational performances. The 'xz' term in (1) is called interaction term. We used a hierarchical regression procedure, Table 3 and Table 4 display the results of the analysis. We considered firm size and sector as control variables. The size was measured by the number of firm's employees. The sector was insert in the model, by creating dummy variables (Electronics and Transportation components). For every operational performance, firstly, we studied the main effects of independent variables - i.e. lean manufacturing and JIT links with suppliers - , then, we introduced in the model the product term xz (LM X JITsup) to analyze the interaction effects. If the coefficient of the product term (β_3) is statistically significant and R^2 increases when this term is introduced in the model, the existence of a moderated effect on x-y relationship is demonstrated [17].

4 Results

As shown in Table 3 and Table 4, firm size and sector control variables don't result significantly related to operational performances. The non-significant values of both β_3-coefficients exposed in Table 3 do not confirm hypotheses H1 and H2 about the moderating role of JIT links with suppliers on the relationship between lean manufacturing and efficiency and throughput time performances. To the contrary, the significant and positive β_3-coefficient shown in Table 4 suggest that it is possible to confirm the existence of the moderating role of JIT links with suppliers on the relationship between lean manufacturing and on time delivery performance (hypothesis H3). Additional support is the significant increase of R^2 when the interaction effect was introduced in the model (from 0.084 to 0.126).

The promising results exposed in Table 4 led us to a detailed study on the marginal effect of the Lean manufacturing (variable x) on the on time delivery performance (variable y), for different values of JIT links with suppliers (variable z), as suggested by [16] and [17].

We calculated that the marginal effect of LM on OTD depends on JITsup, according to the following formula:

$$\partial OTD/\partial LM = -0.469 + 0.256 JITsup \qquad (2)$$

T-test reveals that equation (2) is significant at a 0.05 level for the values of JITsup greater than 2.57. Figure 1 shows how the marginal effect of LM varies when JITsup increases. It is easy to see that LM has an increasing impact on OTD performance when the level of JITsup is greater than 2.57.

Table 3. Hierarchical regression analysis (efficiency and throughput time)

	EFF		TT	
	Main effects	Interaction effects	Main effects	Interaction effects
Constant (β_0)	0.849*	0.318	0.952*	1.753
Size	0.000	0.000	0.000	0.000
Electronics	-0.280	-0.276	-0.014	-0.020
Transp. Comp.	-0.091	-0.086	-0.121	-0.127
LM (β_1)	0.583***	0.671*	0.499***	0.337
JITsup (β_2)	-0.085	0.070	0.020	-0.215
LM X JITsup (β_3)		-0.031		0.047
R^2 Adjusted	0.187	0.183	0.192	0.190
F test	9.097***	7.568***	9.198***	7.712***

The value reported are unstandardized regression coefficients
* p-value <.05 level; ** p-value <.01 level; *** p-value <.001 level

Table 4. Hierarchical regression analysis (on time delivery)

	OTD	
	Main effects	Interaction effects
Constant (β_0)	1.703***	6.060***
Size	0.000	0.000
Electronics	-0.019	-0.048
Transp. Comp.	0.064	0.029
LM (β_1)	0.414***	-0.469*
JITsup (β_2)	0.020	-1.253**
LM X JITsup (β_3)		0.256**
R^2 Adjusted	0.084	0.126
F test	4.249**	5.224***

The value reported are unstandardized regression coefficients
* p-value <.05 level; ** p-value <.01 level; *** p-value <.001 level

To gain an intuitive understanding of the interaction effect between LM and JITsup, we computed and graphed the slope of OTD performance on LM at few different values of JITsup. Our strategy was to evaluate the effects of LM on OTD at "low" and "high" values of JITsup, where "low" is defined as one standard deviation below the JITsup mean (i.e. = 2.598), and "high" as one standard deviation above the JITsup mean (i.e. = 4.616) [18]. Starting from the relation found out from the hierarchical regression analysis (ODT = 6.060 − 0.469LM − 1.253JITsup + 0.256LMJITsup) and using the two mentioned values of the variable JITsup, two linear equations of OTD performance, depending on LM, were created. Figure 2 reports the graph of the equations. Jaccard and Turrisi classifies this trend as 'disordinal interaction' [17], an interaction in which the regression line that regresses y onto the focal independent variable for a given level of the moderator (high JITsup)

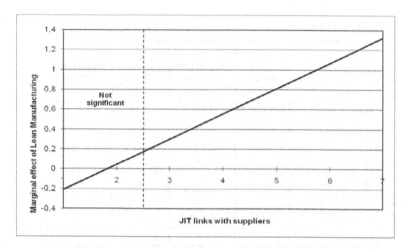

Fig. 1. The influence of JIT links with suppliers on the marginal effect of lean manufacturing

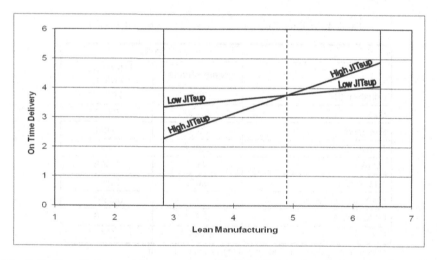

Fig. 2. On Time Delivery performance slope at low and high levels of JIT links with suppliers

intersects with the correspondent regression line for a different level of the moderator (low JITsup). The intersection corresponds to a level of lean manufacturing of 4.89 (49% of the sample is below this score). Within the LM range (2.83 - 6.50), all values of OTD are above the minimum acceptable level (2.26 > 1.00) and below the maximum acceptable level (4.91 < 5.00).

5 Discussion and Conclusions

The multiple regression analysis demonstrates several key findings:

Finding 1: companies adopting lean manufacturing don't show an additional contribution to efficiency (unit cost of manufacturing) and throughput time by implementing also JIT linkages with suppliers. Both performances are significantly explained by the implementation of lean manufacturing.

Finding 2: JIT linkages with suppliers moderate the impact of lean manufacturing on punctuality. For a company that has high values of LM (e.g. LM = 5.60) and medium values of JITsup (e.g. JITsup = 3.61), a one-point increment of LM increases OTD of about 11%; whereas a one-point increment of JITsup increases OTD of about 4.4%. It is always better to increase LM rather than JITsup to improve OTD. However, the hierarchical regression highlights a "disordinal interaction" (Figure 2). This interaction suggests to implement only lean manufacturing practices firstly, and then (when LM overpasses the 4.89 value, which corresponds to the intersection point) implement both lean manufacturing and JIT links with suppliers practices.

Finding 3: the effect of LM could be even negative for levels of JITsup lower than 1.83 (Figure 1). This means that, when companies have not JIT links with suppliers, Lean Management effects on punctuality could be counterproductive. Nevertheless this result is not statistically significant, therefore this finding would be interesting to test on a wider sample of companies in a future study.

In conclusions, the study presents implications both for academics and practitioners. Our work confirms most of the previous literature contributions and provides to fill the lack of literature concerning how JIT with suppliers impacts lean manufacturing and operational performances. It also suggests the correct sequence to implement Lean Manufacturing inside a company and JIT with suppliers to obtain maximum levels of punctuality (OTD). As a matter of fact, data analysis reveals that for companies which haven't good levels of lean manufacturing is better to improve these practices first, and then direct their efforts also towards JIT links with suppliers.

The research is subject to the normal limitations of survey research. The model tested in this study used a selection of medium and large enterprises operating in machinery, electronic and transportation components sectors. Thus, future studies should include firms operating in other industries or small enterprises.

References

1. Wafa, M.A., Yasin, M.M., Swinehart, K.: The impact of supplier proximity on JIT success: an informational perspective. International Journal of Physical Distribution & Logistics Management 26(4), 23–34 (1996)
2. Swanson, C.A., Lankford, W.M.: Just-In-Time manufacturing. Business Process Management Journal 4(4), 333–341 (1998)
3. Tan, K.C.: A framework of supply chain management literature. European Journal of Purchasing & Supply Management 7, 39–48 (2001)
4. Spencer, M.S., Guide, V.D.: An exploration of the components of JIT: case study and survey results. International Journal of Operations & Production Management 15(5), 72–83 (1995)
5. Zhu, Z., Meredith, P.H.: Defining critical elements in JIT implementation: a survey. Industrial Management and Data Systems 95(8), 21–28 (1995)
6. Mistry, J.J.: Origins of profitability through JIT processes in the supply chain. Industrial Management & Data Systems 105(6), 752–768 (2005)

7. Matson, J.E., Matson, J.O.: Just-In-Time implementation issues among automotive suppliers in the southern USA. Supply Chain Management: An International Journal 12(6), 432–443 (2007)
8. Flynn, B.B., Schroeder, R.G., Flynn, E.J., Sakakibara, S., Bates, K.A.: World-class manufacturing project: overview and selected results. International Journal of Operations & Production Management 17(7), 671–685 (1997)
9. Bagozzi, R.P., Yi, Y.: On the evaluation of structural equation models. Academy Marketing Science 16(1), 74–94 (1988)
10. Nunnally, J.C.: Psychometric Theory. McGraw-Hill, New York (1994)
11. Harris, R., Rother, M.: Creating Continuous Flow, An Action Guide for Managers, Engineers and Production Associates. The Lean Enterprise Institute, Cambridge (2001)
12. Shingo, S.: A revolution in manufacturing: The SMED system. Productivity Press (1985)
13. Coleman, B.J., Vaghefi, M.R.: Heijunka: a key to the Toyota production system. Production and Inventory Management 35(4), 31–35 (1994)
14. Nicholas, J.: Competitive Manufacturing Management. Irwin/McGraw-Hill, New York (1998)
15. Womack, J.P., Jones, D.T.: Lean Thinking: Banish Waste and Create Wealth in your Corporation. Simon and Schuster, New York (1996)
16. Brambor, T., Clark, W.R., Golden, M.: Understanding Interaction Models: Improving Empirical Analyses, vol. 14, pp. 63–82 (2006)
17. Jaccard, J., Turrisi, R.: Interaction effects in multiple regression, 2nd edn. Sage Publications, Thousand Oaks (2003)
18. Cohen, J., Cohen, P.: Applied Multiple Regression for the Behavioral Sciences. Lawrence Erlbaum, Hillsdale (1983)

Type Toyota Management Systems (MSTT) of Small and Medium-Sized Enterprises in Mechanical and Electrical Industry

Stefan Kluge, Andreas Rau, and Engelbert Westkämper

Institute of Industrial Manufacturing and Management (IFF), University of Stuttgart, Nobelstr, 12, D-70569 Stuttgart, Tel.: +49 (0)711 / 685-61862; Fax: +49 (0)711 / 685-51862
sjk@iff.uni-stuttgart.de
www.iff.uni-stuttgart.de

Abstract. This paper gives an overview and considers the most recent aspects of a study, dealing with the topic of Type Toyota Management Systems. In the survey SMEs in mechanical and electrical industry have been asked. On the one hand, a questionnaire for a mass evaluation was used and on the other hand specialists have been interviewed orally for the specific evaluation. The paper shows the methodology of the survey and some of the highlights of the results. Additionally, some approaches to face future challenges are introduced.

Keywords: Production Systems, Lean Management, Holistic Production Design.

1 Introduction

Since basic conditions, such as shorter technology and product life cycles, are changing faster and faster, and due to increasing globalization and growing dynamics of the markets, the requirements for enterprises have increased with regard to product and service quality. Due to the worldwide growing competition, enterprises are faced with a stronger pressure. The companies' tasks are frequently hard to accomplish with conventional organizational methods [1, 2]. At the beginning of the nineties of the last century, the "International Motor Vehicle Program" of the M.I.T. in Cambridge aroused automotive industry in Germany and Europe [3]. The use of production systems was proven in studies [8, 9] and in practice [5, 6] and is qualitatively visible through downsizing the process chains. The profit potentials developed with holistic production systems are remarkable and quantified in practice with the following details: Increasing productivity by an average of 40%, reduction of processing time by an average of 60%, and stock minimizing by an average of 40%. With the keyword Lean Production, the American scientists Womack, Jones und Roos describe the method of automotive production which they had seen in the Toyota company in Japan in their book "The machine that changed the world" [4, 5]. They write about the effective and quality-oriented production which looms large for competitiveness, management concepts like the integrated production system or Lean Production were introduced in enterprises [5, 6]. These concepts mainly exist in automotive enterprises and also in large companies from other sectors. They rarely exist in SME [7].

B. Vallespir and T. Alix (Eds.): APMS 2009, IFIP AICT 338, pp. 97–104, 2010.
© IFIP International Federation for Information Processing 2010

2 Study in Type Toyota Management Systems

Type Toyota Management Systems (MSTT) are management approaches such as the Toyota production system, holistic production systems, lean production, business reengineering or management concepts which contribute a positive approach to the changing market conditions. MSTT are still focused on the automotive and supply industry. MSTT are predominantly used in large enterprises and only slowly arrive in other industries. Due to the fact that in branches like the mechanical and electrical industry only less experience and awareness had been documented the Institute of Industrial Manufacturing and Management of the University of Stuttgart realized a study. Relating to enterprise typological classifications, leading enterprises develop customer-specific products, standardized products with customer-specific variants as well as standard products with variants (86%). Standard products with variants only exist in a minority of the surveyed enterprises of the mass evaluation. The leading enterprises apply manual (51%), industrialized (71%) and also automated work techniques. However, the enterprises surveyed in the mass evaluation apply only 21% automated work techniques. The leading enterprises supply a high product variety, work mainly with automated processes and have a highly standardized product range. These are aspects of the leading position of enterprises of the specific evaluation. The following questions in this study were to be answered from the perspective of science and practice:

- What is the actual state of MSTT? Holistic production systems and management concepts have been analyzed which have potential to develop substantial solutions for new and changing challenges
- Which methods and tools are included in effective MSTT? Examples from automotive industry show that methods and tools like Just-in-Time-Logistic (JIT), the continuous improvement process (CIP), the process standardization and the visual management belongs to MSTT [11]
- Are there any enterprise-specific conditions for the usage of MSTT?
- Which general conditions are important for the success of MSTT?
- What should MSTT be able to do in future apart from what they can do today?

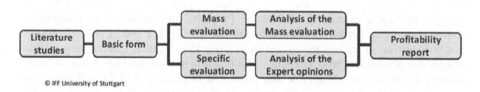

© IFF University of Stuttgart

Fig. 1. Research design (IFF, University of Stuttgart)

Based on literature studies which cover the current research and practice status a basic form was developed (figure 1). In this basic form all relevant questions were summarized in a question pool, including open and closed questions. For getting funded data and information, a combined procedure with extensive surveys (mass evaluation) and several detailed expert opinions in the form of interviews (specific evaluation) were chosen. In the mass evaluation more than 100 enterprises within the mechanical and electrical industry were interviewed. The specific evaluation covers so-called leading enterprises which come from the target group and have experience within the scope of the MSTT. In a conclusive step, the results were consolidated and prepared for the report.

2.1 Mass Evaluation

The majority of the polled enterprises follow the trend of the big companies which often belong to the automotive industry with a time gap to implement MSTT.

Approximately 20% of the enterprises have planned "no implementation". Almost 50% of the enterprises have started with the implementation later than 2005. The implementation of such systems started in the automotive industries from the beginnings up to the mid-nineties of the previous century. For a few years now MSTT has been in the improvement and optimization phase [6, 7]. Contrary to this situation, enterprises which are actually implementing MSTT are in the starting phase.

2.1.1 Specific Tools of Work Organization
The methods of the work organization (figure 2) are consistently often implemented and applied, which is an argument for these methods. Analyzing the results of the survey, the methods of "Job-Enlargement", "Job-Enrichment" and "Job-Rotation" are less often used than expected according to their degree of popularity. The same is true for the method "ergonomic evaluation of operating processes". The target of these four methods is to improve the working conditions for employees in assembly. There are important aspects in comparing the success and the implementation of these methods. For example, many enterprises mention "flexible working hours" as very

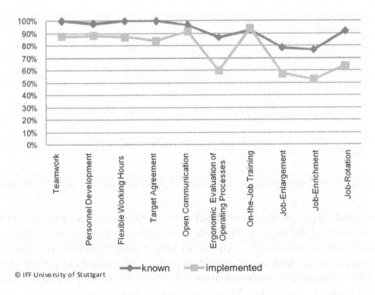

Fig. 2. Popularity and implementation of methods of work organization (IFF, University of Stuttgart)

successful. Accordingly, this tool is implemented very often. The method "ergonomic evaluation of operating processes" is in a completely different situation. This method is mostly seen as successful but the implementation is only realized by few of the interviewed enterprises [10].

For "Job-Enlargement", "Job-Enrichment" and "Job-Rotation" the above mentioned effect is even stronger, so that not used potentials could be identified.

2.1.2 Specific Tools of CIP and TQM Methods

Analyzing the methods of the CIP (continuous improvement process) and TQM (total quality management) it can be stated that "Six-Sigma" and "Line-Stop Concept" are well-known but rarely used. Regarding the evaluation of the CIP and TQM methods, it shows that some methods are categorized as successful but the implementation is rarely mentioned (figure 3).

"Poka-Yoke" and "Fast Problem Detection and Resolving" are also well-known and evaluated as very successful. At the same time the implementation of "Poka-Yoke" is not very distinct. The implementation of "Fast Problem Detection and Resolving" is on a higher level.

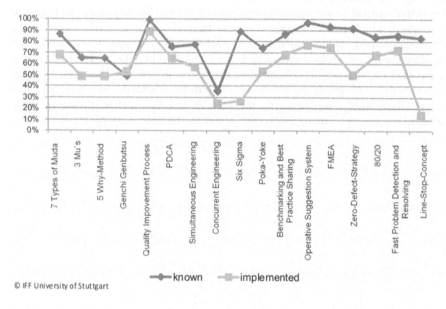

© IFF University of Stuttgart

Fig. 3. Popularity and implementation of CIP and TQM methods (IFF, University of Stuttgart)

An important aspect of the survey results are the mentioned most successful methods. In the sector of the target group there is no method which accords to all requirements and could be universally used for all ranges of application. This means that each enterprise has to develop an individual package of methods to get the expected benefit after a successful implementation. The base for such a package should be universally usable methods like "5S or rather standardized clean-up".

The result of the mass evaluation to methods which can support MSTT in enterprises (multiple choices were possible) is a ranking of the most important methods. The two main methods are "exchange of experiences with the partners" and "special implementation guide for SME".

2.2 Specific Evaluation

The majority of the leading enterprises have started with the implementation of MSTT later than 2001. 43 %, however, started between 1990 and 2000. The realization and implementation level in enterprises is very high. More than half of the enterprises have implemented more than 50% of their MSTT. The results show, that the interviewed enterprises have good experience within the scope of the MSTT, through early introduction and extensive implementation.

2.2.1 Specific Tools of Production Control

The specific tools of production control have been analyzed concerning their usability from the experts' point of view. In these interviews the "Pull-System" has been identified as well-known and as an important method. But still this method has been evaluated to 100% as "little", respectively "rather little" realized. The same applies for the methods of "synchronized production", "value stream design" and "flow production". The indicators of "relevance" and "realization" of "Just-in-Time" are relatively balanced.

2.2.2 Specific Tools of Robust Processes

The evaluation of the methods of "robust processes" based on experts interviews shows for "Jidoka" that the implementation and application is to 100% specified as being "little", although it is rated as rather important by 75%. The like applies for other methods like "standardized methods and processes" and "supplier standardization". This means that enterprises see high potential for these methods.

2.2.3 Specific Tools of Visual Management

The methods of visual management are known by 100% of all specialists but this is no guarantee for a successful implementation in the enterprises. A good example is the method "standardized clean-up at a workplace". Although it has a high relevance (80%) and a high degree of notification, the implementation rate is rather small. Similar values and relations are evaluated for "Andon-Boards" and "lettering on bottom, marking und labeling" or "communication boards".

The leading enterprises have identified the two methods "exchange of experiences with the partners" and "implementation guide especially for small and medium-sized enterprises" as especially important for the support for the realization of the MSTT.

2.3 Comparison between Mass and Specific Evaluation

The question whether the interviewed enterprises from the target group are actually leading enterprises, was to be answered through the comparison of the essential results from the mass and specific evaluation. Also it was to be analyzed, how leading enterprises are characterized. Therefore, all relevant similarities and differences from the interviewed enterprises were compared in this study with the results of the mass evaluation.

The enterprises of the mass evaluation for the most part (40%) use individual methods from a MSTT. The leading enterprises, however, confirm their special position by the implementation of complete systems. Additionally, the leading status of the interviewed enterprises can be established with the implementation of MSTT with 43% between 1990 and 2000 and 57% between 2001 and 2005 and the fact that the degree of implementation of MSTT in enterprises is not smaller than 10%. However, 45% of the enterprises from the mass evaluation have started with the implementation after 2005 and 22% see the degree of the realization smaller than 10%. 50 % of the suppliers are involved in the MSTT according to enterprises from the mass evaluation but this is true for only 29% of the enterprises of the specific evaluation. The analysis of the used methods shows that the percentage distribution of the differences between the general popularity and the actual implementation of individual methods is nearly identical in enterprises of the mass and the specific evaluation. Differences exist especially in methods like Just-in-Time, One-piece-flow, flow shop, synchronic production, supplier standardization, Six Sigma, Poka-Yoke or Line-stop-concept / trigger line which require a higher standardization level and/ or implementation effort. It seems that it is more complicated to implement these methods in enterprises of the target group than in the automotive industry. The popularity and the actual implementation of CIP and TQM methods are relatively high in both the mass and specific evaluation. This indicates that the target group chooses selectively generally known methods instead of all existing methods. The methods of work organization and business culture/environment were both mainly used in the target group and in the enterprises of both evaluations. To identify the reasons for the low realization level of the MSTT in the target groups, the enterprises were asked about potential barriers. "Limited personnel resources" and "work overload high performer" were mentioned as the highest barriers in the interviews. The enterprises in the mass and specific evaluation agree on the fact that business culture and support from the management facilitates the implementation of MSTT. Essential is the participation of the employees. The integration of the employees is the core aspect which underlines the leading role of the interviewed enterprises. This is confirmed by the fact that the leading enterprises use a bigger spread of learning styles to convey MSTT to their employees.

2.4   Study Results

The aim of this study was to analyze the level of experience and developmental status of MSTT within the target group for SME. The mass evaluation was necessary to show the level of experience of a high number of enterprises in comparison to enterprises with proven know-how. Through the specific evaluation, the core questions could be considered in detail with the leading enterprises [12].

The study could prove with the results of the expert discussions by the leading enterprises, that the implementation of MSTT could be successful in the target group. The leading enterprises are working actually on the further development of their MSTT. However, many enterprises are in the implementing phase of their first MSTT. 67% of the enterprises from the mass evaluation are planning or implementing an MSTT today. Only 11% say that they have already finished the implementation.

The importance of this topic is obvious because 79% of the enterprises are working on the implementation of a MSTT. By the comparison with the leading enterprises, less successful users of MSTT can identify potentials for their own further MSTT and use the leading enterprises for orientation. They have potentials in the administrative, development and service fields. The study shows that the use of MSTT in the enterprises, can lead to success and can receive and improve their competitiveness. Thus, there is need for action for the interviewed enterprises. They need instruments to be able to control an MSTT with little effort. According to the results of the interviews, the enterprises mainly require more exchange of experiences with partners from industry, a major regard of the general conditions of SME and special adaptive solutions of MSTT. The main potentials, for the target group as well as for enterprises of other industries in Germany, are a stronger integration of the employees, a better management support, and an enterprise-specific adaptation of MSTT. Therefore, business culture has to change substantially. In summary, the study results confirm the benefit of MSTT in enterprises of the interviewed group. The implementation should be less complex and regard the enterprise-specific circumstances.

3 Forecast

In the specific evaluation the enterprises had been asked "what MSTT should be able to do in the future, where they are unfit today" and "where the unexhausted applications" are. These questions are the base for the following optimization potential of MSTT:

The management has to be committed stronger to the MSTT, methods have to be designed easier, MSTT should be adaptive to enterprise-specific circumstances, prove integration of employees and customers and better preserve resources. Potential exist in administration, in the supplier integration, in development and service.

For the future, it will be necessary to develop branch and firm-specific solutions. Therefore, the characteristic basic conditions of the interviewed enterprises must be considered. However, the further question shouldn´t be how to reproduce Toyota, but rather "What is beyond Toyota?" Already today researchers and increasingly also enterprises in Germany and Europe concentrate on this question. Production systems which are adaptive for the site-specific requirements are necessary. For the long-term protection of Europe and Germany as a location for manufacturing industry, a further development to a knowledge-based production system is essential. Based on this, the idea of a European production system occurred [2, 3]. This advanced knowledge-based production system, has to be beyond the scope of the typical aspects from the TPS. It has to be adjusted to the structures of transformable production, without renouncing the benefits of the TPS [1, 3]. Modern production systems must regard that production takes place in global networks. The sustainable and efficient usage of resources such as energy, air, water and finally the employees should be a part of the production system and thus the base for middle and long-term strategic decisions [2, 3]. The application of all value added potentials demand a relevant build-to-order strategy and also the integration of modern ICT- technologies, to exploit strategic and long-term competitive advantages for production in Europe [2, 3].

References

1. Westkämper, E., Zahn, E. (Hrsg.): Wandlungsfähige Produktionsunternehmen: Das Stuttgarter Unternehmensmodell. Springer, Berlin (2009)
2. Jovane, F., Westkämper, E., Williams, D.: The ManuFuture Road: Towards Competitive and Sustainable High-Adding-Value Manufacturing. Springer, Berlin (2009)
3. Womack, J.P., Jones, D.T., Roos, D.: The machine that changed the world: The Story of Lean Production. Harper Perennial, New York (1991)
4. Ditzer, R.: Toyota: Managementsystem des Wandels und Kultur der Verbesserung. Japan Markt, Wissenschaft und Praxis (2004); Köln (2005)
5. Ohno, T.: The Toyota Production System: Beyond Large-Scale Production. Productivity Press, Portland (1998)
6. Liker, J.: The Toyota Way: 14 Management Principles from the World's Greatest Manufacturer. McGraw-Hill, New York (2004)
7. Lay, G., Neuhaus, R.: Ganzheitliche Produktionssysteme (GPS) – Fortführung von Lean Production. Angewandte Arbeitswissenschaften 185, 32–47 (2005)
8. Lay, G., Dreher, C., Kinkel, S.: Neue Produktionskonzepte leisten einen Beitrag zur Sicherung des Standortes Deutschland. In: Mitteilungen aus der Produktionsinnovationserhebung, vol. 1. Fraunhofer ISI, Karlsruhe (1996)
9. Sautter, K., Meyer, R., Westkämper, E.: Mehr Erfolg durch professionellen Methodeneinsatz? Ergebnisse und Handlungsfelder einer empirischen Untersuchung des Fraunhofer IPA und des REFA-Verbandes in 226 produzierenden Unternehmen, Stuttgart und Darmstadt (1998)
10. Spath, D.: Ganzheitlich Produzieren – Innovative Organisation und Führung, LOGIS, Stuttgart (2003)
11. Feggeler, A., Neuhaus, R.: Ganzheitliche Produktionssysteme; Gestaltungsprinzipien und deren Verknüpfung. Institut für angewandte Arbeitswissenschaft, Wirtschaftsverlag, Köln (2002)
12. Westkämper, E., Kreuzhage, R., Hummel, V., Kluge, S., Wiese, S.: Managementsysteme vom Typ Toyota: In kleinen und mittelständischen Unternehmen des Maschinenbaus und der Elektroindustrie mit 100 bis 1500 Mitarbeitern. State of the art, Entwicklungs- und Erfahrungsstand, Forschungs- und Handlungsbedarf. Studie im Auftrag der KSB-Stiftung (KSB-Nr. 1254) Stuttgart, März (2008)

Production Leveling (Heijunka) Implementation in a Batch Production System: A Case Study

Luciano Fonseca de Araujo and Abelardo Alves de Queiroz

Federal University of Santa Catarina, Department of Manufacturing, GETEQ Research Group,
Caixa Postal 476, Campus Universitário, Trindade, 88040-900, Florianópolis, SC, Brazil
lfaraujo2005@gmail.com, abelardo@emc.ufsc.br

Abstract. This paper presents a case study of an implementation of a new method for Production Leveling designed for batch production. It includes prioritizing criteria of products and level production plan. Moreover, it was applied on a subsidiary of a multinational enterprise located on Brazil, which manufacturing processes comprise batch production in a make-to-stock policy. Regarding a qualitative assessment, evidences show that the company had deficient practices related to Operations Planning. Thus, based on a case study approach, proposed method was applied as well empirical data were analyzed. Results were measured before and after this implementation by performance indicators of Costs (inventory), Speed (lead time), Mix flexibility (monthly set up operations) and Reliability (service level). Evidences confirm improvements in operational efficiency as expected. Researchers and practitioners can evaluate general applicability of this method by applying it in different companies that share similarities related to batch processing operations.

Keywords: Batch Production, Heijunka, Operational Efficiency, Production Leveling.

1 Introduction

Nowadays international markets feature keen competition among both established and emerging companies that operate at global value networks. For this reason, enterprises must redesign existing methods for Operations Planning (OP). Such decision becomes more complex as product variation increases. Moreover, researchers advocate that Production Leveling – a Lean Manufacturing concept for OP – enables basic conditions to minimize the Bullwhip Effect, a dynamic phenomenon that *amplifies* and transmits the variability of customers´ demand across a supply network [8], [9], [10]. Indeed, Production Leveling improves operational efficiency by means of flexibility, cost and service level [1], [9].

Production Leveling aims to achieve a much more stable schedule for mixed-model production, by combining two well known concepts of Lean Manufacturing: Kanban System and Heijunka. The former means pull signaling of production based on concept for replenishment of supermarket to control work-in-process inventory. The latter means a smother pattern for daily production sequencing at assembling lines [7], [8], [9].

B. Vallespir and T. Alix (Eds.): APMS 2009, IFIP AICT 338, pp. 105–112, 2010.
© IFIP International Federation for Information Processing 2010

In spite of well known relevance of such concepts, recent research evidences a sparse number of cases of implementation of Production Leveling outside automotive networks. Additionally, one can question whether Lean Manufacturing concepts can be generally applicable [5]. Hence, three main gaps of literature review can also be used to support such statement. Beginning with conceptual models focused on problem solving of mixed model assembling lines [2]. Secondly, it can be said that batch production is very suitable to a wide variety of manufacturing processes, even in an automotive supply network [3]. Finally, regarding that Production Leveling is often described as simple models and examples [8], [9] there w no particular method based on Production Leveling designed for batch production processes and its variations related to many supply networks [1].

Based on those exposed gaps, the purpose of this paper is to present a case study of a new method for Production Leveling implementation in batch production system. A case study is a good opportunity to test emergent theories aiming to validate them empirically [4]. Additionally, this qualitative research was done in early 2008 in a large company, located on state of São Paulo, Brazil [1]. Hence, this paper is structured as follows. In section 2, a literature review of the main concepts is presented, including the framework for implement Level Production as well its main activities. In section 3, research methodology is briefly explained. Section 4 comprises a case study, before and after implementation. Results of the implementation of this method are commented in the section 5. This paper ends with conclusions in section 6.

2   Literature Review

This section summarizes the main activities of the new method [1] designed particularly to level the production of batch manufacturing systems. Additionally, it is expected to suit in a wide variety of value networks. That is, aiming to explain the general applicability of this method, a classification of batch production processes was briefly explained (see Appendix A). Hence, those elements were combined into a proposed framework, as showed in section 4.

2.1   Activities Related to Production Leveling

This section briefly explains the new method that was applied for the first time on case study and it includes the following activities [1]:

- Monthly Planned Demand: comprises the first activity of Tactical Level and is based on inventory data, bill of materials and customers´ ordering book, materials planners must set, for every product model, its planned volume for the next month. After that, the Level Production Plan is a decision that starts with monthly planned demand and means the design of a leveled production pattern taking into account production mix, production batch size, set up time and a planning interval that can be set as six or more days [1], [6]. Required capacity named as total lot processing time (´production pitch´ or ´pitch´) is also calculated for every product model. That is, it comprises a better balance between both required and available capacity of process and also provides inputs to two important activities: Supermarket sizing and Load-capacity analysis. The former is related to materials and the latter comprises decisions concerning direct and indirect labor and overhead.

- Daily order entering: named as Operational Level and contains five activities of production control: loading, sequencing, scheduling, dispatching and control. In such activities, visual controls are set to improve visibility for Production personnel, such as operators and supervisors. This activity features Kanban Board, Electronic Kanban, Heijunka Board and Production Rate Control Board [1].

It is worth highlighting that the implementation of Production Leveling starts with product prioritization that usually recommends make-to-stock production must be focused on high volume ('A' items") and medium volume ('B' items) whereas make-to-order production is better suitable for low volume ('C' items) [9].

3 Research Methodology

Based on objectives of this paper, the methodological approach comprises a qualitative research that was done in early 2008 [1] by using appropriate roadmap for case studies [4]. To accomplish this work, author visited the studied company from December´07 to June´08. Hence it was divided into two phases. The first one, named 'Previous State' comprises the scenario before implementation of the new method. Secondly, 'Future State' means the condition after the implementation. Regarding those criteria, the Previous State of the company was analyzed and evidences emphasize the need for change in OPC practices. During the first month, data was gathered from direct observations, interviews, archives analysis and corporate presentations. The next month comprised a seminar for training was presented to managers, supervisors, planners and process engineers. Finally the method was applied on February´08 as well visual controls and an electronic kanban. Such operational tools will be presented in a future paper. Hence, data were gathered and results were analyzed including October´07 to December´07 and March´08 to May´08. Such work is briefly described as follows.

4 A Case Study of an Implementation

4.1 Company "A" at Previous State

The researched company, hereinafter named Company "A", is a subsidiary of a North American multinational enterprise located on Brazil. There are three industrial facilities on state of São Paulo which its manufacturing systems produce a wide variety of products for many industrial applications. However, only one facility was studied which value chain is described as a make-to-stock batch production system which parts processing are typically disjunctive operations (See appendix A).

4.1.1 Features of Products and Pacemaker Process
Due company policy for information confidentiality, it was necessary to change the name and the type of manufacturing processes as well its products types. Additionally, the last productive stage, focus of this paper, is similar to a stamping press process and comprises two identical machines that convert different types of hot rolled steel coils into up to 130 product models. At downstream side, there is an automatic

packing machine that operates in two steps. First, parts are grouped into 200 units each and secondly there is a non automated palletizing machine to group 250 packages in a single pallet. In this Previous State, there was no problem concerning neither packing process nor standard packages.

Based on Lean Manufacturing concept, the daily production schedule was generated by scheduling software and daily schedules reports were sent only for both press machines. That is why such productive stage can also be named as the 'pacemaker process' because they set the production pace of upstream processes. Both press machines run at three shifts a day and six days a week. Furthermore, every day has 3 breaks for shift which comprises 10 min for shift reporting and 1 hour for lunch each. Moreover both machines have 98% of average Uptime, each of them can be operated 20.25 hours a day, from Mondays to Fridays; and 15 hours on Saturdays.

4.1.2 Problems Concerning the 'Previous State'
Based on previous analyses of gathered data from interviews, direct observation and archives analyzing, the new method was proposed because there was no strategy for continuous improvement. Evidences revealed that company had many operational problems such as uneven pattern of daily production related to overproduction using big-sized production batches related to three or four hot rolled steel coils at once. Additionally, there were no visual controls as well a huge amount of finished goods inventory and a non suitable condition for using kanban cards for pull system triggering. Finally, there was neither prioritization of products nor a consistent inventory reduction plan [1].

4.2 'Future State' Planning

Based on presented framework, a Level Production Plan must be set to provide a further analysis of available capacity. Those decisions are summarized as follows.

4.2.1 Prioritization of Products ('A' and 'B' Items)
The proposed method includes the criterion for classification of products based on monthly demand, namely 'ABC analysis' previously explained. By using it, it was found that among up to 130 product models, only 22 items correspond to 80% of average demand in value. So, the Production Leveling can be applied to be focused in a few items. After that, instead of running all products in both machines, 22 items were divided in two groups of 11 items each and one group was set for each machine. Remaining 108 low volume items corresponds to 20% of monthly average demand shall be produced once a month in both machines.

4.2.2 Production Leveling Planning
After the previously explained activity, a Level Production Plan was designed to both machines. Operations Planner has set a monthly planned demand for every product model as the average of the last three months and the next two forecasted monthly demand. After the training seminar, manager and supervisors decided that the Level Production Plan should be set as a six days week for time horizon. Such decision was made to provide a direct connection between planning interval and normal working time interval.

After selecting prioritized items, project team designed a Level Production Plan for both machines by leveling the required capacity using three information types: Set up time, production lot size and production rate at the pacemaker process. For both machines, average set up time was equal to nine minutes for every product model. Batch sizes were set as the minimum possible value related to the length of one single hot rolled steel coil. This criterion diverges on previous condition of 'Previous State' and each product model has a different 'minimum-size lot' due differences in length in hot rolled steel coils. Thus, based on results, managers stated it was a great contribution of the method. Finally, production rate comprises the pace that machines are able to produce parts per unit of time (parts per minute). For its turn, production rate also vary as product model does, for instance, for a generically named Model 'E' it is equal to 417 parts per minute.

The first decision features a calculation of production cycle within a given interval. That is a relation between average monthly demand and production lot size. By dividing the former by the latter, it defines a theoretical number of monthly set up operations. Second decision includes calculating the required capacity ('production pitch' or 'pitch') for each product model. In other words, is necessary to evaluate the total processing time elapsed from setting up machine till concluding a complete lot for a given product model. At last, the level production plan gives a visual distribution as shown in Fig. 1 as follows.

Product Model	Mon	Pitch (min)	Tue	Pitch (min)	Wed	Pitch (min)	Thu	Pitch (min)	Fri	Pitch (min)	Sat	Pitch (min)
J	84,000	177			84,000	177			84,000	177		
E	69,300	175			69,300	175	69,300	175			69,300	175
A	69,300	148			69,300	148			69,300	148		
C	63,000	135					63,000	135				
S											105,000	189
L									150,000	219		
M			105,000	219								
B											94,500	198
U			63,000	198								
D							52,500	114				
V			25,200	85								
Daily Required Capacity (min)	635		502		500		424		544		562	
Daily Available Time (min)	1,215		1,215		1,215		1,215		1,215		900	
Daily Remaining Time (min)	580		713		715		791		671		338	
Utilization of Capacity (%)	52%		41%		41%		35%		45%		62%	
Daily Number of Set up	4		3		3		3		3		3	

Fig. 1. Level Production Plan for Machine #2 with six days of time horizon

Fig. 1 depicts a Level Production Plan with six days of planning time interval. First left column has selected product model grouped in Machine #2 whereas every week day has production batches (columns labeled as days of week) and its related required capacity in minutes ('Pitch'). On bottom left side there are five rows namely 'Daily Required Capacity' is the sum of daily production pitch. For its turn 'Daily Available Time' is the normal daily available working time. Moreover, 'Daily Remaining Time' is the difference between the first two previous rows and 'Utilization of Capacity' is set as 'Required Time' divided by 'Available Time'. Finally, 'Daily Number of Set up' is the result of leveling of required capacity of high volume items within planning interval, aiming to get an even pattern for production schedule in terms of daily utilization of capacity. Furthermore, Fig. 1 also depicts that utilization of capacity was set varying from 35% to 62% for 'A' and 'B' items which implies an opportunity to review actual normal working time. Finally, this level production plan enabled team to decrease production lot size to as small as possible to a minimum value. After implementing this method, due high mix variety, team members developed an electronic Kanban by combining four key elements: an inventory management system based on 'Reorder Point' or 'Fixed Quantity' model (logical feature), bar codes and bar code readers for production back flushing (data input), an inventory system managed by a MRP software (data base) and an electronic spreadsheet combined with Visual BasicTM routines for data transferring (data output). Such tool as well new visual controls have improved Operational practices.

5   Research Findings

Results were analyzed in terms of performance indicators of Mix Flexibility (number of monthly Set up), Costs (inventory), Speed (days of stock) and Reliability (service level). Data was gathered and divided into two intervals: three months before the implementation ('Previous State') and three months after the implementation ('Future State'), as shown in Fig. 2 as follows:

PERFORMANCE INDICATORS	OBJECTIVE	PREVIOUS STATE				FUTURE STATE				VARIATION (%)
		Oct/07	Nov/07	Dec/07	AVERAGE	Mar/08	Apr/08	May/08	AVERAGE	
MONTHLY DEMAND (THOUSANDS OF PARTS)	REVENUE	11,086	11,702	11,883	11,5571	13,357	9,914	10,617	11,2959	-2%
PLANNED INVENTORY (THOUSANDS OF PARTS)	COST	4,447	4,694	3,991	4,3774	5,196	5,289	5,923	5,4691	25%
ACTUAL INVENTORY (THOUSANDS OF PARTS)	COST	5,118	3,868	3,925	4,3035	3,368	3,421	3,195	3,3282	-23%
ACTUAL INVENTORY (DAYS OF STOCK)	SPEED	14.1	9.3	9.9	11.1	8.4	8.4	8.7	8.5	-23%
AVERAGE LOT SIZE (PARTS)	FLEXIBILITY	72,207	70,008	73,087	71.767	57,626	66,962	51,710	58,766	-18%
MONTHLY SET UP (SET UP PER MONTH)	FLEXIBILITY	173	158	168	166.3	200	178	171	183.0	10%
SERVICE LEVEL (%)	RELIABILITY	99.6	99.1	98.9	99.20	98.0	98.4	99.0	98.46	-1%

Fig. 2. Summary of total achieved results regarding 'A' and 'B' items

Fig. 2 shows that even on a steady average monthly demand, production planner increased planned inventory in 25% regarding demand forecasting. However, results evidence that actual inventory decreased in 23% in average monthly values after proposed method. Also, 'days of stock' decreased at the same rate as expected. By setting lot size as a minimum possible value fig. 2 shows that average lot size has also been decreased by 18% in monthly average value. This evidences that the number of monthly set up has also increased in 10%. Indeed it is worth stating that results could be better for smaller lot sizes. Finally, service level has not been changed indicating that there was no negative effects in this case.

6 Conclusions

After analyzing 'Previous State', data evidence that company should improve existing methods for Operations Planning regarding Lean Manufacturing principles. The 'Future State' began with changes at ˝Tactical Level˝ and monthly planned demand was set as well a Level Production Plan. By leveling the required capacity of both 'A' and 'B' items, team members were able to set a minimum size criterion for production batches. Indeed, utilization of capacity now varies from 35% to 62% with implies an opportunity to evaluate changes in normal working time. Based on that, findings evidence that method leaded to improvements in operational efficiency. Thus proposed method was accepted by top and middle management as well Production personnel. Additionally, visual controls and electronic Kanban were also implemented but such tools will be presented in a future paper. Finally, based on research limitations, researchers and practitioners can review these concepts aiming to test its general applicability in different batch production systems in make-to-stock policy with high product mix variety.

Acknowledgements

We would like to thank Conselho Nacional de Desenvolvimento Científico e Tecnológico (CNPq) of Brazil for financial support. We would also like to thank the company where this research has been developed.

References

1. Araujo, L.F.: Method for application of Production Leveling in repetitive manufacturing systems with batch production (Master of Science Dissertation). Federal University of Santa Catarina. Department of Mechanical Engineering, p. 169 (2008) (In Portuguese).
2. Boysen, N., Fliedner, M., Scholl, A.: Sequencing Mixed-Model Assembly Lines: Survey, Classification and Model Critique. Jena Res Papers in Bus and Econ. Friedrich-Schiller-University Jena (February 2007), http://www.jbe.uni-jena.de
3. Cooney, R.: Is Lean a Universal Production System? Batch Production in the Automotive Industry. Int. J. Op. & Prod. Man. 22(10), 1130–1147 (2002)
4. Eisenhardt, K.: Building Theories from Case Study Research. The Academy of Management Review 14(4), 532–550 (1989)
5. Godinho Filho, M., Fernandes, F.C.F.: Lean Manufacturing: a literature review which classifies and analyses papers indicating new research. Gestão & Produção 11(1), 1–19 (2004) (in Portuguese)
6. Liker, J., Meier, D.: Toyota Way field book: a practical guide for implementing Toyota's 4Ps. McGraw-Hill, New York (2007)
7. Monden, Y.: Toyota Production System: An Integrated Approach, 3rd edn. Engineering & Management Press, New York (1998)
8. Slack, N., Chambers, S., Johnston, R.: Operations Management, 2nd edn., Atlas (2002) (in Portuguese)
9. Smalley, A.: Creating Level Pull. Lean Enterprise Institute, São Paulo (2004) (in Portuguese)
10. Lee, H.L., Padmanabhan, V., Whang, S.: The bullwhip effect in supply chains. Sloan Management Review 38(3), 93–102 (1997)

Appendix A: Classification of Batch Processing Operations

Production Leveling is expected to be generally applicable in batch production systems featuring processing operations [1] as described as follows:

- Disjunctive type I – Processing operation that converts a single piece of material into several ones. For instance, a press stamping like process that transform hot rolled steel coils to generate multiple purpose parts.
- Disjunctive type II – Processes that convert either powders or pellets into a batch of parts such as extruder machine as well sintering and injection molding.

Towards a Maintenance and Servicing Indicator

Pascal Vrignat[1], Manuel Avila[1], Florent Duculty[1], and Frédéric Kratz[2]

[1] Orleans University, Institut PRISME, IUT Indre,
2 Av. François Mitterrand
36000 Châteauroux, France
{pascal.vrignat,manuel.avila,florent.duculty}@univ-orleans.fr
[2] ENSIB, Institut PRISME,
88 boulevard lahitolle
18020 Bourges, France
frederic.kratz@ensi-bourges.fr

Abstract. This paper deals with a tool which may help maintenance manager to schedule maintenance activities. To help him, we show that by using events which can be observed on a process, like maintenance events, we can predict failures before they occur. Principles are based on the hypothesis that failure is preceded by a typical sequence of events. We also show that Hidden Markov Models can be used according to a good choice of parameters.

Keywords: Preventive Maintenance, Maintenance planning, Hidden Markov Model, Failure detection.

1 Introduction

Newspaper headlines often present incidents or accidents caused by industrial activities. In some cases, events may be prevented by applying a correct maintenance policy. Some tankers may not have sunk if some maintenance had been correctly applied. Factory should not have exploded with some preventive control or maintenance. In a more classical context, industrial tools may be more useful if they were maintained efficiently. Today, we have sufficient background about maintenance to improve tool effectiveness [1]. In this work, we propose a model that can anticipate the arrival of an accident. If the events can be "learned" by the model, then we can make **prediction** which can be used to help maintenance manager to schedule maintenance actions (Fig. 1).

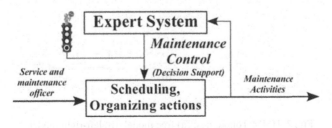

Fig. 1. Maintenance monitoring

B. Vallespir and T. Alix (Eds.): APMS 2009, IFIP AICT 338, pp. 113–120, 2010.

In more general cases, we try to model a sequence of events which should indicate a failure to come. We assume that a typical failure has a typical temporal or sequential signature which should be learned by Hidden Markov Models (HMM). Our approach can be compared with Zille's work [2]. These works are based on the Stochastic Petri networks and Monte Carlo simulation. In the next part, we recall some bases about HMM. Then, we present our study which is a part of an industrial continuous food process. Finally, we focus on help to be brought to maintenance manager in order to schedule his maintenance actions.

2 Hidden Markov Models

2.1 Introduction of HMM

The aim of this paper is not to present exhaustively the Hidden Markov Model. For readers interested in more details, we recommend to read Rabiner's paper [3] which is already a good tutorial and which presents HMM general problems. In this paper, we use the same notation for models. A model $\lambda = (A, B, \Pi)$ is described by three matrices:

- $A = \left[...a_{ij}...\right]$ corresponding to transition probabilities between hidden states,

- $B = \left[...b_j(k)...\right]$ corresponding to probabilities of observations considering states,

- $\Pi = \left[....\pi_i...\right]$ corresponding to initial state probabilities.

$O = \left\{O_1, O_2, ..., O_T\right\}$ is the sequence of observations which can be made onto the process. HMM have been used in several domains and applications since algorithms to compute easily HMM have been proposed [4], [5], [6]. We can list several applications that use HMM: speech recognition [3], [7]; biosciences [8], [9]; climatology [10]; handwritten word recognition [11], [12]; writer identification [13]; medicine [14]. HMM are characterized by several parameters. One of them is topology as we can see Fig. 2. The choice of topology will influence behavior of the model. Free topology should be used to model some process which may "turn around" like weather estimation. When needs are to match model with an oriented sequence, left to right topologies are better to absorb information. It is the case with speech recognition or handwritten word recognition.

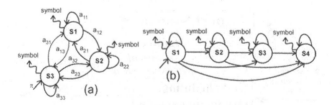

Fig. 2. HMM Topologies: (a) free model, (b) left-right model

Another determining parameter is the number of states that may be chosen arbitrarily. There is no rule to find this number, experiment is often used to find a number of states providing some good results. In some cases, we can use the mean value of observation sequences lengths. A good estimation of parameters is the main difficulty for using HMM.

2.2 Implementation of HMM

In literature, there are three problems to solve before using HMM. They consist in computing easily and quickly: $P(O|\lambda)$. Considering a sequence O={$O_1,O_2, ... O_T$}, and the model $\lambda = (A,B,\Pi)$, it consists in computing the probability of the observation sequence, given the model, given a sequence O={$O_1,O_2, ... O_T$}, how do we chose the corresponding state sequence Q={$q_1,q_2, ... q_T$} which "best" explains the observations ? How do we adjust the parameters (A, B, π) of the model λ to maximize $P(O|\lambda)$? The solution to the first problem can be found in [3]. We do not use it in this study. To solve the second problem, i.e. find the state sequence which has the maximum probability, we use the Viterbi algorithm [6], [3], [15]. The last problem consists in "learning" some observation sequences to provide a model estimation of (A, B, Π). We use the classical algorithm of Baum-Welch [4], [5], [16]. The principle of the algorithm is Expectation and Modification (EM). It consists in starting with a set of matrices (chosen randomly or arbitrary). Then, likelihoods of sequences are computed. The model is recalculated to maximize likelihood and then parameters are re-estimated. The more frequent a sequence is, the higher the transition probability associated becomes.

3 Study Case: Part of a Continuous Food Process

To test our method, we use data coming from a part of a continuous food process. The data were provided by an industrial baker. Maintenance activities for the process can be preventive or remedial. Maintenance policy consists in cleaning or replacing some "critical" parts of machines to prevent failure. But in some cases, maintenance team is to repair the failure situation. In this case, priority is given to remedial maintenance. In some other cases, capacity of maintenance team being fixed to enable production going on and preventive maintenance cannot be done on time. All maintenance actions are collected and stored in a database (Table 1).

3.1 Situation of the Study

The studied part, in this work, is located in the middle of a complete line of bread production (Fig. 3). At the beginning of the process, there is a storing zone where different ingredients are weighted according to the cooking recipe. Then, all products are mixed according to the recipe. Then, pancake mixture can be weighted with accuracy to form bread or others bakery products. Our study deals with this part. After this stage, dough balls are placed in moulds. Moulds pass through an oven and then get cold to enable bread to be extracted of mould. Finally, the bakery product is prepared to be sent with several controls and conditionings, with an adequate packaging.

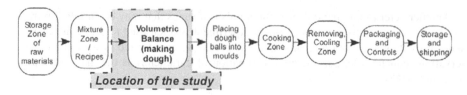

Fig. 3. Continuous food process

Table 1 shows a part of collected information on the scale of line called M2. This database is composed of maintenance activities. Like name of maintenance worker, day, kind of work, activity code, time spent, etc...

Table 1. Database sample

Number in the list	NAME	TEAM	DATE	LINE	NAME OF THE MACHINE	WORK PERFORMED	OBS	CODING OF THE MAINTENANCE ACTIVITIES	TI (min)	PARTS CHANGED	REF
1	M.Dupond	PM	03/01/2005	M2	Balance	The incharge request		Pro-Adj	20		

Entire production line can be stopped by a failure occurring on one of the subsystems placed previously on the line. These situations should involve loss of several hours of production (some hundred kg of bakery products). To prevent such cases, preventive maintenance is scheduled. We dispose of about two years of recording - between January 2005 to March 2007 - which represent about a thousand of events. The model was trained using the database from "2005" recording. We used 2006 and 2007 data for testing.

3.2 Description of Model vs. System

The aim of this study is to show that Hidden Markov Model should correctly learn specific sequences of maintenance activities to provide a failure detector. Events collected in database will form observations of a Hidden Markov Model. The model

Table 2. Events list

Symbolic Codes: Observations	State process RUN STOP	Description interventions (comments)									
		Rep (Repairing / Ending production)	Pro-Adj (Process Adjustment)	Ano (Another)	Obs (Observation)	Pre (Preventive maintenance work)	Sec (Security)	Dis (Discount level)	Mak (Making clean)	Pre-visit (Preventive maintenance visit)	Not (Nothing to report)
		1	2	3	4	5	6	7	8	9	10

states can inform us about the availability level of the studied part. Table 2 lists different events that may be observed on recordings. Each of them is explained in the table. Some events can be grouped: maintenance actions (Pro-Adj, Pre, Pre-visit, Dis and Mak); observing actions (Obs, Ano, Sec); repairing action (Rep which means system is stopped); no action (Not).

In order to provide a daily evaluation of our indicator, we insert a specific symbol Not (Nothing to report) every day when no event is recorded (Fig. 4). If more than one symbol is observed during a day, it means that the estimated state can change several times in the same day and consequently increase the sensibility of our indicator.

Pro-Adj	Pro-Adj	Sec	Not	Not	Not	Sec	Pre	...
2	2	6	10	10	10	6	5	...

↑　　↑　　↑ Daily Insertions

Fig. 4. Symbols insertion

Fig. 5 shows estimated states on the system (hidden layer) from visible observations.

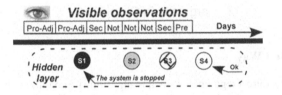

Fig. 5. Hidden layer and visible observations

We want the model to give us information about maintenance and servicing level. To do this, we force model at learning stage. Starting (or restarting after maintenance action) of the machine must take place at the state which represents the "max level" of maintenance and servicing (S4). In the same way, when we observe a remedial maintenance action, it means that the system stopped. This is represented by the "stop" state (S1). According to these conditions: we train model on training database.

3.3 Choice of Topology

The maintenance service manager should use servicing indicators to schedule dynamically preventive maintenance. After several tests, we chose a left to right topology which correctly fit observation sequences (Fig. 6). The reader can refer to the paper [17].

We chose four states. This is the choice made in a common situation. For example: "Plan vigipirate" in France with four levels; "Plan canicule" in France with four levels; ...

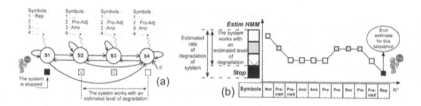

Fig. 6. Left to right topology (a), results with left to right topology (b)

3.4   Training the Model

To train the model, we use one year of recording (2005). We test the model with "unknown" sequences of year 2006 or 2007. To initialize training phase, we choose arbitrary parameters in model matrix. We use same initial probability for each element of matrix except for some specific symbols or a topology i.e. zero probability. For example: the symbol "Rep" will be plugged only on state S1 (Remedial action means that machine is stopped); probability from state S4 to state S1 is fixed to zero; ... Baum-Welch algorithm is used to estimate the model iteratively. This algorithm provides a model which maximizes probability $P(O|\lambda)$.

$$\lambda^* = \text{argmax}_\lambda P\big(O = o\big|\lambda\big) \qquad (1)$$

3.5   Find the Best Way

The Viterbi procedure (segmental k-means algorithm) maximizes the probability of observations sequences by the basic learning only along the optimal way obtained by Viterbi decoding. The variable $\delta(t,i)$ is defined as the maximum probability:

$$\delta(t,i) = \max_{q1...qt-1} P(o_1...o_t, q_1...q_t = i|\lambda) \qquad (2)$$

3.6   Some Results

In Fig. 7(a) and Fig. 7(b), we can see results provided by our model on two different sequences of test database. In these graphs, abscise is graduated with day scale. The most likelihood state is calculated each day using event provided by the test database or using Not symbol in case of no action. In Fig. 7(a), first, we begin at state S4. We can suppose that when system is started, probability that a failure occurs is low. On the third day, indicator begins to go down which means that the failure probability failure is growing. We can note that two Pre-visit events (preventive control) are observed. Model has learnt that these events preceded a failure. But when maintenance actions are provided (Pre) indicator goes up because of constraints use to learn model; Rep associated to state S1; State S1 will always be proposed by the model when Rep is observed. But it's too late. Preventive maintenance cannot be scheduled. What we need to evaluate is presence of state S2 days before failure occurs. Then maintenance manager can schedule specific actions. A quick remedial maintenance is needed to avoid losses of production. Tests on database do not allow prevention of the failures. We cannot go back to the future, but the model should have predicted the state the day before. Performance of our method can be evaluated on estimation days before failure: not too late but not too early either. In test database, all stop state (S1) was preceded by state S2.

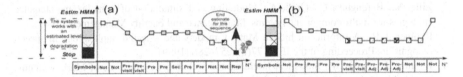

Fig. 7. Test on a first observation sequence (a), test on a second observation sequence (b)

In Fig. 7(b), analysis is different. We can observe a serie of Pre events. When many preventive actions are effectively done, it means that maintenance planning has been modified because of some doubts about availability of the system. Pre-visit events' following confirms the maintenance manager's doubts. Then Pro-Adj events (regulating of the machine) that follows and "Not symbol" (event number 10, Table 2) show that the system has been correctly repaired as indicated by the high level of servicing.

4 Conclusion

In this paper, we try to perform maintenance and servicing indicator using a Hidden Markov Model. Results show that our method can give a good level of system availability. As it has been shown earlier, choosing correctly model parameters (topology, …), can lead to a good prediction of failure. But how to use this information to help maintenance manager ? As we can see it in Fig. 8, servicing indicator is at S2 state which means that failure risk is important. What can the manager decide, a preventive action coming soon ?

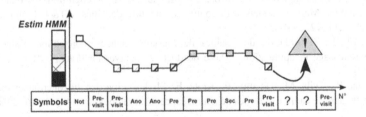

Fig. 8. Which decision to make?

If we have same indicators for different parts of the entire process, we could help the manager comparing values of different indicators. In this example, the manager of maintenance team has a constant volume of maintenance activity. These indicators should help him to better organize his maintenance actions.

References

1. Vrignat, P., Avila, M., Duculty, F., Kratz, F.: Conventional approaches to the modelling of a dysfunctional process in the context of maintenance activity. IEEE Melecon Region 8, t1-sf0008 (2008)
2. Zille, V., Bérenguer, C., Grall, A.: Modelling and simulation of complex maintenance strategies for multi-component systems. Maintenance and Facility Management (2007)
3. Rabiner, L.R.: A tutorial on hidden Markov models and selected applications in speech recognition. Proceeding of the IEEE 77(2), 257–286 (1989)
4. Baum, L.E., Petrie, T.: Statistical inference for probabilistic functions of Markov chains. Annals Math. Stat. 37, 1554–1563 (1966)
5. Baum, L.E.: An inequality and associated maximisation technique in statistical estimation for probabilistic functions. Inequalities 3, 1–8 (1972)
6. Viterbi, A.J.: Error bounds for conventionnal codes and asymptotically optimum decoding algorithm. IEEE Trans. on Information Theory 13, 260–269 (1967)
7. Doss, M.M.: Using Auxiliary Sources of Knowledge for Automatic Speech Recognition, Thèse de doctorat, Ecole Polytechnique Fédérale, Lausanne (2005)
8. Grundy, W.N., Bailey, T.L., Baker, M.E.: Meta-MEME: Motif-based Hidden Markov Models of protein families. Computer Applications in the Biosciences 13(4), 397 (1997)
9. Schbath, S.: Les chaînes de Markov cachées: présentation et usage en analyse de séquences bioliques. In: Unité Mathématique, Informatique & Génome, INRA (2007)
10. Hugues, J.P., Guttorp, P.: A hidden Markov model for downscalling synoptic atmospheric patterns to precipitation amounts. Climate Research 15(1), 1 (2000)
11. Avila, M.: Optimisation de modèles Markoviens pour la reconnaissance de l'écrit, Thèse de doctorat, Université, Rouen (1996)
12. Belaïd, A., Anigbogu, J.: Hidden Markov Models in Text Recognition. International Journal of Pattern Recognition 9(6) (1995)
13. Schalapbach, A., Bunke, H.: Using HMM-based recognizers for writer identification and verification. In: Proc. 9th Int. Workshop on Frontiers in Handwriting Recognition, pp. 167–172 (2004)
14. Vialatte, F.B.: Aide au diagnostic d'anomalies cardiaques, mémoire de DEA de Sciences Cognitives, Paris VI, Paris (2002)
15. Rabiner, L.R., Juang, B.H., Levinson, S.E., Sondhi, M.M.: Recognition of isolated digits using hidden Markov models with continuous mixture densities. AT&T Technical Journal 64, 1211–1222 (1986)
16. Brouard, T.: Hybridation de Chaînes de Markov Cachées: conception d'algorithmes d'apprentissage et applications, Thèse de doctorat, Université François Rabelais, Tours (1999)
17. Vrignat, P., Avila, M., Duculty, F., Kratz, F.: Modélisation des dysfonctionnements d'un système dans le cadre d'activités de maintenance. Communication 4A-1, lm16 (2008)

Monitoring of Collaborative Assembly Operations: An OEE Based Approach

Sauli Kivikunnas, Esa-Matti Sarjanoja, Jukka Koskinen, and Tapio Heikkilä

VTT Technical Research Centre of Finland, Networked Intelligence, Kaitoväylä 1,
FI-90570 Oulu, Finland
{Sauli.Kivikunnas,Esa-Matti.Sarjanoja,
Jukka.Koskinen,Tapio.Heikkila}@vtt.fi

Abstract. In this paper we present requirements and concept generation principles for performance monitoring of a collaborative assembly task. Life cycle aspects are considered and an Overall Equipment Efficiency (OEE) based monitoring scenario for a developed passive collaborative robot (COBOT) test system is presented. In this case main benefits of applying COBOT are expected to be: improved productivity, improved quality, reduced production cost and improved ergonomics. Since human and COBOT are working co-operatively human actions have also affects on process performance, i.e. OEE. However a human's and machines or a COBOT's efficiency are undistinguishable directly from OEE factors. It is possible to infer cause of lower efficiency from the variables from which OEE factors are calculated. One such variable is cycle time, which is used to define performance efficiency.

Keywords: OEE, car rear screen installation, COBOT.

1 Introduction

Business environments are changing continuously leading to needs for changes in production and manufacturing. Production strategies need to be revised to be better able to satisfy changing customer needs. These demands can be met with technologies introducing different types of flexibilities into production.

Technologies for achieving these flexibilities imply changes in software, machinery and layouts. This paper contributes to increasing flexibility by introducing a performance monitoring concept for new machines or robots for assisting humans in assembly tasks.

Many current industrial manual assembly tasks could be fully automated with conventional robots, but high flexibility is often difficult to be achieved cost-effectively with conventional robot systems [1]. Robotic systems are usually cost-effective in assembling high volume products, but flexibility in these assembly lines is low. Low and medium volume products are typically customized for customer needs and production times and volumes may vary depending of a product demand. Therefore for low and medium volume products high product and mix flexibility are required by manufacturing systems. High flexibility can be achieved by co-operative robot-human systems, rather than by autonomous robots.

B. Vallespir and T. Alix (Eds.): APMS 2009, IFIP AICT 338, pp. 121–127, 2010.
© IFIP International Federation for Information Processing 2010

In collaborative task operations the human operator takes care of controlling interactively all the critical operations with required accuracy targeting also to better quality. The effect of new device or any improvements on the assembly line performance should always be evaluated, also in the case of collaborative task execution. An increasingly common method for this is to use Overall Equipment Efficiency (OEE). It is an indicator how well equipment or machinery are performing or are being utilized at a time period and it indicates, which parts of assembly line or machinery are not performing well. OEE is a tool which helps in focusing improvement activities.

Life cycle costs are evaluated in planning and designing of manufacturing line or machines whereas OEE is typically used for benchmarking, evaluating and continuously improving performance of a manufacturing line or machines (process performance aspect). Co-operative assembly robots sharing a workplace with humans are called assistant robots. Such a robot can be guided physically by a human or it assists human worker without any physical guidance. In the previous case the robot can be called as a passive collaborative robot (COBOT) [2] and the latter case intelligent assists robots. A typical example of a COBOT application is an assembly task where human lifts a heavy load co-operatively with COBOT: human introduces motion intelligence and the COBOT produces power assistance. An assembly system that executes and monitors tasks where a robot and a human work co-operatively needs to be flexible. The systems should recognize and recover from abnormal situations, like safety risks or system malfunctions.

This paper presents requirements and a concept for performance monitoring of a collaborative assembly task. Life cycle aspects are considered and an OEE based monitoring scenario for a developed COBOT test system is presented.

2 Theoretical Background

According to [3] OEE can be used at three levels of manufacturing: manufacturing plant, manufacturing line and machine process level. In the manufacturing plant OEE can be used as benchmark before (initial performance) and after changes. At the manufacturing line level OEE can be used to indicate performance of the production line. In the machine process level OEE indicates performance levels of the machines.

Overall equipment efficiency is defined as product of three factors: availability, performance rate and quality rate.

2.1 Causal Chain to OEE

OEE can be linked to major equipment losses. Major equipment losses can be categorized as six big losses. The linkages between OEE factors [3, 4] and the six big losses are illustrated in Fig. 1. Time losses can be divided into downtime, speed and quality losses. [5].

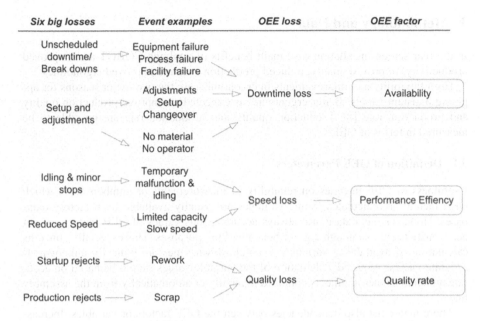

Fig. 1. Linkage between OEE factors and six big losses. (adapted from [3, 4]).

2.2 OEE Extended to Operations Performance Assessment

OEE is not an explicit index of performance of a manufacturing process. OEE can be seen as an indicator how well equipment or machinery are performing or are been utilized at a specified time frame and indicate, which parts of assembly line or machinery is not performing well. As stated in [6]: "the most important objective of OEE is not to get an optimum measure, but to get a simple measure that tells the production personnel where to spend their improvement resources".

OEE can be used to fully automated and semi-automated manufacturing lines. In automotive industry type of manufacturing lines vary from fully automatic to manually operated stations, thus there are possibilities to utilize OEE as a tool. In OEE, the machinery is assumed to generate a fixed ideal cycle time and due to changing resources in manual assembly, accurate measurement is challenging.

The purchase price of equipment is just one cost element in the comparison [7]. Total Cost of Ownership (TCO) methodology has shown how important it is to analyse all the cost, direct and indirect, incurred throughout the life cycle of an equipment, including acquisition and installation, operations and maintenance, and end-of-life management. TCO methodology pinpoints costs that could be easily underestimated, such as quality and rework as well as all the costs of running the system. The methodology is useful in system integrator and end-user collaboration, where both can use similar formulae in system evaluation and trade-off analysis.

3   Methodology and Data

In the rear screen installation case main benefits of applying COBOT are: improved productivity, improved quality, reduced production cost and improved ergonomics.

High flexibility and improvements in ergonomics are the two major reasons for applying assistant robots. Better ergonomics is expected to improve production quality and production rate [8]. Production quality and production rate are possible to be measured in terms of OEE.

3.1   Definition of OEE Parameters

Usefulness of OEE in relies on reliability of measurements or numbers from which OEE factors are calculated. Some variables are usually available from factory databases. However this data is not always accurate, thus values of OEE factors are not necessarily accurate enough e.g. for benchmarking purposes. This especially concerns calculation of availability variables; accurate down times are typically unknown. If accurate OEE is required, calculation of the variable values should be based on accurate numbers or measurements collected manually or automatically from the assembly line.

There may exist also dependencies between the OEE factors or variables. Increasing performance efficiency may decrease quality and lower availability may also be seen as lower performance efficiency. Raising efficiency of one factor in cost of another is not always acceptable. For instance, increase in performance efficiency in cost of quality is typically unacceptable.

An improvement of one variable may also be insufficient. For instance, decreasing only planned cycle time would decrease performance efficiency, if number of manufactured products were not increased. If this is not possible, availability efficiency should be increased by reducing set-up times and down times. In flexible assembly lines where product volumes or type may vary it is important to affect to several variables to maintain good performance level of the line. A practical way to increase the performance of the line is to focus continuous improvements in one variable at a time (availability parameters) i.e. improvements are focused to reduce first setup times, then down time etc.

Especially important in this context is to have tools for human-COBOT cooperation life cycle monitoring. The concept should enable the validation of benefits of new COBOT solutions and give clear indications for continuous development processes. Special emphasis should be put on generating, delivering and using information about human-COBOT cooperation performance. Human creativity, intelligence, knowledge, flexibility, and skills are hardly directly transformed to performance indices. Instead, indirect asset utilisation and operational efficiency indicators must be found.

Since human and COBOT are working co-operatively human actions have also affects on process performance, i.e. OEE. However a human's and machines or a COBOT's efficiency are undistinguishable directly from OEE factors. It is possible to infer cause of lower efficiency from the variables from which OEE factors are calculated. One such variable is cycle time, which is used to define performance efficiency. In addition, availability of operators affects calculation of availability.

3.2 Measuring of OEE Parameters

The automatic measurement of accurate availability parameters such failure times and limited availability of operators and material can be difficult. For instance, there is no way to directly measure availability of an operator. Many cases down times are thereby collected manually in order to calculate accurate values. In manual collection operators write down times and their reasons into paper forms or records them into a computer program. This is carried out along with their normal activities. Manually collected down times can also be inaccurate [9]. Operators can be unmotivated for recording these times, there is no time to record them or the operators forget to record them as well as measuring of the down times can be difficult.

Automatic data collection of down times would be much more attractive. Down times could be defined indirectly from machine measurements or events. Sensors can measure conveyor speeds, electric motors on/off times, passing time of a part or a component passing through an assembly station etc. Many of these variables are already available from factory automation systems or data bases. However, installation of new sensors is probably needed. The sensors for measuring above mentioned information are usually inexpensive. Cost of installation of sensors and their hard wiring could be minimized by using wireless data transfer and feeding power from batteries. Also moving of wireless sensors nodes to other locations is easy. Fig. 2 represents OEE data collection, where production data management gives information about defects in manufacturing. Production line is not usually stopped when defects occur, and so those events are stored into a database on a later phase. Therefore that information is not available real time. Automation systems give information about time-based productivity measurements. Unscheduled downtimes are manually entered to the information system at the COBOT cell.

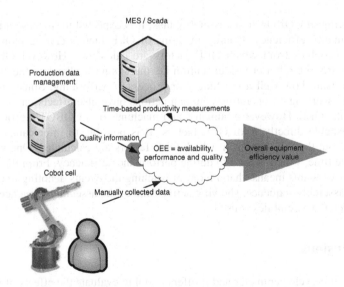

Fig. 2. Collecting OEE variables from different sources

What to measure in order to define cycle times? The rear screen installation case is used here as an example. Cycle time of rear screen installation could be defined as follows:

The window installation process begins when the COBOT grabs a window from a panel supply and begins to move towards a vehicle with its suction pads attached to a window panel. COBOT trajectories and its events are possible to be stored into a database. Cycle time can be measured from the database by using the preceding terms.

What to measure in order to define down times? Down times have been separated into two categories in the six big losses -definition. Breakdowns consist of tooling failures, unplanned maintenance events and general breakdowns. Down times regarding setup and adjustment consist of setup and changeover tasks, material shortages, operator shortages, major adjustments of the equipment and warmup-time of the equipment.

A way to define operating times is to subtract a machine's down time from loading times [3]. Loading time is the time when the machine is in productive use. In practice measuring of several machines or their components states may be needed in order to calculate operating times. An inferences mechanism for defining states of the machines may also be needed.

Down times can be measured by using the COBOT trajectory database. Some reasons for idle times and down times may be derived also from the COBOT trajectory database. For example a person entering the COBOT's safe area will halt the COBOT. The reason for halting is stored into the database.

4 Findings

By introducing of COBOT to an assembly task, it is expected to increase quality rate and performance efficiency. Quality in terms of OEE factors can be monitored by measuring variables from which OEE factors are calculated. However OEE is not used for controlling robot or task execution i.e. there is no feedback to the systems. It is just a measure how well a machinery or process is performing. Since human and COBOT are working co-operatively human actions have also affects on process performance, i.e. OEE. However a human's and machines or a COBOT's efficiency are undistinguishable directly from OEE factors. It is possible to infer cause of lower efficiency from the variables from which OEE factors are calculated. One such variable is cycle time, which is used to define performance efficiency. From the monitoring point of view this means, that a monitor catching the events denoting the start and end of the assembly sequence, showing active time of the assembly sequence and idle time between the assemblies is used.

5 Conclusions

OEE is one life-cycle parameter and it offers a tool to evaluate the effects of introducing new machinery in the performance of a manufacturing line. Especially OEE offers a tool to evaluate effects of continuous improvements i.e. where to focus maintenance and improvements activities. The actual suitability of OEE in selected case (car rear screen assembly) should be tested in the real work environment with an OEE tool.

Acknowledgements. This work is partially funded by the European Union as part of the NMP-2004-3.4.3.12 PISA project.

References

1. Hägele, M., Schaaf, W., Helms, E.: Robot Assistants at Manual Workplaces: Effective Co-operation and Safety Aspects. In: Proceeding of the 33rd International Symposium on Robotics 2002, Stockholm, Sweden (2002)
2. Bernhardt, R., Surdilovic, D., Katschinski, V., Schreck, G., Schröer, K.: Next Generation of Flexible Assembly Systems. In: Innovation in Manufacturing Networks IFIP International Federation for Information Processing, vol. 266, pp. 279–288. Springer, Boston (2008)
3. Dal, B., Tugwell, P., Greatbanks, R.: Overall equipment effectiveness as a measure of operational improvement – A practical analysis. International Journal of Operations & Production Management 20, 1488–1502 (2000)
4. Pomorski, T.: Managing Overall Equipment Effectiveness (OEE) to Optimize Factory Performance. In: 1997 IEEE International Symposium on Semiconductor Manufacturing Conference Proceedings, pp. A33–A36. IEEE, New York (1997)
5. Högfeldt, D.: Plant Efficiency. A value stream mapping and overall equipment effectiveness study, Master's thesis, Luleå University of Technology (2005)
6. Tangen, S.: An overview of frequently used performance measures. Work Study 52, 347–354 (2003)
7. Heilala, J., Montonen, J., Helin, K.: Selecting the right system - assembly system comparison with total cost of ownership methodology. Assembly Automation 27, 44–54 (2007)
8. Akella, P., Peshkin, M., Colgate, E., Wannasuphoprasit, W., Nagesh, N., Wells, J., Holland, S., Pearson, T., Peacock, B.: Cobots for the automobile assembly line. In: Proceedings of the 1999 IEEE International Conference on Robotics & Automation, pp. 728–733. IEEE, New York (1999)
9. Ljungberg, O.: Measurement of overall equipment effectiveness as a basis for TPM activities. International Journal of Operations & Production Management 18, 495–507 (1998)

The Value of Sampling Inspection in a Single-Period Remanufacturing System with Stochastic Returns Yield

Christos Zikopoulos, Sofia Panagiotidou, and George Nenes

Department of Mechanical Engineering, Aristotle University of Thessaloniki,
54124 Thessaloniki, Greece,
Tel.: +30 231 0995914; Fax: +30 231 0996018
cziko@auth.gr, span@auth.gr, gnenes@auth.gr

Abstract. We examine a reverse supply chain consisting of a collection site, where consumers return used products, and a remanufacturing facility. Some of the returned products are transported to the remanufacturing facility in order to be remanufactured and used to satisfy the stochastic demand for remanufactured products. The quality of returns is characterized by uncertainty, and therefore, before the procurement quantity determination, the remanufacturer has the alternative to inspect a sample drawn from the collected quantity in order to evaluate more accurately returns' quality. Using general assumptions for returns quality and remanufactured products demand distributions, we formulate the expected profit function for both sampling and no-sampling cases and we examine numerically the economic effectiveness of sampling. A key characteristic of the current paper is that returns' yield is expressed as the probability of a unit to be remanufacturable.

Keywords: reverse supply chain, random yield, sampling inspection, binomial yield, value of information.

1 Introduction

One of the most important issues in Reverse Supply Chain Management is the quality of returned used units. Returns quality is associated with the ability of a unit to successfully undergo a recovery process, such as remanufacturing, refurbishing, repair, etc. Firms engaged in value-recovery activities employ a number of different practices in order to obtain information on returns quality. There are two main dimensions regarding this information: accuracy and timing. Usually, the acquisition of timely returns quality information requires the shift of inspection operations at the collection sites. Some remanufacturing firms introduce certain nominal metrics based on specific product characteristics and assign to the supplier the task of inspecting and grading the returned units, e.g. ReCellular [1]. Consequently, the supplier provides information regarding returns quality to the remanufacturer. Another way to obtain timely information is by incorporating electronic devices in the products that record basic usage data, e.g. Bosch [2], HP [3], which provide some information usually indirectly related to the quality of each unit upon its return. Both these practices permit an initial classification of returns according to their quality, before the investment

B. Vallespir and T. Alix (Eds.): APMS 2009, IFIP AICT 338, pp. 128–135, 2010.

of significant resources by the remanufacturer. The disadvantage of these methods is that the accuracy of the information is generally limited. On the other hand, when the accuracy of the returns quality assessment is important, remanufacturing firms prefer to transfer the collected quantity to the remanufacturing site, disassemble all available units and inspect them, e.g. NEC-CI [4], Mercedes-Benz [5]. The obvious disadvantage of this practice is that it can result in a considerable waste of time and effort because of the delayed identification of inferior-quality lots.

In the current paper we propose a different practice; that is to examine a sample taken from the collected quantity and base the procurement decision on the inspection outcome. To the best of our knowledge, sampling inspections in a reverse supply chain context has been initially proposed in [6]. In the current paper we extend the work of [6] for the case of stochastic demand for remanufactured products. The advantage of sampling inspection is that quality assessment can be carried out using a fairly accurate method while the total inspection cost is kept bearable. Of course, due to sampling there are inherent statistical errors.

The uncertainty in returns quality is the main issue in a number of papers as for example in [7], [8], [9], [10] and [11]. The main objective in the aforementioned contributions is either the determination of procurement and remanufacturing decisions or the evaluation of the value of advanced information on returns quality. Other relevant contributions include [12] and [13] in which apart from the procurement and remanufacturing decisions, the impact of grading errors is explored, as well.

The scope of the current paper is to study the advisability of establishing sampling inspection in reverse supply chains. The yield (i.e. the probability that a unit can be remanufactured successfully) of returns is considered stochastic and it is formulated as a continuous random variable. Before determining the procurement quantity, a sample from the collected quantity is inspected. Based on the outcome of this inspection, the prior belief about returns' quality is updated and the optimal procurement quantity is defined. Under general assumptions, we formulate the expected profit functions corresponding to the cases that procurement quantity is decided with or without conducting previously a sampling inspection. The optimal sampling, procurement and remanufacturing decisions are evaluated numerically.

There are two characteristics of the current paper that have not been studied extensively in the reverse supply chain literature:

a) For each returned unit in the procurement lot, it is assumed that there is a specific probability to belong to a certain quality category. Therefore, the number of remanufacturable units in the quantity received is defined as a Binomial random variable. Although this type of random yield model can be found in conventional supply chain literature, e.g. [14], it is rare in the reverse supply chain context.

b) The advisability of conducting sampling inspection is explored, taking into account that the decision of the procurement quantity is based on the inspection outcome. The issue of simultaneous determination of procurement quantity and sampling scheme has already been examined in the context of forward supply chains, e.g. [15] and [16]. Contrary to existing contributions, we examine this issue in the reverse supply chain context. In addition, we treat the sample size as a decision variable and we allow the procurement quantity to vary with respect to the outcome of sampling inspection.

The remainder of the paper is organized as follows. In the next section we describe in detail the problem setting and we define the basic assumptions. In Section 3 we present the formulation of the expected profit function for the cases without and with sampling inspection. Section 4 presents a numerical study and discusses the findings regarding the impact of the problem parameters on the optimal policy. Finally, Section 5 summarizes and concludes the paper.

2 Problem Setting and Assumptions

The reverse supply chain examined consists of a single collection site (CS) and a remanufacturing facility (R). At the collection site, end-users return used products. Each returned unit can be in one of two possible quality states, remanufacturable or non-remanufacturable. Although the actual condition of each unit is unknown, there is a rough knowledge about the quality of the lot collected at the CS. Specifically, we assume that all returned units in the lot have a specific but unknown probability, q, to be remanufacturable. This probability is considered a random variable, which follows a known distribution with density and probability functions $g(q)$ and $G(q)$, respectively.

The remanufacturer, in order to decide the exact amount of returned units to procure, Q, has two alternatives: either to rely on the initial knowledge of returns yield distribution or to inspect a sample of size n drawn from the quantity collected, at a cost of c_n per unit, evaluate the yield in the sample and consequently update the distribution of q based on the ratio of number remanufacturables in the sample to the sample size (Q_n/n). In either case, when R procures some quantity of returned units, which cost c_a per unit, upon reception it implements a thorough inspection procedure to the total quantity received (e.g. disassemble every unit and check each of its components) in order to identify all remanufacturable units in the procurement quantity. The respective cost at this stage is set equal to c_{da}.

After disassembly, the exact number of available remanufacturable units, Q_a, is revealed, and the remanufacturer reaches at a second decision stage which is related to the number of remanufacturable units that will undergo the remanufacturing procedure, Q_r, taking into account the relative cost and revenues as well as the demand characteristics. All units that after disassembly were classified as non-remanufacturables as well as the excess remanufacturables are disposed of at a cost, c_d and c_{dr}, respectively. The remanufacturing process costs c_r per unit. It is assumed that all remanufactured units can be considered suitable to satisfy demand for remanufactured products.

Demand for remanufactured products is considered a random variable, x, with mean equal to $E(x)$ and with $f(x)$ and $F(x)$ used to denote the density and probability functions, respectively. The sales revenue equals v per remanufactured unit sold. We assume that $v > c_r$, in order to assure that it is worth considering remanufacturing of returns as a profitable option. If demand exceeds the number of available remanufactured units, a cost equal to c_s per unit short is incurred. Unsold remanufactured units also incur cost, denoted by c_u per unit. We assume that $c_r + c_u > c_{dr}$, since otherwise it would be profitable just to remanufacture returns without the intention to sell them. Table 1 summarizes the notation used throughout the paper.

Table 1. Notation

v	Sales revenue per unit	n	Sample size
c_a	Acquisition cost per unit	Q	Procurement quantity
c_{da}	Disassembly cost per unit	Q_r	Number of units to remanufacture
c_d	Disposal cost per non-remanufacturable unit	Q_n	Remanufacturable units in the sample
c_{dr}	Disposal cost per remanufacturable unit	Q_a	Available remanufacturables in Q
c_r	Remanufacturing cost per unit	q	Probability of a unit to be remanufacturable
c_s	Shortage cost per unit short	x	Demand for remanufactured units
c_u	Cost per unsold remanufactured unit	g(q)	Probability density function of q
c_n	Inspection cost per unit in the sample	f(x)	Probability density function of x

3 Expected Profit Function Formulation

Regardless of the establishment of sampling inspection, after disassembling the procurement quantity the only remaining factor of uncertainty is demand. In that stage, having resolved quality uncertainty the remanufacturer can determine the optimal quantity that should be remanufactured. The expected profit function at this stage can be written as:

$$TP(Q_r) = (v + c_s + c_u) \int_0^{Q_r} (x - Q_r) f(x) dx + (v + c_s + c_{dr} - c_r) Q_r - c_{dr} Q_a - c_s E(x) \quad (1)$$

It is easy to show that (1) is maximized for Q_r^*, which satisfies:

$$F(Q_r^*) = (v + c_s + c_{dr} - c_r) / (v + c_s + c_u). \quad (2)$$

Since the quality of returns is uncertain, it is not assured that at the second decision stage there will always be adequate remanufacturable units for processing. Therefore, the optimal policy at this stage is to remanufacture-up-to Q_r^* units and dispose of the remaining, if there are adequate remanufacturable units. Otherwise, i.e. if $Q_a \le Q_r^*$, all available units should be remanufactured.

When there is not the alternative of sampling inspection, the lot-sizing decision is based on the prior knowledge for the returns quality. The formulation of the expected profit function is carried out separately depending on the relationship between the values of the procurement quantity, Q, and the optimal remanufacturing quantity, Q_r^*. For simplification of exposition we introduce the function B, defined as follows:

$$B_a^b(y) = \sum_{Q_a=a}^b y \binom{Q}{Q_a} q^{Q_a} (1-q)^{Q-Q_a}$$

Taking into account all relevant costs and revenues and after some algebraic manipulation and using (2), the expected total profit is written as follows:

$$TP[Q|g(q)] = (v + c_s + c_u) \int_0^1 B_0^Q \left(\int_0^{Q_a} (x - Q_a) f(x) dx \right) g(q) dq + (v + c_s + c_d - c_r) Q E(q)$$

$$- (c_d + c_a + c_{da}) Q - c_s E(x), \quad \text{for } Q \le Q_r^*, \text{ and} \quad (3)$$

$$TP[Q|g(q)] = (v + c_s + c_u) \int_0^1 B_0^{Q_r^*} \left(\int_{Q_r^*}^{Q_a} (x - Q_a) f(x) dx \right) g(q) dq + (v + c_s + c_u) \int_0^{Q_r^*} x f(x) dx$$

$$+ (c_d - c_{dr}) Q E(q) - (c_d + c_a + c_{da}) Q - c_s E(x), \quad \text{for } Q > Q_r^*. \qquad (4)$$

Given the distribution of the yield, the optimal procurement quantity, Q^* can be evaluated using (3) and (4).

When sampling inspection is in effect, the sampling outcome is used to update the estimation regarding the quality of the collected quantity using Bayes theorem. The lot-sizing decisions are based on the posterior distribution of the returns quality. The form of the expected profit function given the sampling outcome is identical to the case without sampling inspection, substituting for g(q) the posterior distribution that is derived based on the sampling inspection outcome and subtracting the cost of the sample inspection. Thus, given the values of n and Q_n, and the posterior distribution $g_{n,Q_n}(q)$, (3) and (4) apply for the expected profit function,

$$TP[Q|n, Q_n] = TP[Q| g_{n,Q_n}(q)] - c_n n. \qquad (5)$$

The expected profit for any possible outcome of the sampling inspection can be computed as the expected value of the profit weighted over all possible outcomes of the inspection, which are based on the prior distribution of the yield,

$$E_{Q_n}[TP(Q)] = \int_0^1 \sum_{Q_n=0}^n \left\{ TP\left[Q^* | g_{n,Q_n}(q_{n,Q_n}) \right] b(Q_n; n, q) \right\} g(q) dq - c_n n, \qquad (6)$$

where b(x; y, z) stands for the probability that a random variable that follows the Binomial distribution with parameter z takes the value x after y Bernoulli trials.

4 Numerical Illustration and Discussion

In this section we present a numerical experiment which investigates the economic effectiveness of sampling inspection as well as its interaction with the mean and variance of the yield and the costs of remanufacturing, disassembly and sampling inspection. The random yield is modeled using 6 different distributions of the Beta family. The Beta parameter values were selected so as to examine 3 levels of yield mean, i.e., low (E(q) = 1/3), medium (E(q) =1/2) and high (E(q) = 2/3), and two levels of yield variance, low (V(q) = 0.03) and high (V(q) $\simeq$ 0.07). Remanufacturing and disassembly costs are examined in two levels. Specifically, c_r is set equal to 10 or 20, while c_{da} = 0.25c_r or c_{da} = c_r. The demand is modeled using normal distribution with mean and standard deviation equal to μ = 100 and σ = 10, respectively. The sales revenue, v, is set in all examples equal to 100, while the shortage cost, c_s, is assumed negligible. Disposal costs (c_d, c_{dr}) as well as cost of unsold remanufacturable units, c_u, are set equal to 1. Finally, acquisition cost, c_a, is set equal to 15. Table 2 summarizes the 24 parameter sets used in the numerical investigation.

Table 2. Parameter values and optimization results

	Parameter values				No sampling		Sampling (low c_n)		Sampling (high c_n)	
#	E(q)	V(q)	c_r	c_{da}	Q^*	TP	n^*	%	n^*	%
1	low	low	10	2.5	205	1918.7	42	16.6	26	13.1
2	low	low	10	10	153	579.8	17	44.8	10	37.8
3	low	low	20	5	167	850.2	27	31.7	15	26.1
4	low	low	20	20	0	0.0	4	100.0	0	0.0
5	low	high	10	2.5	170	1595.2	44	30.2	29	27.4
6	low	high	10	10	127	488.8	16	61.0	9	57.2
7	low	high	20	5	138	711.0	26	48.3	14	44.7
8	low	high	20	20	0	0.0	5	100.0	3	100.0
9	medium	low	10	2.5	189	4022.0	40	4.2	22	2.5
10	medium	low	10	10	165	2696.3	0	0.0	0	0.0
11	medium	low	20	5	170	2723.3	18	1.6	0	0.0
12	medium	low	20	20	125	513.3	7	18.7	2	8.9
13	medium	high	10	2.5	154	3202.2	44	13.8	25	11.9
14	medium	high	10	10	130	2144.9	14	16.6	10	12.8
15	medium	high	20	5	134	2163.0	23	16.0	15	13.0
16	medium	high	20	20	101	423.3	6	59.5	4	55.3
17	high	low	10	2.5	154	5173.1	36	4.0	19	2.9
18	high	low	10	10	140	4073.6	7	0.9	0	0.0
19	high	low	20	5	142	3874.3	16	2.3	7	1.0
20	high	low	20	20	119	1928.7	0	0.0	0	0.0
21	high	high	10	2.5	147	4838.5	34	6.1	24	4.8
22	high	high	10	10	131	3802.1	12	2.8	6	0.7
23	high	high	20	5	133	3616.2	18	4.5	10	2.6
24	high	high	20	20	111	1808.0	5	3.7	0	0.0

Each of the 24 sets is optimized assuming that no sampling inspection is in effect. Table 2 reports the optimal procurement quantity along with the corresponding expected profit. Moreover, assuming that there is the alternative of conducting a sampling inspection before the determination of Q, we specify the optimal sample size, n^*, using the same 24 parameter sets including the sample inspection cost, c_n, which is examined in two levels, low ($c_n = c_{da}$) and high ($c_n = 2c_{da}$). The resulting optimal values of n and the corresponding profit increase as compared to the no-sampling case are also shown in Table 2. It should be noted that when sampling inspection is allowed, the optimal procurement quantity value depends on the inspection outcome, Q_n. Thus, for a given sample size, Q^* is a function of Q_n, and it is evaluated through the maximization of (5).

Examination of Table 2 reveals that the introduction of sample inspection may increase the profitability of remanufacturing. This improvement is attributed to the fact that after inspection the additional information on returns' yield allows the more precise determination of the procurement quantity. For example, for set #12 (high c_n) with $n^* = 2$, if $Q_n = 2$ the optimal procurement quantity is $Q^* = 130$, if $Q_n = 1$, then $Q^* = 129$ and if $Q_n = 0$, then $Q^* = 0$. On the other hand, based solely on the prior to inspection knowledge, the optimal decision would be to procure $Q^* = 125$ units. This effect is more pronounced for sets #4 (low c_n) and #8 (for both low and high values of

c_n). For these sets in the no-sampling case $Q^* = 0$, while with sampling inspection there can be the opportunity to procure some quantity leading to positive expected profit (45.6 for set #4 and 253.5 or 171.0, respectively for set #8). However, in set #4 (high c_n) the value of information from sampling vanishes because of the high value of c_n. Another consequence of inspection sampling is that it can prevent remanufacturing firms from procuring inferior-quality lots. For example, in case #1 (low c_n) without sampling $Q^* = 205$, while when sampling is allowed, for $Q_n < 8$ it is optimal not to procure at all ($Q^* = 0$).

Based on the results, we conclude that high sampling cost decreases the value of n^*, reducing sampling discriminatory power; thus, the value of sampling decreases. Sampling inspection is more advisable, in terms of percentage profit improvement, when the expected yield of returns is rather low. On the contrary, when yield variability is low, the benefits of sampling inspection decrease or even vanish. The impact of c_{da} differs depending on the expected yield of returns. Specifically, for low or medium values of $E(q)$, the value of sampling inspection increases with c_{da}, since performing an initial quality assessment of the returns decreases the amount of non-ramanufacturable units disassembled and disposed of. On the other hand, when the returns' expected yield is high, the percentage profit improvement due to sampling inspection is perceivable only for low values of c_{da} (mainly as a result of lower c_n values). Finally, based on the numerical examples studied we conclude that the value of c_r does not influence notably the results.

5   Summary and Future Research

In the current paper we examined the advisability of establishing sampling inspection prior to the determination of the procurement quantity in a reverse supply chain. We formulated the expected profit functions for the cases with and without sampling inspection and evaluated the optimal decisions under different values of the problem's parameters.

The most important contribution of the current paper is that it proposes a new method for resolving, at a certain extent, the uncertainty regarding returns' quality which is inherent in reverse supply chains. Moreover, it enables the evaluation of the economic benefits of sampling inspection and the determination of the optimal values of the sample size and the procurement quantity with respect to the sampling outcome.

It has been shown that the establishment of sampling inspection can substantially improve the profitability of a reverse supply chain. The outcome of sampling inspection allows the remanufacturer to refine the procurement quantity decision and also to avoid procurement of lots characterized by low returns' yield. The optimization results provide insights on the factors that affect the value of sampling inspection before the procurement of returns. Specifically, through the numerical investigation presented we found that the advisability of establishing sampling inspections is increasing as the quality uncertainty and the disassembly cost increase and as the expected yield of returns and the sampling inspection cost decrease.

Interesting extensions of the proposed model include the investigation of the impact of different degrees of sampling inspection accuracy and of the advisability of sampling inspection when multiple returns quality states and recovery options exist. In the latter case the inspection outcome would define, apart from the procurement quantity, the appropriate recovery process, as well.

References

1. Guide Jr., V.D.R., Van Wassenhove, L.N.: Managing product returns for remanufacturing. Production and Operations Management 10(2), 142–155 (2001)
2. Debo, L.G., Savaskan, R.C., Van Wassenhove, L.N.: Coordination in closed-loop supply chains. In: Dekker, R., Fleischmann, M., Interfurth, K., Van Wassenhove, L.N. (eds.) Quantitative Models for Closed Loop Supply Chains, pp. 295–311. Springer, Berlin (2004)
3. Guide Jr., V.D.R., Souza, G.C., Van Wassenhove, L.N., Blackburn, J.D.: Time value of commercial product returns. Management Science 52(8), 1200–1214 (2006)
4. Geyer, R., Neeraj, K., Wan Vassenhove, L.N.: Reverse logistics in an electronic company: the NEC-CI case. In: Flapper, S.D.P., Van Nunen, J.A.E.E., Wan Vassenhove, L.N. (eds.) Managing Closed-Loop Supply Chains, pp. 33–39. Springer, Berlin (2005)
5. Driesch, H.M., Van Oyen, Flapper, S.D.P.: Recovery of car engines: the Mercedes-Benz case. In: Flapper, S.D.P., Van Nunen, J.A.E.E., Wan Vassenhove, L.N. (eds.) Managing Closed-Loop Supply Chains, pp. 157–166. Springer, Berlin (2005)
6. Nenes, G., Panagiotidou, S., Zikopoulos, C.: Procurement and sampling decisions under stochastic returns yield in reverse supply chains. Working Paper (2009)
7. Ferrer, G.: Yield information and supplier responsiveness in remanufacturing operations. European Journal of Operational Research 149, 540–556 (2003)
8. Ferrer, G., Ketzenberg, M.E.: Value of information in remanufacturing complex products. IIE Transactions 36, 265–277 (2004)
9. Aras, N., Boyaci, T., Verter, V.: The effect of categorizing returned products in remanufacturing. IIE Transactions 36, 319–331 (2004)
10. Galbreth, M.R., Blackburn, J.D.: Optimal acquisition and sorting policies for remanufacturing. Production and Operations Management 15(3), 384–393 (2006)
11. Ketzenberg, M.E., Van der Laan, E., Teunter, R.H.: Value of information in closed loop supply chains. Production and Operations Management 15(3), 393–406 (2006)
12. Souza, E.A., Ketzenberg, M.E., Guide Jr., V.D.R.: Capacitated remanufacturing with service level constraints. Production and Operations Management 11(2), 231–248 (2002)
13. Tagaras, G., Zikopoulos, C.: Optimal location and value of timely sorting of used items in a remanufacturing supply chain with multiple collection sites. International Journal of Production Economics 115, 424–432 (2008)
14. Yano, C.A., Lee, H.L.: Lot sizing with random yields: A review. Operations Research 43(2), 311–334 (1995)
15. Lee, H.L., Rosenblatt, M.J.: Optimal inspection and ordering policies for products with imperfect quality. IIE Transactions 17(3), 284–289 (1985)
16. Ben-Daya, M., Noman, S.M.: Integrated inventory and inspection policies for stochastic demand. European Journal of Operational Research 185, 159–169 (2008)

The Impact of Behavior-Based Strategies on Supply Uncertainty

Pirola Fabiana and Pinto Roberto

CELS – Research Center on Logistics and After-Sales Service
University of Bergamo
Viale Marconi, 5 - 24044 Dalmine, Italy
{fabiana.pirola,roberto.pinto}@unibg.it

Abstract. Today's economical environment encompasses a high level of uncertainty, which affects decision makers capability in predicting future events, their occurrence probability and possible decision outcomes. A common way to guard against uncertainty is holding inventory in order to ensuring business continuity and on-time delivery to customer, buffering the effect of the risk. This method belongs to the buffer-oriented techniques that represent only a shield against uncertainty and contribute to raise the overall costs. A more effective way to reduce supply uncertainty is to deeply analyze its sources and try to reduce its occurrence probability adopting behavior-based strategies. A Systems Thinking model, aiming at explaining the logical relationships among different strategies and at analyzing their impact on supply uncertainty and total costs, is presented.

Keywords: Supply uncertainty, behavior-based strategy, buffer-based method.

1 Introduction

Effectively manage a supply chain has become a complex and challenging task because of today's economical environment, characterized by rapid technological changes, shorter product lifecycles, demanding customers and global competitors. This context encompasses a high level of uncertainty, which affects decision makers capability in predicting future events, their occurrence probability and possible decision outcomes. Davis [5] recognizes three sources of uncertainty in the supply chain: demand, manufacturing process and supply. Demand uncertainty depends on customer orders variability, manufacturing uncertainty is due to internal problems arising during the manufacturing process, while the latter is associated with supplier failure in delivering products as required by customer. This leads to a variability in delivery lead time and then to uncertainty about supply availability. Consequently, disruption in firm production scheduling, increased inventory costs and reduced service level can occur. In their study Boonyathan et al. [1] showed that supply uncertainty is a more significant determinant of organizations performance than demand uncertainty. Therefore, managing supplier uncertainty becomes a relevant factor in developing supply chain strategies. This paper focuses on supply side of the risk and on strategies

B. Vallespir and T. Alix (Eds.): APMS 2009, IFIP AICT 338, pp. 136–143, 2010.

followed to deal with this risk. Common methods employed to manage supply uncertainty are buffer-oriented methods [26] that include holding stocks to reduce the stock-out probability in case of delays in supplier deliveries. Since buffers increase total cost, according to Zsidisin et al. [26], a more effective method to reduce supply uncertainty is to deeply analyze its sources and consequently undertake behavior-based strategies in order to eliminate or reduce this risk, focusing on supplier process rather than on its outcomes.

Hence, the main research questions are (i) which are the main sources of supply uncertainty, (ii) which are the main behavior-based strategies an organization could undertake to attempt to reduce or eliminate it and (iii) which are the relationships among these strategies, the uncertainty level and the overall costs.

In order to pursue these objectives, the following section provides a literature overview about supply uncertainty, its main sources, buffer-based methods and behavior-based strategies. In section 3, Systems Thinking methodology is introduced and, based on this methodology, in section 4 a model analyzing the relationship among buffer-based methods, behavior-based strategies and supply uncertainty is proposed. The last section concludes the paper with some remarks and indications for further researches.

2 Literature Overview

Due to recent increased interest in decision making under uncertainty and risk, Samson et al. [19] stated that there is no general definition for these terms but rather many discipline and context dependent definitions. For the purpose of this paper, we consider risk and uncertainty as two different but related concepts. In particular, according to Willet [19], we define risk as the "objective uncertainty regarding the occurrence of an undesirable event", while the subjective uncertainty "resulting from the imperfection of man's knowledge" is uncertainty. Consequently, considering risk as the occurrence probability of an undesirable event, uncertainty is the greatest when this probability is ½ because the decision maker completely does not know which will be the outcome (the undesired event has the same probability of occurring or not). The uncertainty level decreases when the probability increases or decreases and it is null when the probability is 0 or 1. This paper focuses on supply uncertainty, that, accordingly with the above definitions, is related to supply risk. Referring to Zsidisin [27], supply risk is defined as "the probability of an incident associated with inbound supply from individual supplier failures or the supply market occurring, in which its outcomes result in the inability of the purchasing firm to meet customer demand or cause threats to customer life and safety". In a study about uncertainty in supply chain, Ho et al. [8] stated that supply uncertainty sources are related to complexity, quality and, especially, timeliness of delivered products. In fact, the more complex is a product the more human intervention is required; this increases the errors probability and the time needed to resolve them and can lead to delivery delays. Relating to quality, two different cases can occur: in the first one, defects are detected by the supplier before the shipment so it can quickly repair it; in the second one, the quality problem is identified by the buying firm and a supplier intervention is required in order to repair or substitute the defective product. In both cases, delays in delivery can occur, especially when problems come out at the company's plant. Consequently, both complexity and quality can be referred to the time dimension of deliveries that disrupt company's processes and schedules.

A common way to guard against uncertainty is holding inventory to ensuring the continuation of the business and on-time delivery to customer ([2], [5], [10], [26]), buffering the effect of the risk. This method belongs to buffer-oriented techniques, as defined by Zsidisin [26], where buffers represent an outcome-based approach to dealing with risk that attempts to reduce its detrimental effects, rather than decrease its occurrence probability. Apart from representing only a shield against uncertainty and do not attempting to eliminate it, the main drawback of this kind of methods is that they contribute to raise overall costs due to storage space, potential obsolescence and capital investment in inventory. A more effective way to reduce supply uncertainty is to deeply analyze its sources and try to reduce the occurrence probability adopting behavior-based strategies [26]. From a literature review, this kind of strategies can be divided in *supplier development* and *supplier integration* [23].

Supplier development is defined by Krause [14] as "any effort by a buying firm to improve a supplier's performance and/or capabilities to meet the buying firm's short and/or long term supply needs" and it can be characterized by different levels of buying firm commitment. Krause identified six main activities: (i) formal supplier evaluation, (ii) visits to the supplier's site by buying firm representatives, (iii) certification programs, (iv) bringing supplier representatives on-site at the buying firm to further enhance interaction, (v) supplier award programs, and (vi) training of supplier's personnel by buying firm representatives. Modi et al. [17] added also capital and equipment investments made from procuring firms in supplier operations and partial supplier acquisition from buying firm. Investing in supplier development, the buying firm may reduce transaction costs [14] and, depending on the investment level, may obtain different rewards [13], such as more responsive suppliers and more certainty and continuity in buyer-seller relationship. Obviously, these investments are non transferable and benefits are unrecoverable if the relationship is prematurely dissolved. So, increasing the investment level increases benefits but increases also the firm dependence on suppliers and then the associated risk.

The second strategy available is *supplier integration* that leads to increase communication and information sharing between buying firm and its supplier and encompasses ([4], [23]): (i) joint problem solving, (ii) direct communication between buyer and supplier production schedulers and (iii) integration of information technology. Wilson [25], applying system dynamics methodology to investigate the effect of supply disruption on a 5-echelon supply chain, showed that the impact is less severe in a supply chain with vendor managed inventory system than in a traditional supply chain, characterized by lower integration level. This behavior is due to information sharing because the retailer does not overreact to disruption by placing an excessive order to warehouse, as in the traditional structure (the traditional behavior is also demonstrated in [21]). Moreover, supplier integration practices reduce both transaction and production costs [4]. In fact, increasing the coordination level through goal and information sharing, increases familiarity and trust between the two companies and decreases supplier opportunistic behavior, leading to a reduction in transaction costs; from production cost standpoint, integration with a few number of suppliers allows to take advantage of economies of scale and scope. The main drawbacks of supplier integration are the coordination and inflexibility costs, where the first one arises because the need of coordination can increase response times and human capital requirements, while inflexibility comes up because firm is locked into a partner's technology and the supplier is not incentivized to innovate with new product or services [4].

In conclusion, referring to supply uncertainty and risk field, usually qualitative and descriptive studies ([1], [11], [26]) are carried out, especially through surveys and case studies, in order to give some insights into the actual employment of different strategies to deal with risk and their perceived benefits. An effective comparison among these strategies is still missing as well as a model that considers systems complexity to address organizations in strategy selection, based on market and firm characteristics and their evolution along the time. Thus, the aim of this paper is to define factors that favor and hinder these possible investments and identify the impact of these strategies in term of risk, uncertainty and overall costs. In order to analyze these relationships, a model is proposed and discussed in the next sections.

3 Methodology

The proposed model is realized using Systems Thinking methodology, that focuses on the way that a system's parts interrelate and how systems work over time and within the context of larger systems. The approach of Systems Thinking is different from the traditional form of analysis. While traditional analysis focuses on separating the parts of what is being studied, Systems Thinking, in contrast, focuses on how the thing being studied interacts with other constituents of the system. This means that instead of isolating smaller and smaller parts of the system, Systems Thinking works by expanding its view to taking into account larger and larger interactions. This broad view can help a decision maker to quickly identify the real causes of issues in organizations and allow to solve the most difficult types of problems. As referred by Senge [20], Systems Thinking discipline aims at seeing interrelationships among system parts rather than linear causal-effect chains and seeing processes of change rather than snapshots. In fact, Systems Thinking methodology is based on causal loops diagram [22]: they can be self-reinforcing (R) or self-correcting (B) and they consist of variables connected by arrows denoting causal influences, describing what would happen if there were a change. In the next section, a model attempting to describe how behavior-based strategies and buffer-based methods impact on supply uncertainty will be proposed, using Systems Thinking methodology.

4 The Proposed Model

The supply process involves the coupling made up by a company and its supplier which can be seen as the smallest supply chain entity. For this reason, this model will be developed from a firm point of view, considering the relationship with its main suppliers. Modi et al. [17] showed that knowledge transfer activities, and then supplier development and integration activities, are undertaken by the procuring firm especially with suppliers that satisfy a high percent of buyer requirements. Consequently, behavior based strategies make sense in case of relevant suppliers. A useful way to identify these suppliers may be the Kraljic matrix [12], where items are classified based on strategic importance and on supply risk. Therefore, behavior-based strategies can be addressed to suppliers providing strategic and bottleneck items, namely the ones with high supply risk.

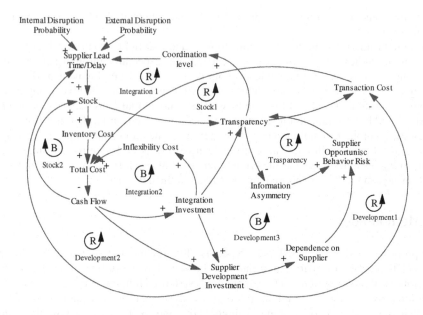

Fig. 1. The proposed model

The model represented in Figure 1 attempts to show the relationships among supplier performance, supply uncertainty, supplier development investments, integration investments, stock holding for a selected supplier. As shown in the literature review section, uncertainty sources depend on product complexity, quality and timeliness. Given that both complexity and quality can be referred to time dimension of deliveries, in this paper supply risk is represented by supplier delivery delay that gives rise to uncertainty because firm does not know exactly when product will be available in the factory plant. Delivery delays depend on supplier internal and external disruption probability. For each available strategy two or more casual loops has been identified, both balancing (B) and reinforcing (R) ones:

- *Buffer-based methods* ([1], [2], [3], [8], [18], [21], [26]): on the one hand, delays in supplier deliveries increase the quantity stocked by the company, the inventory and total costs, and decrease the cash flow needed to make further capital investment in inventory (Stock2); on the other hand, increase in inventory level decreases the transparency and coordination in the relationship and then even more stocks are taken to buffer uncertainty (Stock1).
— *Integration investments* ([4], [6], [9], [11], [16], [17], [23], [24], [25]]): cash flow gives the chance to make integration investments; through this kind of investments, a firm can increase transparency and coordination level with its supplier and, hence, decrease delivery delays, buffer size and costs, raising the cash flow needed to make new investment (Integration1); on the contrary, these investments increase the inflexibility costs, raising total costs and decreasing cash flow availability (Integration2). Referring to transparency loop (Transparency), increasing transparency decreases the information asymmetry between buying

firm and supplier and, consequently, decreases the supplier opportunistic behavior risk and raises the willingness to achieve a more transparent relationship.

— *Supplier development investments* ([7], [9], [13], [14], [15], [17], [23]): cash flow availability increases the chance to make supplier development investments to reduce both delay probability and transaction cost and achieve a cash flow increase (Development1 and Development2); on the other hand, supplier development investments raise the company dependence on supplier and the supplier opportunistic behavior risk, reducing transparency and increasing delay probability, stock requirement, costs and decreasing cash flow availability (Development3). Additionally, integration degree between the two firms is positively correlated to an effective supplier performance increase.

5 Conclusion

Supply risk has become one of the major concern companies are facing. In this paper, methods and strategies to deal with supply risk are identified and classified in buffer-based methods and behavior-based strategies. A Systems Thinking model, aiming at explaining the logical relationships among these different strategies and at analyzing the impact of different investment mix on supply uncertainty reduction and total cost minimization, is presented. The main limitation of this model is that it does not consider all variables influencing supply uncertainty and the adoption of different strategies. Moreover, relationships among variables are given only by a logical point of view. To solve this last problem System Dynamics methodology can be useful, because it is based on Systems Thinking, but takes the additional steps of constructing and testing a computer simulation model.

Thus, the model presented in this paper is only a first step towards a more comprehensive one, where more variable will be considered and a System Dynamics simulation will be carried out. In order to shift the present model in a System Dynamics one, quantitative relationships among variables should be added to allow a computer simulation. Finally, model validation will be realized through simulation and policy analysis in organizations belonging to different industries to evaluate its value in environment with different risk and uncertainty degrees. Since the supply risk level and the strategy impact depend on firm and market characteristics, this will not be a prescriptive model and it will not suggest a standardized firm behavior and a unique strategy mix. At the contrary, based on context characteristics, it will be possible to set the different parameter values and their reactions to strategies in order to understand the system behavior, its sensitivity to initial and boundary conditions.

References

1. Boonyathan, P., Power, D.: The Impact of Supply Chain Uncertainty on Business Performance and the Role of Supplier and Customer Relationships: Comparison between Product and Service Organizations. In: DSI Mini Conference on Services Management, Pittsburgh, USA (2007)
2. Caputo, M.: Uncertainty, Flexibility and Buffers in the Management of the Firm Operating System. Production Planning and Control 7, 528–538 (1997)

3. Christopher, M., Lee, H.: Mitigating supply chain risk through improved confidence. International Journal of Physical Distribution & Logistics Management 34, 388–396 (2004)
4. Das, A., Narasimahn, R., Talluri, S.: Supplier Integration – Finding an Optimal Configuration. Journal of Operations Management 24, 563–582 (2006)
5. Davis, T.: Effective Supply Chain Management. MIT Sloan Management Review 8, 35–46 (1993)
6. Frohlich, M.T., Westbrook, R.: Arcs of integration: an international study of supply chain strategies. Journal of Operations Management 19, 185–200 (2001)
7. Hallikas, J., Karvonen, I., Pulkkinen, U., Virolainen, V.-M., Tuominen, M.: Risk Management Process in Supply Network. International Journal of Production Economics 90, 47–58 (2004)
8. Ho, C.-F., Chi, Y.-P., Tai, Y.-M.: A Structural Approach to Measuring Uncertainty in Supply Chain. International Journal of Electronic Commerce 9(3), 91–114 (2005)
9. Humphreys, P.K., Li, W.L., Chan, L.Y.: The Impact of Supplier Development on Buyer–Supplier Performance. Omega 32, 131–143 (2004)
10. Hung, Y.-F., Chang, C.-B.: Determining Safety Stocks for production planning in uncertain manufacturing. International Journal of Production Economics 58, 199–208 (1999)
11. Kaipia, R.: The Effect of Delivery Speed on Supply Chain Planning. International Journal of Logistics: Research & Applications 11, 123–135 (2008)
12. Kraljic, P.: Purchasing Must Become Supply Management. Harvard Business Review 61, 109–117 (1983)
13. Krause, D.R., Handfiel, R.B., Scannell, T.V.: An Empirical Investigation of Supplier Development: Reactive and Strategic Processes. Journal of Operation Management 17, 39–58 (1998)
14. Krause, D.R.: The Antecedents of Buying Firms' Efforts to Improve Suppliers. Journal of Operation Management 17, 205–224 (1999)
15. Lee, P.K.C., Yeung, A.C.L., Cheng, T.C.E.: Supplier Alliances and Environmental Uncertainty: An Empirical Study (2008) (in Press)
16. Lee, H.L.: Aligning Supply Chain Strategies with Product Uncertainties. California Management Review 44, 105–119 (2002)
17. Modi, S.B., Mabert, V.A.: Supplier Development: Improving Supplier Performance Through Knowledge Transfer. Journal of Operation Management 25, 42–64 (2006)
18. Molinder, A.: Joint Optimization of Lot-Sizes, Safety Stocks and Safety Lead Times in an MRP System. International Journal of Production Research 35, 983–994 (1997)
19. Samson, S., Reneke, J.A., Wiecek, M.M.: A Review of Different Perspectives on Uncertainty and Risk and an Alternative Modeling Paradigm. Reliability Engineering and System Safety 94, 558–567 (2009)
20. Senge, P.M.: The Fifth Discipline: The Art & Practice of the Learning Organization, Doubleday, New York (1990), ISBN: 0385472560
21. So, K.C., Zheng, X.: Impact of Supplier Lead Time and Forecast Demand Updating on Retailer's Order Quantity Variability in a Two-Level Supply Chain. International Journal of Production Economics 86, 169–179 (2003)
22. Sterman, J.D.: Business Dynamics: System Thinking and Modeling for a Complex World. McGraw-Hill/Irwin (2003)
23. Wagner, S.M., Johnson, J.L.: Configuring and Managing Strategic Portfolios. Industrial Marketing Management 33, 717–730 (2004)

24. Wilding, R.: The 3 Ts of Highly Effective Supply Chains. Supply Chain Practice 3, 30–99 (2003)
25. Wilson, M.C.: The Impact of Transportation Disruption on Supply Chain Performance. Transportation Research Part E 43, 295–320 (2005)
26. Zsidisin, G.A., Ellram, E.L.: An Agency Theory Investigation of Supply Risk Management. Journal of Supply Chain Management 39, 15–27 (2003)
27. Zsidisin, G.A.: A Grounded Definition of Supply Risk. Journal of Purchasing & Supply Management 9, 217–224 (2003)

MRP Offsetting for Assembly Systems with Random Component Delivery Times: A Particular Case

Mohamed-Aly Louly[1,*] and Alexandre Dolgui[2]

[1] King Saud University
College of Engineering - Industrial Engineering Department
P.O. Box 800, Riyadh 11421, Kingdom of Saudi Arabia
louly@ksu.edu.sa
[2] Ecole des Mines de Saint-Étienne
Centre for Industrial Engineering and Computer Science
158 cours Fauriel, 42023 Saint Etienne Cedex 2, France
dolgui@emse.fr

Abstract. This paper considers component supply planning for assembly systems where several types of components are needed to produce one finished product. The actual component lead times have random deviations. The aim of this study is to find the optimal MRP offsetting when the Periodic Order Quantity (POQ) policy is used. The proposed model and algorithms minimize the sum of the setup and average holding costs for the components, while satisfying a desired service level for finished product.

Keywords: Assembly Systems, Inventory Control, Stochastic Component Lead Times, Periodic Order Quantity, MRP offsetting.

1 Introduction

Material Requirements Planning (MRP) is a commonly accepted approach for replenishment planning in major companies. The practical aspect of MRP lies in the fact that this provides a support clear and simple to understand, as well as a powerful information system to decision making [1], [9], [10].

Nevertheless, MRP is based on the supposition that the demand and lead times are known. However, most production systems are stochastic. This is because there are some random factors and unpredictable events such as machine breakdowns, transport delays, etc. which can cause random deviations from planning [4]. Therefore, actually, the deterministic assumptions of MRP are often too restrictive. Thankfully, the MRP approach can be tailored to uncertainties by searching optimal values for its parameters [3], [11]. Thus, one of essential issues is MRP parameterization for real life companies in industrial situations. This is commonly called MRP offsetting under uncertainties.

* This work has been partially supported by Princess Fatimah Alnijris's Research Chair of Advanced Manufacturing Technology.

B. Vallespir and T. Alix (Eds.): APMS 2009, IFIP AICT 338, pp. 144–151, 2010.
© IFIP International Federation for Information Processing 2010

Some MRP parameters are: planned lead time, safety stock, lot-sizing rule, freezing horizon, and planning horizon. There are extensive publications concerning safety stock calculation [5], [8]. In contrast, certain parameters seem not to be sufficiently examined as, for example, planned lead times. Nevertheless, this parameter (differences between due dates and release dates) is especially important for assembly systems, because for these systems all components must be present to begin the assembly, so a delay of a component blocks the entire process. The difficulty of the calculating optimal planned lead times (safety lead times) in assembly systems lies in the interdependence among different component stocks. Certainly, many types of components are needed to produce a single finished item. Therefore, the inventory level of a component depends on the stock levels of other components. Stockout for a component leads to shortage, and so decreases the service level. In addition, as the assembly process is stopped, the stocks of other components increase (because they are not used) and consequently the corresponding holding costs augment.

This problem is the subject of this paper. It was already examined in our earlier work. The case of Lot-for-Lot policy was examined in [2]. In the model proposed, the backlogs are authorized and a unit backlogging cost is supposed to be known. The objective was to minimize the sum of average backlogging and holding costs. A special case was considered in [6], when all components have identical properties, i.e. the same lead time probability distribution and unit holding cost. The optimal planned lead times were obtained using an extension of the Discrete Newsboy. This result was extended to the Periodic Order Quantity (POQ) policy in [7]. However, the assumptions used in the last two publications are relatively restrictive. Moreover, in real life applications the unit backlogging cost is difficult to ascertain. The purpose of this paper is to extend these models to a more general case of POQ policy with service level constraints and different holding and setup costs.

2   Objective of this Study

Each MRP table has several parameters: lot-sizing rule; planned lead time for the time phasing, safety stock, etc.

In this paper, the POQ lot-sizing rule is considered and only the following essential parameters are optimized (due to of their importance):

-    periodicity (p);
-    planned lead times (x_i).

It is clear that, for assembly systems, the parameters x_i and the periodicity p cannot be calculated separately for each component type (if we search for optimal solutions). Indeed, in assembly systems, the difficulty of determining optimal component planned lead times resides in the interdependence among different component inventories. Many types of components are needed to produce one product; therefore, the inventories of the different components become dependent.

In this paper, we consider assembly systems with one-level BOM when the POQ lot-sizing policy is used. Components are ordered every p periods. The periodicity is the same for all component types. The goal is to search for the optimal values of the parameters p and x_i, $i=1,2,\ldots,n$ minimizing the sum of the setup and average holding costs for the components, while satisfying a desired service level for finished product as well as taking into account the interdependence among the inventories of the different components.

3 Cost and Service Level Calculation

The POQ lot-sizing rule is used with periodicity p common for all component types (p is a decision variable). The orders for components are made at the beginning of the periods $kp+1$, $k=0,1,2,...$, and there is no order made in the periods $kp+r$, $r=2,3,...,p$.

The following additional notations are used:

h_i unit holding cost for component i
c setup cost, i.e. the cost incurred each time a replenishment order is made
L_i probability distribution for the component i lead time
u_i upper value of lead time distribution for component i
L_i^k lead time of the components i ordered at the beginning of the period k
D demand for finished product per period
a_i quantity of component i needed to assemble the finished product
p supply periodicity
Q_i supply order quantity for component i
x_i planned lead time for component i
$1-\varepsilon$ objective service level

The demand is constant, therefore, the supply orders Q_i of components i are also constant $Q_i=a_iDp$. The finished products are delivered at the end of each period and unsatisfied part of demand is backordered and has to be satisfied during the subsequent periods.

In the considered model, the quantities ordered are the same, so the planned lead times give also initial inventories. Thus, the aim of this study can be expressed in other terms: to find the optimal values of the initial inventories a_iDx_i and parameter p, where x_i, $i=1,2,...,n$, are the planned lead times.

This approach takes into account the major factors of the supply planning in assembly systems with random lead times to obtain an efficient optimization algorithm for planned lead times and the periodicity calculation.

As aforementioned, a particular case of this model was earlier considered in [7], where all components have identical properties, i.e., the same lead time probability distribution and the same unit holding cost. The new techniques proposed in this paper were developed without these restrictive assumptions.

For the considered model, given that the maximal value of the component i lead time is equal to u_i, only the orders made in the previous u_i-1 periods may not have arrived yet. The orders made before have already arrived. Therefore, the number $N_i^{p,m}$ of orders for the component i which are in waiting at the end of the period $m=kp+r$ is easy to calculate.

Let

$$L_i^{m+1-j}, j=r,\ r+p,\ r+2p,...,\ r+\frac{u_i-1-r}{p}p,$$

be the lead times of the orders made at the beginning of the periods $kp+1$, $(k-1)p+1,\ldots, (k-\frac{u_i-1-r}{p})p+1$.

If $L_i^{m+1-j} > j$, then the order made in the period $m+1-j$ is delivered after the end of the period m.

Let 1_E be the binary function equal to 1 when the expression E is true and equal to 0 otherwise. Therefore, if $1_{L_i^{m+1-j}>j}$ is equal to 1, then the order made at the period $m+1-j$ is delivered after the end of the period m. Thus, the random variables $N_i^{p,m}$ can be represented as follows:

$$N_i^{p,kp+r} = \sum_{j=0}^{\frac{u_i-1-r}{p}} 1_{L_i^{(k-j)p+1}>jp+r} \qquad i=1,\cdots,n \tag{1}$$

$$k \geq 0, \; p \in \{1,2,..,u_i-1\}, \; r \in \{1,2,..,p\}$$

The variables $N_i^{p,m}$ are independent for different types of components, and also independent from the decision variables x_i. Thus, they can be used to derive closed forms for the shortage level and cost [7].

The average cost has the following closed form:

$$C(X,p) = \frac{1}{p}\sum_{r=1}^{p} E\left(C(X,p,N^{p,kp+r})\right) = \frac{c}{p} +$$

$$\frac{p-1}{2}H + \sum_{i=1}^{n} h_i\left(x_i - E(N_i^p)\right) + H\sum_{k\geq 0}\left(1 - \frac{1}{p}\sum_{r=1}^{p}\prod_{i=1}^{n}F_i^{p,r}(\frac{x_i+k-r+p}{p})\right) \tag{2}$$

The average number of shortages has the following closed form:

$$S(X,p) = \frac{1}{p}\sum_{r=1}^{p}\Pr\left[\max_{i=1,\cdots,n}(pN_i^{p,kp+r}+r-p-x_i)^+ > 0\right] =$$

$$1 - \frac{1}{p}\sum_{r=1}^{p}\prod_{i=1}^{n}F_i^{p,r}(\frac{x_i-r+p}{p}) \tag{3}$$

4 Cost Optimization under Service Level Constraint

The optimization problem can then be written as follows:

$$\text{Minimize } C(X,p) \tag{4}$$

Subject to:

$$\frac{1}{p}\sum_{r=1}^{p}\prod_{i=1}^{n}F_i^{p,r}(\frac{x_i-r+p}{p}) \geq 1-\varepsilon \tag{5}$$

$$N_i^p = \sum_{r=1}^{p} N_i^{p,r} \tag{6}$$

$$F_i^{p,r}(x) = \Pr(N_i^{p,r} \le x) \tag{7}$$

$$H = \sum_{i=1}^{n} h_i \tag{8}$$

$$0 \le x_i \le u_i - 1, \quad i = 1, \dots, n \tag{9}$$

$$1 \le p \le u - 1 \tag{10}$$

The optimization problem (4)–(10) seems difficult to solve because of the nonlinearity of the objective function and the fact that the decision variables are integers. Nevertheless, in an earlier work [12] we already solved a similar problem: minimizing the sum of holding, setup and backlogging (instead of the service level constraint) costs. The approach was based on the partial incremental functions defined as follows:

$$G_i^+(X, p) = C(x_1, \dots, x_i + 1, \dots, x_n, p) - C(x_1, \dots, x_i, \dots, x_n, p),$$

$$G_i^-(X, p) = C(x_1, \dots, x_i - 1, \dots, x_n, p) - C(x_1, \dots, x_i, \dots, x_n, p).$$

It was proved that $G_i^+(X, p)$ is increasing on x_i and decreasing on x_j for j different from i. Inversely, $G_i^-(X, p)$ is decreasing on x_i and increasing on x_j for j different from i.

These properties can be easily extended for the objective function considered in this paper (the sum of holding and setup costs) with service level constraint and used to prove the following dominance properties:

If $G_i^+(A, p) < 0$, then each solution (X, p) with $x_i = a_i$ is dominated,

If $G_i^-(B, b) < 0$ and the vector $(a_1, \dots, a_{i-1}, b_i - 1, a_{i+1}, \dots, x_n)$ satisfies the desired service level, see constraint (9), then each solution (X, p) with $x_i = b_i$ is dominated.

In addition, the following lower bound on the objective function in the space $[A, B] \times \{p\}$ can be proven:

$$LB(p) = C(A, p) + \sum_{i=1}^{n} (b_i - a_i) \min\left(G_i^+(b_1, \dots, b_{i-1}, a_i, \dots, a_n, p), 0\right) \tag{11}$$

Let us present the space of all possible values of x_i by $[A, B]$, where $A = (a_1, a_2, \dots, a_n)$, $B = (b_1, b_2, \dots, b_n)$, and a_i, b_i are minimal and maximal possible values for x_i, respectively, i.e. $a_i \le x_i \le b_i$.

A Branch and Bound (B&B) approach can be used. Each node of the Branch and Bound tree represents a solution space $[A, B] \times p$. Two cut procedures are developed based on the aforementioned dominance properties. They are applied to each current solution space $[A,B]\times p$ (to each current node). The forward cut procedure replaces A by a larger vector, while the backward cut procedure replaces B by a smaller vector. A procedure is also developed to calculate lower bounds for any solution space $[A,B]\times p$, i.e., any branch tree node, using $LB(p)$ see (11). To calculate an *Upper Bound* for a given node $[A,B]\times p$, a heuristic method consisting in a variant of depth first search can be used. It partitions the solution space (current node) into two subspaces (nodes) and chooses as current node the node that has the best feasible solution at one of its two extremities, and so on. A root upper bound is also calculated by exploring all the promising values of the parameter p.

Algorithm B&B:
For each periodicity p **do:**
- Activate the solution space corresponding to the periodicity p. This initial space is represented by one node corresponding to all possible lead time values.
- Reduce the size of this node using dominance properties.
While the solution space is not empty **do:**
-    Activate the node corresponding to the subset having the largest number of solutions.
-    Divide this node into two new nodes (subsets).
-    Reduce the size of the new nodes using dominance properties.
-    **If** the reduced subsets contain feasible and not dominated solutions, **then:** add them to the solution space.
-    **If** the processing of the new nodes gives a better solution than the current best one, **then:** update the current best solution and delete the nodes having their lower bound larger than the current best solution.
End while
End for

The algorithm is applied for each value of p whose initial solution space $[A,B]\times p$ is not dominated. This B&B algorithm is a variant of width first search that consists in choosing for extension the node that contains the maximum number of solutions.

We studied an example with $n=10$ different types of components. The maximum value of the lead time was equal to 10 ($u=10$). The unit holding costs h_i were chosen as follows: 9, 2, 4, 6, 4, 3, 10, 5, 6, and 2. Setup (ordering) cost c was equal to 100. The required service level was 0.99.

For this example, the optimal solution was obtained after 301 iterations of the B&B algorithm, where, the cost is equal to 266.652, periodicity p is 2, and values of planned lead times for the considered ten types on components are 8, 9, 9, 8, 8, 8, 8, 7, 7, 8, respectively.

5 Conclusions

This paper further develops the models of our previous publications while considering the case of POQ policy. The objective is to determine the values of the following two types of MRP parameters for all components: order periodicity and planned lead times, minimizing the sum of average holding cost for the components and setup costs. There are no restrictive assumptions on the probability distributions and unit holding costs. In addition the backlogging cost is replaced with a service level constraint, which is a more realistic parameter.

The model presented in this paper uses less restrictive assumptions than previous models known in literature. This is a multi-period model with no restriction on the number of components and where lead time density function for each component may differ from the density functions of other components. All possible distributions can be used for component lead times. The decision variables are integer; they represent the periodicity and planned lead times for components. Branch and Bound approach is developed. The experimental study shows that the proposed B&B algorithm is very fast. It will always find the optimal solution within a very short computing time.

The proposed model and algorithms can be used in many industrial situations. For example, often security coefficients are introduced to calculate the planned lead time for unreliable suppliers in an MRP environment. In this case, planned lead times are equal to contractual (or forecasted) lead times multiplied by the security coefficients. These coefficients are empiric but anticipate the delays by creating safety lead times. The more unreliable a supplier is, the larger its coefficient. The model and algorithms suggested in this paper can be used to better estimate these coefficients basing on statistics on the procurement lead times for each supplier and taking into account the holding and setup costs, as well as a service level constraint.

Nevertheless, the model proposed keeps some restrictive assumptions as: fixed and constant demand for the finished product (for a given period), one-level bill of material, same order cost and periodicity for all components, etc. Therefore, for some actual industrial cases, the solution obtained can be approximate and not optimal. Future research will be focused on the study of how to relax some of these assumptions, for example, examining multi-level bills of material (BOM).

Concerning the assumption of constant demand, note that this model should be used with different possible values of the demand to examine the sensitivity of the obtained parameters to said values. If the parameter values are significantly different for the given demand levels, the approach by scenarios can be applied to choose the parameter values. In addition, the demand variations can be decoupled from planned lead time calculation by using safety stocks. This is another perspective for future research.

References

1. Axsäter, S.: Inventory Control, 2nd edn. Springer, Heidelberg (2006)
2. Dolgui, A., Louly, M.A.: A Model for Supply Planning under Lead Time Uncertainty. Int. J. Prod. Econ. 78, 145–152 (2002)
3. Dolgui, A., Prodhon, C.: Supply Planning under Uncertainties in MRP Environments: A State of the Art. Ann. Rev. Contr. 31(2), 269–279 (2007)
4. Koh, S.C.L., Saad, S.M.: MRP-controlled Manufacturing Environment Disturbed by Uncertainty. Robot. Comput. Integr. Manuf. 19, 157–171 (2003)
5. Lee, H.L., Nahmias, S.: Single-product, Single-Location Models. In: Graves, S.C., Rinnooy Kan, A.H.G., Zipkin, P.H. (eds.) Handbooks in Operations Research and Management Science, vol. 4, pp. 3–57. North-Holland, Amsterdam (1993)

6. Louly, M.A., Dolgui, A.: Newsboy Model for Supply Planning of Assembly Systems. Int. J. Prod. Res. 40, 4401–4414 (2002)
7. Louly, M.A., Dolgui, A.: The MPS Parameterization under Lead Time Uncertainty. Int. J. Prod. Econ. 90, 369–376 (2004)
8. Porteus, E.L.: Stochastic Inventory Theory. In: Heyman, D.P., Sobel, M.J. (eds.) Handbooks in Operations Research and Management Science, vol. 2, pp. 605–652. Elsevier Science Publishers, Amsterdam (1990)
9. Sipper, D., Bulfin Jr., R.L.: Production: Planning, Control and Integration. McGraw Hill, New York (1998)
10. Tempelmeier, H.: Inventory Management in Supply Networks: Problems, Models, Solutions, Books on Demand GmbH (2006)
11. Whybark, D.C., Wiliams, J.G.: Material Requirement under Uncertainty. Dec. Sci. 7, 595–606 (1976)
12. Louly, M.A., Dolgui, A.: An Optimization Approach for Time Phasing in MRP Systems. In: Preprints of the Fifteen International Working Seminar on Production Economics, Innsbruck, Austria, March 3-7, vol. 3, pp. 273–280 (2008)

From Product End-of-Life Sustainable Considerations to Design Management

Natalia Duque Ciceri[1], Marco Garetti[1], and Severine Sperandio[2]

[1] Politecnico di Milano, Department of Management, Economics and Industrial Engineering,
Piazza Leonardo da Vinci 32, 20133 Milano, Italy
{natalia.duque,marco.garetti}@polimi.it
[2] IMS, Department LAPS, University of Bordeaux
351, cours de la Liberation, 33405 Talence cedex, France
severine.sperandio@u-bordeaux1.fr

Abstract. Better understanding of the current product End-of-life sustainable practices leads to important feedback for the design of more "sustainable" so called eco-products, by identifying the design improvements that reduce the impact of manufactured goods on the environment and society. In this paper, we propose a way to assess the impact on product design that ultimately helps on deciding the product characteristics required for a desired End-of-life (EOL) practice (i.e. reuse, recycle, remanufacture, etc). Categories and criticality scales of impacts of these practices on the product design stages are proposed. Then, a framework is proposed to provide designers with guidance on how to proceed towards taking into account the impact of the sustainable requirements.

Keywords: Product End of Life, Product Design, Sustainable Development.

1 Introduction

Currently, we are at one of the booms of a "green era" often connected with the term sustainability (perhaps one of the words with the most attempts to be conceptualized and misused nowadays). Though, sustainability has an environmental, social, and economic connotation, its achievement is a matter of practical implementations, with the objective being that of minimizing the impact on the environment and society. Our current model of industrial and economic growth has become (unfortunately) the most damaging for the environment and the ecosystem in which we live. This impact from industrial practices is seen in the form of waste (hazardous/solid), overuse of natural resources (materials and energy), overproduction, toxic release, water emissions among many others. Only in terms of Greenhouse Gas (GHG) emissions, for instance, the world sources institute reported in 2005 that energy-related and industrial processes account for 64.7% of GHG emissions world-wide[1]. With this at stake, companies and product manufacturers are being faced with great challenges in their industrial practices. The greater challenge is that often performance measures are

---

[1] The World Bank Data and Statistics http://siteresources.worldbank.org

B. Vallespir and T. Alix (Eds.): APMS 2009, IFIP AICT 338, pp. 152–159, 2010.
© IFIP International Federation for Information Processing 2010

based on cost, quality and productivity. However, with the current "boom" more and more companies are voluntarily or required to consider sustainable practices.

The idea proposed in this paper is not to provide with ultimate solutions, but rather with a tool and an overall perspective. This tool is addressed mainly for designers when taking into account the "sustainable" considerations during the new product development process and transfer them to the different phases of design management. The focus of this work is in the considerations related to the End-of-Life (EOL) of the product: reuse, recycle, remanufacture or dispose (landfill or incineration) and their impact during product design. Categories of impacts are proposed, as well as, criticality scales associated to a decisional framework connecting the risk management and the strategic design planning processes. The paper is organized as follows: in Section 2, concepts and role of product lifecycle and EOL sustainable options are introduced; categories and criticality scales of impacts of sustainable considerations on the product design stages are proposed in Section 3; then, a framework to manage the design and to provide designers with guidance on how to proceed so as to take the impact of these requirements into account is provided. Some conclusion remarks and discussions are provided in the last section.

2   Closing the Loop from End-of-Life to Beginning-of-Life

This work deals with the strategic dimension of sustainable development within an industrial context, as the objectives are to understand how sustainable considerations influence the future product design stages. Indeed, rapid technological changes of these last years and the increasing competition have already led companies to modify their products development activities. Also, there are now several categories of "new" product introduction: completely new, repositioning, new product lines, core product revision, etc. For example, the paradigm of product platforms (i.e. a grouping of individual products sharing a common technology) permits to classify different categories of product developments. A strategy of products platform allows reducing pieces and components, costs relative to the design of products and investments necessary for new manufacturing processes. But how do sustainable considerations coming from other phases, such as the EOL, impact the beginning of the product lifecycle? How these sustainable strategies or requirements lead to changes in design stages? Figure 1 illustrates this graphically, while showing the entire product lifecycle and the activities related to the three main phases: from Beginning-of-Life (BOL), through Middle-of-Life (MOL) until End-of-Life (EOL).

The EOL phase starts at the point of disposal by a customer (consumer or business) and includes different end routes, ranging from *reuse* of the product without any structural changes (i.e. lifetime extension) [1]; *remanufacturing* where a discarded, non-functional, or traded-in product is restored to like-new condition [2]; *recycling*, which involves the collection and treatment of waste products for use as raw material in the manufacture of the same or a similar ones; *incineration*, where combustible wastes are burned and changed into gases (with or without energy recovery); dumping waste underground or *landfill* [3]; or else simply ends up in *emission or leakage* into the environment.

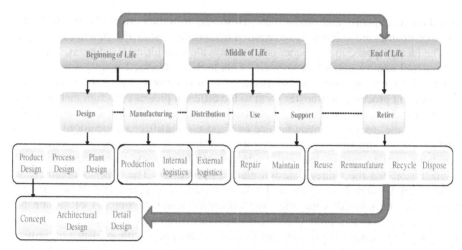

Fig. 1. Closing the loop from End-of-Life to Beginning-of-Life

It may be said that these options are presented in a traditional order of preference from an environmental point of view. However, this statement could be controversial among different EOL options and it varies from product to product and their application. This paper does not aim at evaluating how sustainable is a certain EOL practice or whether each one of them is sustainable or not. Therefore, for the purpose of this paper, the following assumptions are made on what the "sustainable" considerations are (i) defined by the single company or product manufacturer; (ii) encouraged either by internal influences (company-based) or external (suppliers, customers, government); (iii) implemented voluntarily or enforced (regulations, legislations). To illustrate such considerations that would require being transferred to the design stages, let us mention some examples:

- The regulated targets that the European Commission has established for different industries. For instance, WEEE *(Waste of electrical and electronic equipment)*: mandatory collection targets equal to 65% of the average weight of electrical and electronic equipment placed on the market over the two previous years [4]. Similarly, with regulations such as ELV *(End-of-Life Vehicles)* [5]; RoHS *(Restriction of use of certain Hazardous Substances)* [6] among others.
- The increasing demand for eco-products by environmentally-conscious customers has forced companies to incorporate "green" initiatives to meet the demand of this growing market. For instance, recently a computer manufacturer has determined "reducing the environmental impact of their products within their design phase". For this, they redefine "the quantity of raw materials, as well as, the type and recyclability of materials used"[2] to minimize waste at the end of a product's life. Besides these established visions and in the midst of improving their brand image, many companies have adopted such strategies as part of their "Corporate Social Responsibility"[3] programs.

---

[2] http://www.apple.com/environment/design/
[3] A concept whereby companies voluntarily integrate social and environmental concerns in their business and the way they interact with stakeholders. [3].

Behind each of these considerations, there are tremendous amount of decisions to be made by engineers, designers and other product/process decision-makers. How does each of these requirements affect the design of new products? How are they translated to the product functionality, customer needs, product architecture, marketability, reliability, performance, etc? Product development requires time. Very few products can be developed in less than one year, many require 3-5 years, and some may take as long as 10 years [7]. For the first example taken, each of these illustrated EU Directive requirements should be incorporated in today's product development plans for a company to stay in business in the upcoming years. The idea is to understand the present "sustainable" product to be able to predict the future "sustainable" product, and also identify changes to be introduced during the future design stages. For example, recycling and dismissal activities require and provide useful information on product components, materials and resources from/to the design and manufacturing stages. A visualization of this proposition is depicted in Figure 2:

- Along the x-axis there is time. The first aim is to understand "What is needed TODAY for "W" product to be in the market?" where product "W" is the product being analyzed. This is in relation with the different "requirements" (e.g. regulations, limited material resources, energy-related). The second aim is to understand "What type of EOL product-related information will be needed in the year "X" for a sustainable product? Where year "X" is any future year (e.g. 2015, 2020, etc).
- Along the y-axis, the "sustainability level" which can be determined by: manufacturing regulations/legislations, energy and materials use, emissions reduction, hazardous materials use and waste, and labor standards, et cetera. To illustrate this level, we take the example of a regulation already into place in the automotive industry in Europe: 85% recycling/recovery rates in terms of weight by 2006 and 95% by 2015.

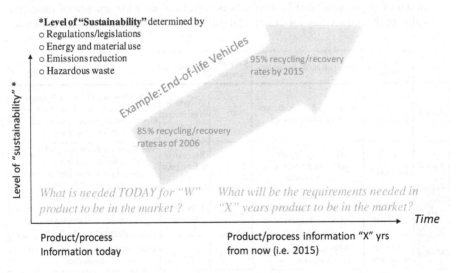

Fig. 2. Illustration of current and future sustainable requirements of products

3   Impact of EOL Sustainable Considerations in Product Design

Many authors recognize that product design proceeds roughly (though not strictly) in stages or phases. Hence, models relative to design process intend to provide the designer with guidance on how to proceed from the recognition of a need to preliminary, abstract ideas on how that need could be met, and on to detailed, concrete solutions [8]. While no two design process models are exactly alike, they all seem to explicitly include a problem definition / information gathering / need recognition phase, a concept design phase, and a detail design phase. The majority also include a transition phase of some kind between concept and detail design. For example, Ulrich and Eppinger [7] define concept, system-level, and detail design phases of product development; Dym and Little [9] present concept, preliminary, and detailed design as key stages; Pahl and Beitz [10] identify concept design, embodiment or architectural design, and detail design as distinct design phases. In accordance with this last proposition, we decide to categorize the impact of an EOL sustainable practice strategy on the design process into four groups. Considering the different types of impact on the design process, we also establish four criticality classes associated with the actions to be carried out for the process to succeed:

- A "slight adjustment" leads to changes of resource capacities or operational constraints (e.g. constraints of precedence, temporal or cumulative constraints, etc). To take an example, some companies have opted for selling their brand remanufactured or reused guaranteed products, encouraging a good EOL sustainable option. This choice extends the life of the product and has a slight impact in the design phase (i.e. type of adjustments for this change are mostly operational-based).
- A "fair adjustment" entails modifications of capacities and / or competences of human and technical resources, legislated constraints, etc. For instance, reducing the amount of waste generated by products is correlated with the amount of materials used in each product. Say for example, the amount of plastic to make a water plastic

Case	Impact category	Impact on the design process	Criticality classes	Level of risk	Decision
Case 1	"Slight adjustment"	No impact on the architecture of the current product	C1	Acceptable in the present state	No action or modification at the functional level. Follow-up, monitoring and review. Risk assessment. Success probability of the design closed to 1
Case 2	"Fair adjustment"	Acts upon the organic or architectural definition of the current product	C2	Reasonable under regular control	Modification at the organic level. Follow-up, monitoring and review. Risk assessment. A significant success probability of the design.
Case 3	"Large adjustment"	Requires strategic adjustments of the current product impacting its functional or conceptual characteristics	C3	Difficult to tolerate	Modification at the functional level. Follow-up, monitoring and review. Risk assessment. A moderated success probability of the design.
Case 4	"Critical adjustment"	Makes the current product obsolete.	C4	Highest	Change of strategy. Total reengineering of the product.

Fig. 3. Impact of sustainable considerations on the design process (adopted from [11])

bottle is changed and to achieve this, the shape of the bottle has changed, then some technical changes have to occur during product and process design (i.e. architectural design and therefore different molds in the manufacturing phase).

- A "large adjustment" requires changes of the industrial activity, integration of new technologies, etc. Let us take the example of a cell phone, which its current recycling rate is roughly 11% [12]. Part of the reason why it is quite low is for the high material mixing content, which at the time of recycle, makes it rather difficult to separate these materials. If the recyclability desired is uplifted to 50% or more, depending on the changes designers decide to make to meet this target, it may require the integration of new materials or, for instance, reduction to only one type of plastic. If most of the functional components are kept, this change will compromise the conceptual design of the product (as many of its main characteristics are changed), but an acceptable amount of design content of the product can be kept as it is.

- In a "critical adjustment" it is necessary to remake all the design stages, including the problem definition / information gathering / need recognition phase.   Let us say, the company is a nickel-cadmium rechargeable batteries manufacturer. Due to the poisonous nature of cadmium, which constitutes dangerous toxic waste, it is banned under the RoHS [5]. For this manufacturer, the redesign of the product is affected in all stages. This requires new technologies, materials and the design content of the previous product is unable to be kept.

Determination of these criticality classes, evidently, depends on specificities of each product or particular industry. Future "adjustments" due to sustainable objectives require an early diagnosis and management in the design process. To this purpose, a methodology is proposed by the authors, based on the framework illustrated in Figure 4, which will be described with a quick simple example through the steps.

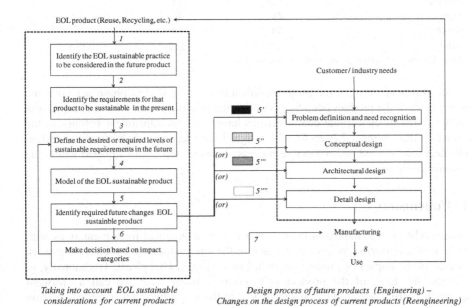

*Taking into account EOL sustainable
considerations for current products*
*Design process of future products (Engineering) –
Changes on the design process of current products (Reengineering)*

Fig. 4. Methodology: EOL sustainable considerations in the design process

Let us consider the following EOL practice in the design of a TV product: 65% of the average weight of the TV is collected and at least 30% is recycled material and used as raw material in the manufacture of the same or a similar product. In this case, the present and future targets/levels of sustainability are given (step 2 and 3). Assuming that the product is manufactured or imported into Europe, where 65% of the average weight of a WEEE is collected [4]; we call this the present requirement. The future level is aimed at 30% of the average weight of the TV being material recycled. For step 4, it is decided by the product designers that in order to meet this target, the current design can be modified in this way: steel parts will be made out of aluminum, which accounts for about 20% of the average product weight. The glass content is recycled along with the cooper accounting for 46% and 5% respectively. Assuming that at least half of these materials' content is actually recovered after the recycling process, which in the case of aluminum, cooper and glass is reasonable; then the resulting material recycled is about 35%, resulting in the achievement of the desired target. Plastics and wood are not taken into consideration, given that their recycle fraction in current supply is less than 10% [13]. This constitutes the model of the EOL sustainable product design, summarized as follows:

Table 1. Model of the EOL sustainable product design

Billl of Materials - TV (% average weight)	Current Product*	EOL sustainable product	Material Recycled
Steel	17	-	-
Copper	5	5	2.5
Aluminium	3	20	10
Plastics	11	11	-
Glass	46	46	23
Wood	18	18	-
Total	100	100	**35.5**

Bill of Materials of current product are taken from [14].

The pertinent changes for these modifications on the design phase act upon the architecture of the product (step 5), given that the material contents have changed, but no functional or conceptual characteristics have, such an adjustment belongs to the criticality class number 2 (step 6), with a significant success probability of the design. The decision is made and respective process changes (step 7) are adjusted within the manufacturing phase.

4   Conclusion

Sustainability in the industrial context is a matter of practical implementations with the aim of minimizing its counter impact on the environment and society. Our work focuses in the impact of products at their End-of-Life (EOL) phase. Traditionally, in practice, the EOL of the product is determined using what we call a "forward approach": from the product characteristics to the respective EOL practice decision (i.e. reuse, remanufacture, recycle, and dispose), which in the end is taken in terms of profitability. The methodology proposed provides a way to assess the impact on product design that ultimately helps on deciding the product characteristics required for a desired EOL practice. For instance, a company wants to sell a product to be at the end of its life x% recyclable, what impact on the design of the product would this entail? We transfer these considerations to the industrial design context. The result allows designers to identify the impact of these requirements and assist during the product development process.

Acknowledgments. The paper is the results of a research which is partially funded the EC project LeanPPD Lean Product and Process Development NMP-LA 2008-214090.

References

1. Huisman, J.: The QWERTY/EE Concept Quantifying Reciclability and Eco-Efficiency for End-of-life Treatment of Consumer Electronic Products. PhD thesis, Delft TU, The Netherlands (2003)
2. Lund, R.T., Hauser, W.: The Remanufacturing Industry: Anatomy of a Giant. Department of Manufacturing Engineering, Boston University, Massachusetts (2003)
3. EEA (European Environmental Agency) Glossary. Obtained through the Internet, http://glossary.eea.europa.eu/ (accessed on July 2009)
4. EU Directive 2002/96/EC on Waste Electrical and Electronic Equipment (WEEE) (2002), http://ec.europa.eu/environment/waste/weee/index_en.htm (accessed on July 2009)
5. EU Directive 2000/53/EC on End-of-Life Vehicle (2002), http://ec.europa.eu/environment/waste/elv_index.htm (accessed on July 2009)
6. EU Directive 2002/95/EC on RoHS (Restriction of Hazardous Substances) (2002), http://ec.europa.eu/environment/waste/weee/index_en.htm (accessed on July 2009)
7. Ulrich, K.T., Eppinger, S.D.: Product design and development, 4th edn. McGraw-Hill Higher Education, Boston (2008)
8. Sobek, D.K.: Transitions: From Conceptual Ideas to Detail Design. In: Proceedings of the 2005 American Society for Engineering Education Annual Conference & Exposition (2005)
9. Dym, C.L., Little, P.: Engineering Design: A Project-Based Introduction. John Wiley & Sons, New York (2000)
10. Pahl, G., Beitz, W.: Engineering Design: A Systematic Approach. Springer, New York (2001)
11. Sperandio, S., Robin, V., Girard, P.: Management of risk caused by domino effect resulting from design system dysfunctions. In: Joint ESREL 2008 and 17th SRA-EUROPE Conference, September 22-25. Universidad Politecnica de Valencia, Spain (2008)
12. Dahmus, J., Gutowski, T.: What Gets Recycled: An Information Theory Based Model of Product Recycling. Environmental Science and Technology (41), 7543–7550 (2007)
13. Ashby, M.F.: Materials and the Environment: Eco-informed Material Choice. Elsevier Science & Technology/Butterworth-Heinemann
14. Truttmann, N., Rechberger, H.: Contribution to resource conservation by reuse of electronical and electronic household appliances. Resource Conservation and Recycling 48(3), 249–261 (2006)

A Conceptual Framework for Sustainable Manufacturing by Focusing on Risks in Supply Chains

Masaru Nakano

The Graduate School of System Design and Management, Keio University,
Kyosei Building, 4-1-1, Hiyoshi, Kohoku-ku, Yokohama, Kanagawa, 223-8526, Japan
m.nakano@sdm.keio.ac.jp

Abstract. Sustainable manufacturing is becoming a popular concept. However, the definition is not clear, and technical approaches are not specified in conventional studies.

This study proposes a conceptual framework for understanding sustainable manufacturing from the viewpoint of risks in manufacturing enterprises and supply chains. Two aspects of sustainable manufacturing are defined: manufacturing for a sustainable society and sustainability of the manufacturing sector.

A technical approach is relevant to visualization techniques in systems engineering. The study categorizes risk and sustainability factors of manufacturing enterprises into four sections: internal, supply chain, manufacturing, and global society. Inter-sectional analysis is important for resolving environmental issues. In addition, this study categorizes methods for risk management corresponding to different time scales and frequencies.

Keywords: Sustainable Manufacturing, Supply Chain, Risk Management.

1 Introduction

The concept of sustainable manufacturing is becoming an important issue in the context of concern about the environment. Many studies, such as Jovane et al. [1] and Westkämper et al. [2], described the background, needs, and major conceptual steps from economic growth to sustainable development. However, the definition of sustainable manufacturing is not clear. In this study, two aspects of sustainable manufacturing are defined: manufacturing for a sustainable society and sustainability of the manufacturing sector. The definition is consistent with a well-known definition of sustainability that combines economic, environmental, and social dimensions (for example, see Sutherland et al. [3] and Seuring and Muller [4]).

Studies on sustainable supply chains have increased recently regarding the risk of supply chain disruption and green supply chains [4]. A survey with case studies related to disruption and resilience in supply chains is provided by Sheffi [5] by considering a combination of risk and competence in enterprises. Nakano [6] discusses mid-term flexibility, adaptability, and changeability in designing manufacturing systems against market risk. A conceptual framework for inverse manufacturing (see Srivastava [7]) is provided with economic criteria of a focal company for a green

B. Vallespir and T. Alix (Eds.): APMS 2009, IFIP AICT 338, pp. 160–167, 2010.
© IFIP International Federation for Information Processing 2010

supply chain. This paper not only considers an enterprise or a supply chain but also emphasizes collaboration of industrial sectors, and proposes a conceptual framework by focusing on risks in enterprises and supply chains in the two aspects of sustainable manufacturing. The idea goes from sustainable society to sustainable enterprise through sustainable manufacturing and sustainable supply chains. The conceptual relationship is illustrated in Figure 1.

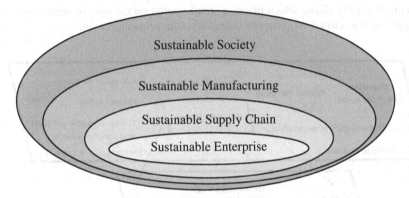

Fig. 1. Conceptual relationship between concepts relevant to sustainable manufacturing

Section two categorizes the risks of manufacturing enterprises from different per-spectives. A sustainable supply chain is defined in this study as a value chain in manufacturing for the sustainability of society, industrial sectors, and manufacturing enterprises under constraints of social needs and supply networks. The study also categorizes methods for risk management corresponding to different cases in terms of timescale and frequency.

Section three proposes methods to visualize and analyze problems in sustainable manufacturing by using systems engineering techniques (see Haskins et al. [8] and Forsberg et al. [9]). Section four describes a method for inter-sectional analysis of sustainable manufacturing. The topic connects sustainable manufacturing and sustain-able supply chains. Section five concludes the paper and describes future work.

2   Risk and Sustainability of Manufacturing Enterprises

Figure 2 illustrates four categories of risks and sustainability for manufacturing enter-prises. The enterprise has dishonesty risks such as fraud and leaks, which may lead it to sudden death. Upstream or downstream risks exist in supply chains. They include disruptive risks from social catastrophes such as natural disasters, civil war, and fi-nancial crisis, and competitive risks in business such as M&A and innovation by competitors. There may be dishonesty for intellectual property rights (IPR) in devel-oping countries. In addition, we should also consider risks related to social factors such as global warming, shortage of energy and material resources, and an aging society. Most public sectors concern risks to the manufacturing sector in their regions. Another risk is change in the industrial structure. Green policies may change the structure dramatically and threaten specified sectors.

Consider Figures 1 and 2. Sustainable manufacturing consists of two issues: green manufacturing, which is manufacturing with a low burden on the natural environment, and sustainability of the manufacturing sector. Green manufacturing employs energy-efficient, material-efficient, and pollution-free technologies in manufacturing. Similarly, a green supply chain, which places a small burden on the environment, employs techniques such as closed-loop supply chains and lifecycle engineering.

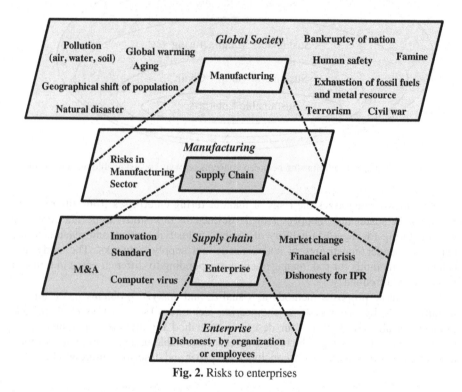

Fig. 2. Risks to enterprises

Risks in global society, such as global warming and material shortages, are long-term risks, which are supposed to predict future occurrences and their timing. Collaborative efforts to design and improve the social system should be made to mitigate these risks, because delayed actions may be too late for recovery. Risks for manufacturing sectors are also predictable if you look at the history of the automobile sector. On the other hand, the exact timing of disruptive and competitive risks, such as financial crises and natural disasters, cannot be predicted, and therefore monitoring capability and quick response are more important. We call this kind of risk unpredictable risks. As for risks arising inside enterprises, continuous management is essential. Table 1 summarizes risks and appropriate responses. Because

Table 1. Main approaches to avoiding risks and fostering sustainability

Risks	Main Approach	Management	Monitoring and Resilience	Prediction and System Design
Inside Enterprise		●	▲	
Supply Network	Disruptive		●	▲
	Competitive		●	
	Green			●
Manufacturing	Green			●
	Sector		▲	●
Society			▲	●

internal risks also occur in non-manufacturing enterprises, the following sections exclude internal risks.

3 Systems Engineering for Sustainable Manufacturing

This section considers a methodology to mitigate risks and foster sustainability of manufacturing enterprises. The underlying approaches come from systems engineering. A V-shaped model (Vee) is well known as a process model to design and manage systems, and includes the following steps: problem definition and requirement analysis, system design and decomposition, component design, development and implementation, integration, verification, and validation. A Vee model to evaluate technologies and policies in green manufacturing is proposed, as shown in Figure 3.

Global warming and material exhaustion are risks that we already understand, and it may be too late if we tackle them in the future. Therefore, as the first step, the stakeholders should estimate future risks, set a goal to prevent catastrophe, and collaboratively design a social system and a supply network. A technology road map should be made to develop a new system design for sustainable manufacturing. The dotted lines suggest that the left box is a starting point and the right box is the corresponding end point. The deliverable will be a proposal to the public in most cases.

A Vee model for monitoring and resilience in supply chains is proposed, as shown in Figure 4.

It is important to monitor occurrences of risks and use simulations to prepare for quick recovery because you cannot estimate the exact timing. The author proposes a multi-view modeling technique to visualize the problem's mechanism and design new supply chain architecture. The multi-view model consists of an event model, a risk model, and a management model, as shown in Figure 5.

The event model represents the relationship between causes and problems by investigating past cases, and provides scenarios for what can happen in the future. The dotted arrows represent risk mitigation factors while fault tree analysis FTA represents only paths that cause problems. The risk model evaluates risks mathematically by computing the probability of occurrences and multiplying by the cost of damage. The risks, occurrences, and damages are provided in probabilistic distribution. The arc represents probability of transition. The management model has the corresponding tasks and organization to monitor risk occurrences and respond quickly.

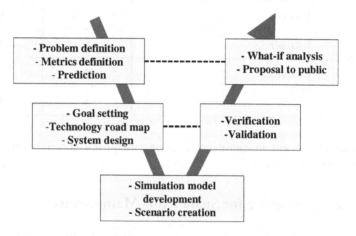

Fig. 3. A Vee model for system design in green manufacturing

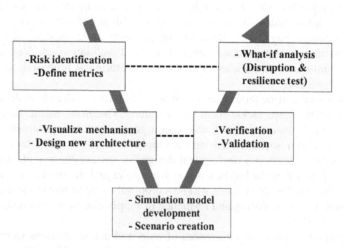

Fig. 4. A Vee model for monitoring and resilience in supply chains

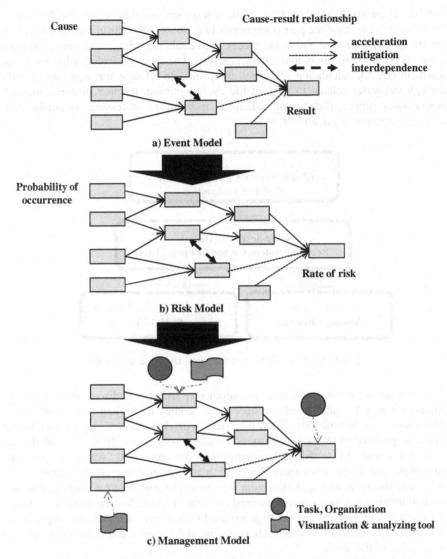

Fig. 5. A multi-view model to mitigate risks in supply chains

4   Inter-sectional Analysis of Green Sustainable Manufacturing and Green Supply Chains

Figure 6 shows a concept for analyzing green sustainable manufacturing and green supply chains. Forecasting of macro-economic concerns, such as global warming, energy shortages, and material exhaustion, is necessary for goal-setting. The micro-stakeholders are consumers and enterprises. Enterprises have the role of designing environmentally friendly products in terms of product life cycle management (PLM) and life cycle engineering (LCE), while consumers regulate enterprise behaviors. However, the intermediate part is important to connect macro-level prediction regarding the global economy and environment with goals regarding time, space, and life cycle on which consumers and enterprises rely. The analysis includes life cycle assessment (LCA), calculation of carbon footprints, and design for recycling systems through industries related to product life cycles: mining, refining, material making, power/water supply, distribution, chemical, machining, processing, assembly, construction, transportation, and so on.

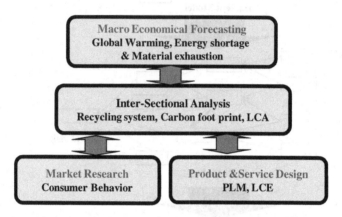

Fig. 6. System design for green sustainable manufacturing

A material selection problem in the automotive industry is discussed as a sample. Aluminum may be substituted for steel in car bodies more than is currently done. Aluminum is environmentally better than steel in driving due to its lighter weight, but worse to produce in terms of energy and water resource use. It is essential that all aluminum is recycled to the primary material. A dedicated study was done by NEDO [10] using life cycle assessment. Exhaustion of copper resources is threatened by increasing use in motors, and aluminum is expected to substitute for copper. However, more aluminum use may cause a material shortage. To visualize the triple relationship in the context of systems engineering, we need to deal with demand and supply in the future and collect data on items such as trading and accumulated volumes, which can be recycled in the future.

To encourage a recycling society, we may change our habit of product possession to that of rental or lease because the rental system is good for guaranteeing recycling. The industrial sector faces big risks because the change of our habit can cause a dramatic change in industrial structure in the future. We have three views, time-wise, space-wise, and life-cycle-wise: when a metal material approaches exhaustion and when other metals should be substituted, that is, time-wise; which countries should be affected by the crisis and what policy can be effective to mitigate the risk worldwide, that is, space-wise; and which sectors should collaborate in providing their data, that is, life-cycle-wise. To analyze this issue, data are needed to estimate accumulated stocks in used products, demand/production forecasting, and recycling technology from many sectors such as mining, automobiles, electrical appliances, and construction.

5 Conclusion

The study discusses multiple views of sustainable manufacturing and proposes a conceptual framework to visualize and analyze relevant research topics. The discussion includes sustainable society, sustainable supply chains, and risks, as well as sustainable manufacturing. In addition, this study proposes three views, time-wise, space-wise, and life-cycle-wise, and three approaches, management, monitoring and resilience, and forecasting and system design.

The studies included in the paper remain conceptual in this field. Therefore, a future work will be a case study to verify and improve this concept.

Acknowledgments. This work was supported in part by a Grant in Aid from the Global Center of Excellence Program for "Center for Education and Research of Symbiotic, Safe and Secure System Design" from the Ministry of Education, Culture, Sport, and Technology in Japan.

References

1. Jovane, F., Yoshikawa, H., Alting, L., Boer, C.R., Westkamper, E., Williams, D., Tseng, M., Seliger, G., Paci, A.M.: The Incoming Global Technical and Industrial Revolution towards Competitive Sustainable Manufacturing. CIRP Annals – Manufacturing Technology 57, 641–659 (2008)
2. Westkämper, E., Alting, L., Arndt, G.: Life Cycle Management and Assessment: Approaches and Visions towards Sustainable Manufacturing. Proceedings of Institution of Mechanical Engineering, Part B 215, 599–626 (2001)
3. Sutherland, J.W., Rivera, J.L., Brown, K.L., Law, M., Hutchins, M.J., Haapala, K.R.: Challenges for the Manufacturing Enterprise to Achieve Sustainable Development. In: The 41st CIRP Conference on Manufacturing Systems, pp. 15–18 (2008)
4. Seuring, S., Muller, M.: From a Literature Review to a Conceptual Framework for Sustainable Supply Chain Management. Journal of Cleaner Production 16, 1699–1710 (2008)
5. Sheffi, Y.: The Resilient Enterprise: Overcoming Vulnerability for Competitive Advantage, pp. 1--352. MIT Press, Cambridge (2005)
6. Nakano, M., Noritake, S., Ohashi, T.: A Lifecycle Simulation Framework for Production Systems. In: Lean Business Systems and Beyond, pp. 327–335. Springer, Boston (2008)
7. Srivastava, S.K.: Network Design for Reverse Logistics. Omega-International Journal of Management Science 36, 535–548 (2008)
8. Haskins, C., Forsberg, K., Kruger, M. (eds.): System Engineering Handbook - A Guide for System Life Cycle processes and Activities, version 3.1, International Council on System Engineering, INCOSE (2007)
9. Forsberg, K., Mooz, H., Cotterman, H.: Visualizing Project Management: Models and Frameworks For Mastering Complex Systems, pp. 1–480. John Wiley & Sons Inc., Chichester (2005)
10. NEDO committee report (Japanese), Life Cycle Assessment of Aluminum for Automotive Material (2005),
    http://www.nedo.go.jp/iinkai/kenkyuu/bunkakai/17h/jigo/
    10/1/4-1_9.pdf

Introducing Energy Performances in Production Management: Towards Energy Efficient Manufacturing

Alessandro Cannata and Marco Taisch

Politecnico di Milano, Department of Management, Economics and Industrial Engineering,
Piazza Leonardo da Vinci, 32 – 20133 Milano, Italy
{alessandro.cannata,marco.taisch}@polimi.it

Abstract. Energy consumption is one of the main economic, environmental and societal issues. As stated by recent researches, manufacturing plays a major role in energy consumption. To react to this situation and to go towards Energy Efficient Manufacturing, several initiatives are on-going. One relevant lever that is discussed in this paper and that should be taken into consideration is production management. Present production planning and control policies, which are used to optimize manufacturing processes, do not take into consideration energy efficiency. In this paper, we investigate energy efficiency performance indicators on one side and production scheduling and control practices on the other side. The purpose is to highlight this research gap in literature and start defining next steps towards Energy Efficient Manufacturing.

Keywords: sustainable manufacturing, energy efficiency, production management, key performance indicators, energy efficient manufacturing.

1 Introduction

Nowadays, energy consumption is one of the main economic, environmental and societal issues. As stated by recent researches on energy use [6], manufacturing plays a major role in energy consumption. As a matter of fact, 33% of the global energy consumption is due to manufacturing, representing a main issue both due to increasing and volatile price of energy sources, and to the environmental impact (38% of the total CO_2 emissions are due to manufacturing).

In order to react to this situation and to go towards sustainable production, several initiatives on energy efficiency are on-going. Most of them are developing innovations in production processes and technologies, and policy regulations.

One relevant lever that is not yet considered enough to go towards Energy Efficient Manufacturing is Production Management. Production Management is core in order to ensure proper and efficient operation of production systems. Hence, one of the new challenges, which Production Management Systems are facing, is the proper inclusion of Energy Efficiency as a core objective. Moreover, considering the possibility to exploit information available at shop floor level (thanks to pervasive Information and Communication Technologies), innovative production management systems can be adopted to support energy efficient manufacturing.

B. Vallespir and T. Alix (Eds.): APMS 2009, IFIP AICT 338, pp. 168–175, 2010.
© IFIP International Federation for Information Processing 2010

In this paper, we investigate energy efficiency performance indicators on one side and production scheduling and control practices on the other side. The purpose is to highlight this research gap in production management literature and start defining next steps towards Energy Efficient Manufacturing.

2 Research Focus in Manufacturing Domain: IMS2020

Energy Efficiency is core for manufacturing, and this can be also shown by looking at the results coming from foresight studies that focus on the identification of future topics/challenges to be addressed by the scientific and industrial community. In the manufacturing domain, some research activities are on-going (e.g. ManuFuture [18]): among them there is IMS2020 (www.ims2020.net/ - IMS2020: Supporting Global Research for IMS2020 Vision).

IMS2020 is a European funded project, whose aim is to support global European-centric research under the IMS scope. Intelligent Manufacturing Systems (IMS) is an international research & development initiative established to develop next-generation manufacturing technologies.

In particular, IMS2020 project maps and analyzes on-going major research activities and conducts foresight analyses to derive a set of recommendations for future manufacturing research. In the project, the following key areas are identified:

- **Sustainable Manufacturing:** in this key area, the focus is manufacturing approaches and technologies towards sustainable development, i.e. "a development that meets the needs of the present without compromising the ability of future generations to meet their own needs" [1]. Specific topics addressed are: innovative manufacturing technologies for environmentally benign production and measurement/assessment technologies to ensure occupational safety (e.g. ergonomics, industrial disaster prevention, etc.).

- **Energy Efficient Manufacturing:** this key area focuses on efficiency improvement and carbon footprint reduction in energy utilization for manufacturing and operational processes. In this area, different approaches for energy measure, control, and management are investigated in order to define future research streams.

- **Key technologies:** this area refers to the development of manufacturing and information and communication technologies for supporting next-generation manufacturing including new materials. .

- **Standards:** in this key area the focus is on manufacturing research issues that can benefit from standardization to create open manufacturing and product standards that are accessible to everyone, enhancing innovation globally.

- **Education:** educational programs for an information based knowledge worker environment that will support manufacturing. Research topics in this key area address the development of a coherent vision of manufacturing education.

In each of these five areas, IMS2020 is preparing a coherent roadmap for future manufacturing research, suitable to IMS cooperation. Being one of the five main pillars of this foresight activity, the central role in the future of Energy Efficient Manufacturing is stressed. In the next section, a literature review is conducted on research efforts spent in the area of Energy Efficient Manufacturing, in order to find out some gaps to be bridged.

3 Approaches to Energy Efficient Manufacturing

In our literature review, we mapped several research activities that proposed advances for energy efficiency in the industrial domain. Here, we propose the most relevant ones clustered homogeneously in terms of objectives and approaches.

Some research activities have been performed in order to analyze and control energy efficiency in energy-intensive sectors [14]-[16]-[17]. These analyses are mostly driven by economic evaluations; as a matter of fact, in these sectors energy is responsible for a major part of the total production cost. This stream of research focuses mainly on process technology improvement, as a mean to reach energy efficiency. However, as stated by [13]-[16] studies of the non-energy intensive sector are scarce. And since non-energy intensive industry accounts for a non-negligible part of total industrial energy consumption [13], there is a need for research also in this area.

With regards to the development of performances indicators [19], some researchers addressed this topic identifying new methods to assess energy efficiency in industrial domain. However, most of these works are focused on aggregate performances suitable to be used at the top level of enterprise hierarchy. Indeed, investigation of performance indicators to be adopted at different hierarchical level in the enterprise seems to be missing.

Another relevant stream of research in Energy Efficiency [20]-[21] is related to policy and standardization. Even if this is an extremely interesting area of research, it is slightly far from traditional production management research but should be taken into consideration in order to have a holistic view on the issue Energy Efficiency.

Looking at production management as a research area, some scientific initiatives have been mapped. Most of them include energy efficiency consideration, in particular in relation to eco-efficiency analysis or environmental analysis. Methods developed from these literature streams are Life-Cycle Assessment [10]-[12], Environmental Management Systems [3], and Total Quality Environmental Management [2].

Even if these methodologies have been applied successfully, they present also some drawbacks already emerged from literature. Concerning LCA, [2] noted that "LCA has been recognized as extremely information intensive, difficult to implement, somewhat subjective and difficult to defend". Indeed, to adopt LCA much effort is required to find and analyze data. Hence, this approach could be difficult to implement in everyday operation management.

Concerning Environmental Management Systems, similar drawbacks have been identified. Moreover, some authors argue that Energy Management is not enough integrated in Environmental Management Systems: as stated by [23], "Even though Energy Management should be integrated in EMS, empirical data indicates that it is not".

TQEM can be considered an evolution of Total Quality Management, where environmental aspects are taken into consideration. Even if this approach was developed some years ago, some barriers are limiting its adoption [2]. Indeed, [2] states that managers have difficulty assessing the impact of TQEM programs, because of the lack of appropriate measures. Even if in [2], the authors perform an analysis in order to show impacts of TQEM, little attention is put on energy aspects; furthermore the analysis is mainly cost-based.

At present, few consolidated techniques are available to perform energy efficiency analyses and (near real-time) control of production systems' operation (especially in non-energy intensive industries). Only three works, which slightly address this topic, have been found: [4]-[5]-[9]. However these works still leave many open questions about production management improvements for energy efficiency.

Concluding, from this initial literature review we highlighted that performance indicators need to be further discussed in particular focusing on cross-layer adoption of different indicators for addressing Energy Efficient Manufacturing. Moreover, production management practices with focus on energy efficiency seem not to be addressed yet, e.g. production planning and control.

4   Introducing Energy Efficiency in Production Management

In Production Management, i.e. field of study that includes techniques and practices adopted in industrial domain to define how (when, in which sequence, by which resource, etc.) products should be manufactured, two pillars are required to support smooth and efficient operation of manufacturing systems: production planning & control practices and performance assessment.

With regards to performance assessment, three different layers of performances can be defined [22]: aggregate performances, set of indicators, and specific indicators (see Fig. 1). These three layers can be respectively linked to different hierarchical levels in the company. This means that if top management is usually interested in aggregate performances, middle management (such as plant managers, etc.) are instead more interested in set of indicators and so on. This structure could be adopted for different business performance; however, in this paper, we will focus only on relevant performances in the production management scope.

Traditionally, at the aggregate performances level, production management looked at performance such as Cost, Quality, and Speed [11]. These performances can be considered the most relevant drivers seen by the customer, among those drivers affected by production management decisions. More recently, one new dimension is more and more considered relevant: Environment. As a matter of fact, several stakeholders such as customers, policy-makers and industries themselves are highlighting this aspect.

Passing to the lower level, i.e. set of indicators, we identified some indicators categories that are widely adopted. They can be clustered in Time, Utilization, Internal Quality, and Inventory Level. As said, these are considered categories of indicators that can be represented through different specific indicators (lowest layer in Fig. 1) with slightly similar aims. For example, Overall Equipment Effectiveness (OEE) [8] is a specific indicator that includes both Internal Quality and Utilization aspects, but Utilization could be also assessed through the sole indicator Availability (i.e. the ratio between operating time and loading time of a manufacturing system).

This performances structure, adapted depending on the industry and on the specific manufacturing company objectives, could be used to assess production management practices and decisions, at all layers. As a simple example, by introducing Kanban in a manufacturing company, WIP can be analyzed in order to assess its reduction [7]. However the plant manager, will be interested at looking at the inventory level reduction (both in economic measures and not). Finally the top management will look at the cost reduction due to lower inventory.

Looking at the middle and lowest layers in Fig. 1, in this paper we will focus on Energy as one of the main important drivers affecting Environmental and Cost performances. Indeed, energy is becoming an important issue to be tackled, and this has been stressed in the first two section of this paper.

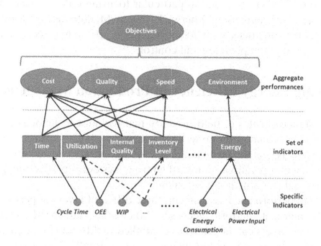

Fig. 1. Performance measurement structure

In industrial domain, a well-known indicator that can be measured and controlled is the Electrical Energy Consumption. This indicator is measured in kWh. We consider this indicator since it is simple to be calculated/measured, it represents a relevant part of the total energy consumed by industries (especially in non-energy intensive industries) and finally, it allows elaborations in terms of both Cost and Environment (e.g. one typical environmental indicator at aggregate level is CO_2 emission that can be derived from the energy consumption). However, this indicator is required to be differentiated depending on the source of Electrical Energy. As a matter of fact, industries are more and more adopting heterogeneous sources to procure energy (and with different cost and environmental impacts): power plants, proprietary power generators, photovoltaic cell, etc. Indeed, in order to properly assess costs and environmental impact of energy consumption, the indicator Electrical Energy Consumption needs to be constructed accordingly.

Having detailed data on Energy consumption, energy efficiency indicators can also be defined as the ratio between production level (e.g. number of products processes by a production line) and energy consumption (e.g. kWh consumed). These indicators need to be assessed to describe production efficiency from the energy point of view. However, they should be analyzed thoroughly and in a comprehensive way to avoid drawbacks such as rebound or backfire effects [21].

Moreover, for effective near real-time control on the energy performance of production systems, another indicator should be considered: Electrical Power Input. With this indicator we refer to the power input required by production systems, measured in kW. Indeed, there are two aspects that affect cost and environmental impact: (i) different prices of energy consumption depending on the time-window during the day and on the instantaneous power required, (ii) different impacts depending on the type of source of electrical energy (gas, oil, wind, etc.). Hence, controlling the electrical power input is required in order to assess how different production practices may have different outputs. For example a plant manager may decide to avoid peaks of power consumption, and exploit the proprietary power generators, reducing the workload in specific time-windows and spreading the workload production on more appropriate moments (e.g. night production).

This concept is becoming more impactful with the exploitation of real-time information, available thanks to Information & Communication Technologies (ICT).

5   Energy Efficient Manufacturing in Real-Time Enterprise Context

As said in section 4, the other pillar of production management is production planning & control. Nowadays, production planning and control systems usually take into consideration time and cost in order to define specific plans and they do not take into consideration energy efficiency as an objective or as a decision driver. To go towards energy-aware factories this aspect need to be included.

Without performing a thorough analysis on energy requirements due to production, energy availability, and related impact, production planning and control cannot be appropriately performed with respect to energy efficiency.

As an example, we consider loading rules that define when material should be loaded in a manufacturing system. Instead of using traditional rules based on time requirements, new energy-driven rules could be adopted in order to avoid energy peaks, and to better distribute energy consumption. Dispatching rules could also be constructed to reduce energy consumption due to set-up activities (i.e. activities performed to prepare a specific machine for the next production). Moreover, exploiting the possibility of switching off machines instead of keep them in stand-by mode, reduction of energy consumption can be obtained through appropriate production scheduling. It is interesting that this could lead to define batch production, with possible drawbacks (i.e. time or cost) that should be assessed in a holistic way.

Thanks to availability of information enabled by ICT, production management practices for energy efficient manufacturing could be more easily implemented. Indeed, nowadays through ICT, near-real time information can be provided to interest targeted persons in the enterprise [24]. As an example, a scenario is depicted in Fig. 2. In this scenario a plant manager exploits real-time information coming from the field, through appropriate indicators such as WIP, Cycle Time, but also Electrical Energy Consumption and Electrical Power Input, in order to take proper decision in terms of production planning and scheduling. The plant manager needs to adopt modeling techniques in order to support his decision-making process, and on the other side will compare different production management practices (i.e. different schedules, different production plans, etc.) in order to assess them in terms of energy efficiency.

This kind of ICT support will be fundamental due to variability and dynamicity of energy consumption in complex manufacturing systems operation.

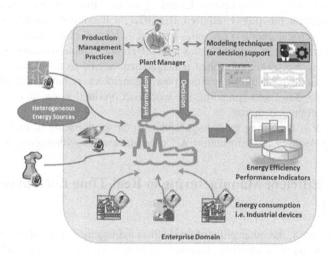

Fig. 2. Energy Efficient Manufacturing in Real-time Enterprise. Adapted from [24]

6 Conclusions

We highlighted in this paper the need to introduce Energy Efficiency in Production Management. As a matter of fact, it is clear that energy consumption is a core issue that industries have to face nowadays, and on the other hand from literature review it emerged that this aspects is not completely tackled in the context of production management.

Several further research actions are needed in three main streams: modeling techniques for production processes, production planning and control practices, performance indicators. Modeling techniques for production processes need to be investigated in order to include energy performances aspects. Moreover, best suited models for energy performance representation in manufacturing domain should be identified and validated. Finally, production planning and control need to be further investigated in terms of energy efficiency together with performance evaluation in order to find out trade-off among performances and improve present practices.

Acknowledgments. The authors would like to thank the European Commission and the partners of the IST FP6 project "Service-Oriented Cross-layer infRAstructure for Distributed smart Embedded devices" (SOCRADES - www.socrades.eu) and of the NMP FP7 project "IMS2020: Supporting Global Research for IMS2020 Vision" (IMS2020 – www.ims2020.net) for their support.

References

1. Brundtland, Report at World Commission on Environment and Development (1987)
2. Curkovic, S., Sroufe, R.: Total quality environmental management and total cost assessment: An exploratory study. Int. J. of Production Economics 105(2), 560–579 (2007)
3. Rondinelli, D., Vastag, G.: Panacea, common sense, or just a label? - the value of iso 14001 environmental management systems. European Management Journal 18, 499–510 (2000)
4. Devoldere, T., Dewulf, W., Deprez, W., Willems, B., Duflou, J.: Improvement potential for energy consumption in discrete part production machines (2007)
5. Dietmair, A., Verl, A.: Energy consumption modeling and optimization for production machines. In: Proc. IEEE International Conference on Sustainable Energy Technologies, ICSET 2008, pp. 574–579 (2008)
6. IEA, Worldwide trends in Energy Use and Efficiency, Energy Indicators (2008) http://www.iea.org/Textbase/Papers/2008/indicators_2008.pdf
7. Khojasteh-Ghamari, Y.: A performance comparison between kanban and conwip controlled assembly systems. Journal of Intelligent Manufacturing 20, 751–760 (2009)
8. Muchiri, P., Pintelon, L.: Performance measurement using overall equipment effectiveness (OEE): literature review and practical application discussion. International Journal of Production Research 46(13), 3517–3535 (2008)
9. Gutowski, T., Dahmus, J., Thiriez, A.: Electrical energy requirements for manufacturing processes. In: Proceedings of the 13th CIRP Int. Conf. on Life Cycle Engineering (2006)
10. Pennington, D.W., Potting, J., Finnveden, G., Lindeijer, E., Jolliet, O., Rydberg, T., Rebitzer, G.: Life cycle assessment part 2: Current impact assessment practice. Environment International 30(5), 721–739 (2004)
11. Hopp, W.J., Spearman, M.L.: Factory Physics, 2nd edn. McGraw-Hill Int., New York (2000)
12. Rebitzer, G., Ekvall, T., Frischknecht, R., Hunkeler, D., Norris, G., Rydberg, T., Schmidt, W.P., Suh, S., Weidema, B.P., Pennington, D.W.: Life cycle assessment: Part 1: Framework, goal and scope denition, inventory analysis and applications. Environment international 30(5), 701–720 (2004)
13. Rohdin, P., Thollander, P.: Barriers to and driving forces for energy efficiency in the non-energy intensive manufacturing industry in Sweden. Energy 31(12), 1836–1844 (2006)
14. Solding, P., Petku, D.: Applying energy aspects on simulation of energy-intensive production systems. In: WSC 2005: Proceedings of the 37th Conference on Winter Simulation, Winter Simulation Conference, pp. 1428–1432 (2005)
15. Sun, H., Hong, C.: The alignment between manufacturing and business strategies: its influence on business performance. Technovation 22(11), 699–705 (2002)
16. Thollander, P., Karlsson, M., Sderstrm, M., Creutz, D.: Reducing industrial energy costs through energy-efficiency measures in a liberalized european electricity market: case study of a swedish iron foundry. Applied Energy 81(2), 115–126 (2005)
17. Utlu, Z., Sogut, Z., Hepbasli, A., Oktay, Z.: Energy and exergy analyses of a raw mill in a cement production. Applied Thermal Engineering 26(17-18), 2479–2489 (2006)
18. ManuFuture website, http://www.manufuture.org
19. Veleva, V., Ellenbecker, M.: Indicators of sustainable production: framework and methodology. Journal of Cleaner Production 9, 519–549 (2001)
20. Geller, H., Schaeffer, R., Szklo, A., Tolmasquim, M.: Policies for advancing energy efficiency and renewable energy use in Brazil. Energy Policy 32, 1437–1450 (2004)
21. Herring, H.: Energy efficiency—a critical view. Energy 31, 10–20 (2006)
22. MESA Metrics that Matter Guidebook & Framework - International Guidebook (2006)
23. Amundsen, A.: Joint management of energy and environment. Journal of Cleaner Production 8, 483–494 (2000)
24. Karnouskos, S., Colombo, A.W., Lastra, J.L.M., Popescu, C.: Towards the energy efficient future factory. In: 7th International Conference on Industrial Informatics - INDIN (2009)

Part II

Supply Chains

Supply Chain Reactivity Assessment Regarding Two Negotiated Commitments: Frozen Horizon and Flexibility Rate

Aïcha Amrani-Zouggar, Jean-Christophe Deschamps, and Jean-Paul Bourrières

IMS - LAPS/GRAI, University of Bordeaux, UMR 5218CNRS
351, Cours de la libération, 33 405 Talence Cedex, France
{aicha.amrani,jean-christophe.deschamps,
jean-paul.bourrieres}@ims-bordeaux.fr

Abstract. The problem addressed in this paper is the supply chain reactivity assessment through numerical experimentations regarding specifically two negotiated commitments within supply contract: the frozen horizon and flexibility rate. Analysis of impact of these commitments on each partner will be depicted in term of storage costs, reliability and reactivity indicators. The decision making inside each partner is operated under rolling horizon planning and based on production linear programming model wherein different contractual commitments are included. To carry out experimental scenarios, simulation platform is developed from which expecting numerical results afford deciders to get more understanding about the commitments that should be contracted and the relevant dimensioning of them.

Keywords: Supply chain, Tactical production planning, supply contract commitments, simulation.

1 Introduction

In increasingly competitive context where the customer's requirements are still growing and the demand is highly volatile, many risks are threatening the order fulfilment process. One way to cope with these risks is to extend the partner's network that brings some stability to the network. The deciders are aware that collaborative approaches constitute a strong axis of reducing surrounding risks. However, if the network may constitutes a response to some risks, it generates other ones [1] therefore it becomes essential to achieve the challenging aim of ensuring whole supply chain performance. Our current work is based on collaborative relationships that are framed by supply contracts among the partners. Indeed, contractual agreement of supplying products from the suppliers if accurately designed may provide the required enhancement of performance. Negotiate specific clauses of collaboration with suppliers through contract commitments becomes an excellent coordination mechanism [2] stabilizing the relationship over certain horizon of time and minimizing industrial risks (such as high inventory level, backorders, delay of deliveries, unsatisfying customer and rush orders).

B. Vallespir and T. Alix (Eds.): APMS 2009, IFIP AICT 338, pp. 179–186, 2010.
© IFIP International Federation for Information Processing 2010

In our previous works, we have shown in [3] the intrinsic relationship between risks and the negotiated clauses. Further, we have revealed through simulation an effective quantified sensitivity of buyer and supplier performance to different quantity commitments contracts [4]. In this paper, our proposition focuses on the analysis of supply chain reactivity regarding two negotiated commitments: Frozen horizon and flexibility rate. The purpose of this study is beyond the simple checking of sensitivity leading to *show explicitly to which partner do the commitment benefit and how explain it?*

The remainder paper is organized as follows. The related work of supply contracts is presented in Section 2. In Section 3, description of tactical production planning model is provided with an overview of contractual agreements (frozen horizon and flexibility rate) subjected to the study. Section 4 is devoted to discussing the reactivity of supply chain regarding two evoked commitments. The analysis is done inside a buyer-supplier relationship. In Section 6, further experimentations come to reinforce our contributions and conclusion comes to end this paper.

2   Literature Review

Great attention is granted to collaborative approaches which are widely studied. Supply contracts constitute part of them and consist in agreements between buyer and supplier, that aim at protect their respective own and joint interests, describe the limits of risk, enounce terms and conditions of fulfilment. Once clauses clearly identified, monitoring of order fulfilment process becomes possible at the operational level. In literature, we distinguish for example [5], [6] where the authors aim through their research to get optimal purchasing policy. We notice that majority of works are optimization models under contractual context based on stochastic modelling [7] or continuous modelling [8]. Our research is quite different in term of problem modelling and objective, in one hand we propose a discrete planning model (like [9]) rather infrequently used in this field. In the other hand, the simulation that will be carried out is the basis of quantitative analysis to oversee simultaneous impact on performance of varying two commitments.

The aim of our work is rather to check the impact of each commitment (frozen horizon and flexibility rate) on own and overall performance than to assess the numeric value of the optimisation.

3   Tactical Production Planning Model

Each actor of considered supply chain SC is assimilated to a DMU (Decision Making Unit) with carrying out the calculation of production, replenishment and delivery plans and the levels of necessary stocks to each period. The model concerns multi-product (p), multi periods (t), with finished nominal capacity that accommodates adjustment by additional capacity represented here by the decision to resort to overtime (additional hours). Planning process is dynamically depicted according to the principle of rolling horizon planning. Any modification that occurs either on the demand or on operational execution can be taken into account at the next planning occurrence.

We make the assumption that Demand is deterministic and known along the planning horizon. The production planning process developed is based on linear programming modelling with a criterion to maximize under a set of constraints.

3.1 Model

The table 1 summarizes various notations adopted to formalize the production planning process.

Table 1. Notation list

Decision variables		Parameters of rolling horizon planning	
$F_{p,t}$	Quantity of products (p) performed at period (t)	H	Planning horizon length (number of periods)
$I_{p,t}$	Level of inventory of product (p) at the end of period (t)	PP	Planning Periodicity
$I_{j,t}$	Level of inventory of component (j) at the end of (t)	i	Step of planning
A_t	Additional hours to carry out at period (t)	φ	Period of next planning = $i.PP$
$B_{p,t}$	Level of backorders recorded of product (p) at the end of period (t)	FH	Frozen horizon
		α%	Flexibility rate
$R_{j,t}$	Quantity of component (j) received from supplier at period (t)	$t = \varphi, ..., \varphi + H\text{-}1$	Planning period
$L_{p,t}$	Quantity of delivered product (p) at period (t)		
$C_{j,t}$	Purchasing quantity of component (j) to transmit to supplier at period (t)		
$D_{p,t}$	Global demand of finished product (p) at period (t)		
PV_p	Selling price of product (p)		
Costs		**Other parameters**	
$\hat{f}p$	Production unit cost	p	index for product, p =1,...,n
$\hat{i}p$	Inventory unit cost of product (p)	j	index for component, j =1,....,m
$\hat{b}p$	Shortage unit cost of product (p)	CAPN	Nominal capacity limitation
$\hat{l}p$	Delivery unit cost product (p)	CAPA	Additional capacity limitation
$\hat{h}$	Additional hour unit cost	θ%	Percentage of authorized capacity extension
$\hat{i}_j$	Inventory unit cost of component (j)	Dliv	Delivery time from supplier
$\hat{a}_j$	Purchase unit cost of component (j)		
$\gamma_{p,j}$	Bill of materials coefficients, linking product (p) to component (j) consumption.		
α_p	Processing time of product (p)		

The objective function (1) tends to maximize the profit resulting from the difference between the sales and the various undergoing costs:

$$\max \sum_{t=\varphi}^{\varphi+H-1} (\sum_{p=1}^{n} PV_p \cdot L_{p,t} - (\hat{f}p.F_{p,t} + \hat{i}p.I_{p,t} + \hat{b}p.B_{p,t} + \hat{l}p.L_{p,t} - \hat{h}.A_t) - (\sum_{j=1}^{m} \hat{i}j.I_{j,t} + \hat{a}j \cdot R_{j,t}))$$

Under the constraints

$$I_{p,t} = I_{p,t-1} + F_{p,t} - L_{p,t} \qquad \forall p = 1,...,n \qquad (2)$$

$$B_{p,t} = B_{p,t-1} + D_{p,t} - L_{p,t} \qquad \forall p = 1,...,n \qquad (3)$$

$$I_{j,t} = I_{j,t-1} + R_{j,t} - \sum_{p=1}^{n} \gamma_{p,j}.F_{p,t} \qquad \forall p = 1,...,n, \forall j = 1,...,m \qquad (4)$$

$$\sum_{p=1}^{n} \alpha_p.F_{p,t} \le CAPN + A_t \qquad \forall p = 1,..,n \qquad (5)$$

$$A_t \le CAPA \,| CAPA = \theta\% .CAPN \qquad \forall p = 1,...,n \qquad (6)$$

These constraints are valid $\forall t = \varphi,..., \varphi + H - 1$.

The equation (2) is a quantity conservation equation; it links the level of stocks and the produced quantity. The equation (3) links the level of shortages to the demand and deliveries. The equation (4) calculates the level of stocks of components according to the receptions, the production and bill of materials coefficients. The constraint (5) gives the limits of production quantities according to the normal capacity and additional capacity. The constraint (6) guarantees limitation of overtime in such way that additional capacity is equal to a certain percentage (θ%) of the normal capacity.

3.2 Contractual Constraints

The specificity of this contribution is to check the potential impact on reactivity of partners when varying two commitments negotiated during the design of supply contract. In this section we introduce more deeply these clauses and formalize them in order to integrate them into the production planning process.

3.2.1 Frozen Horizon (FH) and Flexibility Rate (α%)

In fluctuant demand context, rolling horizon planning often comes to palliate the uncertainty impact giving the possibility to the deciders to update their planning process including new information (demand fluctuation, delivery disturbance...). However, the industrial reality shows the necessity to stabilize the activities during certain amount of time called "frozen horizon" (FH) in [10], or "freezing time". When a frozen horizon is negotiated through supply contract between two adjacent partners, the value of purchasing quantities over frozen horizon have a commitment values and could not be modified with next planning occurrence. Over a frozen horizon, a rate of flexibility (α %) is negotiated to enable the buyer to modify demand among two planning occurrences (Fig.1). Flexibility rate concept has been studied in literature. These are some definitions founded: for [7], it is an upside and downside flexibility bounds of order quantity. Bassok & Anupindi in [8] considers a model in which the amount of increase or reduction in the order for a given period is limited to a percentage of the current order for the period. We notice that these definitions converge to the same idea, flexibility rate (α%) consists in two bounds allowing adaptation to the uncertainty of the market.

These commitments constitute a kind of constraints that each partner has to model, to formalize and take into account during each occurrence of the planning process. Our work consists on modelling these commitments and introduces them in a tactical planning model. Over seven periods of FH in (Fig.1), the producer starts a certain production volume. Indeed, the necessary purchasing quantities $C^i_{j,t}$ from supplier for executing orders will have a commitment value. They could not be modified at next planning moments.

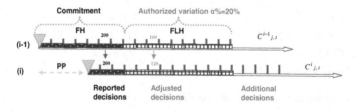

Fig. 1. Frozen horizon and flexibility rate

Beyond the frozen horizon of the producer, we find the flexible horizon (FLH) which is by definition less rigid. On this horizon the producer is approved to vary his orders of over or under certain percentage ($\alpha\%$) at the next planning occurrence (example: $\alpha\%=20\%$ means from 100 units to 120 units). After planning period PP, additional decisions come to complete the length of horizon.

We claim that it should be taken care that the quantity of purchasing orders ($C_{j,t}$), belongs to the intervals authorized by negotiated (α %). Constraints of this context may be written as follows:

$$R^i_{j,t} = C^i_{j,(t-Dliv)} \qquad \forall t = \varphi,..., \varphi + H - 1 \qquad (7)$$

$$F^i_{p,t} = F^{i-1}_{p,t} \qquad \forall t = \varphi,.., \varphi + (FH - PP - 1) \qquad (8)$$

$$At^i = At^{i-1} \qquad \forall t = \varphi,.., \varphi + (FH - PP - 1) \qquad (9)$$

$$C^i_{j,t} = C^{i-1}_{j,t} \qquad \forall t = \varphi,.., \varphi + (FH - PP - 1) \qquad (10)$$

$$C^{i-1}_{j,t}(1-\alpha\%) \le C^i_{j,t} \le C^{i-1}_{j,t}(1+\alpha\%) \qquad \forall t = \varphi + FH - 1,..., \varphi + FLH - 1 \qquad (11)$$

To ensure the arrivals of ($R_{j,t}$) the purchasing quantity ($C_{j,t}$) have to be transmitted to supplier some periods (D_{liv}) in advance; it is expressed through equation (7). Equations (8), (9), (10) express the report of the frozen decisions. For example, Produced quantities $F^i_{p,t}$ at step (i) will be assigned the value of previous produced quantities $F^{i-1}_{p,t}$ of previous planning step as long as $t = \varphi,..., \varphi + (FH - PP - 1)$. See Fig.1: At planning step (i-1), we report decisions of ($C^{i-1}_{j,t}$) over periods 5,6,7. The constraints (11) expresses the flexibility commitment, as long as $t = \varphi + FH - 1,..., \varphi + FLH - 1$, the orders transmitted at planning step (i) $C^i_{j,t}$ might vary within the interval plus or less (α %) from a previous order $C^{i-1}_{j,t}$.

4 Experiments and Analysis

The simulation platform dedicated to perform different scenarios has been detailed in our previous contribution [4]. In this experimental section, based on our simulation platform, we test different configurations of flexibility rate, and frozen horizon between a buyer OEM and supplier PRODU. The results will be expressed in terms of different performance indicators, as *the profit* (criterion to maximize), the *costs* of adaptation (including finished product inventory costs, delivered components inventory costs, backorders and additional hours costs); the *reactivity* is then expressed by the number of required periods by the partner to satisfy the entire demand and the reliability is calculated as the ratio of real delivery and expected delivery products. These indicators allow a better understanding of supply chain behaviour according to the point of view of decision maker. At first, buyer supplier view is analyzed in order to give off global trends. To depict accurately the impact of parameters on both partners, more focused analysis will be carried out. Demand disturbance would be tested at period t=11 with enhancement of 600 products.

4.1 Buyer-Supplier View: Global Trends

Global trend shows (Table 2.) that the supply chain behaves differently according to the adopted configuration of FH and α %. More the FH is high better it is for supplier

(PRODU) but not to the buyer. More the flexibility rate increases, better it is for the buyer (OEM) but unfortunately not so benefit for supplier PRODU. Further, we achieve a detailed analysis on each partner to perceive the mechanism that leads the partner to record these performances.

Table 2. Buyer & supplier performance trend

	FH= 6			FH = 7			FH = 8		
	OEM	PRODU	Overall	OEM	PRODU	Overall	OEM	PRODU	Overall
α=13%									
Profit ($)	2038071	817440	2855512	2033776	820402	2866602	2023002	825112	2848114
Costs ($)	40679	23359	64039	46287	20398	66688	58465	15688	74152
Reactivity (period)	4.00	3.00		6.00	2.00		7.00	3.00	
Reliability (%)	98.18	99.51		97.48	99.69		96.06	99.68	
α=20%									
Profit ($)	2045910	815802	2861712	2045424	816644	2871616	2045262	816557	2861819
Costs ($)	40341	24998	65339	40341	24155	64496	40503	24243	64746
Reactivity (period)	4.00	2.00		4.00	2.00		4.00	2.00	
Reliability (%)	98.13	99.61		98.13	99.61		98.11	99.64	
α=35%									
Profit ($)	2051684	81689	2868578	2051198	817737	2868934	2049457	821106	2871868
Costs ($)	36001	34705	70706	36000	33863	69864	37694	30493	68187
Reactivity (period)	4.00	1.00		4.00	1.00		4.00	1.00	
Reliability (%)	98.13	99.69		98.13	99.69		98.13	99.69	

According to these results, we may notice that these two clauses are antagonists. That's why it becomes important to relevantly negotiate them. Another interesting observation that simulation shows is that a compromise of performance (by regulating two parameters) could be obtained to achieve expected performance. It doesn't mean that maximum value of flexibility only achieve accepted performance. Configuration of (α =20%, FH=8) records less overall costs than configuration (α=35%, FH=7) it underlines the fact that the best configuration of commitments compromises can be obtained by simulation and the best configurations aren't particularly obviously expected.

4.2 Analysis of Local Performance Per Partner

What happens with varying frozen horizon, why is it benefiting for supplier?
We highlight the undertaken points to make our analysis; it consists on observing the costs of inventory levels, backorders levels and required additional hours. Let us consider the scenario where flexibility between two partners is equal to 13%; we focus on the differences of costs generated by two configurations of frozen horizon FH=6 and FH=7. (Fig.2)

The observation shows that for OEM more frozen horizon is high, more he will be constrained to freeze also his production planning according to the arriving components from suppliers, less periods remains for performing the smooth of the load so less production could be done. (FH=7) generates by this way more backorders, huge costs and smaller reactivity. FH seems not to be benefit to the buyer at all, it prevents

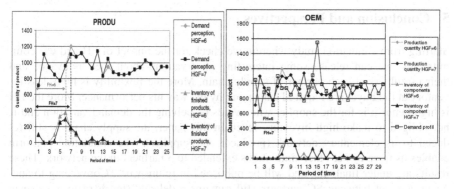

Fig. 2. Profiles with varying FH at producer (OEM) and supplier (PRODU)

him from smoothing and do not allows the transmission of the real demand changing, limited to only what supplier would like to perceive. Whereas for PRODU, more the frozen horizon is high (FH=7) better it is, the supplier hasn't ever to perceive the demand pick, he considers previously planned production and is not obliged to make high inventory of ended product (as it is the case for FH=6). Indeed, if frozen horizon decreases, (Fig.2) shows the necessity to anticipate by preparing more inventory level generating high adaptation costs for supplier.

What happens with varying flexibility rate, why is it benefiting for buyer?

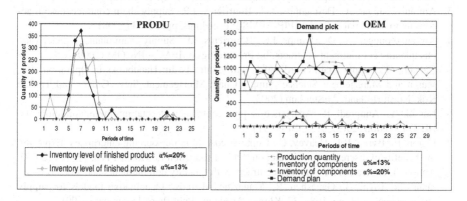

Fig. 3. Profiles with varying α% at buyer (OEM) and supplier (PRODU)

We carry out an analysis in scenario with (α =13%, FH=6) and (α =20%, FH=6) configurations of commitments. The results enable us to show that increased α % granted by the supplier benefits to OEM and penalise PRODU.

In (Fig.3), we may notice with increasing α % that inventory level of components at OEM decreases. In deed, with increasing flexibility rate, more deliveries can be expected avoiding cumulating inventory stocks at the buyer OEM. Whereas at the supplier, more inventories of finished products becomes required to be reactive to buyer pick; therefore, we see that the smooth of inventory load becomes bigger in scenario α =20% configuration.

5 Conclusion and Perspectives

Starting from simulation study wherein we check for the impact of FH and α% commitments, we can release some interesting observations about their relevance and their usefulness at each partner of supply chain. More the flexibility is high, less inventory at the buyer are required enhancing by the way his performance. More the FH is high better it is for the supplier who avoids perceiving the demand variation and is not obliged to make high inventory level. In this paper, the supply chain is still reduced to its elementary network (producer and supplier). The simulation platform enables us to carry out other simulations extended to 3 partners in the network. These results are under finalizing and will be published in future work. Converging to adequate contract between SC partners still remains a delicate step hard to achieve in industrial reality. This study wishes to provide deciders with more visibility about the commitments able to protect them or on contrary threat their interests in order to guide them to thoroughly consider them during negotiation process.

References

1. Christopher, M.: Logistics and Supply Chains management. In: Financial Times. Prentice Hall, Englewood Cliffs (2005)
2. Mentzer, J.T., Foggin, J.H., Golicic, S.G.: Supply chain collaboration: enablers, impediments and benefits. Supply Chain Management Review 4(4), 52–58 (2000)
3. Amrani-Zouggar, A., Deschamps, J.C., Bourrières, J.P.: Supply chain contracts design according to industrial risks. In: IFIP-APMS Proceedings, pp. 22–33 (2008)
4. Amrani-Zouggar, A., Deschamps, J.C., Bourrières, J.P.: Supply chain planning under various quantity commitment contracts. In: Proceedings of IFAC – INCOM (2009)
5. Cachon, G.: Supply chain coordination with contracts. In: Handbooks in Operations Research and Management Science: Supply Chain Management. Steve Graves and Ton de Kok. North Holland, Amsterdam (2003)
6. Bassok, Y., Anupindi, R.: Analysis of supply contracts with total minimum commitments. IIE Transactions 29(5), 373–381 (1997)
7. Liston, P., Byrne, P.J., Heavey, C.: Contract costing in outsourcing enterprises: Exploring the benefits of discrete-event simulation. Int. J. Production Economics 110, 97–114 (2007)
8. Anupindi, R., Bassok, Y.: Supply contracts with quantity commitments and stochastic demand. In: Tayur, S., Ganeshan, R., Magazine, M. (eds.) Quantitative models for supply chain management, pp. 198–232. Kluwer Academic Publishers, Dordrecht (1999)
9. Schneeweiss, C., Zimmer, K., Zimmermann, M.: The design of contracts to coordinate operational interdependencies within the supply chain. Int. J. Production Economics 92, 43–59 (2003)
10. Millart, H.H.: The impact of rolling horizon planning on the cost of industrial fishing activity. Computers Operational Research 25(10), 825–837 (1998)

Principles for Real-Time, Integrated Supply Chain Control: An Example from Distribution of Pharmaceuticals

Heidi C. Dreyer[1], Jan Ola Strandhagen[2], Anita Romsdal[1], and Annette Hoff[2]

[1] Norwegian University of Science and Technology, Department of Production and Quality Engineering, NTNU – Valgrinda, N-7491 Trondheim, Norway
[2] SINTEF Technology and Society, Department of Industrial Management, S.P. Andersens veg 5, N-7465 Trondheim, Norway
Heidi.c.dreyer@sintef.no, jan.strandhagen@sintef.no, anita.romsdal@sintef.no, annette.hoff@sintef.no

Abstract. This paper investigates how to control an integrated supply chain based on demand-driven principles and sharing of real time information. A set of principles to support a unified supply chain control model is proposed based on theory and previous and ongoing research and illustrated in a case example from the pharmaceutical industry. Essential elements include application of pull-based control principles, automated decision support, advanced visualisation, and automated replenishment concepts. Expected effects include improvement of supply chain speed and reliability, and reduced resource consumption. However, implementation challenges associated with financial, political and trust issues in supply chain relationships remain.

Keywords: Supply chain control, real-time information, demand-driven.

1 Introduction

Integrating and coordinating supply chain operations is today widely considered a prerequisite for achieving high efficiency and competitiveness. Focusing on the performance and competitiveness for the supply chain rather than the single company is a trend in several industries. Operating supply chains is challenging due to the heterogeneous system characteristics, the diversified product and material flow structure, the trade-off situations, and the conflicting interests and goals of the participants. Products vary in value, volumes and shelf life. Offering high customer service either means maintaining a high inventory level or frequent deliveries. In order to deal with these trade-off situations and challenges, and to be able to adjust the supply chain according to customer demand, supply chain approaches have become more focused on utilising real-time information and modern information and communication technology (ICT). The research challenge of this paper is therefore *how to control an integrated supply chain – based on the assumption that all relevant information is made available to all partners in real-time.* The objective is to establish a set of principles to be applied in the related control processes. Based on a number of Norwegian

B. Vallespir and T. Alix (Eds.): APMS 2009, IFIP AICT 338, pp. 187–194, 2010.

research and development (R&D) projects including Automed, Norman, Smart Vare-flyt and Origo, this conceptual paper addresses real-time supply chain operations and the control principles which should support a unified and real-time supply chain control model. The scope of the paper is on the replenishment and inventory processes of the supply chain and on how these should be integrated with the manufacturing and retailing processes. The paper builds on a concept for intelligent and real-time supply chain control and proposes a number of principles which are illustrated through a case supply chain in the pharmaceutical industry.

2 Methodology

This paper combines the insights from an R&D project called Automed with practice and theory from operations management, logistics and supply chain management (SCM). Data from the case has been gathered through personal participation, observation, discussions with industrial and academic participants, project reports and presentations, secondary documentation, other R&D projects, and relevant literature. Following an action research strategy building on the perspectives of Coughland and Coghlan [1] and Greenwood and Levin [2], focus and activities in the project were determined and carried out in close cooperation between practitioners and researchers based on the specific challenges facing the participating organisations and their supply chain. New solutions in the project were developed using the *control model methodology* (Alfnes, 2005). A control model is a formalised way to describe the material and information flows in a supply chain and can be used as a foundation for reengineering and improvement processes. The model describes resources, materials, information, processes, organisation, and the detailed principles and rules used to control material flows. The control perspective describes how operations are organised and controlled in manufacturing and distribution, outlining control principles and methods, main processes, buffers/inventories, operations areas, and material and information flows. Initially, an AS IS control model describing the starting point for the supply chain was developed in order to make all involved actors aware of and agree on the structures and policies currently used to control the supply chain. After an analysis of the AS IS control model and a mapping of improvement opportunities, a TO BE control model was collaboratively developed specifying how the supply chain could be controlled in the future.

3 Theoretical Background

Supply chain operations extend the control span and increase the complexity of the planning and control task which emphases the need for coordination, integration and collaboration among companies. A holistic and unified manufacturing planning and control (MPC) approach should therefore be applied in order to guide the flow of products and information through the supply chain. The MPC task in a supply chain involves determining what, who, when and how to act in order to meet customer demand with exact supply in a coordinated chain [3, 4]. Each node in the chain cannot be managed in isolation [5], and the MPC system must support cross-company processes in a manner that avoids increasing amplifications, inventory levels, and lead and response times [6]. Most planning and control systems used in supply chain operations today are based on the traditions of make-to-stock (MTS) and MRP/MRP II, where forecasts and expectations of future demand are the main inputs [7]. Additionally, the main planning and control logic of ERP systems is still based on aggregation, optimal batch sizes, order quantities, transport frequencies, sequencing, etc. [8]. The consequences are that a number of supply chain operations are decoupled from actual end customer demand and that inventories are used as a buffer against uncertainty and fluctuating demand.

The next generation supply chain MPC models, however, are derived from the principle of sharing demand information with all actors in the supply chain, changing the planning and control processes towards more make-to-order (MTO) strategies. Access to and sharing of information contributes to reduced demand variability and uncertainty in the supply chain and consequently reduction of the bullwhip effect. The more actors in the supply chain that have an undistorted and near real-time view of the consumer buying behaviour, the more responsive the supply chain as a whole is [9].

In order to develop demand-driven MPC models, several models for orchestrating supply chain and network activities have developed. The aim of models such as collaborative planning, forecasting and replenishment (CPFR), vendor managed inventory (VMI) and automated replenishment programs (ARP) is to achieve seamless inter-organisational interfaces by specifying control principles and operations models for the flow of materials and information [see e.g. 10, 11, 12]. The main principle is to tie and adjust network operations to customer demand and MTO strategies instead of the traditional forecast and MTS approaches.

The ability to utilise real-time information in supply chain operations will be a significant contributor to improving performance. Real-time information in this context refers to immediate and continuous access to information without time lag. An important enabler for the realisation of real-time supply chain operations will be technology such as radio frequency identification (RFID), sensor technology and Electronic Product Code Information Services (EPCIS). Performance monitoring is essential to ensure efficient optimization of operational processes and over the last few years focus has shifted to incorporate a supply chain perspective [e.g. 13, 14]. Supply chain performance measurement requires a consistent and comparable holistic hierarchy of indicators, based on agreed upon strategies, performance targets and priorities. Both reactive and proactive indicators are required [15, 16].

Methods and tools for advanced decision support have seen tremendous developments over the last decades [17], supporting decision makers in strategic, tactical, and operational decision making [18]. Common for these applications is that they are still mainly used off-line, creating plans daily or hourly. As data processing capabilities are constantly increasing, and modelling capability pushed forward by research achievements, the possibilities for on-line and automated decision support based on real-time information is increasing. Recently, so-called automated decision systems have appeared, making decisions in real-time after weighing all the relevant data and rules [19]. Such systems often make decisions without human intervention and are used for decisions that must be made frequently and very rapidly, using on-line information [19]. Opportunities for decision support with a very short (immediate) planning horizon include [20]: improving deployment of finished goods inventory, minimizing transportation costs, real-time tentative rescheduling of production and reconfiguring of orders to meet date requests.

Building on theory and previous research a number of elements have been identified as essential in the creation of real-time and demand-driven supply chains. In order to capture a more holistic picture of supply chain planning and control that will support future developments in industrial business cases a conceptual framework and methodology for intelligent and demand-driven supply chain control have been developed. The main elements of the concept are shown in Fig. 1.

Fig. 1. Concept for intelligent and demand-driven supply chain control [adapted from 21]

4   Example: The Automed Supply Chain

In the following, the simplified case of a supply chain in the Norwegian pharmaceutical/pharmacy industry is used to illustrate the control concept described in Fig. 1, leading to a set of principles for its realisation. The case stems from a three-year R&D project called Automed (automated replenishment of medicine), which ended in 2008. The project's objectives included development of a control model for automatic replenishment from manufacturer through wholesaler to pharmacies and a control dashboard prototype.

Norwegian pharmacy legislation is among the most liberal in the world, and a new law in 2001 opened up for extensive vertical and horizontal integration. Today, the Norwegian pharmacy market consisting of approx. 500 pharmacies is dominated by three pharmacy chains – which are each owned by three major European wholesalers. Thus, the wholesaler and pharmacy chain in the Automed supply chain are owned by the same European group. The manufacturer is among the world's largest pharmaceutical suppliers and manufactures most products for the Norwegian market in a plant located near Oslo. The plant makes prescription and non-prescription drugs (tablets, mixtures, sprays, lotions, etc.), skin care products and other commercial goods sold in pharmacies, in total 750 different finished goods. The wholesaler keeps an inventory of approx. 10.000 stock keeping units (SKU), which are distributed to pharmacies in the retail chain nationwide from a warehouse in the Oslo area. Each of the approx. 140 pharmacies in the chain typically carries approx. 3-4.000 SKUs.

At the start of the project each pharmacy manually placed daily orders to the wholesaler, for delivery the next day. Orders were mainly based on daily sales and current inventory levels. The wholesaler manually placed orders with the manufacturer once a week, for delivery one week later. Orders were based on historic sales to pharmacies, forecasted demand and current wholesaler inventory levels. Manufacturing was MTS based on forecasted demand from wholesalers and current levels of finished goods in inventory. Orders for raw materials typically had a lead time of three months and were placed monthly.

A number of challenges faced the supply chain actors in Automed at the start of the project. Some were results of government regulations, while others were a result of sup-optimisation and a lack of overall supply chain control. Main challenges related to supply chain operations included traditional MTS and batch manufacturing, large inventories at wholesaler level, low ingoing service levels from manufacturers to wholesaler, limited flexibility in manufacturing due to strict government regulations regarding approval of manufacturing batch sizes, long lead and throughput times, very little value creating time, limited information sharing between actors, little focus on logistics parameters in performance measurement, and high administrative costs in order handling, purchasing and forecasting. During the project, a number of possible improvements to the AS IS situation were identified and a unified supply chain control model containing principles and decision rules for real-time integrated supply chain control was collaboratively designed. Table 1 illustrates a number of principles applied in the design of this TO BE model. Some of these were implemented during the project, while others reflect the ideal control model for the Automed supply chain.

Table 1. Principles for TO BE control in the Automed supply chain

	Topic and main principle
1	Real-time information: fixed-frequency, manual order placement and confirmation replaced by automated replenishment and shipping based on real-time information on point-of-sale (POS) data, inventory levels, marketing plans and transport status.
2	Placement of CODP: CODP at manufacturer moved back to packing with replenishment of wholesaler based on POS, downstream inventory levels and marketing plans.
3	Pull and product based control: manufacturing and shipment based on principle of "buy one – produce and deliver one". Control by product, demand and market characteristics.
4	Replenishment responsibility: wholesaler responsible for pharmacy replenishment, manufacturer responsible for replenishment of wholesaler.
5	Automation and decision support: traditional purchasing and order fulfilment replaced by automated replenishment systems. Human decision making changed to status monitoring and exception handling facilitated by a supply chain control dashboard.
6	Roles and cooperation: roles in sales, marketing, forecasting and replenishment organised by product groups. Cooperation within product groups across company boarders.
7	Information availability: a supply chain control dashboard established for collection, communication and visualisation of relevant information from all actors. Companies can access information on appropriately aggregated levels for all participants in the chain.

Some of the elements of the TO BE control model are illustrated in Fig. 2. The most important changes involved replacing the traditional forecast-based control principles with integrated supply chain control based on real-time information on end-customer demand, inventory levels and marketing plans. Other key changes include the elimination of a number of administrative processes and the integration of IT systems across the supply chain, made possible through a supply chain dashboard.

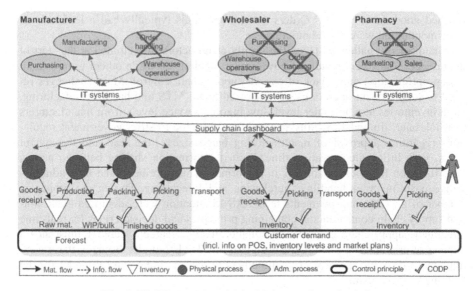

Fig. 2. TO BE control model in the Automed supply chain

5   Discussion

In terms of achievement of research objectives, the Automed project was considered successful. Important improvement areas were identified and solutions developed in order to increase integration and the use of real-time demand information to better balance demand and supply. Knowledge and new insights enriched the organisations, the relationship between the companies was strengthened and the understanding of the dynamics of the supply chain was increased.

Although the proposed solutions are technically possible to implement today, a number of other implementation challenges were identified related to the companies' interests and motivation for entering into such extensive supply chain collaboration. Implementing a new control concept such as the one proposed in this paper would require changes to a number of company processes, considerable capital investments, training and other changes that could be perceived as threatening to the companies' commercial interests and competitive advantage. Financial, political and trust issues of supply chain collaboration are well known and require development of solutions where benefits and costs are fairly distributed among the participants. Even though all participants agreed that the new control model would have led to major improvements for each company and the entire supply chain, the proposed model was not implemented. An essential element of this was the project's failure to achieve its ambition of utilising POS information in manufacturing operations control. From a scientific point of view the lack of follow-through of such implementation initiatives is an interesting aspect worth reflection.

The proposed supply chain control model assumes that real-time demand information is captured, distributed and shared among participating companies so that companies further up the supply chain gain insight into the needs of the end customer.

This would improve the manufacturing and supply processes and provide a better balance between demand and supply. At least two critical aspects related to this were identified. Firstly, the wholesaler, represented through its marketing function, was highly unwilling to make market information available to its suppliers. Sharing of this type of information was considered to weaken the wholesaler's bargaining position. Secondly, the manufacturer had limited knowledge on how to utilise real-time demand information in improving its internal planning and control processes.

Another implementation obstacle was the structure of the manufacturing industry. The vast majority of pharmaceutical manufacturers are dominant actors operating on a global scale supplying heterogeneous markets. For some products and markets the MTS model is most efficient, while for other segments a MTO model would be more appropriate. Also, the proposed control model assumes a VMI type principle where the manufacturer is responsible for the replenishment process, involving a new planning paradigm, a number of new processes and investment in ICT solutions; changes which were difficult to justify in a small market such as Norway.

6 Conclusion

This paper has demonstrated how a unified supply chain control model based on application of real-time information and changes in manufacturing operations can improve supply chain efficiency. The main contribution is the set of principles for real-time operations of supply chains. These principles have been demonstrated through a case within the pharmaceutical industry, showing the potential for improving speed and reliability of the supply chain, combined with reduced resource consumption for the administrative processes and reduced inventory levels.

The paper has not described the implementation challenges related to these issues in detail, nor are the potential effects measured and evaluated as a part of this research. These are two of the main research areas still to be pursued. A third issue for further research is the development of the detailed rules and algorithms for control as an integral part of the automated decision support facilities. A final challenge is that of integrating the control model description into the ICT architecture and infrastructure in the form of a fully operational supply chain dashboard.

Acknowledgements

The research in this paper was financed by the Norman project (see www.sfinorman.no) and the Research Council of Norway.

References

1. Coughlan, P., Coghlan, D.: Action Research for Operations Management. In: Karlsson, C. (ed.) Researching Operations Management. Taylor & Francis, New York (2008)
2. Greenwood, D.J., Levin, M.: Introduction to Action Research: social research for social change, 2nd edn. Sage Publications, Thousand Oaks (2007)

3. Jonsson, P., Lindau, R.: The supply chain planning studio: utilising the synergic power of teams and information visibility. In: Solem, O. (ed.) NOFOMA Annual Conference for Nordic Researchers in Logistics: Promoting Logistics Competence in Industry and Research, pp. 115–130. Norwegian University of Science and Technology, Trondheim (2002)

4. Vollmann, T.E., et al.: Manufacturing Planning and Control for Supply Chain Management. McGraw-Hill, Boston (2005)

5. Shi, Y., Gregory, M.: International manufacturing networks - to develop global competitive capabilities. Journal of Operations Management 16(2, 3), 195–214 (1998)

6. Dreyer, H.C., et al.: Global supply chain control systems: a conceptual framework for the global control centre. Production Planning & Control 20(2), 147–157 (2009)

7. Zijm, W.H.M.: Towards Intelligent Manufacturing Planning and Control Systems. OR Spektrum 22, 313–345 (2000)

8. Alfnes, E., Strandhagen, J.O.: Enterprise Design for Mass Customization - the Control Model Methodology. International Journal of Logistics 3(2) (2000)

9. Mason-Jones, R., Towill, D.R.: Using the Information Decoupling Point to Improve Supply Chain Performance. The International Journal of Logistics Management 10(2), 13–26 (1999)

10. Daugherty, P.J., Myers, M.B., Autry, C.W.: Automatic replenishment programs: an empirical examination. Journal of Business Logistics 20(2), 63–82 (1999)

11. Sabath, R.E., Autry, C.W., Daugherty, P.J.: Automatic replenishment programs: The impact of organizational structure. Journal of Business Logistics 22(1), 91–105 (2001)

12. Mattsson, S.-A., Jonsson, P.: Produktionslogistik, Lund, Studentlitteratur (2003)

13. Chan, F.T.S., Qi, H.J.: Feasibility of Performance Measurement System for Supply Chain: A process-based approach and measures. Integrated Manufacturing Systems 14(3), 179–190 (2003)

14. Lapide, L.: True Measures of Supply Chain Performance. Supply Chain Management Review, 25–28 (July/August 2000)

15. Bititci, U.S., Turner, T., Begemann, C.: Dynamics of Performance Measurement Systems. International Journal of Operations & Production Management 20(6), 692–704 (2000)

16. Neely, A., et al.: Performance Measurement System Design: Developing and Testing a Process-Based Approach. International Journal of Operations & Production Management 20(10), 1119–1145 (2000)

17. Power, D.J.: Decision Support Systems: Concepts and Resources for Managers, Westport, Connecticut: Quorum books (2002)

18. Simchi-Levi, D., Kaminsky, P., Simchi-Levi, E.: Designing and Managing the Supply Chain. In: Concepts, Strategies and Case Studies, 3rd edn. McGraw-Hill/Irwin, Boston (2008)

19. Turban, E., et al.: Decision support and business intelligence systems, vol. XXVIII, p. 772s. Pearson/Prentice Hall, Upper Saddle River (2007)

20. Sodhi, M.S.: Applications and opportunities for operations research in internet-enabled supply chains and electronic marketplaces. Interfaces 31(2), 56–69 (2001)

21. Bjartnes, R., et al.: Intelligent and Demand Driven Manufacturing Network Control Concepts. In: The Third World Conference on Production and Operations Management, JOMSA, Editor, Tokyo, Japan (2008)

Capacity Adjustment through Contingent Staffing Outsourcing

Gilles Neubert[1] and Philippe Adjadj[2]

[1] Liesp Laboratory School of Management ESC, 51-53 cours Fauriel,
BP29 42009 Saint Etienne cedex
gilles_neubert@esc-saint-etienne.fr
[2] Procurement manager Wincanton, 38291 la Verpillière – France
philippe.adjadj@wincanton.fr

Abstract. For a long time, contingent staffing was considered as the responsability of the Human Resource department. The high needs of workforce flexibility combined with disseminated agencies have led some companies to a great number of labor suppliers. This situation has produced important cost variation, poor quality of service, and important risk due to the mistunderstanding by local managers of legal considerations. To face this situation, companies have started to move from a HR consideration to a purchasing one. This paper deal with the problem of sourcing contingent workers as a supply chain mangement issue: to secure and optimise the sourcing of non permanent workers, companies need to involve different departments within the organisation and to develop an optimise business process with some prefered suppliers. A case study developped with Wincanton finally illustrates the benefit of identifying the needs and outsourcing to a unique service provider such a sourcing process.

Keywords: Supply Chain management, capacity adjustment, contingent workforce management, Logistic Service Provider.

1 Introduction

Today, globalization and technological innovations call for improved organizational adaptability and more flexible and advanced systems relative to manufacturing, logistics, engineering, information and process technology (Momme, 2002). In this environment, many enterprises have taken bold steps to break down both intra and inter enterprise barriers to form alliances, with the objective to increase the financial and operational performance. A closer relationship enables the partners to achieve cost reductions and revenue enhancements as well as flexibility in dealing with supply and demand uncertainties (Bowersox 1990, Lee et al. 1997, Bowersox et al. 2000).

To increase their performance in the supply chain, enterprises tend to focus now on their own business and to outsource non core competencies activities. Outsourcing is an approach that consists in making carry out by an external partner an activity, which has been carried out until then internally. It first concerned general company departments and services, such as office cleaning, and progressively, it impacted more sophisticated activities such as IT or logistics. For Abdel-Malek et al. (2005),

B. Vallespir and T. Alix (Eds.): APMS 2009, IFIP AICT 338, pp. 195–202, 2010.

outsourcing targets, on one hand, the concentration of the company on its key competencies and, on the other hand, economies of scale.

Rabinovich et al. (1999) made a study on the outsourcing of different logistics activities and found that customer service could be improved and costs reduced by outsourcing diverse logistics functions such as internal logistics of production sites or transport management. The growing rate in exhanges of goods, especially logistics-intensive industries that require reactivity and flexibility, has led to an increasing sophistication of the needs in supply chain channel. In this context, an important component to the supply chain development was the emergence of third-party logistics providers that are specialized in providing logistics services.

The performance of a Logistic Services Provider (LSP) relies on its flexiblility and reactivity, which means its ability to meet various and fluctuating demands, while ensuring a good service level to requests from a variety of clients. LSP actually work side by side with industrial and distributor clients to best meet requirements for a drastic reduction of stocks and lead times.

The sharing of the data base information with their partners concerning demand, planning, products and locations, inventory, etc. is of major importance for the optimisation of the operations in complex supply chain. In many of these relationships, they have to face with different business processes, different IT solutions, and different organisations, which lead to important interoperability and synchronisation requirements. Even these technological aspects are important to deal with the great variety of partners; one other key point for LSP's efficiency is their capability to adapt their capacity to the fluctuating demand.

With the high level of labor in logistics operations and constant pressure to reduce costs, properly managing the labor supply chain has become an important challenge. To deal with this labour-intensity characteristic, LSP require significant labour flexibility to deal with the fluctuation in supply chain demand. In this contex, the way LSP's workforce is managed, especially the way they ensure capacity flexibility through contingent labor, has a direct impact on the logistics cost and the quality of service.

Contingent Staffing has traditionnaly been the Human Resource Department responsabilitiy, but in recent years it evolves to a multi actor's decision. After developping risk and benefits of non permanent workforce management, the next paragraph will describe contingent staffing as an integrated, cross fonctional process, that involves the collaboration of various department of the company.

2 Contingent Workforce: A Multi Actor's Decision

Global competition is affecting nearly every industry. And it comes harder than ever for companies to forecast their staffing needs. The cost of overstaffing can reduce profitability and viability for a company while the cost of understaffing can lead to missing business opportunities and decreasing of Customer Service Level. In 1999, the report from the U.S. Department of Labor (USD, 1999) found "Employers that have flexibility in adjusting labor requirements to meet product and service demands have a competitive edge over those with less flexible human resource policies. The contingent work force that accommodates fluctuations in labor requirements has become an increasing segment of the labor market". That's why, use of temporary employees to smooth labor needs has grown substantially and why companies determined to make their staffing team fully responsive to market changes are using more contingent workers. With a contingent labor strategy, in which a portion of the workforce is easy to scale back or ramp up, it's easier to rapidly expand when business is growing, and to shift resources as the business changes. Instead of hiring everyone as permanent; companies have developed a flexible approach: depending on the level of operations, as demand is changing, the percentage of the workforce is adjusted.

As mentionned by Phillips (2005), increased competition and the need for cost-efficiency require that employers have flexibility in adjusting employment levels and employment costs to demand for its product or services, both of which might be constantly changing and volatile. A permanent full-time workforce does not permit that. Advantages and Disadvantages of Using the Contingent Workforce have been exposed by Phillips (table1).

Table 1. Advantages and Disadvantages of Using Contingent Workforce Phillips (2005)

Advantages	Disadvantages
Flexibility.	Perceived lack of loyalty
Savings in the cost of taxes and benefits.	Lack of knowledge of the organization's culture, policies, and procedures
Access to expertise not internally available.	Potential for overall higher costs, depending on the situation
Potential savings in overall compensation costs.	Concern with disclosure of organizational proprietary information
	Impact on morale of permanent workforce
	Loss of internal capabilities
	Potential for increased training costs when contingent workers must be trained on unique or unusual processes or procedures used by the organization

While many firms currently use some forms of contingent labor, few have developed a strategy to help ensure that such deployments maximize the organization's return (Sullivan, 2008).

2.1 Contingent Workforce: A Sourcing Problem

In their paper, Pac et al. (2007) classified the production capacity under two main categories: permanent capacity and contingent capacity formed by the workers that can be acquired temporarily from what they call an External Labor Supply Agency (ELSA). Their paper investigates different supply uncertainty in ELSA responses to workforce request. As indicated in Table1, the main advantage in using non permanent staff is cost reduction and flexibility, but manufacturer's requests for contingent workers may be totally or partially unmet by the ELSA due to the lack of availability and/or skill requirements.

As indicated in Taleo (2004), Contingent Workforce Management is part Human Resource (HR), part Procurment, part Finance, IT, Security/Compliance/Risk management. It does not reside comfortably in any one traditional corporate department. The same point of view is developped in the special report from Workforce Management (2007), saying that managed staffing provider contracts are a growing trend, driven by security concerns, compliance issues, costs, the desire for tighter control over spending and shortage of skilled labor for specific position.

In this context, because temporary labor involves sourcing workers from External Labor Supply Agencies, negociating rates and contracts, many HR departments prefer not to deal it. Moreover, identifying the needs for contingent workers in the company, finding the right supplier, reducing the time for candidate sourcing, monitoring their presence, adapting their number to the level of demand, etc., are activities that can be supported and improved using supply and purchasing techniques. Pac et al. (2007) identified the risk and wrote that, in case there is a high demand for contingent workers in the market at the time of the request, or if the manufacturer requires the workers in short notice, the risk of the request not being met in full terms is highter. They identified different risk factors such as the size of available temporary worker pool, capability of finding skilled workers, competition in the environment, demand structure of different customers, and opportunities in alternative options. Moreover, ELSAs may not be willing to fulfill a specic request at a specic time, considering potentially better options.

The next paragraph will describe the problem of sourcing contingent workers as a multi actor issue: to secure and optimise the sourcing of non permanent workers, companies need to involve different corporate departments and to develop an optimise business process with some prefered suppliers.

2.2 Contingent Workforce: A Multi Actor Perspective

Todays, many enterprises are changing their organisation in order to better integrate their activities. The concept of integration can be approached through different perspectives (functional, business process, Information System, etc.), but in all cases, it aims at shifting from local management to system management. From literature, it emerges that integration can support business processes at two different levels (Romano, 2003), intra-company integration, aiming to overcome the functional silos boundaries, and inter-companies integration, aiming to overcome the individual company boundaries.

Sourcing of temporary workers has to be considered as a cross fonctional process. It needs to plan the needs, to identify the knowledge, skills and abilities of contingent workers, recruit and select them accordingly, to schedule their arriving (start and stop times), and identify the tools, equipment and information that will be needed, to supervise their activity, and specify the procedures and methods to follow. As it includes all these activities, the process of sourcing contingent workers involves different actors from various departments within the company, and need their interaction and their close collaboration:

- HR: qualification, legal and practical considerations ,
- Operation: capacity planning, skill and knowledge of the workers, etc.
- Quality/security: safety wear, equipment, procedures, etc.

- Purchasing: contracts, sourcing of the external labor agency
- Finance: invoice paiement, cost regulation, etc.

But, as mentioned by Rice (2004), in many organizations, individual hiring managers manage their own contingent workforce needs, resulting in multiple, redundant vendor relationships, non-uniform pricing and tremendous overall losses in time and money. Moreover, in big groups, with numerous location and agencies, sourcing of temporary workers often use different external labor supply agency (ELSA) as shown in figure 1.

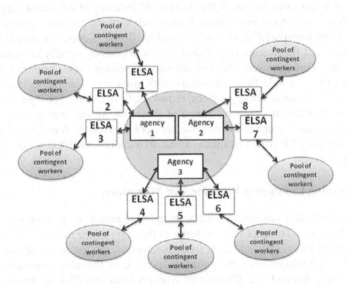

Fig. 1. Network of labor supply agencies for contingent workforce sourcing

This organisation, based on decentralised decision, is closed to local market but it leads to some major inconvenience:

- The pool of skilled employees in each aerea is limited and shared by all the companies that need contingent workers. One agency of the group is generally a small structure that, in many situations, is not considered as a prefered customer by the ELSA.
- The number of requests from one agency to one ELSA can be limited. This lead to cost variation in contingent workers sourcing.

In many cases, legal and practical considerations are not well known by the managers in the agencies. This situation can lead to dramatic consequence for the group.

As there is a competition among companies to attract and develop their non permanent workforce, big groups have to start establishing longer-term relationships with preferred providers to ensure proper leveraging of contingent labor volumes and a continuous flow of qualified candidates (Falgione, 2008). To be more efficient, they have to standardize their interaction with their labor suppliers.

To achieve the goal, the process of managing contingent workers can be outsourced to a service provider. That means that activities and best pratices have to be defined, actors have to be identified, inside (manager in the company's department) and out side the company (ELSA), and Key Performance Indicators have to be chosen to evaluate the performance of the process.

3 Case Study: Wincanton

Wincanton is a European leader in the design and delivery of advanced supply chain solutions. Wincanton operates a comprehensive range of supply chain solutions for its customers; from transportation of simple product flows to complex freight management solutions and from temporary shared user warehousing to fully automated dedicated solutions. Through every stage of the supply chain process, from raw materials to recycling, they provide their customers with solutions: warehouse management, transport and distribution, barge services, removals, outsize loads, or logistics consulting. Wincanton offers an extensive range of warehousing and transport services including national and European distribution services. In France, Wincanton has built a distibuted network of logistics facilities: about 30 locations, 600 000 sq. m, 300 trucks and 1500 employees.

3.1 Outsourcing Contingent Workforce at Wincanton

Because many of their customers have a changing demand, Wincanton has to face a fluctuating business. To adapt its workforce to the level of the demand, Wincanton is using contingent labor. Depending on some parameters, the logistics platform's needs are different: specialisation of the paltform, periode in the year, seasonality of the major customers demand, etc. Contingent workers represent 25% of the expenses of the group and 30% of the total number of employees and mainly concern: fork-lift truck driver, picking and warehouseman. With its distributed complex of logistics platform, Wincanton had built a network of agency labour suppliers that was so large it was no longer possible to be sure that their needs were being met. Further more, with a contingent labor representing up to 10% of the total cost of a contract, and with an increased pressure on supply chain managers to reduce costs, Wincanton has decided to redesign the sourcing of its contingent workforce.

Based on the considerations described in paragraph 2, the first point was the constitution of a cross-functional group to rationalise the process. Under the control of the purchasing department the objective was not to reduce the cost, but rather to secure the quality of service to their customers by better understanding the requirements of all the persons concerned in the group. As previously described, included in the team were representatives from all the departments involved in the labour supply: HR, IT, Quality Health and Safety, Legal, Finance and Operations with the sponsorship of the senior management.

The long term goal was to outsource the management of the temporary workers in order to get down from 65 different external labor suppliers that have contract with the local Wincanton agencies around France, to a unique centralised managed service supplier (MSP) as shown on figure 2.

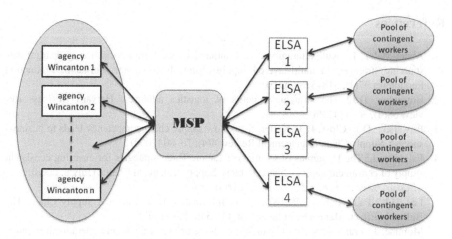

Fig. 2. outsourcing of temporary workers' management to a unique managed service supplier

The main benefits of this new organisation are the folowing:

- All the agency needs for all the French sites are centralized and managed by the dedicated ONESYS team,
- A centralized French work legislation control,
- A full electronic recruitment process for a much lighter administrative load,
- A 97% fulfilment rate completed in the first month of operation,
- A 30 min average time to find a suitable agency worker across France,
- Improved payment processes between the operational sites and the supplier through the innovative eprocurement.

4   Conclusion

To achieve the competitive advantage that results from high performance, companies must develop their ability to anticipate demand trend and to react to pontual demand fluctuation. This adjustment is based on a permanent workforce and a contingent one, formed by workers that can be acquired temporarily.

For a long time, this contingent staffing was considered as the responsability of the Human Resource department, but it has recently shifted to Purchasing departments. The fact is that to secure and optimise the sourcing of non permanent workers, companies need to involve different actors within the organisation and to develop an optimised integrated business process with a few number of prefered suppliers.

Wincanton France decided to do so during 2008, and the satisfactory roll-out of their programme encourages other countries to deploy this strategy.

One limitation is that this study was conducted in a specific area of competencies, where the variability of request to the service provider is not so wide. Applying this method to specific skill workers will probably need to integrate more sophisticated tools to specify compenties for the contingent workers.

References

1. Abdel-Malek, L., Kullpattaranirun, T., Nanthavanij, S.: A framework for comparing outsourcing strategies in multi-layered supply chains. International Journal of Production Economics 97(3), 318–328 (2005)
2. Bowersox, D.J.: The strategic benefits of logistics alliances. Harvard Business Review 68(4), 36–43 (1990)
3. Bowersox, D.J., Closs, D.J., Keller, S.B.: How supply chain competency leads to business success. Supply Chain Management Review 4(4), 70–80 (2000)
4. Falgione, J.: The Dynamics of Contingent Labor: Three strategies for ensuring consistent supply of contingent labor at "market" rates. Supply & demand Chaine (July 8, 2008), http://www.sdcexec.com/publication/
5. Lee, H.L., Padmanabhan, V., Whang, S.: Information Distortion in a Supply Chain: The Bullwhip Effect. Management Science 43(4), 546–558 (1997)
6. Momme, J.: Framework for outsourcing manufacturing: strategic and operational implications. Computers in industry 49, 59–75 (2002)
7. Pac, F., Alp, O., Tan, T.: Integrated workforce capacity and inventory management under labour supply uncertainty, 29 pages (2007), 978-90-386-0885-3
8. Phillips, L.: Senior Professional in Human Resources, 720 pages (2005), ISBN-10: 0-7897-3497-4
9. Rabinovich, E., Windle, R., Dresner, M., Corsi, T.: Outsourcing of integrated logistics function: an examination of industry practices. International Journal of Physical Distribution and Logistics Management 29(6), 35–37 (1999)
10. Rice, E.: Best Practices to Effectively Manage the Contingent Workforce (2004), http://www.innovativeemployeesolutions.com/knowledge/articles
11. Romano, P.: Co-ordination and integration mechanisms to manage logistics processes across supply networks. Journal of Purchasing and Supply Management 9(3), 119–134 (2003)
12. Sullivan, J.: Having a contingent staffing strategy helps HR avoid traditional (and flawed) cost-cutting approaches such as the freezing of hiring, promotions, pay or budgets. Workforce Management, 58 (July 14, 2008)
13. Taleo Contingent Workforce Management: strategies for results, White Paper, 23 pages (2004), http://www.taleo.com
14. Toshinori, N., Koichiro, T.: Advantage of Third Party Logistics in Supply Chain Management, Working Paper, vol. 72. Graduate School of Commerce and Management, Hitotsubashi University (2002)
15. USD, Report on the American Workforce, U.S. Department of Labor, Alexis M. Herman, Secretary (1999), http://www.bls.gov/opub/rtaw/pdf/rtaw1999.pdf
16. Workforce Management, contingent staffing, special repport, 10 pages (February 2007), http://www.workforce.com

Coordination in Supply Chains:
From Case Studies to Reference Models

Yue Ming[*], Raymond Houé, and Bernard Grabot

University of Toulouse, INPT, LGP-ENIT
47, avenue d'Azereix, BP1629
F-65016 Tarbes Cedex, France
{yue.ming,rhoue,bernard}@enit.fr

Abstract. Intensive competition has forced companies to focus on their core business and as a consequence to participate to more and more complex supply networks. The necessity to preserve the autonomy of each partner makes such networks usually managed in a decentralized way. Consequently, problems and conflicts emerge during the coordination processes. This paper describes some coordination problems identified through interviews and locates them within the activities of the coordination processes. Interpretations of the aspects influencing coordination are suggested, allowing to better explain the origins of these problems.

Keywords: Supply Chain; Coordination; Modeling; Performance.

1 Introduction

Nowadays, the growing intensive competition has forced enterprises to focus on their core business and participate in more and more complex Supply Networks (SNs). To build an efficient partnership, the crucial element is the coordination between partners, including selecting a suitable partner, executing and measuring the performance of coordination.

For years, various literatures have related efforts in giving mechanisms, models and tools of coordination in order to improve the overall performance of a supply chain. In the marketing literature, coordination mechanisms have mainly focused on pricing decisions, for instance linked to contract [1], demand [2] and advertising [3]. In the operations research literature, most of works on coordination of supply chain are related to the optimal process parameters and policy, such as inventory policy [4], delivery [5] or order processing [6]. Besides, works on tools and techniques for supporting coordination are widely presented, such as agent-based frameworks [7], attribute-based approach [8] or Virtual e-Chain [9]. Commonly, coordination in a supply chain can be interpreted as exchanging information, plans and executions which have been performed in isolation but may take into account the partner's constraints and expectations. Building a consistent coordination framework on that base is a

---

[*] Corresponding author.

B. Vallespir and T. Alix (Eds.): APMS 2009, IFIP AICT 338, pp. 203–210, 2010.

complex process, not only dealing with models and techniques but also related to other aspects, such as characteristics of partners, types of supply chains, or communication means. Marcotte et al. [10] suggest for instance coordination models based on the mutual influence of the partner and network. However, as a first step, it is critical to track the problems linked to the various activities of the cooperation process. Identifying possible dysfunctions, diagnosing reasons and tracing the resources which may facilitate coordination are basic but critical issues. This paper focuses on identifying real problems in coordination processes, based on case studies, and at identifying the causes of these problems.

The communication is organized as follows: in section 2, is introduced the background of the case studies. The typical structure of the Supply Networks of the interviewed companies is given. In section 3 are introduced two models giving an overview of the activities involved in typical cooperation processes and allowing to localize some coordination problems. We then list the aspects which influence coordination, in order to better explain the origin of these problems. In section 4, we propose two models that interpret the relationships according to these aspects in order to provide directions for a better cooperation.

2   Case Studies in the Aeronautic Industry

As stated above, more attention is usually paid to supply chain planning rather than to coordination models. Coordination processes are more than the juxtaposition of purchasing, production and delivery, which are the main operational processes in a supply chain. In order to approach real industry situations, we have conducted interviews in various contexts, all aiming at analyzing problems arising in the coordination between large and small companies belonging to supply chains in the aeronautic sector of the South-West region of France. Interviews in more than thirty companies of various sizes have allowed to identify a considerable list of problems, either linked to technical or behavioral issues [10],[11]. Only some of them will be discussed here.

From the case studies, it is first clear that the structure of a supply chain is in practice more complex than a unidirectional flow (see Figure 1): it also includes loops which may be the origin of internal conflicts. Usually, the coordination in the interviewed companies is managed at three levels, namely long term, middle term and short term. The long term coordination process focuses on the definition of the partnership and dimensioning of the chain without any detailed information. This long term process defines average flows and provides information for all the partners in the chain, while forecasts are exchanged at middle term in order to adjust the capacities. The short term level is more operational and includes information such as purchasing orders or production orders. However, uncertainty of forecast in the middle term process and urgent orders at short term induce much instability. The changes between different slide planning are also source of conflicts during coordination. Considering the case studies, it is apparent that managing partnerships and eliminate barriers are critical elements that indeed exist in each activity of coordination. Problems usually emerge during coordination since actors are sometimes focusing on their own interpretation and benefits, without consideration of a win-win mechanism which would sometimes require negotiation. This point will be addressed in next section.

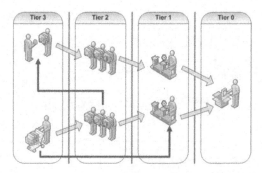

Fig. 1. Typical structure of a Supply Chain

3 Qualitative Models of Coordination Processes

Many models have already been suggested in the literature for describing logistic processes in supply chain (see SCOR [12], ASLOG [13], etc.), with the idea that applying these processes would allow increasing performance. We would like to show in this section that whenever the processes are "correct", problems may arise due to other aspects which are not included in these models. We have here used the ARIS [14] formalism for describing our process models.

3.1 Long Term Coordination

In the long term coordination process, the main activities can be identified as in Figure 2. When selecting a sub-contractor for a given long-term relationship, the customer defines its own standards, which are more and more elective. A result is that a multiplication of certifications is required from the sub-contractors, since standard certifications are often particularized by the customers to their own case. The customer also takes into account the results of his previous relationships with the sub-contractor, for instance through its key performance indicators (KPIs) (service ratio, etc.). As a consequence, the sub-contractors complain about the high cost and work induced by this over-assessment, which can in some cases hardly be linked to real performance.

Reaching a common agreement may be difficult since it usually includes not only conditions on price and cycle times, but a commitment for constantly decreasing these values through time. A problem often related is that the people involved at the customer's are more and more buyers, with a poor experience in technical aspects. Therefore, most of the discussion concern prices, which may induce at short term technical problems. Once the contract has been signed, the sub-contractor has to perform local adjustments (investments, contacts with its own sub-contractors or suppliers) for being able to execute the contact. The availability of efficient information systems and production management tools play an important role in making plans in long term, middle term and short term. Indeed, this complex task requires the sub-contractor to be capable of processing forecasts from his customer, using his information tools and assessing risk due to forecast uncertainty. Tools are here an issue, but also the competence and motivation of sub-contractors for tasks that they consider as "administrative", not belonging to their core business.

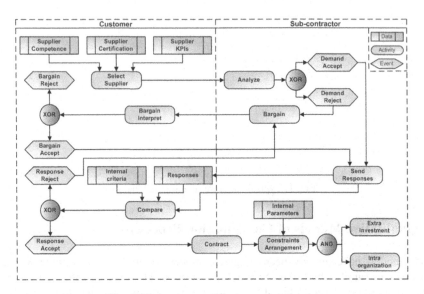

Fig. 2. Long term coordination process model

3.2 Short Term Coordination

In the short term coordination process (see Figure 3), the sub-contractor usually tries to improve its internal efficiency for being able to decrease its costs through time. This necessity makes that different orders having similar characteristics are often grouped, resulting in problems for meeting the due dates and decreasing the cycle times. In addition, planning is often disturbed by urgent orders or returned goods. In many cases, the urgency of the orders is questionable (and may rapidly change through time) while parts are often returned due to cosmetic reasons (aspect of the parts, not linked to functional issues), to over-tolerances or to different interpretations from the customer and the sub-contractor. On the other hand, sub-contractors often have some difficulty for performing their internal planning, and as a consequence for not being able to control their own suppliers. Therefore, it is very usual that a

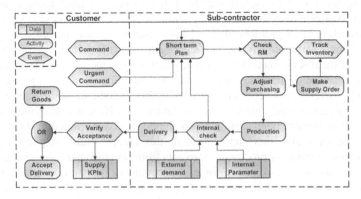

Fig. 3. Short term coordination process model

sub-contractor only detects a problem concerning the availability of an order when the delivery has to be performed.

On the customer side, measure of performance indicators may become more important than good sense: several sub-contractors mentioned cases when their performance was good, but considered as poor according to the customer's performance indicators, and conversely.

3.3 Concepts to be Added to the Coordination Models

From the coordination models and the described problems, we suggest interpreting some influence aspects that impact the coordination performance and are not usually taken into account.

Trust. Trust is interpreted as the degree of partners' confidence in each other for accomplishing behaviors and achieving benefits as the agreements. In supply chain coordination, partners need to trust each other for exchanging internal information, such as purchase lead time, internal costs or inventory level. Both coordination actors are confident that exchanging information leads to better cooperation rather than losing confidential data or competitive advantages. In practice, trust has a strong influence in the cooperation processes since it allows each partner to share information and to have a positive view on the partner's behave.

Common Understanding. Common understanding is a kind of agreed interpretation between customers and sub-contractors, which is required in several issues in which misunderstanding often occur, like uncertainty of forecasts, urgency, standards of quality and etc.

Willing to Cooperate. As an individual entity that pursues benefits, enterprise, in certain case, chooses to concentrate on its own interests without the considerations of the overall chain. For instance, the customer sends a consultant to its sub-contractor in order to improve the supply performance. However, the consultant only pays attention to the works related to his employer, or even raises the priority of these works ignoring the overall plan of its sub-contractor. These self protective activates of the customer possibly reduce the willing of cooperate of the sub-contractor.

Balance of Power. Balance of power is a very important condition of cooperation in a supply chain, and may result from various issues: size of the partner, specialty (critical for the partner or not), power in the whole supplier chain, competence, access to markets etc.

It is clear that these aspects are interrelated. For instance, balance of power strongly impacts the communication atmosphere and accordingly influences common understanding between partners. We shall try in next section to investigate these relationships at a quite global level, and then try to correlate them with some of the problems observed during the case studies.

4   Towards and Extended Model for Cooperation

From the case studies, we introduce four main concepts that could be taken into account when considering the cooperation not only focusing on formalized processes but also tracing the influence issues of the conflicts. It is also apparent that these aspects are interrelated and relevant to certain cooperation processes. In this section, we suggest two simplified models to presents the relationships at a global view, from both the customer and the sub-contractor's points of view.

In Figure 4 are positioned the relationships between the concepts suggested in the previous section with the customer's point of view. A key point is that the customer has a very positive view on all his incentives towards his suppliers: for him, audits, certification, and competition with other suppliers are good means for increasing the motivation of the partner, and so its performance. Similarly, having a common understanding with the suppliers mainly comes from common standards, brought by certification. Balance of power is only of interest for allowing sharing risk, which is one of the ultimate goals of large companies within supply chains.

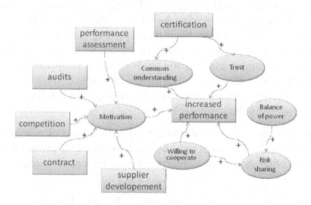

Fig. 4. Relationships between concepts – the customer's side

On the opposite, the same concepts are positioned in Figure 5 according to the sub-contractor point of view. Most of the initiatives of the customer aiming at improving its maturity and motivation are considered as a proof of distrust, and have a negative influence on motivation and willing to cooperate. The idea of mutual respect is here of prime importance, since the small companies want to be recognized for their skills. This need for mutual respect is struck by the tentative of the customer to change their suppliers (in his view, "increase its maturity"). The origin of most of these misunderstandings is certainly in a lack of dialogue: in the customer's mind, standardization of the relationship leads to performance (through the use of common tools, common processes, etc.). For the small and medium enterprises, dialogue and actions are more important than standards. Balance of power is here only pursued in order to have an influence on the contracts, which is clearly not the idea of the large companies.

These two simplified models provide a first interpretation of the relationships between suggested concepts according to the interviews from the case studies. The results suggest that influence concepts that induce conflicts during the cooperation play opposite roles in different sides of partners. The same concepts which are considered as positives issues for cooperation in the customer's point of view are reversely treated as negative facts from the sub-contractor side. Only an increased dialogue could solve such an issue.

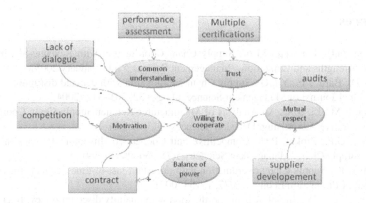

Fig. 5. Relationships between concepts – the sub-contractor's side

5 Conclusion

In this paper, we suggest reference models to describe the cooperation processes according to real case studies. These processes are close to the main activities described in existing models, such as SCOR etc. Accordingly, the purpose of proposed models is locating problems that may arise due to other aspects which are not included in the existing models. Then, we focus on interpreting the concepts that induce the cooperation problems allowing better explaining the origin of these problems. Based on the interpreted concepts, two models are proposed in order to draw attention to global view of relationships among these concepts and the relevance between concepts and cooperation processes.

Due to the case studies in aeronautical industry, the results from the reference models are approach to real cooperation situations, showing that problems during cooperation may be induced by interrelated non-technical concepts such as trust, common understanding, willing to cooperate, balance of power and so on, which are not considered in other models for supply chain cooperation. In addition, the same concepts which are considered as positive points for cooperation in the customer's side are in opposite considered as negative facts from the sub-contractor side. This is a key point that impacts the cooperation in supply chain.

As perspectives in future work, we suggest that cooperation models could consider these interrelated concepts as the "input" or "data" in order to improve the cooperation from partnership rather than standard processes. A possible way to ameliorate the proposed models using ARIS is that "data" are classified according to its influence to the customer and the sub-contractor. For instance, concept "trust" acts as a "support data" in the models of the customer, in opposite, "trust" plays as a "constraint data" in the models of the sub-contractor. In that way, both the customer and the sub-contractor are legible about the conflicts and commons, furthermore to improve the cooperation between partners.

References

1. Cachon, G.P., Lariviere, M.A.: Supply Chain Coordination with Revenue-Sharing Contracts: Strengths and Limitations. Management Science 51(1) (January 2005)
2. Qi, X.D., Bard, J.F., Yu, G.: Supply Chain coordination with demand disruptions. The International Journal of Management Science, Omega 32, 301–312 (2004)
3. Huang, Z.M., Li, S.X.: An Analysis of Manufacturer-Retailer Supply Chain Coordination in Cooperative Advertising. Decision Sciences 33(3) (2002)
4. Cachon, G.P., Zipkin, P.H.: Competitive and Cooperative Inventory Policies in a Two-Stage Supply Chain. Management Science 45(7), 936–953 (1999)
5. Zimmer, K.: Supply Chain coordination with uncertain just-in-time delivery. International Journal of Production Economics 77, 1–15 (2002)
6. Li, J.L., Liu, L.W.: Supply Chain coordination with quantity discount policy. International Journal of Production Economic 101, 89–98 (2006)
7. Xue, X.L., Li, X.D., Shen, Q.P., Wang, Y.W.: An agent-based framework for supply chain coordination in construction. Automation in Construction 14, 413–430 (2005)
8. Xu, L., Beamon, B.M.: Supply Chain Coordination and Cooperation Mechanisms: An Attribute-Based Approach. Journal of Supply Chain Management 42(1), 4–12 (2006)
9. Manthou, V., Vlachopoulou, M., Folinas, D.: Virtual e-Chain (VeC) model for supply chain collaboration. International Journal of Production Economics 87(3), 241–250 (2004)
10. Marcotte, F., Grabot, B., Affonso, R.: Cooperation models for supply chain management. International Journal Logistics Systems and Management 5(1/2), 123–153 (2009)
11. Galasso, F., Mercé, C., Grabot, B.: Decision support framework for supply chain planning with flexible demand. International Journal of Production Research 47(2), 455–479 (2009)
12. SCOR 9.0 Reference Guide, http://www.supply-chain.org
13. Association française pour la logistique, http://www.aslog.org
14. Davis, R.: ARIS Design Platform: Advanced Processes Modeling and Administration. Springer, Heidelberg (2008)

Construction Logistics Improvements Using the SCOR Model – Tornet Case

Fredrik Persson, Jonas Bengtsson, and Örjan Gustad

Department of Science and Technology
Linköping University, Campus Norrköping
S-601 74 Norrköping, Sweden
fredrik.persson@liu.se

Abstract. The cost for house production is rising in Sweden. Compared with other consumer goods, the cost for houses have had a steeper increase over the last decades. Initiatives such as Lean Construction and Prefabrication have emerged in the construction industry to reduce the cost of house production and thereby the cost of the house itself. These initiatives have collected a lot of ideas and tools from the automotive industry and a lot of good examples are emerging that leads to cost reductions in construction. In this strive towards improvement, logistics activities are emerging as important processes and a potential for cost savings. This paper reports on a project at the construction company Peab where the SCOR-model (Supply Chain Operations Reference Model) have been utilized in order to find processes with high cost saving potential. The result reports on cost savings from the logistics perspective in different areas of the logistic system.

Keywords: Construction Industry, Construction Logistics, Supply Chain Management, SCOR.

1 Introduction

During the last decade, construction logistics have become more and more in focus both from academia but also from practitioners. It is believed that much can be gained by implementing the ideas and theories from the very broad logistics filed. All that is needed is a little tweaking to make the theories suitable for the construction industry. Although there is an increasing interest for research in construction logistics, one can notice a clear trend in publications. That is the division of, on the one hand logistics from raw materials to the construction site, rather a supply chain management initiative, and on the other hand, the construction site logistics, more internal logistics on the actual site. This research originates in the idea that these two logistics initiatives cannot and should not be divided, but that the uniqueness of construction logistics is the incorporation of site logistics into the whole supply chain management theory. With this in mind, this study of supply chains in the construction industry is a step forward, both for the definition of construction logistics, but also for the supply chains in the construction industry.

B. Vallespir and T. Alix (Eds.): APMS 2009, IFIP AICT 338, pp. 211–218, 2010.
© IFIP International Federation for Information Processing 2010

The logistics systems in the construction industry take up a large part of the total costs and affect the total lead time in any construction project. Large amounts of money can be saved if supply chain operations can be made in a more standardised way, learning from previous projects or using standard solutions. Today, however, it seems that every new building project is reinventing the management of supply chains.

The construction industry is in some countries considered as the backbone of their economy. This large sector with a highly traditional business approach is closely interlinked with the rest of the economy [1]. In Sweden (during 2007), more than 73.000 companies compete in the industry with a total turnover of approximately EUR 37 billions and 225.000 employees [2]. The construction industry is basically a project based industry. Every construction site is considered a project and many projects are performed simultaneously. The productivity development in the construction industry is slow compared to other industries [3]. Much of the blame for the slow productivity gain is the high cost levels throughout the industry. According to Vrijhoef and Koskela [3] the high costs are to be blamed on the supply chain and its involvement of many subcontractors and both local and global suppliers.

Vrijhoef and Koskela [3] propose four roles of supply chain management in the construction industry covering the supply logistic part of the chain. To some extent their model has provided useful information regarding coordination between supply chain and construction site but the model is limited to supply chains and does not cover supply networks. Vidalakis and Tookey [4] use simulation to study a supply chain in the construction industry. They draw on the similarities between a manufacturing supply chain and a construction supply chain. Differences are functional and located at the end of the supply chains; otherwise they find no major parts where the two supply chains differ.

The purpose of this paper is to analyse a construction site with a supply chain management view utilising common supply chain analysis tools, in this case the SCOR model [5]. For the case company, the purpose is to evaluate the use of the SCOR model and to find areas of improvement that can reduce costs or in any other way increase profitability or reduce the environmental impact of a construction project.

The paper is structured as follows. Chapter 2 presents the case company Peab and the building project Tornet. Chapter 3 is a theoretical outlook into the area of construction logistics. Chapter 4 is the case study. Chapter 5 ends the paper with some conclusions and acknowledgements.

2 The Case Company Peab

Peab AB (Peab) is one of the largest companies on the Swedish construction market. The company has about 11,000 employees and an annual turnover of about EUR 3.6 billions, for 2008 [6].

The building called *Tornet* (the Tower) is the final stages of construction work during the summer of 2009. The building is located in Tornby city in Linköping, Sweden. Peab started to build *Tornet* in September 2007 and it is planned to be finished in summer of 2009. The 19 storey high building will rise 64 meters off the ground, which for Linköping is quite high, only shadowed by the Cathedral. . *Tornet* will accommodate offices, business apartments and conference facilities.

Material that arrives at construction sites requires human resources for unloading; mostly there is also need for handling equipment as an aid in this process. This handling equipment often needs to be rented. When delays occur the equipment cannot be used, they will generate unnecessary costs. At the construction site The Tower this has been solved with a nearby handling equipment rental service. Peab has the opportunity to rent the handling equipment when needed. A bad delivery performance results in interruptions of the work, the personnel need to unload the material instead of finishing their planned tasks. Personnel who wait for delayed deliveries lead to an increased waste of time of the human resources, time that could be used for value adding tasks. Another problem that can occur is that nobody is able to receive the delivery.

The products which will be included in this study are plasterboards, doors and kitchens. The reasons why these particular products have been chosen are the following: plasterboards are chosen because of the common use of this product in the construction industry. Doors and kitchens are also chosen based on their commonality. Also, they have been subjected to delivery disturbances and quality problems for the examined construction site.

Fig. 1. Tornet (The Tower) during construction

3   The Supply Chain in the Construction Industry

The supply chain in the construction industry varies from the traditional supply chain in the manufacturing industry, where raw material is delivered to a production site for further transformation to a finished product and later distributed to the costumers. The construction industry is characterized by the production site being built up around the building that is about to be manufactured. The construction industry is also characterized by temporary supply chains with fragmentation and instability as a result. Even though some processes in the construction industry seem to be similar, there tends to be no standard in them [3]. According to Vrijhoef and Koskela [3] the construction industry is an example of make-to-order, MTO. Other authors consider the construction industry to be a typical example of engineer-to-order, ETO [7].

The supply chain in the construction industry is in need of change according to Xue et al. [8]. There are, however, barriers and problems that prevent coordination and integration of the supply chain. Examples of problems are attitude-related problems, myopic focus, lack of understanding for suppliers and subcontractors. Furthermore the lack of communication in the construction industry contributes to inferior transparency in the supply chain. Tight schedules and unrealistic lead-time requirements for material and equipment lead to further problems [8]. Many of the problems are caused in earlier stages in the supply chain than where they discovered [3].

During the work with the case, it became obvious that construction logistics needed a unique definition since several issues made it difficult to solely rely on common definitions of logistics for other industries. It became also very clear that logistics is a too narrow term for the purpose at hand. Although the work still focuses on logistics improvements, a glance at supply chain management was needed. Stadtler [9] defines SCM such as: "The task of integrating organizational units along a supply chain and coordinating materials, information and financial flows in order to fulfill the (ultimate) customer demands". Construction SCM can be defined, following Stadtler's [9] definition, as: The task of integrating organizational units along a supply chain, *including the construction site and subcontractors*, and coordinating materials, information and financial flows *with the project site plan* in order to fulfill the (ultimate) customer demands".

4   SCOR Mapping of the Supply Chain

A mapping of the material flow of plasterboards, doors and kitchens have been performed with SCOR in levels 2 and 3. First, the material flow for these particular items, from supplier to the construction site, has been analysed in the SCOR methodology in level 2, see Figure 2. The mapping was used to visualize and identify possible problems within the material flow. To identify further problems in the supply chain processes at the construction site, secondly, a mapping at SCOR level 3 has been made for each of the three product types, see Figure 3 for plasterboards. The mapping for plasterboards is presented in detail in this paper in the following subchapters.

4.1 Plasterboards

When Peab has been assigned a building project, the process to develop a production schedule (D3.3) begins, see also Figure 3. The production schedule is based on backward planning by using a Gantt chart. As the project continues, work on developing construction plans (M3.1) takes place. The plan enables scheduling of production activities (M.3.2).

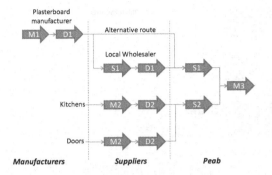

Fig. 2. SCOR mapping in level 2

The schedule of production activities (M3.2) is used as a support for the call off process (S1.1). Another process that supports the call offs is the delivery plan (P2.4). Call offs for plasterboards are made by mail to the local retailer. The retailer delivers orders that are below five tonnes in weight, bigger orders will be shipped directly from the manufacturer. When the plasterboards arrive, the product is considered received (S1.2). The reception of plasterboards takes place at a nearby yard because of the lack of space. As the products are received, verification (S1.3) is performed. After the verification the products are transferred to the construction site with rented machines. At the construction site, the plasterboards are distributed to the right floor for assembly (S1.4). The invoice is then compared to the delivered quantity (S1.5). When needs arise on a floor due to miscalculations, plasterboards are, if possible, transferred from floors above (M3.3). Assembled boards are inspected by craftsmen (M3.4). Waste is thrown in a container for landfill (M3.8).

At *Tornet* construction site most of the deliveries were not time bound. With current costs, for rental of machines and time bound deliveries, the rent for machines exceeds the cost for time bound deliveries when delays exceed one hour.

Perfect order fulfilment. The data was hard to collect because of the lack of access to documentation. Some of the gathered data did not include all the desired metrics. This applied to all the investigated products. Data was gathered from delivery notes that were compared to the call offs and order acknowledgements; additional complementary data were obtained from the manager at the construction site. The results for the plasterboards are as follows:

- *% of ordered Delivery in Full.* All orders contained the right products, 95 percent of them also arrived in the right quantity.
- *Delivery Performance to Customer Commit Date.* All orders were shipped to the right geographical location, but only 50 percent were delivered on time. All the orders that arrived on time were also delivered in full, according to the first level 2 metric.
- *Documentation Accuracy.* The investigation for this metric only included plans for assembly. This was, however, not relevant for plasterboards.
- *Perfect Condition.* There was no information of damaged plasterboards; however this is not a likely scenario and indicates a lack of documentation.

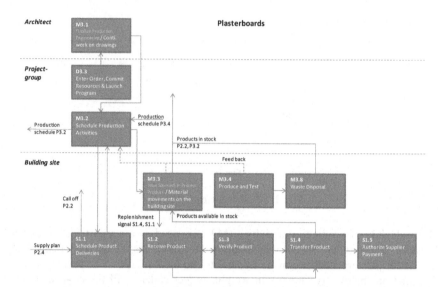

Fig. 3. SCOR mapping of plasterboards at Tornet

Because of the lack of documentation when it comes to damaged products, the results for perfect order fulfilment tend to be higher than the actual value for plasterboards. The results for doors and kitchens will not be explained in detail but the result is presented in Table 1.

Supplier plasterboards. Figure 2, that illustrates the material flow to the *Tornet* construction site, indicates that Peab is using unnecessary intermediaries. This extra step in the supply chain generates unnecessary costs. Even though larger orders are shipped directly from the supplier, the call off is made to the retailer who wants his share. The majority of the call offs are performed by mail, even though Peab has a purchase and procurement system. If Peab used the purchase and procurement system (EDI) when ordering gypsum boards, they would acquire an EDI-discount. With the EDI and quantity discounts, which they receive when using direct deliveries, Peab obtains a total discount of 24 percent compared to the retailers' price. Even though only ten percent of the plasterboard deliveries are ordered from the retailer, there is still a potential saving, see Table 2.

Table 1. Perfect order fulfilment

	Plasterboards [%]	Doors [%]	Kitchens [%]
Orders Delivered in Full	95	57	0
Delivery Performance to Customer Commit Date	50	57	33
Documentation Accuracy	-	100	100
Perfect Condition	100	86	100
Perfect Order Fulfilment	**50**	**57**	**0**

Table 2. Savings when using the EDI system and direct deliveries (Costs in SEK)

	EDI System	Direct deliveries	Total savings
Tornet	16 000	22 000	38 000 (~4 %)
Total 2007*	106 000	147 000	253 000 (~4%)

* For region Linköping, 2007.

Handling of plasterboard waste. Peab's supplier of plasterboards receives and recycles plaster waste as well as damaged boards. This service is provided without fees as long as the moisture level for the plaster is less than seven percent. For higher moisture levels a small fee is charged for each tonne. Currently all plaster waste is sent to landfill. Although the cost for landfill is almost 1000 SEK per tonne of waste it is currently cheaper than recycling because of the significant transportation costs.

4.2 Other Suppliers and Products

The deliveries of doors have often been incomplete and are subjected to delays. The incomplete orders have generated more deliveries and increased costs due to increased administration. Another problem with the incomplete orders is that it has been impossible to follow the production plan. When Peab fails to follow the production plan, they are forced to keep the received doors in stock. Stocks lead to increased time spent on searching for the desired product as well as decreased space and increased risk for damages to the products.

The deliveries of kitchens have also been subjected to delays and incomplete orders. The most frequent problem concerns the kitchen doors or rather the lack of them. Not a single delivery that was examined contained the ordered kitchen doors. In addition the supplier of kitchens has not informed Peab when delays have occurred. To get the information about the deliveries, the construction site manager was forced to contact the supplier by himself. These circumstances make it impossible to follow the production plan and Peab is forced to do a time consuming rescheduling, since the installation of the kitchens cannot be completed.

Perfect order fulfilment for these two products, doors and kitchens, are presented in Table 1.

4.3 Consolidation Point, Terminal

Highly frequent products, such as plasterboards, wood products and isolation, which are often standardized, can with advantage be kept in stock at a consolidation point, in this case in a terminal. Using the purchasing and procurement system the call offs in the region should be consolidated. This would give Peab economy of scale towards their suppliers. The terminal enables the possibility to consolidate different products at the construction site, which leads to increased filling ratio in the trucks and fewer deliveries to the construction sites. Another advantage is the closeness of the terminal with the possibility of increased delivery precision. Not all the products need to be kept in stock since the point also enables cross docking.

The establishment of a terminal is a step towards centralization. Centralization would decrease the total amount of products kept in stock. Fewer products at the construction site leads to increased space and decreased search time for desired products. The terminal also becomes a natural consolidation point for the plasterboard waste. When the waste is gathered, Peab will get economy of scale in the transports to the manufacturer. The cost for recycling will then be lower than the current costs for landfill. The greatest benefit from the recycling is, though, the environmental aspect.

5 Conclusions

This case study in the construction industry pinpoints some of the problems construction logistics (or rather construction SCM) are facing in order to help the business as a whole to be more productive and to reach lower costs in the future. The SCOR model proved a useful tool in this case study. However, the use of SCOR was not straight forward. It is obvious that the SCOR model is not developed and maintained with the construction industry in mind. The authors would like to thank Brains and Bricks (B^2) who made this research possible (www.liu.se/b2/).

References

1. Olsson, F.: Supply Chain Management in the Construction Industry – Opportunity or Utopia?, Licentiate Thesis, Lund University, Department of Design Sciences, Logistics (2000)
2. SCB: www.scb.se (accessed July 8, 2009)
3. Vrijhoef, R., Koskela, L.: The four roles of supply chain management I construction. European Journal of Purchasing & Supply Management 6 (2000)
4. Vidalakis, C., Tookey, J.E.: Conceptual functions of a simulation model for construction logistics. In: Joint International Conference on Computing and Decision Making in Civil and Building Engineering, pp. 906–915 (2006)
5. SCC (2009), http://www.supply-chain.org (accessed July 8, 2009)
6. Peab AB (2009), http://www.peab.se (accessed July 8, 2009)
7. Persson, F., Engevall, S.: The shift from construction site to prefabrication in the construction industry: A case study. In: APMS 2008 (2008)
8. Xue, X., Wang, Y., Shen, Q., Yu, X.: Coordination mechanisms for construction supply chain management in the Internet environment. International Journal of project management 25 (2007)
9. Stadtler, H.: Supply Chain Management – An Overview. In: Stadtler, H., Kilger, C. (eds.) Supply Chain Management and Advanced Planning, pp. 7–28. Springer, Berlin (2000)

Interoperability Constraints and Requirements Formal Modelling and Checking Framework

Vincent Chapurlat and Matthieu Roque

LGI2P - Laboratoire de Génie Informatique et d'Ingénierie de Production
site EERIE de l'Ecole des Mines d'Alès, Parc Scientifique Georges Besse, F30035 Nîmes
cedex 5, France
{Vincent.Chapurlat,Matthieu.Roque}@ema.fr

Abstract. This paper aims to present and formalize the foundations of a modeling and checking framework for system requirements management. It is illustrated by the study of interoperability requirements having to be respected all along collaborative (private or public) processes.

Keywords: System requirement, modeling, verification, interoperability requirement.

1 Introduction

For a long time, System theory has proposed paradigms and concepts (complexity vs. complication, system, system of systems, abstraction, multi views representation, interaction, processor, etc.) [1] in order to support and to help an actor involved in a process (engineering, decision, control) focusing on complex system. These paradigms allow:

- to acquire and to formalize knowledge about this system and,
- to acquire knowledge allowing to manage the process itself and,
- to define and to argue what are the most relevant actions having to be done regarding first, the objectives the studied system must reach in terms of performance, integrity and stability (safety, security, etc.) and second, the process environment, resources and context.

Various technical, industrial and scientific domains such as system engineering [2] or enterprise modeling [3, 4] for example, have declined and specialized these concepts and paradigms in order to take into account their specificities. Modeling frameworks, methods, languages and tools have been defined and developed. However, a question appears to have been treated unequally, or even completely forgotten by some domains because of its apparent disinterest or poor understanding of the actors. This question is: how the requirements of the studied system are really and efficiently defined, handled and verified all along the process and for doing what?

This paper aims to present the foundations of a system requirements modeling and verification framework. This framework is applied here to describe and formalize interoperability requirements when the considered system is a collaborative process in

B. Vallespir and T. Alix (Eds.): APMS 2009, IFIP AICT 338, pp. 219–226, 2010.
© IFIP International Federation for Information Processing 2010

which various companies aim to be involved and work together. The illustrative example presented has been developed with the support of CARNOT-Mines Institute during the CARIONER project[1] [5].

2 Problematic

All along an engineering process, the resulting product or service (the target system) but also the process itself (the management system) must respect several needs. A need can come logically from the customer of the target system or from the stakeholders having to interact with the target system during its life-cycle or during the engineering process itself (management rules...). It can be formalized by the use of languages such as SysML but remains usually described informally by actors with possible ambiguities in meaning of words, omissions or repetitions. Thus, to prove that the target system or the process satisfy a need become then difficult.

The proposed framework aims to help actors (customers, stakeholders, engineers, managers) involved in the process first to formalize a need i.e. to list requirements, second to check these requirements on the different models. This work takes into account next hypothesis:

- As proposed in Model Based System Engineering paradigm, and more generally Model Driven Engineering [6], engineering process is led by the use and implementation of models. This induces first to define a requirement model able to formalize needs. Second, it is necessary to enrich existing modeling frameworks, languages, methods and tools considering this requirement model.
- Checking a requirement may use several techniques more or less formal [7, 8]: expertise of the model by a human expert, test on a prototype followed by an expertise, simulation e.g. for evaluating the system performances, formal proof for achieving and improving trust into a model. Some techniques remain difficult to use or not well suited for different kinds of systems (technical, socio-technical). This requires then to rethink partially or to adapt some of these techniques taking into account necessary skills to be able to use it, required delays, required re-working phases to transform a given model into another ones, ...

3 Proposed Approach

The proposed framework aims to:

- Provide a requirement model for describing a need and focusing on what can or what must be proved by using given techniques.
- Provide automatic mechanisms for models transformation, requirement re-writing considering different potential checking techniques and tools. Provide conceptual enrichments for adapting existing modeling languages respecting Model Driven Engineering context and,

---

[1] French translation of characterization and improvement of organizational interoperability in enterprises processes.

– Methodology for system requirements modeling and verification process in relation with existing system modeling enriched languages and frameworks.

This approach is illustrated in this paper by an application to interoperability requirements modeling and checking problematic.

Requirement Model

A requirement is considered as an unambiguous, but may be partial, description of the pointed out need concerning customer, stakeholders, process management and models management. Customer describes what the system must do. Stakeholder describes what they require in order to interact with the system. Last, some constraints and rules have to be respected during the process for example when some technological or organizational choices have been made or when reusing existing models. This work takes consideration to the reference model [2] summarized in Figure 1.

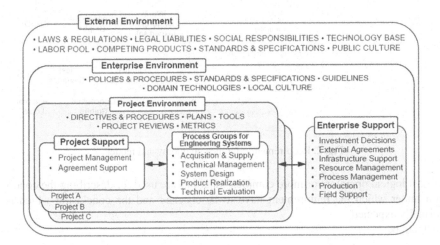

Fig. 1. Requirement reference model [2]

In other words, a requirement formalizes a expected functional (what the system must do) or non-functional (how the system must do in terms of constraint, performance, integrity and stability or more commonly security, safety, availability, etc.) characteristic of the system. Each need has then to be described by a list of identified requirements related to various aspects of the system (behavior, function, structure) before being allocated to the components forming parts of the system. The requirement model proposed is inspired first by the reference requirement tree model proposed in Figure 2 and by the property model [9] as follows. A property describes rules and constraints to verify the correctness, the coherence and the relevance of a model. In this work, a requirement is defined as a property i.e. as a causal and typed relation (Figure 2) between two sets called respectively cause (condition) and effect (conclusion). In all cases, a requirement is described from a recursive manner and a given cause can induce different effects.

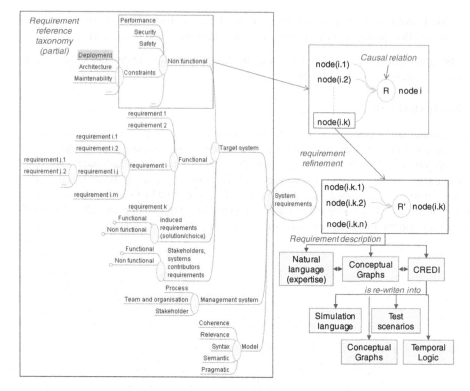

Fig. 2. Requirement reference taxonomy and model

Last logical operators or more complex functions are used for describing the condition under which the requirement have to be checked and the conclusion which is normally expected.

It can be:

- Temporized: requirement depends from time evolution and concerns system behavior.
- A-temporal: requirement characterizes only the structure or the functional aspect of the system without taking into account the time.
- Simple requirement: cause is empty and effect has to be checked in every case.
- Composite requirement: cause and effect are interacting.
  Requirement specification can be done respecting three cases:
- Cause and effect are composed of modeling variables, parameters and predicates extracted from the model to be verified i.e. model has to be transformed in order to dispose of data which compose it. Requirement cause and effect are described by using the CREDI property model and UPSL [9] (Unified Property Specification language) or the Conceptual Graphs as proposed in [10]. They can be formally checked on the pointed out model by using technique as proposed in [10] or re-written into other formal checking tool inputs languages such as Temporal Logic (for example TCTL in the case of temporized composite or simple requirement if the chosen checking tool is UPPAAL [11]) or simulation scenario description language.

– Cause and effect are composed of other properties allowing then to refine requirements from more complicated or complex ones to most simple ones. Their specification can use then Natural Language to allow users to be more autonomous and creative but this limits usable checking techniques to expertise.

The Figure 3 shows a partial view of the interoperability reference taxonomy proposed in CARIONER project. It takes into account different levels and nature of interoperability problems such as proposed in interoperability reference models defined by the research and industrial communities [12, 13, 14, 15, 16].

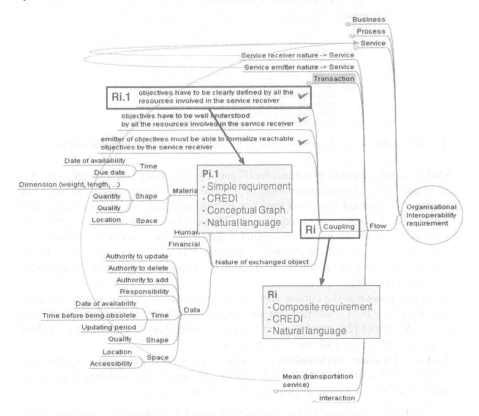

Fig. 3. Interoperability requirements reference taxonomy (partial view)

The Figure 4 shows a very simple example of composite requirement described by using each of the three provided modeling languages.

Other Elements of the Approach

The conceptual enrichments, model transformation principles and checking mechanisms are rapidly defined and illustrated in the case of CARIONER project as follows:

– **Conceptual modeling enrichments:** numerous methodologies, frameworks and tools have been developed for enterprise modeling [4]. They provide adapted concepts, modeling languages and reference models. In the current state of the work, the proposed approach focuses on the BPMN language (Business Process Modeling Notation) [17] enriched by the formal interoperability requirement reference taxonomy model related concepts and relations presented before. These enrichments have been introduced in [6].

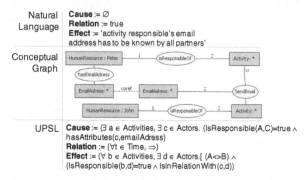

Fig. 4. Example of a requirement described by using three different provided languages

- **Model transformation mechanisms** (Figure 5): this study intent to take into account the limited formalization level of a majority of used modeling languages in industry, the limited requested time for system modeling but also modeling and checking different natures of requirement. The checking technique used in the next phase is based on the use of conceptual graphs [19]. So, a set of re-writing rules under development will be defined respecting MDA [18] principles in order to translate the enriched version of BPMN into Conceptual Graphs inducing a limited loss of information.

- **Proof mechanisms:** the current state of the project focuses only on requirements described by using Conceptual Graphs. Analysis mechanisms are then issued from COGITANT tool [20] and based on three conceptual handling mechanisms called projection, constraint and rule as proposed in [10].

- **Tool development methodology:** six steps are required for developing the supporting set of tools. In CARIONER context, Eclipse GMF modeling framework and COGITANT are used (Figure 6) [6, 21]. These steps are:

    1 - Define a meta model (concepts and relations) describing the required system modeling languages and modeling framework employed.

    2 - Establish the requirement taxonomy model related to the domain and process engineering purpose taking into account the meta model(s) established in step 1.

    3 – Choose checking tools and formalize input languages a new meta model.

    4 – Enrich the modeling languages meta model from step 1 taking into account the requirement taxonomy from step 2.

    5 - Formalize model and requirements transformation rules models.

    6 - Proceed to the development of the tool platform including system and requirement modeling, model transformation, requirement re-writing and other handling functionalities required by users.

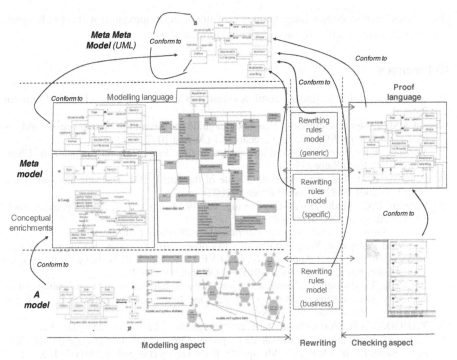

Fig. 5. Meta modeling rules and paradigm

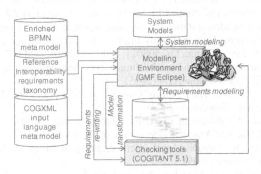

Fig. 6. CARIONER platform

4 Conclusion and Perspectives

This article presents how a requirement model based on property concept can be used all along a system engineering process for improving quality and interactions between actors involved in the process. Indeed, sharing a common requirement taxonomy model, handling our own modeling languages but become able to use checking tools can help collaborative works between actors from different domains to ameliorate their processes. The main perspectives of this work concern now the temporal requirements checking in a multi languages and multi view modeling environment. A research work about multi agents systems integration is now under development. It will provide simulation mechanisms taking into account behavioral models.

References

1. Le Moigne, J.-L.: La modélisation des systèmes complexes, Paris, Dunot (1990) (in French)
2. INCOSE, Systems Engineering Handbook: a guide for system life cycle processes and activities, Incose-Tp-2003-002-03.1, version 3.1 (August 2007)
3. Vernadat, F.B.: Enterprise Modelling and Integration: Principles and Applications. Chapman & Hall, Boca Raton (1996)
4. Petit, M., et al.: Enterprise Modelling State of the Art. UEML Thematic Network. Contract: IST–2001–34229. Work Package 1 (2002)
5. Schmidt, D.C.: Model-Driven Engineering, vol. 39 (2), pp. 25–31. IEEE Computer Society, Los Alamitos (2006), 0018-9162/06,
   http://www.cs.wustl.edu/~schmidt/PDF/GEI.pdf
6. Roque, M., Chapurlat, V.: Interoperability In Collaborative Processes: Requirements Charactersisation And Proof Approach. In: PRO-VE 2009, 10th IFIP Working Conference on Virtual Enterprises, Thessaloniki, GREECE, October 7-9 (2009)
7. Chapurlat, V., Braesch, C.: Verification, Validation, Qualification and Certification of Enterprise Models: statements and opportunities. Intl. Journal on Computers in Industry, 5th issue of the 59th volume (Mai 2008)
8. YAHODA verification tools data base, http://anna.fi.muni.cz/yahoda/
9. Lamine, E.: Définition d'un modèle de propriété et proposition d'un langage de spécification associé: LUSP, PhD thesis, Montpeiller II University (December 2001) (in French)
10. Kamsu-Foguem, B., Chapurlat, V., Prunet, F.: Enterprise Model Verification: a Graph-based Approach. In: International IEEE/SMC multiconference on Computational Engineering in Systems Applications, CESA 2003, Lille, France (July 2003)
11. UPPAAL documentation and tool are available online at, http://www.uppaal.com/
12. INTEROP, Enterprise Interoperability-Framework and knowledge corpus - Final report, INTEROP NoE, FP6 – Contract n° 508011, Deliverable DI.3 (May 21, 2007)
13. ATHENA, Framework for the establishment and management methodology, Integrated Project ATHENA, deliverable A1.4 (2005)
14. Tolk, A., Muguira, J.A.: The Levels of Conceptual Interoperability Model. In: Fall Simulation Interoperability Workshop (2003)
15. C4ISR, Levels of Information Systems Interoperability (LISI), Architecture Working Group, United States of America, Department of Defence (1998)
16. Clark, T., Jones, R.: Organisational Interoperability Maturity Model for C2, Australian Department of Defence (1999)
17. BPMN, Business Process Modelling Notation, V1.2 (2009), http://www.bpmn.org/
18. Miller, J., Mukerji, J. (eds.): MDA, Model Driven Architecture (MDA), Architecture Board ORMSC (2001)
19. Aloui, S., Chapurlat, V., Penalva, J.-M.: Linking interoperability and risk assessment: A methodological approach for socio-technical systems. In: Dolgui, A., Morel, G., Pereira, C. (eds.) Proceedings of INCOM 2006, 12th IFAC Symposium on Information Control Problems in Manufacturing, Information Control: a Complex Challenge for the 21st Century, Saint Etienne, France, hal-00354778 (2006), ISBN: 978-0-08-044654-7
20. CoGITaNT Version 5.2.0: Reference Manual (2009),
    http://cogitant.sourceforge.net
21. Rebai, A.S., Chapurlat, V.: System interoperability analysis by mixing system modelling and MAS: an approach, Agent-based Technologies and applications for enterprise interOPerability (ATOP). In: Eighth International Joint Conference on Autonomous Agents & Multi-Agent Systems (AAMAS 2009), Budapest, Hungary (May 12, 2009)

A Study on VMI-Based Supply-Chain System by Simulation Analysis

Shigeki Umeda

Musashi University
1-26 Toyotama-kami Nerima Tokyo 176-8534 Japan
shigeki@cc.musashi.ac.jp

Abstract. This paper discusses performances of VMI-based supply-chain systems by using simulation. Two types of VMI system will be discussed in this paper: "Single-manager stock-driven model" and "Dual-managers schedule-driven model". Several scenarios would be introduced and tested by using typical example models.

Keywords: Supply-chain management, Business process engineering, Inventory Management, Vender-Managed Inventory, Simulation.

1 Introduction

A supply-chain is a network of autonomous and semi-autonomous business units collectively responsible for procurement, manufacturing, distribution activities associated with one or more families of products. Supply-chain system is, in a sense, a business system for the chain members to collaborate with each other by communication. Constructing of supply-chain is, as it were, a implementation of complex communication mechanisms among suppliers.

Evolutions of information and communication technologies such as internet have enabled frequent high-volume data changes in business communication. Internet-based environment, in particular, has provided low-cost data communication for all kinds of companies, including manufacturers, retailers, and distributors. Such communication environments have renovated inter/inner-enterprise communication mechanisms, and enabled information sharing of various types of data, such as products data, production management data, and demand trends data in market.

Vender Managed Inventory (VMI) system is currently one of the hottest topics in supply-chain management world. VMI systems utilize shared common demand data directly between downstream suppliers and upstream suppliers [1][2]. The upstream supplier (vendor) provides materials for its downstream supplier (customer) independently of customer's detail ordering. The vender continuously observes transitions of parts usage in customer's warehouses, and it independently decides volume and time of which it provides to customer. This system needs well-organized information sharing mechanisms between the vendor and the customer [3][4][5].

B. Vallespir and T. Alix (Eds.): APMS 2009, IFIP AICT 338, pp. 227–234, 2010.

Another methodology is possible to implement VMI systems. This method is that a vendor periodically uses data how much parts the customer used. A Simple communications between vendors and a prime contractor can be also implemented by using information cards attached with inventory stocks. A well-known "Kanban" system is a typical example of this type [6]. A kanban card is a trigger of an inventory pull-signal from a downstream supplier to an up-stream supplier in a material-flow.

Based on the above discussions, the authors are developing a new simulation-modeling framework for VMI-based supply-chain systems. The models are based on a hybrid modeling approach, which combines discrete-event models representing processes in each business unit with system dynamics models representing external management environment such as marketing, transportations, and technological evolutions.

This paper, first, discusses VMI-based supply-chain systems. Second, two types of VMI models would be represented. The models include detail descriptions of business process activities. Third, the paper represents a modeling framework and implementations of simulation models. Finally, the paper discusses requirements specification to implement VMI-based supply-chain systems.

2 Methodologies and Models

2.1 VMI (Vendor Managed Inventory) Methodologies

There are many discussions of VMI system's implementation. These include from a simple re-order-point system to a complex system that shares data by using common databases. Meanwhile, there are very few discussions of VMI system models and their evaluation. VMI system is based on the concept of "consolidated inventories" between vendors and vendees. VMI uses various methods to realize minimum operational cost for inventory management and maximum reliance. Multilateral scheme is needed.

VMI system is essentially an inventory control system that vendors take initiative in delivery of goods. In usual business style, the vendors deliver materials according as received orders from vendees. Meanwhile, in VMI, the vendors deliver ones to vendees by their own decisions. The vendors and vendees must share demand data of final products in market by fully utilizing information network terminals.

We, first, consider a configuration of a simple supply-chain system to model information sharing mechanisms. This small system is composed of a "parts-supplier", "product-manufacturer", a set of consumers (market), a "product-manufacturer's manager", and a "parts-supplier's manager". The materials start   parts-supplier, and arrives market by way of product-manufacturer. And, second, we discuss two types of modeling to utilize past demand data in market: "Single-manager Model", and "Dual-Managers Model".

2.2 Single-Manager Model

"Single-manager model" is a model that a part-supplier (Stock-driven supplier) gives orders to itself by using "Stock-driven" control method [6]. This supplier, located downstream in material-flow, uses two parameters to send materials to upstream: stock-replenishment level and stock-volume level. These two parameters of input material stock in down-stream are determined by the manufacturer's manager, which observes the changes of demands. Stock-driven supplier automatically replenishes material inventories based on these two parameters.

The supplier continuously observes stock volume at the "Product- manufacturer. It starts to produce products when stock volume is smaller than the stock-replenishment level, and it continues to work until the stock volume is equal to or greater than the stock-volume level. This stock-driven supplier generally works according to the following operational sequences.

(1) It periodically observes stock-volume data of a particular chain member.
(2) It starts producing when the stock volume goes down below the stock-replenishment level.
(3) It stops producing when the stock volume reaches the stock-volume level.

Product-manufacturer's manager predicts demands by using past demand data, and it also calculates Stock-driven data (Stock-volume level and Stock-replenish level) to set on. The details of activities of each member are as follows:

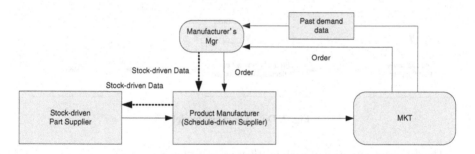

Fig. 1. Single Manager model

- Tasks of manufacturer's manager

(1) It receives orders from customers in Market.
(2) It gives orders to product manufacturer.
(3) It predicts demands by using past demand data.
(4) It calculates Stock-driven data (Stock-volume level and Stock-replenish level), and it set on these data.

- Tasks of product-manufacturer

(1) It receives production orders from Suppliers Manager.
(2) It withdraws parts and starts operations.
(3) It waits until parts arrival, if it does not have enough parts to start operations.
(4) It puts products for deliverer to carry them to customers in Market.

- Tasks of stock-driven part supplier

(1) It periodically observes stock-replenish level.
(2) It starts to work to provide parts, when the part volume becomes smaller than Stock-replenishment level in product manufacturer.
(3) It finishes to work, when the part volume becomes larger than Stock-volume level in product manufacturer.

2.3 Dual-Managers Model

The model consists of a parts supplier and a product manufacturer. Both of these are schedule-driven suppliers, which work according as production orders from their own managers. These managers give production orders to their subordinates independently with each other. It is important that these managers use common dataset of past demands in market.

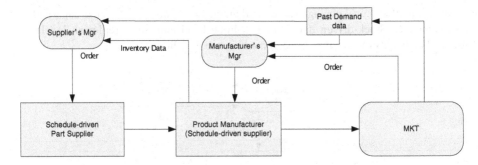

Fig. 2. Dual-Managers model

The details of activities of each member are as follows:
- Tasks of supplier's manager
  (1) It receives orders from customers in Market
  (2) It gives orders to product manufacturer
- Tasks of product manufacturer
  (1) It receives production orders from Suppliers Manager
  (2) It withdraws parts and starts operations
  (3) It waits until parts arrival, if it does not have enough parts to start operations
  (4) It puts products for deliverer to carry them to customers in Market
- Tasks of product manufacturer's manager
  (1) It predicts demands by using both part inventory data at Product Manufacturer and the past demand data in market.
  (2) It gives order to Schedule-driven part manufacturer
- Tasks of Schedule-driven part supplier
  (1) It receives production orders from Vendors Manager
  (2) It puts parts for deliverer to carry them to Product manufacturer

3 Simulation Experiments

3.1 Simulations Parameters

Table.1 represents major run-parameters of simulation. "Replication" is a method to consider that single-run simulation often produces the result that is extremely different values from normal status by the effect of random numbers' seed. N(10,1) means, for an example, the normal distribution, which its mean is 10 lots and its variance (standard deviation) is 1 lot, respectively. In this method, the results of multiple runs with the different seeds are used to evaluate simulation results.

Table 1. Simulation parameters

Items	Value
Simulation duration	100 days
Replications	5 times
Demand volume distribution	N(10,1) or N (10,3)
Interval of purchase-orders from Market to Manufacturer's manager	10 days
Interval of supply-orders from Supplier's manager to Part-supplier	10 days
Interval of Manufacturing-orders to Manufacturer's manager	10 days
Initial volume of parts in Product-manufacturer	50 lots
Stock-replenishment volume	
Supplier lead-time	1 day / lot
Manufacturer lead-time	1 day / lot
Initial part-volume at Product-manufacturer	50 lots
Transportation lead-time between suppliers	0.5 days

3.2 Simulation Results

We used two types of simulation model previously described. Each model used two values of input parameter s that represent standards deviations. We cannot find large difference in major system performance indices, such as resource utilization, throughput, elapse time of entities, and inventory volume average. The difference has been shown in variance (standard deviation) of inventory volume data in product manufacturer.

The following four figures represent time-series changes of parts inventory volumes at product manufacturer. Fig.3 and Fig.4 show the case of stock-driven replenishment model, and Fig.5 and Fig.6 show the case of dual manager model. While the former shows obvious waved curves, the latter shows roughly straight-line. This result explains the reason why the variance of inventory in stock-driven model is larger than ones in dual manager model.

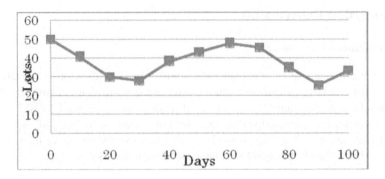

Fig. 3. Parts inventory volume at Product manufacturer in single-manager model simulation (Case: Demand distribution = N(10,1))

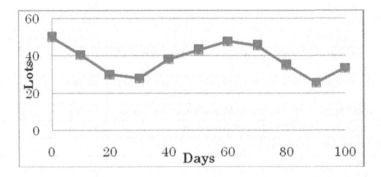

Fig. 4. Parts inventory volume at Product manufacturer in single-manager model simulation (Case: Demand distribution = N(10,3))

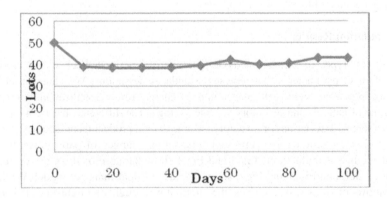

Fig. 5. Parts inventory volume at Product manufacturer in Dual-manager model simulation (Case: Demand distribution = N(10,1))

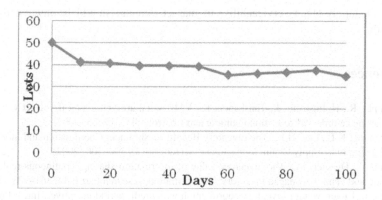

Fig. 6. Parts inventory volume at Product manufacturer in Dual-manager model simulation (Case: Demand distribution = N(10,3))

4 Consideration

In single-manager model, up-stream supplier basically does nothing, while the parts volume in down-stream supplier is between "Stock-volume level" and "Stock-replenishment level". The vendor starts to supply parts to down-stream, when the inventory volume becomes lower than the predefined "Stock-replenishment level". Further, the up-stream continues to supply parts until the volume reaches "Stock-volume level", regardless of actual consumption of parts in the down-stream. The waved curves in Figure.3 and 4 represent such shaker phenomena.

Meanwhile, in dual-manager model, two managers predict demand of down-stream by using common demand data. Accordingly, the supplier harmonizes with consumption of down-stream. Furthermore, the mean of demand volume is constant in this experiment. Accordingly, the supplier provides parts for it's down-stream manufacturer synchronizing with its consumption in respective of its variance of demand.

5 Concluding Remarks

Design and implementation of VMI (Vendor Managed Inventory) system are difficult tasks. Effective assessment methods are needed. This paper has discussed methodologies of VMI system, and it has proposed two types of simulation models: single-manager model using a stock-driven replenishment method model and dual-manager model using common demand data. Characteristics of these models have been discussed through simulation experiments.

These two models stand for a difference in time-series data of part inventory volumes at the prime contractor. The mechanism of the dual-manager model denotes one of system advantages of VMI systems.

Communication mechanism proposed in this model still stays at a primitive stage to embody the whole feature of VMI systems. The detail design of communication model will be needed. Demand prediction logics, inventory management logics, and effects of supply-chain serviceability to market demand should be integrated in a monolith.

References

1. Kaipia, R., Holmstrom, J., Tanskanen, K.: VMI: What are you losing if you let your customer place orders? Production Planning and Control 13(1), 17–25 (2002)
2. Chenung, K.L., Lee, H.L.: The Inventory Benefit of Shipment Coordination and Stock Rebalancing in a Supply Chain. Management Science 48(2), 300–306 (2002)
3. Yao, Y., Dresner, M.: The inventory value of information sharing, continuous replenishment, and vendor-managed inventory. Transportation Research Part E 44, 361–378 (2008)
4. Luo, J.: Buyer–vendor inventory coordination with credit period incentives. Int. J. Production Economics 108, 143–152 (2007)
5. Achabal, D.D., Mcintyre, S.H., Smith, S.A., Kalyanam, K.: A Decision Support System for Vendor Managed Inventory. Journal of Retailing 76(4), 430–454 (2000)
6. Monden, Y.: Toyota Production System: An Integrated Approach to Just-In-Time, IIE (1998)
7. Umeda, S., Lee, T.: Integrated Supply Chain Simulation System – A Design Specification for a Generic Supply Chain Simulator, NISTIR 7146. National Institute of Standards and Technology (2004)

How do the Key Determinants of a Distributed Planning Process Impact on the Performance of a Supply Chain?

Julien François[1], Uche Okongwu[2], Jean-Christophe Deschamps[1],
and Matthieu Lauras[3]

[1] University of Bordeaux, IMS
351 cours de la Libération, 33405 Talence (France)
julien.francois@ims-bordeaux.fr,
jean-christophe.deschamps@ims-bordeaux.fr
[2] Toulouse Business School
Department of Industrial Organisation, Logistics and Technology
20 Boulevard Lascrosses
BP 7010, 31068 Toulouse Cedex 7 (France)
[3] Université de Toulouse, Mines Albi
Department of Industrial Engineering
Route de Teillet, 81013 Albi Cedex 9 (France)

Abstract. As firms search to maximise value through the effective management of their various business activities, it is increasingly important to identify and understand the key factors that can significantly impact on the performance of the supply chain. The Supply Chain Operations Reference (SCOR) model enables to identify four distinct processes (plan, source, make and deliver) that constitute a supply chain. If many researchers have studied the last three processes (source, make and deliver), the relationship between the determinants of the planning process and supply chain performance has not been sufficiently explored. This paper therefore aims to identify and analyse the determinants of a distributed planning process that impact on the performance of a supply chain, including both financial and non-financial elements. It proposes a conceptual framework and a simulation model that can be used to improve the performance of a supply chain in terms of efficiency, flexibility, effectiveness and responsiveness.

Keywords: Planning process; supply chain management; performance measurement; flexibility; efficiency; effectiveness; responsiveness.

1 Introduction

Supply chains (SC) are facing growing pressures due to globalisation, harsh competition, fluctuating energy prices and volatile financial markets. Their strategic goals are set to reduce costs, improve customer services, increase reliability and efficiency of operations, and fast delivery of products to markets. These strategic goals can be achieved by effectively designing, monitoring and controlling the various processes that constitute the SC. The Supply Chain Operations Reference (SCOR) model enables to identify four main processes (plan, source, make and deliver) that constitute a

B. Vallespir and T. Alix (Eds.): APMS 2009, IFIP AICT 338, pp. 235–242, 2010.
© IFIP International Federation for Information Processing 2010

supply chain. The determining factors of each of these processes can impact on the performance of the supply chain.

If many researchers have studied the relationship between the various determinants of the last three processes (source, make and deliver) and supply chain performance, the determinants of the planning process have not been sufficiently explored. Moreover, the few studies that have been done on this topic are generally limited not only to manufacturing (Wacker and Sheu, 2006; Olhager and Selldin, 2007) but also to the financial aspect of performance (Reiner and Hofmann, 2006). This paper aims to study how the determining factors of the planning process impact on both the financial and non-financial elements of supply chain performance.

We will start by developing our research framework before presenting the simulation model. Then, the results of the simulation will be discussed with respect to the determining factors and performance criteria identified in the framework.

2 Research Framework

For the purpose of our study, it can simply be said that "a supply chain links production units, one unit's outputs providing inputs into another unit or multiple units" (De Man and Burns, 2006). It follows that supply chain management (SCM) has to do with the planning, execution and coordination of the production units.

A thorough literature review (Chase et al., 2004; Stevenson, 2005; Slack et al., 2007) enabled us to identify 10 determining factors of the planning process (see Table 1). These are: forecast accuracy and stability, planning horizon, time bucket, frozen time fence, manufacturing capacity, lot sizing, inventory management, cycle time, sequencing and scheduling.

Table 1. Determining factors of the planning process

1. Planning horizon - Small (e.g. monthly) - Medium (e.g. quarterly) - Large (e.g. yearly)	2. Time bucket - Small (e.g. daily) - Medium (e.g. weekly) - Large (e.g. monthly)	3. Frozen time fence - Small (e.g. 1 week) - Medium (e.g. 1 month) - Large (e.g. 1 quarter)
4. Manufacturing capacity - Constant output rate - Chase demand - Mixed strategy	5. Lot sizing - Lot-for-lot - Fixed Lot size - Fixed-period quantity	6. Inventory management - Low safety stock - Medium safety stock - High safety stock
7. Sequencing - Earliest Due Date - First In, First Out - Last In, Last Out - Longest Processing Time - Shortest Processing Time	8. Scheduling - Forward - Backward 9. Cycle time - Slow - Fast	10. Forecast accuracy and stability - Low confidence - medium confidence - high confidence

These determining factors can positively or negatively impact on the performance of the supply chain (SC). Walters (2006) and Rainbird (2004) argue that while the upstream part of the SC lays emphasis on efficiency (which consists of minimising operational cost), the downstream part lays emphasis on effectiveness (which entails an effective response to customer expectations). In other words, the upstream SC tends to be "lean" (efficient) by eliminating wastes while the downstream SC tends to be "agile" (effectively responsive) by providing speedy and accurate response to customer expectations. The expression "effectively responsive" could be broken down into two components: effectiveness (which measures the completeness of the order) and responsiveness (which measures the speed at which the order is delivered). Speed and completeness can be obtained by incorporating flexibility in the design of the supply chain.

It follows that a supply chain can be designed, planned and controlled such as to maximise efficiency, effectiveness or responsiveness. On the other hand, the aim could be to achieve a balance between any two or all of these criteria. A system that aims simultaneously for efficiency and effectiveness/responsiveness/flexibility is termed to be "leagile". Naylor et al. (1999) defined leagility as: "the combination of the lean and agile paradigms within a total supply chain strategy by positioning the customer order decoupling point so as to best suit the need for responding to a volatile demand downstream yet providing level scheduling upstream from the decoupling point." Partial leagility can be achieved by searching for a trade-off between efficiency and effectiveness or between efficiency and responsibility.

For the purpose of this paper, we will adopt the following restrictive and one-dimensional (or single factor) definitions:

- Flexibility is the range (number) of options available to do things and this can be defined as the range of options designed into the supply chain, which will enable it to fulfil customer orders.
- Efficiency is doing things right (Zokaei and Hines, 2007) and this can be defined as the cost of fulfilling customer orders.
- Effectiveness is doing the right thing (Zokaei and Hines, 2007) and this can be defined as fulfilling orders exactly as they are requested by customers (that is, the completeness of customer orders).
- Responsiveness is doing things quickly and this can be defined as the speed at which customer orders are fulfilled.

Given that flexibility (as we have defined it) is a rigid capability initially designed into the supply chain, only the last three criteria can be used to measure the performance of the supply chain. If leanness is linked to efficiency, agility is linked to effectiveness and/or responsiveness, and leagility is linked to all three. This leads to seven possible supply chain strategies

1) Efficiency
2) Effectiveness
3) Responsiveness
4) Agility (effectiveness, responsiveness and flexibility)
5) Partial effective leagility (efficiency, effectiveness and flexibility)
6) Partial responsive leagility (efficiency, responsiveness and flexibility)
7) Leagility (efficiency, effectiveness, responsiveness and flexibility)

In a nutshell, we can say that these performance criteria and strategies are based on the following supply chain objective: *the supply chain should aim to deliver the right quantity ordered by the customer, at the right time and at minimum cost*. In this paper, we simply use *efficiency* to measure the cost component of the above definition, *effectiveness* to measure the "right quantity" component and *responsiveness* to measure the "right time" component.

This framework is represented graphically in Figure 1. It can be used by the planning manager to determine the set of factors that would enable to achieve specific performance objectives, depending on the desired supply chain strategy.

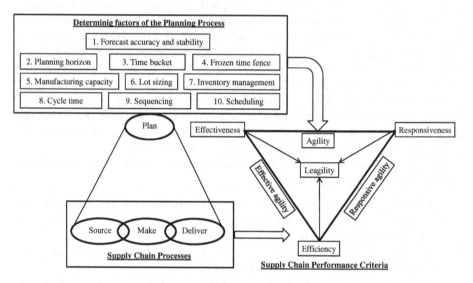

Fig. 1. Linking the determining factors of the planning process to supply chain performance

3 Planning Process Modelling

The distributed planning process simulation is based on a generic linear programming model developed by Francois et al. (2005). The model plans production, inventory levels, replenishment and delivery according to customer demand. In a summarized form, we show hereafter the notations and mathematical model used to describe decision making with respect to the planning process of each of the SC industrial partners. Equations number 2 characterize stock levels while expressions number 3 model product backorders (late deliveries) and shortages (considered as never delivered at the end of the delivery lead time acceptable to the customer). Constraints number 4 represent capacity restrictions with an additional capacity for production while constraints number 5 correspond to the two lot-sizing strategies studied in this paper. A "lot-for-lot" strategy (rule 1) is active for B=0 and a "fixed-period-quantity" strategy (rule 2) is applied for B=1, with a minimum amount (LS^r_p) of manufactured products. Equations number 6 represent the upper bound of the additional capacity and expressions number 7 are non-negativity contraints for all the variables.

Planning model

$$\min C_f = w_1 \left(\sum_t \left(\sum_{r'} \sum_r \sum_p (q_{p,t}^{r,r'}.CA_p^r) + \sum_r \left(\sum_{p'} i_{p',t}^r.CS_{p'}^r + \sum_p (f_{p,t}^r.CP_p^r + b_{p,t}^r.CB_p^r + x_p^r.CR_p^r) \right) \right. \right.$$

$$+ \sum_r \sum_p Ac_t^r.y_t^r \right) + w_2 \sum_p \sum_t \sum_p \sum_{p'} b_{p,t}^{r,r'} \quad (1)$$

$$\begin{cases} i_{p,t}^r = i_{p,t-1}^r + f_{p,t-DP_p^r}^r - \sum_{r'} l_{p,t}^{r,r'} \quad ; \quad i_{p,t}^r = i_{p,t-1}^r + \sum_{r'} q_{p,t}^{r',r} - \sum_{p'} (K_{p,p'}^r * f_{p',t}^r) \qquad \forall p,t,r \quad (2) \\[3mm]

b_{p,t}^{r,r'} = b_{p,t-1}^{r,r'} + d_{p,t}^{r,r} - l_{p,t}^{r,r'} - x_{p,t}^{r,r'} \qquad\qquad\qquad \forall p,t,r,r' \quad (3) \\[3mm]

\sum_p \left(\alpha_p . \sum_{\tau=1}^{DP_p^r} f_{p,t-\tau+1}^r \right) \le CapR_t^r + y_t^r \;\; ; \;\; \sum_{p \in P^r} \delta_p\, i_{p,t}^r \le CapS^r \;\; ; \;\; \sum_{p \in \tilde{P}^r} \beta_p . l_p^{r,r'} \le CapT^{r,r'} \qquad \forall r,r' \quad (4) \\[3mm]

f_{p,t}^r \ge B * LS_p^r \qquad\qquad\qquad\qquad\qquad \forall p,t,r \quad (5) \\[3mm]

y_t^r \le CAP_{SUPP}^r \qquad\qquad\qquad\qquad\qquad \forall t,r \quad (6) \\[3mm]

q_{p,t}^{r,r'}, i_{p,t}^r, b_{p,t}^{r,r'}, l_{p,t}^{r,r'}, d_{p,t}^{r,r'} \ge 0 \qquad\qquad\qquad \forall p,t,r,r' \quad (7) \end{cases}$$

Notations

PARAMETERS				INDEXES	
H	Planning horizon	$CapS_t^r$	Storage capacity	r, r'	Index of PU
$K_{p,p'}^r$	Bill of materials coefficients	$CapT_t^{r,r'}$	Transport capacity	p, p'	Index of products
DP_p^r	Production delay	PV_p^r	Unitary purchase mean cost	t	Index of planning period
$DL^{r,r'}$	Transport delay	CA_p^r	Unitary sale price		
α_p	Quantity of resource required	CS_p^r	Unitary inventory mean cost	w_1, w_2	Criteria weights
β_p	Unitary weight or volume	CP_p^r	Unitary production mean cost	LS_p^r	Product p lot-size in PU_r
δ_p	Space for stocking a unit p	CB_p^r	Unitary backorder cost		
$CapR_t^r$	Production capacity	CR_p^r	Unitary shortage cost		

VARIABLES	
$i_{p,t}^r$	Inventory level of product p in the PU_r at the end of period t
$b_{p,t}^{r,r'}$	Amount of products p in the PU_r delivered in late for its customer r' at the end of period t
$b_{p,t}^r$	Final customers' backorders of product p in the PU_r at the end of period t
x_p^r	Amount of products p never delivered to customer r
$f_{p,t}^r$	Production quantity of product p to launch in the PU_r during period t
$d_{p,t}^{r,r'}$	Demand of product p during period t from PU_r to $PU_{r'}$
$l_{p,t}^{r,r'}$	Delivery quantity of product p launching during period t from PU_r to $PU_{r'}$
$q_{p,t}^{r',r}$	Quantity of component p received during period t at the PU_r from $PU_{r'}$

The criterion (C_f) includes financial and non financial aspects of the performance of the supply chain, mainly ensuring efficiency through the minimization of costs and good service quality (effectiveness) if backorders are reduced. The responsiveness of the supply chain is studied according to the variation of the planning period value.

4 Experimental Setup and Results

A supply chain (SC) instance is defined to assess the sensitivity of the performance of the SC in response to the variation of different parameters. The instance studied in this paper is a multi-stage supply chain structure that produces tables and shelves. Figure 2 shows the key parameters that can enable to understand the discussion of the experimental results. Readers interested in a detailed description of the case study are referred to François et al. (2005).

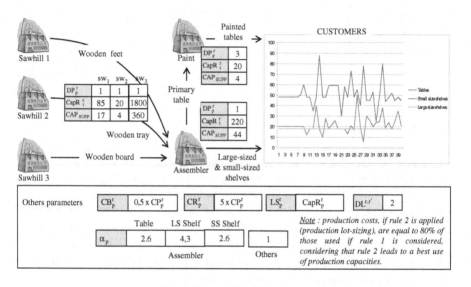

Fig. 2. The studied SC instance

We consider this paper to be a preliminary work that will prepare the ground for a more extensive research in the future. Therefore, of the ten determining factors identified in section 2 (see Table 1), we have tested the impact of only two of them on SC performance. The two factors tested are lot sizing and frozen time fence. For lot sizing, we looked at two strategies: Lot-For-Lot (LFL) and Fixed-Period-Quantity (FPQ); and for frozen time fence, we also looked at two cases: a small fence of 5 periods and a large fence of 10 periods. The impact of these determinants is analyzed with respect to the three dimensions (efficiency, effectiveness and responsiveness) of SC performance, as presented in section 2. Here, we note that efficiency is measured in terms of the total cost of the production plan, effectiveness in terms of shortages (quantities not delivered at all) and responsiveness in terms of delayed deliveries (quantities delivered but not on time). Table 2 shows the main results obtained from a total of fifteen scenarios that we studied. The first scenario considers the use of the normal capacity while the other fourteen take into consideration the additional capacity.

Table 2. Results of the experiments

Scenario Number	Over-capacity[1]	Lot Sizing	Frozen Time Fence	Criteria[2]	Total Cost	Quantity delayed	Shortages
1	N	Lot-For-Lot	5	C	1 026 492€	3650	743
2	Y	Lot-For-Lot	5	C	835 858€	1441	229
3	Y	Lot-For-Lot	5	D	866 713€	1065	191
4	Y	Lot-For-Lot	5	C+D	840 810€	1094	195
6	Y	Lot-For-Lot	10	C	831 422€	1331	200
7	Y	Lot-For-Lot	10	D	859 650€	889	168
8	Y	Lot-For-Lot	10	C+D	835 190€	967	179
10	Y	Fixed-Period-Quantity	5	C	821 735€	1376	218
11	Y	Fixed-Period-Quantity	5	D	855 839€	1275	233
12	Y	Fixed-Period-Quantity	5	C+D	828 125€	1329	236
13	Y	Fixed-Period-Quantity	10	C	875 353€	1732	323
14	Y	Fixed-Period-Quantity	10	D	913 123€	1641	339
15	Y	Fixed-Period-Quantity	10	C+D	887 358€	1678	352

[1]N = No and Y = Yes   [2]C = Cost and D = Delay

5 Discussion and Conclusion

For each combination of lot sizing and frozen time fence, three simulations are performed: cost minimization (C), delay minimization (D) and cost and delay minimization (C+D). We can see clearly from Table 2 that the most economic scenarios are those where simulation is done with respect to cost. We notice that when simulation is done with respect to delay, total cost deteriorates where as the quality of service improves (less shortages and late deliveries). If this sounds normal, an intriguing observation lies rather in the various combinations of lot sizing and frozen time fence. These first exploratory results seem to imply that when lot-for-lot (LFT) is used, a large frozen time fence is a better strategy since all three performance criteria (efficiency, effectiveness and responsiveness) are better than in the case of a small frozen time fence. On the contrary, when a fixed-period-quantity (FPQ) is used, it is better to go for a small frozen time fence. We think that a LFL strategy tries to quickly adapt production to variations in demand, even when these variations are forecasts. Consequently, in order to avoid a bullwhip effect and have a better supply chain performance, it is important to balance this responsiveness capability with a minimum of stability within the inputs. On the other hand, the FPQ strategy tries to optimize production capabilities irrespective of demand variations. It then seems to be more important for a planning manager to track and capture demand variations very frequently in order to be able to use his additional capacity as and when necessary.

In conclusion, as a determining factor, a lot-for-lot strategy can be said to be related more to effectiveness and responsiveness while a large frozen time fence is more inclined towards efficiency. On the other hand, a fixed-period-quantity strategy is related more to efficiency while a small frozen time fence inclines more towards effectiveness and responsiveness. As we have already mentioned, this is an exploratory work; in our further research, we will not only study more determining factors, but will also increase the performance spectrum to include agility and leagility as developed in our framework in section 2.

References

1. Chase, R.B., Jacobs, F.R., Aquilano, N.J.: Operations management for competitive advantage. McGraw-Hill, New York (2004)
2. De Man, R., Burns, T.R.: Sustainability: supply chains, partner linkages, and new forms of self-regulation. Human Systems Management 25, 1–12 (2006)
3. Francois, J., Deschamps, J.C., Fontan, G., Bourrieres, J.P.: Assessing the impact of control architectures on Supply Chains performances. In: 4th International Workshop on Performance Measurement, Bordeaux, France (2005)
4. François, J., Deschamps, J.-C., Fontan, G., Bourrieres, J.P.: Collaborative planning for enterprises involved in different supply chains. In: IEEE SSSM 2006, International Conference on Service Systems and Service Management, Troyes, France (2006)
5. Naylor, J.B., Naim, M.M., Berry, D.: Leagility: interfacing the lean and agile manufacturing paradigm in the total supply chain. International Journal of Production Economics 62, 107–118 (1999)
6. Olhager, J., Selldin, E.: Manufacturing planning and control approaches: market alignment and performance. International Journal of Production Research 45(6), 1469–1484 (2007)
7. Rainbird, M.: Demand and supply chains: the value catalyst. International Journal of Physical Distribution and Logistics Management 34(3/4), 230–250 (2004)
8. Reiner, G., Hofmann, P.: Efficiency analysis of supply chain processes. International Journal of Production Research 44(23), 5065–5087 (2006)
9. Slack, N., Chambers, S., Johnston, R.: Operations management. Prentice Hall, London (2007)
10. Stevenson, W.J.: Operations management. McGraw-Hill, New York (2005)
11. Wacker, J.G., Sheu, C.: Effectiveness of manufacturing planning and control systems on manufacturing competitiveness: evidence from global manufacturing data. International Journal of Production Research 44(5), 1015–1036 (2006)
12. Walters, D.: Effectiveness and efficiency: the role of supply chains management. The International Journal of Logistics Management 17(1), 75–94 (2006)
13. Zokaei, K., Hines, P.: Achieving consumer focus in supply chains. International Journal of Physical Distribution and Logistics Management 37(3), 223–247 (2007)

The Application of Lean Production Control Methods within a Process-Type Industry: The Case of Hydro Automotive Structures

Daryl Powell[1], Erlend Alfnes[1], and Marco Semini[2]

[1] Department of Production and Quality Engineering, Norwegian University of Science and Technology, S.P. Andersens veg 5, NO-7465 Trondheim, Norway
[2] Department of Industrial Management, SINTEF Technology and society, S.P. Andersens veg 5, NO-7465 Trondheim, Norway

Abstract. Lean production has lead to substantial improvements in performance across many industries and is widely implemented today. Certain aspects of lean such as the focus on workplace organisation (5S) and total productive maintenance (TPM) have been applied to all types of industrial processes, while lean production control methods have mostly been applied in discrete and repetitive, assembly-type production. We believe that the real benefits of lean, for example throughput time and inventory reduction, are only realised when lean production control methods are implemented effectively. Therefore, we investigate the traditional lean production control methods of Heijunka and Kanban, and evaluate the concept of every product every (EPE) as an alternative lean production control method for the process-type industries.

Keywords: Process Industry, Lean, EPE, Cyclic Planning.

1 Introduction

In line with King (2009), we choose to categorise manufacturing environments into two distinct groups, assembly operations and process-type industries. Success in lean manufacturing has been largely associated with the automotive industry, typically in assembly operations, and has demonstrated improvements in quality, cost and delivery metrics. However, King (2009) suggests that there is a noticeable lack in lean adoption within the process-type industries. Although certain aspects of lean such as workplace organisation (5S) and Total Productive Maintenance (TPM) have been applied to all types of manufacturing environment, lean production control methods such as Heijunka and Kanban have mostly been applied in discrete, repetitive, assembly-type production. This signifies that Heijunka and Kanban are more appropriate for high volume, repetitive production of a low variety of highly standardized products. It is our opinion that the real benefits of lean production, for example throughput time and inventory reduction, are only truly realised when lean production control methods are implemented effectively. Therefore, the purpose of this paper is to demonstrate how to apply lean production control methods to those manufacturing environments less suited to Heijunka and Kanban, i.e. process-type industries. This research focuses on the application of lean production control methods in process-type industries, and

B. Vallespir and T. Alix (Eds.): APMS 2009, IFIP AICT 338, pp. 243–250, 2010.
© IFIP International Federation for Information Processing 2010

is based on collaboration between two research projects funded by the Research Council of Norway, SFI Norman and CRASH. We would like to state that, although several other control methods exist, this paper only addresses those methods directly associated with lean production.

In this paper, we explore the concept of every product every (EPE) in order to introduce lean production control methods in process-type industries. The paper is structured as follows: We first classify manufacturing environments in line with King (2009). Then, we review traditional lean production control methods, which have been mainly applied to repetitive and discrete, assembly-type production. Next, we explore the concept of every product every (EPE). Finally, we demonstrate the application of EPE in a process-type industry through the use of a case study.

2 Assembly Operations vs. Process-Type Industries

Several authors attempt to categorize manufacturing activities (e.g. Hayes and Wheelwright (1979), Wild (1980), Hill (2005), amongst others). For the purpose of this paper, we have chosen a simplified categorization in line with King (2009), who proposes that manufacturing environments can be categorized into two groups: assembly operations and process industries. Many process industries operate in batch environments with likeness to discrete parts manufacture, whilst, on the other hand, many discrete parts manufacturers share characteristics with the process industries, where high volumes and large inflexible machines with long setup and changeover times require a high level of asset utilization.

Table 1 illustrates the distinguishing characteristics that separate the "process-type industries" from "assembly operations":

Table 1. *Distinguishing Characteristics of Process-type Industries* (adapted from King, 2009)

	Assembly Operations	Process-type Industries
Volume vs. Variety	High Volume, often Low Variety	High Volume, often High Variety
Throughput Limited by:	Labour	Equipment
Size of Equipment	Small, Simple, Easy-to-Move	Large, General Purpose, Complex
Cost of Stopping and Restarting	Relatively Low	Relatively High
Product Changeovers	Relatively Simple, Lost Time and Labour	Relatively Complex, Lost Time, Labour AND Process Materials
Material Flow Pattern	Convergent, "A" Type	Divergent, "V" Type

From these characteristics, it is clear that it is not just the continuous process industries (e.g. oil refineries, chemicals, pulp and paper) that can be classed as process-type industries. Many discrete part manufactures also share these characteristics. It should also be noted that in a typical process industry, although there may be some degree of continuous processing, more often than not much of the production will still be performed in batches.

3 Lean Production Control Methods

Lean production is to a large extent based on the manufacturing principles and work processes developed by Toyota in the 1940s. Lean is often defined in terms of waste reduction, hence a major aspect of the lean movement is just-in-time (JIT). JIT entails producing products in exactly the required quantity – just when they are needed, and not before (Shingo, 1989). Although some may consider other control methods within lean, for example two-bin and ConWIP, the traditional lean production control methods considered here are Heijunka and Kanban.

Heijunka is the method used in lean to level production in terms of both product volumes and product mix. Level production is a way of scheduling daily production for different types of products in a sequence to even out peaks and troughs in the quantities produced. Put simply, Bicheno and Holweg (2009) suggest that Heijunka is a post box system for Kanban cards that authorizes production in pitch increment-sized time slots. A typical pitch increment is between 10 and 30 minutes.

Kanban is a method of control designed to maximise the potential of the Toyota production system (Shingo, 1989). Kanban is typically the card that authorizes production of a certain product. When a product has been consumed from the finished goods inventory (or supermarket), a Kanban card is passed upstream (placed in the Heijunka box) to allow for replenishment of the product. Shingo (1989) suggests that Kanban can be applied only in plants involved in repetitive production, i.e. assembly operations. The application of Kanban is considered unsuitable in process-type industries. This is because, in process-type industries, large investments are made in even larger machines, often at the cost of substantial changeover times. With such large changeover times, introducing Kanban would have detrimental effects to the responsiveness of the production system, and may drastically increase production lead-times.

From previous experience, we recognise that although many of the lean tools and techniques have been applied successfully in all types of industrial processes, lean production control methods have rarely been applied to process-type industries, due to the characteristics defined in chapter three.

4 Every Product Every (EPE): A Promising Concept for Process-Type Industries

In the previous chapter, we explained that Heijunka and Kanban are difficult to apply in process-type industries due to the capacities of the production system, where resource utilisation is the key and large batch runs are the answer. To overcome this challenge and make lean flow possible in process-type industries, one approach is to develop a level production schedule, producing every product every cycle, which is also in line with lean production control principles. We suggest that levelled production is possible through the implementation of a fixed cyclic plan known as EPE. This plan coordinates production by assigning set periods of time to each product, in an optimum sequence. The optimum sequence is calculated by considering the changeover times between each of the products (Andersen et al., 1998).

The EPE concept stems as a result of the lean movement of the 1990s and is a descendent of cyclic planning. Rother and Shook (2003) identify EPE as one of several guidelines for creating a lean value stream. Inman and Jordan (1997) and Bicheno and

Holweg (2009) also agree that producing every product every day is a key lean production principle. As EPE has not been properly defined in literature, we propose the following definition:

EPE is a lean production control method that involves creating a fixed cyclic plan through the levelling of product volume and mix, with a continuous focus on setup reduction.

Although in literature it may be unclear as to how EPE differs from Heijunka, we suggest that where EPE delivers a fixed cyclic production plan in terms of product sequence and volume, Heijunka assumes that changeover times are negligible, hence any sequence of products can be produced at any given time. In support of this, Bicheno and Holweg (2009) suggest that Heijunka be regarded as the final lean tool, because so much must be in place for its success, including setup reduction.

We suggest that the EPE concept is more applicable to process-type industries than Heijunka and Kanban as the length of an EPE cycle can be chosen for convenience, and may be a day, a week or longer. In fact, one cycle of an EPE plan could be considered as one column of a Heijunka box, as it is the time period over which the mixed-model quantity of each product is made.

Groenevelt et al. (1992) suggest that cyclic planning (such as EPE), is applicable in many environments and that the benefits range from shorter production leadtimes and lower work-in-process inventories and safety stocks, to improved material handling and material flow and increased customer responsiveness. We suggest that a fixed EPE plan will also deliver greater stability and predictability to the production environment, which results in less fire fighting and simplified coordination across the value-stream. Consequently, more time can be spent on improvement efforts, such as setup reduction.

The basis of EPE is to make each cycle of the plan as small as possible by doing as many changeovers as are feasible, in keeping with lean principles. Figure 1 demonstrates how production of every product every month can be developed into every product every day, assuming that enough capacity can be created by reducing changeover times or acquiring additional work centres:

One limitation of the fixed EPE plan, however, is its effect on a Make-to-Order (MTO) environment. If current setup times only allow for the production of every product every week, in MTO, this may in fact prolong the lead-time. Therefore, unless the capacity exists for the changeovers associated with every product every day, we would suggest that EPE is better suited to make-to-stock (MTS) environments. In addition, EPE may also be criticised for its requirement for a finished goods inventory, in order to deal with day-to-day fluctuations in demand. However, by

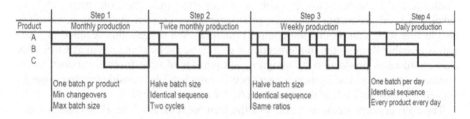

Fig. 1. *Stages of development in EPE* (adapted from Glenday and Sather, 2005)

establishing stability thus reducing the need for fire fighting, the idea is to continuously work on setup reduction, allowing the length of the cycle to be continuously reduced, hence the finished goods inventory can also be reduced in size.

We suggest that three factors must be considered when designing an EPE plan, the first being runners, repeaters and strangers, which is a powerful idea for lean scheduling (Bicheno and Holweg, 2009). This involves dividing the products into those that have high volume, regular demand (runners), intermediate volume (repeaters) and low volume (strangers). Determining the optimum product sequence based on changeover times is the second factor. Finally, optimum batch size (EOQ vs. time available for setups) must also be considered. The design of an EPE plan is demonstrated in the following case study.

5 The Case of Hydro Automotive Structures

The characteristics that distinguish process-type industries, as described in Chapter three (particularly the divergent process structure, large equipment and complex changeovers), are representative of the situation at Hydro Automotive Structures Raufoss (HARA), in Norway. HARA supplies the automotive industry with crash management systems, developing and manufacturing bumper beams for almost all major original equipment manufacturers (OEMs).

This case study is taken from the previous work of Fauske et al. (2008) at SINTEF. In the case, the problems experienced by HARA can be defined as follows:

- Changes in demand and production breakdowns cause frequent plan changes and rush orders.
- Focus on high resource utilisation and large batch sizes results in subsequent high inventories.
- Poor information exchange between processes and lack of collaborative planning leads to confusion and delays in production.

Fauske et al. (2008) mapped the current material and information flows at HARA:

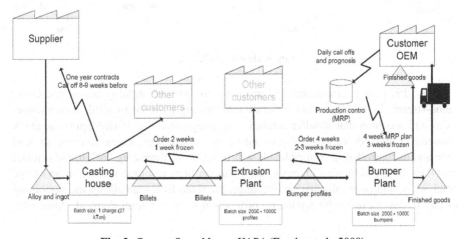

Fig. 2. *Current State Map at HARA* (Fauske et al., 2008)

In order to develop an EPE plan for the bumper plant, HARA's products were divided into runners, repeaters and strangers according to demand volume. A range of cost-effective batch sizes were then calculated for the runners. These calculations were based on EOQ calculations, which are quite insensitive across a large interval. That is, EOQ calculations actually indicate a range of batch sizes for which total costs are approximately the same (see Hopp and Spearman, 2000).

The range of cost-effective batch sizes were used together with demand averages to determine how frequently a product should be produced, for example every week or every day, etc. It was established that an EPE plan with weekly cycles could be developed. As far as sequencing was concerned, similar products were placed after each other in order to simplify changeovers between them. This resulted in a fixed cyclic production plan for runners with short lead times and high responsiveness.

For repeaters, time slots were provided in the EPE plan where no production of runners was planned. Lower demand and more variability made repeaters more difficult to introduce into a fixed weekly cyclic schedule. They are therefore produced at a lower frequency, such as every second or even third week, depending on demand and batch size requirement. It was recommended that strangers be carefully investigated as to whether they are actually profitable, considering both the administrative cost and the production cost incurred from making them.

An example of a levelled EPE plan can be seen in Figure 3:

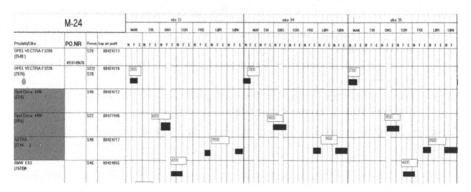

Fig. 3. *HARA's EPE Plan*

This EPE plan is communicated upstream to improve stability across the entire value-stream. In order to achieve the excess capacity required to fulfil more changeovers and accommodate smaller batches, it was suggested that HARA apply the quick changeover methodology (SMED) to reduce the current setup times. In doing so, lead time and uncontrolled inventory levels will be reduced. Returning back to the original problems of frequent plan changes, the focus on high resource utilisation and large batch sizes, and poor information exchange, the fixed EPE plan allows the smoothing of day-to-day variation by balancing production to longer term demand. Also, EPE focuses on batch reduction through continuous setup reduction, and simplifies communication across the entire value-stream.

6 Conclusion and Further Work

The traditional lean production control methods of Heijunka and Kanban are difficult to apply in the process-type industries where resource utilisation and large batch runs are the key due to large machines with significant changeover times. On the other hand, the EPE concept appears to have promising results for applying lean production control methods to process-type industries. Based on cyclic planning, the EPE concept is a descendant of the lean movement and introduces a fixed cyclic production plan in order to increase stability and predictability. The positive effects realised through the application of an EPE plan are as a result of this, and include improved coordination across the entire value-stream and the potential for reduced changeover times leading to reduced batch sizes and increased throughput. In the HARA case, it was illustrated how such a plan can improve stability across the entire value-stream.

A key element in realising a fixed EPE plan is the establishment of a finished goods inventory buffer that absorbs fluctuations in demand. Although this may initially increase inventory, it is essential in creating stability on the shopfloor. This stability enables a greater focus on the reduction of changeover times, which in turn allows for the reduction of batch sizes and inventory.

Future work at HARA will include further analysis and synchronisation of the EPE plan across the entire value-stream. We have shown how the EPE concept has potential for application in an automotive, process-type industry. Another area of future research will involve applying the EPE concept to other process-type industries outside of the automotive arena.

References

Andersen, B., Strandhagen, J.O., Haavardtun, L.J.: Material- og Produksjonsstyring. Cappelen, Oslo

Bicheno, J., Holweg, M.: The Lean Toolbox, 4th edn. PICSIE Books, Buckingham (2009)

Fauske, H., Alfnes, E., Semini, M.: Lean Supply Chain Control in Hydro Automotive Structures. In: APMS 2008 Conference Proceedings (2008)

Glenday, I., Sather, R. (2005), Breaking Through to Flow, http://www.leanuk.org/downloads/LFL_2005/Day2_Plenary_Glenday_Sather.pdf (accessed May 2009)

Groenevelt, H., Johansen, J., Lederer, P.J.: Cyclic Planning. University of Rochester, New York (1992)

Hayes, R.H., Wheelwright, S.C.: Link manufacturing process and product life cycles. Harvard Business Review, 133–140 (January-February 1979)

Hill, T.: Operations Management. Palgrave Macmillan, New York (2005)

Hopp, W., Spearman, M.: Factory Physics. McGraw-Hill, New York (2000)

Inmann, R.R., Jordan, W.C.: Integrated Assembly Line Loading, Design and Labour Planning. Journal of Manufacturing Systems 16(5), 315–322 (1997)

King, P.L.: Lean for the Process Industries. Productivity Press, New York (2009)

Rother, M., Shook, J.: Learning to See. Lean Enterprise Institute Inc, Cambridge (2003)

Shingo, S.: A Study of the Toyota Production System. Productivity Press, New York (1989)

Wild, R.: Production Operations Management. Holt, Rinehart and Winston, New York (1980)

A Data Aggregation Methodology to Assess the Global Production Capacity of Complex Supply Chains

Frederic Pereyrol, Jean-Christophe Deschamps, Julien François,
Pascale Farthouat, and Remy Dupas

University of Bordeaux, LAPS - IMS
351 Cours de la Liberation
33405 TALENCE cedex, France
{Frederic.Pereyrol,Jean-Christophe.Deschamps,Julien.François,
Pascale.Farthouat,Remy.Dupas}@ims-bordeaux.fr

Abstract. Nowadays, no decisional tools allow to assess if an unforeseen customers demand variation should be accepted without creating material disruptions among a supply chain or not. The main difficulty consists in aggregating resources capacities, especially if resources perform different tasks with multiple items. This paper then proposes a data aggregation methodology based on graph analysis in order to assess the global production capacity of complex resources networks, like supply chains.

Keywords: aggregate capacity, networks flows, manufacturing processes.

1 Introduction

In supply chains, decisions individually performed by each decision maker to elaborate its production plans guarantee a local optimal solution (i.e. the best compromise in terms of performances they intend to improve), but do not always ensure the most efficient coordination through the whole supply chain (SC). Many researchers have studied this problematic and have proposed different global solving approaches. Some studies proposed to develop a centralized middle-term planning process applied to the wide supply network. Others showed that performance is better when information (supply, production and delivery plans) is shared between industrial partners [2] [3] [5].

Since practical studies show that a centralized supply chain management represents today a non realistic approach for industrials, SC partners actually begin to share information to propose a common system of aggregated performance indicators. Assuming that this practice will be developed in the future, this paper proposes a data aggregation methodology starting from detailed technical data in order to assess the global production capacity of a supply chain. This study is motivated by the lack of tools allowing to evaluate if an unforeseen customers demand variation should be accepted without creating material disruptions among a SC or not.

In section 2, we will propose useful concepts and models in defining a new approach for assessing aggregated capacities in complex resources networks. Section 3 will describe the methodology used to reduce the complexity of graphs (and data)

B. Vallespir and T. Alix (Eds.): APMS 2009, IFIP AICT 338, pp. 251–258, 2010.
© IFIP International Federation for Information Processing 2010

supporting the aggregate capacities calculation. A numerical example will be presented in section 4 to illustrate the considered approach before concluding.

2   Concepts and Models

The originality of this paper consists in considering multi items performed on operating resources, their capacities being considered as dependant of the nature of the achieved products. The proposed approach consists in estimating an aggregated capacity to implement a global planning process in order to help managers to assess their own production loads in an aggregate way, according to customers' demands. A multi-level decomposition is applied to analyse the physical processes and graphs are used to model the supply chain structure. The proposed approach is defined, considering its application on a single time unit but should be generalized to a whole horizon time.

2.1   Modelling Production Processes by Graphs

The proposed structured analysis framework is based on graph theory in order to assess the capacity of heterogeneous and interdependent production resources performing multiple items.

Let consider a detailed production process composed of a set $\underline{R}$ of operating resources R_r (where r is the index of resource – $\underline{R}=\{R_r \mid r\in[1..R]\}$). These ones perform a set $\underline{T}$ of tasks T_t - $\underline{T}=\{T_t \mid t\in[1..T]\}$. The relations between tasks and resources are expressed through the definition of a matrix Ω: each resource R_r fulfils one or several tasks, and its capacity is defined by a vector $\omega_r = [\omega_{1r}, ..., \omega_{tr}, ... \omega_{Tr}]^T$ ($t\in[1,...,T]$) wherein each component ω_{tr} represents "the maximum number of tasks t performed per time unit when the resource r only executes this type of task". When a resource R_r has no technical competence to perform a task T_t, $\omega_{tr}=0$. The vectors set is synthesized through the matrix $\Omega=\{\omega_r / \forall r\in\underline{R}\}$ which represents the capacities set of all resources involved in production. The production process performs P items (components, intermediate and finished products). Those required for performing the different tasks are defined in matrix $B=[\beta_{pq} \mid p,q \in[1..P]\}$ where β_{pq} is the number of component P_p required to perform the product P_q, i.e matrix B characterizes the bill of materials (BoM) coefficients.

Digraphs (directed graphs) are used to depict two production representations: the resources dependencies and tasks sequencing. Let $\underline{V}$ and $\underline{E}$ be respectively the vertex and edge set of a acyclic graph $G=(\underline{V},\underline{E})$. Depicting the resources network by a graph G allows us to have a flow-oriented representation. Each vertex (or node) $v \in \underline{V}$ is associated to an operating resource R_r and a task T_t (fig 1) according to matrices:

- $D=[d_{vr} \mid v\in\underline{V}, r\in\underline{R}]$ with $d_{vr}=1$ if resource R_r is related to node v, 0 otherwise,
- $L=[l_{vt} \mid v\in\underline{V}, t\in\underline{T}]$ with $l_{vt}=1$ if task T_t is related to node v, 0 otherwise,

Vr should be deduced from matrix D, expressing the vertices set associated to the same resource R_r. Directed edges $e\in\underline{E}$ (also called arcs and noted $e=(u,v)$ $\forall u,v\in\underline{V}$) between nodes model the operating activities sequencing. Fig 1 proposes an example of graph G. Notice that, in this case, task T_2 is performed by resources R_3 or R_4, resource R_2 (respectively R_4) performs tasks T_4 (respectively T_2 and T_5).

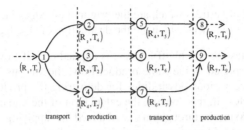

Fig. 1. Production process modelling by graph

In the following, we assume that, in graph G, a transportation activity always separates two production activities; divergence of materials flows is only due to transportation: a transportation task is represented by a node with one incoming arc and various outgoing arcs. Convergence of materials flow is only made in entrance of a production task T_t, which is then modelled by a vertex v with various incoming edges and one outgoing edge (each operation performs one item (one outgoing product) resulting from the production/assembly of one or various components with different quantities).

We also make the hypothesis that a product P_p and the task T_t which accomplishes this one should be assimilated, so that p=t (ex: task T_2 performs a product P_2).Based on this hypothesis, we define a matrix $A=[a_{uv} \mid u,v \in \underline{V}]$ similar to a classical adjacency matrix except that the value a_{uv} associated to each edge (when it exits) is determined as the coefficient β_{pq} such as it is known at the customer's who orders the product p (performed through the task T_t associated to vertex u).

2.2 Calculation of Network Capacities Based on Classical Solving Approaches

The Max-Flow determination in the graph G representing flow interactions between operating resources is one way to assess the network capacity, when each resource r is dedicated to one type of tasks (only one component of vector ω_r is not equal to zero).

In this case, the capacity matrix $C=[c_{uv} \mid u,v \in \underline{V}]$ of the graph G can be easily deduced from the matrix Ω. C is derived from the adjacency matrix of the graph G in which c_{uv} is a weight associated to an edge e outgoing from vertex u and incoming to vertex v. In order to simplify the graph analysis, we assume that bill of materials (BoM) coefficients β_{pq} are taken into account in the definition of capacities c_{uv} expressed on the graph G (through the use of matrix A), so that the unit of measure is "the number of lots":

$$c_{uv}=(\textstyle\sum_r \sum_t l_{ut}.d_{ur}.\omega_{tr})/(a_{uv}) \qquad\qquad \forall u \in \underline{V}, \ v \in Out(u) \qquad\qquad (1)$$

The weight $c_{uv} \neq 0$ of every edge e is completed by a flow f_{uv} such as flows satisfy the classical constraints (2) and (3):

$$f_{uv} \leq c_{uv} \qquad\qquad \forall u,v \in \underline{V} \qquad\qquad (2)$$

$$\sum_{u \in In(v)} f_{uv} = \sum_{w \in Out(v)} f_{vw} \qquad\qquad \forall v \in \underline{V} \qquad\qquad (3)$$

with   In(v)   set of vertices which are the origin of all edges incoming to vertex v
         Out(v)   set of vertices which are the destination of all edges outgoing from v

Expression (3) verifies the Kirchhoff law and is applied only if flows converging to a
vertex v can be interpreted as the same product flow: the various incoming edges of
vertex v represent the various possibilities for delivering the product to the resource
associated to the vertex. In this context, the calculation of the maximum flow through
the graph G (or maximum throughput) is obtained by applying the famous Ford-
Fulkerson algorithm [1] [5] or others analytical approaches [6].

2.3 New Fundaments for Assessing the Network Capacity

Nevertheless, this calculus becomes hard when graphs represent more complex phenomena as operating resources which assemble components in intermediate products
(i.e. several flows of components converge on the resources), or operating resources
which perform multiple items during the same time interval, i.e. the resources capacity is dependent on the product.

The first quoted problem refers to production processes based on bill of materials
with tree structures representing that different components types are required to perform assemblies and multiple material flows income to resources. Basing the calculation of the maximum throughput on the respect of the Kirchhoff law, graphs do not
model these situations. In case of flows convergence representing different components (fig. 2a), the considered sub graph can be simplified to one vertex with one
outgoing weighted arc (u,v). Expression (4) replaces expression (3):

$$f_{vw}=\min_{u\in In(v)}(f_{uv}) \qquad\qquad \forall v\in \underline{V}, w\in Out(v) \qquad (4)$$

Besides, complex production processes should contain resources that (not simultane-
ously) perform multi items, represented by multiple vertices $v\in \underline{V_r}$ ($\underline{V_r}\subset\underline{V}$ is defined
as the vertices subset associated to resource R_r, i.e. $v\in\underline{V}$ | $d_{vr}=1$). We assume that a
constant capacity expressed on the edge outgoing from each $v\in\underline{V_r}$ is not representative of real phenomena when production load on resource R_r relative to a task completion reduces the remaining capacity useful in others tasks accomplishment.

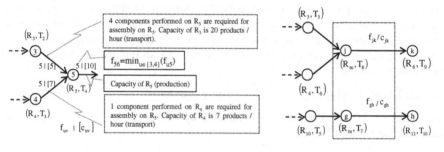

(a) Convergence of different material flows   (b) Resources performing multi items

Fig. 2. Complex phenomena modeled in graphs

Detailed information concerning the coupling of capacities associated to any edge modelling an output flow from a resource R_r should be kept on graphs to assess in the best way the maximum throughput. Considering that capacities on graph G are not always constants, depending on partial loads due to the various tasks execution on a same resource R_r, these variable capacities are dynamically calculated in accordance with any flow on graph describing an output material flow of this resource (fig. 2b). Capacities are updated every time the flows vary, according to the following relation:

$$c_{uv} = \sum_t l_{ut}.\omega_{rt} / a_{uv} - \sum_{g \in V_r - \{u\}} \sum_{h \in Out(g)} \sum_t \frac{l_{ut}.\omega_{rt} / a_{uv}}{l_{gt}.\omega_{rt} / a_{gh}} f_{gh} \qquad \forall u \in \underline{V}, \, v \in Out(u), \qquad (6)$$
$$r \in \{R \mid d_{ur} = 1\}$$

3 A Data Aggregation Methodology to Assess a Global Production Capacity

The proposed methodology based on graphs analysis should be applied recursively at an abstraction level n-1 in order to obtain an aggregate representation at level n. We introduce the notations R_r^n (respectively T_p^n) which reference any resource r (respectively any task t) at the level n. The methodology uses graphs properties and solving algorithms previously mentioned to simplify the graph structure, when it is required to aggregate at the level n (graph G^n), any detailed network defined by a graph G^{n-1} at the level n-1. The aggregation process is decomposed in several steps:

- *Step 1*: any arc e=(u,v) is deleted if $\sum_{w \in In(u)} c_{wu} < c_{uv}$ or $\sum_{w \in Out(v)} c_{vw} < c_{uv}$.
- *Step 2*: based on the detailed graph G^{n-1} describing the resource and task network at the lower abstraction level, a vertices subset $\underline{V}_r$ is defined, considering that the subset $\underline{V}_r$ represents one tasks subsequence (i.e a unique tree/road exists and connects the various nodes $v \in \underline{V}_r$).
- *Step 3*: we define a resource $R_{r'}^n$ (respectively $T_{p'}^n$) which is the encapsulation of resources R_r^{n-1} (respectively tasks T_p^{n-1}) associated to vertices $v \in \underline{V}_r$. $\underline{V}_r$ is then modelled by one vertex u in graph G^n with one weighted outgoing arc e=(u,v) such as its capacity is :

$$c_{uv} = \min_{x,y \in \underline{V}_r} (c_{xy}) \qquad (6)$$

Notice that expression (6) is deduced from expression (4). $\underline{V}_r$ can define graph structures representing parts of a production process with operating resources which assemble different components. Go to step 2 until no new set $\underline{V}_r$ can be identified (any task subsequence is aggregated).

- *Step 5*: on the graph G^{n-1}, we search a vertices subset $\underline{V}_{r'}$ such as this one represents alternative tasks subsequence (i.e $\underline{V}_{r'}$ defines a acyclic sub graph G_s in which multiple roads connect the source to the sink).
- *Step 6*: resources and tasks are aggregated as defined in step 2 and G^n is partially completed. The capacity c_{uv} is deduced from the application of the Ford-Fulkerson algorithm to the sub graph G_s. Go to step 5 until all sets $V_{r'}$ are treated.

Graph G^n results from the reduction and simplification of the graph G^{n-1}, according to the calculation of aggregate capacities. The remaining structure of the graph is then mainly composed of vertices associated to resources performing multi items and should undergo a last reduction in order to keep one vertex associated to each performed product type. The global capacity of the network is then deduced from the graph G^n by calculating the maximum throughputs according to capacities associated to the edges set. The aggregation process should be applied recursively.

4 Illustrative Example

In this section, a SC example is defined to concretely apply the data aggregation methodology.

4.1 Description / Modeling

The studied SC instance is composed of a two coupled multi-stage supply chains structure. Three products are performed: tables (product 1), small-sized shelves (product 2) and large-sized shelves (product 3). For reducing the complexity, transport capacities are supposed infinite, so that only production activities impact the global capacity assessment. Some details concerning the case study from which this numerical example is extracted should be found in [3] [4]. The following graph G^0 models the SC at the detailed level (Fig. 3a).

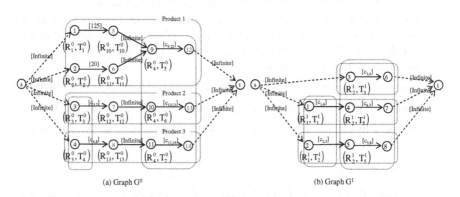

(a) Graph G^0 (b) Graph G^1

Fig. 3. SC modeling by graphs

Arc capacities c_{uv} mentioned on the graph G^0 result from equation (6) such as:

$c_{3,7} = 15 - 1,5f_{4,8}$; $c_{4,8} = 10 - 0,67f_{3,7}$

$c_{9,12} = 20 - f_{10,13} - 1,67f_{11,14}$; $c_{10,13} = 20 - f_{9,12} - 1,67f_{11,14}$; $c_{11,14} = 12 - 0,6f_{9,12} - 0.6f_{10,13}$

According to the proposed methodology, graph G^0 is aggregated leading to the elaboration of graph G^1 (fig. 3b) from which we can deduce the matrix C^1 defining the various capacities of arcs, assimilated to those of the supply chain (represented by a single resource) in relation with the different aggregate tasks (one task for one performed product). Considering a workload vector $W=(w_1\ w_2\ w_3)^T$ in which w_p is the number of products P_p to be performed in the supply chain, we assume that $(f_{1,4}\ f_{2,5})^T$ $= (w_2\ w_3)^T$ represents the order book for the resource R_1^1, and $(f_{3,6}\ f_{4,7}\ f_{5,8})^T = (w_1\ w_2$ $w_3)^T$ represents the order book for the resource R_2^1. The capacity of the aggregate resource (supply chain R) is then a vector, so that:

$$
CAP(R)=\begin{bmatrix} 20-w_2-1,67w_3 \\ min\ (15-1,5w_3,\ 20-w_1-1,67w_3) \\ min\ (10-0,67w_2,\ 12-0,6w_1-0,6w_2) \end{bmatrix} \tag{10}
$$

4.2 Exploitation of the Aggregate Capacity

Each component of CAP(R) is interpreted as the maximum number of each product the supply chain performs, if loads induced by others productions is known. The comparison of CAP(R) with values defined in W allows to verify if orders book W should be performed or not, during the considered time unit. Suppose that the workload vector is $W=(4\ 4\ 2)^T$. Expression (10) leads to assess the supply chain capacity as $CAP(R)=(12.67\ 12.00\ 7.20)^T$. We notice that W<CAP(R) (i.e. the value of every element of W is lower than the value of the corresponding element in CAP(R)), showing that the supply chain may perform the orders book. If we now consider a vector $W=(10\ 5\ 4)^T$, the vector CAP(R) becomes $CAP(R)=(8.33\ 3.33\ 3)^T$. We can observe that 10 products P_1 are required to be performed and only 8 can be completed during the considered time interval (one time unit). If necessary, overloaded resources should then be defined by analysing the capacities on resources R_1^1 and R_2^1: $CAP(R_1^1)=(9$ $6.67)^T$ and $CAP(R_2^1)=(8.33\ 3.33\ 3)^T$ shows that overload is only due to the second resource.

5 Conclusion

The assessment of aggregate capacities in complex resources networks is today a great challenge in developing rapid computational approaches able to show if new orders to perform in a supply chain may cause disruption or not. In this context, we propose first fundaments of a data aggregation methodology, referring to graph theory. Nevertheless, the numerical example being simple, the approach feasibility must be proved through its application to more complex networks. Experiments must also be performed to determinate the inaccuracy of production loads calculations based on aggregated capacities knowledge, relative to results issue from a detailed complex planning process.

References

1. Bertin, R., Bourrieres, J.P.: A multi-level and parametric approach to Max-Flow analysis for networked manufacturing and logistics. Studies in Informatics and Control 13(2), 119–134 (2004)

2. Dominguez, H., Lashkari, R.S.: Model for integrating the supply chain of an appliance company: a value of information approach. International Journal of Production Research 42(11), 2113–2140 (2004)
3. François, J., Deschamps, J.-C., Fontan, G., Bourrieres, J.P.: Assessing the impact of control architectures on Supply Chains performances. In: 4th IFIP International Workshop on Performance Measurement, Bordeaux, June 27-28 (2005)
4. François, J., Deschamps, J.-C., Fontan, G., Bourrieres, J.P.: Collaborative planning for entreprises involved in different supply chains. In: IEEE SSSM 2006, International Conference on Service Systems and Service Management, Troyes, France, October 25-27 (2006)
5. Ford, L.R., Fulkerson, D.R.: Flows in networks. Princeton University Press, Princeton (1962)
6. Huang, G.Q., Lau, J.S.K., Mak, K.L.: The impacts of sharing production information on supply chain dynamics: a review of the literature. International Journal of Production Research 41(7), 1483–1517 (2003)

The Behavior of Suppliers in Supplier-Customer Relationships

Ralph Riedel, Norbert Neumann, Marco Franke, and Egon Müller

Chemnitz University of Technology, Department of Factory Planning and Factory Operations, D-09107 Chemnitz, Germany and Robert Bosch GmbH, Chassis System Control, Blaichach, Germany
ralph.riedel@mb.tu-chemnitz.de, norbert.neumann@de.bosch.com, marco.franke@mb.tu-chemnitz.de, egon.mueller@mb.tu-chemnitz.de

Abstract. Suppliers have become resources for innovation and competitive advantages. To realize those potentials specific competencies have to be developed in a partnership between customer and supplier. The success of those development projects and also the effort that has to be put in depend on several factors. One of those factors is the motivation of the supplier organization. An empirical study shows that the motivation can be described sufficiently exactly by particular characteristics. Moreover particular influencing factors with significant impact on supplier motivation could be extracted. Those findings can be used to control supplier development projects better which in turn will lead to qualitatively better results and a better cost-benefit ratio.

Keywords: Keywords: supplier development, supplier motivation, supplier relations.

1 Introduction

The interface between supplier and customer has seen a constant change over the last three decades. In the 1970s customer focused primarily on reliable supply and price and neglected other criteria for supplier selection. [1] In the following years companies outsourced higher and more complex value adding process steps to their suppliers. [2] This trend intensified the cooperation between customer and supplier. In the beginning customers started to target quality and innovation performance. Later on customers tried to integrate suppliers closer and closer into their product development process. [3] The main objective of this integrated supply management is getting the best value out of the close linkage through optimized product and process design for both parties. Frontrunners of this development are electronics and automotive industry.

As a result the criteria for supplier selection changed over time. Today customers want to know if suppliers are able to act proactively and will recognize their needs. This can be shown for instance by the commitment to zero defects quality processes and best price quotes. [4] In reality customers know that those expectations can rarely be found. [5]

One way to improve the performance level of suppliers in the described direction is supplier development. This is conducted in many industries by the customers itself or

B. Vallespir and T. Alix (Eds.): APMS 2009, IFIP AICT 338, pp. 259–266, 2010.

by consulting companies in close cooperation with the customer. Well known approaches are the activities of Japanese electronics and automotive companies which are accomplished within Keiretsu structures. The outstanding success of the Japanese industry of the last decades is based to a certain extend on this kind of integrated supplier integration into the holistic value adding process. [6]

Although, one aspect is different in Japanese industry compared to Europe or the US. Japanese Keiretsu suppliers are generally motivated for the development by the customer. This results from the special cultural context of Japanese industries. Normally the supplier fears that in a development project the customer acquires too much insider know-how. If this happens it would be possible for the customer to use this know-how price negotiations or, even worse, by transferring it to other companies for building up an alternative supply source.

In this respect it is difficult that the motivation of suppliers with regard to potential development projects cannot be easily verified before the start of a project. Normally both motivated as well as non motivated supplier signal interest in the proposed development projects. In the existing phase of integrated supplier management it is nearly impossible for a supplier to refuse the wish of a customer for a development project. Non motivated suppliers behave comparable to children in front of Santa Claus. They promise to behave according to the wishes of the customer in the next time. Later on they may show a different behavior with the objective to minimize the information flow to the customer during the project which typically lasts between 6 to 18 months. For the customer this behavior means the worst case in respect of his original target. Instead of getting a benefit out of a developed supplier through a stable and productive process and a resulting lower price, better quality, innovations or increased logistics performance the result is the waste of his (the customer's) valuable supplier development resources.

Therefore it is essential to use the supplier development resources efficiently. This must be supported by the identification for the actual supplier motivation before the projects starts. The objective of the study presented here is the development of a method for the analysis and prediction of supplier's motivation for development projects as one important dimension of a supplier-customer-relationship.

2 Supplier Relationship Management

We started this study by searching an existing scientific base for the given context. As we realized that we have to look generally on influencing factors for customer supplier relationship we focused on Supplier Relationship Management (SRM). SRM is a part of overall Supply Chain Management (SCM). [7] The explicit use of the expression Supply Chain Management started in the 1990s in the North American industry. The objective was to realize more optimization potential in the overall value adding process. The main focus at the beginning of the activities was in many cases the optimization of logistic processes of information and materials. [8] This was also one reason for the establishment of the term Supply Chain Management. Defined and standardized steps should support the realization of the idle potentials in the total value adding process. Hereby Supplier Relationship Management focuses on part of direct interaction with potential and defined suppliers. Since for a long time a static consideration of customer supplier relationships was used these considerations became more and more dynamic at the end of the 1990s. [9] Thus these premises changed the role of a supplier from an unchangeable element of the value adding process towards a potential resource which can be influenced through defined actions. [10] Here we also find the starting point for supplier development activities outside of Japan.

One momentum for doing this was the study about the "Second revolution of the automotive industry", which showed systematically advantages of Japanese carmakers versus their American and European competitors. [11] These considerations showed positive as well as negative impacts of supplier behavior on the customer. Negative effects mainly occur by one sided dependencies of a supplier from a customer or vice versa. This can be identified in reality by supplier or customer monopolies. Generally these situations lead to opportunistic behavior which reduces the overall value of the whole supply chain. [12] The theoretical basis for those considerations is provided by institutional economics and transaction cost theory. [13-15]

Fig. 1 shows the important elements of Supply Chain Management and Supplier Relationship Management.

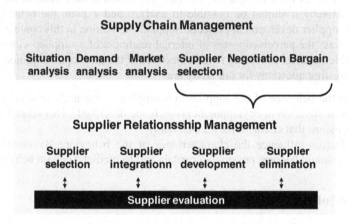

Fig. 1. Elements of Supply Chain and Supply Relationship Management

An important basis for Supplier Relationship Management is the instrument of supplier evaluation. [16] A systematic approach for supplier evaluation should deliver all relevant information a customer needs to start, develop, continue or end a business relationship with a supplier. Since many customers use the instrument of supplier evaluation at the starting point of a relationship it is only rarely used during an already established relationship. [17] Especially as an instrument for defining candidates for supplier development processes there is no method in practical use.

3 Research Question

Based on the discussion above, it becomes obvious that for all partners involved in a supplier-customer-relationship it would be essential to know the factors that influence the quality of the relationship. Of special interest are the factors that influence the quality, effectiveness, efficiency and sustainability of supplier development projects. Sustainability means in this context that the process improvement is adapted and autonomously maintained by the supplier after the project initiated by the customer and processed with the support of customer's resources ended.

As was discussed too, the behavior of the partners, especially the supplier, in development projects may be driven by its motivation. Motivation plays an important role in explaining human behavior. Motivation is seen as the internal condition that activates behavior and gives it direction; energizes and directs goal-oriented behavior.

Motivation is the psychological feature that arouses an organism to action toward a desired goal; the reason for the action; that which gives purpose and direction to behavior. [18] Motivation is a multivariate concept for the explanation of behavior. [19] The concept consists of the variables person, environment and transaction and its scope covers cognitive as well as behavioral aspects. For the analysis and explanation of motivation several models exist, see for instance [20-22].

Since organizations are led by people, processes and projects are carried out by people it seems to be reasonable to apply the concept of motivation also to a supplier organization. It needs to be recognized that this application is only valid in the scope of this study. Hereby it should be possible to analyze and explain the behavior of the supplier in supplier development projects. Supplier motivation in this context therefore was defined as "the perceived status of internal readiness of a supplier with respect to its sustainable behavior according to the objectives of the development project."

The interesting questions for our study are

1. How can the behavior of the supplier in a supplier – consumer relationship, especially the motivation in development projects, be described? This relates merely to the dimensions that characterize the behavior.
2. Which factors influence the characteristics of the behavior? By knowing those factors is should become possible to explain and to predict a certain behavior.

4 Methodology

As a first step a model for the behavior of a supplier in a supplier customer relationship was developed. This model contained several dimensions and characteristics as well as a scale for the motivation of the supplier which was the main focus. The dimensions of the characteristic were derived from literature and also from a workshop with experts in supplier evaluation and development.

Those dimensions and characteristics were then empirically analyzed. The empirical basis of the study consists of data from 60 suppliers of a leading automotive 1st tier supplier. By a factor analysis those dimensions and characteristics were extracted that were able to reliably describe the behavior of the supplier. As a result is was possible to reduce the amount of items and dimensions for the description of the motivation. At the same time the scale for the motivation was validated.

In a second step possible factors were worked out that might have an influence on the behavior of the supplier in a supplier customer relationship. There has been some research on such factors that could be used in this study, see for instance [23-26]. Those factors were also investigated empirically. The data for those factors were collected for the same 60 suppliers as were used for the aforementioned analysis. By a factor analysis and a discriminant analysis those factors were extracted that significantly influence the behavior of suppliers. As a result those factors could be extracted that have a significant influence on the motivation of the supplier.

The empirical investigation was done with the help of two questionnaires each containing a multitude of items for the different characteristics and dimensions and the influencing factors respectively. Furthermore quantitative data describing particular internal and external factors (size, turnover, portion of turnover with particular customers, etc.) were analyzed.

5 Results

The results gained with the project are interesting and suitable for practical application. They describe motivation in five dimensions or more simple one rating status. The workshop with a brainstorming at the beginning of the process had the objective of finding prospective characteristics and factors that would be able to describe the motivation of suppliers as well as influencing criteria from inside or outside.

For the description of motivation 34 characteristic variables were found e.g. candidness, fair feedback, quality of project management, commitment of the top management and so on. These characteristics were arranged content related in five groups, namely corporate strategy, reliability, credibleness, initiative and cooperation culture.

On the other hand more than 80 influencing factors were initially extracted from the expert workshop as well as from literature. Some of these factors are based on experience e. g. role of the owner, managerial style, and experiences with costumers and corporate projects. Those factors could only be captured subjectively. Some other factors are more measurable or objective e.g. legal form, turnover, market position. These factors were arranged in 14 groups, e. g. products, market, future, strategy and so on. In a later discussion the structure was reduced to six groups. The number of factors could be reduced from 80 to 54 by requirements definition. Requirements had been easy access, objectivity, stability and applicability for statistic evaluations. The objective was the decrease of the number of items regarding to data collection.

The characters and factors were then transformed into items. On average each characteristics variable got three items. Measurable factors were taken from other sources. Experience based factors got one or two items. This means that some 180 items/questions had to be answered during the data collection with the questionnaires. Caused by the quantity of items/questions the data collection was shared into two phases – the first phase for characters and a second one for influencing factors.

After the first phase the data analysis delivered interesting results. The correlation analysis showed that 32 items are suitable for the aspired model. For these items the correlation coefficients differed from 0.369 to 0.511 and for these items the correlation was significant on a 0.01 level. A factor analysis arranged the items in 3 new groups. They differed completely from the original content related groups. The groups got new designations as "holistic acting and understanding", "quality of cooperation" and "systematic of acting".

During the statistic analysis of phase one's data the second data collection phase took place. After its finish the same statistic methods had been used to analyze these data. The results were astonishing. The results show that only the factors based on experiences are suitable. The correlation coefficients differed from 0.351 to 0.552 and the correlation was significant. Regarding the measurable factors no significant correlation could be shown. That's why only 10 items from the factors part were used for the model. They were arranged in two groups called "experience and perception" and "initiative and business acting" as a result of the factor analyses. As well as the characteristic variables those groups are completely new regarding their composition.

Both analyses showed that the suppliers can be classified only in "motivated" or "not motivated". "Possibly motivated" suppliers could not be found.

After the configuration a prototype of the model had been validated in two steps. For the first step the original data had been used. The objective was to show the consistence of the model. The reliability achieved some 80 %. That means that 80 % of the suppliers were classified in the right way. In the second step the model was applied to evaluate the same suppliers that were used for the study for the second time. The results revealed that 60 percent had been classified like in the original way.

Furthermore the validation results showed that the range of rating is characterized by overlaps between "not motivated" and "motivated" suppliers. With respect to this situation and to the desired validity the range of overlaps is now called "possibly motivated". As a consequence for practical application most of the suppliers (namely 21) are classified as "motivated". Only four suppliers are classified as "not motivated". Caused by the aforementioned different ranges between "motivated" and "not motivated" a number of 10 suppliers are "possibly motivated". The following spider graph (Fig. 2) shows the average rating across all suppliers arranged in the five new groups classified form "not motivated" to "motivated".

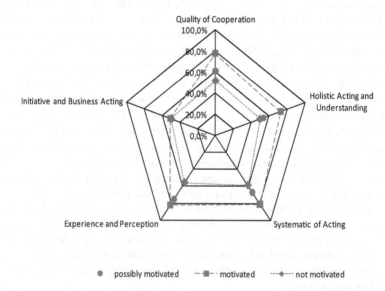

Fig. 2. Classification of Suppliers according to the developed model

6   Conclusion and Outlook

With the study we could show that it is possible to identify the motivation of suppliers in development projects and to describe those factors having an impact on the motivation. Hereby it will be possible to evaluate and to measure the influencing factors. These insights in turn can be used

1. to predict the probability for the success of development projects under given circumstances
2. to actively influence factors with a hindering characteristic
3. to predict the effort needed to make a project successful

The results of the motivation and factor evaluation could be included into Supplier Relationship Management. By using the evaluation results development projects can be focused on those that promise the most success or the best cost-benefit ratio. Moreover it would be possible to give some feedback to the supplier regarding his motivation so that certain characteristics, factors or the whole relationship can be specifically changed.

References

1. Theisen, P.: Grundzüge einer Theorie der Beschaffungspolitik. Berlin (1970)
2. Arnold, U., Eßig, M.: Sourcing Konzepte als Grundlage der Beschaffungsstrategie. In: WiST 2000, pp. 122–128 (March 2000)
3. Van Weele, A.: Purchasing & Supply Chain Management, London (2005)
4. Glatschnig, E.: Merkmalsgestützte Lieferantenbewertung, Köln (1994)
5. Bratzler, M.: Technologiekooperation mit Lieferanten. In: Boutellier, R., Wagner, S.M., Wehrli, H.P. (eds.) Handbuch der Beschaffung, pp. 603–629. Carl Hanser Verlag, München (2003)
6. Imai, M.: Gemba Kaizen. Wirtschaftsverlag Langen Müller/Herbig, München (1997)
7. Ballou, R.: Business Logistics/Supply Chain Management. Planning, Organizing and Controlling the Supply Chain, Upper Saddle River (2004)
8. Wildemann, H.: Supply Chain Management, TCW, München (2000)
9. Knapp, T., Bichler, K.: Permanente Bewertung von Lieferanten. In: Beschaffung Aktuell 2000, pp. 42–47 (December 2000)
10. Ahlström, P.: Presenting qualitative research: convincing through illustrating the analysis process. Journal of Purchasing & Supply Management 13, 216–218 (2007)
11. Womack, J., Jones, D., Roos, D.: The machine that changed the world. Rawson Associates, New York (1990)
12. Ellram, L., John, N.: The Role of the Purchasing Function: Toward Team Participation. The International Journal of Purchasing and Materials Management 3, 3–9 (1993)
13. Neumann, v.J., Morgenstern, O.: Theory of Games and Economic Behaviour. University Press, Princeton (1944)
14. Williamson, O.: The Economic Institutions of Capitalism, New York (1985)
15. Stölzle, W.: Industrial Relationsships. Oldenbourg Verlag, München (1999)
16. Monczka, R., Trent, R., Handfield, R.: Purchasing and Supply Chain Management. South Western, Mason (2005)

17. Gofin, K.: Supply base management - an empirical investigation. Cranfield School of Management, Cranfield (1996)
18. Princeton University, http://wordnetweb.princeton.edu
19. Katzell, R.A.: Attitudes and Motivation. In: Meltzer, H., Nord, W.R. (eds.) Making Organizations humane and productive, New York (1981)
20. Klein, H.J.: An Integrated Control Theoy Model of Work Motivation. Academy of Management Review 14(2), 150–172 (1989)
21. Hackman, J.R., Oldham, G.R.: Motivation through the design of work: test of a theory. Organizational Behaviour and Human Performance 16, 250–279 (1976)
22. Ajzen, I.: The theory of planned behavior. Organisational Behavior and Human Decision Processes 50, 179–211 (1991)
23. Bakkera, E.F., Kamann, D.-J.F.: Perception and social factors as influencing supply management: A research agenda. Journal of Purchasing & Supply Management 13, 304–316 (2007)
24. Das, T.K., Teng, B.: Between trust and control: Developing confidence in partner cooperation in alliances. Academy of Management Review 23, 491–512 (1996)
25. Lee, C.W., Kwon, I.-W.G., Severance, D.: Relationship between supply chain performance and degree of linkage among supplier, internal integration, and customer. Supply Chain Management: An International Journal 12(6), 444–452 (2007)
26. Li, S., Lin, B.: Accessing information sharing and information quality in supply chain management. Decision Support Systems 42, 1641–1656 (2006)

Multi-supplier Systems with Seasonal Demand⋆

Ekaterina Bulinskaya and Larisa Afanasyeva

Department of Mathematics and Mechanics,
Moscow State University, Moscow 119991, Russia,
ebulinsk@mech.math.msu.su

Abstract. Multi-supplier inventory systems with seasonal demand are investigated via queuing theory methods in the framework of cost approach. Optimal distribution of replenishment orders between suppliers is obtained under assumption of make-to-order strategy. To this end asymptotic analysis of systems behavior is performed. We apply various mathematical tools such as weak convergence and use properties of regenerative, doubly stochastic Poisson and Markov processes.

Keywords: Multi-supplier systems, seasonal demand, queuing theory approach.

1 Introduction

The aim of this research is twofold. On one hand, we would like to further develop the investigation of inventory systems via queuing theory methods. One of the first interpretations of inventory models as queuing ones was given in the book [4]. Since then many researchers have used such analogies, see, e.g., [2], [7]. On the other hand, we are interested in the study of seasonal demand impact on the inventory policies in systems with many suppliers. A single supplier is assumed to be available in many inventory control models. However, there exist such situations in which more than one supplier is necessary to reduce the total system cost or to sustain a desired service standard. Multi-supplier strategies can create a suppliers competition and ensure their providing faster delivery, see, e.g., [5]. The models considered below can be applied to logistics in agriculture or fuel supply in countries with continental climate. Due to lack of space we omit almost all proofs. Moreover, we consider only make-to-order (MTO) strategy.

2 Model Description

The system consists of one dealer (or producer) and N suppliers. Let customers (each demanding a unit of product) arrive according to a Poisson flow with intensity $\lambda(t)$. To take into account the seasonality of demand we assume $\lambda(t)$ to be periodic function with the period T. A customer arriving at time t is satisfied immediately if inventory on hand is positive, waiting otherwise. It is

---

⋆ The research was supported by RFBR grant 10-01-00266a.

B. Vallespir and T. Alix (Eds.): APMS 2009, IFIP AICT 338, pp. 267–274, 2010.

also supposed that each time when a product unit is demanded an order is sent to the i-th supplier with probability α_i, $\alpha_i \geq 0$, $\sum_{i=1}^{N} \alpha_i = 1$. Such a procedure is the result of application of continuous-review $(S-1, S)$ policy for any S.

Each supplier has a random delivery time. Suppose that arriving orders are served according to FIFO rule (First In First Out). The order processing time of the i-th supplier has a distribution function $B_i(x)$ with finite mean $b^{(i)}$ and second moment $b_2^{(i)}$. It is well known that under above assumptions the input flow of orders to the i-th supplier is a Poisson one with periodic intensity $\alpha_i \lambda(t)$. Thus, we have an open queuing network consisting of N independent queuing systems of type $M(t)|GI|1|\infty$ working in parallel.

There exists a limit cyclic distribution $\mathsf{P}_j^{(i)}(t) = \lim_{n \to \infty} \mathsf{P}(q_i(nT + t) = j)$ iff $\rho_i = \alpha_i \lambda b^{(i)} < 1$, $i = 1, \ldots, N$, where $\lambda = T^{-1} \int_0^T \lambda(y)\, dy$ and $q_i(t)$ is the orders number in the i-th node of network at time t, see, e.g., [1].

2.1   Objective Function

We consider optimization of the system performance from the dealer view-point. Namely, the objective function we are going to minimize is the long-run average costs per unit time under MTO strategy $(S = 0)$. We take into account only unit stock-out cost c_s and want to choose α_i, $i = 1, \ldots, N$, providing the minimum of the function

$$W(\alpha_1, \ldots, \alpha_N) = c_s \sum_{j=1}^{\infty} j \mathsf{P}_j$$

with $\mathsf{P}_j = T^{-1} \int_0^T \mathsf{P}_j(y)\, dy$, here $\mathsf{P}_j(y) = \mathsf{P}\left(\sum_{i=1}^{N} q_i(y) = j\right)$.

A model of this type was considered in [2] under assumption that Poisson input has a constant intensity λ and each of the nodes is $M|M|1$ system.

2.2   Seasonal Demand and Periodic Orders Processing

Taking into account the seasonal demand we get, in the simplest case, the system of the type $M(t)|M(t)|1|\infty$ in each node. Thus, the input flow to the network is Poisson with intensity $\lambda(t)$. Service intensity $\nu_i(t)$ in the i-th node also depends on time. Moreover, functions $\lambda(t)$ and $\nu_i(t)$ are periodic with period T. The cyclic limit distribution exists if $\alpha_i \lambda < \nu_i$, $i = 1, \ldots, N$, with $\lambda = T^{-1} \int_0^T \lambda(y)\, dy$ and $\nu_i = T^{-1} \int_0^T \nu_i(y)\, dy$. A system $M(t)|M(t)|1|\infty$ was investigated in [6] under assumption that initially the system has k orders. Introducing a time transformation $\tau =: \tau(t) = \int_0^t \nu(y)\, dy$ one can obtain the following system of differential equations for the probabilities $Q_j(\tau) = \mathsf{P}(q(\tau) = j)$

$$Q_0'(\tau) = -Q_0(\tau) + \gamma(\tau)Q_1(\tau),$$
$$Q_j' = -(1 + \gamma(\tau))Q_j(\tau) + Q_{j-1}(\tau) + \gamma(\tau)Q_{j+1}(\tau), \quad j > 0, \tag{1}$$

where $\gamma(\tau) = \nu(\tau)\lambda^{-1}(\tau)$.

If $\nu_i(t) = \beta_i\lambda(t)$ then for the i-th node we have $\gamma_i(t) = \beta_i$ and (1) is a system of differential equations with constant coefficients. It is easily shown that, for $\alpha_i < \beta_i$, $i = 1, \ldots, N$, there exist

$$\lim_{\tau \to \infty} Q_j^{(i)}(\tau) = \lim_{n \to \infty} \mathsf{P}(q_i(nT + t) = j) = \rho_i^j(1 - \rho_i), \quad j \ge 0 \;.$$

Thus, the cyclic distribution does not depend on time and coincides with that considered in [2]. If $\gamma_i(t) \ne \beta_i$ it is possible to propose an algorithm for solving (1), hence, for calculation of objective function and its minimization.

2.3 Arbitrary Service Times

To analyze a system of type $M(t)|GI|1|\infty$ with an arbitrary service distribution function $B(x)$ having two finite moments b and b_2 it is useful to study the Markov process $(q(t), \zeta_t)$. Here $q(t)$ is the customers number in the system and ζ_t is the time a customer has been already served (if $q(t) > 0$). Introducing $\mathsf{P}_j(t, x) = \mathsf{P}(q(t) = j, \zeta_t \le x)$ and densities $p_j(t, x) = \partial \mathsf{P}_j(t, x)/\partial x$ we get, as usual, the differential equations for the functions $g_0(t, x) = p_0(t, x)$ and $g_j(t, x) = p_j(t, x)/[1 - B(x)]$, $j > 0$. Solving the system one obtains the cyclic distribution.

Considering MTO strategy we can use the following procedure to calculate the objective function. Denote by $V(t)$ virtual waiting time. As shown in [1], in cyclic regime $m(t) = \mathsf{E}V(t)$ has the following form

$$m(t) = \frac{\lambda b_2}{2(1 - \rho)} - \frac{T(1 - \rho)}{2} + \pi(t) - \frac{1}{T(1 - \rho)} \int_t^{t+T} \pi(y)\mathsf{P}_0(y) \, dy$$

with $\pi(t) = b\Lambda(t) - t$, $\Lambda(t) = \int_0^t \lambda(y) \, dy$.

According to Little's formula, see, e.g., [9]

$$\mathsf{E}q = T^{-1} \int_0^T \mathsf{E}q(t) \, dt = \lambda T^{-1} \int_0^T m(t) \, dt + \rho \;.$$

In some cases it is possible to take $1 - \rho$ as a first approximation for $\mathsf{P}_0(y)$.

Since it is impossible, with rare exceptions, to find the explicit form of cyclic distribution an important role belongs to the asymptotic analysis.

3   Asymptotic Analysis of Systems with Periodic Input

Considering approximations of cyclic distributions there arise a lot of questions to answer, among them the following:

- how one obtains the estimates of approximation precision using instead of initial periodic intensity $\lambda(t)$ a simpler one, for example, a step-function,
- whether it is possible to estimate the fluctuation of system characteristics, in particular $\mathsf{E}q(t)$, on interval T (period) because that enables us to decide when we can disregard the dependence of intensity on time,
- it is useful to get some limit theorems concerning the heavy ($\rho \approx 1$, $\rho < 1$) or light ($\rho \approx 0$) traffic, moreover, we can take into account such properties of intensity as its being slow or quick varying function and so on.

3.1   Sensitivity Analysis

In order to find a class of functions $\lambda(t)$ for which one can use a certain approximation calculating the cyclic distribution it is necessary to answer the above mentioned questions. Moreover, for different values of parameters α_i, $i = 1, \ldots, N$, some of the network nodes may be in conditions of heavy traffic, the others having light traffic. Sensitivity analysis of queuing systems with respect to their input intensities is based on the paper [8] where it is established that the function $H(t, x) = \mathsf{P}(V(t) \leq x)$ is a probability of non-crossing a certain boundary by a compound Poisson process. Below we formulate one of the results using this function.

Consider a family of periodic intensities $\{\lambda_\varepsilon(t), \ \varepsilon > 0\}$. All the characteristics for the system with intensity $\lambda_\varepsilon(t)$ will be labeled by ε. Assume also that $\rho < 1$, $\rho_\varepsilon < 1$. For any $t \in [0, T]$, $x \in [0, \infty)$ and $\varepsilon > 0$ there exists

$$h(t, x, \varepsilon) = \sup_{v \geq 0, \, |x-v| \leq \lambda_*^{-1}\varepsilon, \, 0 \leq t-u \leq \lambda_*^{-1}\varepsilon} \partial H(u, v)/\partial v \ ,$$

where $\lambda_* = \inf_{t \in [0,T]} \lambda(t)$.

Theorem 1. *Let $\lambda_\varepsilon = \lambda$ and $\max_{t \in [0,T]} |\Lambda_\varepsilon(t) - \Lambda(t)| < \varepsilon$ then, for any $t \in [0, T]$ and $x \geq 0$, the following inequality is valid*

$$|H(t, x) - H_\varepsilon(t, x)| \leq 2\lambda_*^{-1}[h(t, x, 2\varepsilon) + \lambda^*]\varepsilon, \qquad \lambda^* = \sup_{t \in [0,T]} \lambda(t) \ .$$

In particular, for $\lambda(t) \equiv \lambda$ one has $|H_\varepsilon(t, x) - \Phi_\lambda(x)| \leq 2\varepsilon$, here $\Phi_\lambda(x)$ is a stationary distribution of virtual waiting time $V(t)$ in a system $M|GI|1|\infty$ with input intensity λ.

Theorem 1 gives sufficient conditions for using the stationary distribution $\Phi_\lambda(x)$ as approximation of cyclic limit distribution.

3.2   Limit Theorems

Heavy Traffic. Consider a family S_ε of single-server queuing systems with service distribution function $B(x)$ and Poisson input with intensity $\lambda_\varepsilon(t)$ depending on time t. Heavy traffic means that $\rho_\varepsilon \nearrow 1$, as $\varepsilon \to \varepsilon_0$. Denote by $q_\varepsilon(t)$ the customers number in S_ε at time t and $G_\varepsilon(t, x) = \mathsf{P}(q_\varepsilon(t) \leq x)$ its cyclic distribution.

Theorem 2. *Let $\lambda_\varepsilon(t) = \varepsilon\lambda(t)$ and $\rho = bT^{-1} \int_0^T \lambda(y)\,dy < 1$. Then*

$$G_\varepsilon(t, x(1 - \varepsilon\rho)^{-1}) \to 1 - \exp(-2b^2 x/b_2), \qquad as \quad \varepsilon \to \rho^{-1} \ .$$

Proof. Asymptotic behavior of $V_\varepsilon(t)$ and $bq_\varepsilon(t)$ is the same, as $\varepsilon \to \rho^{-1}$. Therefore it is sufficient to investigate the function $H_\varepsilon(t, x) = \mathsf{P}(V_\varepsilon(t) \leq x)$. This function satisfies the Takacs equation, see, e.g., [9]. Hence, using the periodicity, it is possible to obtain for the Laplace transform $H_\varepsilon^*(t, s) = \int_0^\infty e^{-sx} H_\varepsilon(t, dx)$ the following expression

$$\frac{s \int_0^T H_\varepsilon(u+t, 0) \exp\{-su + \varepsilon(1 - b^*(s))(\Lambda(t+u) - \Lambda(t))\} \, du}{1 - \exp\{(-s + \varepsilon\lambda(1 - b^*(s))T\}}$$

with $b^*(s) = \int_0^\infty e^{-sx} \, dB(x)$.

This enables us to establish that $H_\varepsilon^*(t, s(1 - \varepsilon\rho)) \to (1 + sb_2/2b)^{-1}$, whence easily follows the desired statement. $\square$

The result of Theorem 2 can be used to obtain the representation of $\mathsf{E}q_\varepsilon(t)$, as $\varepsilon \nearrow \rho^{-1}$, in the form $\lambda b_2[(2b^2(1 - \varepsilon\rho) + u(t) + O(1 - \varepsilon\rho)]^{-1}$. Here $u(t)$ is given by

$$c_1 \lambda^{-2} T^{-1} \int_t^{t+T} \lambda(y)[\Lambda(y) - \Lambda(t)] \, dy + (\rho T)^{-1} \int_t^{t+T} (y - t)\lambda(y) \, dy + c_2$$

where $c_1 = (T - b + be^{-T/b})[Tb(1 - e^{-T/b})]^{-1}$ and c_2 is a constant that can be calculated. It is worth noting that points of extrema for $u(t)$ are obtained by solving the equation $\lambda(t) = \lambda$. This lets us estimate the fluctuation of the function $\mathsf{E}q_\varepsilon(t)$ on interval of length T (period) and decide whether it is possible to approximate it by a constant when the traffic intensity is close to 1.

Light Traffic. Let $\lambda_\varepsilon(t) = \varepsilon\lambda(t)$ and $\varepsilon \to 0$. It is not difficult to establish that

$$\mathsf{P}_0^\varepsilon(t) = \mathsf{P}(q_\varepsilon(t) = 0) = H_\varepsilon(t, 0) = 1 - \varepsilon \int_0^\infty \lambda(t - x)[1 - B(x)] \, dx + o(\varepsilon) \,.$$

This is useful for obtaining the term of order ε in expression of the virtual waiting time mean as well as the mean customers number. For getting the terms of higher order in ε it is necessary to use the following theorem proved in [3].

Theorem 3. *Let $\int_0^\infty x^{n^2+1+\delta} \, dB(x) < \infty$ for some $\delta > 0$ and positive integer n. Then there exist functions $F_i(t, y)$, $i = 1, \ldots, n$, such that*

$$H_\varepsilon(t, y) = 1 - \sum_{i=1}^n \varepsilon^i F_i(t, y) + o(\varepsilon^n) \,.$$

An algorithm for obtaining functions $F_i(t, y)$ is also provided.

Slowly Varying Intensities. It is natural to suppose intensity to be slowly varying treating the seasonal demand. As above we consider a family of systems S_ε with intensity depending on ε. However now we assume $\lambda_\varepsilon(t) = \lambda(\varepsilon t)$ with periodic $\lambda(t)$. Thus period of $\lambda_\varepsilon(t)$ is equal to $T\varepsilon^{-1}$ and grows, as $\varepsilon \to 0$.

The main role in cyclic distribution analysis plays now function $\mu(t)$ given by

$$\mu(t) = \max_{0 \le y \le t} [\mu(0) + \pi(t), \pi(t) - \pi(y)].$$

If $b\lambda(y) \leq 1$ for all y, setting $\mu(0) = 0$ we get $\mu(y) \equiv 0$. Otherwise we move the origin to the point of absolute minimum of $\mu(y)$ on interval of length T, getting $\mu(0) = 0$ and $\mu(t) = \pi(t) - \min_{0 \leq y \leq t} \pi(y)$.

Theorem 4. *Let $\lambda(t)$ be piecewise continuous, $\rho = \lambda b < 1$ and $b_2 < \infty$. If t_0 is a continuity point for $\lambda(t)$, moreover, $\lambda(t_0) > 0$ and $\mu(t) = 0$ in some neighborhood of t_0, then $\Pi_\varepsilon(\varepsilon^{-1} t_0, z) \to P_{\lambda(t_0)}(z)$, as $\varepsilon \to 0$. Here $\Pi_\varepsilon(t, z)$ is a probability generating function of customers number in system S_ε, whereas $P_\lambda(z)$ corresponds to the system $M|GI|1|\infty$ with constant input intensity λ and has the form*

$$P_\lambda(z) = (1 - \rho)(1 - z)[b^*(\lambda(1 - z)) - z]^{-1} .$$

Moreover,

$$\mathsf{E}q_\varepsilon(\varepsilon^{-1} t_0) \to m(\lambda(t_0), b, b_2), \quad as \quad \varepsilon \to 0,$$

where $m(\lambda, b, b_2) = [2(1 - \rho)]^{-1}[\lambda b_2 + 2b(1 - \rho)]$.

Proof is based on the relation obtained for $H_\varepsilon^*(t, s)$ in Theorem 2.

Thus under assumptions of Theorem 4 one can use the stationary distribution for the system with input intensity $\lambda(t_0)$ as approximation for the cyclic distribution. The error of such approximation depends on the convergence rate to stationary distribution in system $M|GI|1|\infty$ with input intensity $\lambda(t_0)$.

Assume $\lambda(t)$ to be slowly varying step-function and $\lambda^* > b^{-1}$. In practice that means $b \ll T$. If $\lambda(t_0) > b^{-1}$ then $q(t_0)$ is well approximated by $\mu(t_0)/b$ according to the following

Theorem 5. *If $\rho = \lambda b < 1$ then $\hat{q}_\varepsilon(t) = \varepsilon q_\varepsilon(\varepsilon^{-1} t)$ converges in probability to $\mu(t)$, as $\varepsilon \to 0$, for any $t \in [0, T]$.*

Proof can be found in [1].

4   Application of Limit Theorems to Objective Function

Recall that under MTO strategy objective function is equal to

$$c_s \sum_{i=1}^{N} \mathsf{E}q_i = c_s T^{-1} \sum_{i=1}^{N} \int_0^T m(\alpha_i \lambda(t), b^{(i)}, b_2^{(i)}) \, dt .$$

The choice of approximation for $m(\cdot, \cdot, \cdot)$, as we have already seen, depends on values of $\rho_i = \alpha_i \lambda b^{(i)}$ and behavior of $\lambda(t)$ on interval T. Theorem 1 enables us to estimate the fluctuations of $m(\alpha_i \lambda(t), b^{(i)}, b_2^{(i)})$ and decide whether it can be replaced by the stationary mean $m(\alpha_i \lambda, b^{(i)}, b_2^{(i)})$ where $\lambda = T^{-1} \int_0^T \lambda(t) \, dt$ and expression for $m(\lambda, b, b_2)$ is given in Theorem 4.

If the answer is negative, it is necessary to use Theorem 2 for $\rho \approx 1$, that is, take $\mathsf{E}q_i = \lambda b_2^{(i)} (b^{(i)})^{-2}[2(1 - \alpha_i \lambda b^{(i)})]^{-1}$. For α_i such that $\rho \approx 0$, according to Theorem 3, we set $\mathsf{E}q_i = \alpha_i T^{-1} \int_0^\infty \lambda(t - y)[1 - B_i(y)] \, dy$. For ρ_i sufficiently far from 0 and 1 it is possible to apply Theorems 4 and 5. Thus, if $\alpha_i \lambda(t) b^{(i)} < 1$ for all $t \in [0, T]$ and $i = 1, \ldots, N$ the objective function has the form

$$W(\alpha_1, \ldots, \alpha_N) = c_s T^{-1} \sum_{i=1}^{N} \int_0^T \frac{\alpha_i \lambda(t) b_2^{(i)} + 2b^{(i)}(1 - \alpha_i \lambda(t) b^{(i)})}{2(1 - \alpha_i \lambda(t) b^{(i)})} \, dt \ .$$

If $\alpha_i \lambda(t) b^{(i)} > 1$ for some i and t, then in a neighborhood of this point it is necessary to use $\mu(t)/b^{(i)}$ instead of corresponding $m(\alpha_i \lambda, b^{(i)}, b_2^{(i)})$.

Thus asymptotical analysis of systems behavior gives the possibility to propose an effective algorithm of $W(\alpha_1, \ldots, \alpha_N)$ calculation and to find numerically the optimal policy of orders placement under seasonal demand. We can also use the reliability approach and choose parameters α_i, $i = 1, \ldots, N$, maximizing the service level of customers.

4.1   Example

Assume the input intensity to be a constant λ. Each supplier processes the orders as $M|GI|1$ system.

Objective function $\sum_{i=1}^{N} [\alpha_i \rho_i - \alpha_i^2 \rho_i^2 + (\alpha_i^2 \lambda^2 b_2^{(i)}/2)](1 - \alpha_i \rho_i)^{-1}$ is convex in $\alpha_1, \ldots, \alpha_N$. We minimize it introducing the Lagrange multiplier β. Thus, we have to solve equations

$$\rho_i - \beta + \frac{\lambda^2 \alpha_i b_2^{(i)}(2 - \alpha_i \rho_i)}{2(1 - \alpha_i \rho_i)^2} = 0, \quad i = 1, \ldots, N,$$

under assumptions $0 \leq \alpha_i \leq 1$, $\sum_{i=1}^{N} \alpha_i = 1$, $\alpha_i \rho_i < 1$, $i = 1, \ldots, N$.

Proposition 1. *Optimal probabilities α_i^*, $i = 1, \ldots, N$, have the form*

$$\alpha_i^* = \rho_i^{-1} \left(1 - \lambda \sqrt{b_2^{(i)}} (2\rho_i(\beta - \rho_i) + \lambda^2 b_2^{(i)})^{-1/2} \right) \ .$$

Here β is the solution of the following equation

$$\sum_{i=1}^{N} \rho_i^{-1} \left(1 - \lambda \sqrt{b_2^{(i)}} (2\rho_i(\beta - \rho_i) + \lambda^2 b_2^{(i)})^{-1/2} \right) = 1$$

satisfying additionally $\rho_i \leq \beta \leq \rho_i + \lambda^2 b_2^{(i)}(2 - \rho_i)/2(1 - \rho_i)^2$, if $0 \leq \rho_i < 1$, and $\beta \geq \rho_i$, if $\rho_i \geq 1$.

Proposition 2. *The optimal α_i^*, $i = 1, \ldots, N$, can be obtained solving the Lagrange problem iff $\sum_{i=1}^{N} \rho_i^{-1} > 1$.*

Using Maple 12 it is possible to calculate the optimal parameters.

Some numerical results are given below for $N = 2$, $\lambda = 2$, $b_2^{(1)} = b_2^{(2)} = 0.1$.

Case $\rho_1 < 1 < \rho_2$			
ρ_1	ρ_2	β	α_1^*	α_2^*
0,4	1,2	1,217325411	0,9597951872	0,04020481317
0,6	1,1	1,298578981	0,7194120625	0,2805879374
0,6	1,4	1,523859202	0,8084692052	0,1915307944
0,6	2	2.028167863	0,9416522358	0,05834776480
0,9	1,1	1,591743594	0,5632300892	0,4367699110

Case $\rho_1, \rho_2 < 1$			
ρ_1	ρ_2	β	α_1^*	α_2^*
0,2	0,4	0,5487697400	0,6947230170	0,3052769835
0,2	0,7	0,7222398081	0,9474492070	0,05255079300
0,4	0,8	0,9326329628	0,7603895062	0,2396104938
0,6	0,8	1,086054229	0,6036417640	0,3963582371
0,7	0,8	1,164767915	0,5471213116	0,4528786881

Case $\rho_2 > \rho_1 > 1$			
ρ_1	ρ_2	β	α_1^*	α_2^*
1,2	1,3	2,223372271	0,5214712735	0,4785287270
1,2	2,0	3,603736818	0,6211347510	0,3788652492
1,2	4,0	24,07589991	0,7624608414	0,2375391590

Other examples as well as results concerning make-to-stock strategy, omitted due to lack of space, will be published in the next paper.

References

1. Afanas'eva, L.G.: On Periodic Distribution of Waiting Time Process. In: Stability Problems for Stochastic Models. Lecture Notes in Math., pp. 1–20 (1985)
2. Arda, Y., Hennet, J.-C.: Inventory Control in a Multi-supplier System. Int. J. Prod. Econom. 104, 249–259 (2006)
3. Bashtova, E.: The Queue with Doubly Stochastic Poisson Input in the Light Traffic Situation. In: Trans. XXV Int. Sem. Stability Probl. Stoch Models, Maiori, Salerno, Italy, pp. 32–37 (2005)
4. Buchan, J., Koenigsberg, E.: Scientific Inventory Management. Prentice-Hall, Inc., Englewood Cliffs (1963)
5. Bulinskaya, E.V.: Inventory Control in Case of Unknown Demand Distribution. Eng. Costs and Prod. Econom. 19, 301–306 (1990)
6. Clarke, A.B.: A Waiting Time Process of Markov Type. Ann. Math. Stat. 27, 452–459 (1956)
7. Gupta, D., Weerawat, W.: Supplier-Manufacturer Coordination in Capacitated Two-Stage Supply Chains. Eur. J. Oper. Res. 175, 67–89 (2006)
8. Harrison, J.M., Lemoine, A.: Limit Theorems for Periodic Queues. J. Appl. Probab. 14, 566–576 (1977)
9. Takacs, L.: Combinatorial Methods in the Theory of Stochastic Processes. Wiley, New York (1967)

A Concurrent Newsvendor Problem with Rationing

Pinto Roberto

CELS – Research Center on Logistics and After-Sales Services
University of Bergamo
Viale Marconi, 5 - 24044 Dalmine, Italy
roberto.pinto@unibg.it

Abstract. The model proposed in this paper aims at identifying the best allocation of a limited quantity of product to a group of retailers supplied by a unique supplier, considering the variability of the demands faced on the market. The proposed approach aims at reducing the problem of demand inflation, inherent to many rationing policies, by considering the mean and the standard deviation of the demand faced by each retailer. Moreover it could provide managerial insights for managing concurrent retailers under availability constraints.

Keywords: Newsvendor problem, rationing, probabilistic demand, stock allocation, inventory management.

1 Introduction

The newsvendor (or newsboy, or single-period) problem (NVP hereafter) is a well-known operations research model for controlling the inventory of a single item with stochastic demands over a single period i.e. when there is a single purchasing opportunity before the start of the selling period and the demand for the item is random.

It is assumed that a retailer places an order to a supplier for a finite quantity. In such a setting the size of the order should be carefully determined: in fact, if the order quantity is smaller than the realized demand, the newsvendor forgoes some profit. On the other hand, if any inventory remains at the end of the period, a discount is used to sell it or it is disposed of. Hence, the trade-off for the retailer is between the risk of *overstocking* (forcing disposal below the unit purchasing cost) and the risk of *understocking* (losing the opportunity of making a profit) [4]. The NVP aims at finding the order quantity that either maximizes the expected profit or minimizes the expected costs of overestimating and underestimating probabilistic demand when there is a single purchasing opportunity before the start of the selling period [9]. Indeed, both approaches yield the same results [8].

The importance of this problem is reflective of many real life situations and is often used to aid decision making in the fashion and sporting industries, both at the manufacturing and retail levels. Moreover, the NVP is not limited to inventory control: it can also be used in managing capacity and evaluating advanced booking of orders in service industries such as airlines and hotels [8].

B. Vallespir and T. Alix (Eds.): APMS 2009, IFIP AICT 338, pp. 275–282, 2010.

Several extensions of the classical single-period / single product problem (dating back to early '50 with the contributes of Arrow et al. [1] and Morse and Kimbal [10]) have been proposed, in order to deal with multiperiod / multiproduct / multistage problems, different objectives and utility functions, different supplier pricing policies, different newsvendor pricing policies and discounting structures, different states of information about demand, constrained multi-products, multiple-products with substitution, random yields, and multi-location models [8].

However, the general NVP does not take into account the interaction of several newsvendors that can generate shortage at supplier level when a limited product quantity is available, with the consequent impossibility to completely fulfill the demand. For this reason, the present paper deals with a problem that can be considered as a further extension to the classical NVP: we consider several concurrent retailers (newsvendors) that face probabilistic demands expressed as probability density functions (for the sake of simplicity, in this paper we consider the Normal distribution). These retailers submit their orders for the same product to the same (unique) supplier.

In turn, the supplier has a limited quantity available for selling: when demand is uncertain and capacity is costly, a supplier will not build an amount of capacity sufficient to cover every possible demand realization. Hence problems arise when the overall amount of received orders from retailers exceeds the available quantity. In such a setting, the supplier must employ a rationing mechanism to allocate the available quantity among the retailers in order to maximize the expected profit (or minimize the expected cost) of the whole distribution system under probabilistic demand [3].

We implicitly assume that the objective of the supplier is to capture as much demand as possible at the customer level, considering that the selling price is the same for all the retailers. A typical example of the system described above is found when a franchise contracts between supplier and retailers are in place.

Several rationing policies have been proposed in literature. For example, *proportional allocation* based on percentage of total orders is perhaps the most intuitive scheme for dividing capacity, but it incentives the inflation of the order size: retailers order more than they desire in an attempt to ensure that their ultimate allocation is close to what they truly want [3].

The proposed model aims at overcoming this problem: in fact, the proposed model allocates the quantity considering the distribution of the demand faced by the retailers, instead of the actual size of the orders they could place.

In general rationing schemes, there is a rank of the incoming demand, such that these demand classes may have different values, so that it is more important to satisfy one class than the others; when the inventory is low, it is reasonable to ration inventory by rejecting demand from the less valuable classes in anticipation of future demand from the more valuable classes.

Even though this is quite a common setting, we focus our attention on the case where the value of each demand (retailer) is the same, and the only objective is to capture as much demand as possible at the customer level. Hence, in the described case we reject order from retailers that have less probability of selling the entire, requested quantity, the probability being based on the demand distribution expressed as known mean and standard deviation.

The rationing decision naturally depends on the current inventory level as well as the operating characteristics of the system. For example, if the production leadtime is long and hence inventory cannot be replenished quickly, rationing will be more critical [5].

1.1 The General Newsvendor Problem

Formally, the general newsvendor problem is stated as follows. A decision maker (a retailer) places an order for a quantity Q, which arrives before the start of the selling period. Let D be the stochastic demand during this period and let μ be its mean. Let F be the distribution function of demand and f the density function. For simplicity, assume F is continuous, differentiable and strictly increasing. Hence, we can write:

$$F(Q) = Prob(0 \le D \le Q) = \int_0^Q f(x)dx \tag{1}$$

Further, assume that the decision maker has an unbiased forecast of the demand distribution and knows F. The decision maker purchases each unit for cost c and sells each unit at price $p > c$. When $Q > D$, each unit remaining at the end of the period can be salvaged for $s < c$ (notice that in the case the units are simply disposed, $s = 0$). In case of shortage the company incurs a penalty cost per unit v.

If Q units are ordered, then $min(Q, D)$ units are sold and $max(Q - D, 0)$ units are salvaged (disposed).

Hence, we define

$$\pi(x) = \begin{cases} (p - c) \cdot Q - v \cdot (x - Q) & if \; x \ge Q \\ p \cdot x + s \cdot (Q - x) - c \cdot Q & if \; x < Q \end{cases} \tag{2}$$

as the realized profit, and let

$$E[\pi(x)] = (p + s - c) \int_Q^\infty Qf(x)dx - v \int_Q^\infty xf(x)dx + \\ +(p - s) \int_0^Q xf(x)dx - (c - s) \int_0^Q Qf(x)dx \tag{3}$$

be the expected profit. Using Leibniz's rule to obtain the first and second derivatives it is possible to show that $E[\pi]$ is concave; hence the sufficient optimality condition is the well known fractile formula [8], [11]:

$$F(Q^*) = \frac{p + v - c}{p + v - s} \quad \rightarrow \quad Q^* = F^{-1}\left(\frac{p + v - c}{p + v - s}\right) \tag{4}$$

2 Design of the Proposed Approach

The problem we are considering is a *single period / 1-warehouse / N-retailer* inventory system where demand occurs at all locations with the same probability distribution (but with different mean and standard deviation). We assume that demands coming from different retailers are equally important; hence, the inventory manager have to apply some type of rationing policy based on the probability of reaching as much demand as possible at customers level, when the total quantity required exceeds the available quantity at the supplier level.

For the sake of clarity, we distinguish two stages. The first stage is called *ordering stage*: each retailer places its own order (solving its own NVP) of size Q_i. Hence, from the supplier's standpoint this is comparable to N instances of independent NVPs (being N the number of ordering retailers). The solutions of these independent problems represent the best order size for each retailer and a bound for the overall solution.

Since each retailer makes his decision independently, there is no guarantee that the sum of the order sizes does not exceed the supplier's availability A. Therefore, if $\sum_i Q_i > A$ a rationing procedure takes place in the second stage.

In the second stage, called *rationing stage*, a set of constraints is imposed in order to bind the independent solutions to the available quantity A. From a mathematical standpoint we can state the problem as:

$$\min E[c, s, v, \bar{Q}] \quad \text{s. t.}$$
$$\sum_i Q_i \leq A \quad and \quad Q_i \geq 0 \quad \forall i = \{Q_i \in \bar{Q}\} \tag{5}$$

The mathematical formulation appears really simple, indeed, but since it generally implies a non-linear distribution function in the expected value operator, the problem is non-linear. Hence, an alternative approach has been devised. In the remainder we present the procedure for the rationing stage.

2.1 Rationing Stage

In the rationing stage, the order sizes proposed by retailers are modified in order to take into account the availability at the supplier level. In doing this we want to assure to cover as much demand as possible at the customer level, allocating the right portion of A to each retailer.

We start expressing the demand as:

$$Q_i = \mu_i + k_i \cdot \sigma_i \tag{6}$$

where μ_i and σ_i are the mean and the standard deviation of the demand faced by the i-th retailer and k_i a multiplicative factor, not yet know at this point. We use this representation according to the Chebyshev inequality:

$$Prob(|D - \mu| < k \cdot \sigma) \geq 1 - \frac{1}{k^2} \tag{7}$$

In other words, given a set of values $D = (d_1, ..., d_n)$ and a number k, at least a percentage of $1 - 1/k^2$ falls in the interval $(\mu \pm k \cdot \sigma)$. Hence, maneuvering k according to (7) we can assure that a given proportion of the demand will be covered.

In order to find k_i we have to solve the following equation:

$$\sum_i Q_i = A \quad \rightarrow \quad \sum_i k_i \cdot \sigma_i = A - \sum_i \mu_i \tag{8}$$

Hence we have N incognitos (k_i) and only 1 equation. No others intuitive equations seem to be available in order to close the equation system, therefore other numerical approaches have been tested.

A first attempt was performed using a Monte Carlo simulation, by randomly generating the value of k_i in a given range (i.e. [0; 4] in order to cover at least 93% of demand, according to (7)). But in this way we cannot assure that the constraint expressed in (8) holds.

Hence, in order to solve this system we have to close it by letting an incognita depending by the other values. We can rewrite (8) as:

$$k_j = \frac{A - \sum_i \mu_i - \sum_{i \neq j} k_i \cdot \sigma_i}{\sigma_j} \qquad (9)$$

where j is the index of one of the N retailers.

At this point, the mean μ_i are known and we can try different values of k_i (for i ≠ j) being sure that the overall constraint (8) will be always satisfied. In other words, k_j is assumed as a *balancing variable* that assure the satisfaction of the constraint.

In the Monte Carlo simulation we can draw *N-1* values for k_i ($i \neq j$) and then calculate k_j in order to satisfy the constraint. Clearly we do not accept the solutions in which $Q_i < 0$; in fact, only the sum of Q_i is checked against the availability A, while no check is performed in order to assure that $Q_i > 0$.

While Monte Carlo simulation allows the exploration of the search space, it does not assure a monotone descent towards the minimum (since the solution are drawn randomly, there is no a monotone sequence of solutions towards the optimum).

Hence we decided to devise and test a Genetic Algorithm (GA) approach. In the GA, a population of solutions evolve from one iteration to the following improving quasi-monotonically (that is, there could be cases where the best solution in the $m+1$ iteration is the same of the best solution in the m-th iteration).

3   Improving the Solution Procedure Using GA

Genetic algorithm (GA) is a well known method for solving optimization problems that mimic natural selection, repeatedly modifying a population of individuals that represent solutions to the problem at hand. Each individual encodes a solution. At each step, the genetic algorithm selects individuals from the current population and uses them produce the children for the next generation. Over successive generations, the population evolves towards an optimal solution. It is recognized that in some classes of problem it makes possible to explore a far greater range of potential solutions to a problem than do conventional programs.

The GA uses three main types of rules at each step to create the next generation from the current population: *(i) selection rules* to select the individuals, called parents, that contribute to the population at the next generation; *(ii) crossover rules*, used to combine two parents to form children for the next generation; *(iii) mutation rules* that apply random changes to individual parents to form children, allowing to expand the search space introducing stochastic variability.

We implemented the GA using the Matlab GA Toolbox™. Several options are available for the most important parameter: we briefly report only the best choices for the GA parameters as resulted from an extensive test run:

- *Encoding:* the population is encoded as a vector of *N-1* double values, representing the maneuvered k_i. This seems the most reasonable choice in this case, but at the same time it implies other constraints in the choice of other operators such as mutation and crossover [6].
- *Selection:* the Stochastic uniform function lays out a line in which each parent corresponds to a section of the line of length proportional to its value. The algorithm moves along the line in steps of equal size. At each step, the algorithm allocates a parent from the section it lands on.
- *Mutation:* the Gaussian mutation function adds a random number taken from a Gaussian distribution with mean 0 to each entry of the parent vector.
- *Crossover:* the crossover function creates children by taking a weighted average of the selected parents.

For the sake of clarity, although these choices stem from a test run, at present we only exploited Matlab™ built-in functions: it could be possible to obtain better results implementing custom operators, but this aspect goes beyond the scope and purpose of this paper.

4 Computational Results

The proposed approach has been tested on different problem settings, from small (10 retailers) to medium (50 retailers) to large (100 retailers). We just report some main results on three specific settings that differ in the values of the mean and standard deviation. Each setting is run with increasing values of A in the interval [$\sum \mu - \sum \sigma$; $\sum \mu + \sum \sigma$]. For each value of A the GA determines the optimal allocation between N retailers. For the sake of simplicity, we present the results for $N = 3$.

Setting 1: retailers with same mean and same standard deviation

When all retailers face the same type of demand (i.e. they face the same demand distribution with the same mean and standard deviation) the best solution appears to be the one that maximize imbalance between retailers when availability is below a threshold; after such threshold, the best solution is obtained by minimizing the imbalance. From the test executed, the threshold can be empirically set at about $N \cdot \mu + \sigma$, but this value deserves a deeper analysis.

Setting 2: retailers with same mean and different standard deviation

When all the retailers face the same demand distribution with the same mean but with different standard deviations, the best solution is to give higher priority to retailers that face demand with lower standard deviations. As in the previous case, it has been empirically observed that as the availability A increases, the imbalance in the allocation tends to decrease.

Setting 3: retailers with different mean and different standard deviation

In this case we considered two sub cases: in the first one the standard deviation is proportional to the mean, while in the second case the standard deviation is inversely proportional to the mean.

In the first sub case, as the availability increases, the proportion allocated to the retailers with higher standard deviation increases, while the proportions allocated to other retailers remains almost constant.

In the second sub case, the retailer with highest mean demand and lowest standard deviation is favored, while retailer with lowest demand and highest standard deviation is backlogged. As the availability increases, the quantity given to the latter rapidly increases, while the quota devoted to the others is kept almost constant.

Convergence issue on large problems

The approach has been tested on large instances (with 50 and 100 retailers). As expected, the GA converges to a solution slower as the number of retailer increases. Moreover, depending on the shape of the fitness landscape, the convergence to global optima is generally not assured.

5 Conclusion, Research Limitations and Extensions

In its present form, the paper presents a formulation and a solution procedure based on Genetic Algorithm to a problem where several newsvendors compete for the same resource provided by a unique supplier.

GA may have a tendency to converge towards local optima or even arbitrary points rather than the global optimum of the problem; hence further solution heuristics are currently under development and testing.

The presented problem does not consider cooperation or information sharing among retailers (which is considered in other, recent works, such that of Huang and Iravani [7]): retailers operate as isolated entities and should decide on their own the size of the order before the beginning of the selling season (ordering stage).

The proposed formulation of the problem is limited by the fact that it only considers the cost of inventory neglecting the service level at the retailer and customer level. Further extensions of the proposed model will encompass the possibility to set different service levels for each retailer (as in [2]). Another extension would encompass the possibility to handle several demand classes with different values so that it is more important to satisfy one class than the others.

References

1. Arrow, K.A., Harris, T.E., Marschak, J.: Optimal inventory policy. Econometrica 19, 250–272 (1951)
2. Axsäter, S., Kleijn, M., De Kok, T.G.: Stock Rationing in a Continuous Review Two-Echelon Inventory Model. Annals of Operations Research 126, 177–194 (2004)
3. Cachon, G.P., Lariviere, M.A.: An equilibrium analysis of linear, proportional and uniform allocation of scarce capacity. IIE Transactions 31, 835–849 (1998)
4. Gallego, G., Moon, I.: The distribution free newsboy problem: review and extensions. Journal of operational research society 44(8), 825–834 (1993)
5. Ha, A.Y.: Inventory Rationing in a Make-to-Stock Production System with Several Demand Classes and Lost Sales. Management Science 43, 1093–1103 (1997)

6. Herrera, F., Lozano, M., Verdegay, J.L.: Tackling Real-Coded Genetic Algorithms: Operators and Tools for Behavioural Analysis. Artificial Intelligence Review 12, 265–319 (1998)
7. Huang, B., Iravani, S.M.R.: Optimal production and rationing decisions in supply chains with information sharing. Operations Research Letters 35, 669–676 (2006)
8. Khouja, M.: The single-period (news-vendor) problem: literature review and suggestions for future research. Omega International Journal of Management Science 27, 537–553 (1999)
9. Kogan, K., Lou, S.: Multi-stage newsboy problem: A dynamic model. European Journal of Operational Research 149, 448–458 (2003)
10. Morse, M.P., Kimbal, G.E.: Methods of Operations Research. MIT Press, Cambridge (1951)
11. Schweitzer, M.E., Cachon, G.P.: Decision Bias in the Newsvendor Problem with a Known Demand Distribution: Experimental Evidence. Management Science 46(3), 404–420 (2000)

A Model for Vendor Selection and Dynamic Evaluation

Raffele Iannone, Salvatore Miranda, Stefano Riemma, and Debora Sarno

University of Salerno, Department of Mechanical Engineering
Via Ponte don Melillo,
84084 Fisciano (SA), Italy
{riannone,smiranda,sriemma}@unisa.it, deborasarno@hotmail.it

Abstract. The present paper proposes an evaluation model able to integrate the selection phase with the monitoring and the continuous analysis of the vendor performances. The vendor evaluation process is realised through an opportune methodology which puts beside qualitative judgements (i.e. the adequacy of the organisation or the maintenance management policies) and performance data (i.e. delivery delays, number of non conformities, discrepancies in the delivered quantities, etc.) and builds the database which will support the daily decisions of the buyers. Thanks to its generality and customisability, together with the use of basic managerial tools, the system represents an appropriate trade-off between implementation costs and obtainable benefits.

Keywords: Vendor Evaluation, Vendor Selection, AHP, Supply Management.

1 Introduction and Literature Review

The success of an enterprise into the global market is even more strictly conditioned by the competitiveness of the supply chain in which it is positioned: however effective and efficient in pursuing its targets a company is, it can be in serious troubles if has to interact, along the chain, with ineffective actors, which operate far to the real needs of the market, because this will have severe repercussions on the output offered to the final customer.

The global trend, as largely confirmed in literature and by the practice, advises the enterprises to focus on their own core activities, with consequent aiming to the outsourcing, which represents the tool able to reduce the enterprise overall dimensions. The higher flexibility, obtained by the transposition of the fixed costs in variable costs, is accompanied by the transferring to external actors of all the activities not directly related to the core business. Obviously, these actors must be able to sustain the quality levels which before were a peculiarity of the enterprise.

The purchasing function, therefore, assumes a fundamental role, in terms of both incidence on the total costs and strategic relevance [1]. For these reasons, its positioning into the organisational macrostructure has been progressively redefined, up to the creation of interfunctional teams able to guarantee a systemic vision of the process and more decisional power. This has been targeted to satisfy a series of new necessities: to monitor the suppliers performances, in order to verify their ability to

B. Vallespir and T. Alix (Eds.): APMS 2009, IFIP AICT 338, pp. 283–290, 2010.

assure the required levels of excellence; to optimise the even more complex purchasing process, through careful comparisons and by reducing the set of available suppliers to the most virtuous ones; to understand the real potentialities of the suppliers in order to establish with them strict and durable relationships [2].

The process of Vendor Evaluation (VE) is characterised by:

- *Vendor selection*: vendor knowledge and evaluation of its potentialities in order to elaborate a list of qualified vendors;
- *Performance evaluation*: rectified measurement during the supplying. Together with the selection phase it constitutes the *vendor rating*, which ratifies or denies the final approval of a vendor;
- *Vendor ranking*: comparison of the results of all the vendors;
- *Periodic review* of the potentialities evaluation.

To support the new strategic role of the purchasing function, during the last decades numerous methods of vendor evaluation have been proposed. In literature the Multiple Criteria Decision Making nature [3,4] of the VE is commonly accepted, as well as the extremely diversified data the models have to manage, reflecting the logic of the specific decision maker. As concerns the analysis criteria, different studies have been carried out [5,6], but most of them have demonstrated their applicability under specific constraints only and, then, scarce practical interest.

The experience matured on the field leads the authors to affirm that these models have been scarcely appreciated and utilised in the industrial practice (especially in small and medium enterprises). This can be principally explained with the traditional reticence towards complex mathematical models for choices that can be left to the intuition of the buyer. In the rare cases in which such reticence has been surmounted, these methods have been seen as not very reliable black boxes, due to the reduced number of considered variables.

This paper proposes a model able to guarantee **completeness**, by taking into consideration a wide range of aspects, and **easiness**, by avoiding the adoption of a high number of mathematical modellings, contrarily to what found in literature [7].

2 The Proposed Vendor Evaluation Method

In this section a VE model, based on the Linear Weighting Method (LWM), is presented. Starting from a hierarchical structuring of all the evaluation criteria, the model provides for a procedure which aims to contextualize the general structure to the specific cases. This is obtained through a calculation method based on the AHP logic which assigns opportune weights to the criteria, basing on experts judgment. The general scheme of the model is shown in Fig.1. Objectives and details of the steps will be described in the next paragraphs.

The batching in homogeneous classes. The classification of the provisions in clusters for which the same rules are valid enables to contextualize the evaluation structure for a limited number of categories. This can be performed by means of the material merchandise data.

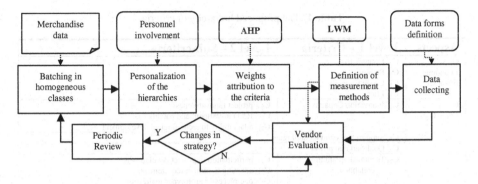

Fig. 1. Logical scheme for the implementation of the model

The hierarchy of the evaluation criteria. In order to permit a complete evaluation of the vendors, a wide set of analysis aspects, subdivided in criteria, sub-criteria and indicators has been defined (Fig.2). This structure represents the hierarchy of the evaluation criteria. The passing from a level to the lower implies a detail increase of the analyzed information. In Table 1 the detail of the evaluation criteria is proposed. It is important to underline that the evaluation has subjective nature, whether it is based on quantitative data or it arises from qualitative judgments.

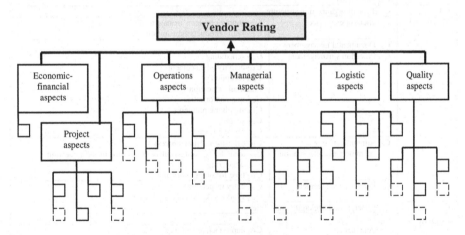

Fig. 2. The criteria hierarchical structuring

The personalization of the hierarchy. The hierarchy of criteria is extremely generic: to guarantee the right trade-off between implementation efforts and benefits of the model, it has to be contextualized according to the company strategy and to the cluster of the considered materials. The method proposes to selecting the criteria by submitting the maxi-hierarchy to at least two figures with specific competences on the provisioned products/services. In particular one member of the Engineering Department and one of the Quality Assurance Department should be involved. They are called to cut/supplement the list of criteria, realising in this way a specific hierarchy for each cluster of materials. The cutting is performed by defining a lower

Table 1. The proposed hierarchy of criteria

Aspects	Level 1 – Criteria	Level 2 – Sub-criteria
C_1 Economic-financial	C_{11} Country Risk C_{12} Stability C_{13} Credit Capacity C_{14} Price	
C_2 Project	C_{21} Innovation Capacity	C_{211} project innovativeness C_{212} R&D investment and patents C_{213} adaptability to technological development
	C_{22} Support tools and technologies	
	C_{23} Qualified manpower	
	C_{24} Technical –planning collaboration	C_{241} participation in project development C_{242} adapting to project requirements C_{243} one-pieces or prototypes realization
C_3 Operations	C_{31} Manpower	C_{311} available C_{312} overtime capacity C_{313} skill C_{314} independence on the job C_{315} technical/social integration
	C_{32} Machinery and equipment	C_{321} adequacy C_{322} maintenance policies
	C_{33} Structures	C_{331} plants C_{332} warehouses C_{333} service equipment
	C_{34} Flexibility	C_{341} ability to reduce lot dimensions C_{342} flexibility to mix and selling volume
	C_{35} Punctuality	
C4 Managerial	C_{41} Type of organization structure	
	C_{42} after--sales service	C_{421} supply problems management C_{422} faulty products substitution
	C_{43} Documental management	
	C_{44} Procedures management	C_{441} scheduling C_{442} activity advancement C_{443} reception C_{444} final inspection C_{445} non conformities C_{446} supplying problems C_{447} security C_{448} process reviews
	C_{45} Administrative – commercial collaboration	C_{451} offer formulation process C_{452} availability, professionalism and timeliness in question answering C_{453} time for order confirmation
	C_{46} Purchase management	C_{461} entry inspections C_{462} vendor selection and evaluation
C_5 Logistic	C_{51} Coherence in packaging modalities	
	C_{52} Flexibility	
	C_{53} Punctuality	C_{531} unproductive working hours C_{532} increase of interest charges on capital invested in WIP C_{533} delivery delay on estimated times C_{534} reminders for shipments
	C_{54} Respect of ordered quantities	
	C_{55} Geographical localization	
C_6 Quality	C_{61} Quality certification	C_{611} application of the quality management system C_{612} skill of quality control operators
	C_{62} Quality costs	C_{621} checks in acceptance C_{622} cost of audits C_{623} cost of reworking
	C_{63} Quality problems	C_{631} non conformities C_{632} damaged products C_{633} claims

limit for the judgments of preference obtained by each criterion. The criteria whose mean judgment is below that limit will be excluded by the hierarchy. A further reduction can be effected by other company figures directly involved in the vendor evaluation process [8].

Weights attribution to the criteria. Not all the evaluation methods require the definition of the weights for the criteria – see DEA [9], OR methods [10,11], total cost of ownership methods [12]. Given the numerousness of the considered criteria and the easiness aim, the model is based on the LWM which receives as input weights and scores of the evaluation parameters. In order to convert in numbers the decision maker perceptions about the relative importance of the criteria, the AHP method, already adopted by Narasimhan [13], is utilized. This differs from the traditional application of the AHP, which is generally used to choose among different alternatives [14]. According to this method, the comparison matrices will be compiled. They are not necessarily consistent (unit rank): forcing the compilers to be perfectly coherent in their judgments, inappropriately obliges them to respect the principles of preference and indifference transitivity. The error will be therefore reduced through the Power Method and subsequently by verifying the consistence through the calculation of the relative index (see [15] for the explanation of the steps to follow). The procedure will be executed at the first implementation of the model as well as at each change of the company strategy [16].

The evaluation model. The relative weight vectors obtained through the AHP are disposed beside the indicators into a worksheet, so as to constitute the global evaluation form for each cluster of materials. The decision makers will be able to complete the form for each vendor by assigning their score to each criteria or sub-criteria of the hierarchy. Through the LWM, the global rating A_i of the ith vendor for a specific cluster of material will be calculated by the following formula:

$$A_i = \sum_{j=1}^{n} w_j a_{ij} \cdot \tag{1}$$

where: w_i = weight relative to the jth aspect; a_{ij} = score obtained by the ith vendor on the jth aspect; n = number of considered aspects.

In (1) the score a_{ij} is in its turn given by:

$$a_{ij} = \sum_{k=1}^{m_j} w_{jk} a_{ijk} \cdot \tag{2}$$

where: w_{jk} = weight relative to the kth criterion of jth aspect; a_{ijk} = score obtained by the ith vendor on the kth criterion of the jth aspect; m_j = number of considered criteria of the jth aspect.

The same relation of (2) is valid for the score a_{ijk} as a function of its sub-criteria. At each level the weight vectors are defined according to the following conditions:

$$\sum_{j=1}^{n} w_j = 1 \quad \text{and} \quad \sum_{k=1}^{m_j} w_{jk} = 1 \; \forall j \cdot \tag{3}$$

As concerning the score attribution, for qualitative judgments a 1-10 range (10 is the optimum) will be adopted; for quantitative data specific formulas have been created. Starting from them, opportune membership functions can be defined, in such a way as it is possible to convert the performance measured through the formula in a score included in the 1-10 range.

This method avoids the problem of the uncertainty in the weights attribution, typical of the pure LWM. The other controversial issue, the possible offsetting among the criteria, has been solved by fixing a score which represents the lower limit for the approval: if a score goes under this limit (i.e. 6/10) the vendor cannot be considered qualified, independently to its final score.

Data Collection. In order to implement the method, data have to be procured in different ways and moments of the supply process. For the evaluation of the potentialities in the Selection Phase, the *Auto Evaluation Form* (an opportunely developed questionnaire to be sent to each vendor) and the predisposition of test samplings have to be used. After the first selection, the proper qualification consists of the analysis of all the data, through the compilation of the *Preventive Evaluation Form*. The supplies evaluation is performed through the *Rectified Evaluation Form*. The two evaluations, preventive and rectified, constitute the global rating of the vendor, whose total score determines the eventual approval. The preventive evaluation has to be updated at each change in strategy (**Periodic Review**) and, in any case, at least every 3-5 years; the rectified evaluation, on the contrary, has a time-limited validity which strongly depends on the kind of supply.

3   The Case Study

A first validation of the model has been carried out on a company leader in the engineering industry. The high number of vendors and the relative importance of the purchases on the total expenses (70%) have offered a valid test field for the validity of the proposed model. After unstructured interviews and the analysis of the data resident into the ERP of the company, all the steps of the model have been implemented. Subsequently, a comparison between the obtained results and the actions undertaken by the buyers, basing on their experience, in a period of six months has been done. As instance, the comparison for a particularly critical mechanical component, present in all the products, is reported. The characteristics analyzed for a vendor of this component are resumed in the ad hoc hierarchy shown in Fig.3. According to the model, the hierarchy has been adapted to the specific case with the elimination of some criteria and the addition of others.

The purchase department, in the analyzed six months, has confirmed orders for 80 pieces, distributing them on 5 accredited vendors. The diagram of Fig.4 shows such distribution together with the global rating obtained by each vendor through the application of the proposed model. The coherence between obtained results and buyers choices appears evident. The same coherence has been confirmed for all the main clusters of the materials provisioned by the company.

The buyers are surely facilitated in their choices by the implementation of the proposed VE system: by reading on the database the scores obtained by the vendors for the specific aspects of evaluation and the relative global ratings, they can

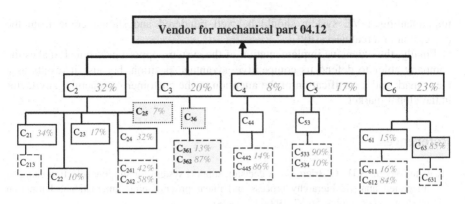

Fig. 3. Hierarchy of criteria for the analyzed mechanical component

immediately take their decisions. In this way they avoid the long and laborious process of data acquisition, which often requires numerous consultations with different company figures, without losing effectiveness in their final choices.

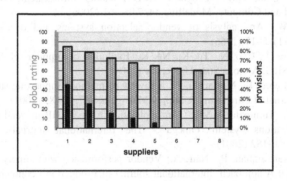

Fig. 4. Comparison between global ratings of the model and buyers choices

4 Conclusions

The paper presents an easy and versatile VE model which can be utilized by every kind of company. Its information power can be a basic tool for the management in supporting the company strategies in the medium period, because it assures a complete outline of the vendors and facilitates considerations about the instauration of more evolved contractual relationships. In addition it allows the buyers to make studies on historical series, sensitivity analyses and also make the evaluation parameters known to the vendors (which can in this way steer better their efforts).

The implementation and the continuous use of a VE system requires great care of the decision makers: retrieving the necessary data and taking coherent evaluations from time to time are not banal problems. For these reasons, the system, even if well conceived, can result in some cases limited or lacking. Other problems can be the underutilization or the crystallization of the system. Therefore, the choice of implementing a VE system should be well pondered and should come from the perception of a real necessity.

Finally, the extensive implementation of the system, opportunely tuned, makes the company abler to defend its competitive advantage position, because it results as a merit mark and a certification of the attention to the customer satisfaction, key factor in the global market.

References

1. Ghodsypour, S.H., O'Brien, C.: A decision support system for supplier selection using an integrated analytic hierarchy process and linear programming. International Journal of production economics, 56-57, 199–212 (1998)
2. Ragatz, G.L., Handfield, R.B., Scannell, T.V.: Success factors in integrating suppliers into new product development. Journal of Production Innovation Management 14, 190–202 (1997)
3. Weber, C.A., Current, J.R., Benton, W.C.: Vendor selection criteria and methods. European Journal of Operational Research 26, 35–41 (1991)
4. Shyur, H.J., Shih, H.S.: A hybrid MCDM model for strategic vendor selection. Mathematical and Computer Modelling 44, 749–761 (2006)
5. Dickson, G.W.: An analysis of vendor selection systems and decisions. Journal of Purchasing 2(1), 5–17 (1966)
6. Zhang, Z., Lei, J., Cao, N., To, K., Ng, K.: Evolution of supplier selection criteria and methods. PBSRG, Arizona State University (2004)
7. de Boer, L., Labro, E., Morlacchi, P.: A review of methods supporting supplier selection. European Journal of Purchasing & Supply Management 7, 75–89 (2001)
8. Tam, M.C.Y., Tummala, V.M.R.: An application of the AHP in vendor selection of a telecommunications system. Omega - The International Journal of Management Science 29, 171–182 (2001)
9. Talluri, S., Narasimhan, R., Nair, A.: Vendor performance with supply risk: A chance-constrained DEA approach. International Journal of Production Economics 100, 212–222 (2006)
10. Ng, L.W.: An efficient and simple model for multiple criteria supplier selection problem. European Journal of Operational Research 186, 1059–1067 (2008)
11. Wadhwa, V., Ravindran, A.R.: Vendor selection in outsourcing. Computers & Operations Research 34, 3725–3737 (2007)
12. Roodhooft, F., Konings, J.: Vendor selection and evaluation. An activity based costing approach. European Journal of Operational Research 96, 97–102 (1996)
13. Narasimhan, R.: An analytical approach to supplier selection. Journal of Purchasing Material Management Winter, 27–32 (1983)
14. Noorul Haq, A., Kannam, G.: Fuzzy analytical hierarchy process for evaluating and selecting a vendor in a supply chain model. International Journal of Advanced Manufacturing Technology 29, 826–835 (2005)
15. Saaty, T.L.: Foudamentals of decision making and priority theory with the analytic hierarchy process. The AHP series, vol. VI. RWS Publications, Pittsburgh (1994)
16. Dulmin, R., Mininno, V.: Supplier selection using a multi-criteria decision aid method. Journal of Purchasing & Supply Management 9, 177–187 (2003)

Customer Driven Capacity Setting

Alexander Hübl, Klaus Altendorfer, Herbert Jodlbauer, and Josef Pilstl

Upper Austria University of Applied Science, School of Management,
Wehrgrabengasse 1-3, 4400 Steyr, Austria
{alexander.huebl,klaus.altendorfer,herbert.jodlbauer,
josef.pilstl}@fh-steyr.at

Abstract. The purpose of this article is to develop a method for short and medium term capacity setting decisions for providing a market oriented level of available capacity for the investigated machine groups. An MTO (make to order) production system is considered. The basic concept is that the cumulative available capacity of the machine group has to be greater than or equal to the cumulative needed capacity influenced by the customer orders. The cumulative needed capacity is corrected with an operation characteristic which defines the slack of the production system, in order to include enough capacity for short term orders.

Keywords: Capacity setting, cumulative capacity, Make To Order (MTO), market driven production planning.

1 Introduction

Many industries are facing strong global competition where product life cycles are shortened, time to market decreases and customers require fast deliveries of a variety of products of an appropriate quality (see [6]). Therefore it is absolutely necessary that a company ensures that the right product of the right quality is available to the customer in the right quantity at the right time (see [10]). Companies have to adjust their available capacity on customer needs and methods for estimating the needed capacity are crucial for being successful.

If it is not possible to increase the needed capacity then it is essential in terms of customer satisfaction to know what the earliest possible due date is. A high service level can be achieved if due date negotiation is possible, which is according to [14] and [13] a difficult task to perform.

The purpose of this article is to develop a method for short and medium term capacity setting decisions. Reference [7] developed a method where the required customer order lead time and production capacity needed to fulfill customer orders are combined. The basic idea for capacity setting according to [1], [5], [2] as well as [16] is that the cumulative available capacity of the machine group has to be greater than or equal to the cumulative needed capacity for all customer orders which are already in the system.

B. Vallespir and T. Alix (Eds.): APMS 2009, IFIP AICT 338, pp. 291–298, 2010.
© IFIP International Federation for Information Processing 2010

2 Literature Review

In literature many methods for setting or promising due dates exist, which are directly related to the delivery reliability of orders. In order to promise or set due dates, the available capacity has to be allocated in an MTO environment according to the received customer orders. If the available capacity of the production system is higher than the needed capacity influenced by customer orders, then the difference between the two is wasted capacity (see [4]). But if the available capacity is less than the needed capacity, then the due dates promised to the customer cannot be met. Therefore this paper presents an approach for capacity allocation in an MTO environment.

In [11] a mixed integer programming model with dynamic characteristics is presented for capacity allocation in a supply chain. Moreover heuristics are presented and compared to the results of the mixed integer program in order to demonstrate that the heuristics work well.

Reference [12] developed an analytical model for a capacity allocation problem. The authors assumed a stochastic production capacity and have implemented frequent and occasional customers demanding the capacity. In this paper the expected total income including the penalty costs is maximized. Product mix and sensitivity information allow a guideline for online control systems.

In [17] and [18] a model is published where the production orders are processed by the bill of material (BOM) from the finished goods down to the raw material delivered by the suppliers. At each level of the BOM the inventory is checked if enough material for the orders is available. Missing material is then produced or ordered. This approach supposes deterministic material availability data and no processing times are considered.

Reference [9] developed a mathematical model for a route-independent analysis of available capacity in flexible manufacturing systems whereby the approach is based on the concept of operation types. Moreover a sensitivity analysis is developed to analyze the feasibility of the production system when production requirements and machine capacities changes.

Reference [3] introduced a model which supports decision makers by verifying a customer required due date, whereby potential and already confirmed orders with different probabilities are compared with the actual level of available capacity. A two stage capacity check is applied, where in the first step all resources required by the new order are checked for occurring overloads without the new order. This is followed by a second overload test by including the additional capacity of the new order. Moreover [3] assumed deterministic processing times.

As seen, many methods are available in literature. Reference [11] presented a mixed integer programming model. Reference [12] published an analytical approach for optimizing the total expected income. Reference [9] developed a model for a route-independent capacity analysis. Reference [17] and [18] developed a material based approach. Reference [3] established a model where orders are divided into different probabilities of occurrence.

In our paper the probability of the occurrence of capacity needed based on customer orders depends on the slack between order due date and order date. The difference to [3] is that no explicit future orders are considered but only certain future capacity leads are used for the capacity setting. This means we anticipate future demand also with shorter customer required lead time than the orders already being in the production system. As shown in the literature review most of the authors discussing capacity setting assumed a deterministic processing time. Hence, the processing time is supposed to be deterministic in this paper as well.

3 Model

At the beginning of this section the concept of operations characteristic (OC) is explained and adapted. This is followed by the development of a capacity allocation model. In the main part of this paper the connection between the concepts of OC and capacity allocation is presented. Finally a short numerical example is given.

3.1 Model Assumptions

The model assumes an operation earliest due date (see [15]). Stochastic distributions for interarrival time of customer orders and customer required lead times are assumed. In this model processing times are supposed to be deterministic as argued in the literature review. The machines are clustered into machine groups which fulfill the same processing step.

3.2 Operations Characteristics

The concept of applying the operations characteristic (OC) is based on [7], whereby this OC defines the relationship between the customer required lead time and the capacity needed at a machine group. For a one-machine-model the OC shows how much of the customer required capacity is known how many periods in advance. Figure 1 shows such an OC.

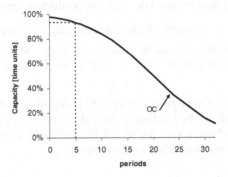

Fig. 1. Operations characteristics

The horizontal axis of Figure 1 shows the required customer order lead time. The vertical axis indicates the cumulated workload of the customer orders at the investigated machine group. The example shown in Figure 1 is based on a normally distributed required customer order lead time where the mean is 20 periods and sigma is 10 periods. Five periods before the due date, on average 93.3% of the required capacity of a machine group is known for the production system in the given example. Moreover the integral over OC up to a certain time period returns the average production lead time if all customer orders which have a customer required lead time smaller then the investigated time period (used in the integral) are released to the production system immediately.

In [7], the OC concept encompasses the concept of a constant remaining processing time. This time can be the transportation time to the customer in a one-machine production system or the remaining processing and handling time in a multi machine production system. Since this time is assumed to be constant in [7], which especially for job shop production systems does not hold, the OC concept is slightly changed in this paper. The following definition shown in (1) to (3) is used:

$$OC_j(t) = 1 - F_{l_s(j)}(t) \tag{1}$$

$$l_s(j) = d_{i,j} - o_i \tag{2}$$

$$d_{i,j} = d_i - l_{min}(i,j) \tag{3}$$

Whereby:

- $OC_j(t)$ ... Operations characteristic, stating what percentage of capacity is, on average, already known t periods before the due date at machine group
- $F_{l_s(j)}(t)$ ... cumulated distribution function of $l_s(j)$
- $l_s(j)$ ... stochastic variable for the slack between machine dependent due date $d_{i,j}$ and order date o_i
- d_i ... customer required due date for production order i
- $l_{min}(i,j)$ ... minimum technical remaining time to finish the order i after being finished at machine group j, includes the processing times of the following processing steps as well as the handling time but no waiting time

The difference between the original concept of [7] and the one applied here is that in [7] the l_{min} just depends on the machine group but not on the order itself. Especially in cases of job shop production systems with different lot sizes and routings, this additional dependence on the order leads to advantages.

3.3 Capacity Allocation

The following section describes the model for capacity setting, which compares the cumulated needed capacity and the cumulated available capacity. The cumulated needed capacity is calculated by summing up the processing and setup times at the machine group j of all orders at their due date as shown in (4) and (5). $A_j(t)$ is a non negative monotonically increasing function, which describes how much capacity is needed at the investigated machine to fulfill the customer demand on time.

The needed capacity of a machine group for producing a final product depends on the bill of material, the routing data, the lot sizes and the standard processing times. Instead of a classical backward scheduling the proposed approach determines the latest possible date for capacity allocation for each machine in the production system by subtracting from the customer confirmed due date only the remaining process-, set up- and transport times (defined as minimum technical remaining lead time l_{min} (i,j). If a backlog exists at machine group j then $A_j(t)$ will not start at zero, because all the late jobs are cumulated into $A_j(0)$.

The OC converges asymptotically to the abscissa. Hence, orders with long and extremely long customer required lead times are treated almost identically by the OC correction. Therefore, the work-ahead window w, where only those orders are taken into consideration which have a smaller customer required lead time than w, is introduced as seen in (5). The work-ahead window is introduced to reduce the finished goods inventory (see [8]) and to set a border for which time frame the short and medium term capacity planning is performed.

$$A_j(t) = \int_0^t a_j(\tau)\, d\tau + A_j(0) \tag{4}$$

$$a_j(t) = \sum_{\substack{d_{i,j}=t \\ d_{i,j} \le w}} a_{i,j} \tag{5}$$

Whereby

- $A_j(t)$ ... capacity needed until time t at machine group j

- $A_j(0)$ ... backorder capacity at time 0 at machine group j

- $a_{i,j}$ ... capacity needed at the machine group j to finish order i (each production order consists of one customer order)

- $a_j(t)$ ... capacity needed with due date t at machine group j

- w ... work-ahead window

The cumulated available capacity is calculated by integrating over the planned machine group capacity as seen in (6).

$$X_j(t) = \int_0^t x_j(\tau)\, d\tau \tag{6}$$

Whereby

- $x_j(t)$ ... capacity available at time t

- $X_j(t)$ ... capacity available until time t

The model presented in section 3.3 corresponds to the work published in [1] and [5].

3.4 Model Extension

By applying the classical approach developed in [1] and [5] no securities for short term capacity allocation exist, because only the capacity for already fixed customer orders is included. However, the concept of the operation characteristics developed by [7] and adapted in this paper explains that with a certain probability short term orders, which will decrease over the length of the customer required lead time, will enter the production system. The model developed in this paper combines those two concepts in order to include short term orders.

The problem of implementing enough capacity for short term orders is solved by producing fixed customer orders earlier in order to get free capacity for short term orders. The OC describes exactly how much workload of the orders has to be produced earlier by applying the integral of the OC. Therefore, integrating the OC up to the investigated customer required delivery time indicates how much earlier a capacity for an order has to be provided as seen in (7). This leads to $G_j(t)$, which shows the cumulative needed capacity corrected by the OC.

$$G_j(t) = A_j \left(\int_0^t OC_j(\tau) d\tau \right) \tag{7}$$

Whereby $G_j(t)$ refers to the corrected capacity needed until time t.

To set the capacity in a proper way it is necessary to compare the cumulative available capacity $X_j(t)$ provided by the machine group with the corrected cumulative needed capacity $G_j(t)$ for producing the customer orders. If $G_j(t)$ exceeds $X_j(t)$ then orders cannot be produced on time. There are several possibilities for the management to handle this problem, such as, flexible working hours, splitting the lot size or negotiating new due dates for customer orders according to [8]. But, if $X_j(t)$ is bigger than $G_j(t)$ then the company wastes money because more capacity is provided than needed. In this case it is possible to reduce $x_j(t)$ in order to save money.

3.5 Numerical Example

A machine group somewhere in the production process is investigated in this numerical example, whereby the customer required due dates are calculated according to (3). In the numerical example $x_j(t)$ is assumed to be 3 capacity units per period, whereby preventive maintenance is planned for periods 8 to 10 as illustrated in Figure (2). $A_j(t)$ indicates the cumulated needed capacity for all fixed customer orders until time 30, whereby the due date and the required capacity for each order is shown in the table on the right in Figure 2.

Due to the fact that the production system will receive further customer orders according to the OC the system has to provide enough capacity to produce these short term customer orders on time as well. Therefore $G_j(t)$ represents the cumulated corrected needed capacity for the investigated machine group, whereby the OC parameters from Figure (1) have been applied. For example the capacity with the due date at time 10 has to be provided until time 9.25, because the integral of the OC from 0 to time 10 is equal to the corrected latest possible date for capacity allocation time. Figure 2 shows the correction of $A_j(t)$ which results in $G_j(t)$.

If no short term orders are included for capacity planning, then $X_j(t)$ is always bigger than $A_j(t)$. That means the company is not able to accept orders until time 11 in order to guarantee the due dates negotiated with customers. All orders are fulfilled on time.

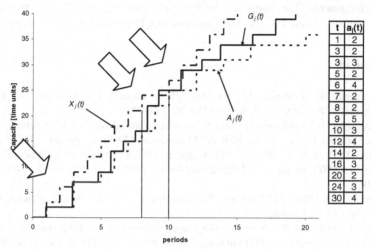

Fig. 2. Capacity checking

Due to the OC it is known that short term orders will enter the system with shorter due dates than the existing orders. Hence capacities are planned earlier than the original due date as seen in Figure 2. After applying the OC the production system cannot produce existing orders or new short term orders on time as shown by the three highlighted crossings of $X_j(t)$ and $G_j(t)$ in Figure 2. Now actions like flexible working hours, lot size splitting and delaying customer orders can be implemented in advance by the management to increase delivery reliability based on the anticipated future needed capacity.

4 Conclusion

In MTO environments it is necessary to allocate production capacity according to customer demand. This paper uses the approach of comparing the cumulated available capacity of the production system and the cumulated needed capacity demanded by the customer. The major drawback of this method is that no capacities for short term orders are included. Therefore, the concept of the operations characteristics, which describes the relationship between customer required lead time and needed capacity, is implemented to calculate how much earlier the needed capacity has to be provided, so that short term orders can be included.

Based on the corrected needed capacity the available capacity of a production system can be adjusted. This can be done by management decisions. If the cumulated available capacity is much higher than the cumulated needed capacity, then reducing the capacity by a reduction of shifts or redundancies can be an option. But if the cumulated needed capacity is higher than the cumulated available capacity the available capacity has to be increased by increasing for example the workforce by personnel leasing otherwise the promised due date cannot be adhered to. Further research should extend this concept to a stochastic processing time.

Acknowledgments. This paper was written within the framework of the project "Embedded Conwip" funded by the Austrian Research Promotion Agency (FFG).

References

1. Altendorfer, K., Jodlbauer, H.: An Approach for Capacity Checking and Due Date Adjustment. In: Proceedings FH Science Day 2007 (2007)
2. Altendorfer, K., Jodlbauer, H.: Simple cumulative model for Due Date Setting. In: Leobener Logistic Cases – Supply Network Management (2009) (to appear)
3. Corti, D., Pozzetti, A., Zorzini, M.: A capacity-driven approach to establish reliable due dates in a MTO environment. International Journal of Production Economics 104, 536–554 (2006)
4. Edwards, J.N.: MRP and Kanban – American Style. In: APICS 26th Conference Proceedings, pp. 586–603 (1983)
5. Hübl, A., Jodlbauer, H.: A combined approach for capacity checking, due date setting and stock availability in an MTO environment. In: Proceedings FH Science Day 2008 Linz, Austria, pp. 372–381 (2008)
6. Javalgi, R.G.W., Thomas, W., Ghosh, A.K., Young, R.B.: Market orientation, strategic flexibility, and performance: implications for services providers. Journal of Services Marketing 19(4), 212–221 (2005)
7. Jodlbauer, H.: Customer driven production planning. International Journal of Production Economics 111(2), 793–801 (2008a)
8. Jodlbauer, H.: Produktionsoptimierung – Wertschaffende sowie kundenorientierte Planung und Steuerung, 2nd edn. Springer, Wien (2008b)
9. Koltai, T., Stecke, K.: Route-Independet Analysis of Available Capacity in Flexible manufacturing Systems. Prod. and Operations Management 17, 211–223 (2008)
10. Lambert, D.M., Stock, J.R., Ellram, L.M.: Fundamentals of Logistics Management. McGraw-Hill, New York (1998)
11. Li, H., Hendry, L., Teunter, R.: A strategic capacity allocation model for a complex supply chain: Formulation and solution approach comparison. Int. J. of Prod. Econ. (March 24, 2007) (in Press, Corrected Proof)
12. Modarres, M., Sharifyazdi, M.: Revenue management approach to stochastic capacity allocation problem. Europ. J. of Op. Res. 192(2), 442–459 (2007)
13. Moses, S., Grant, H., Gruenwald, L., Pulat, S.: Real-Time due-date promising by build-to-order environments. Int. J. Prod. Res. 42, 4353–4375 (2004)
14. Özdamar, L., Yazgac, T.: Capacity driven due date settings in make-to-order production systems. Int. J. Prod. Econ. 49, 29–44 (1997)
15. Panwalkar, S.S., Wafik, I.: A Survey of Scheduling rules. Operations Research 25(1), 45–61 (1977)
16. Taylor, S., Plenert, G.: Finite Capacity Promising. Production & Inventory Management Journal 40(3), 50–57 (1999)
17. Xiong, M., Tor, S.B., Khoo, L.P., Chen, C.-H.: A webenhanced dynamic BOM-based available-to-promise system. Int. J. Prod. Econ. 84, 133–147 (2003a)
18. Xiong, M., Tor, S.B., Khoo, L.P.: WebATP: a Web-based flexible available-to-promise computation system. Prod. Plan. & Control 14, 662–672 (2003b)

Decision Making Tool for the Selection of Urban Freight Transport Project

Nicolas Malhéné and Dominique Breuil

EIGSI – Ecole d'Ingénieurs en Génie des Systèmes Industriels,
26, rue des Vaux de Foletier La Rochelle Cedex 1 17041
{nicolas.malhene,dominique.breuil}@eigsi.fr

Abstract. The control of transport is a very current preoccupation in a context of sustainable development. Nuisances associated to Urban Freight Transport (UFT) force politicians to propose measures relevant to sustainable development of the city. Nevertheless they should keep in mind the efficiency of UFT which renders the implementation of new projects quite difficult. We propose to transpose systemic approach to UFT problematic and to develop a global approach for the management of the evolution of City Logistics. Our first propositions in the domain conduce to the development of a tool allowing politicians to determine UFT solution coherent with their objectives.

Keywords: Urban Freight Transport, Evolution, innovative solutions for UFT.

1 Introduction

COST 321 Actions [1] show that freight transport contributes about 20 % in the total traffic within urban areas but represents 40% of the pollution. Recent and convergent surveys (ex "Sustainable Urban Transport Plans" in 2007, French national surveys in 2004 or Bestufs indicators) gave UFT's quantified situation in the city flows and its evolutions in next coming years; the growing importance of these flows will be more and more worrying. The importance of UFT has also been highlighted by the cost distribution within the freight transport chain. The weight of these costs is further increased by the reduction of stocks, the smaller size of consignments and the increase in their number [2]. UFT challenges can be classified in four categories [3]:

- Functional ones address the city as a whole and more particularly the integration of goods flows in global sustainable transport plans and the sharing transport facilities with passengers flows;
- Economics, since UFT efficiency directly impacts the performances of supply chains and influences indirectly the commercial or crafts activities of a city;
- Urban planning ones because the frequentation and the occupation of space are indeed closely related to his accessibility both for the people and the goods;
- Societal and environmental ones have direct effects on the quality of life.

Considering resulting complexity, it is quite difficult for politicians to optimize UFT. Furthermore, even if they succeed in implementing a so called optimized UFT

B. Vallespir and T. Alix (Eds.): APMS 2009, IFIP AICT 338, pp. 299–306, 2010.

system, the fast evolution of the economic environment makes this system quickly obsolete. The evolution of UFT system must be controlled together with the evolution of its environment. The first part of the paper proposes a reference framework to study UFT in medium size cities and to formalize the associated problematic. The second part shows how innovative works relevant to the production systems domain may be transferred towards UFT systems in order to conceptualize the management of their evolution. The last part of the paper presents the prototype of a software tool to support such approach.

2   Reference Framework for the Study of Urban Freight Transport

2.1   Concept of System .

The framework should be global in order to include all stakeholders, resources, constraints associated to UFT and to underline relationships between previous elements. Widely exploited in production systems domain, systemic approach fits our criteria. It proposes a conceptual framework, a set of knowledge and tools to understand phenomena in a global way. A system is defined as a group of elementary processors of various natures connected and interconnected, in order to satisfy one or several defined objectives or finalities.

By definition, the environment of the system contains all that the modeler does not wish to integrate into the system. In particular, the environment contains the entity which wishes to consume for its own activity one or several Objects that it can not produce itself. The identification of such a relation brings to the foreground a system.

2.2   Characterization of the UFT System

To transpose systematic paradigm into the urban transport problematic, we could define the environment of our system as being composed of all the entities wishing to be moved by a A point towards a B point at time t given. In our proposition, A or/and B correspond(s) to location(s) in the city when entity is a specific good. Our environment wishes to consume an Object which we shall define as the service of transport necessary for this movement. Thus UFT Transport system is depicted through fig. 1:

Systematic paradigm [4] stresses the need for a system to be able to evolve in order to adapt itself permanently to the modifications of its environment. The system's variety is function of the potential number of relations between system's elementary processors and depends directly on the number of processors of the system. By the way, variety represents the capability of the system to evolve. One closed system can not import or exchange processors: its variety growths till a maximum $V_{max} = 2^{N^2}$ where N is the number of processors of the system. This value determines the end of the evolution process. This is not the case for an open system: the variety of the system continues to grow while the system is able to import new processors. On an etymologic point of view, the system should stay a coherent group in order to fulfill the finality. The importation and the integration of new processors have to be controlled then the evolution of the system can be managed.

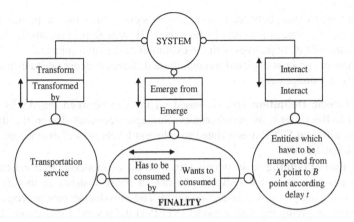

Fig. 1. Emergence of the system dedicated to transport of entities

3 Management of the Evolution of UFT System

3.1 Conceptual Approach of the Evolution Trajectory

Our work is mainly based on techniques developed by the GRAI Laboratory on the coherence analysis and on the performance evaluation in manufacturing systems [5]. This research conduces to characterize the evolution of the system as a continuous process based on a combination of "steps". Each step represents the evolution of the status of the system [6].

SHOULD-BE corresponds to the idealist vision of the UFT system at time t. It is expressed through the vector of operational performances expected by stakeholders. Associated to a strategic horizon this state will not be reached; during this lead time system environment will be modified requiring definition of different vector of performances. AS-IS corresponds to representation of the UFT system at time t. It gives a model of actual UFT system as well as the actual vector of operational performances. Successive STEP-n draw the evolution trajectory of the UFT system. The

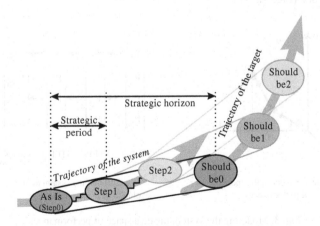

Fig. 2. Evolution process

interval of time existing between two successive steps is the strategic period. It corresponds to the lead time at the end of which the UFT system must reconsider its trajectory (adaptation of its objectives with the evolution of the environment).

The evolution process depicted through these different conceptual states underlines three levels of management.

- The **Strategic Definition** level is based on the gap between the AS-IS and the SHOULD-BE in term of performances. Strategic decisions design the trajectory defining different STEP-n associated to coherent levels of performance which lead to the SHOULD-BE;
- The **Actions Planning** level operates in a world of models. Once existing UFT system has been modeled (AS IS), the design phase consists in modifying this model arranging processors interconnections and introducing new processors. This phase aims at giving the future model (STEP-1) the potential that ensure the UFT system to match operational performances provided by upper level. Actions Planning decisions aim at linking on one side the gap of operational performance between existing and future system and on the other side design objectives;
- The **Projects Management** level has in charge the integration of new processors. This level corresponds to a classical multi-project management system and then all activities usable for such a management find their place within it and in particular activities referring to human resources involvement.

3.2 Proposal for a Formalization of Performance-Based Management of Evolution

The Strategic Definition level operates only in term of performances evolution. The UFT system can be modeled in a space of operational performances. CIVITAS program (cf www.civitas-initiative.eu) identified different performance criteria for such system: Operating costs, Air Quality, Service reliability, Congestion Levels, etc. This level draws the evolution of the system through a vector of performances. For instance, a UFT system is chosen to be evaluated through three performances: P_1, P_2 and P_3. Then the system itself and its evolution will be modeled inside a three-dimension space (Fig. 3).

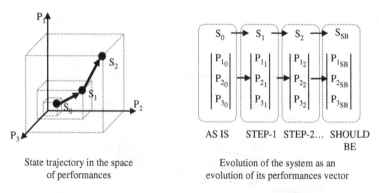

State trajectory in the space   Evolution of the system as an
of performances   evolution of its performances vector

Fig. 3. Modeling the system inside a space of performances

During the evolution process, the repository of performance does not change: the criteria are kept and only their value is modified. If it was necessary to modify it repository, it would mean that the objectives of evolution changed and that a new process must be engaged.

3.2.1 Dynamics and Characterization of Evolution

Each evolution state is associated to a vector of performances. Two following states are linked by a step of evolution called "transition". A transition is characterized by a cost value (regarding one or several criteria like money, environment or social impacts ...) and a time to be fulfilled. cost value and time are strongly linked.

3.2.2 Accessibility

An evolution state is accessible if the associated vector of performances can exist, i.e. if the variables of the vector respect internal and external constraints. Two main kinds of situations explain this notion:

- The first one corresponds to a level of performance which cannot be reached by one or several variables of the vector (for instance, the CO_2 emission variable is likely to be limited by 0 mg regarding the vehicle life cycle);
- The second situation corresponds to the case where one variable of the vector limits other ones (mutual exclusion). The case in which two performances are linked by a trade-off illustrates this situation. As an example, experiments demonstrate that Operating costs and Service reliability limit each other.

3.2.3 Pertinence

A state is pertinent if each performances vector variable participates effectively to the global performance expected by the enterprise. Effective participation of a variable means that the reduction of its value induces global performance reduction.

4 Decision Aided Tool to Support UFT Evolution Process

Our previous theoretical reflections represent the first step for the development of a global approach. Nevertheless to interest politicians and other stake holders to these concepts, it is important to present operational results. For this reason we have initiated the development of a software tool which can support our approach. We had first to identify what are the processors or relevant innovative solutions allowing UFT system evolution.

4.1 Relevant Processors or Innovative Solutions in UFT

UFT's solutions have been studied and experimented for quite some time now. Different categories of innovative solutions have been identified and many of them have been recorded in the European BESTUFS program [7]; several demonstration measures have been conduced in the frame of CIVITAS initiative European program. In France several studies and some solutions have been supported by the PREDIT [8]. Short or medium term evolutions can already be foreseen; some of them linked to the deployment of telematics, others due to development of technologies or of awareness of the stakeholders:

4.1.1 To Develop Infrastructures

This category of solutions reefers to all types of infrastructures. Various actions are engaged from anticipation in land use planning to the adaptation of dedicated lanes. Evolutions will concern mainly access controlled zones and delivery bays. For both of them, new concepts such as status variation during the day (i.e. adapting the finality of the road space during the day) or new technologies (ex. remote control of delivery bays occupation) will bring flexibility in the utilization of the space.

4.1.2 To Facilitate City's Access

Solutions concern all information devices which can be thought of in order to make easier the drivers' job to deliver products in the city. Then signing equipments as well as software participate to these improvements which are linked directly to the progresses of Information & Telecommunication Technologies. In the very next future, specific routing messages will be transmitted to drivers to modify their routes according to traffic situation or global goods distribution will be organize through common information platform shared by haulers. This will also concern the future self routing determination that RFID equipped products will have in the future.

4.1.3 To Implement Proximity Storage Facilities

This topic concerns all types of storage from freight villages' warehouses to logistic boxes, going through Urban Freight Consolidation Centre platforms. Many experimentation cases already showed the various ways of organizing distribution from these facilities. The main evolutions will concern both the management and the global organization of these facilities in the cities, in order to optimize the efficiency of distribution activities and make them really profitable. Then the different types of proximity storages could be combined according to the surroundings activities, on permanent or temporary basis (building construction, specific events...).

4.1.4 To Use Adequate Vehicles

Important developments are yet to be realized in that domain; Apart from existing clean vehicles which are more or less fit for city logistics, new ones are already designed and should be used in the next coming years. Other concepts will be implemented, probably in a combined way in order to adapt the vehicles to the transported goods, final destination and cost effectiveness. Of course these developments are related to the organization of storage facilities.

4.1.5 To Control

To control means both to set up adapted, homogeneous and coherent regulations and the verification of their compliance by concerned stakeholders. The main evolutions will concern more the way the results are analyzed and used for evaluation purpose of other actions than on the regulations themselves for which almost all possible experimentations have been realized.

4.1.6 To Set Up Partnerships

This point is the key factor which is necessarily part of other improvements. This cannot be set alone, for whatever the negotiations between stakeholders deal with, there will be concrete modifications in the goods circulation. Several types of partnerships' building strategies have been experimented (ex FQP, Freight Quality Partnerships in England) involving main transport companies delivering goods in cities. The evolution will be on the ways to involve all stakeholders in the partnerships or the incentive given to increase their motivation.

4.2 Decision Tool for the Importation of UFT Processor

Our objective is to develop a tool which can support the evolution of UFT system. The first version does not aim at integrating all our theoretical proposals. It focuses on two consecutive steps and the associated transition. Respecting principles of accessibility and pertinence, the resulting operational tool aims at directing politicians to several projects, so that they become aware of the largest number of potential solutions. The tool is based on a data base and a qualitative matrix. The data base includes the results of CIVITAS initiative European programme in particular:

– Characteristics of different middle size cities involved in the program,
– Characteristics of several demonstration measures launched by those cities.

The set of city's characteristics corresponds to a basic model of the city. It also corresponds to a vector of performances which guides the evolution of UFT system. Based on these elements, the use of the tool is quite easy. First, the decision maker has to input the characteristics of his city. These characteristics are compared to average CIVITAS data. A score results from this comparison and allows going through the qualitative matrix which is already fulfilled.

This matrix is the kernel of the tool. To highlight the most sensible solution to be set up in a city, we opted for a homemade binary notation. This system of notation allows to increase the note associated to a solution if its contribution is considered as positive with regarding a specific city characteristic. If its contribution is negative or neutral the note is not influenced. By the way the biggest note corresponds to the most pertinent solution in this sense that it positively influences a majority of the city characteristics.

So, the tool informs the decision maker on the opportunity to choose a UFT action among others through a hierarchical presentation. Finally, the decision making tool presents the results of the implementation of similar action in a similar context. It also gives information related to characteristics, advantage and inconvenient of such actions as well as the cost aspects considering the fact that such factor is quite important for this kind of decision.

5 Conclusion

The tool has been validated by politicians of the Urban Community of La Rochelle. It is a first version of a global set of tools which will integrate all the conceptual approach and relevant theoretical proposals. The overall approach itself and in particular the formalization of the evolution process will be widely developed. Recent work related to management of the evolution process of industrial enterprise gives some perspectives. [9] conceptualizes change projects to evaluate associated cost, duration and impacts. The generic framework developed in this work allows evaluating the interest of change projects in order to build a relevant trajectory. This approach could be adapted to our problematic. This will be the next step before considering the global optimisation of urban mobility. In this perspective, an integrated approach will deal with both UFT and Transport of Passengers opening research field toward interoperability and system of systems.

References

1. COST 321 Action, European Commission Directorate General Transport (1998) COST 321 Urban Goods Transport, final report, Brussels (European Commission) (1998)
2. Study material, Inner Urban Freight Transport and City Logistics (2003), http://www.euportal.net
3. Boudouin, D., Morel, C.: Logistique Urbaine – l'optimisation de la circulation des biens et services en ville. In: Programme national "Marchandises en ville", Documentation Française, p. 15 (2002)
4. Le Moigne, J.L.: La théorie du système général. Théorie de la modélisation, Presses Universitaires de France, Paris (1977)
5. Ducq, Y.: Contribution à une méthodologie d'analyse de la cohérence des systèmes de production dans le cadre du modèle GRAI, Thèse de doctorat, Université Bordeaux 1, Février (1999)
6. Malhéné, N.: Gestion du processus d'évolution des systèmes industriels – Conduite et méthode, Thèse de doctorat, Université Bordeaux 1 (Janvier 2000)
7. BESTUFS, Good Practice Guide (September 2007), http://www.bestufs.net/
8. PREDIT, Publications of Operational Group no. 5 (2008) Logistics and Freight Transport, http://www.predit.prd.fr/predit3/goDirect.fo?cmd=go&inCde=5
9. Ben Zaïda, Y.: Contribution à la conduite du changement du système entreprise, Thèse de doctorat, Université Montpellier 2 (Novembre 2008)

Making PROFIT at the Intermodal Terminal – A Research Agenda

Torbjörn H. Netland and Ingrid Spjelkavik

Department of Industrial Management, SINTEF Technology and society,
S.P. Andersens veg 5, 7465 Trondheim, Norway
`torbjorn.netland@sintef.no`

Abstract. Intermodality has been a hot topic in the logistics sector for several decades, but the expected diffusion into business is still limited. The key to increased intermodalism lies at the intermodal terminal. This paper puts forward four literature-based propositions that should be part of the future research agenda for intermodal terminals. In order to realise the intermodal terminal of the future, there is a need to: (P1) develop an effective operative terminal system, (P2) develop a holistic performance measurement system for the terminal, (P3) develop cooperation models for the network actors, and (P4) develop new value increasing services at the terminal.

Keywords: Intermodality, terminal, logistics.

1 Introduction

Due to today's global competition in logistics services and the focus on environment-friendly transport, intermodal transportation is increasingly achieving attention. For intermodal transportation networks to be effective it is required that the main goods flows are routed through centralised nodes where the goods are efficiently transhipped to other carrying units. The transhipment can be between similar modes (rail-rail, road-road etc.) or different modes of transport (rail-road, sea-road etc.). Thus, the terminal is the key to achieve competitiveness in intermodal networks. It is at the terminal that the *"inter"*-aspect of intermodality is realised.

The purpose of this paper is to put forward a set of literature-based propositions that should be part of the future research agenda for intermodal terminals. The paper is written as a conceptual point of departure for the Norwegian research project PROFIT (Project Future Intermodal Terminals) 2009-2011, with a vision to "develop the terminal from a cost centre to a central node for value creation in the future intermodal logistic networks" [1].

The paper presents a literature review on intermodal transport with a focus on terminals and discusses relevant future research areas. Databases such as Bibsys, Ei Compendex, ABI, ISI and other databases were searched for books and papers with the keywords "terminals", "intermodality", "port" and "intermodal transport", combined with "freight transport", "container", "performance management" and "operations management" in title and abstract. Reference lists in the found articles and

B. Vallespir and T. Alix (Eds.): APMS 2009, IFIP AICT 338, pp. 307–314, 2010.

books where searched for additional relevant literature. The theory discussions end into a set of literature-based propositions for the future research agenda on intermodal terminals.

2 Research on Intermodality at Terminals

Research on intermodality at terminals is not new. The invitation programme for the Second Conference on Intermodal Freight Terminal Design, held in New Orleans in March 1986, clearly emphasises a topic that is as relevant today as it was twenty years ago:

> *"There are more and more and larger and larger conferences on the intermodal subject every year. The aim of this conference, however, was to focus appropriate attention to the most costly element of intermodal services: the terminal. The conference theme 'Facing the Challenge – The Intermodal Terminal of the Future', was borne out by a program that featured the latest examples of the technologies involved"* [2].

1.1 Defining Intermodality

A wide variety of definitions of intermodality exists. In this paper we adopt the definition of intermodal transport put forward by OECD [3]: "Intermodal transport indicates the use of at least two different modes of transport in an integrated manner in a door-to-door transportation chain". This definition underpins the distinction between intermodalism and multimodalism: According to Chatterjee and Lakshmanan [4] multimodalism simply means transport by multiple modes, and has existed for hundreds of years since early cargo sea shipment and the first years of the railway. Intermodalism, on the other hand, has grown since the 1980s, and involves standardised and *integrated* interfaces between modes. In other words; intermodal transport is similar to multimodal transport but puts more emphasis on connectivity of different transport modes [5]. It is exactly this connectivity or *interconnectivity* that gives a *seamless* transportation chain that is the key to future success of intermodal transport. Intermodalism as it exists today is far from seamless, and the most important issue is how to build the seams by reducing transaction costs at the transfer points [4]. Thus, the seamless interconnectivity can only be ensured at the terminal.

1.2 Drivers for Increased Intermodal Transport

There are several reasons for the growth of intermodal transportation systems. Chatterjee and Lakshmanan [4] outline four main macro drivers towards increased intermodal transport:

One macro trend is *globalisation*. Globalisation encourages increased intermodal transportation through the growth of international and interregional trade agreements and unions (e.g. GATT, WTO, NAFTA, and EU) that leads to free competition in earlier regulated national markets. In addition global production and global sourcing substantially increase the need for transport in general.

Technological innovation, containerisation in particular, is another macro driver. The container, measured in TEU (Twenty-foot equivalent units), allows for standardisation and gives predictability and robustness in global transportation networks and is the clearly most referred reason for intermodal growth. Other key technological drivers for increased intermodality are advanced container ships and RO-RO-ships, double-stack trains, piggyback rail solutions, general ICT-developments such as web portals, EDI and advanced business software, ITS technologies (Intelligent Transportation System), auto-id technologies giving visibility such as AVL, GPS, DGPS (Differential GPS), and handling technologies and machines such as for example gantry cranes with capacity of 40 container moves per hour.

Some recent political and commercial *reforms in the transportation sector* also encourage the growth of intermodal transport. Deregulation of national transportation markets (in particular road and rail) is a typical example of a *institutional reform* that leads to free competition and the development of competitive intermodal transportation. Other *organisational reforms* have led to new business models, consisting among others of specialised freight forwarders, container leasing companies, consolidators that take LTL (less-than-truckload), custom brokers, intermodal terminal operators, and third party and fourth party logistics providers. Many of these new business models are ready to reap the advantage of better intermodal infrastructure.

Finally, the global trend in manufacturing industry to become more lean and efficient is changing transportation *from push to pull logistics systems.* The Just-in-time principle introduced by Toyota in the 1960s was picked up by the Western manufacturing industry in the 1980s, and is more popular today than ever. Just-in-time production requires smaller volumes and more frequent supply with a track-and-trace and cost efficiency focus.

2.3 Two Main Streams of Research

In particular two streams of research fields are dominating the literature on intermodal terminals today:

(1) Operations Research (OR) on both a macro view (e.g. network optimisation) and a micro view (e.g. crane move optimisation) [e.g. 6, 7, 8, 9]

(2) Transportation infrastructure and communication (often state-funded research with political implications) [e.g. 10, 11, 12, 13]

Intermodal transportation networks have received much attention from Operation Research (OR) disciplines using mathematical programming techniques to optimise the design of location and flow in networks. A reason for this might be that "logistics and transportation have been among the most successful application areas of OR" [6]. OR-research on terminal logistics is concerned with issues such as network optimisation, location analysis, planning algorithms for container stacking, fleet management optimisation, crane utilisation optimisation, berth management optimisation, allocation of storage space, and so on. OR-research indisputable has a powerful contribution in regard to increasing the effectiveness and efficiency of logistics networks and terminal operations, but OR-research alone will not lead to great increase in intermodal transportation.

Intermodal transportation networks has also been heavily analysed from a public perspective on transportation infrastructure and communication. In his rather extensive book on Intermodal Freight Transport, David Lowe [10] recognises the importance of the terminal; "A network of strategically located and fully equipped transfer terminals (...) is critical to the development of international combined transport operations. But yet, throughout his book Lowe put very limited emphasis on the subject; only five out of 276 pages directly discuss the freight interchange at terminals (pages 142-146). Much is written about intermodality from this political macro perspective, but great practical examples of intermodal transport are still relatively rare in these studies.

Common for both research streams is an underlying focus on performance, because improving performance (throughput, cost effectiveness, speed, quality, reliability etc) is the overall remedy of creating competitive intermodal terminals. Altogether there seems to be three reasons for performance measurement in transports according to Meyer [14] and Humphreys and Graham [15]: (1) Measurements of the effects of public investments in transports, (2) measurements as a basis for decision making and strategies for investments in transport, and (3) measurements for following up and identification of improvements within the transporting companies. Fagerhaug and Olsson [13] studied state-of-the-art in performance measurement within railroad, transport and found that the reason for performance measurement in transports is to achieve continuously improvements in operations and results, but what actually is being measured, is productivity in the sense of output in relation to input. Gosling [16] also calls on measuring *outcomes* rather than outputs, to measure customer satisfaction, measures relevant for strategy processes and decision making

3 Discussion on Challenges to Be Met

3.1 Operational Challenges

Despite the political drivers towards increased intermodal transportation, intermodalism is still in its early stages of development [4], and the market share of intermodal transport is still low, and moreover, is not showing a significant increase [17, 18]. There are several reasons for this slow diffusion of intermodality into praxis; First and foremost, the unbiased cost focus in the Europeans transport sector [18] has led to hard entry conditions for new transportation systems such as intermodality. Especially the time- and cost handicap of intermodal transportation due to the transhipment, and it's still inferior frequency, is hindering intermodal growth [11]. Also technological and infrastructural factors are still obstacles [17], as an example there are 37 different combinations of rail gauge, tunnel clearance and power systems in Europe [18]. Another technological challenge is the lack of standardisation of swap bodies [11]. But first and foremost, intermodal competitiveness is tied to operational effectiveness and efficiency at the terminal.

In order to reap the full environmental and corporate benefits of intermodal transportation systems, the successful intermodality at sea must be passed forward to inland transportation modes. While the diffusion of intermodality in the inland transportation systems has been slow, global intermodality has been very successful on sea [19]. The

European inland intermodal success is mainly tied to the Alpine crossing and the transport between the main seaports and their hinterland [11]. Inland intermodal transportation systems are rare in practice. Intermodal shipping has 30 years of success. It is the shipping industry that developed the standardised container, not rail- and road actors. According to Stone [19], successful marine intermodal terminals have passed through four development phases: (1) Making it work, (2) Handling the growth of demand, (3) Reducing the system cost, and (4) Managing the performance. The four suggested phases are maturity levels with thresholds that must be overcome in order to reach the next maturity phase. Now is the time to realise the fact that "containerisation and intermodality have strengthened the symbiotic relationship between foreland and hinterland in the sense that a true foreland-hinterland continuum has come to existence [20]". Making it work implies a first focus on operational effectiveness.

Based on this discussion we propose that a first challenge to solve should be to *(P1) develop an effective operative terminal system.*

3.2 Performance Challenges

Several authors [19, 21, 22] ask for better performance measurement systems at terminals. The terminal must meet the requirements of the transportation *network*. Terminals should change from production-oriented (internal processes) to customer-oriented [21]. Metz [23] and Bustinduy [24] focuses on quality as the key to success. But container terminals have no tradition for quality measurement [21].

In the future development of performance perspective within intermodal terminals we should look for advice in the statements of Konings et al [17] and their three determinants for the performance of intermodal transport and its potential role as an alternative mode for road transport (1) intermodal transport operations, (2) design and modelling and (3) implementation and policy. The development of a performance measurement system for the terminal should provide transparency in the logistic network, and support and emphasise the behaviour that ensures efficiency in the flow of containers. The performance measurement system should be a tool for different users of the future intermodal terminal. There is also a lack of performance indicators for intermodal terminals that should be answered in future research.

Based on this we propose that a second challenge to solve is to *(P2) develop a holistic performance measurement system for the terminal.*

3.3 Network Challenges

One major obstacle to increased intermodalism is that the investments has to be taken by one or two actors (rail infrastructure owners and terminal operators), while the gains are partially reaped by the logistic service companies, and certainly also passed forward to the most powerful actor in the supply chain – the goods owners (retail chains, manufacturing companies etc). The latter group is decoupled from all investments in rail and terminal infrastructure. In short; most cost for quality improvement occurs at the terminal, while most benefits are reaped in the network [21]. Halseth [12] found that it has been extremely difficult to study cooperation models at Norwegain intermodal terminals, because independent transportation providers has sought competition rather than cooperation, and has not been willing to share data and information with researchers and competitors.

Another major obstacle to increase intermodalism is the total absence of cross-actor IT-infrastructure in the transportation industry. Typically transportation service providers mainly have their in-house-developed IT-system, and this system is regarded as one of the competitive advantages of the firm. This is not unlike the situation in manufacturing industries some two decades ago. In today's manufacturing industries all actors use one out of a limited number of available ERP-systems (Enterprise Resource Planning) (e.g. SAP, Microsoft Dynamics, Microsoft Navision, ERP-LN etc.), that are able to communicate almost seamless with each other through EDI-standards (Electronic Data Interchange). Even though the transportation industry increasingly implements EDI-solutions and especially sea ports' IT-systems (yard management systems) are well developed, much can be learned and transferred from manufacturing industries focus on supply chain management to achieve increased intermodal transportation. Halseth [12] stresses that the use of EDI for consignment notes between major Norwegian logistics providers and their customers has grown as a result of a joint industry initiative in the 90s. Thus major innovations in the transportation industry will not succeed if left to single actors.

Based on this we propose that a third challenge to solve should be to *(P3) develop cooperation models for the network actors*.

3.4 Innovation Challenges

The transportation industry has traditionally a very low degree of research and development. New innovative technologies do only have a limited and slow diffusion into terminals [25]. Incremental innovations in transportation networks are probably the best way to proceed [12]. If new services shall become attractive there is need for compatibility with existing solutions. Conservative logistics providers seek quick return on investment. Nevertheless, there is a need for dramatic innovations in order to tempt more goods to intermodal transportation systems.

Risjenbrij [26] discusses how hinterland terminals can expand their services in order to remove operations and improve throughput in even more pressured mainport terminals. Operations that can be "outsourced" include stripping, customs handling etc. This is in line with the Agile Port System [27] that aims to split the port terminal into an Efficient Marine Terminal (EMT) ashore and an Intermodal Interface Centre (IIC) inland. Wiegmans et al. [21] stress that "to make the container terminal – and the transport service it forms part of – more competitive, it is necessary to offer a total service package (...). Terminals should offer a one-stop-shopping total service, that includes pre- and end- haulage, and not only container handling.

Therefore we propose that a fourth challenge to solve is to *(P4) develop new value increasing services at the terminal*.

4 Conclusions and Future Research

Based on the literature reviewed the authors put forward four propositions. In order to realise the future intermodal terminals there is a need to:

(P1) Develop an effective operative terminal system
(P2) Develop a holistic performance measurement system for the terminal

(P3) Develop cooperation models for the network actors

(P4) Develop new value increasing services at the terminal

These four propositions will be addressed in the remainder of the research project PROFIT. While the literature review indicates that the macro perspective is a commonly used approach in transport literature, the approach of the PROFIT project is the micro perspective as working with the cluster of companies involved in the interaction at the terminal. This conceptual paper will be followed by empirical case studies in the business cluster around Oslo port and the Alnabru freight terminal.

References

1. PROFIT web page, http://www.sintef.no/profit
2. US Transportation Research Board: Facing the challenge: The intermodal freight terminal of the future. In: Conference on Intermodal Freight Terminal Design, New Orleans. State-of-the-art report no. 4, Transportation Research Board, National Research Council, USA, p. iii (1986)
3. OECD: Benchmarking intermodal freight transport, Paris (2002)
4. Chatterjee, L., Lakshmanan, T.R.: Inermodal freight transport in the United States. In: Konings, R., Priemus, H., Nijkamp, P. (eds.) The Future of Intermodal Freight Transport. MPG Nooks Ltd., Bodmin (2008)
5. Taniguchi, E., Nemoto, T.: Intermodal freight transport in urban areas in Japan. In: Konings, R., Priemus, H., Nijkamp, P. (eds.) The Future of Intermodal Freight Transport. MPG Nooks Ltd., Bodmin (2008)
6. Andersen, J.: New service network design models for intermodal freight transportation, philosophia doctor thesis, Norwegian University of Science and Technology, Thesis number 2008:41, Trondheim, Norway (2008)
7. Kim, K.W., Günther, H.-O. (eds.): Container terminals and cargo systems – design, operations management and logistics control issues. Springer, Heidelberg (2007)
8. Steenken, D., Voß, S., Stahlbock, R.: Container terminal operation and operations research – a classification and literature review. OR Spectrum 26, 3–49 (2004)
9. Macharis, C., Bontekoning, Y.M.: Opportunities for OR in intermodal freight transport research: A review. European Journal of Operational Research 153, 400–416 (2004)
10. Lowe, D.: Intermodal Freight Transport. Elsevier/Butterworth-Heinemann, Oxford/UK (2005)
11. Woxenius, J., Bärthel, F.: Intermodal road-rail transport in the European Union. In: Konings, R., Priemus, H., Nijkamp, P. (eds.) The Future of Intermodal Freight Transport. MPG Nooks Ltd., Bodmin (2008)
12. Halseth, A.: Strategier og rammebetingelser for intermodal transport – Oppsummeringsrapport, ECON Pöyry Forskningsrapport 2004-014 (2004)
13. Fagerhaug, T., Olsson, N.: PEMRO Arbeidspakke 1.2. State of the art innenfor prestasjonsmåling, Report SINTEF Technology and society (2005)
14. Meyer, M.D.: Measuring System Performance: Key to Establishing Operations as a Core Agency Mission. Transportation Planning and Analysis. Transportation research record (1817), 155–162 (2002)
15. Humphreys, I., Francis, G.: Traditional Airport Performance Indicators: A Critical Perspective. Issues, problems, and performance measures in airports and airspace Transportation research record (1703), 24–30 (2000)

16. Gosling: Aviation system performance measures for state transportation planning. Issues, problems and performance measures in airports and airspace. Transportation research record (1703), 7–15 (2000)
17. Konings, R., Priemus, H., Nijkamp, P.: The Future of Intermodal Freight Transport; an overview. In: Konings, R., Priemus, H., Nijkamp, P. (eds.) The Future of Intermodal Freight Transport. MPG Nooks Ltd., Bodmin (2008)
18. Tsamboulas, D.: Development strategies for intermodal transport in Europe. In: Konings, R., Priemus, H., Nijkamp, P. (eds.) The Future of Intermodal Freight Transport. MPG Nooks Ltd., Bodmin (2008)
19. Stone, B.: Critical success factors: interconnectivity and interoperability. In: Konings, R., Priemus, H., Nijkamp, P. (eds.) The Future of Intermodal Freight Transport. MPG Nooks Ltd., Bodmin (2008)
20. Notteboom, T.: Bundling freight flows and hinterland network development. In: Konings, R., Priemus, H., Nijkamp, P. (eds.) The Future of Intermodal Freight Transport, p. 66. MPG Nooks Ltd., Bodmin (2008)
21. Wiegmans, B., Nijkamp, P., Rietvald, P.: Conatiner ternminal hanling quality. In: Konings, R., Priemus, H., Nijkamp, P. (eds.) The Future of Intermodal Freight Transport. MPG Nooks Ltd., Bodmin (2008)
22. Janic, M.: An assessment of the performance of the European long intermodal freight trains (LIFTS). Transportation Research Part A: Policy and Practice 42(10), 1326–1339 (2008)
23. Metz, D.: Journey quality as the focus of future transport policy, Transport Policy (2005) (article in Press)
24. Bustinduy, J.: More quality in regional transport. In: Public Transport 1995, 51st International Congress. Paris 1995, International Commision on Regional Transport (1995)
25. Kreutzberger, E.: The impacts of innovative technical concepts for load unit exchange on the design of intermodal freight bundling networks. In: Konings, R., Priemus, H., Nijkamp, P. (eds.) The Future of Intermodal Freight Transport. MPG Nooks Ltd., Bodmin (2008)
26. Risjenbrij, J.: Container handling in mainports: a dilemma about future scales. In: Konings, R., Priemus, H., Nijkamp, P. (eds.) The Future of Intermodal Freight Transport. MPG Nooks Ltd., Bodmin (2008)
27. Franke, K.-P.: A technical approach to the Agile Port System. In: Konings, R., Priemus, H., Nijkamp, P. (eds.) The Future of Intermodal Freight Transport. MPG Nooks Ltd., Bodmin (2008)

The Value of Lead Logistics Services

Oliver Schneider[1] and André Lindner[2]

[1] ETH Zurich, Center for Enterprise Sciences (BWI), 8092 Zurich, Switzerland
oschneider@ethz.ch
[2] Kuehne + Nagel Management AG, 8834 Schindellegi, Switzerland
andre.lindner@kuehne-nagel.com

Abstract. Logistics Services are one of the most outsourced functions within a supply chain. This is due to easily transferrable know-how and traceable direct cost reductions, which directly impact the profit and loss statement. However, an effective management of materials and transportations on the supply and deliver side also carries indirect benefits by positively influencing the cash flow and the amount of capital locked up in inventories. Therefore, it also affects the balance sheet and the company's profitability. This paper describes an approach to make these effects transparent and traceable, by linking operational performance to the resulting changes in working capital. Having transparency on the direct and indirect effects fosters the service relationship and allows for new pricing concepts which carry advantages for both service provider and customer. The approach was developed in a collaborative action research project with a world leading provider of lead logistics services.

Keywords: Transportation Management, Enterprise Value, Productivity, Performance evaluation, Economic Value Added (EVA).

1 Introduction

Through the recent decades the idea of international division of labor and outsourcing has been pursued by nearly all companies with a manufacturing background. This has created multiple tier supply chains. Boosted by relatively low costs for transportation and various deregulations in international trade, such supply chains span significant distances and cover various time zones. Global supply chains have become the norm in business, resulting in increased lead times and decreased visibility.

In this context, Supply Chain Management (SCM) services have gained importance in recent years [1]. Not considered as a core competence, manufacturers outsource their supporting functions like the management of warehouses and logistical activities, and start to outsource tactical demand and supply planning.

SCM in its initial understanding tried to integrate information and material flows from the suppliers' suppliers to the customers' customers [2]. In practice, SCM in most cases has been understood as an execution activity running in isolation from sales and operations planning, creating artificial barriers and inefficiencies [3].

The emerging concept of lead logistics services (LLS) tries to cope with these barriers and inefficiencies. An example is the offering of the "supplier and inventory management (SIM)" service by a world leading LLS provider (LSP), which is a set of

B. Vallespir and T. Alix (Eds.): APMS 2009, IFIP AICT 338, pp. 315–322, 2010.
© IFIP International Federation for Information Processing 2010

management services focusing on the dynamic alignment of demand with supply, including the setup and management of third-party logistics (3PL) providers in charge of the execution. It fulfills a given demand profile with a targeted level of inventory in compliance with customer defined constraints. SIM has to be understood as a layered service offering with three service modules, 1) "Execution Management", which is planning and coordination of transportation, 2) "Supply Logistics", dealing with the replenishment of the inbound warehouse, and 3) "End-to-End Demand and Supply Planning", which represents the Best Practice of "Integrated Demand and Supply Planning" of the SCOR-model.

SIM services support several activities at the OEM, namely the sales and operations planning, procurement, and distribution. Such a service is only possible because of recent advances in information technology (IT) [4]. A layered IT-architecture connects the different tiers within the supply chain.

1.1 Objectives of the Paper

This paper presents a method to quantify the value generated by SIM services from the perspective of the service consumer. Having a clear transparency on the value generated is important for several reasons. From the perspective of the service customer, this transparency is required before the decision on whether to buy this service or not, and after an outsourcing decision for an effective controlling of the LSP. From the perspective of the LSP this transparency is the basis for selling the service according to the customer's needs already from a qualitative perspective, and furthermore to define a price which is considered as fair by both service provider and service consumer [5]. The latter aspect is supported by a then possible new mode of logistics contracting. The basic principle is sharing – sharing of costs, revenues and risks, which is a core topic not only in recent supply chain research [6], but also in practice. Operational performance indicators and the resulting financial impact can be used for including incentives, which go beyond direct cost savings.

1.2 Research Method

Following Action Research (AR) principles [7], supplemented by the method of Systems Engineering [8], several contracts of a leading LSP were analyzed. A generic approach of displaying the different service relationships was developed, using the Supply Chain Operations Reference (SCOR-) model. A method to represent the influence of the supply chain operations on the different elements of working capital was developed and agreed upon. This concept is the basis to calculate a changed enterprise value caused by the LSP, in terms of the financial metric of the Economic Value Added (EVA). The concept was approved and implemented by the key actors of the LSP.

2 Value Assessment of SIM Services

Until now, there are only a few and very limited approaches to calculate the economic value which is generated by SCM services for the service consuming company [9]. They often do consider direct benefits (e.g. savings in transportation and administration cost, changes in inventory levels), but do not likewise consider monetary benefits resulting from higher availability, reliability, and shorter lead times. In order to understand these effects, it is important to know the relationship between SCM and financial management.

2.1 Relationship of SCM and Financial Management

The main goal of financial management is to create value for the stockholders through an effective use of capital, in terms of profitability, liquidity, and security [cf. e.g. 10]. From this overall objective, management tasks can be derived. On a daily basis, the working capital needs to be managed, in order to improve its utilization and reduce capital lockup. On an occasional basis, managers need to decide on stock and bond issues, dividends, and have to do capital budgeting for investments in fixed assets or cost reduction projects, in order to reduce operational risks and therefore improve the liquidity and the profitability of the supply chain [11].

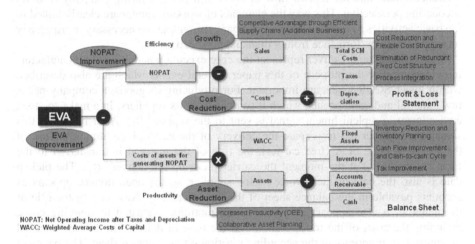

NOPAT: Net Operating Income after Taxes and Depreciation
WACC: Weighted Average Costs of Capital

Fig. 1. Relationship of EVA and SCM improvement strategies

A well-established metric to express the generated value resulting from these management tasks is the Economic Value Added (EVA) [cf. e.g. 12]. The EVA is positive, i.e. value is generated, when an investment activity (in this case, a supply chain) leads to higher profit than the costs related to the utilization of the assets which are needed for performing the activity. The structure of EVA is shown in Fig. 1.

The EVA includes the Weighted Average Costs of Capital (WACC), which represent the investors' perspective in terms of financing costs (interest rates, which also take into account investment risks) and opportunity costs (alternative investments available on the market).

Important element of the EVA is the costs for financing the assets, which include the working capital as current assets. The working capital represents the capital which is "bound" in the operating business, meaning that it transforms its representation in the balance sheet by going through the different stages in a supply chain.

Considering this, the EVA concept merges the aspect of operational performance in the form of sales and costs, and the financial perspective in the form of capital costs. This allows a continuous analysis of the enterprise value generated by its operating business [13]. There are three levers for improving the EVA, 1) sales, 2) costs (of goods sold), and 3) assets, for which financing costs occur. SCM offers improvement strategies and concepts which aim at exactly the three levers for improving the EVA. Therefore, effective SCM directly contributes to enterprise value [14].

2.2 The Relationship of Operational Performance and Working Capital

The core result of the presented research is displayed in Fig. 2. It represents a new way of linking operational supply chain performance to the elements of working capital and provides the basis for translating the performance into enterprise value. The underlying logic combines the use of the SCOR-model as an event-driven process reference model and the known flow of costs in a manufacturing company from an accounting perspective. This way the elements of working capital are clearly linked to the basic activities of a manufacturing company, providing the necessary transparency on supply chain performance from a financial perspective.

Source, Make, and Deliver represent the core execution activities of a manufacturing company. For the purpose of this paper, several events which are also described within lower SCOR levels are important. For producing its goods, a company needs raw material and components, which it sources from its suppliers. In a make-to-stock environment, a replenishment signal is sent to the supplier (t_1). After receiving this signal, the supplier has to prepare the delivery of the material. Assuming the use of the Incoterm code FCA (free carrier), the title of the material is transferred to the focal company (t_3) at the moment the carrier picks up the delivery (t_2). The pickup date is also the date of the invoice of the supplier, so the open invoice appears as accounts payable in the balance sheet of the focal company. Now having the title of the material, it also appears as inventory (in motion), evaluated to sourcing costs, including the costs of the transportation. At the time of delivery to the raw material inventory (t_4), it appears in the according position on the balance sheet. The payment terms with the supplier determine t_5, representing the time when the focal company pays the supplier and has a cash outflow. The invoice is closed and does not appear on the balance sheet anymore. T_6 represents the time when the material is called off for production, then appearing not as raw material anymore, but as work in process. There value is added at every stage of production (with according expenses appearing in the accounts payable), until the assembly is finished and the products are stored in the finished goods inventory (t_7). After the customer order comes in (t_8), the loads are prepared and carriers selected, so that the products can be loaded at t_9. Then they are considered as inventory in motion or in transit, when assuming Incoterm code DDU or DDP, (delivery duty unpaid/paid). From the moment on when the products are delivered and accepted by the customer (t_{10}), and therefore the titles (t_{11}) are transferred, the customer invoice is active. At this moment the products do not appear on the balance sheet of the focal company anymore, but the amount of the invoice appears on the accounts receivable. When the customer pays (t_{12}), the amount disappears and the company has a cash inflow.

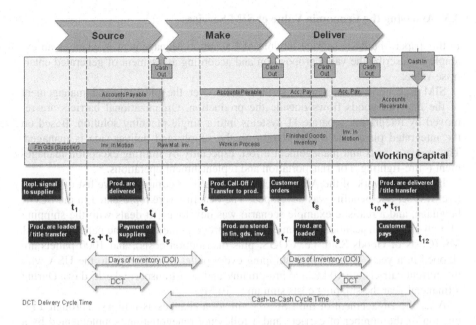

Fig. 2. SCOR level 1, supply chain events, key cycle time indicators, and the relationship to elements of working capital (make-to-stock environment)

As Fig. 2 displays, the time between the payment of suppliers and receiving the money from the customer represents the cash-to-cash cycle time. Additionally, the inbound and outbound delivery cycle times and the days of inventory play an important role. The shorter all the cycle times, the less capital is locked up in the form of inventories.

There is the need to explain the last statement in more detail. All material which is somehow inventory, either in motion, raw material, in process, or finished goods, appears on the balance sheet evaluated to actual total costs. This has two important consequences. First, in case costs per unit are lowered, the evaluation is decreased at the same amount. Second, considering that the balance sheet is a snapshot of the company's asset and capital situation at a given time, there is material in the whole pipeline, which all appears as inventory in the according stage. The shorter the pipeline, the less material adds up in the position of inventory. In Fig. 2, the height of the inventory rectangles represents the evaluation of the material at the particular stage. The widths represent the duration of time (or cycle time) the material remains within the particular stage, and therefore the length of the pipe at a given point of time. The area of the rectangles is the value of the particular element of working capital which appears on the balance sheet. So both cost and cycle time reductions reduce the amount of bound capital within a company.

This relationship provides the basis to show the influence of SIM services on the financial performance of the manufacturer. In the following, an exemplary scenario is given.

2.3 Assessing the Economic Value of SIM Services

In this paper, the basic service module of Execution Management is taken as an example to describe the value proposition and according assessment of generated enterprise value.

SIM Execution Management services take over the planning and management of the material goods flows outside the production. Organizational barriers are removed by integrating separate IT-systems into a single planning solution. Based on the integrated plans, the transportation on the supply and deliver side is managed. This reduces costs and management effort, especially by limiting exception management ("fire-fighting") of transportation and replenishment operations.

In the framework of the AR project with the LSP, a comprehensive list of qualitative SIM service benefits was developed. The benefits were represented in the SCOR language, and a realistic example scenario was developed. It deals with the shipping of high-end pharmaceutical equipment from Europe to the USA. One pallet is worth 1 M€ (Costs of Goods Sold, i.e. COGS, plus distribution costs), and 1000 pallets are shipped in a year. The costs for shipping every pallet from Europe to the USA with the current carriers are 10 k€, and pre-, main-, and post-transport take 15 days. During a financial year the shipping costs sum up to 10 M€.

After the engagement of the LSP, the situation changes as follows. Through a reduction of the number of carriers and a following renegotiation, supplemented by a more efficient use of planners' time, the shipping costs per pallet can be reduced to 8 k€. The faster planning and carrier selection, as well as the selection of better carriers and routes, reduces the outbound delivery cycle time to only 10 days.

Based on the logic of Fig. 2, the financial effects are as follows. Assuming a requirement to ship every day, 2.8 pallets are sent out every day with 42 pallets in transit at the same time in the as-is scenario. The material in transit therefore is worth 42.420 M€, (42 M€ + 420 k€ transportation costs). Because of the reduced shipping costs in the improved scenario, less costs need to be attributed to the COGS. Therefore, one pallet in transit is now evaluated with 1.008 M€ instead of 1.010 M€. Because of the faster delivery cycle time, now only 28 pallets are in transit at the same time, in total evaluated with 28.224 M€ (releasing 14.196 M€ of capital lockup). Because of the reduced shipping costs, the service customer has to pay less to the 3PL, reducing the accounts payable by 20% (from 840 k€ to 672 k€, assuming payment terms of 30d, resulting in open invoices for 84 shipped pallets in one month).

In total, 14.196 M€ capital is released, when compared to the initial situation, and the Earnings Before Interest and Taxes (EBIT) are increased by 2 M€ due to the higher gross profit margin caused by the lower transportation costs. In the logic of the EVA, the amount of released capital can be evaluated against the costs for capital, by using the Weighted Average Costs for Capital (WACC) of the company. Because the accounts payable are part of financing a company's business (as short-term credit from the suppliers), the amount of 168 k€ needs to be deducted from the released capital, because the case company needs to finance this amount through other sources. In the described example and an assumed WACC of 10%, the saved costs of capital therefore are 1.403 M€. Using the EVA calculation logic, this amount can be added to the 2 M€ EBIT improvement. Neglecting probable changes in safety stock levels due to the shorter lead times and changes in tax expenses, the resulting EVA is 3.403 M€.

3 Summary, Practical Implications and Outlook

It was shown, that for calculating the financial impact of transportation management services in the more comprehensive manner of the EVA "classic" indicators as costs and cycle time already qualify. Within the described AR project, the other service modules were examined as well. It was identified that two other key performance characteristics come into play, when providing an even more comprehensive lead logistics solution, namely the reliability in the form of the key metric "Perfect Order Fulfillment", and the "Ability to Commit" in the form of lost sales. A detailed description of these relationships exceeds the limited frame of this article.

The transparency on the generated financial impact provides benefits for both the service provider and service consumer. The latter is supported in doing his make-or-buy decision, by making realistic assumptions on the prospected changes in working capital, and later in controlling the effectiveness of the service provider based on actual performance. The service provider can use information on prospected changes in the working capital of the potential customer as a sales argument, displaying the differentiation value.

The yearly control of the financial impact can be used as an essential element for pricing the service, for instance by implementing gain and risk sharing elements. When applied in an appropriate manner, such service pricing results in the strong incentive for both sides to continuously improve operations, in order to benefit more and more from the generated value.

The proposed concept also carries some limitations. For instance, some changes will be required, in order to implement the service as described. This applies to the organization itself, and the employed IT-infrastructure. Therefore aspects of Change Management must be considered, supplemented by a strong focus on information flows and the according master data within the IT system. A strong requirement in this regard is a high level of trust between the partners.

Moreover, an important requirement for the method is a clear filtering of effects of changes at the customer which are not caused by the service provider, for instance, changes in shipping volumes, the product characteristics, or regions in scope. The experiences of the LSP with gain share contracts show that it is necessary to agree on a clear scope of the influence area and required basic filtering aspects already beforehand. This results in a regular calculation and negotiation effort, which is not to be underestimated. However, this additional effort is considered as worthwhile, because the awareness of the quality and value contribution of collaboration is kept at a constant high level, which builds trust.

The project which developed the described approach focused on assessing the financial impact of lead logistics services. However, it was identified that the concept should also qualify for other types of activities, i.e. basically with any activity related to planning and execution of material and information flows within a supply chain. Therefore the paper provides the basis for further research in the field of SCM and Lean Management, which wants to show a comprehensive and holistic picture on the value of internal improvement projects or make-or-buy decisions.

References

1. Klaus, P., Kille, C.: Die Top 100 der Logistik: Marktgrößen, Marktsegmente und Marktführer in der Logistikdienstleistungswirtschaft (4. Aufl.). Dt. Verkehrs-Verl., Hamburg (2006)
2. Schönsleben, P.: Integral logistics management: Operations and supply chain management in comprehensive value-added networks, 3rd edn. Auerbach Publications, Boca Raton (2007)
3. Sandberg, E.: Logistics collaboration in supply chains: practice vs. theory. Int. J. Log. Man. 18(2), 274–293 (2007)
4. Bauknight, D.N.: The Supply Chain's Future in the e-Economy...: And Why Many May Never See It. Supply Chain Management Review 4(1), 28–35 (2000)
5. Schneider, O., Lange, I., Nitu, B.: Enabling Industrial Service Providers to offer Comprehensive Service Contracts. In: 13th International Conference on Concurrent Enterprising (ICE), Sophia-Antipolis, pp. 295–304 (2007)
6. Melnyk, S.A., Lummus, R.R., Vokurka, R.J., Burns, L.J., Sandor, J.: Mapping the future of supply chain management: a Delphi study. Int. J. Prod. Res. 47(16), 4629–4653 (2009)
7. Greenwood, D.J., Levin, M.: Introduction to Action Research: Social research for social change. Sage Publ., Thousand Oaks (1998)
8. Haberfellner, R., Daenzer, W.F.: Systems Engineering: Methodik und Praxis (11. durchgesehene Auflage). Verlag Industrielle Organisation, Zürich (2002)
9. Sennheiser, A., Schnetzler, M.: Wertorientiertes Supply Chain Management. Springer, Berlin (2008)
10. Stührenberg, L., Streich, D., Henke, J.: Wertorientierte Unternehmensführung: Theoretische Konzepte und empirische Befunde. Dt. Univ.-Verl., Wiesbaden (2003)
11. Garrison, R.H., Noreen, E.W., Brewer, P.C.: Managerial Accounting, 11th edn. McGraw-Hill/Irwin, Boston (2006)
12. Ehrbar, A., Mühlfenzl, I.: EVA, Economic Value Added: Der Schlüssel zur wertsteigernden Unternehmensführung. Gabler, Wiesbaden (1999)
13. Kames, C.: Unternehmensbewertung durch Finanzanalysten als Ausgangspunkt eines Value Based Measurement. Lang, Frankfurt am Main (2000)
14. Lambert, D.M., Burduroglu, R.: Measuring and selling the value of logistics. Int. J. Log. Man. 11(1), 1–17 (2000)

Part III

Interoperable and Distributed Systems

High Resolution Supply Chain Management – Resolution of the Polylemma of Production by Information Transparency and Organizational Integration

Tobias Brosze[1], Fabian Bauhoff[1], Volker Stich[1], and Sascha Fuchs[2]

[1] Research Institute for Operations Management (FIR) at RWTH Aachen University,
Pontdriesch 14/16, 52064 Aachen, Germany
Tobias.Brosze@fir.rwth-aachen.de,
Fabian.Bauhoff@fir.rwth-aachen.de,
Volker.Stich@fir.rwth-aachen.de
[2] Laboratory for Machine Tools and Production Engineering
(WZL) at RWTH Aachen University,
Steinbachstr 19, 52056 Aachen, Germany
Sascha.Fuchs@wzl.rwth-aachen.de

Abstract. High Resolution Supply Chain Management (HRSCM) aims to stop the trend of continuously increasing planning complexity. Today, companies in high-wage countries mostly strive for further optimization of their processes with sophisticated, capital-intensive planning approaches [3]. The capability to adapt flexibly to dynamically changing conditions is limited by the inflexible and centralized planning logic. Thus, flexibility is reached currently by expensive inventory stocks and overcapacities in order to cope with rescheduling of supply or delivery. HRSCM describes the establishment of a complete information transparency in supply chains with the goal of assuring the availability of goods through decentralized, self-optimizing control loops for Production Planning and Control (PPC). By this HRSCM pursues the idea of enabling organizational structures and processes to adapt to dynamic conditions. The basis for this new PPC Model are stable processes, consistent customer orientation, increased capacity flexibility and the understanding of production systems as viable, socio-technical systems [1, 2].

1 Introduction

Within today's manufacturing business the ability to produce individualized goods for a price close to a mass product is one of the key challenges to keep production in high-wage countries. Additionally companies have to be able to adapt themselves and their processes to dynamic environment conditions like shifts in customer's demand, reschedules in supply as well as turbulences in networks without loosing the high objective synchronization enabled by today's planning approaches. These two challenges constitute the polylemma of production, which's resolution is the goal of the German Cluster of Excellence on "Integrative Production Technology for High-Wage Countries" at Aachen University (RWTH) (www.production-research.de). "High

B. Vallespir and T. Alix (Eds.): APMS 2009, IFIP AICT 338, pp. 325–332, 2010.
© IFIP International Federation for Information Processing 2010

Resolution Supply Chain Management" is part of this national initiative funded by the German Research Foundation (DFG).

"High Resolution Supply Chain Management" focuses to solve the dilemma between a high grade of adaptivity (value orientation) and a high objective synchronization (planning orientation). The final aim is to enable manufacturing companies to produce efficiently and be able to react to order-variations at any time, requiring process structures to be most flexible.

2 Methodological Approach

To achieve a higher flexibility and a better value-orientation of inter- and in-company PPC processes, it is necessary to replace the present static arrangement of the central-controlled processes [1, 2]. In consequence, self-controlled and self-optimizing supply chains based on decentralized production control mechanisms must replace the classic approach of PPC. Goal of the decentralized PPC is a higher robustness of the system by distributed handling of complexity and dynamics [6].

Technological Preconditions: The higher the knowledge about the facts, the more sophisticated decisions can be made. Thus, a higher information transparency on all levels of the PPC is a precondition for the implementation of a decentralized planning system. The information transparency enables decision makers or intelligent objects to act adequately. Advantages in miniaturization, sensor systems and communication technology enable the paradigm shift of centralized information handling to intelligent objects with mobile capabilities (cp. Fig. 1) [5].

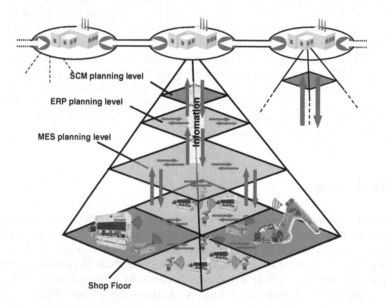

Fig. 1. HRSCM – Vertical and horizontal information transparency in production networks

Organisational Preconditions: Producing companies are complex organizational systems. They consist of sophisticated, technological subsystems, constitute a social structure with individuals having own values and goals, interact with a dynamic environment, and last but not least are adapting or are adapted.

HRSCM aims not only for the technological advantages in production systems, but chiefly for the efficient organization of production systems. In order to understand production systems as socio-technical systems methods of management cybernetic are used to establish a new model of the PPC widening the current perspective and leaving beaten tracks [7,10]. One of the most proven corporate-cybernetic approaches which orientates itself explicitly towards the living organism is the „Viable Systems Model" by Stafford Beer [2] (cp. Fig. 2).

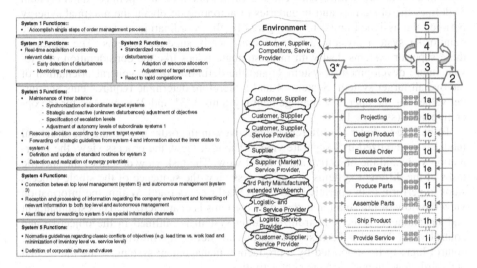

Fig. 2. The order management process as a socio-technological, viable production system

3 Findings

The Viable System Model (VSM) is conceived in analogy to the human nervous system which has proven its reliability due to the evolutionary process of billions of years to be the most reliably organized and most adaptable system. The VSM specifies the necessary and sufficient constraints for the viability of complex organizations. These constraints can be subsumed as completeness and recursivity of the system structure. This leads to the requirements of the basic model:

First, all specified managerial and operative functions must be present and networked in a way that every function has access to the necessary information. Second, every viable system has to be subsystem of a superior viable system and has subordinate viable subsystems itself. Preconditions for this recursive structure are integrated, synchronized target systems, which can be concretized top-down consistently.

The application of the VSM to the order process in manufacturing companies constitutes the structure of the reference model for a Viable Production System (VPS). The reference model is characterized by an explicit process orientation and comprises the whole order processing from the processing of an offer, over the PPC- control loop to the production and delivery of the final product [9]. Within this scope the model incorporates the organizational view and the process view in one holistic enterprise modeling method.

Figure 2 shows the top level of the reference model applied to the case of a project producer including exemplary tasks of the different systems. Together with the following explanations it outlines the general structure of the model:

Semi-autonomous operative units (systems 1) are embedded in a superordinate multi-level managerial structure. The operative units plan, carry out and control the assigned tasks based on a given target system and act autonomously within defined boundaries. In cases exceeding the usual grade of dynamics the coordinating system (system 2) is taking action. The central control system of the operative units (system 3) defines the objectives and boundaries of autonomy to obtain the maximal synergy between the assigned units. It is triggered by the coordinating system as well as the monitoring system (system 3*) and hierarchically superior systems. The duties of these superior systems deal with more strategic issues like the consideration of relevant future developments (system 4) and the definition of the general orientation of the overall target system. Systems 4 and 5 therefore determine requirements and target values for the operative management (systems 3, 3* and 2) as well as for the operative units (systems 1).

To be able to cover all different perspectives on the order processing the structural model is concretized in 4 separate views: The task view, the process view, the information view and the objective and control view. The task view describes the specific tasks of the different systems. In the process view the sequence of the single process steps to perform both operative and control tasks are defined. Within the information view the flow of information between the systems is characterized. The establishment and sustainment of the synchronized target system is outlined in the objective and control view. Thereby the first and fourth view define the information items and the control logic to be supported by a production management system, while the second and third view support management activities.

To get a more precise impression of the design of such a cybernetic based enterprise model, exemplarily the process and information view are concretized within a use case. Object of the described case is the process "Inventory Management" as a representative process to be performed and controlled within a semi-autonomous operative unit (system 1).

Ensuring the self-optimizing character of the operative units they are designed consisting of two elements: A process designed according to the logic of a control loop (cp. Fig. 3) is embedded in an organization for process control (cp. Fig. 4). The control loop character enables the process to cope with a certain level of dynamics by adapting the respective process parameters. In the case of consumption-driven inventory management the whole control loop consists of the three sub-loops forecasting, inventory control and procurement. The first control loop forecasting minimizes the forecasting error by an appropriate parameterization of the applied forecasting method. The highly accurate forecast enables the inventory control loop to determine a dynamic reorder level taking the replenishment time and the required internal service level into account. Initiated by an inventory level lower than the reorder level the optimal order quantity is calculated and compared to the economic order quantity. Based on this calculation the order is placed.

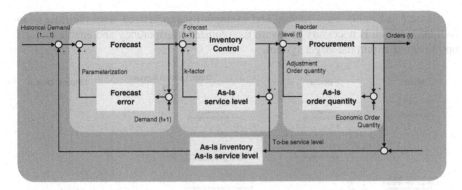

Fig. 3. Control loop for dynamic, consumption-driven inventory management

The process internal absorption of dynamics (e.g. variations of replenishment time or shifts in customers demand) avoids an overload within the organization of process control. In times of normal dynamics the organization of process control's activities can be limited to the calculation and monitoring of performance indicators, the supply of the process with the relevant information as well as forwarding of performance information to other processes (cp. Fig. 5). Thus a cross-process transparency is assured and the process owner (e.g. material planner) is able to focus on critical products which are for example subject to a high level of dynamics.

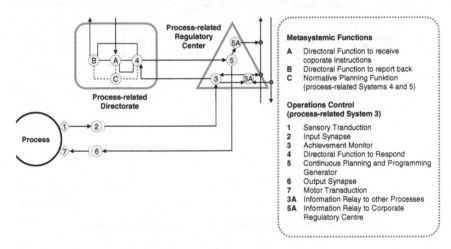

Fig. 4. Organization of process control

In those cases when the level of dynamics is exceeding the absorption capability of the process, the organizational process control detects deviations between the performance indicators and the target values. As a consequence countermeasures like an external adjustment of the process are necessary. This could mean the adjustment of one or more process parameters or even the necessity to reconfigure the whole process. Concerning the case of inventory management this dynamics could be caused for example by a planned marketing action.

Figure 5 subsumes on a general and exemplarily concretized level the flow of information which is necessary to assure the required transparency and enable the self-optimization within the target system.

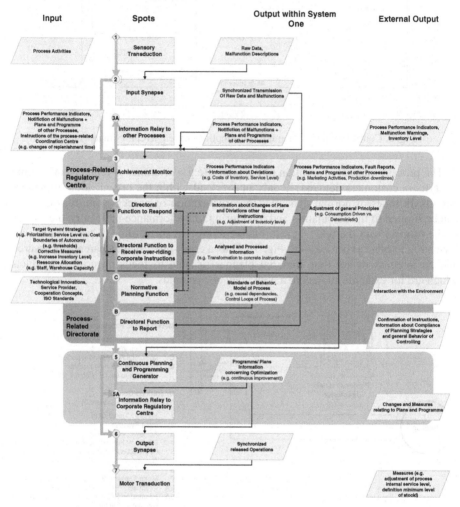

Fig. 5. Information flow within the organization of process control

4   Findings and Practical Implications

In order to assure the practical relevance of HRSCM several industry workshops have been accomplished. Within these workshops branch-specific problems have been derived and are further analyzed within use cases. These use cases as well as best practices of the participating companies are incorporated in the HRSCM approach [8]. As one example implications for the process and process control of inventory management have been derived by applying the reference model for a Viable Production

System. Configuring the process and its control according to the principles of the reference model leads to a better handling of dynamics and thereby higher process stability and efficiency. Furthermore the definition of escalation levels stops the continuous firefighting of the organization of process control. In practice the process owner e.g. material planner is enabled to use the saved time to deal with critical issues and the continuous improvement of the operative unit. The establishment of the flow of relevant information between the processes improves the planning quality and enables process control to take anticipatory measures.

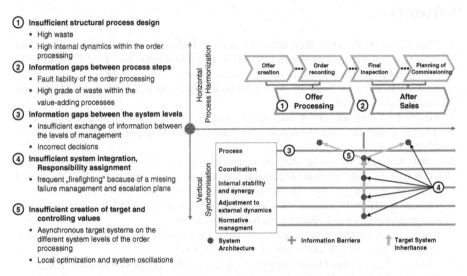

① Insufficient structural process design
  • High waste
  • High internal dynamics within the order processing
② Information gaps between process steps
  • Fault liability of the order processing
  • High grade of waste within the value-adding processes
③ Information gaps between the system levels
  • Insufficient exchange of information between the levels of management
  • Incorrect decisions
④ Insufficient system integration, Responsibility assignment
  • frequent „firefighting" because of a missing failure management and escalation plans
⑤ Insufficient creation of target and controlling values
  • Asynchronous target systems on the different system levels of the order processing
  • Local optimization and system oscillations

Fig. 6. Solution competences of the reference model for a Viable Production System

Figure 6 systematizes the solution competences of the reference model for a Viable Production System to horizontal process harmonization and vertical synchronization. Widely spread practical problems are related to these two dimensions and thus can be solved by benchmarking with the proposed reference model. While the horizontal process harmonization is mainly enabled by adaptive processes and cross-process information transparency, the key factors to improve the vertical synchronization are synchronized target systems. A methodology to synchronise target systems in decentralised organizations is currently being developed as the next steps towards the viable production system.

5 Conclusion

In this paper the application of Stafford Beer's Viable System Model (VSM) on the order process has been discussed as a holistic regulation framework for production systems. The technological and organizational preconditions as well as the general structure of such a cybernetic based production management model have been described. Within a practical use case a self-optimizing control unit based on information transparency, escalation levels and adaptive processes has been implemented.

The resulting benefits are an increased level of adaptability and stability leading to a higher efficiency of the process. The establishment of a synchronized target system over the whole order processing avoids the nullification of these effects on both horizontal and vertical level. Thus it can be stated that the application of HRSCM will contribute to the resolution of the polylemma of production by reducing the dilemma between planning and value orientation. Thereby high-wage countries will be supported in keeping a competitive edge.

References

1. Fleisch, E., et al.: High Resolution Production Management – Auftragsplanung und Steuerung in der individualisierten Produktion. In: Wettbewerbsfaktor Produktionstechnik: Aachener Perspektiven, pp. 451–467. Apprimus Verlag, Aachen (2008)
2. Beer, S.: Brain of the Firm. In: A Development in Management Cybernetics. Herder and Herder, New York (1972)
3. Meyer, J., Wienholdt, H.: Wirtschaftliche Produktion in Hochlohnländern durch High Resolution Supply Chain Management. In: Supply Chain Management, III, vol. 7, pp. 23–27 (2007)
4. Scholz-Reiter, B., Höhns, H.: Selbststeuerung logistischer Prozesse mit Agentensystemen. In: Schuh, G. (ed.) Produktionsplanung und -steuerung – Grundlagen, Gestaltung und Konzepte, 3rd edn., pp. 745–780. Springer, Berlin (2006)
5. Fleisch, E.: High Resolution Management, Konsequenz der 3. IT-Revolution auf die Unternehmensführung. Schäffer-Poeschel Verlag (2008)
6. Espejo, R., et al.: Organizational Transforming and Learning. In: A Cybernetic Approach to Management. John Wiley & Sons, Chichester (1996)
7. Malik, F.: Strategie des Managements komplexer Systeme. Haupt Verlag, Bern (2002)
8. Meyer, J., Wienholdt, H.: High Resolution Supply Chain Management, Ergebnisse aus der Zusammenarbeit mit Industrieunternehmen. In: Unternehmen der Zukunft, Aachen, pp. 11–13 (January 2008)
9. Balve, P., Wiendahl, H.-H., Westkämper, E.: Order management in transformable business structures – basics and concepts. Robotics and Computer Integrated Manufacturing 17, 461–468 (2001)
10. Thiem, I.: Ein Strukturmodell des Fertigungsmanagements: Soziotechnische Strukturierung von Fertigungssystemen mit dem "Modell lebensfähiger Systeme". Shaker Verlag, Aachen (1998)

Superior Performance of Leagile Supply Networks by Application of Autonomous Control

Bernd Scholz-Reiter and Afshin Mehrsai

c/o BIBA GmbH, Hochschulring 20,
28359 Bremen, Germany
{bsr,meh}@biba.uni-bremen.de

Abstract. In the paper, a special approach to supply networks' material flows is posed. The considered strategy is based on the both principles of Lean and agility, beside push and pull of materials. Here, the trade off between positioning of decoupling point throughout an exemplary network, and reduction of inventory level along throughput time is examined. Moreover, autonomous control for material routing and lot-sizes is taken into account. To do so, a discrete-event simulation model is developed to show the performances.

Keywords: Leagile, Production Network, Autonomous Control, Dynamic.

1 Introduction

Dynamic complexities, constraints in performances, interactions between heterogeneous interests, competitions, and requirements in the current business environment force enterprises to undertake more innovative strategies for their supply chains. This should be done in order to meet customized demands in markets on time with less cost to keep own market share or even expand it.

To be on time and cost efficient in performances are two competitive necessities at the present market circumstance. While enterprises move toward cost efficiency, they are pledge to meet customer demands at the right time with their exact customized requirements [1]. From an isolated enterprise to broader scales like supply networks, several disparate performance targets confront enterprises with several difficulties to coordinate their effective processes. For instance, reductions in time and cost of production activities have been considered as two incongruent targets for supply chains (SC).

In general, two production approaches exist; mass production and mass customization. In case of mass production the higher priority was with cost reduction and other activities had to be aligned to comply with that objective. On the contrary, in mass customization (i.e., the ability of manufacturer to quickly design, produce and deliver product to the customer with its specific requirements by the lowest possible price), time reduction and responsiveness beside reduction in cost are taken into account [2]. In fact, cost reduction is a result of time efficiency and agility in performances.

Normally, mass production is based on make-to-stock (MTS) strategy, which by clustering the production activities in a straightforward format (distinct from its inventory cost), causes less effort for production of the same products and consequently

B. Vallespir and T. Alix (Eds.): APMS 2009, IFIP AICT 338, pp. 333–341, 2010.
© IFIP International Federation for Information Processing 2010

reduction in finished cost. On the other hand necessity of customizing products according to customer needs bring about the requirements of becoming enough flexible, agile, responsive, effective, and also efficient in supply networks. In contrast to mass production, mass customization seeks built-to-order (BTO) or assemble-to-order (ATO) strategies for fulfilling customers. Yet, employment of the both approaches, simultaneously, throughout a supply network is possible. For the mentioned purposes, it requires some arrangements to configure such a network. Modular design of products, flexible resources [3], agility, and positioning of a decoupling point (DP) between front-end (with MTS strategy) and back-end (with ATO strategy) [4], are some of those arrangements. These types of hybrid networks are known as leagile supply networks that combine two material flow strategies; push of the materials with the same platform up to DP, while pulling of semi-finished products according to customers' customized orders.

In a supply network, members from several tiers, and via a virtual network, are closely connected to each other. This brings coordination and integration to their logistics processes. Monitoring of inter- and intra- organizational processes causes better accomplishments throughout the network in terms of material and information flow [4]. However, this integrity and high volume of information exchange in a mass customized system leads to another problem which is complexity and overloading in information analysis as well as less flexibility for members.

Autonomous control is a new approach to decline the complexities of information mass processing. Although the input information to an autonomous object (e.g., products, machines, transporters) could be a collection of data about global and local targets, but the decision maker is the object itself and no hierarchy dominate that. In general, autonomous control means: "a decentralized coordination of intelligent logistic objects and the routing through a logistic system by the intelligent objects themselves" [5]. Regarding the characteristics of autonomous systems, this state-of-the-art is assumed suitable to realize customized systems' goals.

In the paper, firstly, it is addressed the features of supply networks as well as its contribution to mass customized products. Secondly, autonomous control vs. conventional planning will be discussed. Thirdly, the simulation scenario is introduced and the results are compared. Finally, followed by the results the conclusion is explained.

2 Supply Networks

Markets environment, competitions, scarce resources, globalization, and requirement of the right product to the right customer within the right time by the lowest cost, persuade organizations to go toward managing their supply networks instead of optimizing their own processes. Today, there is no isolated organization which is successful in the market. That led to higher integration between supply networks and consequently appearance of the art of supply chain management (SCM). Focusing on logistics processes and transportation, SCM interpreted as integrated logistics systems. Thus main concentration is on inventory reduction both within and across organizations in supply networks [6].

Integration between members of supply chains brings about higher complexity in terms of processes' coordination. Simply, consideration and coordination of all effective processes of a supply network burden a tough controlling task to the entire network. Moving from the initial concept about supply chain management, which considers intra and inter-organizational processes, some new approaches exist. They try not to integrate and coordinate all effective units' processes, but just the interfacing processes to get the global consistency. In this approach the members or units of the network perform autonomously in their internal processes [4]. This tactic decreases the existing complexity of entire networks' coordination.

It is noticeable that supply chains are usually assumed as series of suppliers and manufacturers aligned in a successive order. Nonetheless, supply networks address those supply chains that configure some networks via virtual interconnections rather than configuration of successive unites. Here supply chain and network could be used alternatively.

2.1 De-coupling Point

In a system with modular products, procurement of materials is going to be easier. Final products are constructed based on similar (even the same) platforms with just some variations in final assembly. This contributes to the both requirements of customization and efficiency of products [12]. In addition, the supply network could benefit from this modularity by allocating two different strategies to two sides of its chain. This will be happened by application of postponement concept. Postponement could be explained as differentiation of products' types at the closest point to the customer [13].

Separation of supply networks, into two divisions of material push and material pull, makes a drop in complexity of information and material flow. By means of this strategy, demand's information penetrates from downstream of the chain up to a specific level of supply chain. This point called information DP. However, there exists another DP that separates the flow strategy of goods and called material DP [7], [8]. Both DPs could be shifted from downstream of a SC to upstream of that concerning the product varieties, types and SC structure. Necessarily, information DP and material DP are not coupled in the same location of a supply network.

2.2 Leagility

In those supply networks with the capability of decoupling, employment of two outstanding capabilities as lean and agile principles is facilitated. According to some literatures [9], [10] from upstream of a chain to the material DP, members are persuaded to follow lean principles into their processes and sustain the waste reduction and value adding activities. On the other side, downstream from material DP should be responsive and flexible to customized demands. Therefore, here, the agile principles are sought by networks [11]. Agility has been introduced to bear required flexibility and responsiveness in term of real-time constraints and demands to the system. Such a favorable combination of two material push-pull strategy as well as lean-agile principles configures leagile networks with the profits of both concepts.

Positioning of material DP in a network, moving from adjacency of final customer toward the upstream of the network, means expanding material pull principle from downstream customers and shrinking of material push from the upstream plants. Obviously, location of this point has a remarkable effect on supply chain performance measures like: throughput time (TPT), WIP, and responsiveness [19].

3 Autonomy

Current supply networks are configured based on coordination of operations and integration of decision makings amongst autonomous units of the network. This context gives flexibility to SC and their members to make their own decisions, while the entire performance complies with global goals of the network [14].

In general, the outbound logistics of SC should disseminate the effective information to the members in order to integrate them to achieve final customer satisfaction. However, autonomy for members and logistics objects seems to be a practical solution for reducing accompanied complexities in supply networks with customized market. Autonomous control for logistics objects is an absolute heterarchical structure; thereby entities with gathering local information act upon global targets of the logistics system. So far, for this imminent structure, some routing control methodologies have been introduced that give the ability to moving units to find their routes through a logistics network, according to some local information and metrics. Among them are queue length estimator (QLE), ant colony, bee's foraging, and due date [15], [16], [17], [18]. Autonomous control (Aut) normally is explained against conventional[1] systems (Conv).

QLE is an autonomous routing control method that accommodates autonomous objects with the competency of estimating their following queues and bottlenecks. By comparing the alternative routes or destination for producing purposes, the one with the lowest processing and waiting time will be chosen by the autonomous object itself.

Furthermore, autonomous control is not limited to routing in production or logistics networks. Flexible lot-sizes (Varlot) and intelligent pallets (IP) from the material DP (the interface of push and pull of materials) bring superiority to leagile networks according to the general performance measures of logistics. In particular, autonomous pallets are in the way of individualization of products in a material pull principle system. Individualization in mass customized systems has a crucial roll to superior operations and results [3], [4].

4 Simulation Scenario

For evaluating the performance of autonomous control for products and pallets as logistics' objects, a discrete-event simulation approach is considered. A simple model of a supply network, with push and pull of materials, is developed to represent a leagile network. For simulating the pull system a special conwip control system is set up here [20]. The network is constructed of two similar source plants in the upstream (P_{11}, P_{12}), two assembly plants with similar capabilities (P_{21}, P_{22}) and one original equipment manufacture (OEM). Within this network, three types of final products are delivered to final customers. Each final product is assembled of two parts that each of them is produced in either sour plant. The final three types of products are pulled by customers within a seasonal effect manner. To simulate this effect a sinusoidal equation is considered as demand rate (1) that each type has a 1/3 phase shift. In order to realize the total flexibility for the supply network, both source plants are connected to

---

[1] Conventional systems: Those dispatching systems of product types based on pre-defined production schedules, regarding general constraints, available capacities and stations' cycle times.

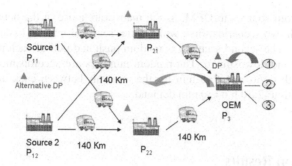

Fig. 1. Exemplary leagile supply network. Each distance is assumed as 140km which is connected via one transporter. Each round trip takes 4 hours for transporters [20].

the both assembly plants, respectively, both assembly plants are connected to OEM. Fig. 1 shows the structure of outbound logistics in this supply network.

Based on a developed model of Scholz-Reiter et al. [18], the inbound logistics' structure for source 1/2 as well as OEM, is constructed of three production lines, each consist of three similar stations. This makes up a 3×3 matrix of stations. To configure a flexible structure, for facilitating autonomous control, every station in the same column is coupled with their successors (see Table 1 for times).

The respective autonomous control for routing the intelligent products and pallets is QLE [5]. This method is taken because of its simple performance to understand and realized.

In addition to routing control, here, pallets in OEM (with pull of material) have the capability to assess the rate of demand versus rate of pushing materials. This aptitude gives the pallets the ability of pro-activity. These proactive pallets continuously get the ratio of demands to upcoming products. In fact, the pallets, between the intervals of coming demands, compare the average of last five intervals of demands with the last five intervals of coming semi-finished products into the entrance of OEM. When the ratio is over one this means the demands are ordered with a higher rate than before. Since over one ratio is kept, respective pallets will be loaded to the entrance of the OEM, to collect the respective product, without any direct demand order.

Table 1. Considered processing times for each product on each line at P_{11}; P_{12}; P_3 and assembly plants P_{21}; P_{22}. The min processing times are equal to the mean intervals of emerging products.

Plant	Processing times [h:min] for each plant			
	P_{11}; P_{12}; P_3			P_{21}; P_{22}
	Line			
Product	1	2	3	1
Type 1	2:00	3:00	2:30	1:00
Type 2	2:30	2:00	3:00	1:00
Type 3	3:00	2:30	2:00	1:00

However, from sources to OEM, as the main warehouse in the network, products are pushed with two scenarios; first, with similar seasonal manner to demand with the same sequence. The second scenario is random push and pull of each product type in both upstream and downstream. The random numbers are accompanied with normal distribution with μ=50 min σ=5 min for the intervals between each upcoming same product and with μ=2:30 h σ=30 min demand.

$$\lambda(t) = 0.4 + 0.15 \sin(t + \varphi) . \tag{1}$$

5   Simulation Results

Following graphs and bar chart are depicted to illustrate the comparison of logistics performance under Aut and Cont systems.

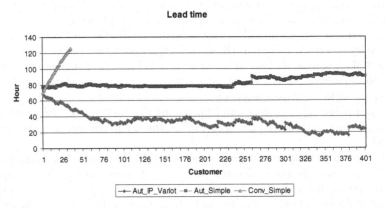

Fig. 2. Comparison between customer lead times under Conv routing, Aut routing and Aut with IP and Varlot

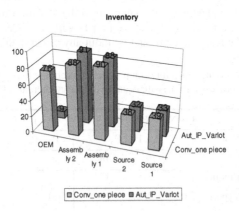

Fig. 3. Inventory comparison between five plants; under Aut with IP and Varlot, and Conv with one piece flow. Both push and pull of materials are subject to seasonal effect (1).

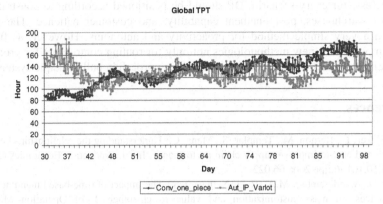

Fig. 4. Global throughput time (TPT) of products starting from source and terminating after OEM. Comparison under Conv and Aut with IP and Varlot.

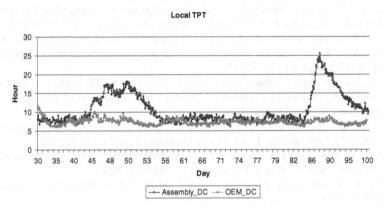

Fig. 5. Local TPT in OEM when the DC is positioned before OEM, and when before Assembly stations

6 Conclusion

In conclusion, simulation results already appeared that the autonomous control in routing has several pluses to logistics performance in comparison with conventional planning. This was proved before under different scenarios. Furthermore, variable lot-sizes and proactive pallet in pull systems (assumed the conwip system works with pallet) proved its contribution to superior performance of logistics measures. Although just TPT, customer lead time, and WIP were used as logistics criteria, but some other metrics should be considered for evaluating the real contributions of methods and technologies.

Here was shown that closer DC to final customer shorter local TPT for end plant, and respectively shorter lead time is resulted. By postponing the consolidation of final product, inventory volume before DC and the stress for individualization decreases.

Nonetheless, for every scenario, DP should be positioned according to constrains in terms of warehouses, postponement capability, and customer patience. The paper assumed a very simple method for proactivity and autonomy. However, as further research potentials, new methodologies not only for routing control, but for proactive and intelligent pallets seem to be a very feasible approach in pull principle systems.

References

1. Whicker, L., Bernon, M., Templar, S., Mena, C.: Understanding the relationships between time and cost to improve supply chain performance. Int. J. Production Economics (2006), doi:10.1016/j.ijpe.2006.06.022
2. Tu, Q., Vonderembse, M.A., Ragu-Nathan, T.S.: The impact of time-based manufacturing practices on mass customization and value to customer. J. of Operation Management 19(2), 201–217 (2001)
3. Fredriksson, P., Gadde, L.E.: Flexibility and rigidity in customization and built-to-order production. Industrial Marketing Management 34(7), 695–705 (2005)
4. Romano, P.: Co-ordination and integration mechanisms to manage logistics processes across supply networks. J. of Purchasing & Supply Management 9, 119–134 (2003)
5. Scholz-Reiter, B., Jagalski, T., de Beer, C., Freitag, M.: Autonomous Shop Floor Control Considering Set-up Time. In: Proc. of 40th CIRP International Seminar on Manufacturing Systems, Liverpool, UK, pp. 1–6 (2007)
6. Li, S., Ragu-Nathan, B., Ragu-Nathan, T.S., Subba Rao, S.: The impact of supply chain management practices on competitive advantage and organizational performance. J. of Management Science, Omega 34, 107–124 (2006)
7. Mason-Jones, R., Towill, D.R.: Using the Information Decoupling Point to Improve Supply Chain Performance. Int. J. of Logistics Management 10(2), 13–26 (1999)
8. Sun, X.Y., Ji, P., Sun, L.Y., Wang, Y.L.: Positioning multiple decoupling points in a supply network. Int. J. Production Economics 113, 943–956 (2008)
9. Hoek, R.I.V.: The thesis of leagility revisited. Int. J. of Agile Management Systems 2(3), 196–201 (2000)
10. Wanddhwa, S., Mishra, M., Saxena, A.: A network approach for modeling and design of agile supply chains using a flexibility construct. Int. J. of Felxible Manufacturing System 19(4), 410–442 (2007)
11. Yusuf, Y.Y., Gunasekaran, A., Adeleye, E.O., Sivayoganathan, K.: Agile supply chain capabilities: Determination of competitive objectives. European J. of Operational Research 159, 379–392 (2004)
12. Lau Antonio, K.W., Yam, R.C.M., Tang, E.: The impact of product modularity on competitive capabilities and performance: An empirical study. Int. J. Production Economics 105, 1–20 (2007)
13. Ernst, R., Kamrad, B.: Evaluation of supply chain structures through modularized and postponement. European J. of Operation Research 124, 495–510 (2000)
14. Avneet, S., Wadhwa, S.: Flexible configuration for seamless supply chains: Directions towards decision knowledge sharing. Robotics and Computer-Integrated Manufacturing 25, 839–852 (2009)
15. Scholz-Reiter, B., Jagalski, T., Bendul, J.C.: Autonomous control of a shop floor based on bee's foraging behavior. In: Kreowski, H.J., Scholz-Reiter, B., Haasis, H.D. (eds.) Dynamics in Logistics. First Int. Conf., LDIC 2007, pp. 415–423. Springer, Heidelberg (2007)

16. Vogel, A., Fischer, M., Jaehn, H., Teich, T.: Real-world shop floor scheduling by ant colony optimization. In: Dorigo, M., Di Caro, G.A., Sampels, M. (eds.) ANTS 2002. LNCS, vol. 2463, pp. 268–273. Springer, Heidelberg (2002)

17. Scholz-Reiter, B., Wirth, F., Freitag, M., Dashkovskiy, S., Jagaslki, T., de Beer, C., Rüffer, B.: Some remarks on the stability of manufacturing logistic networks. Stability margins. In: Proc. of the Int. Scientific Annu. Conf. on Operations Research, pp. 91–96. Springer, Bremen (2006)

18. Scholz-Reiter, B., de Beer, C., Freitag, M., Jagalski, T.: Bio-inspired and pheromone-based shop-floor control. Int. J. Computer Integrated Manufacturing 21(2), 201–205 (2008)

19. Nythuis, P., Wiendahl, H.P.: Logistic Production Operating Curves- Basic Model of the Theory of Logistic Operating Curves. CIRP Annals- Manufacturing Technology 55, 441–444 (2006)

20. Scholz-Reiter, B., Mehrsai, A., Goerges, M.: Handling the Dynamics in Logistics- Adoption of Dynamic Behavior and Reduction of Dynamic Effects. Asian Int. J. of Science and Technology (AIJSTPME) 2(3), 99–110 (2009)

Analysis of the Harmonizing Potential of Order Processing Attributes in Spread Production Systems

Dirk Oedekoven, Volker Stich, Tobias Brosze, and Stefan Cuber

Forschungsinstitut für Rationalisierung e.V. (FIR) an der RWTH Aachen,
Pontdriesch 14/16, 52062 Aachen, Germany
{Dirk.Oedekoven,Volker.Stich,Tobias.Brosze}@fir.rwth-aachen.de

Abstract. The paper discusses an approach how to measure the competitive advantage of harmonized order processing data by making use of knowledge about the interdependencies between related benefit dimensions. Corresponding harmonization projects are all projects that strive for common structures in product attributes, classification systems or product structures. The main objective of the underlying research work is the development of a method for the estimation of the benefit potential of harmonized order processing data.

Keywords: classification systems, attribute and data harmonization, analysis of potential, order processing.

1 Introduction

1.1 Initial Situation

Focusing on core competences, striving for global presence and of course outsourcing sub processes lead to major changes in the set-up of production systems as they became more and more spread all over the world. The increasing number of multi-site enterprises as well as the necessity of integrated coordination throughout supply chains imposes a tremendous challenge to the performance especially of enterprise resource planning (ERP) systems. The support of order processing tasks by IT infrastructure has gained increasing importance since the 80ies [1, 2]. Cross-company processes within the order management are steadily gaining importance. Furthermore a rising number of companies are focussing on efficient communications with their network partners as these actions are more and more understood as strategic instruments of great importance influencing the value of the company [3, 4, 5, 6].

But while efficient order processing turns out to be increasingly important the forces of globalization lead to spread production structures and concurrently to inhomogeneous landscapes of data, attributes and IT-systems. In consequence they face inefficient information flows and processes. The economic and logistic potential within the interfaces of the companies is enormous, independent if it is rooted in intra company networks or between autonomous companies [7, 8, 9]. But although enterprises are eager to harmonize data, attributes and attribute structures they can not evaluate expectable expenses and benefits in advance. This is a major problem for

B. Vallespir and T. Alix (Eds.): APMS 2009, IFIP AICT 338, pp. 342–349, 2010.

initiating projects. In the end projects run out of budget or are not even launched although there is a high potential for improving processes and gaining competitiveness.

The underlying research work of this paper investigates how to estimate the competitive advantage of harmonization projects by making use of knowledge about the interdependencies between benefit dimensions.

1.2 Problem Definition and Motivation

Within operational order processing actions system discontinuities inhibit efficiency. This fact can be differentiated by two different causes: On the one hand supply relations between the entities of a production network exist but the use of different ERP systems cause physical incompatibility of the interfaces. This case can be described as the integration gap. On the other hand compatible ERP systems are used, but semantic differences in the order processing data lead to incompatibilities what can be summarized as the standardization gap. Identical products are not automatically a guarantee for synchronized process- and attributes structures. Not standardized processes lead to inadequate ERP system support, even if the objectives are consistent.

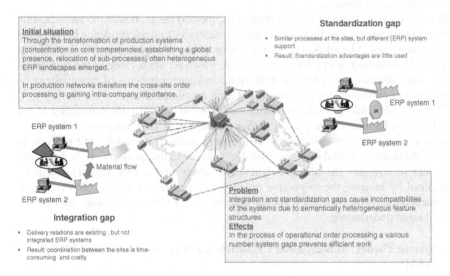

Fig. 1. Initial situation

The results are inefficient information flow and poor transparency. The coordination between the different facilities is time-consuming and costly because integration and standardization potentials are not utilized. In addition operational and cross-site planning to integrate modern concepts for cooperation remains limited. In the end, the extent of the corresponding influences on the company's key figures (e.g. ROCE) cannot be determined currently.

Because of that, harmonization activities are needed, that create an integrated, accurate and consistent data basis for all company-relevant master data, which is already connected to the existing application landscape through corresponding interfaces or a service-oriented architecture [10].

The closure of integration- and standardization gaps through corresponding harmonization projects is generally promising a significant improvement of logistical performance on the company- and network level. These improvements could not be quantified yet. An investment to a harmonization plan as an IT project remains undone, if only one of the involved entities appreciates the not negliable investment as too expensive, project risks as too high and the profitability ex ante not to be identified [11]. In times of intense global competition it is these days of particular importance, to ensure the plausibility of costly large-scale projects in terms of their real potential benefits. Otherwise companies are risking their existential business actions through wasting liquid funds.

1.3 Objective of Research Work

The objective of this research work is the development of a method for the identification and estimation of the benefit potential of harmonized order processing attributes and data in companies which act within the frame of distributed production structures. The method should be useable to support decision processes regarding investments into harmonization projects.

Because of many partners and parameters the method has to, beside the identification of the complex structure of benefits, include an analysis of interdependency between the single dimensions of benefits. The analysis is necessary to explore the different effects, whether in reinforcing or in inhibiting affection, which occurs because of the correlation of the single dimensions of benefit. Finally the qualitative benefits of potential can be quantified to a certain degree by the usage of such functional chains.

The method should provide an assistance to enable and raise the rationality of the decision for a harmonization project within a company, a group or a network. That is mandatory to thereby provide the basis of modern methods of cost-benefit analysis to make a dedicated profitability analysis for harmonization projects. It is explicitly important to consider the induced dynamics, variety and complexity. This will be guaranteed by locating the respective processes in a reference model that fits the requirements. Lastly the procedure should give assistance to estimate monetary benefits despite some uncertainties.

1.4 System Theory, Management Cybernetics and the Viable System Model (VSM)

Existing assessment approaches usually focus on the implementation of specific systems such as SCM or ERP applications only. Indeed, harmonization projects should not only be qualified by verifying their contribution to a systems implementation. Furthermore it is essential to become aware of the total impact of harmonization activities on all strategic goals.

All possible interfaces in the order processing procedure have to be identified in a first step. To narrow the scope of investigation contract manufacturers of products with variants are the initial point of work. Furthermore it is necessary to stick to processes that are suited as references of real actions. An analysis of the reference processes ensures a complete enumeration of all interfaces that may suffer from heterogeneous data and attribute landscapes in and between enterprises. Accordingly for each interface a number of potentials can be identified and structured in terms of a set-up benefit model. By developing a coherent target system connecting subordinate objectives of data harmonization with superior objectives such as cycle time reduction, the interdependencies can be evaluated.

The conventional methods of the model theory do not provide fitting approaches to face the system-immanent complexity of production systems. Systems theory and cybernetics specifically start at this point. In contrast to the general approach of engineering or business sciences, these approaches do not exclude the complexity through restrictions and simplifying assumptions, but are setting the focus on it. The discipline of management cybernetics founded by Beer [12] delivers receipts and methods to manage the company effectively because of a system oriented approach.

According to the ideas of management cybernetics the viable systems model (VSM) provides a framework that allows designing reference processes that can cope with real world requirements such as dynamic control loops and mutability. VSM was developed by Beer as a tool for managers to cope with complex systems. Beside Ashbys law, the viable design of a company is in the focus. Viability in Beer's opinion does not mean a „survival at the subsistence level", but the continuous preservation of the system identity during environmental changes [13]. The generalized question in the focus is, if a specific configuration of the system can be maintained for a certain time period. In addition, the principle of recursiveness as one of the most important principles for structuring says, that irrespective from the level in which the system is actually located, every system shows a homogenous structure. The basic set-up of a system hierarchy following the principle of recursiveness has the design of systems nested into each other and not the organization theory's well known pyramidic structure [14].

Within the research work a system is considered following Beer as a group of entities, which are dynamically and time-dependent correlated to each other and thereby showing a coherent and connected behaviour.

2 Research Design

The following individually described steps are based on the approach to applied research according to Ulrich [15]. The aim is the description and explanation of the impact potential of harmonized order processing data on the company's success. The steps of the research process include terminological-descriptive, empirical-inductive and analytical-deductive components [16].

2.1 Embedding the Problem within the Viable Systems Model

The high number of potential interfaces in the order processing procedures are difficult to neglect, and for a scientific analysis not readily to handle. That is why in literature various models occur trying to structure the order processing activities and to provide a uniform description of information interfaces. Nevertheless existing models allow no adequate classification and differentiation of the different starting points for harmonization projects due to their focus and / or their level of detail. In order to succeed in an approach to identify potential benefits, the viable systems modelling (VSM) is used and further developed considering the needs of the research work. The development is focusing especially the consideration of dynamic effects in terms of management cybernetics. Accordingly, it serves as a fundamental part of the description model. Basis for the model are given by the spadework of the FIR.

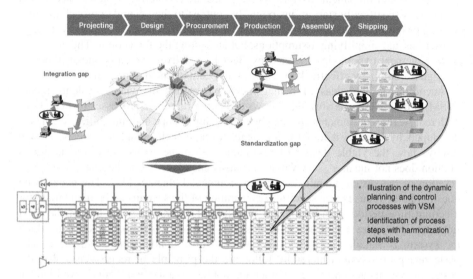

Fig. 2. Embedding the problem within the Viable Systems Model

2.2   Analysis of the Potential Benefits

To assess harmonizing potentials in terms of objective economic activity, the implementation of the implied benefit analysis is essential. The objective of economic activity is the maximization of the ratio of a target performance (benefit) for deployment of funds (expenses) [44]. Although therefore the fundamental aspects of economic analysis are relatively simple (design and comparison of expected costs and benefits), a practical implementation is not readily available. So the task is to deal with the six basic problem areas in the benefit analysis of harmonization [45, 46]:

- The problem of holism
- The problem of measurement
- The problem of situation
- The problem of allocation
- The problem of interconnection
- The problem of innovation

As a quintessence of the described problems, it should be noted that the designated benefit provided has to be seen as a potential benefit as far as the uncertainty about its characteristics and probability of occurrence exists.

2.3 Development of the Target System and the Utility Model

The target system that has to be developed is used as a basis for the identification and mapping of benefits of the harmonization project. Among the general business objectives as well as the resulting target and ratio systems numerous approaches in the literature exist from which the relevant work for this system is primarily synthesized [49]. The weighting and possibly the omission of individual goals allows within the application of the description model the individual adjustment of goals.

2.4 Functional Chain-Based Analysis of the Influence of the Potential Benefits to the Target Elements

The aim of creating the functional chains is to identify the most important, in a harmonization context occurring interdependencies between potential benefits and target elements in order to assess and to estimate them adequately. The functional effect chains perform as a first step on the path to monetary estimation of the potential benefits. Therefore, they have to be covered as completely as possible [36]. According to the nature of reference models selected connections can be further specified due to cases of application. The top level chains of benefit potential are defined by the relations of the target system. In this respect, the chains of benefit potentials have to be extended with potential benefits which influence the target elements significantly.

2.5 Design of a Procedure for Identification and Assessment of Potential Benefits in Harmonization Projects

The final method has to meet different requirements. To meet users expectations and the objectives of the research receivables certain qualities and attributes have to be present. Thereby formal and substantive requirements are to be differentiated, which arise from the problem itself and the objective of the desired method [50]. These requirements should be defined in terms of literature based findings about challenging areas of the benefit analysis. Formal requests describe the general requirements for a method. For example, the utility is an essential formal requirement. Content requirements result analytical-deductively from the objective of the research work; which is in turn empirical-inductively derived from shortcomings in operational practice.

The method that has to be developed for the identification and assessment of potential benefits in harmonization projects finally results out of several activities: the description and positioning of the various potential benefits and costs, the systematic analysis of the interdependencies and by the reference to an integrated target system.

3 Conclusion

The challenge for enterprises of being efficient and effective in using their IT infrastructure is gaining more and more importance. Yet a promising approach to evaluate potential benefits in advance is missing. In the field of profitability analysis of order processing in spread production structures the difficulty lies more within the estimation of benefits rather then in the estimation of the efforts. The monetary analysis of benefit potentials is so far limited to quantitative dimensions, while the qualitative aspects, which are more difficult to estimate, are often neglected or analyzed only on a general level.

The analysis of the status quo in knowledge has shown that many authors are working on the approaches of the (cybernetic) organizational theory but that there is no attempt to make use of it for evaluating the value proposition of IT. An application of the cybernetic principles to the analysis of system supported processes of order processing activities has not been carried out in the sense of a regulatory framework yet. Nevertheless this seems to be a promising approach as it enables to deal with complexity as well as with dynamics.

Because the mediate potentials of benefit at harmonization projects have a high total ratio, the validation of the effects on a monetary key figure for those systems is highly relevant. The interdependencies between the dimensions of benefit were so far only analyzed isolated and without regarding of cross-sites effects. Therefore the analyzed functional chains do not give a detailed description of the influencing mechanisms, apart from positive/negative influence. But to use functional chains to estimate developments of benefit, the paths of effects can be explored and defined.

By that it can be stated that so far no systematic, scientifically founded derivation of the benefit potentials of harmonized data landscapes of specifying attributes with regard to the perspectives, company, network and the complete supply chain exists. A corresponding possibility to efficiently assess potential benefits and exemplify their interdependencies is missing as well.

The underlying and in this paper described research work addresses these gaps and will provide a solution which meets the relevant requirements. The benefit assessment will be comparable to the cost elements, by providing an adequate economic analysis. Therefore, the focus of this research work lies on the one hand on the identification, categorization and assessment of potential benefits and costs of corresponding harmonization investments and on the other hand on the consideration of the interdependencies between the various benefits. In addition, current methods of economic analysis and to their suitability for the use in specific cases of the harmonization projects are evaluated and adapted.

References

1. Kernler, H.: PPS der 3. Generation: Grundlagen, Methoden, Anregungen, Hüthig, Heidelberg (1995)
2. Krcmar, H.: Informationsmanagement. Springer, Berlin (1997)
3. Schuh, G., Friedli, T., Kurr, M.A.: Kooperationsmanagement. Hanser, München (2005)
4. Arnold, B.: Strategische Lieferantenintegration. Dissertation Technische Universität Berlin. Deutscher Universitäts-Verlag, Wiesbaden (2004)
5. Lee, H.L.: Creating value through Supply Chain Integration. Supply Chain Management Review 4(4), 30–36 (2000)
6. Ihde, G.: Lieferantenintegration. In: Kern, W., Schröder, H.-H., Weber, J. (eds.) Handwörterbuch der Produktionswirtschaft: Enzyklopädie der Betriebswirtschaftslehre, vol. VIII, pp. 1086–1095. Schäffer-Poeschel Verlag, Stuttgart (1996)
7. Schuh, G.: Referenzstrategien in einer vernetzten Welt. In: Milberg, J., Schuh, G. (eds.) Erfolg in Netzwerken, pp. 17–34. Springer, Berlin (2002)

8. Schönsleben, P., Luczak, H., Nienhaus, J., Weidemann, M., Schnetzler, M., Roesgen, R.: Supply Chain Management: Monitoring-Lösungen auf dem Vormarsch. IT-Management (5), 10–17 (2003)

9. Busch, A., Lange, H., Langemann, T.: Marktstudie zum Collaborative Supply Chain Management. Heinz Nixdorf Institut, Paderborn (2002)

10. Möbus, D., Richter, G.: Stammdatenstrategie: Nur ein IT Thema? http://www.cio.de/_misc/article/printoverview/index.cfm?pid=181&pk=851640&op=1st

11. Rautenstrauch, T.: SCM-Integration in heterarchischen Unternehmensnetzwerken. In: Busch, A., Dangelmaier, W. (eds.) Integriertes Supply Chain Management, pp. 341–361. Gabler, Wiesbaden (2002)

12. Beer, S.: Kybernetik und Management. Fischer, Frankfurt (1959)

13. Thiem, I.: Ein Strukturmodell des Fertigungsmanagements. Soziotechnische Strukturierung von Fertigungssystemen mit dem Modell lebensfähiger Systeme. Shaker, Aachen (1998)

14. Malik, F.: Strategie des Managements komplexer Systeme: Ein Beitrag zur Management-Kybernetik evolutionärer Systeme, Haupt, Bern (2002)

15. Ulrich, H.: Die Betriebswirtschaftslehre als anwendungsorientierte Sozialwissenschaft. In: Geist, N., Köhler, R. (eds.) Die Führung des Betriebes, Poeschel, Stuttgart, pp. 1–15 (1981)

16. Hill, W., Fehlbaum, R., Ulrich, P.: Organisationslehre 1: Ziele, Instrumente und Bedingungen der Organisation sozialer Systeme. Haupt, Bern (1994)

17. Zangemeister, C.: Erweiterte Wirtschaftlichkeits-Analyse: Grundlagen und Leitfaden für ein 3-Stufen-Verfahren zur Arbeitssystembewertung. Wirtschaftsverlag NW, Bremerhaven (1993)

18. Schumann, M.: Wirtschaftlichkeitsbeurteilung für IV-Systeme. Wirtschaftsinformatik 35(2), 167–178 (1993)

19. Reichwald, R.: Modell einer Wirtschaftlichkeitsrechnung: Einsatz moderner Informations- und Kommunikationstechnik. CIM-Management 3, 6–11 (1987)

20. Lücke, T.: Koordination von intra-organisationalen Produktionsnetzwerken. Shaker, Aachen (2005)

21. Linß, H.: Integrationsabhängige Nutzeffekte der Informationsverarbeitung: Vorgehensmodell und empirische Ergebnisse. Deutscher Universitäts-Verlag, Wiesbaden (1995)

22. Friedrich, M.: Beurteilung automatisierter Prozesskoordination in der technischen Auftragsabwicklung. Shaker, Aachen (2002)

HLA Multi Agent/Short-Lived Ontology Platform for Enterprise Interoperability

Gregory Zacharewicz[1], Olivier Labarthe[2], David Chen[1], and Bruno Vallespir[1]

[1] LAPS / GRAI, Université de Bordeaux – CNRS, 351, Cours de la Libération,
33405 TALENCE Cedex, France
[2] CIRRELT, Université Laval, 2325 rue de la Terrasse, bureau 2535,
Québec City, Québec, Canada
{gregory.zacharewicz,david.chen,
bruno.vallespir}@ims-bordeaux.fr, olivier.labarthe@cirrelt.ca

Abstract. This paper aims at proposing an specification of the Federation oriented Enterprise Interoperability concept, using Multi Agent / HLA paradigm and the rising notion of Short-Lived Ontology. We give first, a review of Enterprise Interoperability. Then, we recall on Artificial Agent Concept and HLA Standard that appear to be adequate to support execution of the studied concept. Indeed, on the one hand Agent dialogue fits the concept of information exchange in a federated enterprise interoperability approach, on the other hand the HLA standard, initially designed for military M&S purpose, can be transposed for enterprise interoperability at the implementation level, reusing the years of experiences in distributed systems. From these postulates, we propose the first Agent/HLA Short-Lived Ontology framework for distributed enterprise interoperability solution in the federated enterprise approach.

Keywords: Enterprise Interoperability, Multi Agent Systems, Distributed Simulation, HLA, Ontology.

1 Introduction

In the globalised economic context, the competitiveness of an enterprise depends not only on its internal productivity and performance, but also on its skill to collaborate with others. This necessity led to the development of a new concept called interoperability that allows improving collaborations between enterprises. No doubt, in such context where more and more networked enterprises are developed; enterprise interoperability is seen as a more suitable solution to total enterprise integration. Since the beginning of 2000, several European research projects have been launched to develop enterprise interoperability (e.g. INTEROP [1]). Three main research themes or domains that address interoperability issues were identified, namely: (1) Enterprise Modeling (EM) dealing with the representation of the internetworked organization to establish interoperability requirements; (2) Architecture & Platform (A&P) defining the implementation solution to achieve interoperability; (3) Ontologies (ON) addressing semantics necessary to assure interoperability.

B. Vallespir and T. Alix (Eds.): APMS 2009, IFIP AICT 338, pp. 350–357, 2010.
© IFIP International Federation for Information Processing 2010

This paper proposes a new contribution of Information Technology (IT) architecture and platform to implement Enterprise Interoperability. In the first part, we present the various approaches of interoperability and the current consideration of interoperability stated as conclusion of the Interop Network of Excellence (FP6, 508011). Then, we recall the concepts of software Agent and the High Level Architecture (HLA) [2], i.e. a standard for distributed simulation.

Next, from our experience, we propose to investigate three aspects of interoperability: time management, Enterprise Ontologies and the privacy of data. Indeed. Computer science Ontologies, Artificial Agent language, and Object / Interaction in HLA can give keys to two first considerations. As well, the experience coming from Information Systems (IS) and M&S programming can be studied to keep data safe to address third point. From these postulates, we specify a plat-form implementation using HLA and Software Agents' autonomous dialogue concepts, to the concern of distributed federated Enterprise Interoperability models.

2 Basic Concept of Interoperability

Enterprise Interoperability refers to the ability of interactions between enterprise systems. The interoperability is considered as significant if the interactions can take place at least at the three different levels: data, services and process, with a semantics defined in a given business context. Establishing interoperability means to relate two systems together and remove incompatibilities. Our goal is to tackle interoperability problems through the identification and passing barriers which prevent interoperability to happen. The interoperability has been historically established as:

Integrated approach. there exists a common format for all models. This format must be as detail as models. The common format is not necessarily a standard but must be agreed by all parties to elaborate models and build systems.

Unified approach. there exists a common format but only at a meta-level. This meta-model is not an executable entity as it is in the integrated approach but provides a mean for semantic equivalence to allow mapping between models.

Federated approach. there is no common format. To establish interoperability, parties must accommodate on the fly. Using federated approach implies that no partner imposes their models, languages and methods of work.

Today, most of the approaches developed are unified ones. Using the federated approach to develop Enterprise Interoperability is most challenging and few activities have been performed in this direction. The federated approach aims to develop full interoperability and is particularly suitable for an inter-organizational environment (such as networked enterprises, virtual enterprises, etc.).

3 HLA Recalls

The High Level Architecture (HLA) is a software architecture specification that defines how to create a global execution composed of distributed simulations and software. This standard was originally introduced by the Defense Modeling and Simulation Office (DMSO) of the US Department Of Defense (DOD). The original goal was reuse and interoperability of military applications, simulations and sensors.

In HLA, every participating application is called federate. A federate interacts with other federates within a HLA federation, which is in fact a group of federates. The HLA set of definitions brought about the creation of the standard 1.3 in 1996, which evolved to HLA 1516 in 2000 [2] The interface specification of HLA describes how to communicate within the federation through the implementation of HLA specification: the Run Time Infrastructure (RTI). In order to respect the temporal causality relations in the execution of distributed computerized applications; HLA proposes to use classical synchronization mechanisms [2].

An HLA federation is composed of federates and a Run Time Infrastructure (RTI).A federate is a HLA compliant program, the code of that federate keeps its original features but must be extended by other functions to communicate with other members of the federation. The RTI supplies services required by distributed executions, it routes messages exchanged between federates. A federate can, through the services proposed by the RTI, "Publish" and "Subscribe" to a class of shared data.

4 Agent-Based Distributed Simulations

The Multi-Agents System (MAS) [3] concentrates on the study of the collective behavior which results from the organization and interactions of agents for the resolution of problems. A MAS is a distributed system in which there is generally no centralized control or global point of view. A MAS is composed of agents which act in an autonomous way but do not locally have the knowledge, the resources or the information required to ensure the coherence of the concerted actions in a MAS. This section is dedicated to the presentation of the agent definition and the introduction of distributed simulations of Agent-Based Systems.

4.1 Agent Definition

Actually, there is no consensus in the scientific literature on the definition of an agent. Disciplines, in which reference is made, are numerous and various authors have proposed different definitions as for example Ferber [3]. However, the definition proposed in Jennings et al. [4] is commonly used within the MAS community: "an agent is a computer system, situated in some environment that is capable of flexible autonomous action in order to meet its design objectives...».

Agents and MAS constitute an active research field in which numerous applications are developed. In Nwana [5], the authors propose surveys of the agents according to various application domains (cognitive agents, software agents, mobile agents, etc.). Agents perceive the modifications of their environment and perform actions on it. Among the possible actions, agents have to determine the most suitable decisions that can reach their objectives. In addition to the application domain, environment, interaction and organization influence the design of the agent.

5 Perspectives to Interoperability

From the state-of-the-art of federated enterprise interoperability and implementations experiences presented in § 2, we can define several directions for, almost natural, interoperability barrier removal with Agent and HLA concepts in the following domains.

The first direction concerns the definition of commonly recognized paradigms and data structure able to evolve during run time. The second not addressed requirement at the enterprise modeling level is the data synchronization. The data exchanged order is crucial; ignoring this can lead to not desired indeterminist model behavior.

Finally, the enterprise modeling must consider the confidentiality management of data. The interoperability can be considered between concurrent enterprises in that context, a strategy of data sharing/not sharing between these must be defined. We present, in the following, propositions to address these requirements.

6 Federated Enterprise Agents

In the federated Enterprise Interoperability approach, no common persistent ontology is supposed to exist; the communication must be accommodated on the fly. In consequence, the ontology that structures the messages exchanged must be short-lived, (i.e. non-persistent). We state that the communication mechanism, in this approach, can be informally illustrated as follow in figure 1. We mainly distinguish two cases.

In case a., the enterprise 1 sends information and the ontology to decode it at the same time. This ontology is supposed to be only valid for this information.

In case b., the enterprise 1 sends only the information to enterprise 2. Once enterprise 2 receives the information, it checks within its local ontology if it is able to decode the information. If not, it asks for the ontology associated to the message to the sender of the message. The new received ontology can be conserved to be reused with further data sent by the same emitter.

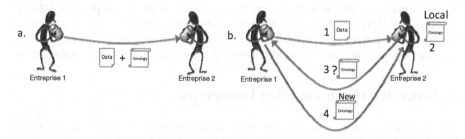

Fig. 1. HLA Federated Interoperability Data Exchange

In the first solution, the information size exchanged is more important, it can be intercepted and the confidentiality can be broken. In the second case, the confidentiality is enforced but it can require more exchanges between the two partners and consequently overlapping the communication duration. Nevertheless, for confidentiality (i.e. §5.) and accuracy to the definition of §2., we choose to focus in this article, on the second solution. From that postulate, we introduce the concept of "short lived" ontology, where ontology can be, in some case, suppressed after use or have finite duration validity. It maps on-the-fly accommodation requirement of federated interoperability.

6.1   Agent for Short-Lived Ontology Concept

From the concept presented in the preceding point, we state that the autonomous dialogue between Agents, from Multi Agent System (MAS) [3] and Agent Based Simulation [6], can map properly the "on the fly" concept of federated interoperability at process level. We propose to use the dialogue mechanism algorithm of Agent programming, introduced in [3] and [6], to solve at computerized level the problem of federated Enterprise Interoperability. This dialogue between Agents, aims at establishing communication (e.g. two enterprises that discuss to agree on domain ontology), it is based on Agents cooperation behavior settings, and messages exchanged language (ontology).

On the one hand, (Ferber in [3] specifies the communication behavior algorithms of Agents' with Petri Nets (PN). On the other hand, Zacharewicz in [7], have tailored the use of DEVS/HLA (introduced as a generalized M&S language (including PN) for distributed systems, gaining accuracy and flexibility (these models communicate within a distributed environment by message passing). Thus, we state that DEVS/HLA synchronized communication can support a unified, reusable and interoperating implementation of distributed Agents' dialogue.

On behalf of previous paragraphs propositions, we propose to develop a MAS simulator in the aim of validating Enterprise Interoperability concepts, studying the performance by simulation and implementing a concrete solution for Enterprise Interoperability ISs.

The research for developing MAS distributed Platforms is wide (as can denote for e.g. a repository of Agent-Based Simulation Platforms proposed in [8]), and actual MAS simulators are powerful (i.e. [6]). Nevertheless, they mainly do not tackle the problem of interoperability and reuse of components at coding level (e.g. heterogeneity of syntax, semantic, time management, etc.). In consequence, to preserve Interoperability at all levels of Enterprise Modeling including execution level; we propose to implement an Enterprises Federated Agents System that will be HLA compliant (to guaranty also run time interoperability between heterogeneous software components).

7   Federated Communication Framework

The proposition starts from the statement on interoperability needs on interfacing enterprises IS in the context of project cooperation. The figure 2 depicts the requirement on exchanging data from heterogeneous Information Systems, it can include vendor tools such as SAP and other specific developed solutions. It is issued by generalizing study case of [9], various enterprises are involved in a common project and their heterogeneous components need to be interfaced. Existing interoperability between components is represented with plain arrows and in demand interoperability with dotted arrows. Labarthe et al. in [10] reports on solution to establish interoperability using MAS in the communication of enterprises IS (i.e. figure 2 long dotted set); they have implemented an agent communication mechanism using JADE platform facilities. Zacharewicz et al. in [9] defined an interoperable Workflow using DEVS / HLA. By joining these approaches, this paper introduces the basis for a generalized approach to realize interoperability between heterogeneous components. A way of research is envisaged. The first requirement is solving the interoperability of data and services, HLA can be part of a solution.

For instance in the practical case of figure 2, a solution is to establish links to an "Interoperability Service Bus", referring to Enterprise Service Bus of Chapel [11] concepts, to connect new features with already connected components, (e.g. DEVS/HLA Anylogic, HLA...). We detail next point how an HLA compliant platform can facilitate the integration of all required components.

Different levels of ontology are required in our approach. From low level with poor semantics associated to HLA objects to information transport level (HLA bus). Agent KQML [12] will be used as an intermediate level able to match from low level description to high level description used in heterogeneous platforms, software or enterprise models involved in the system using reference to domain Ontologies.

Information System Services Layer. The distributed implementation requires the extension of two add-ons to the local enterprise IS to define HLA Enterprise Federate Agent (HEFA). We present in the figure 2, the elements of this new architecture. The respective local enterprise ISs remain unchanged, HLA only required to add components to interface with input output messages of the IS.

Multi Agent Coding / Decoding Layer. All agents involved in the data ontology matching are detailed:

The **Agent 1 (Storing data)** is employed to store the received information and will check the capacity to decode information using a communication with ontology agent. Receiving the agreement to use the data, it sends to the information system the data and the ontology. **The Agent 2 (Ontology)** is linked to a repository of local ontology; it checks the consistency of the information regarding the local ontology and decides if the data can be exploited. If yes, it sends back to the storing data agent the information and the ontology to use. If not, it asks to the communication agent to start dialog to obtain the appropriate ontology. **The Agent 3 (Communication)** will start a conversation with the respective agent of the data sender to deal on the modality to receive the appropriate ontology. We propose, in the following, that this dialog will be established using HLA message communication protocol but from a conceptual consideration it can be considered as a general approach where HLA is just one practical technical solution.

Local RTI Component Layer. This level is the lower level; it is the service and data level. It deals with technologies employed to exchange computerized information. The first component is the Local RTI component (LRC). We illustrate in figure 2, the use of two instances of our structure connected to a Workflow monitoring tool. This tool is employed to run a simulation of a Supply chain or of a document, exchanging process and is triggering right in time the information systems of the interoperating enterprises.

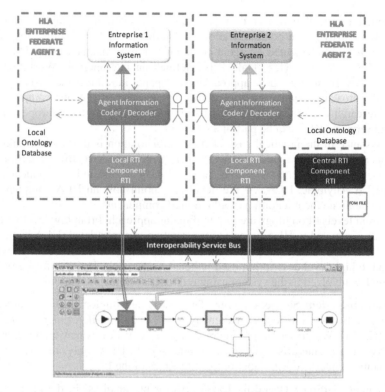

Fig. 2. Federated Interoperability Data Exchange

7.1 HLA Interaction and Object Class Model

The idea is to propose a new mapping for data to be exchanged in a HLA compliant distributed system between Interoperable Enterprise Agents. We proposed in [9], a generic HLA FOM that will support the descriptions of the data required to insure the exchange of information in the figure 1. case b.

Information to exchange. Information exchanged between enterprises information systems will be mapped with HLA Object class models (that handle persistent information in the distributed execution). The enterprise IS federates will publish and subscribe (PS) to these classes of information. An information channel Object represents the informational link between at least two enterprises. We notice that communication channels preserve confidentiality.

Ontology. Ontologies exchanged between enterprises are not persistent in the studied approach; they will be mapped into HLA Interactions (that are non persistent information exchanged). Enterprise IS Federate Agents will publish and subscribe (PS) to these classes of information. One Ontology class is associated to each information channel; each Ontology definition can change during run time. Eventually, validity duration can be set for each Ontology.

The structure of the generic ontology and of the messages will be implemented in the FOM presented in [9]. Because of generic concepts introduced in this paper, HLA interaction parameters and HLA object attributes are not fully specified; they will be in more detailed depending on the applications. It gives flexibility to the data structures exchanged.

8 Conclusion and Future Work

This article has given a state of the art of Enterprise Interoperability concepts and illustrated the use of Agent concepts and HLA standard for the implementation of enterprise applications federations.

From the new concept of short-lived enterprise ontology for federated Enterprise Interoperability, we proposed a specific implementation of distributed enterprise models for simulation or real time information exchange. At the end, the keys for implementation given by Agent dialogue mechanism has helped to bridge the gap from Enterprise Interoperability concepts to HLA compliant distributed implementation in the field of Enterprise Modeling by following a new standardized and systematic approach.

References

1. INTEROP: INTEROP Home Page, INTEROP NoE (2005),
   http://www.interop-vlab.eu/
2. IEEE std 1516.22000: IEEE Standard for Modeling and Simulation (M&S) High Level Architecture (HLA) - Federate Interface Specification. IEEE, New York (2000)
3. Ferber, J.: Multi-agents Systems. In: An Introduction to Distributed Artificial Intelligence. Addison Wesley, London (1999)
4. Jennings, N.R., Sycara, K., Wooldridge, M.: A Roadmap of Agent Research and Development. Autonomous Agents and Multi-agents Systems 1(1), 7–38 (1998)
5. Nwana, H.S.: Software agents: An overview. Knowledge Engineering Review 11(3), 205–244 (1996)
6. Huang, C.Y., Nof, S.Y.: Autonomy and viability measures for Agent-based manufacturing systems. International Journal of Production Research 38(17), 4129–4148 (2000)
7. Zacharewicz, G., Frydman, C., Giambiasi, N.: G-DEVS/HLA Environment for Distributed Simulations of Workflows. Simulation 84(5), 197–213 (2008)
8. Marietto, M.B., David, N., Sichman, J.S., Coelho, H.: Requirements Analysis and Agent-Based Simulation Platforms: State of the Art and New Prospects. In: Sichman, J.S., Bousquet, F., Davidsson, P. (eds.) MABS 2002. LNCS (LNAI), vol. 2581, pp. 125–141. Springer, Heidelberg (2003)
9. Zacharewicz, G., Chen, D., Vallespir, B.: Short-Lived Ontology Approach for Agent/HLA Federated Enterprise Interoperability. In: IEEE Proc. of International Conference I-ESA Interoperability for Enterprise Software and Applications, Beijing (2009)
10. Labarthe, O., Espinasse, B., Ferrarini, A., Montreuil, B.: Toward a Methodological Framework for Agent-Based Modelling and Simulation of Supply Chains in a Mass Customization Context. Simulation Modelling Practice and Theory 15(2), 113–136 (2007)
11. Chappell, D.A.: Enterprise Service Bus. O'Reilly, Sebastopol (2004)
12. Finin, T., Fritzson, R., McKay, D., McEntire, R.: KQML as an agent communication language. In: Proc. of the Third International Conference on Information and Knowledge Management, Gaithersburg, Maryland, USA (1994)

Model Based on Bayesian Networks for Monitoring Events in a Supply Chain

Erica Fernández[1], Enrique Salomone[1], and Omar Chiotti[1,2]

[1] INGAR – CONICET, Avellaneda 3657, Santa Fe, Argentina, 3000
[2] CIDISI- UTN FRSF, Lavaisse 610, Santa Fe, Argentina, 3000
{ericafernandez,salomone,chiotti}@santafe-conicet.gov.ar

Abstract. The execution of supply process orders in a supply chain is conditioned by different types of disruptive events that must be detected and solved in real time. This requires the ability to proactively monitor, analyze and notify disruptive events. In this work we present a model that captures this functionality and was used as the foundation to design a software agent. A reactive-deliberative hybrid architecture provides the ability to proactively detect, analyze and notify disruptive events that take place in a supply chain. For the deliberative performance of the agent, a cause-effect relation model based on a Bayesian network with decision nodes is proposed.

Keywords: supply chain, event management, agent, Bayesian Networks.

1 Introduction

Current planning and execution systems are rather limited in their ability to automatically respond to changes caused by disruptive events in the supply chain [1]. This is a shortage of these systems because the execution of supply process orders is conditioned by different types of disruptive events. These unexpected events (cancellation of an order, failure in a process, change in a process capacity, etc.) must be detected and solved in real time. This requires ability to proactively monitor, analyze and notify disruptive events. In this scenario, Supply Chain Event Management Systems (SCEM) [1], [2] have been proposed. SCEM is defined as a business process in which significant events are timely recognized, reactive actions are suddenly executed, flows of information and material are adjusted, and the key employees are notified. In other words, SCEM can be seen as a complex control problem. SCEM systems emphasize the need of managing the exceptions by means of short term logistics decisions, avoiding frequent re-planning processes.

Montgomery [3] defines 5 functions that a SCEM system should perform. These are: *Monitoring* (to provide data in real time about processes, events and current states of the orders and parameters); *Notification* (to alert the occurrence of exceptions to take decisions proactively); *Simulation* (to evaluate the effect of actions to be taken); *Control* (if an exception takes place, to evaluate the changes in the processes proactively); *Measurement* (to evaluate the supply chain performance).

In this work, based on a SCEM model defined as a network of resources and supply process orders, we propose a model for monitoring, analysis and notification of

B. Vallespir and T. Alix (Eds.): APMS 2009, IFIP AICT 338, pp. 358–365, 2010.
© IFIP International Federation for Information Processing 2010

events. Based on this model a software agent has been designed. A reactive-deliberative hybrid architecture provides the ability to proactively detect, analyze and notify disruptive events that take place in a supply chain. For the deliberative performance of the agent, a cause-effect relation model based on a Bayesian network with decision nodes is proposed.

This paper is organized in the following way. Section 2 discusses related works. Section 3 presents a SCEM model. Section 4 presents a model for monitoring, analysis and notification of events. Section 5 presents an example and section 6 presents conclusions and future work.

2   Related Works

In order to provide a SCEM solution, several contributions have been proposed, among them: Tai-Lang [4] proposed a method to analyze and manage the impact of an exception during order execution; Chin-Hung [5] developed a model based on cause-effect relationship to represent the disruptive exception caused by unexpected events in a supply chain. Liu [6] presented a methodology that uses Petri nets to formulate supply chain event rules and analyze the cause-effect relationships among events. Maheshwari [7] described the events that throw exceptions through business processes. In Zimmermann [8], the orders to be monitored are initialized by different triggers: queries from customers, alerts from suppliers and critical profiles. The critical profiles are the orders with high probability of being affected by disruptive events. This SCEM solution is based on a multi-agents architecture to proactively monitoring orders, integrating and interpreting several data gathered from the supply chain members to evaluate and distribute the results. Kurbel [9] proposed a mobile agent-based SCEM system to collect and analyze data provided by a supply chain monitoring system. Here, the monitored resources are considered to be important to anticipate unexpected events. To detect exceptions, his approach is not only based on target-state comparison, but it includes statistical analysis as well.

Hofmann [10] proposed an agent based system that allows customers track and trace their orders. In order to know the status of an order, the requirement must be entered by the user. The system is proactive regarding notification of unexpected events. Kärkkäinen [11] presented an agents based system to manage the information flow related to a tangible object. It offers information about the state of an order but it does not consider disruptive events management. These last two approaches are limited to functions of Tracking and Tracing while SCEM is not.

A common feature of these contributions is that the proposed SCEM models are focused on orders and not on resources, when in fact, the resources are the ones affected by disruptive events in a direct way and the orders are the ones affected by the exceptions triggered by such events.

3   The SCEM Model

We have defined a SCEM Model (Figure 1) as a network of *resources* linked among them by *supply process orders*. The *schedule* (provided by the planning system) defines the execution timetable of a set of orders and determines the *resources* (with their parameters values) that are linked to *supply processes*. This representation shows the origin and propagation of an exception, allowing the monitoring actions focus on resources where the unexpected events can occur. The monitoring of resources during the plan execution can help to anticipate the occurrence of exceptions and proactively take decisions [9]. Resources are control points with a set of parameters that must be monitored to detect the occurrence of an event. This event must be analyzed using a *cause-effect relation network* to determine if an exception occurs. Different from other approaches described in Section 2 (Related Works), in which the control actions or the monitoring actions are centered in the orders, in our approach, the monitoring actions focus on resources because they are directly affected by the disruptive events. This allows us to generate a model to monitor and analyze exceptions with a higher predictive quality.

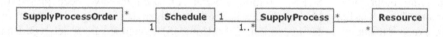

Fig. 1. SCEM Model

4   Model for Monitoring, Analysis and Notification of Events

Based on the defined SCEM model, we have developed a reference model (Figure 2) satisfying the following requirements: ability of reasoning out uncertain scenarios and with partial observations; ability of preventing potential exceptions caused by unexpected events, and ability to predict future states (potential unexpected events) based on past and present observations.

The *Monitor* (Figure 2) is the main component of the model, which is responsible of the information required by monitoring, analysis and notification functions. Each *SupplyProcess* has assigned a *Monitor*. Each *Resource* linked to a *SupplyProcess* (Figure 1) is a control point with a set of *Parameters* that must be monitored to detect the occurrence of an event. This event must be analyzed using a *cause-effect relation network* to determine if an exception occurs. A network defines a causal relation among parameters. Each parameter can take a *Value* in a discrete or continuous domain. The network topology represents temporal causality. Causality refers to the impact or influence among the parameters. Temporal refers to the ability to proactively detect events and evaluate their impact. A *Parameter* has two disjunctive *State* values: *Observed*, the parameter is observed and its value is captured; and *Inferred*, the parameter value is calculated from the value of precedent parameters. Although a causal network has a lot of parameters, only one (the root) is used to evaluate if an exception occurs. Initially, all parameters of the network have the state value inferred, which is calculated with a priori information. During the plan execution, an *ActivationCondition* defines the parameter that has to be observed to incorporate an evidence. Based on this evidence, the *CausalModelAnalizer* uses the causal network to infer an upgrade value of the root parameter. Based on this inferred value and using the *PlannedValue*, the *Monitor* evaluates if an exception occurs. When it predicts an exception, the *Notifier* reports the *DisruptiveEvent*. It can be: change in the requirements of an order (quantity of material, deadline), and/or change in the parameters of a resource (transition time between states, available capacity).

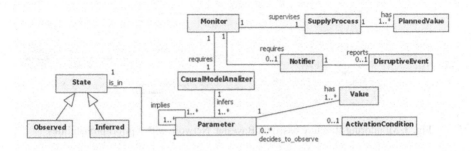

Fig. 2. Reference Model for monitoring, analysis and notification of events

5   An Application Example

As has been said above, the main functions of the model are: *monitoring, analysis* and *notification*. Based on this model, we have designed a hybrid agent responsible of the three functions. It has two components: a *reactive* component for the *monitoring* and *notification* functions; and a *deliberative* component for the analysis function, which allows the agent to make complex reasoning and to make plans and to take decisions. This last agent ability has been implemented by means of a Bayesian Network model. Bayesian networks [12] are a method to represent uncertain knowledge, which allows reasoning based on probability theory. Each node of a Bayesian network is composed by a random variable X, which can take values x_i in a continuous or discrete range. The values are exclusive and exhaustive and they have an associated probability $P(x_i)$. Then, each node is represented by X: (x_i, $P(x_i)$) and direct conditional dependences are the directed edges in the graph.

An example of a cheese production plant is described to show the behavior of the agent. The agent, based on the SCEM model (Figure 1), receives a schedule where an order requires producing a quantity of a cheese type. It links the SupplyProcessOrder: *cheese_production_process* with Resource:*milk*, Resource:*cheese_type* and Resource: *cheese_production_plant*. It performs this function through the *reactive* component.

Milk acidity is a parameter that can affect the cheese quality. High acidity can produce sandy cheese, bitter cheese or increase the curdling rate causing surface cracks. Low acidity can produce insipid cheese. Normal acidity produces cheese with required quality. The agent, based on the reference model (Figure 2), defines the monitoring structure by means of a Bayesian Network with a priori probabilities (Figure 3). These probabilities are obtained from statistical data of previous results. This monitoring structure is composed by the following *Parameters*, whose possible *Values* are represented in braces: *acidity* {normal, low, high}, which is a parameter of resource:*milk*; *time_of_curdle* {normal, low, high}, *fresh_cheese_texture_quality* {good, bad}, *fresh_cheese _texture* {no_granulated, granulated}, *surface_cracks* {no, yes}, *fresh_cheese_taste* {good, insipid, bitter} and *fresh_cheese_taste_quality* {good, bad}, which are parameters of the resource:*cheese_production_plant*; and *cheese_type_quality* {good, bad}, which is a parameter of resource:*cheese_type*. The *ActivationCondition* are: *test_ time_of_curdle*, *test_fresh_cheese _texture* and *test_fresh_cheese _taste*.

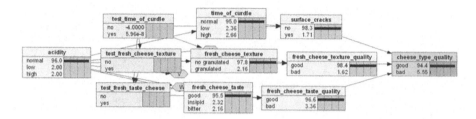

Fig. 3. Monitoring structure based on Bayesian Network with a priori probabilities

The agent notifies changes in the requirement of the order if the probability of the product will be outside the specification is greater than a threshold value; it performs this function through the *reactive component*. In this example *threshold* = 97.0. The total process time depends on the type of cheese to be produced. In this example *cheese_type* = soft cheese is considered, and the total process time is 240 hours.

Thus, the monitoring structure of the agent (Figure 3) initially includes the observed parameter *acidity*. The *acidity* is monitored at the beginning of the process and for each of the three possible values; the agent will define different plans of action which arise from *deliberative component*:

1.   If *acidity* == *high*, the agent inserts this evidence in the net (Table 1, row 1) assigning *acidity:(high, 100)* and propagate it. As a result, the agent obtains the expected value of the parameter, *cheese_type_quality:(bad, 85.1)*. Since, *P(bad)* = *85.1* < *threshold*, it decides to analyze the inferred parameters *surface_cracks:(yes, 50.7)*, *fresh_cheese_texture_quality:(bad, 45)* and *fresh_cheese_ taste_quality:(bad, 45)*. The three parameters explain the value of the parameter *cheese_type_quality*:

1.1   *surface_cracks:(yes, 50.7)* indicates the probability that the cheese has surface cracks caused by a low time of curdle. Based on this information, the agent decides to monitor this parameter. This is done by assigning to the *Activation-Condition test_ time_of_curdle == YES* (Table 1, row 2). This test is made 2 hours after the process has been started. The test has two possible results {*normal, low*} (Table 1, row 1):

1.1.1 If *time_of_curdle == low*, the agent inserts this evidence in the net (Table 1, row 2) assigning *time_of_curdle:(low, 100)* and propagates it. The result is *cheese_type_quality:(bad, 98.5)*. Since *P(bad)* = *98.5* > *threshold*, which implies high probability that product will be outside the specification, so the agent decides to notify the value of the parameter, *cheese_type_quality*, and to FINISH the monitoring process. This allows the agent to predict the result 238 hours before the process ends.

1.2   If *time_of_curdle == normal*, the agent inserts this evidence in the net (Table 1, row 3) assigning *time_of_curdle:(normal, 100)* and propagates it. The result is *cheese_type_quality:(bad, 69.7)*. Since *P(bad)* = *69.7* < *threshold*, the agent decides to analyze the parameters *surface_cracks:(yes, 0.0)*, *fresh_cheese_texture_quality: (bad, 45.0)* and *fresh_cheese_taste_quality: (bad, 45.0)*. The first parameter indicates that there is no risk that the product will have surface cracks. The two last parameters explain the value of the parameter *cheese_type_quality*.

1.3 *fresh_cheese_texture_quality:(bad, 45.0)*, indicates the probability that the cheese results granulated and, therefore, not satisfying the quality specification. Based on this information, the agent decides to monitor this parameter. This is done by assigning to the *ActivationCondition test_ fresh_cheese _texture == YES* (Table 1, row 4). This test is made 48 hours after the process has been started. The test has two possible results {*no_granulated, granulated*} (Table 1, row 3).

1.3.1 If *fresh_cheese _texture == granulated*, the agent inserts this evidence in the net (Table 1, row 4) assigning *fresh_cheese_texture:(granulated, 100)* and propagates it. The agent is certain that the product will be outside the specification, so it decides to notify the value of the parameter, *cheese_type_quality*, to the resource:*cheese_type*, and to FINISH the monitoring process. This allows the agent to predict the result 192 hours before the process has been finished.

1.3.2 If *fresh_cheese _texture == no_granulated*, the agent inserts this evidence in the net (Table 1, row 5) assigning *fresh_cheese_texture: (no_granulated, 100)* and propagates it. Since *P(bad) = 45.0 < threshold*, the agent decides to analyze the parameters *surface_cracks:(yes, 0.0)*, *fresh_cheese_texture_quality:(bad,0.0)* and *fresh_cheese_taste_quality:(bad, 45.0)*. The first two parameters indicate that there is not risk that the product will have surface cracks or texture problems. The last parameter explains the value of the *cheese_type_quality* parameter:

1.4 *fresh_cheese_taste_quality:(bad, 45.0)*, indicates the probability that the cheese has taste problems and, therefore, not satisfying the quality specification. Based on this information, the agent decides to monitor this parameter. This is done by assigning to the *ActivationCondition test_ fresh_cheese _taste ==YES* (Table 1, row 6). This test is made 120 hours after the process has been started. The test has two possible results {*good, bitter*} (Table 1, row 5).

1.4.1 If *fresh_cheese _taste == bitter*, the agent inserts this evidence in the net (Table 1, row 6) assigning *fresh_cheese_taste:(bitter, 100)* and propagates it. The result is *cheese_type_quality:(bad, 100)*; the agent is certain that the product will be outside the specification, so it decides to notify the value of the parameter, *cheese_type_quality*, to the resource:*cheese_type*, and to FINISH the monitoring process. This allows the agent to predict the result 120 hours before the process ends.

1.4.2 If *fresh_cheese_taste == good*, the agent inserts this evidence in the net (Table 1, row 7) assigning *fresh_cheese_taste:(good, 100)* and propagates it. The result is *cheese_type_quality:(good, 100)*; the agent is certain that the product will not have taste problem, so it decides to FINISH the monitoring process.

2. If *acidity == low*, the agent inserts this evidence in the net (Table 1, row 8) assigning *acidity:(low, 100)* and propagates it. As a result, the agent obtains information of the expected value of the parameter, *cheese_type_quality: (bad, 51.0)*. Since *P(bad) = 51.0 < threshold*, it decides to analyze the parameters *surface_cracks: (yes, 0.0)*, *fresh_cheese_texture_quality:(bad, 0.0)* and *fresh_cheese_taste_quality: (bad, 51.0)*. The last explains the value of the *cheese_type_quality* parameter:

2.1 *fresh_cheese_taste_quality:(bad, 51.0)*, indicates the probability that the cheese has taste problems and, therefore, not satisfying the quality specification. Based on this information, the agent decides to monitor this parameter. This is done by assigning to the *ActivationCondition test_ fresh_cheese_taste == YES*

(Table 1, row 9). This test is made 120 hours after the process has been started. The test has two possible results {good, insipid} (Table 1, row 8).

2.1.1 If *fresh_cheese_taste == insipid,* the agent inserts this evidence in the net (Table 1, row 9) assigning *fresh_cheese_taste:(insipid, 100)* and propagates it. The result is *cheese_type_quality:(bad, 100),* the agent is certain that the product will be outside the specification, so it decides to notify the value of the parameter, *cheese_type_quality,* to the resource:*cheese_type,* and to FINISH the monitoring process. This allows the agent to predict the result 120 hours before the process ends.

2.1.2 If *fresh_cheese_taste == good,* the agent inserts this evidence in the net (Table 1, row 10) assigning *fresh_cheese_taste:(good, 100)* and propagates it. The result is *cheese_type_quality:(good, 100),* the agent is certain that the product will not have taste problems, so it decides to FINISH the monitoring process.

3. If *acidity == normal,* the agent inserts this evidence in the net (Table 1, row 11) assigning *acidity:(normal, 100)* and propagates it. As a result, it obtains the the expected value of the parameter, *cheese_type_quality (good, 97.1). Since P(good) = 97.1 > threshold,* the agent decides to FINISH the monitoring process.

Table 1. Bayesian Network inference process

Row	A	TC	testTC	SC	FCTa	testFCTa	FCTaQ	FCTe	testFCTe	FCTeQ	CTQ
1	normal 0 / low 0 / high 100	normal 30 / low 70 / high 0	no / yes	no / yes	49.2 / 50.7	good 40 / insipid 0 / bitter 60	no / yes	good 55 / bad 45	no_granulated 40 / granulated 60	no / yes	good 55 / bad 45	good 14.9 / bad 85.1
2	normal 0 / low 0 / high 100	normal 0 / low 100 / high 0	no / yes	no / yes	5 / 95	good 40 / insipid 0 / bitter 60	no / yes	good 55 / bad 45	no_granulated 40 / granulated 60	no / yes	good 55 / bad 45	good 1.51 / bad 98.5
3	normal 0 / low 0 / high 100	normal 100 / low 0 / high 0	no / yes	no / yes	100	good 40 / insipid 0 / bitter 60	no / yes	good 55 / bad 45	no_granulated 40 / granulated 60	no / yes	good 55 / bad 45	good 30.2 / bad 69.7
4	normal 0 / low 0 / high 100	normal 100 / low 0 / high	no / yes	no / yes	100	good 40 / insipid 0 / bitter 60	no / yes	good 55 / bad 45	no_granulated 0 / granulated 100	no / yes	good 0 / bad 100	good 0 / bad 100
5	normal 0 / low 0 / high 100	normal 100 / low 0 / high	no / yes	no / yes	100	good 40 / insipid 0 / bitter 60	no / yes	good 55 / bad 45	no_granulated 100 / granulated 0	no / yes	good 100 / bad 0	good 55 / bad 45
6	normal 0 / low 0 / high 100	normal 100 / low 0 / high	no / yes	no / yes	100	good 0 / insipid 0 / bitter 100	no / yes	good 0 / bad 100	no_granulated 0 / granulated 0	no / yes	good 100 / bad 0	good 0 / bad 100
7	normal 0 / low 0 / high 100	normal 100 / low 0 / high	no / yes	no / yes	100	good 100 / insipid 0 / bitter 0	no / yes	good 100 / bad 0	no_granulated 100 / granulated 0	no / yes	good 100 / bad 0	good 100 / bad 0
8	normal 0 / low 100 / high 0	normal 15 / low 0 / high 85	no / yes	no / yes	100	good 32 / insipid 68 / bitter 0	no / yes	good 49 / bad 51	no_granulated 100 / granulated 0	no / yes	good 100 / bad 0	good 49 / bad 51
9	normal 0 / low 100 / high 0	normal 15 / low 0 / high 85	no / yes	no / yes	100	good 0 / insipid 100 / bitter 0	no / yes	good 0 / bad 100	no_granulated 100 / granulated 0	no / yes	good 100 / bad 0	good 0 / bad 100
10	normal 0 / low 100 / high 0	normal 15 / low 0 / high 85	no / yes	no / yes	100	good 100 / insipid 0 / bitter 0	no / yes	good 100 / bad 0	no_granulated 100 / granulated 0	no / yes	good 100 / bad 0	good 100 / bad 0
11	normal 100 / low 0 / high 0	normal 98 / low 1 / high 1	no / yes	no / yes 0.72	99.3	good 98 / insipid 1 / bitter 1	no / yes	good 98.5 / bad 1.5	no_granulated 99 / granulated 1	no / yes	good 99.3 / bad 0.75	good 97.1 / bad 2.96

A: acidity; TC: time_of_curdle; testTC: test_time_of_curdle; SC: surface_cracks; FCTa: fresh_cheese_taste; testFCTa: test_fresh_cheese_taste; FCTaQ: fresh_cheese_taste_quality; FCTe: fresh_cheese_texture; testFCTe: test_fresh_cheese_texture; FCTeQ: fresh_cheese_texture_quality; CTQ: cheese_type_quality.

6 Conclusions and Future Work

In this work we have proposed an approach to proactively monitor, analyze and notify disruptive events that take place in a supply chain. The new SCEM Model proposed, based on a network of *resources* linked among them by *supply process orders,* allowed to focus the monitoring actions on resources where unexpected events can occur. Thus, the generated model for monitoring, analysis and notification of events that has two advantages: 1) ability to dynamically change the *network of analysis.* That is to say, after an unexpected event is detected, the monitoring strategy can be extended including other parameters and increasing its monitoring frequency; 2) the model can be used to monitor any process provided the monitoring structure is composed of causal relations. Based on this last model, we proposed a software agent with hybrid architecture. This architecture allows the agent to perform the model functions, defining a Bayesian network with decision nodes representing temporal causality. The agent proposed, has the ability of anticipating, based on evidence, changes in the values of the parameters of the resource or in the requirements of an order.

As future works, our objective is to add the agent ability to learn from the new experiences. This will allow the agent updating its knowledge base. For the particular causal model implemented in this work, it implies updating the probabilities associated to the Bayesian network.

References

1. Masing, N.: SC Event Management as Strategic Perspectiva – Market Study: SCEM Software Performance in the European Market. Master Thesis. Universitié du Québec en Outaouasis (2003)
2. Zimmermann, R.: Agent-based Supply Network Event Management. In: Walliser, M., Brantschen, S., Calisti, M., Hempfling, T. (eds.). Whitestein Series in Software Agent Techonologies (2006)
3. Montgomery, N., Waheed, R.: Event Management Enables Companies To Take Control of Extended Supply Chains. AMR Research (2001)
4. Tai-Lang, Y.: An Exception Handling Method of Order Fulfillment Process in the i-Hub Supported Extended Supply Chain. Master's Thesis, National Central University, Institute of Industrial Management, Taiwan (2002)
5. Chin-Hung, C.: Assessing Dependability of Order Fulfillment in the i-Hub Supported Extended Supply Chain. Master's Thesis, National Central University, Institute of Industrial Management, Taiwan (2002)
6. Liu, E., Akhil, K., Van Der Aalst, W.: A formal modeling approach for Supply Chain Event Management. Decision Support Systems 43, 761–778 (2007)
7. Maheshwari, P., Sharon, S.: Events-Based Exception Handling in Supply Chain Management using Web Services. In: Proceedings of the Advanced International Conference on Internet and Web Applications and Services (2006)
8. Zimmermann, R.: Agent-based Supply Network Event Management. Verlag (2006)
9. Kurbel, K., Schreber, D.: Agent-Based Diagnostics in Supply Networks. Issues in Information Systems VIII(2) (2007)
10. Hoffmann, O., Deschner, D., Reinheimer, S., Bodendorf, F.: Agent- Supported Information Retrieval in the Logistic Chain. In: Proceeding of the 32nd Hawaii International Conference on System Sciences, Maui (1999)
11. Kärkkäinen, M., Främling, K., Ala-Risku, T.: Integrating Material and Information Flows Using a Distributed Peer-to-Peer Information System. In: Collaborative Systems for Production Management, Boston, pp. 305–319 (2003)
12. Jensen, F.: An Introduction to Bayesian Networks. Springer, New York (1996)

Simulation Model Driven Engineering for Manufacturing Cell

Hironori Hibino[1], Toshihiro Inukai[2], and Yukishige Yoshida[2]

[1] Technical Research Institute of JSPMI(Japan Society for the Promotion of Machine Industry),
1-1-12 Hachiman-cho, Higashikurume, Tokyo, Japan
hibino@tri.jspmi.or.jp
[2] DENSO Wave Incorporation, 1 Kusaki, Agui-cho, Chita, Aichi, Japan

Abstract. In our research, the simulation model driven engineering for manu-facturing cell (SMDE-MC) is proposed. The purposes of SMDE-MC are to support the manufacturing engineering processes based on the simulation model and to extend the range of control applications and simulation applications us-ing the PC based control. SMDE-MC provides the simulation model which con-trols and monitors the manufacturing cell directly using PC based control in the manufacturing system execution phase. Then when the simulation model acts in response to its behaviors, the manufacturing system is controlled by synchroniz-ing the simulation model behaviors. In the manufacturing system implementa-tion phase, the simulation model is mixed and synchronized with real equipment, real controllers, and management applications under a condition where parts of equipment, control programs, and manufacturing management applications are not provided in a manufacturing system.

Keywords: Manufacturing Cell, Simulation, Model Driven, PC Based Control, network middleware, and Engineering Process.

1 Introduction

Recently, PC (personal computers) based control is slowly becoming easier to be examined and used in industries, as open control platforms are getting advancing such as development of open interfaces for equipment and development of middleware for manufacturing systems [1]. It is possible to control equipment in manufacturing cells with stability and flexibility using the PC based control. The industries expect to ex-tend the range of control applications using the PC based control beyond the traditional control using PLC (programmable logic controller).

The other hand, the industries need to design and make new products for the market in rapid succession, as it is becoming harder to keep the high value of a product in the market as a long seller [2][3]. It is important to reduce the lead-time for manufactur-ing engineering processes from the manufacturing system design and implementation phase to the manufacturing system execution phase. One of the solutions to realize the requirements is the front-loading method, which finds problems in advance and solves the problems at an earlier phase in the manufacturing engineering processes while limiting wasteful periods to the minimum by reducing the number of times needed to

B. Vallespir and T. Alix (Eds.): APMS 2009, IFIP AICT 338, pp. 366–373, 2010.
© IFIP International Federation for Information Processing 2010

go back and refine the design. The front-loading method using simulation technologies has attracted the attention of the industries. However as the purposes of the present manufacturing system simulation do not include evaluation of manufacturing system implementation by mixing and synchronizing simulation, real equipment, real controllers, and management applications, there are many limitations concerning simulation applications in the manufacturing engineering processes. Therefore it is necessary to extend the range of simulation applications in the manufacturing engineering processes.

In our research, the simulation model driven engineering for manufacturing cell (SMDE-MC) is proposed. The purposes of SMDE-MC are to support the manufacturing engineering processes based on the simulation model and to extend the range of control applications and simulation applications using the PC based control. SMDE-MC provides the simulation model which controls and monitors the manufacturing cell directly using PC based control in the manufacturing system execution phase. Then when the simulation model acts in response to its behaviors, the manufacturing system is controlled by synchronizing the simulation model behaviors. In the manufacturing system implementation phase, the simulation model is mixed and synchronized with real equipment, real controllers, and management applications under a condition where parts of equipment, control programs, and manufacturing management applications are not provided in a manufacturing system.

In this paper, the environment of the simulation model driven engineering for manufacturing cell (E-SMDE-MC) is proposed. The necessary functions for E-SMDE-MC are defined and developed. E-SMDE-MC consists of our developed manufacturing model driven simulator (EMU), our developed soft wiring system, and the industrial network middleware which is one of the semi-standard middleware. The validation of E-SMDE-MC was carried out through a case study.

2 Typical Manufacturing Engineering Process and Its Problems

Based on our analysis for the typical manufacturing engineering processes, manufacturing systems are established through four phases [4]. Figure 1 shows the typical manufacturing engineering processes.

Phase 1: This phase is the planning phase to define fundamental manufacturing requirements such as target production volumes, location and so on.

Phase 2: This phase is the manufacturing system design phase to fix manufacturing specifications such as the numbers of equipment needed, layout, manufacturing management as with the Kanban system and so on.

Phase 3-1: This is a period prior to the manufacturing system implementation phase. In this period, engineers implement hardware such as special machines, transfer machines, and software such as ladder programs, robot programs, operation panels, and production control programs.

Phase 3-2: This is a later period of the manufacturing system implementation phase. In this period, in order to undertake the manufacturing system trial operations, engineers partially operate hardware execution and software execution and accurately evaluate their executions from the viewpoints of the manufacturing systems.

Phase 4: This phase is the actual manufacturing system execution phase.

In phase 1 and phase 2, a manufacturing system simulator plays an important role in designing and evaluating manufacturing systems by using a virtual factory model [5][6][7][8]. In phase 3-1, engineers separately develop hardware such as robots and special machining devices, and software such as ladder programs and production control programs. Then they independently evaluate their developed hardware or software in their place. In phase 3-2, the developed hardware or software is gathered together and adjusted in a real plant. If the delivery of the hardware is late, it is not possible to evaluate the software. If problems occur in this phase, it is necessary to go back to the previous phases. The problems are usually fatal and sometimes cause a delay of production [4][9].

As the purposes of the present manufacturing system simulation do not include evaluation of manufacturing system implementation by mixing and synchronizing simulation, real equipment, real controllers, and management applications, there are many limitations concerning simulation applications in the manufacturing engineering processes [4][9][10]. This difficulty has hindered precise and rapid support of a manufacturing engineering process. Consequently the lead-time is not reduced. Therefore it is necessary to extend the range of simulation applications in the manufacturing engineering processes.

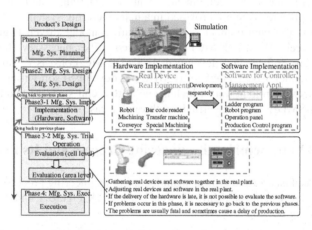

Fig. 1. Based on our analysis for the typical manufacturing engineering processes, manufacturing systems are established through four phases. This figure shows the typical manufacturing engineering process and its problems.

3   Environment of Simulation Model Driven Engineering for Manufacturing Cell

In our research, the simulation model driven engineering for manufacturing cell (SMDE-MC) is proposed. The purposes of SMDE-MC are to support the manufacturing engineering processes based on the simulation model and to extend the range of control applications and simulation applications using the PC based control.

SMDE-MC provides the simulation model which controls and monitors the manufacturing cell directly using PC based control in the manufacturing system execution phase. Then when the simulation model acts in response to its behaviors, the manufacturing system is controlled by synchronizing the simulation model behaviors. In the manufacturing system implementation phase, the simulation model is mixed and synchronized with real equipment, real controllers, and management applications under a condition where parts of equipment, control programs, and manufacturing management applications are not provided in a manufacturing system. Figure 2 shows an outline of our proposed SMDE-MC.

To realize the environment of the simulation model driven engineering for manufacturing cell (E-SMDE-MC), the following functions are necessary.

1. A function to define simulation model behaviors in the simulation model.
2. A function to control real equipment in response to simulation model behaviors.
3. A function to monitor information from real world such as real equipment, and to drive the simulation model in response to the monitored information.
4. A function to display simulation model behaviors using three-dimensional animation.

To realize the first function for E-SMDE-MC, the following modeling methods are proposed.

1.1 A modeling method to define equipment motion behaviors programs using the tree structure.
1.2 A modeling method to define parallel processing programs.
1.3 A modeling method to define specification control programs using a script type programming language.

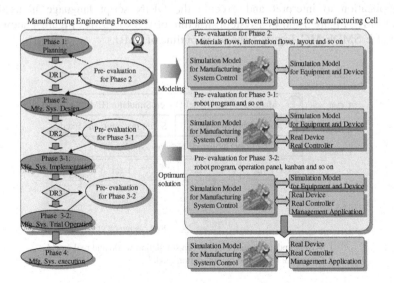

Fig. 2. This figure shows an outline of our proposed environment of the simulation model driven engineering for manufacturing cell (SMDE-MC)

To realize the second function for E-SMDE-MC, the following mechanisms are proposed.

2.1 A mechanism to synchronize with several tasks such as control tasks for equipment and monitor tasks for equipment concurrently.

2.2 A mechanism to run specification control programs using a script type programming language.

2.3 A mechanism to synchronize simulation model behaviors in accordance with monitored information from real world such as robot state information, inspection equipment state information and so on.

To realize the third function for E-SMDE-MC, the soft wiring mechanism that has the following functions is proposed.

3.1 A wiring function to logically wire data on real world and data on the simulation model.

3.2 A transmission function to transmit signals and data between the simulation model and the real world.

To realize the forth function for E-SMDE-MC, the following function is proposed.

4.1 An animation function to visualize the three-dimensional simulation model by synchronizing the results of manufacturing cell behaviors.

In order to implement the first function, the second function, and fourth function, the manufacturing model driven simulator (EMU) is proposed and developed. In order to implement the third function, the soft wiring system is proposed and developed. ORiN (Open Resource interface for the Network) [11] is used as the semi-standard manufacturing middleware in E-SMDE-MC. The ORiN script language, which is provided as the standard script language on ORiN, is used to realize the 2.2 function. The application to interpret and execute the ORiN script language is used in E-SMDE-MC. Figure 3 shows a system structure of E-SMDE-MC. Figure 4 shows an outline of E-SMDE-MC. Figure 5 shows an outline of EMU.

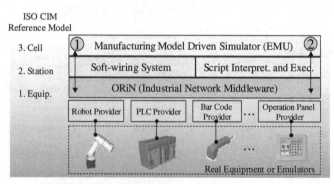

1. Wiring and transmission between simulation world and real world.
2. Control of real world by simulation models.

Fig. 3. This figure shows a system structure of our proposed environment of the simulation model driven engineering for manufacturing cell (E-SMDE-MC)

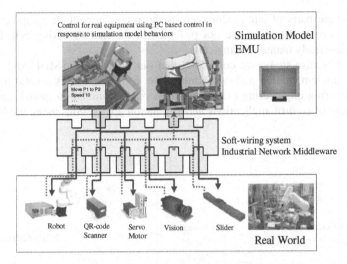

Fig. 4. This figure shows an outline of our proposed environment of the simulation model driven engineering for manufacturing cell (E-SMDE-MC)

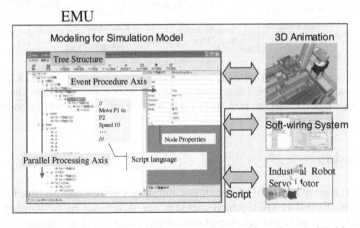

Fig. 5. This figure shows an outline of our proposed manufacturing model driven simulator (EMU) and its relationships with virtual model and real world

4 A Case Study

A case study was carried out using a small size of a manufacturing cell which consists of a robot, inspection equipment, vision equipment, servo motors, conveyors, a QR-code scanner and so on. It was confirmed that the simulation model for the case study manufacturing cell could be made on the manufacturing model driven simulator (EMU). It was also confirmed that the simulation model in EMU could control and monitor the manufacturing cell directly using PC based control. It was also confirmed that the simulation model in EMU could be synchronized with real equipment under a condition where parts of equipment such as the robot, inspection equipment, servo motors, conveyors and so on are not provided in the manufacturing cell. Figure 6 shows the case study manufacturing cell.

Through this case study, we confirmed that our proposed E-SMDE-MC could be used in the implementation and execution phase. E-SMDE-MC is a valid to support the manufacturing engineering processes based on the simulation model, and to extend the range of control applications and simulation applications using the PC based control.

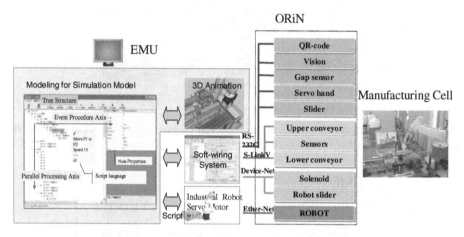

Fig. 6. A case study was carried out using a small size of a manufacturing cell which consists of a robot, inspection equipment, vision equipment, servo motors, conveyors, a QR-code scanner and so on. This figure shows the case study manufacturing cell and the simulation model on EMU.

5 Conclusion

In this paper, the environment of the simulation model driven engineering for manufacturing cell (E-SMDE-MC), which includes our developed manufacturing model driven simulator (EMU), our developed soft wiring system, and the industrial network middleware which is one of the semi-standard middleware, is proposed.
The results were:

1. To summarize the roles to extend the range of simulation applications based on our analysis for typical manufacturing engineering processes.
2. To propose E-SMDE-MC, which realizes to support the manufacturing engineering processes based on the simulation model and to extend the range of control applications and simulation applications using the PC based control.
3. To clarify necessary functions for E-SMDE-MC.
4. To confirm through a case study that the simulation model for the case study manufacturing cell could be made on the manufacturing model driven simulator (EMU) and the simulation model in EMU could control and monitor the manufacturing cell directly using PC based control.

5. To confirm through a case study that the simulation model in EMU could be synchronized with real equipment under a condition where parts of equipment such as the robot, inspection equipment, servo motors, conveyors and so on are not provided in the manufacturing cell.

Acknowledgments. This research is a part of the research project on manufacturing support systems using industrial standard technologies in JSPMI. This project was supported by funding from JKA.

References

1. Hong, K., Choi, K., Kim, J., Lee, S.: A PC-based Open Robot Control System. Robotics and Computer-Integrated Manufacturing 17, 355–365 (2001)
2. Tanaka, K., Nakatsuka, N., Hibino, H., Fukuda, Y.: Module Structured Production System. In: 41st CIRP Conference on Manufacturing Systems, pp. 303–308. Springer, Heidelberg (2008)
3. Molina, A., Rodriguez, C., Ahuett, H., Cortes, J., Ramirez, M., Jimenez, G., Martinez, S.: Next-generation Manufacturing Systems: Key Research Issues in Developing and Integrating Reconfigurable and Intelligent Machines. I. J. Computer Integrated Manufacturing 18, 525–536 (2005)
4. Hibino, H., Fukuda, Y.: Emulation in Manufacturing Engineering Processes. In: 2008 Winter Simulation Conference, pp. 1785–1793 (2008), ISBN:978-1-4244-2708-6
5. Hibino, H., Fukuda, Y., Fujii, S., Kojima, F., Mitsuyuki, K., Yura, Y.: The Development of an Object-oriented Simulation System based on the Thought Process of the Manufacturing System Design. I. J. Production Economics 60, 343–351 (1999)
6. Hibino, H., Fukuda, Y.: A User Support System for Manufacturing System Design Using Distributed Simulation. Production Planning and Control 17, 128–142 (2006)
7. Hibino, H., Fukuda, Y., Yura, Y., Mitsuyuki, K., Kaneda, K.: Manufacturing Adapter of Distributed Simulation Systems Using HLA. In: 2002 Winter Simulation Conference, pp. 1099–1109. Institute of Electrical and Electronics Engineers, Inc., New Jersey (2002)
8. Hibino, H., Fukuda, Y.: A Synchronization Mechanism without Rollback Function for Distributed Manufacturing Simulation Systems. J. Japan Society of Mechanical Engineers 68, 2472–2478 (2002) (in Japanese)
9. Hibino, H., Inukai, T., Fukuda, Y.: Efficient Manufacturing System Implementation based on Combination between Real and Virtual Factory. I. J. Production Research 44, 3897–3915 (2006)
10. Hibino, H.: Simulation Environment for Efficient Manufacturing System Design and Implementation Using Network Middleware ORiN and HLA. J. Society of Instrument and Control Engineers 46, 545–560 (2007) (in Japanese)
11. Inukai, T., Sakakibara, S.: Impact of Open FA System on Automobile Manufacturing. J. Automotive Engineers of Japan 58, 106–111 (2004) (in Japanese)

VirtES (Virtual Enterprise Simulator): A Proposed Methodology for Enterprise Simulation Modeling

Giovanni Davoli , Sergio A. Gallo, and Riccardo Melloni

Department of Mechanical and Civil Engineering (DIMeC)
University of Modena and Reggio Emilia
via Vignolese 905, 41100, Modena, Italy
giovanni.davoli@unimore.it

Abstract. In this paper a methodology to develop simulation models is presented. The methodology is based on a multi-level simulation model which allows flexibility and process analysis. The present work starts from applied researches in different SME enterprises. Enterprise management often needs easy and fast developed tools to increase production capacity and flexibility. In many cases performances increase is possible only adopting a BPR (business processes reengineering) approach. Nevertheless the resistance to a BPR approach is underlined in recent bibliography. The proposed approach consists of a three stages methodology, named VirtES (Virtual Enterprise Simulator). VirtES methodology was first applied to ceramic tiles enterprises. The results achieved encourage the adoption to other industrial field.

Keywords: BPR, process, simulation, tile, SME.

1 Introduction

The economic scenario today is highly competitive in terms of number of competitors and costs. To remain competitive, companies have to maintain a high-level of performance by maintaining high quality, low cost, low manufacturing lead times, and high customer satisfaction [1].

Enterprise management often needs easy and fast developed tools to increase production capacity and flexibility, even in a SME (Small Medium Enterprises) contest. Usually SMEs are organized by function and for achieving the expected results it is not enough to improve the performance of a single function. In many cases performances increase is possible only adopting a BPR (Business Processes Reengineering) approach. Nevertheless this approach meets mostly two objections from management. First of all the resources and the time involved represent an important investment, secondly it is not possible to exactly quantify the predictable results. The resistance to the most known BPR methodology is underlined in recent bibliography [2].

It could be argued that the development of simulation models is an useful approach to quantify the expected results before adopting any BPR action. In fact, because of its great versatility, flexibility, and power, simulation is one of the most widely used operations research techniques from the early eighties [3]. However several studies

B. Vallespir and T. Alix (Eds.): APMS 2009, IFIP AICT 338, pp. 374–380, 2010.

show that there is a low usage of simulation by industries [4], especially simulation has not been widely applied to SMEs (Small Medium Enterprises) [5].

To support BPR activities, a model of the whole enterprise is needed. Carry on the development of such a simulation model is a very expensive activity, in term of resources and time consumption, adopting a commercial simulation tool (for example: AutoMod™, Arena™, em-Plant™). Moreover the developed model for a specific enterprise is not adaptable to another enterprise, because the model has to be very detailed. For this reason SMEs are prevented to develop simulation model in order to support BPR activities.

2   The Proposed Methodology

The proposed methodology was developed during several applied researches carried on in the last years. These researches were focused on the improvement of production – logistic systems performances in SMEs. To achieve the goal BPR activities were undertaken and simulation models were developed to support and drive the BPR process. The SMEs involved operate on different industrial fields such as: ceramic and tile, automotive, wood products and large distribution. Facing these activities a methodology was developed to answer the main common requests coming from different enterprises, this methodology is named VirtES (Virtual Enterprise Simulator).

2.1   VirtES

The aim is to provide an easy to use methodology to develop simulation model for supporting BPR in SMEs. A three stages methodology is developed to address the SMEs instances.

The first stage consists of developing a processes based model highly adaptable to manufactures operating in a specific field. The activities of business processes mining and business process analysis starts from one or more specific enterprises and then are enlarged to all company of the same industrial field. This analysis allowed to develop processes based model, for a generic enterprise, that consider the common features of all companies of the same industrial field. The processes model is developed according to the FDM (Factory Data Model) paradigm [6].

In the second stage a simulation model based on the processes model defined is developed. This is a "high level" simulation model that gives an overview of the performances of the enterprise in term of macro KPI (key performances indices). At this stage the behavior of the whole enterprise is simulated starting from order reception to products delivery. SciLab open source platform is adopted to develop the high level simulation model. Detailed simulation and optimization sub – models are provided at the third stage. These are "low level" simulation models, extremely detailed and focused on a specific sub system or process. The "low level" models can be properly developed with the most appropriate mathematical formalism or commercial simulation suite such as: AutoMod™, Arena™, em-Plant™. These models point out results in terms of production capacity, lead time, scheduling algorithm, exc. The three stages structure of VirtES methodology is shown in fig. 1.

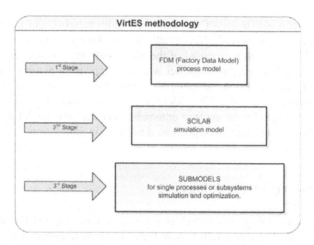

Fig. 1. There stages VirtES methodology structure

2.2 The First Stage

At the first stage, the aim is to develop a process model of the whole enterprise. At this stage a strong cooperation between the modeling team and the human resources of the enterprise is needed. Process modeling is an high resource and time consumption activity and this represent one of the main difficulties in SMEs.

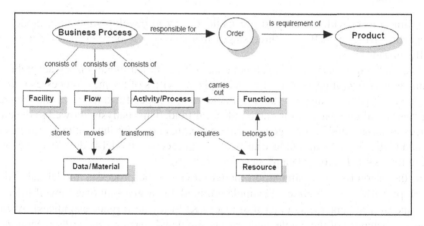

Fig. 2. FDM paradigm [6]

The FDM was introduced by Yu in the 2001 to accelerate the modeling process adopting a scalable and reusable model. The FDM model, belonging to the data model family, was chosen here mainly because of the flexibility of the model and the possibility of its use even when only partially complete. The FDM model paradigm is shown in fig. 2.

The development of the FDM model starts from the study of a specific enterprise. Then the model is compared with the model already available from previous studies and literature review, mainly with model of enterprises operating in the same industrial field. If a reference model is found this can be adapted to suite any particular features of the studied enterprise. Otherwise a new reference model is developed. The reference model has to collect the main characteristics of the studied enterprise and has to be simple to preserve the reusability.

2.3 The Second Stage

At the second stage the FDM process model is implemented on the open – source platform SciLab. An open – source platform was chosen to allow the integration with detailed sub-models developed with specific software at the third stage. The open – source platform SciLab is chosen because of high computational power, statistical and graphic functions useful for results interpretation and the possibility to benefit of the support and the frequent update provided by SciLab Consortium.

VirtES basic rule for code implementation is to develop a single SciLab function for each model process. Each function could be organized hierarchically for a better code design. The process interaction diagram represents also the main flow – diagram of the SciLab code. If the studied enterprise fits with an existing reference model the function already developed for previous studies can be reused. This feature contributes to save resources and time during the model development. The SciLab model is able to simulate the behavior of the enterprise and gives results in term of the chosen macro KPI (Key Performance Indicators).

2.4 The Third Stage

At the third stage sub – models of specific process or sub – system are developed. The most appropriate mathematical formalism and software tools could be used to achieve the expected results. In fact the possibility to interface the sub – models with the main SciLab model is demanded to the open – source platform potential.

3 The Case - Study

VirtES methodology was full developed and firstly applied to ceramic tiles enterprises of the Emilian ceramic cluster. A reference FDM model is developed and coded in SciLab. In the reference model are defined the significant features for the characterization of a tile enterprise and the macro KPI to evaluate the performances.

The models developed by VirtES allowed to quantify for a generic tile enterprise the potential economic benefits related to different BPR actions.

3.1 Model Implementation

The reference model is developed starting from studied enterprises and validated with the evidence found in literature. The description of the manufacture system provided by Andres is confirmed [7]. The model includes also the order process in order to describe the entire enterprise behavior from order collection to costumer satisfaction. The amount of sold tiles (named "SPE") and the average stock level (named "MAG") are chosen as macro KPI, a representation is given in figure 3. The complete tile enterprise reference model is provided in figure 4.

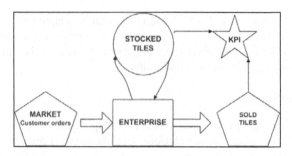

Fig. 3. Tile enterprise KPI

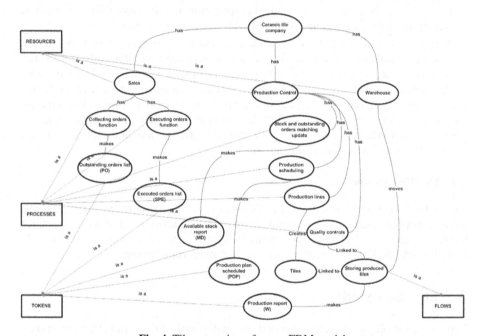

Fig. 4. Tile enterprise reference FDM model

The simulation model is provided and every process is coded in a single SciLab function. The inputs for the FDM model are customer orders, the SciLab simulation model could be feed by real orders from historical data or by a random function that generates orders according to the imposed rules.

The simulation model is set according to the characteristics of the studied enterprise and validated. After validation process the model is used to investigate the effectiveness of the considered BPR actions:

- IT: order process and IT (Information Technology) re – engineering;
- TQ: manufacturing system improvement toward TQ (Total Quality);
- FO: sales forecast optimization (FO).

In the first case the enterprise performances are simulated in the hypothesis of a complete reliability of orders data base information. In the second case the hypothesis of the absolute absence of color tone variation in final products is taken, [8]. In the third case the system behavior is simulated under the hypothesis of total according with sales forecast and real market orders. Simulating the enterprise performance in these extreme condition is useful to evaluate the potentiality of each BPR action.

An integration with the production line sub-model, developed with AutoMod, is provided to evaluate the effect of BPR actions at production line level [9].

3.2 Results

To enable an economic analysis, a simple function is proposed, termed the "Earning function" (1). Maximizing the proposed function means that the performance of the company, as defined in the model, is optimized in terms of enterprise profit. The simulation results are reported in table 1. referring to a period of one year.

$$f(SPE,MAG) = M*SPE - C_m*MAG . \tag{1}$$

- M is the spread between the average sale price and the average production cost for 1 m^2 of tiles;
- C_m is the average stocking cost for 1 m^2 of tiles for 1 year.

High-level simulation results point out the expected improvement in the enterprise profits related to the adoption of any considered BPR action; the results are provided in table 1.

Table 1. Simulation results

BPR actions	Enterprise profits (€)
None, present state	961.211
IT	999.871
TQ	993.151
FO	965.883
IT + TQ	1.095.525
IT + FO	1.010.605

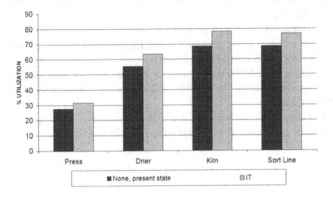

Fig. 5. Sub-model results in term of machineries utilization

The results of the low-level AutoMod model show the improvement in machineries utilization; the results are shown in figure 5.

The most promising single BPR action is IT re – engineering. Also IT re – engineering positive impact on machinery utilization is quantified tanks to the detailed sub – model.

4 Conclusion

The VirtES methodology prevents from developing a very detailed model for the whole enterprise and allows to create and integrate detailed modes for specific sub - systems. The proposed approach requires low resources and matches the instances of SMEs. The implementation of the present approach provides an useful tool for the enterprise to support management in decision-making, investment planning and improvement strategy defining. The results achieved, applying VirtES to the Italian ceramic industry [10] encourage the adoption to other industrial field.

References

1. Al-Aoma, R.: Product-mix analysis with discrete event simulation. In: 2000 Winter Simulation Conference, pp. 10385–10392. WSC Press, Orlando (2000)
2. Vergidis, K., Turner, C.J., Tiwari, A.: Business process perspectives: Theoretical developments vs. real-world practice. Int. J. Production Economics 114, 91–104 (2008)
3. Shannon, R., Long, S., Buckles, B.: Operations research methodologies in industrial engineering. AIIE Transactions 12, 364–367 (1980)
4. Ryan, J., Heavey, C.: Process modelling for simulation. Computer in Industry 57, 437–450 (2006)
5. O'Kane, J., Papadoukakis, A., Hunte, D.: Simulation usage in SMEs. Journal of Small Business and Enterprise Development 14, 512–552 (2007)
6. Yu, B., Harding, J.A., Popplewell, K.: A reusable enterprise model. International Journal of Operations & Production Management 20, 50–69 (2001)
7. Andrés, C., Albarracin, J.M., Torino, G., Vicens, E., Garcia-Sabater, J.P.: Group tschnology in a hybrid flowshop environment: A case study. European Journal of Operational Research 167, 181–272 (2005)
8. Erginel, N., Dogan, B., Ay, N.: The statistical analysis of coloring problems faced in ceramic floor tile industry. In: 8th Conference and Exhibition of the European Ceramic Society, pp. 1693–1696. ECS Press, Istanbul (2003)
9. Davoli, G., Gallo, S.A., Melloni, R.: Analysis of industrial processes based on integration of different simulation tools. In: 10th MITIP International Conference, pp. 38–44. MITIP Press, Prague (2008)
10. Davoli, G., Gallo, S.A., Melloni, R.: Analysing the ceramic sector using processes and simulation models. Ceramic World Review 80, 116–119 (2009)

Part IV

Strategy and Innovation

Measuring the Intangible Aspects of the Manufacturing Strategy – A Case Study from the Automotive Industry

Bjørnar Henriksen[1] and Lars E. Onsøyen[2]

[1] Norwegian University of Science and Technology, 7491 Trondheim, Norway
[2] SINTEF Technology and Society, 7465 Trondheim, Norway

Abstract. In this paper we focus on how manufacturing strategies should be measured in an increasingly complex manufacturing environment where the "traditional" quality and productivity measures are not sufficient. The paper discusses and illustrates measures, quantitative and qualitative, that are relevant for manufacturing strategies based on principles from different paradigms. From our case in the automotive industry we see that the company should measure intangible aspects, but that they could be difficult to measure and there is a risk of just measuring what could be counted. There could easily be a discrepancy between what are actually measured and what should have been measured according to the announced strategy.

Keywords: Performance management, manufacturing strategy, automotive industry.

1 Introduction

The network- and knowledge-based economy is triggering continuous changes in the way companies are organized and the way they do business [1]. This has given us more complex challenges when making strategies, implementing them into operations, and measuring them. We need more information, of a better quality and on other aspects than before. Answering the two basic questions in performance measurement, what- and how to measure, are more and more difficult.

The primary function of a manufacturing strategy is to guide the business in putting together the manufacturing capabilities enabling it to pursue its chosen competitive strategy of the long term [2]. Thus, manufacturing strategy should not only cover quantifiable aspects such as how much-, how- and where- to produce. Stakeholder relations, knowledge and innovativeness, and organizational culture are examples of intangible aspects that are increasingly important in manufacturing strategies.

Performance measurement is normally focusing on quantifications and numbers, with the intention to provide us with an objective, uniform and often complete picture of reality. However, some aspects are not easily quantified, inherently and difficult to

B. Vallespir and T. Alix (Eds.): APMS 2009, IFIP AICT 338, pp. 383–391, 2010.
© IFIP International Federation for Information Processing 2010

measure. These less tangible aspects are often capabilities that increasingly drive our future performance. Some way they have to be assessed and managed. Marr describes three challenges in strategic performance management:

- an incomplete picture of the strategy,
- the wrong performance measures,
- the wrong approach towards managing performance [3, p.1]

In this paper we focus on the second point and discuss how manufacturing strategies should be measured. Our reference for this discussion is manufacturing paradigms and especially how lean manufacturing emphasizes intangible aspects requiring a different way of measuring performance than for example in mass manufacturing. Measuring according to lean strategies is not evident. This is illustrated through a case from a supplier in the automotive industry. The case is based on documents and system descriptions, and in depths interviews with 12 engineers and managers throughout 2008.

The composition of the paper is as follows: First we give a brief introduction to the fields of manufacturing strategy and performance measurement. Chapter 3 is a presentation of the case, which represents a reference for the discussion in chapter 4 of how to measure the manufacturing strategy.

2   How to Measure Manufacturing Strategy

2.1   Manufacturing Strategy

Even though new management concepts often have been abandoned before they are allowed to fully prove their relevance we have seen that each new concept has brought new elements to the table [5]. These elements put into a more coherent and holistic context could be regarded as paradigms [6]. In Table 1 Henriksen and Rolstadås [7] illustrate how paradigms could be identified based on a set of criteria. Paradigms represent principles, methods etc that inspire companies and are reflected in manufacturing strategies.

Hill [8] presents basic principles for the manufacturing strategies based on the more recent paradigms:

- a discretionary approach to change to ensure that scarce development resources are used in those areas that will yield best returns;
- as with process choice, it is necessary to establish and then choose between sets and trade-offs that go hand in hand with each decision;
- the infrastructure design must respond to dynamics of reality and much of necessary change can be achieved incrementally;
- continuous development is easier to bring about where the responsibility for identifying and implementing improvements is locally based

Table 1. Manufacturing paradigms [7]

Aspects		Paradigm			
Field	Criteria	Craft manufacturing	Mass manufacturing	Lean manufacturing	Adaptive manufacturing
Business model	Started	*1850s*	*1910s*	*1980s*	*2000s*
	Customer requirements	*Customized products*	*Low cost products*	*Variety of products*	*Mass customized products*
	Market	*Pull. Very small volume per product*	*Push Demand>Supply Steady demand*	*Push-Pull Supply>Demand Smaller volume per product*	*Pull Globalization, segmentation Fluctiating demand*
Innovations	Process - enabler	*Electricity Machine tools*	*Moving assembly line and DML*	*FMS Robots Modulized products*	*RMS Information technology*
	Innovation process	*Incremental*	*Linear and radical*	*Incremental and linear*	*Incremental and radical*
Knowledge	Behaviour	*Practical oriented (skills Learning by doing)*	*Centralized decisionmaking. Learning by instructions*	*Decentralized decisionmaking. Continuous improvement Learning by doing*	*Decentralized decisionmaking .Knowledge to be applied instantly*
	Knowledge creation	*Tacit knowledge*	*Explicit knowledge*	*Tacit knowledge*	*Tacit and explicit knowledge*
	Knowledge base	*Synthetic*	*Analytical*	*Analytical and Synthetic*	*Analytical and synthetic*
	Knowledge transfer-challenge	*Externalize knowledge communicating with customers*	*Internalize knowledge, for practical use*	*Externalize knowledge, making it more explicit*	*Continuously externalize and internalize knowledge*

2.2 Performance Measurement – Tangible and Intangible Measures

Marr [3] presents three basic and overlapping reasons for measuring performance: reporting and compliance; controlling people's behaviour; and strategic decision making and learning, which has traditionally been based on three principles [9]:

1. performance should be clearly defined,
2. accurately measured and
3. reward should be contingent on measured performance

These principles are still relevant for some purposes and types of measurement but clearly imply risks such as; just measuring what could be counted, data overload or just rewarding behaviour producing quantifiable outcomes.

Measuring performance according to the company's manufacturing strategy requires more than measuring tangible aspects and past performance. This is also reflected in Lebas and Euske's definition of performance: *"performance is the sum of all processes that will lead managers to taking appropriate actions in the present that will lead to measured value tomorrow"* [10, p.68]. Marr defines "strategic performance measurement" as:

The organizational approach to define, assess, implement, and continuously refine organizational strategy. It encompasses methodologies, frameworks and indicators that help organizations in the formulation of their strategy   and enable employees to gain strategic insights which allow them to challenge strategic assumptions, refine strategic thinking, and inform strategic decision making and learning [3, p.4]

Lev [11] describes intangibles as non-physical claims to future benefits, and mentions a patent, a brand and a unique organizational structure as examples. The values of intangible resources are context specific [12]. They are attributed to an organization, supporting capabilities and contribute to the delivery of the company's value proposition [3]. Traditional, accounting based information systems are not able to provide adequate information about corporate intangible assets and their economic impact. One example is the innovation process since much of the economic value created in today's organisations stems from the process of creating new products (and services or processes) and the production and commercialization of these [12].

The intangible aspects normally have to be measured through qualitative methods, or proxies and indirect measures which often only capture a fraction of what we want to measure [13].

Kaplan and Norton [14] and their "Balanced Scorecard" is a well known approach for performance measurement. Lev's [11] "Value Chain Scoreboard" focusing on innovation is another example, but there are many approaches and methods that could guide us towards key measures, and enable us to work more structured on strategic performance measurement (see [15] and [1]).

2.3 Measuring Agile and Lean Manufacturing Strategies

Until 1980 the manufacturing strategies were oriented towards cost reduction through volume, and increasingly towards quality aspects [16]. This resulted in a stream of research on productivity (see [16], [17] and [18]). Authors, such as Bicheno [19] concentrated on contrasting different dimensions of productivity and total factor productivity was a fundamental measure [16].

One of Skinners [20] core arguments was that operations managers had to decide whether to compete on the basis of quality, time, cost, or flexibility, thus measurement of other aspects became more relevant. This was also in line with lean and flexible manufacturing principles that evolved during the 70's and 80's. Liker [21] describe major principles of lean manufacturing through the *"4-P Model of the Toyota Way"*. Womack, Jones and Roos [22] describe similar principles:

1. specify value in the eyes of the customer
2. identify the value stream and eliminate waste
3. make value flow at the pull of the customer
4. involve and empower employees
5. continuously improve in the pursuit of perfection

To measure how well we perform on a strategy based on these principles requires not only measuring those things that are quantifiable and backward looking such as product quality, SMED (Single Minute exchange of Dies9, Just-In-Time, and time to market. The more intangible aspects such as customer relations, knowledge and innovativeness, teamwork and improvement efforts also have to be measured.

3 A Case from the Automotive Industry

Our case is a first tier supplier in the automotive industry where strategy documents refer to lean manufacturing. Empowering employees, continuous improvement in collaboration with customers and waste reduction are emphasized. This should also represent the basic elements of their performance measurement, thus containing a variety of measures to capture both tangible and intangible aspects.

Their performance measurement system is based on the automotive quality system ISO/TS 16949:2002 and their ERP system. The quality system is influenced by lean principles such as customer orientation and continuous improvement. The company states that they actively use their Key Performance Indicators (KPI) developed by "best practice teams", to follow up and support strategy and improvements.

Table 2. KPI's of a supplier in the automotive industry

KPI		Definition	Source
1	**Logistics**		
1.1	Delivery perf. suppliers %	Delivered quantity and date correct=100% or else 0%	ERP
1.2	Delivery perf. customers %	Delivered quantity and date correct=100% or else 0%	ERP
1.3	Delivery perf. inter company %	Delivered quantity and date correct=100% or else 0%	ERP
1.4	Stock raw material, days	Raw/Delivery scheduled	ERP
1.5	Stock semi manufactured, days	W.I.P/Delivery scheduled	ERP
1.6	Stock finished goods, days	Finished/Delivery scheduled	ERP
1.7	Total stock, days	Raw+W.I.P+ Finished/Delivery scheduled	ERP
1.8	Cost of extra ordinary freights	Total cost for all extra ordinary freights	ERP
2	**Manufacturing**		
2.1	Quality administrative PPM	Ad..Claims/Sum of delivered parts	ERP
2.2	Quality product PPM	Product claims/Sum of delivered parts	ERP
2.3	Quality customer PPM	Total=Product+adm.claims/Sum of delivered parts	
2.4	Quality inter company outbound PPM	Product claims/Sum of delivered parts	ERP
2.5	Efficiency % Direct labour	Outcome hours (manufacturing PID's)/Standard hours	Local/ERP
2.6	Overall Equipment efficiency %	Availability*Perfprmance*Quality	Procedure
2.7	Cost center gap	Sum of cost center gaps excl. productivity	ERP
3	**HSE (Health Security Environment)**		
3.1	H-value Injuries/Mhr.	Number of injuries with absence/total hours	Local
3.2	Absence short term %	Absence paid by the company	Local
3.3	Absence long term %	Absence mainly paid by government (Not company)	Local
3.4	Absence unexcused %	Absence for other reasons paid by employee	Local
3.5	Absence total %	Total= short term?long term+Not excused - monthly	Local
3.6	El.energy consumption (Mwh)	Total electricity consumption	Local
3.7	Water consumption (m^3)	Total water consumption	Local
3.8	Oil consumption (m^3)	Lubricants, diesel and fuel oil and gas for heating	Local
3.9	CO2 Emission, fuel oil heating (tons)	Calculated on usage of oil	Local
3.10	SO2 Emissions, fuel oil heating (tons)	Calculated on usage of oil	Local
3.11	Special waste (tons)	Total special waste, not recycled	Local

The performance measurement system has several characteristics to make it a useful strategic tool:

- establish best practice for reporting KPI from operations
- distribute to all concerned through intranet
- data broken down on plant, team level and line/equipment
- reported on a regular basis, based on KPI specification
- accompanied by graphs showing trends over time
- mandatory in team reviews and management meetings

The requirement of their most important customer (OEM[1]), is the premise provider for the measurements where quality- and logistics requirement are emphasized. The majority of the indicators in Table 2 are reported monthly to the OEM. If the measures do not meet the requirements more frequent measurements, deeper investigation and analysis are normally required.

Does the performance measurement systems' focus on logistics, product quality, productivity, HSE and environmental impact cover the main issues of their lean manufacturing strategy?

The company may be accused of being backward looking and measuring what is easy to measure, while intangible aspects such as customer/supplier relations, teamwork, learning and innovativeness are not really measured. Product quality (PPM[2]) and delivery performance to customers are possible indicators of customer relations, but hardly capture the intangible elements such as to which extent they really work together in problem solving, improvements, learning and innovations. The only measures for intangible aspects are within HSE and absence (3.1-3.5), where the measures could indicate working conditions. Interviews with managers showed that the measures that are emphasized and considered important are even fewer than what are reported in the measurement system. One of the senior managers stated that the important measures were: "EBIT[3], net working capital, productivity, customer PPM, delivery precision and investments".

4   How Could the Intangible Aspects of the Strategy Be Measured?

Keeping our example from the automotive industry in mind there are basically two alternative ways of measuring the intangible aspects of the lean strategy; using traditional, objective, quantifiable indicators, or qualitative/subjective measures. A combination of these two would of course be possible.Theory suggests qualitative measures as appropriate performance measures if it is difficult to define objective performance targets or difficult to measure results [24][25]. The problem is their subjectivity and their descriptive nature making it difficult to compare measures in time, space and between respondents.

Indicators are often quantifiable, but less accurate and valid as measures. Qualitative measures are normally quite accurate, since we for example might ask stakeholders how well we fulfil their needs. An indicator of a shareholders satisfaction could be share value or dividend. Measures are far too often imposed on people and involving those people working in the particular field would normally generate good ideas of how to measure.

Defining relevant performance indicators will normally require a way to break down and make more detailed descriptions of the aspects we want to measure. This is illustrated in Fig.1 where the "*pull principle (3)[4].*", and to some extent "*waste reduction (2)*", are detailed into a level where we might derive indicators [23].

---

[1] OEM= Original Equipment Manufacturer e.g VOLVO, GM and IVECO

[2] PPM= Parts Per Million - used as a measure for parts that not having the required quality.

[3] EBIT = Earnings Before Interest and Tax.

[4] Numbers relate to list of lean principles [23] on page 4.

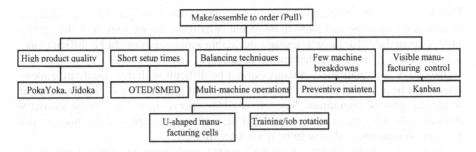

Fig. 1. Logic behind lean manufacturing, based on Skorstad [23]

Even though the measures we derive from Fig.1 are mainly quantitative of nature, there are also intangible aspects for example related to motivation for training, maintenance and Jidoka[5] that are important to capture.

To which degree *"employees are involved and empowered (4)"* could bee measured by indicators such as tasks performed or decisions made by people in the different parts of the organization. The employees themselves have to feel that they have power and are involved in important activities. To capture this subjective data in-depth interviews and questionnaires could help us.

How well the company *"continuously improve in the pursuit of perfection (5)"* is measured through productivity (2.5 and 2.6 in table 2), quality (2.1-2.4) etc over time. But these measures do not necessarily measure the efforts put into improvements or innovations. Number of projects, cross functional team-meetings, improvement suggestions, patents applications could be indicators for improvement efforts. Especially indicators describing knowledge creation could be important for understanding our long term potential. Lev's [11] "Value Chain Scoreboard" proposes a detailed set of disclosures under three headings:

1. Discovery and learning: internal renewal, acquired capabilities and networking
2. Implementation: intellectual property, internet and technological feasibility
3. Commercialization: customers, performance (revenues) and growth prospects

To which extent the lean company in our example *"specify value in the eyes of the customer (1)"* is indicated by the quantitative measures in Table 2: delivery performance customers (1.2) and the quality measures (2.1-2.4). These measures of time and quality have been defined by the main customer, but are they useful as strategic indicators for describing our relations with customers or just to satisfy the reporting regime imposed by the OEMs? Qualitative measures, such as customer surveys and interviews, could be necessary to get the real picture.

5 Conclusion

Measuring performance according manufacturing strategies is essential. Customer orientation, flexibility, partnership, decentralization, continuous improvement,

---

[5] Jidoka (automatic halt of manufacturing if defects occur).

knowledge and innovation, are some of the aspects that have got increased attention in lean manufacturing and other more recent paradigms. To measure how the companies perform they also have to capture intangible aspects, but might be difficult since we have to accept measures that are not accurate.

Indicators and qualitative measures might be difficult to derive. Qualitative measures could be accurate, but also resource demanding and difficult to implement as an integrated part of operations. Since intangible aspects often have to be measured through indicators we must be aware that they often only capture a fraction of what we want to measure, and have to be treated accordingly.

Adding intangible aspects to the performance measurement system increase the risk of having too many metrics. Metrics that no one knows why are being collected, with measures that are not measuring what they are supposed to measure or what really matters, just giving us an administrative burden.We believe that this process will be better off if strategies and performance measurement systems are developed with a broad involvement of employees and partners.

Through a case from the automotive industry we have illustrated how major aspects of lean strategies might be approached and measured. Even though the manufacturing strategy of the case company is defined as lean we see that the performance measurements cover traditional productivity aspects but also quality and delivery precision which is important in lean manufacturing. Even those there are some indicators related to the more intangible aspects, especially within HSE, there is difficult to find answers in the performance measurement system of important lean aspects such as: Do they collaborate well with customers and other stakeholders? Are the employees empowered and is there a culture for continuous improvement? How are the conditions for knowledge creation, innovation, learning and continual improvement?

Measurement directs behaviour. If a company is not able to measure the different facets of the manufacturing strategy there is a risk for pursuing, often unconsciously, mainly the principles and goals that are measured. If the intangible aspects of for example a lean strategy are not measured the issue could be raised to which extent the company really has such a strategy.

References

1. Busi, M.: An integrated Framework for Collaborative Enterprise Performance Management. Doctoral Thesis at NTNU: 48 (2005)
2. Behn, R.D.: Why Measure Performance? Different Purposes Require Different Measures. Public Administration Review 63(5), 586–606 (2003)
3. Marr, B.: Strategic performance management. In: Leveraging and measuring your intangible value drivers. Elsevier, Oxford (2006)
4. Tait, N.: Handling the sourcing decisions: Lowest Cost is not Always the Answer. Financial Times 13 (October 15, 1997)
5. Andersen, B., Aarseth, W., Henriksen, B.: Holistic performance management: an integrated framework. International Journal of Productivity and Performance Management 55(1), 61–78 (2006)

6. Denzin, N., Lincoln, Y.: Introduction: Entering the field of Qualitative research. In: Denzin, N., Lincoln, Y. (eds.) Handbook of Qualitative Research, pp. 1–17. Sage Publications, London (1994)

7. Henriksen, B., Rolstadås, A.: Knowledge and manufacturing strategy - How different manufacturing paradigms have different requirements to knowledge. Examples from the automotive industry. International Journal of Production Research, iFirst, 1–18 (2009)

8. Hill, T.: Manufacturing strategy. Palgrave Macmillan, New York (2000)

9. Austin, R., Hoffer Gittell, J.: When it should not work but does: Anomalies of high performance. In: Neely, A. (ed.) Business Performance Measurement. Theory and Practice. Cambridge University Press, Cambridge (2002)

10. Lebas, M., Euske, K.: A conceptual and operational delineation of performance. In: Neely, A. (ed.) Business Performance Measurement: Theory and Practice, pp. 65–79. Cambridge University Press, Cambridge (2002)

11. Lev, B.: Intangibles: management, measurement and reporting. Brookings Institution Press, Washington (2001)

12. Lev, B., Daum, J.H.: The dominance of intangible assets: consequences for enterprise management and corporate reporting. Measuring Business Excellence 8(1), 6–17 (2004)

13. Blair, M., Wallman, S.: Unseen Wealth. Brookings Institution, Washington (2001)

14. Kaplan, R.S., Norton, D.P.: The Balanced Scorecard. Harvard Business School Press, Boston (1996)

15. Bourne, M., Neely, A., Mills, J., Platts, K.: Implementing performance measurement systems: a literature review. International Journal of Business Performance Management 5(1), 1–24 (2003)

16. Neely, A., Austin, R.: The operations perspective. In: Neely (ed.) Business Performance Measurement. Theory and Practice, pp. 41–50. Cambridge University Press, Cambridge (2002)

17. Kendrick, J.W.: Improving Company Productivity. In: Handbook with Case Studies. John Hopkins University Press, Baltimore (1984)

18. Sink, D.S.: Productivity Measurement – Planning, Measurement and Evaluation, Control and Improvement. John Wiley and Sons, Chichester (1985)

19. Bicheno, J.R.: Cause and Effect of JIT: A Pocket Guide. PICSIE Books, Buckingham (1989)

20. Skinner, W.: Manufacturing - missing link in corporate strategy. Harvard Business Review 50(3), 136–145 (1969)

21. Liker, J.: The Toyota Way. In: 14 Management Principles from the World's Greatest Manufacturer. McGraw Hill, New York (2003)

22. Womack, J.P., Jones, D.T., Roos, D.: The Machine That Changed the World. HarperCollins, New York (1991)

23. Skorstad, E.J.: Produksjonsformer i det tyvende århundre. Organisering, arbeidsvilkår og produktivitet. In: Production in the 20th Century. Organization, Work Conditions and Productivity. AD Notam Gyldendal, Oslo (1999)

24. Bushman, R., Indjejikian, R., Smith, A.: CEO Compensation: The Role of Individual Performance Evaluation. Journal of Accounting and Economics 21, 161–193 (1996)

Managing Innovation: A Multidisciplinary Scenario Development Approach

Esmond Urwin and Michael Henshaw

Systems Engineering Innovation Centre, Holywell Park, Loughborough University,
Loughborough, Leicestershire, LE11 3TU, United Kingdom
{e.n.urwin,m.j.d.henshaw}@lboro.ac.uk

Abstract. The UK Ministry of Defence (MoD) is focusing on and shifting toward a Network Enabled Capability (NEC) approach for improved military effect. This is being realised through the physical networking and coherent integration of existing and future resources including sensors, effectors, support services, and decision makers. This paper is a case study (for NEC) of how the development and use of scenarios for demonstrating academic research can aid and help manage innovation. It illustrates the development, use and application of a multiple stakeholder scenario within the NECTISE research programme that helped establish and exploit a collaborative multidisciplinary working environment and how it helped manage innovative academic research. Our experience suggests that this approach can support the engagement of multiple stakeholders with differing perceptions and priorities and will provide a scenario development strategy for improved research and innovation for many other large systems.

Keywords: Scenario Development, Innovation Management, Scenario Based Planning, Collaborative Working, Multidisciplinary Stakeholder Management.

1 Introduction

In today's commercial and economic environment, only highly innovative organisations will remain competitive. Although it is an easily recognised quality of an organisation, innovation is hard to quantify, articulate and measure. What works for one organisation or situation might not work for another. Much has been written about innovation, its problems and how to approach and tackle these [1]. One of the main factors though seems to be the ability to cope with, and manage, risk. A recent trend is to apply a systems thinking approach to view internal and external influencing factors and help manage innovation [2]. Although some organisations have prescribed innovation methods, inovation is as much about a social process and context as it is a systematic process, thus making it somewhat naturalistic in character [3,4]. How does one manage innovation? With numerous interactions between numerous different stakeholders complexity must surely arise and thus it must concern the ability of people to control such factors [5].

B. Vallespir and T. Alix (Eds.): APMS 2009, IFIP AICT 338, pp. 392–399, 2010.
© IFIP International Federation for Information Processing 2010

Scenario planning is one way to help encourage, plan for and manage innovation. This technique is heavily used for military planning and by the petrochemical industry [6]. Scenarios allow information and knowledge to be modelled and represented for a given context. Doughety *et al.* [7] cite the need for innovative sense making, whereby knowledge of technology and the contexts in which they can be applied are combined to assess and consider possibilities and bring about more successful innovation. Scenarios are an excellent method for enabling this point of view, bringing together disparate sources of information and knowledge that may not be available or on hand to organisations in day-to-day activities. Such an approach allows organisations to accumulate knowledge, transfer that knowledge, explore their environment and consider multiple alternatives as possible routes in which to innovate [8,9,10]. Worthington *et al.* [11] positively argue for scenario planning to enhance innovation.

Network Enabled Capability (NEC) is the UK Ministry of Defence's (MoD) endeavour to enhance [military] capability through the networking of existing and future military assets in order to respond to the rapidly changing conflict environment in which its forces must operate [12,13]. Capability is a key concept and is defined as the enduring ability to generate a desired operational outcome or effect, and is relative to the threat, physical environment and the contributions of joint or coalition forces [14]. At the highest level, capability is described as the seven elements of command, inform, prepare, project, protect, sustain, and operate. These are constructed through planned capabilities such as counter airborne threat, etc. NEC requires the integration of independent components, systems, and networks that can evolve and operate in a collaborative and dependable manner, and manage system and component changes. It makes demands on the overall delivered system that cannot be fulfilled by traditional system engineering design principles addressing independent closed-world systems [15, 16]. NEC is realised through services that form networks of systems of systems that are dynamic, large-scale and subject to continual change and evolution.

This paper describes our experience of developing a scenario for the demonstration of innovative research that addressed the NEC challenge and how such a scenario development process helped to stimulate and manage innovation. Section 2 describes the development of the scenario, the approach, and factors taken into consideration and how such a process managed innovation. Section 3 sets out the developed scenario and section 4 discusses aspects of the approach, draws conclusions and outlines future work.

2 Scenario Development

NECTISE (Network Enabled Capability Through Innovative Systems Engineering) was an integrated research programme in systems engineering that addressed a number of the challenges posed by a networked, capability-based acquisition environment. The programme comprised four topic groups: Through-Life System Management (TLSM), Decision Support, Systems Architectures, and Control and Monitoring. TLSM investigated how the desired capability and the contributory systems should be developed, sustained and evolved. This included aspects such as the adaptable operational effectiveness as well as affordability, safety, qualification and achievability of proposed system elements. The decision support topic group developed an Integrated

Decision Support Environment to support through-life management by enterprises engaged in capability-based acquisition. The Architectures topic group investigated methods of evaluation of systems architectures based on quality of service metrics. The Control and Monitoring group investigated health management, prognostics and reconfiguration of co-operating autonomous systems operating in a NEC environment. The programme was jointly funded by the Engineering and Physical Sciences Research Council and BAE Systems, and included ten UK universities who worked closely with industrial engineers.

Innovation comprises not only the inventiveness that might be termed the 'idea', but also the understanding of how the idea will be used in practice, the selection of those good ideas and the determination to realise the ideas as a benefit (commercial or otherwise), i.e. successfully implement those ideas [1]. Berkum [17] has argued that the eureka moment, which suggests the sudden emergence of an idea is, in reality, often the moment that a number of pieces of the jigsaw come together into the realisation of how an idea might work. In the sections that follow, we shall show how the use of a scenario allows team members to see the larger picture and thus identify the interactions between contributing ideas and systems, leading to integrated solutions; i.e. scenarios help individuals and teams see the whole of the jigsaw. Furthermore, the exhibiting of individual research elements within a realistic context enables stakeholders to understand more clearly how the research may be exploited and, thus, enable the planning of research exploitation across an academic-industry team.

The primary purpose of the NECTISE Scenario was the demonstration and showcasing of the research developed within the programme, in order to promote the research to a range of programme stakeholders. The aim of the series of demonstrations was to show the nature of the research within a meaningful context such that new concepts and ideas could be clearly understood by stakeholders and their views solicited and structured to maximize the opportunities for exploitation. Creating a successful demonstration event that exhibited the research across the NECTISE programme required the development of a scenario that captured the eclectic interests of the stakeholders. Carroll [18] states that scenarios can provide sufficient data, information and context to paint a picture that is wholly believable and real enough to be considered viable for experimentation and analysis. Use of a scenario provides a realistic context through which an audience can engage with and understand the research, explore its benefits and how it can potentially provide value and future advancement for their business. The aim was to create a scenario that satisfied a number of key criteria:

- Include multiple stakeholders' requirements and multiple timeframes.
- Be representative of NEC and its implications for battlespace, the defence industry, UK MoD and the research activities in the programme
- Be sufficiently straight forward to be easily understood by non-experts, but at the same time sufficiently rich to be informative to domain experts.
- Enable the demonstration of multi-disciplinary research outputs.

NECTISE had a range of stakeholders with varied interests. BAE Systems had a number of business streams in the land, air, sea and communications domains engaged with the project. The UK Engineering and Physical Sciences Research Council was a stakeholder with the objective of funding and disseminating good quality and industrially relevant research. In addition, there was the UK MoD, other commercial organisations in the defence supply chain, and academics and industries with interests in improving systems engineering. This wide range of stakeholders naturally results in multiple points of view that had to be accommodated within the demonstration scenario in order to show how the research could be of benefit to all.

When demonstration planning began, there were no public domain scenarios available for NEC, and the team was forced to develop one. Two scenario building tools were used to ensure a disciplined and relevant scenario was developed. The first was The Technical Cooperation (TTCP) Program Guide for Understanding and Implementing Defense Experimentation (GUIDEx) [19] which set out the documentation that would help create a scenario for defence experimentation and enable rigour and structure to be designed into it. The second was the Whitworth *et al.* framework [20] for creating scenarios, which stipulates a number of essential information classes that can be used to elicit, structure and organise the information to enable a coherent approach to scenario writing.

The technical goals, aims and objectives for the scenario were set by the prioritised NECTISE project requirements, thus these were the starting point. A range of factors and techniques were then used to develop the scenario such as goal setting, market forces, stakeholder needs and wants, success criteria and impact analysis [21,22]. From these a set of military scenario examples was created through which researchers could examine their own work. This allowed them to imagine and create potential future states against which to relate their work and to showcase it. Domain experts were invited to regularly assess progress and the content of the scenario.

When the scenario had reached an initial level of maturity, a formal two-day scenario workshop was held with all of the NECTISE researchers and academics, along with invited experts from academia and industry, and representatives from the MoD (military and civilian). The outputs from the workshop established the context of the scenario, four main timeframes, the main concepts and storylines; it allowed all of these to be validated and grounded in reality by domain experts from industry and the UK MoD.

Major design reviews were held at two critical points with the industry partner to assess the approach and planning for the demonstrations. Part of this was to assess the viability of the scenario which considered the use of requirements from all of the stakeholders involved and whether they were fully represented. This helped formalise the scenario and the processes used to create it and ensured that each stakeholder's perspectives and requirements were modelled to explicitly represent all of the inputs to the scenario and act as a completeness check. With this in mind the final assessment involved a NEC expert from the MoD to assess and verify the scenario.

Over a period of time, the regular stakeholder workshops followed the process of innovation, i.e. idea generation, idea selection and idea implementation [1]. The workshops allowed the generation of new ideas and concepts to flourish. Through an extensive process of debate and deliberation the most important ideas were selected by consensus. These determined the constitution of the scenario and how it should be represented (i.e. the 'what' and the 'how'). This not only helped the development of the scenario but also the individual research groups involved. The context and knowledge that had been used to create the scenario was therefore helping the innovative research within NECTISE (both for academia and industry) to focus upon the key customer issues, understand the context within which the research was being carried out and internally relate the components of the NECTISE programme.

The scenario was developed using sound factual evidence, realistic future trends and actual customer and stakeholder needs. It assembled a considerable body of knowledge that would have been difficult to assemble by any other means. Ideas and concepts were continually assessed and validated by domain experts, which created a plausible scenario. Moreover this approach allowed researchers access to industrial knowledge applied to their research and to have it validated and assessed by the multiple stakeholders. The scenario is a unique reference point for NEC research for academics, the MoD and defence industry within the UK.

Figure 1 illustrates the multidisciplinary scenario development approach taken and the benefits that can be gained from it. The process allows academia to establish a context for their research; this enables better understanding of the factors involved, timescales and what is needed by industry from the subject area under review. This allows exploration of the potential possibilities looking at current and future business approaches when conducting impact analysis of external perturbations and internal industrial changes. Performing these de-risks the exploitation potential of the research and allows industry to better understand the research and its applications.

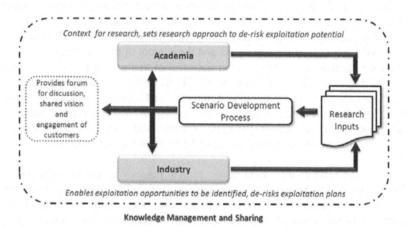

Fig. 1. Scenario Development benefits for academia and industry

Industry can benefit from using a scenario development approach, by highlighting and identifying exploitation opportunities for products, processes and future strategies. Engaging with academic research and participating in such a collaborative development process will enable a more thorough and wider ranging exploration of the factors involved, potential approaches to take and show how business can adapt and evolve to meet market conditions and derive benefit, thus de-risking exploitation plans. The whole development process can act as a knowledge gathering, management and sharing activity allowing different communities to engage with each other, share experiences and provide a forum for discussion.

The scenario development process generated a number of innovative ideas from the programme which were brought about by mixing the research teams during the workshops. An agility framework for systems engineering was developed [23] that can identify processes, tools and techniques to build agility into systems development process. Additionally a number of agile methodologies were developed for service orientated architectures to adapt to changes that can occur in the process of service development, discovery and integration [24]. To complement both of these and other approaches a capability framework for NEC readiness was created, that mapped and formalised relationships between civilian and military domains [15].

3 NECTISE Scenario

The NECTISE scenario needed to provide an exemplar context for research outputs that might be applied to the immediate (short timeframe) situation of a military operation, right up to systems engineering that would be applicable at the long-term capability planning level. The scenario was built up from four vignettes each representing a different period in the capability process, the range of influence of decisions, and different groups of stakeholders.

The basis of the NECTISE scenario is that of a foreign state threatening international airspace with a surface-to-air missile (SAM) weapon system. The operational mission is to neutralise the SAM site to reduce the threat issued against civil air activity. It is composed of four vignettes, each representing a particular stage of capability development and/or use for NEC, and each representing different timeframes. The main question concerns the development of military capability from inception and planning at the government level, development and assessment within the industry-MoD enterprise, through to use by military forces in the battle space. It looks at an incremental increase in surveillance system capability for monitoring no-fly zones.

- *Vignette 4* represents capability planning. At this level, the decisions are taken by the MoD with industry having a supporting role. Systems engineering approaches are studied by which industry can support the MoD's capability planning framework. Typically the timeframe for this level is measured in years.
- *Vignette 3* is the capability development stage where decisions are made about capability change including the development of options, selection, and change plans. This is applicable to industry and the MoD. Typically the timeframe for this is from years to months.
- *Vignette 2* looks at the deployment of new, changed, or updated capability. Again, this is applicable to both industry and the MoD. The timeframe for this vignette is measured in months to weeks.
- *Vignette 1* is concerned with a military operation that is NEC-relevant. This showed how technologies and systems approaches can provide agility benefits at this level; this is also applicable to industry and MoD. The timeframe here is hours and minutes.

The purpose was not to show a consolidated solution to the scenario, but rather to show the focused NECTISE contributions to the overall landscape. The scenario was to set a viable and realistic context in which to view the research outputs and as such did not seek to assert that the described possible future state is more or less likely than another.

4 Discussion and Conclusion

The creation and development of a well formed and plausible scenario is an extremely time consuming and iterative process. Nevertheless, scenarios provide a useful method for conveying ideas and concepts, and also as a platform for exploring potential futures at the evaluation stage of the development process.

For the process of developing scenarios it was highly beneficial to make stakeholders aware of each other's requirements, needs and wants and to properly represent those requirements. By way of regular collaborative workshops the process of people relating their own needs and perspectives against others not only allowed them to better understand the context of the research and assess other stakeholders' perspectives, but also forced them to evaluate their own perspectives and to understand more fully the integration of research elements. This fostered a collaborative environment with which an improved understanding was obtained by industry and academia to develop ideas, and select them in an open and frank manner, helping to develop a realistic scenario and manage innovative academic research.

The NECTISE scenario described herein was used to successfully demonstrate research to audiences around the UK. People engaged easily with the scenario storyline, were able to understand the concepts and ultimately appreciate the benefit of the contextualised research.

This paper portrays the process of scenario development, the factors involved and the resultant scenario. Such an approach can provide benefits to research programmes both for academia and industry, and can be applied in a number of different contexts and areas. The main factor to highlight is that it was the process of development and not the scenario itself that helped to stimulate and manage innovation.

Potential future work is to expand the number and types of processes within each of the vignettes and make them more applicable to different contexts and industries. But in the first instance it would be desirable to better define the stages, populate them with different sets of information and data to develop metrics for the entire scenario so as to improve the potential for analysis and performance measurement.

References

1. Bessant, J., Tidd, J.: Innovation and Entrepreneurship. Wiley, Chichester (2007)
2. O'Connor, G.C., Ravichandran, T., Robeson, D.: Risk Management Through Learning: Management Practices for Radical Innovation Success. Journal of High Technology Management Research 19, 70–82 (2008)
3. Adamides, E.D., Karacapilidis, D.: Information technology support for the knowledge and social processes of innovation management. Technovation 26, 50–59 (2006)
4. Roberts, R.: Managing Innovation: the Pursuit of Competitive Advantage and the Design of Innovation in Intense Environments. Research Policy 27, 159–175 (1998)
5. Sneep, C.: Innovation Management in a Theoretical Perspective. In: Geschka, H., Hubner, H. (eds.) Innovations Strategies. Elsevier Science Publishers BV, Amsterdam (1991)
6. Royal Dutch Shell plc, http://www.shell.com/
7. Dougherty, D., Borrelli, L., Munir, K., O'Sullivan, A.: Systems of Organizational Sensemaking for Sustained Product Innovation. Journal of Engineering Technology Management 17, 321–355 (2000)

8. Gersick, C.J.G.: Revolutionary Change Theories: A Multilevel Exploration of the Punctuated Equilibrium Paradigm. Academy of Management Review 16, 274–309 (1991)
9. Kuhlman, S.: Future Governance of Innovation Policy in Europe: Three Scenarios. Research Policy 70, 953–976 (2001)
10. Kuhlman, S., Edler, J.: Scenarios of Technology and Innovation Policies in Europe: Investigating Future Governance. Technological Forecasting & Social Change 70, 619–637 (2003)
11. Worthington, W.J., Collins, J.D., Hitt, M.A.: Beyond Risks Mitigation: Enhancing Corporate Innovation with Scenario Planning. Business Horizons (2009) (article in Press)
12. UK Ministry of Defence, Network Enabled Capability, Ministry of Defence (2005)
13. UK Ministry of Defence, Understanding Network Enabled Capability, Ministry of Defence (2009)
14. UK, Ministry of Defence, Capability Management Handbook, Ministry of Defence (2007)
15. Neaga, E.I., Henshaw, M.J.D., Yue, Y.: The Influence of the Concept of Capability-based Management on the Development of the Systems Engineering Discipline. In: The Proceedings of the 7th Annual Conference on Systems Engineering Research. Loughborough University, UK (2009)
16. Russell, D., Looker, N., Liu, L., Xu, J.: Service- Oriented Integration of Systems for Military Capability. In: The 11th IEEE International Symposium on Object/component/service-oriented Real-time Distributed Computing, Orlando, USA, p. 33 (2008)
17. Berkun, S.: The Myths of Innovation. O'Reilly Media, Sebastopol (2007)
18. Carroll, J.M.: Five Reasons for Scenario Based Design. Interacting with Computers 13, 43–60 (2000)
19. Guide for Understanding and Implementing Defense Experimentation (GUIDEx): The Technical Cooperation Program (2006)
20. Whitworth, I.R., Smith, S.J., Hone, G.N., McLeod, I.: How do we know that a scenario is 'appropriate'. In: 11th International Command and Control Technology Symposium, Cambridge, UK, September 26-28 (2006)
21. Tuominen, M., Petteri, P., Ichimura, T., Matsumoto, Y.: An Analysis of Innovation Management Systems' Characteristics. International Journal of Production Economics 60-61, 135–143 (1999)
22. Berkhout, F., Hertin, J., Jordan, A.: Socio-economic futures in climate change impact assessment: using scenarios as 'learning machines'. Global Environmental Change 12(2), 83–95 (2002)
23. Mackley, T., Barker, S., John, P.: Concepts of Agility in Network Enabled Capability. In: Conference on Networked Enabled Capability, Leeds, UK (2008)
24. Liu, L., Russell, D., Xu, J., Davies, J.K., Irvin, K.: Agile Properties of Service Oriented Architectures for Network Enabled Capability. In: Conference on Networked Enabled Capability, Leeds, UK (2008)

Industrialization and Manufacturing Steps within the Global Product Lifecycle Context

Anis Ben Khedher[1], Sébastien Henry[2], and Abelaziz Bouras[1]

[1] Université de Lyon, Lumière Lyon 2, IUT Lumière,
LIESP Laboratory, Bron, 69676, France
{anis.ben-khedher,abdelaziz.bouras}@univ-lyon2.fr
[2] Université de Lyon, Claude Bernard Lyon 1, IUT B,
LIESP Laboratory, Villeurbanne, 69622, France
sebastien.henry@univ-lyon1.fr

Abstract. This paper presents and discusses an analysis of the industrialization and production steps within the Product Life cycle Management (PLM) context. Initially, PLM was focused almost exclusively on the product design, but nowadays, it tends to cover all the steps of the product life cycle. In the same time, the industrialization and the production are not sufficiently integrated into the PLM solutions. Currently, there is much to be gained by extending the coverage of PLM to production step. This coverage depends on several features (for instance the frequency of product data modification). It also leads to an information exchange then to a classification of this information into categories. The main purpose of this paper is to study how to extend the PLM coverage of the life cycle steps by defining a mapping among information categories and the Information Systems (IS), which manages product manufacturing, for each feature.

Keywords: Product Lifecycle Management, production management, information systems interoperability.

1 Introduction

Manufacturing enterprises are facing several challenges such as shorten innovation lead-times, reduction of time to market, reduction of costs, mass customization demands, more complex products, improving product quality, geographically dispersed design teams, inventories subject to rapid depreciation and rapid fulfillment needs [1]. Nowadays, the need of deploying PLM system becomes more and more important in order to tackle theses challenges. The PLM is a business strategic approach that leads to develop an attractive system which ensures customer satisfaction. PLM applies a set of business solutions to support the collaborative creation, management, dissemination, and the use of product definition information across the extended enterprise from concept to end-of-life. It integrates people, processes, business systems and information together [2]. The product lifecycle consists of three main phases: the Beginning Of Life (BOL) including requirements, design, industrialization and production; the Middle Of Life (MOL) including logistics, use, and maintenance; and

B. Vallespir and T. Alix (Eds.): APMS 2009, IFIP AICT 338, pp. 400–408, 2010.

End Of Life (EOL) including reverse logistics, remanufacturing, reuse, recycle, and disposal [3]. In fact, with the increasingly demand of complex products and the advancements in Computer Aided Design (CAD), more and more data are being generated. These data are related to the development of products such as CAD drawings, 3D models and the documentation related to the requirements management and development [4]. Currently, design consists of the most developed product life cycle step. Thus, PLM covers requirements analysis, design and industrialization almost total way. In fact, even if it covers all life cycle phases, there are still many interactions not yet resolved such as the interaction with production management. Therefore, PLM focuses mainly on virtual product and process development. The interaction with production management becomes more and more required. The coverage of production management by PLM leads to the full interaction between the two parties. It is dependent on several features such as frequency of product data modification, number of manufacturing systems producing the same product and so on. The definition of these features and its impact on the PLM coverage is also very important to avoid data inconsistencies. The identification of exchanged information between PLM and production management is also important. PLM should support the communication of information to production and consequently information feedback [5]. In order to accomplish the study of the PLM coverage extension, we propose to identify the different exchanged information between PLM and production management and classify this information into categories such as product design, manufacturing process, manufacturing system configuration and manufacturing system design. After defining the features and information categories, we suggest to identify the different IS managing production such as Manufacturing Execution System (MES) and Enterprise Resource Planning (ERP). Therefore, we can establish a mapping among information categories and IS that allows us to define what information can be managed by what IS according to the features defined earlier. This paper describes the PLM coverage of life cycle steps, particularly the production step. We first present the features that impact this coverage and the information categories that can be exchanged between PLM and production management. The mapping among information categories and IS according to the features is also presented before the conclusion.

2 Closed-Loop PLM

During BOL, the information flow is quite complete between design and industrialization. Virtual product and process data such as product design, Electronic Bill Of Material (EBOM), Manufacturing Bill Of Material (MBOM), process plans and so on; are produced within design and industrialization product lifecycle steps. However, the information flow becomes vague or unrecognized after the industrialization step. This prevents the feedback of product-related information such as production status, updated BOM, updated process plans and so on; from production back to engineering [3]. Both design and industrialization steps form the engineering phase within BOL. Sufficient and up-to-date engineering data should be communicated to production management in order to start the product manufacturing. In return, design and industrialization need sufficient and dynamic real-time shop floor data gathered by production to optimize and enhance its engineering data and works. These feedbacks of product information become important in order to allow each lifecycle step to make decisions while having visibility to others lifecycle steps.

To synthesize, we conclude that this data exchange is between high-level information provided by design and industrialization and low-level information provided by production management. It allows forming a closed loop among design, industrialization and production as shown in Fig.1.

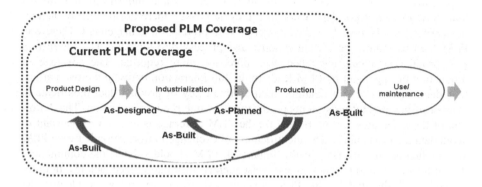

Fig. 1. Closed loop among design, industrialization and production

3   Problem Statement

In an extended enterprise context, PLM support needs to connect the product design and analysis processes to the production and vice versa [5]. In order to realize this goal, PLM should cover design, industrialization and production steps. The coverage of the different steps may vary according to several features. For instance we can identify:

- Frequency of product data modification. When this frequency is high that means that the information flow that begins from design in coming to production become important. This increase of information flow is due to the product-related information modification such as requirements, designs, BOMs and so on. This flow of information is low when the enterprise produces the same products without modifications so the frequency of product data modification becomes low.
- Frequency of making to market of new products. This frequency is high when the enterprise introduces sometimes new products. The creation, development and introduction of this new product imply the creation of new designs, BOMs, process plans and so on. Therefore, the information flow from design to production increases. However this flow of information is low when the enterprise produces the same products for long periods of time so the frequency of making to market of new products becomes low.
- Number of manufacturing systems producing the same product. We distinguish two cases: In the first case, the enterprise has different manufacturing systems located in several countries implying a difference in ways and

means to produce the same product. For example, the cost of labor is low in Asia that promotes manual production. However, in other countries the same product is manufactured by machines and robots. In this case, the coverage of product life cycle steps by PLM cannot exceed the common process plan produced during the industrialization step. Preserving the specificity of each manufacturing site becomes important. In the second case, we have the same manufacturing systems that produce the same product.

To synthesize, the PLM coverage of product life cycle steps should be variable according to these features.

4 Exchanged Information among Design, Industrialization and Production

As we know, the interaction between design, industrialization as a high-level information and production management as low-level information becomes important. Therefore, it seems necessary to classify this information into categories. In fact, we distinguish four categories of product-related information: product design, manufacturing process, manufacturing system configuration and manufacturing system design. Exchanged information among design, industrialization and production is shown in Fig.2.

4.1 Information Required for Production

The most important advantage of data exchange between PLM and production management is to allow production enforcing as-planned record generated by industrialization step and also enforcing manufacturing system configuration data and manufacturing system design data as shown in Fig. 2. All these data should be communicated to production. The as-planned record include the product information provided by CAD tools, such as the attributes of the parts, product design and drawing, structure relationship, EBOM and so on; and the manufacturing process information provided by Digital Manufacturing (DM) and Manufacturing Process Management (MPM) tools, such as process plans, manufacturing proceeding, 3D models, MBOM and so on [6]. The data generated by manufacturing system configuration determine how to produce the product such as routes, work instructions, man-hour, and Programmable Logic Controllers (PLC) code, Compute Numerical Control (CNC) code, manufacturing system parameters, Human Machine Interface (HMI) code and things alike [7]. The manufacturing system design is the step that contains information related on the capacity of manufacturing system to produce the appropriate product. It communicates to production all information about machines notice, materials, machines 3D models, manufacturing system simulations and so on. As we mentioned earlier, all these data should be put into production management in order to manufacture the product using updated engineering data.

4.2 Information Generated by Production

Production management is also critical to engineering when it monitors and reports what currently occurred on the physical factory floor. As-built record is the creation of a virtual counterpart to the physical product [8]. In fact, the as-built record contains three categories of data: data concern manufacturing process, manufacturing system configuration and manufacturing system design. The data concerning process should be the performance indicators of each operation (non-quality and traceability) and so on; this information is useful to update product and process. In order to update the manufacturing system configuration, the data communicated by production should be the PLC & CNC program failures and performance indicators and so on. Finally, data concerning manufacturing system design should be the maintenance operations (curative & preventive), failures and so on. This information are useful modify the physical part of the manufacturing system.

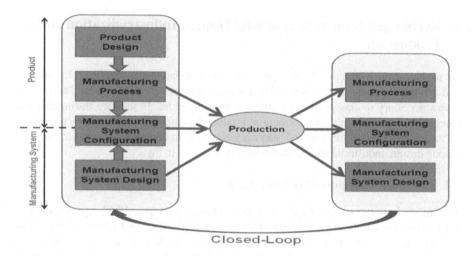

Fig. 2. Exchanged information among design, industrialization and production

4.3 Closed Loop

The described information mentioned earlier form the main contents of the data exchange among design, industrialization and production. The transfer of information from production to design/industrialization forms a closed loop among the information categories generated by production and the information categories provided to production. To synthesize, we conclude that this information exchange allows closing the loop from as-built records to as-designed/as-planned records. Fig.2 shows the closed loop formed by design/industrialization and production exchange.

5   Mapping among Information Categories and ISs

5.1 Industrial Information Systems

In order to lead production operations in the manufacturing enterprise, we distinguish three main IS that manage production. These IS have different tasks and structures. The first system is the PLM that is mentioned earlier. The second is the Enterprise Resource Planning that encompasses a wide range of software products supporting day-to-day business operations [9]. It ensures production process optimization control, optimization operation and optimization management technology that takes production synthesis index as the target [10]. Finally, the Manufacturing Execution System that aims at executing manufacturing plans. It builds a bridge between CNC machine tools and PLCs on the lower level and the ERP system on the higher side [11]. MES has eleven functions, defined by the Manufacturing Execution System Association (MESA), such as resource allocation and status, detailed scheduling, dispatching production units, document control, data and so on [12].

5.2 Mapping Problem

After identifying the different categories of product-related information as well as the different ISs, we have to define which category of information is managed by which IS. Therefore, we suggest defining a mapping among information categories and IS. The coverage of each of the IS varies according to the features mentioned in section 3. We have chosen to realize tables that summarize this mapping according to each feature. In our study, we focus on the case of companies that have the three IS detailed in section 5.1. Indeed, part of the role of the ERP the product-related information that ERP have are limited to items references and manufacture operations sequence without details. For these reasons, the mapping will focus only on the PLM, MES and other possible systems that can manage product information.

5.2.1 Mapping According to the Feature: Frequency of Product Data Modification

When the frequency of product data modification is high, it means that the enterprise produces a customized product. This type of production is characterized by a low volume of production and a high variance of product. Therefore, the enterprise tends to encompass all information categories in PLM system in order to avoid losing product-related information that change rapidly. This is the most ideal mapping that the enterprise can deploy. The MES system is only a user of information. Table 1 shows the mapping according to high frequency of product data modification.

Table 1. Mapping of a high frequency of product data modification

	PLM	MES	Other
Product Design	✓		
Manufacturing Process	✓		
Manufacturing System Configuration	✓		
Manufacturing System Design	✓		

When the frequency of product data modification is low, it means that the enterprise produces the same product for long periods of time. This type of production is characterized by a high volume of production and a low variance of product. The enterprise tends to encompass product design and manufacturing process in PLM, manufacturing system configuration in MES and manufacturing system design in other IS. The question that arises is why we don't use the ideal mapping in this case. In fact, the consideration of costs and gains is important. The enterprises choose this mapping because its advantage is the information consistency provided by PLM / MES interoperability. Its disadvantage is the PLM/MES interoperability costs.

Table 2. Mapping of to low frequency of product data modification

	PLM	MES	Other
Product Design	✓		
Manufacturing Process	✓		
Manufacturing System Configuration		✓	
Manufacturing System Design			✓

5.2.2 Mapping According to the Feature: Frequency of Making to Market of New Products

In fact, the mapping according to the frequency of making to market of new products has almost the same feature as the mapping of high frequency of product data modification. Table 1 and Table 2 show the mapping according to high and low frequency of making to market of new products.

5.2.3 Mapping According to the Feature: Number of Manufacturing Systems Producing the Same Product

We suppose in our study that if there are several manufacturing systems that produce the same product then they are necessarily different. Therefore, we distinguish two cases: one production system and several production systems that produce the same product. The first case means that the enterprise doesn't have a management problem of specificities of the different manufacturing systems that produce same product. Therefore, PLM can encompass all information categories as shown in Table 3.

Table 3. Mapping according to the use of one production system

	PLM	MES	Other
Product Design	✓		
Manufacturing Process	✓		
Manufacturing System Configuration	✓		
Manufacturing System Design	✓		

When the enterprise deploys several production systems to produce the same product, the task of information management of each manufacturing system becomes difficult. Therefore, the local MES system will manage the manufacturing system configuration and the manufacturing system design. Each local MES system communicates with the global PLM. Table 4 shows the mapping when the enterprise produces the same product by several manufacturing systems.

Table 4. Mapping according to the use of several production systems

	PLM	MES	Other
Product Design	✓		
Manufacturing Process	✓		
Manufacturing System Configuration		✓	
Manufacturing System Design			✓

6 Conclusion

The need for a more effective methodology supporting the extension of the PLM coverage of life cycle steps is clearly stated by academics and practitioners worldwide. This coverage depends on several features based on information exchanged among design, industrialization and production. The main purpose of this paper is to contribute in extending PLM to production by proposing a mapping among exchanged information and IS which manages the product manufacturing. This mapping is defined for each feature of the PLM coverage. We have suggested three features: frequency of product data modification, frequency of making to market of new products and number of manufacturing systems producing the same product. Besides, we have defined a mapping among information categories and the different IS for each PLM coverage feature which allows us to distinguish the impacts of this mapping on enterprises. This mapping, however, allows us to think about other combinations such as what can be the PLM coverage when the enterprise has several production systems that produce the same product and the frequency of product data modification is high. Therefore, they are important to choose the technical solution that realizes the interaction between PLM and production management, in other words the PLM/MES interoperability. The Service Oriented Architecture (SOA) may be the best architecture [13]. We have chosen this technique because it offers mechanisms of interoperability that allow different technologies to be dynamically integrated, independently of the system's platform in use [14]. Therefore, the services will be adapted to all mapping combinations.

References

1. Ming, X.G., Yan, J.Q., Wang, X.H., Li, S.N., Lu, W.F., Peng, Q.J., Ma, Y.S.: Collaborative process planning and manufacturing in product lifecycle management. Computers in Industry 59, 154–166 (2008)
2. CIMdata Report, Product Lifecycle Management, Empowering the Future of Business (2002)
3. Jun, H.-B., Kiritsis, D., Xirouchakis, P.: Research issues on closed-loop PLM. Computers in Industry 58, 855–868 (2007)
4. Muhammad, A., Esque, S., Aha, L., Mattila, J., Siuko, M., Vilenius, M., Järvenpää, J., Irving, M., Damiani, C., Semeraro, L.: Combined application of Product Lifecycle and Software Configuration Management systems for ITER remote handling. In: Fusion Engineering and Design (2009)
5. Rachuri, S., Subrahmanian, E., Bouras, A., Fenves, S.J., Foufou, S., Sriram, R.D.: Information sharing and exchange in the context of product lifecycle management: Role of standards. Computer-Aided Design 40, 789–800 (2008)
6. Intercim, Meyer, P., Plapp, J.: Intercim white paper, Extending PLM to the Shop Floor (February 2008)
7. Siemens, Closing the Loop between Engineering and Execution (June 3, 2008),
   http://docs.google.com/gview?a=v&pid=gmail&attid=0.1&thid=12
   1556dd83bd49bb&mt=application%2Fpdf
8. Grieves, M.: Multiplying MES Value with PLM Integration, Whitepaper (March 2007)

9. Botta-Genoulaz, V., Millet, P.-A.: A classification for better use of ERP systems. Computers in Industry 56, 573–587 (2005)
10. Shaohong, J., Qingjin, M.: Research on MES Architecture and Application for Cement Enterprises. In: 2007 IEEE International Conference on Control and Automation ThB5-5, Guangzhou, China, May 30-June 1 (2007)
11. Iassinovski, S., Artiba, A., Fagnart, C.: SD Builder: A production rules-based tool for on-line simulation, decision making and discrete process control. Engineering Applications of Artificial Intelligence 21, 406–418 (2008)
12. MES Explained: A High Level Vision, MESA International White Paper Number 6 (September 1997)
13. Izza, S., Vincent, L., Burlat, P.: Ontology-Based Approach for Application Integration. In: Doctoral Symposium, Pre-Proceedings of the First International Conference on Interoperability of Enterprise Software and Applications: INTEROP-ESA 2005, Geneva, Switzerland, February 23-25 (2005)
14. Jardim-Goncalves, R., Grilo, A., Steiger-Garcao, A.: Challenging the interoperability between computers in industry with MDA and SOA. Computers in Industry 57, 679–689 (2006)

Analysis of End-of-Life Vehicle Processes:
A Case Study in Sardinia (Italy)

Carlo Enrico Carcangiu, Pier Francesco Orrù, and Maria Teresa Pilloni

Università degli Studi di Cagliari
Dipartimento di Ingegneria Meccanica
Piazza D'Armi, 09123 Cagliari, Italy
carloenricocarcangiu@gmail.com, pforru@unica.it,
pilloni@dimeca.unica.it

Abstract. The present work aimed at giving a review of the end-of life phase for motor vehicles, providing accurate process modeling, indicating critical aspects, and finally suggesting improvements. For the study, one of the principal dismantler in Sardinia (Italy) was considered. The main innovation is the bottom-up approach to the problem; this was carried out by field observing the process activities and sharing the criticalities identification with the actors. The study has confirmed that the simplicity of disassembling the components and the ease of identification of the different materials to be separated is fundamental for an efficient dismantling of motor vehicles. It is finally crucial that the dismantling processes, being highly complicated, mainly involve the same manufacturers.

Keywords: ELV, End-of-Life Vehicles, Dismantling, Process Modeling.

1 Introduction

According to modern market strategies, the working life of most goods is expected to keep shortening. Consequently, an increasing amount of waste material is conveyed every year to landfill.

In the automotive field, it has been observed that a huge amount of material is produced from vehicles dismantling, still with high market value (e.g. steel, aluminum, glass and plastics). There is thus an economic drive to the efficient reuse of such matter; in addition, most of them should be carefully handled by reason of their potential environmental impact.

In order to effectively address the problem, the common approach of "use and throw" (i.e. disposable) must be overcome: a new policy of reusing and recycling has to start for the rough materials that form worn out goods.

The strict EU regulations on the matter, which have been recently endorsed by the state members, impose a constraint on the fraction to be reused from a dismantled vehicle. For instance, Directive 2000/53 [1] establishes a number of measures to limit unload of refusal, as well as promote recycling and similar reuse of dismantled cars and their components. In such way the total volume of refusal to be discharged can be

B. Vallespir and T. Alix (Eds.): APMS 2009, IFIP AICT 338, pp. 409–416, 2010.
© IFIP International Federation for Information Processing 2010

diminished; moreover the whole life cycle efficiency of motor vehicles is improving, from both the economical and the environmental points of view.

Currently 75-80% of each end-of-life vehicle is recycled or re-used, the vast majority of which is ferrous metal [2]. These are average numbers, if some European countries have already achieved upper standards (Germany, Belgium), others are far to reach the prescribed targets (Italy above all) [3]. Outside the EU, Japan, Taiwan, and South Korea have instituted similar Extended Producer Responsibility (EPR) legislation, which is also becoming increasingly prevalent in North America [4], [5]. In China, despite the huge number of ELVs, quite a large delay in the ELVs policy and legislation exists when comparing to Europe [6], [7].

The European ELV Directive requires a 15-20% increase in recovery from current average levels by 2015. Such improvements need to come from the 20-25% of the vehicle that is not currently recycled, which consists mainly of polymers, rubber, glass and electronic parts. To reach the 2015 targets roughly half of these materials will need to be recoverable or vehicle composition will need to shift toward materials that are already recyclable.

In addition, the Directive 2000/53 states that vehicle manufacturers should design and produce vehicles that facilitate the dismantling, re-use, recovery and recycling of end-of-life vehicles. Carmakers are therefore taking steps to design for recycling and for disassembly. Increasing the level of re-use and remanufacturing will be a key-part of moving toward sustainable vehicle production. Generally speaking, the higher up the process in the hierarchy the more environmentally friendly it is [2].

The dismantlers are main actors of the reverse logistics processes, i.e. the companies that carry out the separation of vehicles into simple components. In order to abide by the latest directives, the dismantlers are nowadays facing pressing needs of re-engineering their organizational processes. On one side the demand of limiting costs, on the other side thrusts for improving the overall recycling efficiency are. Therefore, such companies are forced to analyze their internal organization, finding and solving critical points, possible sources of errors and wastes.

Many studies have been carried out in the last decade, regarding several aspects of the ELV management. Some of them deal with the legislation and its impact on the sector [2], [8]. Other studies more properly concern the ELV management [9]. A number of papers have been published about the ELV processes technologies [10], [11]. Several works concern ELVs market and economics [12], [13], [14]. Finally, a sub-field of research involves the environmental issues and ELVs sustainability [15].

The present work aimed at giving a review of the end-of life phase for motor vehicles. For the study, one of the principal dismantler in Sardinia (Italy) was considered, providing accurate process modeling, indicating critical aspects, and finally suggesting improvements. The main innovation of the research method is the bottom-up approach to the problem; this was carried out by field observing the process activities and sharing the critical aspects identification with the actors.

The paper is structured as follows. In Section 2 a review of the ELV management techniques and of the dismantling approach is given. In Section 3 the ELV scenario in Sardinia is characterized. Section 4 includes a description of the followed methodology and of the adopted tools: process modeling, process sheets, FMECA. In Section 5 the results of the case study analysis are presented, and the major criticalities are summarized. In Section 6 a possible path of evolution is suggested for the considered case study. Finally, concluding remarks are drawn in Section 7.

2 ELV Management Trends

In order to meet the targets of the European ELV, technological innovation can follow two main paths: upstream or downstream of car manufacturing.

Upstream means modify the design for facilitating the ELV processes, i.e. *design for dismantling*. To this end, several car companies have already made agreements with dismantlers. Upstream operating results clearly in a long term path.

Downstream means modify the recycling operations by developing new techniques. Such improvements need to come from the part of the vehicle that is not currently recycled (fluids, polymers, rubber, glass and electronic parts). On one hand, bigger and more efficient recycling plants will be able to handle wastes coming from different industrial fields, not just the ELVs, with large use of automation. An example of large automated dismantling system is represented by CRS (Car Recycling System) [16], in the Netherlands. On the other hand, small specialized companies will be able to manage with currently non-recycled components.

Car material composition has been evolving during the years, with an increasing use of plastics and aluminum, compared to steel and other metals. Some particular components are still critical with regards to ELV recycling: tyres, batteries and catalysts among others. End-of-Life-Tyres or ELTs dismantling is highly complicated because of their webbed structure, which does not allow fusion and for the presence of metals and fibers for reinforcement. However, the huge amount of ELTs (220 million/year in the EU) imposes to find a solution to the problem. Finally, the recovery of catalysts is still developing, even if the interest in the valuable metals herein contained could be the drive for rapid improvements.

3 ELV Scenario in Sardinia (Italy)

The whole car fleet in the Italian region of Sardinia amounts to 959,946 units [17], one third of which within the Cagliari's district. The 70% of those cars has got a capacity between 800 e 1600 cm^3 (*economy cars*). If you consider the single years of matriculation, a nearly constant amount of new cars was introduced since 1998, about 6-7% of the whole fleet. However, looking at the ELVs for 2007, a peak is evidenced for those matriculated in 1991, which means an average working life of 16 years.

In Sardinia, the dismantlers often operate the essential phases in the ELV process, i.e. drainage and compacting, whereas after the carcass is sent to the rest Italy. Only few of them operate a real dismantling, but keeping for reuse and recycle a small portion of the car components, whilst the rest is compacted and forming the *car fluff*.

When analyzing the process, the first phase (drainage of liquids and hazardous materials) is commonly manual. Afterward, the carcass is made compact by a power press. The car fluff can be ground in Sardinia or shipped to other dismantlers in the rest of Italy, with additional costs. The *car fluff* is anyway sent outside the region, being its amount too small for the sustainability of a dedicated plant in Sardinia.

Some of the dismantlers have direct agreements with one or more car companies. One of them is the analyzed *Case Study* (CS). Despite in the Island there is nearly an absolute lack of recycling plants, the tyres can be conferred for energy recovery or sent to produce acoustic insulator for construction. Oils are transported to two dedicated plants, but only one is able to regenerate the oil. Windscreens are conferred to landfill and the other glass parts remain included into the fluff. In fact, the only company that recycles glass is specialized in bottles and food containers. In a similar way, other plastics are currently recycled, whereas the ELV plastic parts are usually not. Finally, two local companies deal with the recovery of exhaust car batteries.

4 Methodology

4.1 Process Modeling

The analysis of processes, which is key-important for the corrective actions, includes first the identification of the single activities and the process modeling.

The preliminary study was carried out on field, by means of interviews with the process players. Surveys were used to complete this set of information. The followed approach implied that the same people who run the process activities are involved in the analysis (administrative people, workers): with no doubt they know those better.

Flowcharts were chosen for the process modeling, since they represent one of the best tools for the schematic description of processes. Flowchart strength resides in his proper immediacy of direct communication and ease of reading even for non technical readers. When performing process modeling that involves several areas within a company, *functional flowcharts* are more useful for identifying the actors (or groups) responsibilities, also for detecting errors and wastes sources. In addition, the IDEF0 diagrams were thought appropriate for functional modeling, i.e. provide a structured representation of functions, decisions, activities or processes within a system.

4.2 Process Sheets

Process Sheets were filled out for each of the activity in the dismantling process, already identified with the process modeling, and provide the following information: *Phase*: a macro-division of the process, as it appears from the flowcharts; *Activity*: a single operation within the process; *Actor*: the operator who are directly involved in the described activity; *Input*: information/data generated before the single activity; *Description*: summary of the operations performed within the activity; *Time and Duration*: an evaluation of the scheduled time and duration; *Controls*: possible checks done by the operators; *Output*: info/data generated at the end of the single activity; *Criticalities/Errors*: events that could invalidate the effectiveness of the process; *Wastes*: inefficient use of resources and time.

4.3 FMECA

Failure Mode, Effects, and Criticality Analysis (FMECA) is an extension of *Failure Mode and Effects Analysis* (FMEA). In addition to the basic FMEA, it includes a criticality analysis, which is used to chart the probability of failure modes against the severity of their consequences. The result highlights failure modes with relatively high probability and severity of consequences, allowing remedial effort to be directed where it will produce the greatest value.

A FMECA was hence performed, after the required process decomposition into simple activities (i.e. *process modeling*). With the help of the process sheets a list of failure mode was arranged, specifying the possible causes. Those criticalities were grouped into 4 categories, depending on the aspect of the system they affect: *Organizational* (O); *Technical* (T); *Communication and Information* (C); *Layout and Structure* (S). Estimations of the failure frequencies and of their effects on the process were provided and shared with the process players. This resulted into a scale of values: A-*High*: serious, high frequency (can interrupt the process); M-*Medium*: serious, low frequency; B-*Low*: soft, medium-low frequency.

5   Analysis of the *Case Study* (CS)

The *Case Study* (CS) is represented by a dismantling company located in the area of Cagliari, which is the local authorized dismantler of both Citroen and Peugeot. The main activity of such company is car dismantling, but it handles also other wastes, especially hazardous materials. On the whole, the CS deals with: ELVs, ELTs (tyres), plastic packages, ferrous wastes from urban users, electronic equipments, white goods, and more in general metals, paper, wood, plastics.

5.1   The Dismantling Processes

Flowcharts were mainly used for the process modeling. However, for a more compact view is hereby preferred the classical IDEF0 diagram (Fig. 1). The boxes represent the manufacturing functions. The arrows stand for inputs/outputs, controls, and mechanisms.

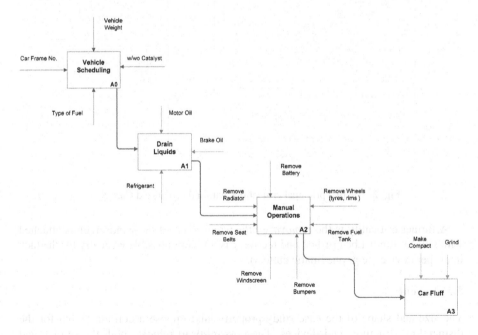

Fig. 1. IDEF0 of the dismantling at WR

Cars arrived with proper trucks directly from dealers, retailers or privates. First, all the office procedures are completed: strike off the Public Car Register (PRA); removal of car frame number. Then, an operator is committed of the car and starts securing the car in the drainage area. All recyclable parts and liquids (motor oil, brake oil, refrigerant) are removed; alike hazardous materials pollutants are extracted. Before raising the ELV with the car deck, the operator annotates the frame number, the weight, if catalyzed or not, fuel (gasoline, diesel, LPG) and all data will be later compared with those registered in the office. Each operator is usually committed of two cars at a time. Manual operations follow in this order: removal of fuel tank, catalyst, radiator, oil filter, bumpers, windscreen, seat belt, battery. All former mentioned materials and liquids are recovered. Later tyres are taken off, to reuse if still in working order. The carcass is moved from the drainage to the compacting area, where is made compact by a power press and ground to the final *car fluff*.

5.2 Main Criticalities

From the FMECA analysis two activities emerge as the most critical (Fig. 2). Operators agree with that outcome, and consistent indications are given by the Gantt diagram of the process. One was found at the beginning of the process, and concerns the *removal of the catalyst*, due to the problematic location and the impossibility of operating in recent cars.

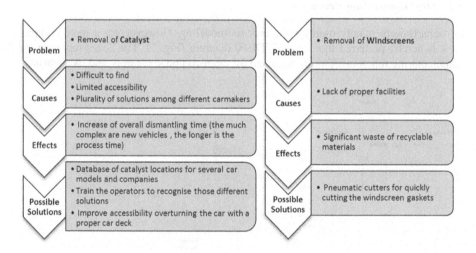

Fig. 2. The two principal criticalities within the analyzed Case Study

A further criticality is the *removal of the windscreen*. If the windscreen is attached with silicon, it must be crushed and recovery is no more possible basically for the lack in proper devices (e.g. pneumatic cutters).

5.3 Layout

The size and shape of the case study property land impose a definite layout for the dismantling structures and devices. The possibility to relocate both the storage and drainage area in one part of the property was analyzed, but even being the surface adequate, difficulties would be faced in collocating the compacting unit as well as the grinding machine. Reducing working spaces would increase risks for people, also because the administrative center would be closer (noise would be secondary but not least drawback).

On the whole, the present layout is reasonable and meets the company requirements. Moreover, any promising modification should be carefully evaluated since it would affect all the company processes, not only those related to dismantling.

6 Suggestions and Improvements

As a general result, fairly good organizational and technological profiles were observed for the case study, especially regarding the rate of ELVs dismantled (2900 per year). In fact, despite the wide diversity of vehicle to be dismantled (i.e. the various company maker and product model) a standard approach is followed for the process and manual operation do not affect the total dismantling time.

Generally speaking, corrections should be directed toward: *Most critical processes:* those that could affect the whole process effectiveness; *Less efficient processes:* those that do not add value (e.g. delays, redundant docs); *Most ease-to-solve criticalities:* corrections cannot affect the overall equilibrium.

For instance, improvements can derive from the removal of valuable parts (e.g. turbocharger, switchboard), which can be sell as spare parts, whereas are now included in the car fluff. Nevertheless, this would cause the increase in time and warehousing costs. Regarding recyclability, car fluff is the worst element, being composed by plastics, gum, and glass. However, the increase of the plastic fraction will reduce the dismantlers income, which mainly come from metals. Concerning sustainability of ELV, the automatic disassembling would reduce costs, but results feasible only for large companies and small companies will be damaged. A mix of small and large companies is more desirable.

7 Concluding Remarks

The study has confirmed that the simplicity of disassembling the components and the ease of identification of the diverse material to be separated is fundamental for an efficient dismantling of motor vehicles.

It is finally crucial that the dismantling processes, being highly complicated, mainly involve the same manufacturers. For this scope, the flow of information within the dismantling process represents a fundamental feedback for the automotive industry; based on such information, the manufacturers can develop specific actions aimed at improving the overall efficiency and sustainability of the vehicles life cycle since from the early design studies.

Acknowledgments. We would like to thank graduate student Fabrizio Ferrante for his help in this work and all the people at the analyzed case study.

References

1. Directive 2000/53/EC of the European Parliament and the council of 18 September 2000 on end of life vehicles. Official Journal of the European Communities (October 21, 2000)
2. Gerrard, J., Kandlikar, M.: Is European end-of-life vehicle legislation living up to expectation? Assessing the impact of the ELV Directive on 'green' innovation and vehicle recovery. Journal of Cleaner Production 15, 17–27 (2007)
3. EUROSTAT, Environmental Data Centre on Waste, ELVs - Key Statistics and Data (2009), http://epp.eurostat.ec.europa.eu/portal/page/portal/waste/data/wastestreams/elvs
4. Toffel, M.W.: The Growing Strategic Importance of End-of-Life Product Management. California Management Review 45(103), 102–129 (2003)
5. Gesing, A.: Assuring the Continued Recycling of Light Metals in ELVs: A Global Perspective. JOM 56(8), 18–27 (2004)
6. Chen, M.: ELV Recycling in China: Now and the Future. JOM 57(10), 20 (2005)
7. Chen, M., Zhang, F.: ELV recovery in China: consideration and innovation following the EU ELV Directive. JOM 61(3), 45 (2009)
8. Edwards, C., Coates, G., Leaney, P.G., Rahimifard, S.: Implications of the ELV Directive on the vehicle recovery sector. J. Eng. Manufacture. 220, 1211–1216 (2006)
9. Mergias, I., Moustakas, K., Papadopoulos, A., Loizidou, M.: Multi-criteria decision aid approach for the selection of the best compromise management scheme for ELVs: The case of Cyprus. Journal of Hazardous Materials 147, 706–717 (2007)
10. Ferrão, P., Nazareth, P., Amaral, J.: Strategies for Meeting EU ELV Reuse/Recovery Targets. Journal of Industrial Ecology 10(4), 77–93
11. Nourreddine, M.: Recycling of auto shredder residue. J. of Hazardous Materials A139, 481–490 (2007)
12. Bellmann, K., Khare, A.: Economic issues in recycling ELVs. Technovation 20, 677–690 (2000)
13. Ferrão, P., Amaral, J.: Assessing the economics of auto recycling activities in relation to European Union Directive on ELVs. Technological Forecasting & Social Change 73, 277–289 (2006)
14. Mazzanti, M., Zoboli, R.: Economic instruments and induced innovation: The European policies on ELVs. Ecological Economics 58, 318–337 (2006)
15. Mildenberger, U., Khare, A.: Planning for an environment-friendly car. Technovation 20, 205–214 (2000)
16. Car recycling Systems BV (2009), http://carrecyclingsystems.com/
17. Automobile Club Italia (2009), http://www.aci.it

Improving Project Control and Guidance through a Time-Frame Simulation Approach

Massimo de Falco and Luisa Falivene

Department of Mechanical Engineering, University of Salerno,
Fisciano (SA), 84084, Italy
{mdefalco,lfalivene}@unisa.it

Abstract. Nowadays projects dynamicity and complexity make the control process highly critical. The existing planning and control techniques have frequently proved inadequacy to manage the present challenge. The paper proposes a simulative approach to managing with more effectiveness projects life cycle. The appositely developed simulation model is populated with both deterministic and stochastic elements: the formers come from the project plan; the stochastic elements have been introduced in order to consider the probabilistic nature of activities duration. In the planning phase the model generates a "baseline pencil" that gives a more confident estimation of the time to complete the project. During the execution phase the model is able to store the data related to the ongoing activities and updates in real-time the estimation of the project completion. Concurrently, it allows the calculation of specific performance indexes which permit to identify in real-time possible occurring "warnings" to users and suggest potential solutions.

Keywords: Project Management; Project control process; Simulation; Stochastic network project; Uncertainty management.

1 Introduction

The flexibility required by tasks coordination as well as the multiple feedback processes and non-linear relationships involved during nowadays projects execution make them highly dynamic and complex. Moreover, the uncertainty and variability due to the lack of knowledge about most factors and variables, especially at the beginning stage, has to be opportunely managed, since projects performances (in terms of reliability and timeliness) principally depend on it. Technical, schedule, cost and political changes as well as mistakes that naturally occur during project execution make aleatory the duration of each activity of the network.

The stricter time boundaries, the lack of information and the high impact of mistakes point out the criticality of the project control process. In these circumstances, the expression "project control" assumes the prevailing meaning of "steering" the dynamic system towards planned targets rather than monitoring its progressive achievement. To control a project means to evaluate the project, identify the required changes and plan interventions. It therefore implies dynamic, active and continuous

B. Vallespir and T. Alix (Eds.): APMS 2009, IFIP AICT 338, pp. 417–424, 2010.

interactions within the "project system" and it consequentially causes an increasing of complexity and uncertainty to be managed [1].

Moreover, the growing need for faster projects advancement requires a closer integration between executing and planning phases and, therefore, it implies the search for new tools able to support the project throughout its whole life cycle.

These observations highlight the inadequacy to manage the present challenges of the existing planning and control techniques, which have not been modified substantially for several decades. Particularly, the deterministic assumptions of the Critical Path Method (CPM) [2] ignore the complexities associated to the uncertainty of the activities. In its turn, the Program Evaluation and Review Technique (PERT) [3] is based on a probabilistic approach but it is limited because it reduces the solution space to a single critical path through the network, ignoring the effects of the complex interactions created by dependent sub-paths.

During the executive phase, project plans are periodically re-evaluated over time as soon as new information become available. This creates a dynamic probabilistic problem whose final solution is a series of partially implemented plans, each one based on the best available information at the moment of the relative evaluation.

The simplifying hypotheses on which the analytical probabilistic approaches are generally based often compromise their reliability degree in the representation of the real problem. In these cases, turning to a simulative approach may result a valid alternative.

Simulation is defined as the manipulation and observation of a synthetic model (which can be described through logical-mathematical functions) representative of a real design that, for technical or economic reasons (such as time constraints), is not susceptible to direct experimentation. The simulation model is developed to represent the essential characteristics of the real system and omits many minor details [4].

Moreover, adopting a simulative approach in projects management consents to consider different characteristics of the networks which can not be otherwise considered: dependences between the durations of activities; alternative ways to follow up depending on significant events occurring during project execution; time-cost links for each activity of the network.

The present paper proposes a simulative approach to manage projects during their whole life cycles. This study incorporates the activities duration uncertainty into the classical analysis of time-costs tradeoffs in project schedules in order to increase the effectiveness of the project control and guidance process.

2 A Simulative Approach to Managing Projects

As previously mentioned, the aim of this paper is to suggest a simulative approach to guide and control projects able to overcome the weaknesses of the existing project management techniques.

A simulation model has been appositely developed through the combination of the Rockwell Software's Arena, the Microsoft's Excel spreadsheet application and the Microsoft's Project. The model is populated with both deterministic and stochastic elements.

The deterministic inputs come from the project plan attained through the commonly used Microsoft's Project software and include a network diagram, a Gantt chart and a cost function defined for each project activity (as the CPM analysis requires). These data are automatically stored in Microsoft's Excel spreadsheets which are opportunely linked with the Arena software, where the simulation is actually performed.

The stochastic elements have been introduced in order to consider that activities durations can not be treated as deterministic but have to be more realistically modelled as probabilistic in order to consider their "natural uncertainty". For this reason the simulation model associates a duration probability function, appositely defined, to each activity of the network.

The definition of the cost functions necessary to carry out the CPM analysis needs a particular attention. The duration of each activity is assumed to be independent from the allocations of the other activities. Each cost function comes from the fitting of the available historical data and is assumed to be deterministic. These functions present a non-increasing trend over the time domain bounded by the normal activity duration T_N (associated to the minimum activity cost) and the crash activity duration T_C (associated to the maximum activity cost), and an increasing trend towards the maximum activity duration T_{MAX}. The latter time domain is a peculiarity of the proposed approach. In fact, it is not considered in the CPM analysis but it has been introduced in order to give completeness to the simulation model.

The figure that follows (Fig. 1) graphically represents the steps of the proposed simulative approach.

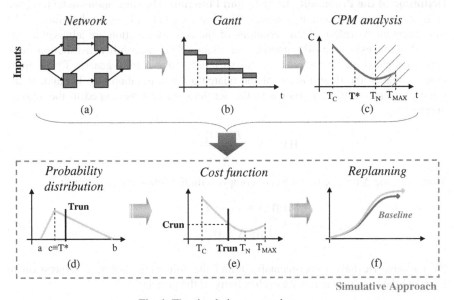

Fig. 1. The simulative approach steps

As previously mentioned, the simulative approach starts from a series of input data coming from the use of the classical project management tools. Once the network diagram (**a**) and the consecutive Gantt chart (**b**) have been built, the CPM analysis can be carried out in order to identify, for each activity of the network, the specific duration (T^* in the figure) which minimises the total cost of the whole project (**c**). The network associated to these durations allows the determination of a project baseline of reference for the simulation replications. In fact, the simulative approach is accomplished by introducing a variability to each duration T* through a specific probability distribution. In this way the intrinsic uncertainty of the activities duration can be fed into the approach. The choice of the probability distribution functions will be afterward explained in detail (see "Definition of the Probability Distribution Function"). At each iteration, for each activity, a duration value is sampled from the probability distribution function (**d**) and the relative cost value is updated (**e**). On the basis of these values the critical path and the whole project duration can be identified (**f**). After a sufficient number of repetitions, determined according to the desired confidence degree for the output variables (see "Choice of the Number of Repetitions"), a "baseline pencil", which portrays the variation field of the project time-cost binomial, can be obtained.

The baseline pencil enables the determination of a probability distribution for the whole project duration (see Section 3) and therefore the estimation of the probability of exceeding prefixed contractual due dates.

The proposed approach can be also used during the execution phase of the project. In this case, the data related to the completely performed activities are considered as deterministic inputs for the simulation model with the consequential reduction of the uncertainty associated to the project duration estimation.

Definition of the Probability Distribution Function. The simulation model has been built considering two main hypotheses. The first - see (1) - allows the definition of the time segment Δ within which variations of the activity duration are admissible; the second hypothesis - see (4) - imposes the shape of the probability distribution function. As regards the first hypothesis, the variation range Δ for a generic T* has to be proportional to the time domain of the related activity duration (T_N-T_C) and, at the same time, inversely proportional to the acceleration cost associated to the activity duration C_a.

$$\mathbf{H1:} \quad \Delta \propto \frac{T_N - T_C}{C_a}. \tag{1}$$

Moreover, the Δ time segment has to comply with the following conditions:

$$\begin{cases} \lim_{C_a \to 0} \Delta = T_N - T_C \\ \lim_{C_a \to \infty} \Delta = 0 \end{cases} . \tag{2}$$

Particularly, we have experimentally found the following analytical expression to calculate the time segment Δ for each activity of the project:

$$\Delta = \frac{T_N - T_C}{e^{k\frac{C_a}{C_c}}} \quad \text{where} \quad k = k_1\left(\frac{C_C - C_N}{C_N}\right). \tag{3}$$

where k_1 is a positive constant ($k_1 > 0$) and (C_C-C_N)/C_N is the cost proportional increase of a generic project activity.

Figure 2 shows the trend of the time segment Δ for a fixed (TN-TC) by varying the acceleration cost Ca.

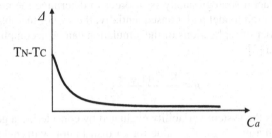

Fig. 2. Trend of the Δ time segment

As regards the choice of the probability distribution for the activities durations (H2), the asymmetric triangular distribution seems to be the most appropriate. There is little in nature that has a triangular distribution. However, it is a good graphical and mathematical approximation to many events that occur in projects. Project management relies heavily on approximation for day-to-day practice. For instance, the approximate behaviour of schedule task durations can be modelled quite well with the triangular distribution.

The asymmetry reflects the unbalance between pessimistic and optimistic events: the pessimistic events (durations higher than T*) is surely more likely than the optimistic events (durations lower than T*) (see Fig. 3).

The triangular distribution parameters for each activity duration T* have been set by imposing the following conditions (4):

$$\textbf{H2:} \quad \begin{cases} \Delta = b - a \\ 2(c-a) = b-c \end{cases} \Rightarrow \begin{cases} a = c - \Delta/3 \\ b = c + 2/3\Delta \end{cases}. \tag{4}$$

The second condition reflects the choice to consider for each activity the pessimistic event more likely than the optimistic event with a two to one ratio.

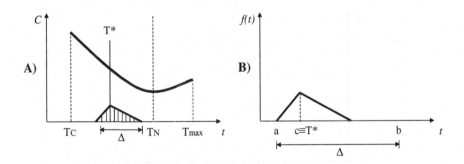

Fig. 3. The cost function (A) and the probability function associated to T* (B)

Choice of the Number of Repetitions. The results of the simulation model are the basis on which the change actions on the real system can be set up. This implies the necessity to know the inaccuracy degree of the reached results and, therefore, the necessity to conduct a strategic analysis in order to determine the number of replications of the simulation model and, consequentially, the size of the observation sample. A sufficient number of replications of the simulation can be accomplished through the following formula [5]:

$$n = \frac{s^2 t_{n-1,1-\alpha/2}^2}{d^2}. \tag{5}$$

where s represents the system variability evaluated by considering a generic number of previously made iterations; t is the value for a t-distribution with (n-1) degrees of freedom for a range of one-sided critical regions; d represents the accuracy of the estimation, that is the biggest difference between the estimated and the real parameters.

Particularly, starting from 100 previously executed simulation replications, the system variability s and the respective value of the t-distribution t have been determined. Therefore, for a confidence interval (1-α) set on 95%, the congruous number of replications to be accomplished has been set on 250.

3   The "Baseline Pencil" to Increase Estimations Confidence

As stated in Section 1, a project "baseline pencil" and the related probability distribution for the project duration are generated by repeating the simulation a congruous number of time (Fig. 4). This probability distribution is based on a time variability more complex than the variability considered in other probabilistic approaches because it depends on the used resources.

The utilisation of a project simulation model in the planning phase forces deeper analysis and understanding of the possible risks occurring during project execution and provides the opportunity to identify, test, and budget potential improvement strategies in advance. This determines a stronger consciousness of both the real and perceived potentials of the selected project proposal which therefore will be more likely to succeed in the subsequent executing phase.

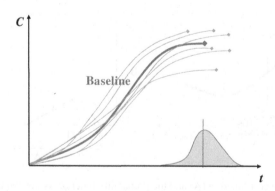

Fig. 4. The probability distribution function of the project completion time

Furthermore, during the planning phase of the project the ability to determine a project length distribution function can provide the organisation with competitive advantages when submitting proposals or negotiating contracts.

Frequently, time contingencies are associated to each activity of the project in order to guarantee that the project plan stays on schedule. However, this solution in most cases turns out to be a tardy approach. Introducing uncertainty in the beginning phase of the project allows the introduction of more effective planning strategies. Particularly, an aggregate "time buffer" from which all the activities can draw time could be introduced. This buffer can be dimensioned by contemporary analysing the behaviour of the probability distribution function of the whole project duration and the probability distribution functions of the durations of each project activity.

4 Real-Time Updating and Change Management

Once the project starts, the use of the proposed simulative approach guarantees a series of interesting advantages. The simulation model is able to store the data related to the ongoing activities and update in real-time the estimation of the project completion. As the project progresses, the data related to the completed activities are now considered as deterministic and a new baseline pencil is created on the updated information. The new baselines may include a set of options different from the not realised options of the baseline pencil identified in the planning phase. This variation may depend on the effects of any previously implemented expediting action, on the differences between expected and actual durations of the completed activities, and/or on changes brought about on the estimated durations of the remaining activities.

In addition, awareness of the completion distribution function during the project execution, allows managers to intervene when required, to test intervention strategies, and to implement those strategies as required in order to improve project outcomes. The model, in fact, enables the calculation of specific performance indexes (based on the classical CPI and SPI indexes) which, compared with previously fixed threshold values, permit to identify in advance possible occurring "warnings" to users. Moreover, potential solutions are suggested on the basis of a particular matrix which links the feasible occurring warnings to appropriate corrective actions [6], [7]. Managers can choose the best solution and implement it by using Microsoft's Project; the project progress curve will be simultaneously updated.

5 Conclusions and Future Research

The proposed simulative approach is characterised by a high flexibility thanks to the suitability of the simulation model to all kind of projects and allows a real-time re-planning together with an efficient change management.

Potential extensions to this research are numerous.

First of all, in this research the cost functions associated to each project activity have been assumed to be deterministic but in practice it is likely that the cost value related to a particular activity duration is considered variable according to a specific probability distribution that can be determined through historical data.

Another interesting extension would be to test the proposed approach in real projects, both to compare its results to more traditional techniques and evaluate users acceptance replies.

References

1. de Falco, M., Falivene, L., Eldomiaty, T.: Controlling fast-forwarding projects: criticalities and innovative decision making perspectives. In: Proceedings of IPMA Conference, Rome (2008)
2. Kelley Jr., J.E., Walker, M.R.: Critical-path planning and scheduling: An introduction. In: Proceedings of the Eastern Joint Computer Conference, pp. 160–173 (1959)
3. Malcom, D.G., Roseboom, J.H., Clark, C.E., Fazar, W.: An application of a technique for research and development program evaluation. Operations Research 7, 646–669 (1959)
4. Salvendy, G.: Handbook of Industrial Engineering, 3rd edn. (2001)
5. Bienstock, C.C.: Sample size determination in logistics simulations. International Journal of Physical Distribution & Logistics Management 26(2), 43–50 (1996)
6. Yates, J.K.: Construction Decision Support System for Delay Analysis. Construction Engineering and Management Journal 119(2), 226–244 (1993)
7. Yates, J.K., Audi, J.H.: Using Decision Support System for Delay Analysis: The Project Management Perception Program. Journal of International Project Management Institute 29(2), 29–38 (1998)

Advanced Topics in Project Management Process

Lucio Bianco and Massimiliano Caramia

Dipartimento di Ingegneria dell'Impresa, Università di Roma "Tor Vergata",
Via del Politecnico, 1 - 00133 Roma, Italy
{bianco,caramia}@disp.uniroma2.it

Abstract. In this paper we present the evolution of project scheduling models with emphasis on temporal constraints.

Keywords: Project scheduling, Generalized precedence relations, Resource constraints, Feeding precedences.

1 Introduction

In today's competitive global environment it is crucial to deliver quality product on time and within an established budget. "Management by projects" has became the principal way to pursue this goal since it is a powerful way to integrate organizational functions and motivate groups to achieve higher levels of performance and productivity. Therefore it is not surprising to see that, in the last few decades, project management has became a hot topic and has been recognized as a central management discipline. Major industrial companies now use project management as their principal management style. Nevertheless the impression is that the contribution that project management can make to management at all is still underrated and poorly known. Moreover, in spite of numerous books on the argument, a very limited number of these put emphasis on the mathematical tools and on the quantitative methods necessary to make project management more effective in dealing with increasing complexity organizations. To better understand this aspect, it is useful to recall that project management is a process which involves the planning, scheduling and control of project activities to achieve performance, cost and time objectives for a given scope of work, while using resources efficiently and effectively (see Lewis, 1995). The *planning phase* involves the following crucial steps: identify the project activities, their interdependencies, and estimate times, resources and costs necessary to perform them. The *scheduling phase* involves the construction of a project base plan which specifies, for each activity, the precedence and resource feasible start and completions times, the amounts of the various resource types necessary during each time period, and, as result, the budget. The *control phase* focuses on the comparison between the project base plan and the actual performance once the project has started. If this comparison reveals some difference on the schedule, or on the budget or also on some technical specifications, a corrective action must be taken to get the project back on the right track.

B. Vallespir and T. Alix (Eds.): APMS 2009, IFIP AICT 338, pp. 425–432, 2010.
© IFIP International Federation for Information Processing 2010

In this paper we mainly focus on project scheduling phase often identified, on the basis of management experience, as the most critical with respect to project failure (Goldratt, 1997, Lewis, 1995). In fact, especially in the case of product innovation and new product development projects, delays in the completion time are more heavily penalized than budget overruns (Goldratt, 1997).

Suri (1998) reports an experience of Hewlett-Packard related to a high-growth market which confirms the greater importance of time schedule than the cost. In fact, Hewlett-Packard found that a delay of six months in a new product project could cause a loss of 33% in profits while, if the project overran its cost by 50% but was completed on time, the loss was only 3.5%. For this reason we consider the project scheduling problem assuming that all input data are know in advance (deterministic case) and that the objective is minimizing project duration. Of course other objective functions, like resource levelling, resource cost, tardiness or earliness, could be considered. In particular, we analyse the evolution of project scheduling models with emphasis on temporal constraints. We start from the well known basic case of resource unconstrained project scheduling with Finish-to-Start precedence constraints and zero time lag (PERT, CPM). Then we analyse the problems arising when other types of precedence constraints with minimum and maximum time lags are considered, that is the "Generalized Precedence Relations" (GPRs).

The next step is Resource Constrained Project Scheduling Problem (RCPSP) with GPRs. With respect to the previous problems, that from the computational point of view are polynomial, the RCPSP is NP-hard and not optimally solvable for large instances, within a reasonable computing time.

Finally a further extension of the classical RCPSP, arising when the activity durations are not defined and known in advance, is considered. This problem happens in that production planning environment, like make-to-order manufacturing, where the resources are often shared among different simultaneous activities in proportion variable over time.

In this case the duration of each activity is not univocally defined, and consequently the traditional Finish-to-Start precedence constraints, so as the GPRs, cannot be used any longer. Then, we need to introduce the so called "Feeding Precedences" (FP) (Kis, 2006) defining in such way a new problem: Resource Constrained Project Scheduling Problem with Feeding Precedences (RCPSP-FP).

2   The Resource Unconstrained Project Scheduling Problem

A project consists of a number of events and activities that have to be performed according to a set of precedence constraints. Each event refers to a stage of accomplishment of a certain activity (in general its starting time or its finishing time). Each activity has a duration and typically requires resources for its execution.

In order to represent activities and their relationships it is a common practice to use networks; the latter allow one to represent precedence relationships more efficiently than other representation techniques like Gantt charts (Clark, 1954), track planning (Herroelen, 1998), and line balance planning (Lumsden, 1968).

A project network is a graph $G = (N, A)$ consisting of a set N of nodes and a set A of arcs. There are two possible representations of a project by means of a graph G. One is the *Activity-On-Arc-representation* (AOA) which uses the set of arcs A to represent the activities and the set of nodes N to represent the events; the other is the *Activity-On-Node representation* (AON) which uses the set of nodes N to denote the activities and the set of arcs to represent the precedence relations, i.e., an arc (i, j) in A means that activity i constrains or is constrained by activity j.

If we assume that resources are unlimited, or are available in huge amounts, a project network is in general used into two fundamental techniques: CPM (Critical Path Method) and PERT (Program and Evaluation Review Technique). These two methodologies study the temporal development of a project taking into account only precedence relations among activities of the so called Finish-to-Start type, i.e., if an arc (i, j) exists in an AON representation then activity j cannot start before the finishing time of activity i. The temporal analysis gives answers to some important questions like how long the project will take, i.e., what is the completion time (makespan) of the project; how early a particular activity may be started; how far an activity can be delayed without causing a delay of the entire project.

It is well known in project scheduling that PERT/CPM methods can be applied under two assumptions. The first one is that resources are available in infinite amounts, and the second is that the precedence relationships between two activities are only of the Finish-to-Start type with time-lags equal to zero; this implies that an activity can start only as soon as all its predecessors activities have finished.

In this context, one can define an acyclic projet network and compute the minimum project completion time as the length of the *critical path*, i.e., the longest path from the initial activity (source node) to the final activity (sink node) in such an activity network (see, e.g., Moder et al., 1983, and Radermacher, 1985).

The computation of the critical path can be accomplished by means of the well-known forward pass recursion algorithm (see, e.g., Kelley, 1963), that is a classical label setting algorithm for longest path calculation. The computational complexity of this algorithm is $O(m)$, where m is the number of arcs of the network; when the graph has a high density, the complexity tends to $O(n^2)$, where n is the number of activities.

However, in a project, it is often necessary to specify other kinds of temporal constraints besides the Finish-to-Start precedence relations with zero-time-lags. Accordingly to Elmaghraby and Kamburoski (1992), we denote such constraints as *Generalized Precedence Relations* (GPRs). GPRs allow one to model minimum and maximum time-lags between a pair of activities (see, e.g., Dorndorf, 2002, and Neumann et al., 2002).

Four types of GPRs can be distinguished: Start-to-Start (SS), Start-to-Finish (SF), Finish-to-Start (FS) and Finish-to-Finish (FF).

A minimum time-lag $(SS_{ij}^{\min}(\delta), SF_{ij}^{\min}(\delta), FS_{ij}^{\min}(\delta), FF_{ij}^{\min}(\delta))$ specifies that activity j can start (finish) only if its predecessor i has started (finished) at least δ time units before.

Analogously, a maximum time-lag $(SS_{ij}^{\max}(\delta), SF_{ij}^{\max}(\delta), FS_{ij}^{\max}(\delta), FF_{ij}^{\max}(\delta))$ imposes that activity j can be started (finished) at most δ time slots beyond the starting (finishing) time of activity i.

In order to better understand GPRs we report some examples. If, for instance, a company must place a pipe (activity j) in a given region, it is necessary to prepare the ground (activity i) in advance. This situation can be represented by a constraint $SS_{ij}^{\min}(\delta)$, since the start of activity j must be δ units of time after the starting time of activity i. In another project, if a company must supply a client with a certain number of products which must be also assembled within 100 days, this relationship can be modeled as $SF_{ij}^{\max}(100)$, which says that the assembly process (activity j) must finish at most 100 days after the starting time of the delivery (activity i) of the products.

GPRs can be represented in a so-called *standardized* form by transforming them e.g. into minimum Start-to-Start precedence relationships by means of the so-called Bartusch et al.'s transformations (Bartusch et al., 1988). Thus, applying to a given AON activity network with GPRs such transformations leads to a *standardized activity network* where associated with each arc is a label ℓ_{ij} representing the time-lag between the two activities i and j (De Reyck, 1988). If more than one time-lag ℓ_{ij} between i and j exists, only the largest ℓ_{ij} is considered.

It should be noted that standardized networks, unlike the networks without GPRs, may contain cycles. This implies that a Resource Unconstrained Project Scheduling Problem (RUPSP) with GPRs and minimum completion time objective:

− cannot be solved by the classical forward and backward recursion algorithm mentioned before;
− can be solved by computing the longest path from the source node to the sink node, whose length is the sum of the time-lags associated with its arcs, using an algorithm working on "general" networks with a worst-case complexity $O(n \cdot m)$ (see, e.g., Ahuja et al., 1993);
− does not admit feasible solutions when the topology of the network and the arc-length function induce one or more directed cycles of positive length (Bartusch et al., 1988).

In Bianco and Caramia (2008, 2010), it has been proposed a new network formulation and a new mathematical program for the RUPSP with GPRs which can be easily solved in $O(m)$ time by means of dynamic programming. Starting from this new complexity result, it has been further proved that, by exploiting the dual formulation of the proposed mathematical program, the minimum completion time can be also computed, with the same computational complexity $O(m)$, by finding an augmenting path of longest length in the proposed acyclic network in which a unit capacity is installed on each arc. An experimental study comparing the performance of the proposed approach and the traditional one confirmed the better performance of the former method also in practice.

3   The Resource Constrained Project Scheduling Problem with GPRs

The basic Resource Constrained Project Scheduling Problem (RCPSP) deals with scheduling project activities subject to Finish-to-Start precedence constraints with zero time-lags and renewable resources under the minimum project completion time objective. The RCPSP is NP-hard in strong sense (see, e.g., Blazewicz et al., 1983). When this kind of temporal constraints are taken into account, an activity can start only as soon as all its predecessors have finished, and, therefore, the resource constraints exist only between two or more independent activities.

As we mentioned in the previous section, when no resource constraint is concerned, GPRs can be represented in a so called "standardized" form by transforming them, for instance, in minimum Start-to-Start precedence relationships obtaining a possibly cyclic network (see Bartusch et al., 1988), or can be represented be means of an acyclic network by transforming them into Finish-to-Start relations (Bianco and Caramia, 2008, 2010).

When resources come into play, the RCPSP with GPRs is strongly NP-hard; also the easier problem of detecting whether a feasible solution exists is intractable (NP-complete, Bartusch et al., 1988). To the best of our knowledge, the exact procedures presented in the literature are the branch-and-bound algorithms by Bartusch et al. (1988), Demeulemeester and Herroelen (1997b), and De Reyck and Herroelen (1998). The paper by Bartusch et al. (1988) reports a limited computational experience on a case study; the paper by Demeulemeester and Herroelen (1997b) is conceived to work on minimum time-lags only; the third approach, that works with both minimum and maximum time-lags, presents results on projects with 30 activities and percentages of maximum time-lags of 10% and 20% with respect to the total number of generalized precedence relations.

Also lower bounds are available for this problem. In particular, two classes of lower bounds are well known in the literature, i.e., constructive and destructive lower bounds. The first class is formed by those lower bounds associated with relaxations of the mathematical formulation of the problem (for instance, the critical-path lower bound and the basic resource-based lower bound; see, e.g., Demeulemeester and Herroelen, 2002). Destructive lower bounds, instead, are obtained by means of an iterated binary search based routine as reported, e.g., in Klein and Scholl (1999). Also De Reyck and Herroelen (1998) proposed a lower bound for the RCPSP-GPRs denoted with $lb3 - gpr$ that is the extension of the lower bound lb_3 proposed by Demeulemeester and Herroelen (1997a) for the RCPSP.

Recently, Bianco and Caramia (2009a) proposed a new lower bound for the RCPSP-GPRs based on a relaxation of the resource constraints among independent activities and on a solution of the relaxed problem suitably represented by means of an AON acyclic network. In particular, for the project scheduling problem with GPRs and scarce resources, the authors exploited the network model proposed in Bianco and Caramia (2008, 2010) and tried to get rid of the resource constraints. The analysis has been restricted to only those pairs of activities for which a GPR exists to determine a lower bound on the minimum project completion time. For each of these pairs it has been verified whether the amount of resources requested exceeds the resource availability, for at least one resource type. In case of a positive answer, some results which allow the reduction of the problem to a new RUPSP with different lags and additional disjunctive constraints have been proved. This last problem can be formulated as an integer linear program whose linear relaxation can be solved by means of a network flow approach (see also Bianco and Caramia, 2008, 2010). Computational results confirmed a better practical performance of the proposed lower bound with respect to the aforementioned ones.

4   Resource Constrained Project Scheduling with Feeding Precedences

More recently, a new variant of the RCPSP appeared in the literature. It is an extension of the classical Resource Constrained Project Scheduling Problem (RCPSP) in which a further type of precedence constraints denoted as *Feeding Precedences* (FP) is introduced. The first authors introducing this problem variant were Kis et al. (2004).

This problem happens in that production planning environment, like make-to-order manufacturing, which commonly requires the so-called project-oriented approach. In this approach a project consists of tasks each one representing a manufacturing process.

Due to the physical characteristics of these processes, the effort associated with a certain activity for its execution may vary over time. An example is that of the human resources that can be shared among a set of simultaneous activities in proportion variable over time. In this case the amount of work per time unit devoted to each activity, and therefore its duration, are not univocally defined.

This kind of problems is in general modelled by means of the so called Variable Intensity formulation, that is a variant of the Resource Constrained Project Scheduling Problem (see, e.g., Kis, 2005). As the durations of the activities cannot be taken into play, the traditional Finish-to-Start precedence relations, so as the generalized precedence relations, cannot be used any longer, and there is the need for the feeding precedences. Feeding precedences are of four types:

- *Start-to-%Completed (S%C) between two activities* (i, j). This constraint imposes that the processed percentage of activity j successor of i can be greater than $0 \leq g_{ij} \leq 1$ only if the execution of i has already started.
- *%Completed-to-Start (%CS) between two activities* (i, j). This constraint is used to impose that activity j successor of i can be executed only if i has been processed for at least a fractional amount $0 \leq q_{ij} \leq 1$.

- *Finish-to-%Completed (F%C) constraints between two activities* (i, j). This constraint imposes that the processed fraction of activity j successor of i can be greater than $0 \le g_{ij} \le 1$ only if the execution of i has been completed.
- *%Completed-to-Finish (%CF) constraints between two activities* (i, j). This constraint imposes that the execution of activity j successor of i can be completed only if the fraction of i processed is at least $0 \le q_{ij} \le 1$.

For this problem, Bianco and Caramia (2009b) proposed a lower bound based on a Lagrangian relaxation of the resource constraints. Regarding exact approaches, only two exact algorithms have been presented in the literature. One is the branch and cut algorithm by Kis (2006), with the objective of minimizing the external resource cost; the other is the exact algorithm by Bianco and Caramia (2009c) based on branch and bound rules.

5   Conclusions

In this paper we presented the main advanced topics emerging in the scheduling phase of the project management process. Our analysis mainly focused on the evaluation of project scheduling models with emphasis on different kinds of temporal constraints.

References

1. Ahuja, K., Magnanti, T., Orlin, J.: Network flows. Prentice Hall, New York (1993)
2. Bartusch, M., Mohring, R.H., Radermacher, F.J.: Scheduling Project Networks with Resource Constraints and Time Windows. Annals of Operations Research 16, 201–240 (1988)
3. Bianco, L., Caramia, M.: A New Approach for the Project Scheduling Problem with Generalized Precedence Relations. In: Proceedings of the 11th International Workshop on Project Management and Scheduling, Istanbul, April 28-30 (2008)
4. Bianco, L., Caramia, M.: A New Lower Bound for the Resource-Constrained Project Scheduling Problem with Generalized Precedence Relations. Computers and Operations Research (2009a), doi:10.1016/j.cor.2009.07.003
5. Bianco, L., Caramia, M.: Minimizing the Completion Time of a Project Under Resource Constraints and Feeding Precedence Relations: a Lagrangian Relaxation Based Lower Bound, RR-03.09 - University of Rome "Tor Vergata" (2009b) (submitted)
6. Bianco, L., Caramia, M.: An Exact algorithm to minimize the makespan in project scheduling with scarce resources and feeding precedence relations, RR-07.09 - University of Rome "Tor Vergata" (2009c) (submitted)
7. Bianco, L., Caramia, M.: A New Formulation of the Resource-Unconstrained Project Scheduling Problem with Generalized Precedence Relations to Minimize the Completion Time. Networks (2010) (in Press)
8. Blazewicz, J., Lenstra, J.K., Rinnooy Kan, A.H.G.: Scheduling subject to resource constraints: Classification and complexity. Discrete Applied Mathematics 5(1), 11–24 (1983)
9. Clark, W.: The Gantt Chart. Pitman, New York (1954)

10. Demeulemeester, E.L., Herroelen, W.S.: New benchmark results for the resource-constrained project scheduling problem. Management Science 43(11), 1485–1492 (1997a)
11. Demeulemeester, E.L., Herroelen, W.S.: A branch-and-bound procedure for the generalized resource-constrained project scheduling problem. Operations Research 45, 201–212 (1997b)
12. Demeulemeester, E.L., Herroelen, W.S.: Project Scheduling - A Research Handbook. Kluwer Academic Publishers, Boston (2002)
13. De Reyck, B.: Scheduling projects with generalized precedence relations - Exact and heuristic approaches, Ph.D. Thesis, Department of Applied Economics, Katholieke Universiteit Leuven, Leuven, Belgium (1998)
14. De Reyck, B., Herroelen, W.: A branch-and-bound procedure for the resource-constrained project scheduling problem with generalized precedence relations. European Journal of Operational Research 111(1), 152–174 (1998)
15. Dorndorf, U.: Project scheduling with time windows. Physica-Verlag, Heidelberg (2002)
16. Elmaghraby, S.E.E., Kamburowski, J.: The Analysis of Activity Networks under Generalized Precedence Relations (GPRs). Management Science 38(9), 1245–1263 (1992)
17. Herroelen, W.: Projectbeheersing in de Bouw, Vlaamse Confederatie Bouw, Vlaamse Ingenieurs-Kamer (1998)
18. Kelley, J.E.: The critical path method: Resource planning and scheduling. In: Muth, J.F., Thompson, G.L. (eds.) Industrial Scheduling, pp. 347–365. Prentice Hall, New Jersey (1963)
19. Klein, R., Scholl, A.: Computing lower bounds by destructive improvement: An application to resource-constrained project scheduling. European Journal of Operational Research 112, 322–346 (1999)
20. Kis, T., Erdős, G., Márkus, A., Váncza, J.: A Project-Oriented Decision Support System for Production Planning in Make-to-Order Manufacturing. ERCIM News 58, 66–67 (2004)
21. Kis, T.: A branch-and-cut algorithm for scheduling of projects with variable-intensity activities. Mathematical Programming 103(3), 515–539 (2005)
22. Kis, T.: Rcps with variable intensity activities and feeding precedence constraints. In: Perspectives in Modern Project Scheduling, pp. 105–129. Springer, Heidelberg (2006)
23. Goldratt, E.: Critical Chain. The North River Press, Great Barrington (1997)
24. Lewis, J.P.: Project Planning, Scheduling and Control. In: A Hands on Guide to Bringing Projects in on Time and on Budget. McGraw-Hill, New York (1995)
25. Lumsden, P.: Line of Balance Method. Pergamon Press, Exeter (1968)
26. Moder, J.J., Philips, C.R., Davis, E.W.: Project management with CPM, PERT and precedence diagramming, 3rd edn. Van Nostrand Reinhold Company (1983)
27. Neumann, K., Schwindt, C., Zimmerman, J.: Project scheduling with time windows and scarce resources. Lecture Notes in Economics and Mathematical Systems, vol. 508. Springer, Berlin (2002)
28. Radermacher, F.J.: Scheduling of project networks. Annals of Operations Research 4, 227–252 (1985)
29. Suri, R.: Quick Response Manufacturing. Productivity Press (1998)

Knowledge Based Enterprise Engineering (KBEE): A Modeling Framework for Enterprise Knowledge Capitalization

Mahmoud Moradi, Mounir Badja, and Bruno Vallespir

IMS-LAPS/GRAI, Bordeaux University, CNRS,
351 cours de la Libération, 33405 Talence cedex, France,
{Mahmoud.Moradi,Mounir.Badja,Bruno.Vallespir}@ims-bordeaux.fr

Abstract. The main objective of this paper is to study the complementarity nature of enterprise modeling and knowledge management within the framework of enterprises. To do so, we evaluate some important methodologies in each domain and then several modeling points of view are explained. By reviewing CommonKADS, MASK, CIMOSA, and GIM methodologies and their modeling views we propose a generic framework to model knowledge in all its aspects. This framework has four modeling views namely, intent modeling, context modeling, content modeling and evolution modeling. These views are classified into several sub-elements brought together by developing meta-model in UML class diagrams. KBEE may possibly be useful both for the practitioners and scientific to deal with knowledge and its modeling in enterprises.

Keywords: Enterprise modeling, Knowledge modeling, Enterprise Engineering, Knowledge Engineering.

1 Introduction

Knowledge is widely recognized as being the key capital of enterprises that contributes to enterprise competitiveness and provides the basis for long term growth, development and existence. Therefore, one of the major questions is how to make more efficient use of knowledge in the enterprise (in terms of sharing or acquiring). It is a well known fact that much of existing information and knowledge, which is extremely valuable, is not made explicit, externalized or formalized and is consequently not available for use by other individuals, and sometimes it can even be lost for the enterprise. Therefore, how can informal enterprise knowledge be captured, formalized, organized, spread and reused?

From the hypothesis that modeling of knowledge and enterprise are imperative tools to manage knowledge in the organizations especially in externalization and integration of knowledge and also for the engineering context, we will propose in this paper a method for engineering the enterprise based on knowledge. This method is a result of synthesis of four main frameworks in Enterprise Modeling (EM) and Knowledge Management (KM). This method put in a shared context approximately all of the aspects concerning knowledge in the enterprises and looks at the knowledge from

B. Vallespir and T. Alix (Eds.): APMS 2009, IFIP AICT 338, pp. 433–440, 2010.
© IFIP International Federation for Information Processing 2010

several point of views and entitled KBEE (Knowledge Based Enterprise Engineering). For the comparison of methods we propose a framework to classify all views into four mains categories as context modeling, intent modeling, content modeling, and evolution modeling. These components together are the basic foundation of reviewed methods. KBEE is a model based enterprise engineering framework that aims at modeling knowledge in all shapes and all sources in the enterprises in the perspective to provide an integrated and multifaceted knowledge base.

As a starting point, we draw on the CommonKADS, MASK, CIMOSA, and GRAI/GIM methodologies which all are intended for supporting and representing several views to model enterprises. These methods together provide an integrated view in enterprise context modeling (Fig. 1).

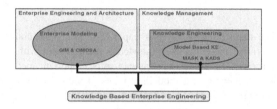

Fig. 1. Theoretic Foundation

2   Meta-modeling

Meta-modeling is the act of modeling applied to languages. The study of intersections between languages for their unification is largely facilitated by meta-modeling. Accordingly, we will use a meta-modeling approach to describe the selected enterprise modeling and knowledge management methods. Each method must be defined through a meta-model. In addition, the meta-modeling language being used is the UML class diagram [1] because it seems sufficient to deal with our problem which is, mainly, to describe the conceptual aspects of the methods. Indeed, for each method, a meta-model is built with a class diagram. With these meta-models, we can compare the constructs of the various methods.

However, it is important to note that the meta-models which we want to build here are not meta-models on the software science point of view. Thus, these meta-models have to be understandable for analysts of the enterprise modeling domain. They have to be clear and not necessarily to be the "best" meta-models, optimized and with the lowest number of classes. Moreover, meta-models are not comprehensive model of methods. This means meta-models developed here are approximately completed ones. Last point about meta-models is that they do not cover all the concepts and formalisms exist in the methods. We use simplified meta-model for the reason which it will cover basic concepts and elements.

3   Knowledge Modeling and Enterprise Modeling Techniques

From modeling point of view, the tools and techniques that help to model knowledge in the enterprises context are the main approaches to share and transfer knowledge. In one part the CommonKADS knowledge engineering methodology and MASK method are two methods that help knowledge sharing and transfer by applying knowledge engineering and knowledge capitalization tools with developing a number of formalisms. In another part CIMOSA and GRAI/GIM methodology are two well-known enterprise modeling framework with several views and formalisms. A point should to be taken into account is that we did not choose these methods for the reason by which they are comprehensive methods in the field.

CommonKADS views knowledge engineering as a modeling activity, where each model is "a purposeful abstraction of some part of reality" [2]. Each model focuses on certain aspects of the knowledge and ignores others. It proposes six models at successively deeper levels of detail: knowledge engineers are encouraged to model the organization in which the system will be introduced; the task (business process) which the Knowledge Based System (KBS) will support; the agents who are or will be involved in the process; required communication between agents during the process; the knowledge which is applied to performing the knowledge-based process; and the design of the proposed KBS. Fig.2 illustrates meta-model of views of Common-KADS.

MASK (Method of Analysis and Structuring Knowledge) offers a flexible environment that allows to success knowledge capitalization projects [3] and [4]. Modeling tools as defined in MASK are generic enough and respond to expert's workspace and cognitive vision. These tools have an important role in knowledge extraction and formalization. They help to structure knowledge under: systemic, ergo-cognitive, psycho-cognitive, historical, and evolution views [5]. These views together construct knowledge modeling in MASK. Detail meta-model of views in MASK is depicted in fig. 3.

CIMOSA (CIM Open System Architecture) provides guidelines, architecture and an advanced modeling language for enterprise modeling covering several aspects of the enterprise [6]. The concept of views allows working with a subset of the model rather than with the complete model providing especially the business user with a reduced complexity for his particular area of interest. CIMOSA has defined four different modeling views: Function, Information, Resource and Organization [7]. See fig.4.

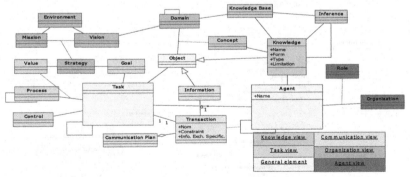

Fig. 2. Meta-model of CommonKADS

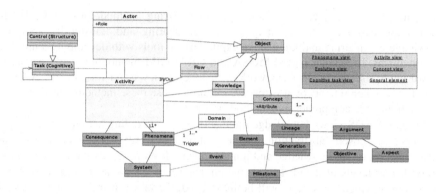

Fig. 3. Meta-model of MASK

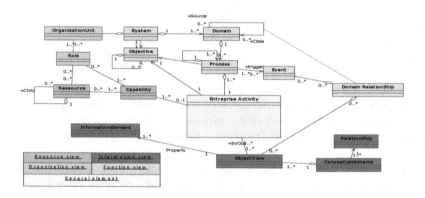

Fig. 4. Meta-model of CIMOSA

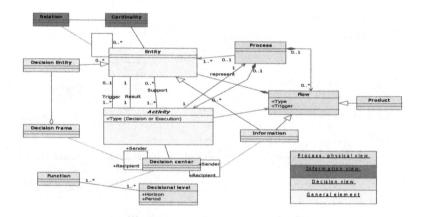

Fig. 5. Meta-model of GRAI/GIM

GRAI/GIM (GRAI Integrated Methodology) is a methodology for design and analysis of production systems based on the GRAI method [8]. It includes modeling languages and focuses on decision system analysis of the enterprise. In GRAI/GIM, an enterprise consists of a physical system, a decision system and an information system. An enterprise can be described using four views: Functional, Physical, Decisional, and Informational [9]. Fig. 5 illustrates meta-model of GRAI/GIM in class diagram of UML.

5 Comparison of EM and KM

Now with a comprehensive look at the methods in modeling both in KM and EM field there are several views. Some of them are common view in all methods like activity and task and some view are unique to each method. Because one of the main objectives of this research is to show and the use the complementary nature of KM and EM here we propose a generic classification to integrate the modeling views and develop the building block of enterprise knowledge modeling (see Fig. 6).

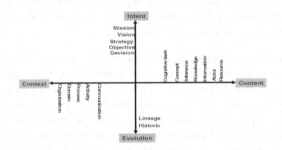

Fig. 6. Views of methods

Both CIMOSA and GRAI/GIM have excellent approach to model organizational context and could provide basic description of operational knowledge context. But they do not provide appropriate explanation of the knowledge being used in the enterprise. Moreover, they do not have any view to model evolution on knowledge and organization. They do not focus on actor or agent directly as a principal source of knowledge. As a matter of intent and intentionality, they provide partial views. For example GRAI/GIM models decision making and CIMOSA partially models the objectives of domain, process, and activities.

Both CommonKADS and MASK provide inclusive views to model knowledge in organization. They provide also advanced approach to content modeling. One weakness of these methods is context modeling. They do not have complete and integrated view to model enterprise context as aforementioned in GRAI/GIM and CIMOSA in meta-model.

6   Knowledge Based Enterprise Engineering (KBEE)

6.1   KBEE Views

We propose four generic view of KBEE. These dimensions assist to model knowledge in the organization from multiple points of view;

Context modeling. One of the important issues to model knowledge is to model the context in which knowledge exists. Several methods in both EM and KM develop views and languages to describe the context. This context includes tasks, activities, and business processes in the enterprises. Moreover, the communication view considered as a dimension of context. Although context modeling is the common point of these two fields but one can find more in detail context modeling in EM methods and there are several good languages to model context in EM domain.

Intent modeling. In the literature of both EM and KM, there are several papers that describe the essential of intentionality of top management to launch a global project in the enterprise. However, only in GIM there is a clear decision modeling. Also some sort of organizational modeling in CommonKADS and CIMOSA exist but there is not a clear modeling of strategy and leadership support for the methods. The concepts like mission, vision, and strategy in the enterprises are the source of knowledge and describe global direction of each organization.

Content modeling. Content is the heart of our classification of knowledge modeling. This dimension includes several aspects that should be modeled. Agent modeling is an important view to model knowledge in enterprise. We know that knowledge exists in some form and somewhere in the organization but a very important part of knowledge is tacit knowledge and this knowledge is with the human and so employees in the enterprises. Inference and concept modeling as other important parts of knowledge exist in KM methods. KM methods take care of information implicitly in throughout of modeling.

Evolution modeling. Even though in the EM context, the researchers talk about evolution management in the company and maturity models but there is the absence of languages or modeling view dealing with evolution modeling in detail. This aspect is well defiled in MASK methodology in two different models; one for pragmatic dimension as historic modeling and another one for the evolution of sense and signification as lineage modeling.

6.2   KBEE Meta-model

Three main elements of KBEE are actor, activity, and artifact (Fig. 7). Artifact includes all elements being used by actor and activity or produced by an activity intended to define what to do. Global objective of the enterprise is the direction of this element. The activity must do by an actor and this actor use the knowledge and some kind of artifact to accomplish that activity.

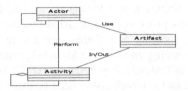

Fig. 7. Three basic components of KBEE

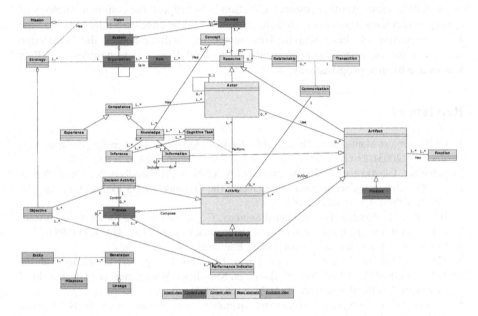

Fig. 8. KBEE meta-model

The elements and concepts being used to KBEE as the results of unification of four methods is described in fig.8. This conceptual meta-model represents essential components of knowledge modeling in the organization. The classed of concepts labeled by green color show the intent concerning concepts. Classes like system, domain, organization and role describe element of context. Communication view and knowledge view in CommonKADS, cognitive task in MASK, and resource view in CIMOSA represent content view in KBEE. Actor, Activity and Artifact here represent the knowledge context for KBEE. Finally evolution view in MASK that originally was intended to model maturity of concepts in the domain is applied to all the classes of KBEE. It means the entire concepts in the context of KBEE will be the object of evolution. To do so, we show evolution as the relation between all the classes that will be subject of evolution.

7 Conclusion and Perspectives

The key idea of KM is to provide a way whereby knowledge contents are created, shared, and utilized in an efficient and effective manner. Therefore, it is critical to analyze these knowledge requirements. Managers need tools to analyze knowledge contents needed in business processes and decision-making. This paper presents the rationale for knowledge modeling as a foundation for successful KM projects. A method is proposed for building an effective knowledge model. As a modeling language of the method, the unified modeling language (UML) has been chosen.

KBEE to be completed and comprehensive need further works. The formalism and proper languages or tools for the dimension and classed are needed. In this paper we developed the conceptual dimensions of KBEE and we did not enter in the detail level of the KBEE view. Another research direction is to propose the common ontology of concepts, elements and views. How to gather the knowledge and information is the next perspective of this research. This perspective will determine the knowledge sources in the organization, implementation methodology and techniques to collect knowledge in an appropriate way.

References

1. OMG : Object Management Group, OMG Unified Modeling Language Specification, Version 1.5. (2003), http://www.omg.org/docs/formal/03-03-01.pdf
2. Schreiber, G., Akkermans, H., Anjewierden, A., de Hoog, R., Shadbolt, N., Van de Velde, W.: Knowledge engineering and management: The Common KADS methodology, 1st edn. The MIT Press, Cambridge (2000)
3. Barthelmé, F., Ermine, J.L., Rosenthal-Sabroux, C.: An architecture for knowledge evolution in organisations. European Journal of Operational Research 109, 414–427 (1998)
4. Ermine, J.L.: La gestion des connaissances, Edition Hermès, Paris (2003)
5. Matta, N., Ermine, J.L., Aubertin, G., Trivin, J.Y.: How to capitalize knowledge with the MASK method? In: IJCAI 2001 Workshop on Knowledge Management and Organizational Memories, Seattle, Washington, USA, August 6 (2001)
6. Vernadat, F.B.: Enterprise modeling and integration: principles and applications. Chapman & Hall, Boca Raton (1996)
7. Abdmouleh, A., Spadoni, M., Vernadat, F.: Distributed client/server architecture for CIMOSA-based enterprise components. Computers in Industry 55(3), 239–253 (2004)
8. Doumeingts, G., Vallespir, B.: A methodology supporting design and implementation of CIM systems including economic evaluation. In: Brandimarte, P., Villa, A. (eds.) Optimization Models and Concepts in Production Management, pp. 307–331. Gordon & Breach Science, New York (1995)
9. Vallespir, B., Merle, C., Doumeingts, G.: GIM: a technico-economic methodology to design manufacturing systems. Control Engineering Practice 1(6) (1993)

The Knowledge Dimension of Production Transfer

Jens O. Riis[1], Brian Vejrum Waehrens[1], and Erik Skov Madsen[2]

[1] Center for Industrial Production, Aalborg University, Fibigerstraede 16, DK-9220 Aalborg,
[2] Department of Industrial and Civil Engineering, University of Southern Denmark,
Niels Bohrs Alle 1, DK-5230 Odense, Denmark
riis@production.aau.dk

Abstract. Empirical studies in three industrial companies have revealed that even companies with many years of experience in production transfer tend to focus attention on planning the physical transfer and on the explicit knowledge associated with normal production. They are uncertain about capturing, transferring and developing tacit knowledge. Supported by studies of the literature it is concluded that there is a need for a more systematic approach to knowledge transfer and development to provide an accelerated ramp-up after the physical transfer. A framework will be structured around a generic set of phases of the transfer process and a distinction between the sending and the receiving organizational unit. A method for capturing the tacit knowledge embedded in a production job has been developed and tested. The framework and the method will provide a basis for preparing a master plan for knowledge transfer and development.

Keywords: Production transfer; Tacit and explicit knowledge; Absorptive capacity.

1 Introduction

Increasingly, industrial enterprises outsource and offshore production to gain from low costs and/or to be close to expanding markets. This implies transferring production facilities and knowledge to another country. Much attention has been given to the choice of new location, design of plant-layout and transfer of physical production facilities, whereas the knowledge transfer and development at the new site remains largely unexplored [1]. In many instances this has become a critical issue, as much of the knowledge determining current operations is tacit and difficult to capture.

This paper will take outset in the thesis that future competitive advantage will not be based on a simple relocation or outsourcing of manufacturing processes to low cost regions; rather it is expected to be found in the company's ability to identify and disseminate best practice, knowledge, market information and capabilities, which are rooted in manufacturing networks [2], [3]. The speed of successful transfer will be important.

1.1 Theoretical Background

Ferdows [1] has developed a valuable classification into four archetypical situations illustrated by selected firms and their way of developing explicit and tacit knowledge

B. Vallespir and T. Alix (Eds.): APMS 2009, IFIP AICT 338, pp. 441–448, 2010.
IFIP International Federation for Information Processing 2010

component. This study along with several studies, however, reports at a general level about the successful relocation of manufacturing activities, but does so without providing a deeper understanding of the tacit knowledge in operation on the shop floor. Few exceptions to this can be found, one being a treatment of the tacit dimension of shop floor activities during different phases of factory maturity [4], and another a discussion of knowledge transfer within a multi-national enterprise [5].

In a comprehensive empirical investigation of knowledge transfer, Szulanski [6] studied eight companies and investigated how best practice was transferred, and he found that the major barriers to internal knowledge transfer were related to internal stickiness, factors like lack of absorptive capacity [7], casual ambiguity and arduousness of the relationship between the source and the recipient.

Knowledge is essentially related to human action [8]. Individuals create knowledge, but organizations create a context for individuals to create and utilize knowledge. The knowledge acquired from a sending plant can be explicit or tacit, and can be grafted to take root into the receiving plant via socialization, internalization, and by combining different types of explicit knowledge to create new knowledge that is useful within the receiving context. The notion of collective knowledge represents the mutual interplay between organizational members when they together perform a task. The Kolb learning circle suggests focus on reflection and experimentation as important elements of transfer of especially tacit knowledge [9].

1.2 Purpose and Outline of the Paper

There is a need for developing a comprehensive framework for dealing with the knowledge dimension of production transfer, and for addressing the issue of capturing, transferring and developing the tacit knowledge associated with operations at the shop floor level, being individual as well as collective in nature.

The paper will address this issue by first presenting a framework for a systematic and comprehensive attention to the knowledge dimension of production transfer. Then a method for identifying tacit knowledge at the sending organizational unit will be presented and discussed. And finally, activities will be proposed for preparing a master plan for knowledge transfer and development.

1.3 Empirical Background

The paper will rest on empirical studies over a period of two years in three large Danish manufacturing companies. All companies have most of their activities outside Denmark and form a wide technological range from manual assembly of industrial components, over semi-automatic production to a fully automated and high-tech electronics production line. In addition, the developed methods have successfully been applied in three minor cases.

The empirical studies have included a survey of documents on the shop floor to uncover the presence of explicit knowledge like work instruction, drawings, maintenance procedures, spare part list etc. Furthermore, a total of 81 semi-structured interviews were carried out at all levels in the organizations in Denmark, Eastern Europe and in Latin America.

For a more detailed exposition of the case studies, as well as the theoretical background, analyses and applied means see Madsen [10].

2 A Framework for the Transfer Process

On the basis of the case studies and pertinent literature we have developed a framework for addressing the knowledge dimension of transfer, cf. fig. 1.

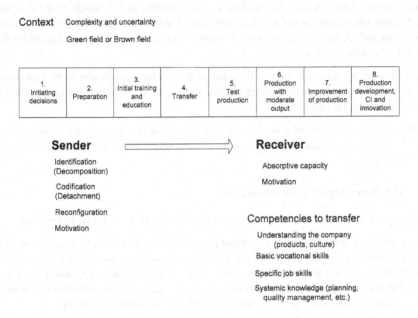

Fig. 1. A framework for planning knowledge transfer and development in production transfer

2.1 A Phased Process

Based on [11] we have extended the four phases proposed by Szulanski [12] to include a training and education phase prior to the physical transfer and additional phases after the transfer to indicate a step-wise development of operation competencies in the receiving unit, cf. fig. 1. Each phase has its distinct set of tasks, the nature and content of which will depend on the actual situation at hand.

Figure 1 shows four different types of competencies. In case of a green field transfer much effort need be devoted to provide an understanding of the corporate culture, and also to introduce operators to the management systems and modes of operations.

Following the Shannon & Weaver model of a transmitter and a receiver of communication [13], two key actors have been identified, namely a sending and a receiving organizational unit.

2.2 The Sending Organizational Unit

Four issues of knowledge transfer are related to the sending unit.

Identification of knowledge in the sending unit. Drawing on systems theory, this involves decomposing the overall task to manageable elements, for example to define the knowledge associated with specific production jobs. A substantial part of operations knowledge is associated with the interplay of several individuals and organizational units, for example in carrying out production planning and quality management. This kind of knowledge cannot easily be decomposed into clearly defined elements.

Codification of knowledge. As pointed out for example in [1], much of the essential production knowledge is not explicit, but tacit. This means that they are only visible when enacted. A special effort, thus, is needed to capture tacit knowledge, to be discussed in a subsequent section.

Reconfiguration. As evidenced in the case studies, a production unit to be transferred is likely to be subjected to a technological update or reconfiguration in an effort to ensure a successful transfer.

Motivation. If a transfer of a production unit implies that operators are to be let off, it may be hard to motivate them to assist in transferring explicit and tacit knowledge to the receiving unit.

2.3 The Receiving Organizational Unit

The empirical studies indicate that in particular two factors should be considered.

Absorptive Capacity. Cohen & Levinthal [7] have made an extensive research of 1719 business units and their ability to recognize the value of new, external information, assimilate it and use it as new knowledge. They call it Absorptive Capacity and suggest that this is largely a function of the company's capacity for absorbing something new related to individual, group, organizational and environmental level.

Motivation. The empirical studies indicate that it is important for a speedy ramp-up in the receiving unit that operators are motivated. Some of the means include a step-wise development of competencies, for example by following the Dreyfus & Dreyfus [14] steps from novice via advanced beginner and competent operator to expert. Another means is to involve operators in improvement initiatives in the new location. In one of the case studies, a Lean program was initiated shortly after the physical transfer. Not only did this help newly appointed operators to systematically be introduced to their jobs, but they became also very much engaged in suggesting improvements, which resulted in a markedly increase in the sense of ownership.

3   Identifying Tacit Knowledge

Observations of practice indicate that managers find it difficult to capture the tacit knowledge embedded in many production jobs. As a result, they tend to focus only on the explicit knowledge part and to leave it to operators themselves to transfer tacit knowledge through application of unstructured peer-to-peer training.

Tacit knowledge may be held by an individual in the company and by a group of persons who are capable of solving complex problems by working together in an informal way using their intuition and mutual experience.

By its very nature, tacit knowledge is difficult to identify. To this end we have developed a method that may help operators and technicians identify significant tacit elements of their knowledge, as a pre-requisite for a systematic transfer [15]. It rests on a model illustrating how different levels of uncertainty and complexity make up four distinctive work situations, which require different competencies, means and institutional support. They also rely on different representations of knowledge, cf. fig.2.

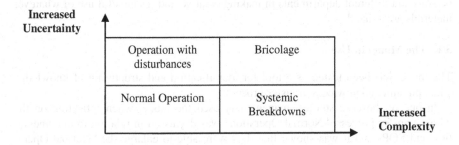

Fig. 2. Dimensions of task situations on the shop floor

A less complex task is expected to be carried out by a single operator whereas a more complex task usually requires the involvement of several operators and specialists with different kinds of knowledge and experience. The uncertainty axis may similarly be divided into a less uncertain and a more uncertain task situation; the former characterized by a high degree of predictability and regularity, and the latter dominated by a lack of knowledge of what incidents may happen and when.

Normal operation constitutes a situation where everything functions as planned and prescribed. The less-experienced operators used drawings, SOPs, maintenance instruction, quality instruction and manuals, all of which also served as a vehicle for discussions between the experienced operator and the new operator.

Operation with disturbances denotes that operators at the individual level experience incidents that occur randomly and call for an extra effort and supplementary knowledge. It could be a spot of rust or a burr on the component to be assembled, which the operator had to let pass, remove or decide if he had to scrap the component. It could also be unplanned stops of a machine due to wear of tooling, stops of a robot or disturbances in connection to sophisticated and automated equipment. The know-how about how to handle these disturbances was possessed by experienced individuals in the sending context.

Systemic breakdowns. In this situation incidents do not readily point to a solution; rather they require a great diagnostic effort, mainly due to a complex set of interactions between technologies and people. In our case studies, the manufacturing equipment combined a large number of different sophisticated technologies, e.g. robots, PLC controls, computer control, pneumatics, hydraulics, electronics, mechanics, CNC tooling machinery with a high degree of complexity. Unskilled operators found it difficult to cope with such situations, and the complexity called for a diverse set of skills, know-how, and a social dimension embedded in the informal task environment of the work place.

Bricolage. Levi-Strauss [16] introduces the term bricolage to denote the social and intuitive dimension where employees use available means when searching for mundane solutions to complex problems. Incidents of this situation are dominated by a high degree of complexity and call for much know-how and experience of each individual within the group. Because of the mutual interplay of different technologies, skills and organizational units, this situation requires a combined effort of several persons and different departments in making creative and resourceful use of whatever materials are at hand.

3.1 The Model in Use

The model has been tested as a tool for identification and structuring of knowledge when planning a knowledge transfer process.

In one of the case studies, management used the model when reflecting on the whole transfer process. "Normal Operation" was discussed in relation to documentation and SOPs and it was shown that they were able to enlarge the "Normal Operation". Most of the tasks related to "Operation with disturbances" and "Systemic Breakdows" were solved by set-up fitters and technicians. However, in cases of "Bricolage" processes and methods were challenged and called for much attention to be able to capture, transfer and develop knowledge, and also to develop a culture at the group level in the receiving unit.

The model was also found useful in another case study where knowledge was to be shared within a group of 15 to 18 planners who were located in groups of two to three persons at different offices in a factory. The model was used by the planners to systemize an internal training process. Tasks of "Normal operation" and "Operation with disturbances" were identified and planned to be trained in such a way that all planners could carry out these tasks. "Systemic breakdowns" should only be solved by a group of five super users. "Bricolage" was identified to include a number of uncertainties that would also call for cooperation with internal and external partners. Therefore "Bricolage" tasks were planned to be managed by two expert planners.

In general we suggest that for a given transfer job 5-10 non-normal situations be defined. Then experienced operators and set-up fitters should discuss how they usually handle these situation, thereby unveiling tacit knowledge. In this way a repository for transfer of tacit knowledge may be established.

4   Preparing a Master Plan for Knowledge Transfer and Development

Outset is taken in the framework model in figure 1 to prepare a master plan for knowledge transfer. It may include the following steps:

Define the overall knowledge transfer and development tasks in a specific production transfer situation. This will include the strategic role and tactical decisions (scope, time frame, what should be transferred and what should not, management approach, etc).

Analysis of jobs to be transferred and the nature of knowledge. As discussed above, it is difficult to identify the tacit knowledge to be transferred. The proposed method (section 3) may help capture both individual and collective tacit knowledge. In addition, analysis of the sending and the receiving organizational unit will provide an idea of the competencies to be developed and the motivation and absorptive capacity in the receiving unit.

Identifying possible means for competence development. Several means exist for training operators on the basis of explicit knowledge, such as instruction sheets, training sessions and exercises. On the other hand, the industrial companies involved in our empirical studies had only a narrow repertoire of means for systematic dealing with tacit knowledge.

The learning circle developed by Kolb [9] provides a background for choosing appropriate means for addressing tacit knowledge transfer and development; for example

Reflection. A common understanding of practice may surface by involving different groups of employees in diagnosing a problem, e.g. around a white board.

Active experimentation. Proposed solutions may be tested as part of an active experimentation process, for example by using games and simulation. The Japanese production philosophy includes Continuous Improvement as a key element, and this has also been adopted in the Lean Thinking.

Preparing a master plan for knowledge transfer and development. On the basis of the above mentioned steps, we shall propose that for each phase of the transfer process to plan what action should be taken for both the sending and the receiving unit. Also the Dreyfus & Dreyfus model of pedagogical steps in competence development may be used to address the question of who (operators, technicians, foremen, etc.), what (which competencies), when, and how [14].

5 Discussion and Conclusion

The empirical studies have revealed that even companies with many years of experience in production transfer tend to focus attention on planning the physical transfer and on the explicit knowledge associated with normal production and are uncertain about capturing, transferring and developing tacit knowledge. These observations initiated development of a more systematic analysis and planning resulting in the proposed framework and method, e.g. figure 1 and 2. Also additional case studies offered opportunities for testing part of the framework.

At the moment, one of the case companies has decided to use the developed framework and method to initiate a concerted and systematic effort to gather and further develop and use the overall experience in the company, recognizing that knowledge transfer and development will be a key competitive factor in future distributed production.

The developed framework and methods will enable an accelerated transfer of knowledge by guiding managers to systematically address key issues. This will provide a more solid background for trying out new training means, especially those aimed at stimulating development of tacit knowledge, individual as well as collective.

Training means that have proven successful in other industries can also benefi-
cially be applied to industrial operations, for example flight simulator. The proposed
framework, in this way, will help managers to address an important issue that have
been neglected so far.

References

1. Ferdows, K.: Transfer of Changing Production Know-How. Production and Operations
   Management 15(1) (Spring 2006)
2. Grant, R.M.: Prospering in Dynamically-competitive environments: Organizational Capability as Knowledge Integration. Organization Science 17(4), 375–387 (1996)
3. Quinn, J.B.: Strategic outsourcing: Leveraging knowledge capabilities. Sloan Management
   Review 40(4), 9–21 (1999)
4. Patriotta, G.: Organizational Knowledge in the Making. Oxford University Press, Oxford
   (2003)
5. Dyer, J., Nobeoka, K.: Creating and Managing a High Performance Knowledge-sharing
   Network: The Toyota Case. Strategic Management Journal 21, 345–367 (2000)
6. Szulanski, G.: Exploring Internal Stickiness: Impediments to the transfer of best practice
   within the firm. Strategic Management Journal 17 (1996) (Winter Special Issue)
7. Cohen, W., Levinthal, D.: Absorptive capacity: A new perspective on learning and innovation. Administrative Science Quarterly 35(1), 128–152 (1990)
8. Nonaka, I., Takeuchi, H.: The Knowledge-Creating Company. Oxford University Press,
   New York (1995)
9. Kolb, D.A.: Experimental learning. Prentice-Hall International, London (1984)
10. Madsen, E.S.: Knowledge transfer in global production, PhD thesis, Aalborg University
    (2009)
11. Maritan, C.A., Brush, T.H.: Heterogeneity and transferring proactice: implementing flow
    manufacturing in multiple plants. Strategic Management Journal 24, 945–959 (2003)
12. Szulanski, G.: The process of knowledge transfer: A diachronic analysis of stickiness. Or-
    ganizational Behavior and Human Decision Processes 82(3), 9–27 (2000)
13. Shannon, C.E., Weaver, W.: The Mathematical theory of communication. The University
    of Illinois Press, Chicago (1949)
14. Dreyfus, H.L., Dreyfus, S.E.: Mind over machine, The Power of Human Intuition and Ex-
    pertise in the Era of the Computer. Free Press, New York (1986)
15. Madsen, E.S., Riis, J.O., Waehrens, B.V.: The Knowledge Dimension of Manufacturing
    Transfers - A method for identifying hidden knowledge. Strategic Outsourcing an Interna-
    tional Journal 1(3) (2008)
16. Levi-Strauss, C.: The Savage Mind. University of Chicago Press, Chicago (1967)

A Framework for Enhancing Responsiveness in Sales Order Processing System Using Web Services and Ubiquitous Computing Technologies

Mokmin Park[1], Kitae Shin[2], Hanil Jeong[3], and Jinwoo Park[1,*]

[1] Department of Industrial Engineering / Automation and Systems Research Institute,
Seoul National University, Seoul, Republic of Korea
{ahrals7,autofact}@snu.ac.kr
[2] Department of Industrial and Management Engineering, Daejin University, Phochon,
Gyenggido, Republic of Korea
ktshin@daejin.ac.kr
[3] Department of Information Technology Business Engineering, Daejeon University,
Daejeon, Republic of Korea
hijeong@dju.ac.kr

Abstract. This study attempts to enhance the responsiveness of enterprises by adjusting the delivery dates taking into account of the production and delivery schedules in a supply chain. To enhance responsiveness, we suggest a due-date assignment method and re-negotiation process for a sales order processing system. The due-date assignment method is designed with the concept of categorized customers' priorities and the re-negotiation process is designed with the concept of the partial delivery and due-date delay allowances. Usually, the due-dates have been considered as customer-assigned exogenous parameters or fixed endogenous variables set by manufacturers. However, those are customary in some industries, e.g. semi-conductor manufacturing, that customers often request changes for their delivery dates after placing an order if something unexpected happens. From these observations, we also propose a new architecture of responsive sales order processing system based on Web Services and Ubiquitous Computing technologies for reliable real-time information.

Keywords: responsiveness, due-date assignment, web services technology, ubiquitous computing technology.

1 Introduction

This study attempts to enhance the responsiveness of enterprises with regard to the production and delivery schedules in a supply chain. According to Christopher [1], the real competitions are not between companies, but rather they are between supply chains. Production cost and quality are not distinctive competencies; they might be necessary conditions for manufacturing firms to survive. Flexibility and responsiveness are becoming distinctive competencies in the age of limitless global competition.

---

* Corresponding author.

B. Vallespir and T. Alix (Eds.): APMS 2009, IFIP AICT 338, pp. 449–456, 2010.
© IFIP International Federation for Information Processing 2010

The sales order processing is one of the most important business processes to enhance the responsiveness of a manufacturing firm [2] and due-dates have great influence on the performance of sales order processing. Therefore, well-structured and flexible due-date managements are expected in responsive sales order processing.

In academia, the due-dates have been considered as customer-assigned exogenous parameters or fixed endogenous variables determined by manufacturers. However, those are customary in some industries, e.g. semi-conductor, that customers often change their due-dates after placing an order by a re-negotiation process if something unexpected happens. From these observations, we propose architecture for responsive sales order processing system based on Web Services and Ubiquitous Computing technologies. And we also suggest due-date assignment methods for three categorized customers based on their priorities and a re-negotiation process.

The remainder of this paper is organized as follows. Section 2 reviews previous studies related on sales order processing. Section 3 presents problem descriptions, due-date assignment methods, and proposed architecture for responsive sales order processing system. In section 4, we describe due-date re-negotiation process. Finally, we give some concluding remarks in Section 5.

2   Literature Review

There have been a great number of articles on sales order processing over the decades. Works on due-date related studies can be categorized into due-date assignment problems and order acceptance/rejection problems.

The due-date assignment problems consider how to quote due-dates which minimize (or maximize) the due-date related objective function. Due-dates had been considered as customer-assigned exogenous parameters in early scheduling studies. Because of finite capacity and lead time management, due-dates were considered as manufacturer-determined endogenous variables. There were several common due-date assignment rules (e.g. CON, NOP, SLK, PPW, TWK, etc.) which are rule-based due-date assignment policies. Gordon et al. [3] presented a review on summarized common due-date assignment studies in single machine and parallel machines. Özdamar and Yazgaç [4] proposed efficient capacity and lead time management in Make-to-Order (MTO) companies using linear capacity planning model to minimize total backorder and overtime costs. ElHafsi [5] considered rush order and partial deliveries allowance. Welker and Vries [6] formalized the ordering process to achieve responsiveness.

Order acceptance/rejection problems focus on the question whether the received order request is beneficial or not to accept. Some studies dealt with rule-based order acceptance/rejection policies ([7], [8]). More recently, several studies focused on Available-to-Promise (ATP) problems ([9], [10], [11]) in Make-to-Stock (MTS) environments and Capable-to-Promise (CTP) problems ([12], [13], [14]) in MTO environments.

There are also several studies that considered multiple priority orders ([15], [16], [17]) and cost model for rush order acceptance [18] in order processing.

There have been considerable studies in the sales order processing problems. But these previous studies considered the due-dates as exogenous parameters or fixed endogenous variables. In this paper, the assigned due-dates with pre-contracted co-operative customers are considered as re-negotiable variables. In the following section, we suggest a framework for responsive sales order processing system using Web Services and Ubiquitous Computing technologies.

3   Responsive Sales Order Processing

As mentioned above, most of the current sales order processing systems do not consider due-date re-negotiations. We can think of several reasons for such phenomenon. They may have come from:

- Contractual responsibility to meet due-dates
- Long response time for re-negotiation
- Unavailability of reliable real-time shop floor and inventory information

So, we are going to propose not only the method for re-negotiating due-dates between collaborating partners but also an information sharing framework for reliable real-time data based on Web Services and Ubiquitous Computing technologies, namely a manufacturing execution system (MES) based on Radio Frequency Identification technology.

In this study, we categorized customers into three types based on their priorities, namely the general, co-operative, and prior customers. General customers have low level profit contributions to the manufacturing firm, relatively small sized order quantity histories, and short term relations. Co-operative customers are different from general customers in the sense that their delivery due-dates are set with shorter buffer time, and they can make special contracts to allow for partial deliveries or due-date re-negotiations. Prior customers are such customers that have shown high level profit contributions and long term business relations. The prior customers have the privilege of asking for rush orders whose due-dates can only be set by preempting previous orders set by current production schedules.

3.1   Description of the Problems Considered

In this study, we assume the following:

1. Make-to-Order environment
2. A bottleneck machine
3. Pre-contracted co-operative customers who are willing to re-negotiate due-dates
4. A scheduling system
5. Web Services-based order management system
6. Reliable real-time shop floor and inventory monitoring system based on Ubiquitous Computing technology

We assumed a single machine case for conceptual descriptions. But, we can also think the single machine as a bottleneck machine or machine at differentiation point (i.e. decoupling point or customization point in postponement) in flow shop environment.

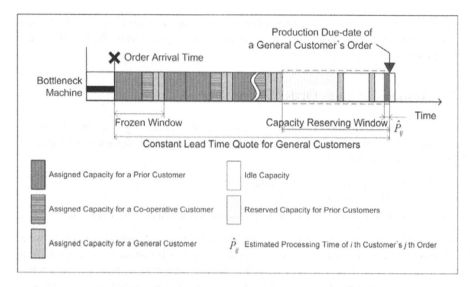

Fig. 1. Due-date Assignment for a General Customer's Order

3.2   Due-Date Assignment Methods

3.2.1   Due-Date Assignment for General Customers' Orders
The general customers' orders are quoted constant lead time with proper buffers as shown in Figure 1. The production due-date of the order is assigned at the end of the capacity reserving window. If there is not enough idle capacity in the capacity reserving window to accept the general customer's order, the order will be delayed or rejected.

3.2.2   Due-Date Assignment for Prior Customers' Orders
The due-date of a prior customer's order is assigned as shown in Figure 2. The scheduling system estimates the most favorable production completion time (i.e. the production due-date of the order) for the prior customer's orders considering current

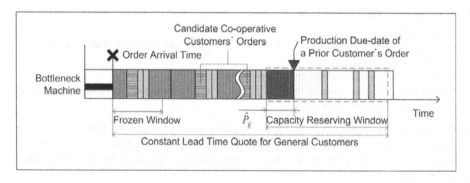

Fig. 2. Due-date Assignment for a Prior Customer's Order

production plans and capacities. In case of a rush order, where the prior customer demands shorter lead time than the time set by the above procedure for prior customers' regular orders, then we need to find some co-operative customer who will re-negotiate their assigned due-dates which have been set already. Depending on whether we can find a co-operative customer who will concede, the prior customer' order may or may not be accepted.

3.2.3   Due-Date Assignment for Co-operative Customers' Orders
Co-operative customers' orders are treated as general customers' one. But their orders are processed in advance among the general orders in the capacity reserving window as shown in Figure 3. In compensation for their cooperativeness, co-operative customers' orders are quoted shorter lead times and lager order quantities than general customers' lead times and order quantities.

3.3   Proposed Architecture for Responsive Sales Order Processing System

Our work proposes architecture for a responsive sales order processing system based on the Web Services and Ubiquitous Computing technologies as shown in Figure 4. The proposed system obtains reliable real-time shop floor status data through an MES based on RFID technology. This framework is important because the proposed flexible sales order processing system depends so much on reliable up-to-date information. The responsive sales order processing system is linked with enterprise resource planning (ERP), supplier relationship management (SRM), customer relationship management (CRM), and ubiquitous shop floor and inventory monitoring systems of the manufacturing firm. And responsive sales order processing system is connected with the customers' order management systems through Web Services.

It is assumed that there is a scheduling system to schedule production plans. The responsive sales order processing system requests to the scheduling system the following information in regular order processing stages:

- Estimated producing time of each customer's order
- Estimated production completion time of each prior customer's order
- Reserved capacity status

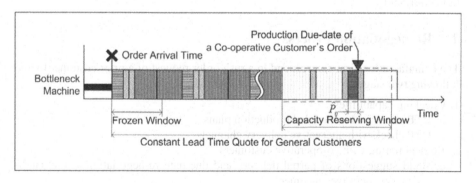

Fig. 3. Due-date Assignment for a Co-operative Customer's Order

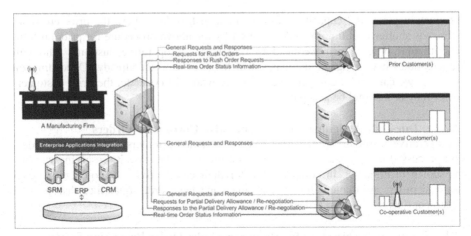

Fig. 4. Proposed Responsive Sales Order Processing System

If a prior customer requests a rush order to the manufacturing firm, the responsive sales order processing system requests to the scheduling system ([19], [20], [21]) the following additional information:

- Capability checks
- Partial delivery and due-date re-negotiation suggestions
- Analysis on the responses from the co-operative customers

Generally, if additional requests are required, customers request to a manufacturing firm through phone, fax, or e-mail. If Web Services technology is adapted in order management systems, order requests and negotiations are automated by XML documents and Web Services. These Web Services technology reduces response time related with the sales order processing and increase the connectivity between a manufacturing firm and customers.

Ubiquitous Computing technology is being shaped up and implementation cases are being reported continually. By adopting this technology in sales order processing, visibility in a supply chain can be improved through the acquisition of reliable real-time information.

4   Re-negotiation Process

The manufacturing firm can respond to a rush order request of a prior customer by the following two stages.

1. Checking capabilities
   a. CTP check with scheduled production plans
   b. CTP check with alternative delivery channels
2. Re-negotiating with co-operative customers
   a. Build suggestions of partial delivery and due-date re-negotiation to the candidate co-operative customers
   b. Analyze the responses from the co-operative customers
   c. Build a rush order acceptance, modified offer or rejection message

In a rush order case, the responsive sales order processing system queries the co-operative customers to allow partial deliveries and due-date re-negotiation through the order management system. The requests will be processed by Web Services-based order management systems of the co-operative customers. If the request is in the predefined allowance level, the order management system responses to the manufacturing firm automatically. Co-operative customers' managers can intermediate the re-negotiation process if necessary.

Because ubiquitous shop floor and inventory monitoring system makes possible the acquisition of reliable real-time shop floor and inventory information, the manufacturing firm and co-operative customers can response quickly and viably. The manufacturing firm can provide real-time order status information (e.g. production, shipping, and delivering status, etc.) to the co-operative customers who have allowed the partial deliveries or due-date re-negotiations. This real-time information ensures minimization of uncertainties to the co-operative customers.

5   Conclusions

A partial due-date re-negotiation concept has been proposed by enhancing the connectivity and visibility of the supply chain using Web Services and Ubiquitous Computing technologies with co-operative customers. The proposed re-negotiation method could help the sales offices of manufacturing firms respond to prior customers' requests flexibly. Rush orders from prior customers, which was not possible previously, can be acceptable by the slacks gained by re-negotiations of co-operative customers' assigned orders. The whole sales order processing system can be automated under the framework proposed thanks to the Web Service and Ubiquitous Computing technologies.

We assumed that the vendors of the manufacturer have enough capacity and flexible enough to adapt to the requested change due to re-negotiation. This assumption may not be acceptable in some cases and vendors' flexibilities may also have to be considered to make this system viable.

References

1. Christopher, M.L.: Logistics and Supply Chain Management. Pitman Publishing, London (1992)
2. Kritchanchai, D., MacCarthy, B.L.: Responsiveness of the Order Fulfillment Process. IJOPM 19(8), 812–833 (1999)
3. Gordon, V., Proth, J.M., Chu, C.: A Survey of the State-of-the-Art of Common Due Date Assignment and Scheduling Research. EJPR 139, 1–25 (2002)
4. Özdamar, L., Yazgaç, T.: Capacity Driven Due Date Settings in Make-to-Order Production Systems. IJPE 49, 29–44 (1997)
5. ElHafsi, M.: An Operational Decision Model for Lead-time and Price Quotation in Congested Manufacturing Systems. EJOR 126, 355–370 (2000)
6. Welker, G.A., Vries, J.d.: Formalising the Ordering Process to Achieve Responsiveness. J. Mfg. Tech. Mgt. 16(4), 396–410 (2005)

7. Wester, F.A.W., Wijngaard, J., Zijm, W.H.M.: Order Acceptance Strategies in a Production-to-Order Environment with Setup Times and Due-dates. IJPR 30(6), 1313–1326 (1992)
8. Philipoom, P.R., Fry, T.D.: Capacity-based Order Review/Release Strategies to Improve Manufacturing Performance. IJPR 30(11), 2559–2572 (1992)
9. Ball, M.O., Chen, C.-Y., Zhao, Z.-Y.: Available to Promise. In: Simchi-Levi, D., Wu, S., Shen, Z.-j. (eds.) Handbook of Quantitative Supply Chain Management: Modeling in the eBusiness Era, pp. 447–482. Kluwer, Boston (2004)
10. Pibernik, R.: Advanced Available-to-Promise: Classification, Selected Methods and Requirements for Operations and Inventory Management. IJPE 93-94, 239–252 (2005)
11. Ervolina, T.R., Ettl, M., Lee, Y.M., Peters, D.J.: Managing Product Availability in an Assemble-to-Order Supply Chain with Multiple Customer Segments. OR Spectrum. Springer, Heidelberg (2007)
12. Taylor, S.G., Plenert, G.J.: Finite Capacity Promising. Prod. Inv. Mgt. J., 3rd Quarter, 50–56 (1999)
13. Bixby, A., Downs, B., Self, M.: A Scheduling and Capable-to-Promise Application for Swift & Company. Interfaces 36(1), 69–86 (2006)
14. Wu, H.H., Liu, J.Y.: A Capacity Available-to-Promise Model for Drum-Buffer-Rope Systems. IJPR 46(8), 2255–2274 (2008)
15. Chung, S.H., Pearn, W.L., Lee, A.H.I., Ke, W.T.: Job Order Releasing and Throughput Planning for Multi-priority Orders in Wafer Fabs. IJPR 41(8), 1765–1784 (2003)
16. Meyr, H.: Customer Segmentation, Allocation Planning and Order Processing in Make-to-Stock Production. OR Spectrum 31, 229–256 (2009)
17. Pibernik, R., Yadav, P.: Dynamic Capacity Reservation and Due Date Quoting in a Make-to-Order System. Nav. Res. Log. 55, 593–611 (2008)
18. Wu, M.C., Chen, S.Y.A.: Cost Model for Justifying the Acceptance of Rush Orders. IJPR 34(7), 1963–1974 (1996)
19. Jeong, H.I., Park, J.W., Leachman, R.C.: A Batch Splitting Method for Job Shop Scheduling Problem in MRP Environment. IJPR 37(15), 3583–3589 (1999)
20. Lee, K.C., Park, J.W., Jeong, H.I., Park, C.K.: Development of a Decision-support System for the Formulation of Manufacturing Strategy. IJPR 40(15), 3913–3930 (2002)
21. Stadtler, H., Kilger, C.: Supply Chain Management and Advanced Planning, 4th edn. Springer, Heidelberg (2008)

How to Foresee and Capture the Effects of RFID Implementation

Kristin Hergot and Lars Skjelstad

SINTEF Technology and Society, Industrial Management, S.P. Andersensv. 5, 7465
Trondheim, Norway
lars.skjelstad@sintef.no

Abstract. RFID technology is, according to both industry and academia, one of the most promising new technologies for improving logistics and manufacturing excellence this decade. This research provides a structured approach for identifying benefits from RFID-implementation, which would be useful for the many manufacturing companies that are still in the phase of considering employing this technology. Based on action research in two Norwegian pilot implementation projects, a framework has been developed for foreseeing, sorting, and capturing the effects of introducing RFID in goods manufacturing value chains. Effects are described in several general performance objective areas, such as cost, time, quality and environment, rather than being calculated in terms of money solely. The key is to systematically highlight possible affected performance areas and the consequences these effects have on each other and on different parts of the value chain.

Keywords: RFID implementation, performance measurement, manufacturing improvement.

1 Introduction

The objective of this research has been to develop a framework for identifying the effects of RFID technology implementation, and to test the framework alongside two pilot implementation cases. In some industries, there is already a demand for RFID technology simply to qualify for being a supplier, or to fulfil governmental rules. However, whether or not to employ the technology for others, off course to a high degree depends on the benefits one can foresee before the decision is made. The technology also allows for some re-engineering, and the challenge is to overview what kind of impact RFID can have on your own business.

The paper suggests how to foresee, sort and capture the effects of introducing RFID in goods manufacturing value chains. The key is to systematically highlight possible effects and the consequences these effects have on each other, in several performance dimensions. A structured approach, both during initial stipulation and later during actual identification of real benefits, would be useful for all companies considering employing this technology. Upfront the implementation project, the technology itself is in focus, and few, if any, in the pilot team can foresee all effects that might follow.

B. Vallespir and T. Alix (Eds.): APMS 2009, IFIP AICT 338, pp. 457–464, 2010.
© IFIP International Federation for Information Processing 2010

Being aware of possible effects in different performance areas before starting RFID implementation projects will influence the possibilities to set goals and reach them. The framework tends to guide the project members in what effects to look for and which ones to avoid.

Since RFID technology primarily is used to *gain more control* or automate processes *related to* the main value creating process, the decision to invest and employ is hard to make in some cases. It is not obvious where effects will occur.

2 Method

The main research method used is action research. Collaboration with two Norwegian industrial companies has given insight in different phases of the RFID-implementation process. The project is funded by the Norwegian Research Council, and the aim has been to implement RFID in pilot areas within the companies in order to learn about the technology and possible effects from it in the value chain, both in the pilot and in a thought future situation where it is rolled out in all processes. In workshops, discussions about possible gain have been initialized at several stages in the development process, from early planning sessions to meetings after the pilot implementation in one of the cases. During the whole process, it has been hard to be conclusive about the effects, but it has been possible to generate discussions about where effects most likely can be expected. This has led to the development of a framework for others to use in similar situations.

Literature reviews have been performed on trade-offs, performance objectives, RFID business cases, decision making under uncertainty and operations management.

This research also includes conceptual development of a new method for a new situation. Results are still under testing and finalizing in the second pilot. The plan is to follow this company throughout implementations and conclusions, to go through all phases of the decision making process.

3 Cases

The research involves two case companies that want to test the RFID technology in order to gain experience with the technology itself and of course to reveal possible effects it might have on their business. Both companies are treated confidentially. One of them is within the food industry, and the other is a manufacturer of sports equipment. In this section, a general description and their strategic goals are referred to. Then, in later sections, the cases serve as examples within the topics discussed.

3.1 Food Manufacturer

The food company is a dairy that makes cheese at two different sites. In the first plant, cheese is made in large blocks, packed and stored for maturation. The cheese is then brought to the other plant where it is split and packed in consumer packages. Finally it is stored and shipped together with other goods.

The main motivation for this producer to investigate possibilities with the RFID technology is the advantage to document the history and origin of the product (traceability). In addition, this producer based its interest in improving price and quality of the products. Also the products have limited lasting ability, and efforts are invested in keeping track of stock. Today's solution is a printed label on every pallet with a bar code on it. In the pilot, RFID tags were introduced as a second label, and put on every pallet in the same operation that puts on the existing label. The existing information system and the RFID test system were used in parallel during the test in order to verify the results. Antennas were mounted on three stocks and both the out gate at the first plant and the in gate at the second.

3.2 Sports Equipment Manufacturer

The sports company manufacture personal sports equipment in a large scale. The products are sold to end users from sports-shops. The end users need to try the products in the shop in order to make sure they get the right equipment. The manufacturer has to make many variants and the stores have to keep stock of different products. The equipment is seasonal, but the production goes around the year. This means that for a long period products are made to stock whilst the plans are based on prognosis. The main motive for employing RFID is quality, price and delivery time. Also to keep track of individual products is a resource demanding task today. In this case, the tags are embedded in the products, and three antennas have been set up in the production.

4 Discussion

Setting the goal to be *identification of all possible effects from employing RFID*, determining the right performance dimensions to look for improvements within is crucial. The traditional way of evaluating an investment, at least in production technology, is to look at the payback time, the net present value and other economic values. These indicate to the decision makers whether the investment is good or not, even compared to alternatives. When it comes to investments in RFID systems however, this paper argues that more performance dimensions must be considered than monetary solely, at least in the beginning and the first part of the employment period. This is due to two reasons mainly. First, the technology is not a direct *process* technology, but rather a *support* technology and an *information handling* technology. Also for such technologies, efficiency effects can be redeemed directly, but other and indirect effects can be expected too. *Other effects* can be found in the environmental-, time-, and quality- dimensions. Long-term aspects should be considered when investing in support technologies such as RFID. Second, what is regarded as a quality- or environmental- effect in the first place (blue, future dollars), can be turned into monetary results (green, current dollars) at a later stage. Customers might find any improvement favourable in time, and hence choose our product in the long run.

When assessing the feasibility of an RFID implementation project, both qualitative approaches, referring to strategy or level of logistics service delivered to customers, and quantitative approaches, assessing costs and savings resulting from the implementation of a to-be scenario or a re-engineered process, can be used [1]. The objectives for an RFID implementation project should be to do something faster or better, and be in coherence with the company's strategic goals and its key performance indicators

[1]. Effects should be sought in different area of the value chain, such as manufacturing, receiving and dispatch, and retail.

Rush [2] uses a quantitative approach and has developed a RFID value calculator to work out RFID's total cost savings and return on investment, based on inventory costs, customer service costs (fill rates) and labour costs. However, financial measures are lagging and can be too narrow-focused on the bottom line, taking the focus off longer-term beneficial improvements [3].

To get a broader picture, one must use qualitative approaches, with focus on strategically important performance areas, in order to get a balanced view of the company [4] and its value chain and to link the company's long-term strategy with its short-term actions. Several authors have for different purposes defined their own sets of measures (RFID benefit identification [5], general performance measuring [6, 7, 8] and designing for manufacture [9]), and a comparison of these can be seen in the table below. The overall performance relies on all these aspects and consequences are expected in them all, whether they are considered or not, and looking at all of them will allow a complete evaluation and prevent problems from being shifted from one area to another [9]. In this research, 9 dimensions are selected based on previous work;

Table 1. Selected performance dimensions to identify RFID-benefits within

	Fabricius [9]	Slack et al [6]	Supply-Chain Council [7]	Kaplan et al [8]	Rhensius et al [5]
Cost	Production costs	Cost	Cost, Asset	Financial	Turnover, Depreciation, Failure cost, Capital commitment
Efficiency	Efficiency			Internal business process, Customer	Process performance
Time	Lead time	Speed	Responsiveness		
Precision		Dependability	Reliability		
Flexibility	Flexibility	Flexibility	Flexibility		
Quality	Quality	Quality			
Environment	Environmental effects				
Risk	Risk				
Developement				Learning and growth	Personnel

Costs may include inventory costs, labour costs, waste or shrinkage costs, and administrative costs. RFID may reduce costs through reducing the need for inventory through better control and reduced safety stock. It also enables information sharing in real-time, and may therefore prevent the bullwhip effect and reduce cycle stocks [10]. RFID may result in reduction of labour and administrative costs due to reduced manual registration. Increased control might also reduce waste and shrinkage costs [11]. In the food case, manual labour can be reduced at goods reception. In the sports case manual labour was found to be reduced in production.

Efficiency is one of the major effects of RFID implementation [12]. Automation of information collection reduces work, and more information can be collected without disturbing other work. Both in the food and sports case automatic inventory counts is expected to be realised.

Focus on *time* is still important in today's competitive environment. Shortened lead times is a direct improvement. RFID can improve lead times through reduction of manual labour. Delivery lead time is one of the most important performance dimensions in the sports manufacturer's case. In the food manufacturer's case, shorter lead times will increase the shelf times of perishable goods.

Precision is a major competitive determinant [13] and an important factor in logistics performance. It is often more important to be able to deliver to the customer at the promised time (not to late or to early) than to be able to deliver fast. RFID can help increase precision, transparency and visibility of information through timely and accurate data. In the food case, improved recalls is important both to health risk and cost. In the sports case, more precise information about inventories will improve planning and shipping.

RFID can help increase *flexibility* through providing real-time information. Real time information helps improve balancing of processes and hence the manufacturer's flexibility in handling new or changed jobs [12].

Lowest possible level of *quality* control, rework and scrap, is important [9]. RFID can help visualise potential problems at an early stage [12]. RFID may also ease documentation of quality of the products (temperature sensitive products). Quality is of strategically importance and one of the most central performance dimensions in the sports manufacturer's case. With RFID, dynamic expiration dates can be enabled.

Environmental friendliness can be a competitive advantage [14] as well as an ethical factor. RFID can be employed to reduce waste from perishable products due to more precise recalls. Tags might help end-of-life operations.

Risk can be reduced through accurate tracking of the goods. More accurate and fast recalls reduces the risk for possible bad reputation. The risk of obsoleteness and stock-outs can be reduced through increased control of product whereabouts [15].

Development work is part of the daily business. Automatic documentation of operations and material flows throughout the value chain forms the best basis for further improvements on all the above mentioned dimensions.

As can be seen in the above discussion, direct effects on one dimension can also have indirect effects on other dimensions.

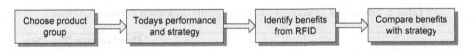

Fig. 1. Process to secure that improvements gained are in line with company strategy

A framework to identify improvements must consider if they are aligned with the company strategy.

This can be shown in figure 1, where step 3 is the use of the framework, and step 2 and 4 compare with the strategy.

1) Choose product group for your pilot implementation.
   RFID technology can be used in many areas, and perhaps be rolled out in the entire organisation over time. However, during the introducing project it is recommended to focus on one single product group.
2) What is your strategy in this market segment, and how well are you performing?
   This step will give you an idea of what you need to improve. The gap between your goals and your performance should be known.

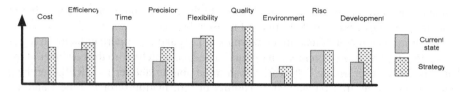

Fig. 2. Current performance compared to strategic goals (example)

3) Use the framework to consider possible benefits from employing RFID.
   By using the framework, possible gains from RFID will be highlighted.
4) Compare to your strategy, and see if investment in RFID is the right action.

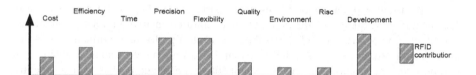

Fig. 3. Contribution from employing RFID (example)

5   Results

A framework to foresee and capture improvements likely to be achieved from employing RFID is suggested using many performance dimensions. In the table below, a single sample is given for the dimension of *quality*. The information in the table is from the food company.

Table 2. Framework example showing the quality dimension from the food case

Advantage / disadvantage	Direct effect or consequence	Pos. eff.	Neg. eff.
The registrations will give statistics for improvement projects	D	x	
Possibility to document quality (temperature) and times in the value chain	D	x	
Receipt of goods at the second plant. Quality assurance and time saving	D	x	
Crew in reception plant 2 can be reduced with 0,5 – 1 man-labour year	C (cost)	x	x
Temperature is an important theme for further development of solutions	D	x	

In addition to the advantages listed, it should be denoted if it is a direct advantage or a consequence from an advantage listed in one of the other dimensions. In the example, reduced staff is registered as a consequence from an advantage listed as a direct effect in the cost dimension. It can also be seen that in the quality dimension, reduced staff could actually be a disadvantage. Loosing the operator in the receiving area can represent a risk and a threat with respect to quality. Of course the framework consists of one table per performance dimension.

To produce the list of possible advantages or disadvantages, one has to go through three steps;

> a) Brainstorming session with every involved person in the project. This will cover benefits that people think about first, and what might follow from other persons input. The list must than be sorted according to the performance dimensions.
> b) For each performance dimension, discuss general and known effects. This sets the mind to think of one focused theme at a time.
> c) Check if the identified effects have consequences on one or several of the other performance dimensions. For example cost savings on personnel might represent a risk or a negative effect when it comes to quality.

The team must consist of persons from all parts of the value chain. Effects that occur in one part of the value chain are considered with respect to consequences in another part and in other dimensions. One then need to look in detail at the positive and negative effects at the operational level to get a true and balanced picture. With the final list of possible effects, created and shared by the whole implementation team, it will be easier to reap the foreseen effects and reach company goals.

6 Conclusion

Participation in two pilot RFID implementation projects has gained insight about possible effects this new emerging technology might have on a manufacturing business. Project focus shift from pure technology interest in the beginning, to performance focus towards the end. It seems as if the participants need to overcome the basics of the RFID technology as such, before knowledge about how to exploit the technology in future business models are considered.

Findings show that implementing RFID technology influences on several performance criteria. Opportunities for process reengineering create additional positive effects, and a certain amount of such reengineering is in fact necessary to get maximum results. To separate effects from the introduction of new technology and the reengineering effort can be challenging, but also in some cases uninteresting.

The framework is developed and used in pilots with a food company and a sports equipment company. Future research should be conducted on complete implementations and include other industries to gain valuable feedback. As more companies follow up their implementations in a similar manner, generic knowledge about what to anticipate from exploiting this technology will be improved. There is still work to be done on how to estimate the effects once they are identified. This is suggested done with trade-off techniques.

References

1. Bottani, E., Hardgrave, B., Volpi, A.: A methodological approach to the developement of RFID supply chain projects. International Journal of RF Technologies: Research Applications 1(2), 131–150 (2008)

2. Rush, T.: How to Calculate RFID's Real ROI. Presentation at RFID Journal Live. Orlando USA (2009)
3. Henricson, P., Ericsson, S.: Measuring construction industry competitiveness: A holistic approach. Paper Presented at the Research Week International Conference. The Queensland University of Technology, Brisbane (2005)
4. Tangen, S.: An overview of frequently used performance measures. Work Study 52(7), 347–354 (2003)
5. Rhensius, T., Dünnebacke, D.: RFID Business Case Calculation. RFID Systech, Bremen (2009)
6. Slack, N., Chambers, S., Johnston, R.: Operations Management, 4th edn. Pearson Education, London (2004)
7. Supply-Chain Council: Supply chain Operations Reference Model SCOR Version 8.0 (2006), http://www.supply-chain.org/resources/scor
8. Kaplan, R.S., Norton, D.P.: Using the Balanced Scorecard as a Strategic Management System. Harvard Business Review (January-February 1996)
9. Fabricius, F.: Design for manufacture DFM Guide for improving the manufacturability of industrial products. Eureka, Lyngby (1994)
10. Netland, T.H., Dreyer, H., Strandhagen, J.O.: Demand driven control concepts – foresight in the effects of RFID. In: 15th International Annual EurOMA Conference, Groningen, The Netherlands (2008)
11. Tajima, M.: Strategic value of RFID in supply chain management. Journal of Purchasing & Supply Management 13, 261–273 (2007)
12. Shibata, T., Tsuda, T., Araki, S., Fukuda, K.: RFID-based production process monitoring solutions. NEC Tech. J. 1(2), 77–81 (2006)
13. Alfnes, E., Strandhagen, J.O.: Enterprise design for mass customisation: The control model methodology. International Journal of Logistics: Research and Applications 3(2) (2000)
14. Andersen, B., Fagerhaug, T.: "Green" performance measurement. International Journal of Business Performance Management 1(2) (1999)
15. Fleisch, E., Tellkamp, C.: Inventory inaccuracy and supply chain performance: a simulation study of a retail supply chain. International Journal of Production Economics 95(3), 373–385 (2004)

Network Compatibility Blocs as Basis of Partner's Selection

Salah Zouggar, Marc Zolghadri, Xin Zhang, and Philippe Girard

IMS - LAPS/GRAI, University of Bordeaux, UMR 5218CNRS
351, Cours de la libération, 33405 Talence Cedex, France
{Salah.Zouggar,Marc.Zolghadri,Xin.Zhang,
Philippe.Girard}@ims-bordeaux.fr

Abstract. The aim of this paper is to contribute to partner's network design beyond the common partner's selection process usually made in the literature. The originality of our approach lies in compatibility concept that comes to consolidate the ordinary approach of partner's selection. We suggest the use of product architecture to extract its related network of partners that would be analyzed with paying attention not only to the efficiency of each required partner within the network, but also to its compatibility with other actors. The gBOMO (generalised Bill Of Materials and Operations) concept becomes significant tool that we intensively use in order to detect the imperatives of realization phase of manufactured product. We will develop exploratory ideas about the network compatibility blocs. These ideas allow a better understanding of partner's compatibility requirements within network.

Keywords: Network design, product architecture, partner selection.

1 Introduction

The partners' selection was extensively studied in the scientific literature since several decades see for instance [1]. However, still remains the need for those firms, called Focal Company (FC), which initiate a product development project to improve their understanding of partnership and the relevancy of their partner selection procedures.

The partner's selection process for any company requires much more attention and know how than what was required in the past [2]. Indeed, the complexity of products and their components is growing everyday. This induces companies to be careful about their partners [3]. Nevertheless, partner's selection is highly risky because of their weaknesses could be propagated to the whole network.

The architecture of the partners' network is not independent from the product that it aims to manufacture. Starting from this observation, we claim that simultaneous analysis of product architecture and network architecture is of upmost importance for the selection process of relevant partners. This could be done by considering partners potential exchanges and/or dependencies.

B. Vallespir and T. Alix (Eds.): APMS 2009, IFIP AICT 338, pp. 465–472, 2010.
© IFIP International Federation for Information Processing 2010

The paper is organized as follows. In section 2 a brief state-of-the-art reviews some existing works in the field of product and network modularity. In section 3, we evoke the product architecture and explore its links with the associated partners' network architecture. Section 4 treats the partners' selection process. In section 5, network compatibility blocs approach is developed. Finally, some conclusions and perspectives end the paper.

2   Related Works

The architecture of any product can be more or less modular. In recent years, several author's publications see benefits in adopting modular product design [4], [5], [6]. In fact, in modular product architecture, components are interchangeable, autonomous, loosely coupled, and individually upgradeable thanks to standardized interfaces [7]. In this case, mapping between functions and components becomes easier. For a modular product, two major factors are: dependence of components and their interfaces. The dependence refers to the way that one component needs some inputs coming form another while the interface defines precisely how this exchange is performed. Obviously, exchanges between components could be and are, quite frequently bilateral.

Focusing on the network, the modularity is measured through *proximity* concept defined by [7] along the following dimensions: 1- *geographic proximity* that can be measured by physical distance; 2- *organizational proximity* which deals with ownership, managerial control and interpersonal and inter-team interdependencies, 3- *cultural proximity* that captures commonality of language, business mores, ethical standards and laws, among other things, and finally, 4- *electronic proximity* that can be captured by e-mail, EDI, intranets, video conferencing, etc. These measures are of great indicators for network modularity. But, here authors consider hat they are not enough to characterise exactly the network. The complementarity and dependence of partners are considered to be of high importance.

3   Network Architecture Extracted from Product Architecture

To clearly define these concepts, we use the gBOMO, generalised Bill Of Materials and Operations, developed in [8], adapted from Jiao BOMO [9]. This representation gathers jointly technical data of BOO (Bill Of Operations) and BOM (Bill Of Materials) of a considered product. gBOMO looks for perceiving the connection between the focal company and a subset of its major partners (cf. Fig 1).

gBOMO allows representing the realization phase as workflows involving partners at various stages. This highlights the exchanges which should take place from one partner to another directly (if they should collaborate together) or indirectly (their collaboration is structured through the FC).

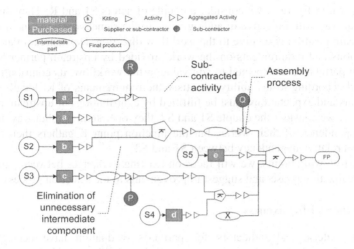

Fig. 1. gBOMO of product

4   Partner's Selection in the Network

Our analysis on partner's selection process is based on information got from gBOMO, we quote the number of partners, the adjacent partners and the kind of relationship (subcontractor, supplier, service providers....)

gBOMO allows a visual understanding of executive operations of manufacturing product during realization phase to perceive those partners that are directly involved in the same workflow. Therefore, hereafter we talk about dyadic relationships to start gradually our analysis on neighbor partners and extend the analysis to effectively and really linked partners in the network by highlighting hidden links.

4.1   Dyadic Relationship

Each couple of adjacent partners detected within the gBOMO might be dependent on their work contributions.

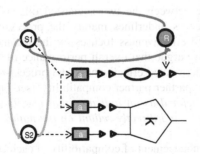

Fig. 2. Dyadic partners' relationship

As shown in figure 2, we consider a couple of actors S1 and R. They operate in a sequential way with objective of adding value to the same workflow; the upstream or downstream position is relative to the workflow direction. Downstream Partner R has expectations and requirements on the work provided by upstream partner S1. As the upstream partner S1 is expected to add value to the workflow, its contribution can be evaluated according to his ability to satisfy the requirements of R. Ideally, these requirements and expectations must be fulfilled by contributions of upstream partner S1 at 100%. If we consider the couple S1 and S2, they operate in parallel way, there is no direct dependency of their works, but the junction point K gathers their flows and generate a relative dependency between S1 and S2.

In the following points, we will focus on existing exchanges between partners during the realization phase, and suggest improvements to the selection process.

4.2 Partner's Effectiveness

Different criteria and indicators for partner's evaluation have been suggested throughout the literature. According to mostly known library of indicators of Huang and Keskar in [1], we achieve to distinguish two evaluation dimensions of partners:

1. *Product-related effectiveness:* that we define as the technical capability of a partner to design or realize given product parts.
2. *Process-related effectiveness:* it reflects the organizational capability of the partner and its ability to perform activities following the network dynamics.

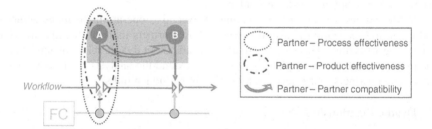

Fig. 3. Framework of compatibility analysis

The distinction made between the two suggested dimensions is that the partner process-related effectiveness underlines mainly the processing abilities of partners while the product-related effectiveness focuses on the technical aspects of the partner's abilities. In [10], we argue that overall performance of the partners' network is not only linked to product-related effectiveness and process-related effectiveness but it depends also closely to partner-partner compatibility. (see Figure. 3)

The compatibility is defined as an indicator that qualifies the collaboration efficiency between two actors and directly reliant on the nature of interactions and exchanges between partners.

The objective is the enhancement of compatibility of each couple of linked partners in the network. Once the technical and technological aspects of the product are guaranteed and the networking dynamics are ensured, it seems obvious that higher is the compatibility better could be the added value to the workflow and as a consequence better would be the performance recorded by the network.

Hereafter a categorization of collaborative situations corresponding to the effective networking is proposed.

4.3 Categorization of Collaborative Situations

Let us take two partners A and B belonging to the same workflow. Their contributions are considered as an added value expected by the focal company. To classify their coupled contributions, we suggest considering two dimensions. In one hand, partners' effectiveness (product and process related) and on the other hand their compatibility (exchanges and interactions quality). Potential collaboration situations are classified in Fig. 4.

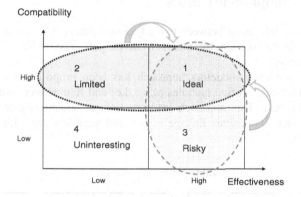

Fig. 4. Categorization of collaborative situations

Four collaboration categories maybe highlighted. They are ranked from the "ideal" collaboration situation (1) to the worst one (4):

1. *Ideal.* The category (1) corresponds to the ideal case, because the concerned partners have the best expected effectiveness and their compatibility is high. This situation has necessary but not sufficient conditions for optimal performance.
2. *Limited.* In category (2), partners have a low-level effectiveness but their compatibility is high. The use of this collaboration situation is limited and might be suitable only for non critical tasks.
3. *Risky.* In category (3), high-level effectiveness of partners is ensured but their ability to work together is not satisfying. This case is called risky because the high-level of technicality could not guarantee by its own the success of the project.
4. *Uninteresting.* In category (4), partners have limited effectiveness and they are not efficient in working together. This case is uninteresting because dysfunctions could appear in both product and partners interactions.

As the expected objective of each company is to achieve the ideal case, the adaptation of categories (2) and (3) allows achieving that.

Category (2) requires the improvement of the partners' effectiveness, this represents product and process oriented improvements which are often expensive to acquire, long to understand and difficult to implement.

For the third category (3), the effectiveness is proven; the only improvement to make is to enhance the compatibility which can be achieved, either by a better adaptation of the partners to the needs of each other, or by looking for new partners with expected effectiveness and a better compatibility.

In order to exploit these improvements based on compatibility, partners selection process has to be adapted and include a third dimension treating of partners links. These links are not always obvious and some of them could be hidden. Hereafter we focus on partners' dependencies to indentify the real links between all the partners of the network.

5   Network Compatibility Blocs

The study of the relationship between two adjacent partners as it was done until now seems obvious. In this section, the idea is to investigate relationships beyond not directly linked partners.

In [11] a dependency modeling approach has been proposed, the studied case concerns product made up five modules (a,b,c,d,e) and five partners within gBOMO (S1, S2, S3, S4, S5). This approach leads to linkage situations categorization by comparing product components linkage matrix and suppliers' strengths dependency matrix, (table 1).

Table 1. Linkage situations

	S1	S2	S3	S4	S5
S1	∞	1	0	0	1/2
S2		∞	1/2	1/2	1/2
S3			∞	1/2	1/2
S4				∞	1/2
S5					∞

Suppliers strengths dependency matrix

	a	b	c	d	e
a	-	1	1	0	0
b		-	0	0	0
c			-	1	0
d				-	1
e					-

Components linkage matrix

Links types Category	Supplier links	Components links
Category 1	Don't exist	Don't exist
Category 2	Don't exist	Exist
Category 3	Exist	Don't exist
Category 4	Exist	Exist

Based on the linkage situations, the first remark that we can make is the rising of two main situations: linked partners (directly or not) and not linked partners. According to this observation and the previous collaboration categorization of section 4.3, we deduce that categories 3 & 4 of partners linkage (linked partners) require considering the compatibility of corresponding partners while for categories 1 & 2, no compatibility is required among the unlinked partners.

5.1   Blocs Extraction

From supplier strength dependency matrix, we can identify for each partner the imperative compatible partners based on their link (table 2). We distinguish two kinds of links: the strong link (equals 1) and the weak one (less than 1).

Table 2. Compatible partners' identification

	S1	S2	S3	S4	S5		Partner	Strong link	Weak link
S1	-	1	0	0	1/2		S1	S2	S5
S2		-	1/2	1/2	1/2		S2	S1	S3, S4, S5
S3			-	1/2	1/2		S3		S2, S4, S5
S4				-	1/2		S4		S2, S3, S5
S5					-		S5		S1, S2, S3, S4

Each group of partners where all the partners are linked constitutes a bloc (fig. 5). It is possible to identify subsets of partners, belonging to the network, which form *network compatibility blocs* because of their internal imperative synergy.

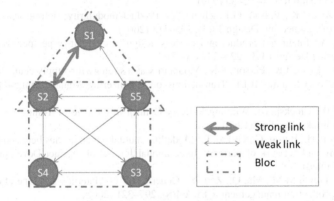

Fig. 5. Network compatibility blocs

Once all the blocs identified, partners' selection process can be improved by evaluating the compatibility in each bloc. This evaluation has to be done according to the kind of the links between partners and based on measures and criteria to be defined.

6 Conclusion

In a high versatile environment, the focal company needs more partnership flexibility to adapt its activities without creating costly dysfunctions. Thanks to suggested approach, for each product module and each new project, the FC would be able to select the suitable sub-contractors and suppliers, looking at the existing network. Modularity of product once correctly understood and coherently handled can brings significant benefits to the focal company, since it serves as support and basis to developing different groups of partners to carry out the most effective partnership and most flexible as possible.

Our analysis focused on the partners' compatibility improvements and partners' dependency links. As a result network compatibility blocs suggest new developments to adapt selection process and enlarge the scope to a third dimension of partners exchanges and relative dependencies that have to be considered specifically beyond the usual partners' selection process based on Product/Process related effectiveness.

Compatibility evaluation based on measures and criteria require a deep analysis of the linkage situations and necessitate further developments.

References

1. Huang, S.H., Keskar, H.: Comprehensive and configurable metrics for supplier selection. International Journal of Production Economics 105, 510–523 (2007)
2. Petersen, K.J., Handfield, R.B., Ragatz, G.L.: Supplier integration into new product development: coordinating product, process and supply chain design. Journal of Operations Management 23(3/4), 371–388 (2005)
3. Junkkari, J.: Higher product complexity and shorter development time continuous challenge to design and test environment. In: Design, Automation and Test in Europe Conference and Exhibition, pp. 2–3 (1999)
4. Gershenson, J.K., Prasad, G.J., Zhang, Y.: Product modularity: definitions and benefits. Journal of Engineering Design 14(3), 295–313 (2003)
5. Kusiak, A.: Integrated product and process design: a modularity perspective. Journal of Engineering Design 13(3), 223–231 (2002)
6. Ro, Y.K., Liker, J.K., Fixson, S.K.: Modularity as a strategy for supply chain coordination: the case of US auto. IEEE Transactions on Engineering Management 54(1), 172–189 (2007)
7. Fine, C.H.: Clockspeed: Winning Industry Control in the Age of Temporary Advantage. Perseus Books, Reading (1998)
8. Zolghadri, M., Baron, C., Girard, P.: Modelling mutual dependencies between products architecture and network of partners. International Journal of Product Development (2008) (to be printed)
9. Jiao, J., Tseng, M.M., Ma, Q., Zou, Y.: Generic Bill-of-Materials-and-Operations for high variety production management. CERA 4(8), 297–321 (2000)
10. Zouggar, S., Zolghadri, M., Girard, P.: Performance improvement in supply chains through better partners' selection. In: Proceedings of 13th IFAC Symposium on Information Control Problems in Manufacturing (2009)
11. Zouggar, S., Zolghadri, M., Girard, P.: Modelling product and partners network architectures to identify hidden dependencies. In: Proceedings of CIRP Design Conference (2009)

Knowledge Based Product and Process Engineering Enabling Design and Manufacture Integration

Matthieu Bricogne, Farouk Belkadi, Magali Bosch-Mauchand, and Benoît Eynard

Université de Technologie de Compiègne,
Mechanical Systems Engineering Department,
CNRS UMR6253 Roberval
BP 60319, rue du Docteur Schweitzer,
60203 Compiègne Cedex, France
{matthieu.bricogne,farouk.belkadi,magali.bosch,
benoit.eynard}@utc.fr

Abstract. After presenting reminders about product and process knowledge, this paper describes a specific knowledge called in this paper "shared knowledge", which is built from a mapping between both these knowledge. Then, a specific approach based on "workers" is proposed to extract data from the different IT components, to create this shared knowledge and to capitalize for the future development projects. Finally, different industrial examples are presented to illustrate the shared knowledge capitalization interest.

Keywords: PLM, MPM, CAD/CAE, ERP, Knowledge Sharing.

1 Introduction

Nowadays artifacts have to meet high performance functions integrating various technologies and numerous components. To cope with this increasing complexity, the development of new methods and techniques has lead to an improvement of the results of engineering activities.

Design process takes an increasingly high importance in the whole product development and industrialization. First, the design process is one of the most complex phases while designers generate new knowledge. They integrate heterogeneous existing knowledge and they transform a set of requirements and constraints into a technical solution. Second, the different choices and decisions taken during the design phase strongly impact the other development phases, the production steps and more generally the whole product lifecycle.

Two main types of knowledge can currently be considered to get a successful result for the design of a product: product and process knowledge. However, another kind of knowledge is crucial to guarantee consistency between the product design's decisions and decisions related to the process. This transversal knowledge, called in this paper "shared knowledge", can be built from the mapping between product and process knowledge.

B. Vallespir and T. Alix (Eds.): APMS 2009, IFIP AICT 338, pp. 473–480, 2010.
© IFIP International Federation for Information Processing 2010

The purpose of this paper is to describe a new approach taking advantage of PLM (Product Lifecycle Management) systems for extracting product and process knowledge from different IT systems. This knowledge is used to generate the shared knowledge.

2 Knowledge Management

The knowledge management is an interactive process that aims to transfer the knowledge throughout its different life states [1] [2]; Sainter distinguishes six steps for the knowledge management process from the knowledge identification to the knowledge reuse [3]. Each of them involves several actors coming from various fields.

Product development project is a source of new knowledge. For the achievement of his activities, the expert needs to reuse existing knowledge for the generation of new knowledge, which has to be integrated back in the management cycle. There is a large range of knowledge that designers use to match the ever-increasing complexity of design problems. Generally, design knowledge can be classified into two categories: product knowledge and process knowledge [4]. The next sections present the description of both kinds of knowledge and their properties.

2.1 Product Knowledge

The commonly accepted approach for structuring product knowledge has been through the construction of Product Models [5]. Several knowledge models reflecting the characteristics of the product are developed in the literature. One of the most usual modelling approaches is the "Function-Behaviour-Structure" (FBS) [6]. Various models are developed as an extension of the FBS method to cope with specific needs [7].

Therefore, regarding to the diversity of product knowledge, five knowledge categories might be distinguished in the building of a product model:

- Function: describes a formalization of the users' requirements according to their needs.
- Structure: describes the technical architecture of the product. The most used representations of this knowledge are the eBOM and mBOM (engineering / manufacturing Bill of Material).
- Behaviour: describes with different formalisms how the product fulfils different functions to cope with the user need regarding the constraints of its various lifecycle phases.
- Properties: complete the definition of the product structure by a set of characteristics such as: material, geometry, technology, etc.
- Life situations: include all constraints generated from the interaction of the product with its environment in each phase of its lifecycle.

In order to represent and share explicit product's knowledge, experts use different information system's components. IS tools are used to store, manipulate and manage data and information. For example, requirements engineering tools propose different tools to assist the designer in the description and the structuring of the product's functions. PDM systems are used to manage the eBOM structure, constituted of components, parts and sub parts. The corresponding product's structure for manufacturing view (mBOM) is stored in the ERP server.

2.2 Process Knowledge

During a product development project, the associated process knowledge is created during the whole lifecycle and different IT systems are involved [8] [9]. It permits to define the contribution of each activity and related resources to the various project goals and to make the connection between the different processes. This knowledge is useful for the IT systems requirements definition and to drive the information sharing mechanisms.

The process knowledge definition is based on activity models: activities allow creating the link between products, resources (facilities, humans...) and their characteristics (behaviour, task, properties...). They structure and define the behaviour of the processes. An activity aggregates several kinds of knowledge such as sequences, functions, rules, states... [10]

In order to formalize this knowledge, several tools such as ERP modules, MPM system [11] and Virtual Factory tools are involved. PLM, ERP and MPM [12] systems are used to manage it (store, manipulate, organize and capitalize). The diversity and the heterogeneous data models of software increase the complexity of the knowledge management process.

In the product development process, two types of activities can be set to support the process knowledge: design activities and, manufacturing and process planning activities. Information's nature and skills requirements are used to differentiate them. In this context, the aim is to make relevant decisions on product and / or on process.

During industrialization process, manufacturing process knowledge is used to create manufacturing data: the resource allocation, the part masters, the mBOM, the NC/Robot programs, the operation sequences, the manufacturing process sheets, the shop floor documents... The manufacturing knowledge is contained in standard and specific processes, the set of resources at disposal (human resources, machines, tools and tooling), the organisation of the manufacturing unit (work centres), the manufacturing know-how. All the knowledge aims to provide coherency between products, resources and processes [13].

So process knowledge has specific properties, such as: the company's specificities; expert knowledge that is owned by individual beings and provided by different departments (Design, Methods, Quality, Manufacturing, Purchasing ...); the necessity of statistical analyse and update for certain data; the fact that specific activities are not yet formalized and then cannot be involved in data capitalization. Moreover, process knowledge defines the mapping between the product and the value chain.

2.3 PLM Approach and Knowledge Building

One of the major properties of knowledge is the capacity to generate a new kind of knowledge from existing one, by using data stored in engineering systems and mapping methods [2] [14].

In the case of explicit knowledge, the information system encapsulates knowledge's representation. An efficient way to extract knowledge is to use communication and information functionalities provided by the different IT tools. Because of their distributed and multi IS connections properties [15], PLM approach gives more advantages to support the knowledge extraction stage.

Indeed, PLM is defined as a systematic concept for the integrated management of all product and processes related information through the entire lifecycle, from the initial idea to end-of-life [16]. In [17], PLM is considered as a strategic business approach that applies a consistent set of business solutions in support to the collaborative creation, management, dissemination, and use of product information across the extended enterprise. At the technical level, the IT solutions to support PLM approach result from the integration of heterogeneous systems such as ERP, PDM and MPM [18], etc.

3   Approach for Shared Knowledge Capitalization

One of the biggest challenges for the companies when they integrate new methodology, new system or new software is to reduce the cost of the solution's deployment project and to minimize the disruption on people's way of working. One of the advantages of the proposed approach is the fact it will not disrupt the global Information System (IS) of the company. Whatever the software used, the way they are interconnected, the data models they are based on, the approach is able to adapt to any configuration. Unlike traditional approach, the purpose is not to integrate some data coming from specific software to another based on a different data model, or to try to define a generic data model able to make different software working together. So the purpose of this approach is to propose a flexible infrastructure (Fig. 1) which should take advantage of the different information system components and which should extract the necessary data for building the shared knowledge.

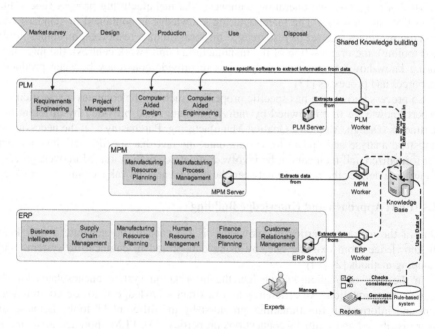

Fig. 1. Information system integration

3.1 Knowledge Extraction: The Workers

For each involved information system's components, the goal is to extract the required data and to store it in the Knowledge Base (KB). This job is performed by a specific machine, called in this paper a worker. Each worker is dedicated to an IS component: it takes advantage of the extension's capabilities of every component in terms of chosen programming language, available Application Programming Interface (API), data model, etc... Sometimes, the data stored in the IS component need to be opened by specific software. In this case, this specific software can be installed in the worker in order to extract the desired information and to store it in the KB. For instance, in a PDM system, CAD data can be retrieved, opened and analyzed in order to store the proper information (e.g. the mass of the product) in the KB (Fig. 2).

In order to not disrupt the put in place components, the workers have to make their jobs during the periods of use less (for instance during the night if the system is not used in other countries).

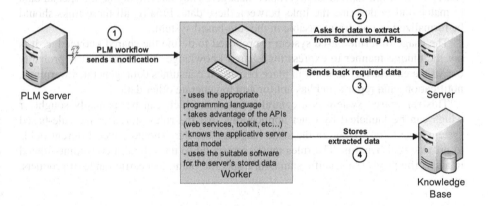

Fig. 2. Workers' processes for data extraction

3.2 Knowledge Base Building and Update

As explained above, the data retrieved from all the IS components thanks to the different workers are all stored in the KB. They can be some generic data, i.e. usable by the whole company for every project, or can be specific to a product, a product range, a step of a process, etc... The chosen structure for the heterogeneous information coming from the different systems is dependant of the company way of working and of the "shared knowledge deployment" goal.

This Knowledge Base can be a unique database or can be fragmented on several computer, for instance on the workers.

One of the most important challenges for this approach is to ensure that the data stored in the KB are up-to-date at the right moment. The update frequency is in-deed completely dependent of the data stored and of the product development / production stage. To pilot the updates of the different data, this paper suggests using the PLM workflow mechanism. The different workflows used send some "up-date required" notifications to the workers at the desired timing. Only necessary information is updated, avoiding surcharging the different system if it is not necessary.

3.3 Shared Knowledge Building

The way of using the extracted data constitutes the shared knowledge: it is a mapping between knowledge coming from different sectors of the company such as legal, research or manufacturing department. During every product's project progress, different meetings are organized in order to evaluate the different constraints of the stakeholders and to find solutions to the coming problems. A great part of the problems solved during these meetings could be avoided by formulating earlier the different actors' requirements. The most difficult work concerning this formulation is to give facts based on data stored in the different experts' software / applications. In order to extract the proper information, to analyze it and to use it, experts of the company's different departments must be brought together under the responsibility of shared knowledge capitalization project manager. They have to define the special data to match and to describe the links between these data. Finally, all these links should be formalized as constraints usable in the rule-based system.

The usage of a rule-based system is proposed to define the shared knowledge. It is not the unique manner to express this shared knowledge. Nevertheless it is probably one of the easiest way to put it in place because it consumes data, generates warnings, notifications and reports and has not for aim to generate other data.

This rule-based system is a central referential which can be manually sought or which can be launched by other applications. All the rules stored in the rule-based system have to be written in the same language but they should cover different fields to provide real benefits. The rules must correspond to the different constraints linked to a specific project, a specific standard, a specific plant, a specific range of products, etc…

3.4 Case Study: Heavy and Civil Engineering Machines

The main example of "shared knowledge capitalization" project deployment provided in this paper comes from a company working in the civil engineering and roadwork machines production. Its main job is to assemble the different machine parts comings from suppliers located all around the world. The purpose of the project was to manage the configuration of these machines depending on different objectives. The first goal was to respect the different standards imposed by the customer's legislation. The second intention was to propose to the customer the allowed marketing options. These options are mainly deduced from the legal and from the manufacturing (assembly line) constraints. The number of marketing options is huge, making it extremely difficult to manage.

The project has been started during the launch of a specific new machine. First of all, the legal department has to express the requirements linked to the specific standards they want to compliant with. These requirements have to be factual or numeric data in order to be easily usable by the rule-based system. Second, all the marketing options have to be mapped with the corresponding technical option(s). Third, the incompatible options have to be listed: the research department has to precise its constraints (mainly based on geometric models) and the manufacturing department has to clarify its restrictions according to its production's plans (e.g. 2 models of the same machine cannot be produced successively...).

Most of this knowledge is usable for other machines, other projects. It is a shared knowledge, a transversal knowledge. So it is important to store the application scope with the extracted data. For example, the scopes could be linked to: a prod-uct, a range of product, etc; a specific manufacturing plant, production line, tool used to assemble the product, etc; a specific standard concerning materials used or the re-quirements of the product, etc.

These data have also their own lifecycle and update timescale. This is why the PLM workflow could help to determine when the data has to be update depending on the project progress...

4 Conclusion

In this paper, the utility of the PLM approach has been underlined in order to support data extraction. The extracted data are used for the shared knowledge building. Shared knowledge is a new kind of knowledge, based on product and process knowl-edge. Its main purpose is to assess managerial and technical decisions.

The role of the experts still remains essential for this approach. For each involved information system's component, a key user has to be defined to determine which data is interesting to be extracted and to be used in the rule-based system. Then, they have to agree about the rules to define and the application field of these rules. The required competences for achieving such an implementation are multiple: software and network engineering to use the different provided APIs, different sections' exper-tise, project management to make all the experts working together, etc...

References

1. Liao, S.H.: Knowledge management technologies and applications - literature review from 1995 to 2002. Expert Systems with Applications 25, 155–164 (2003)
2. Studer, R., Benjamins, V.R., Fensel, D.: Knowledge Engineering: Principles and methods. Data and Knowledge Engineering 25, 161–197 (1998)
3. Sainter, P., Oldham, K., Larkin, A., Murton, A., Brimble, R.: Product Knowledge Man-agement within Knowledge-Based engineering systems. In: ASME 2000 (2000)
4. Zha, X., Du, H.: Knowledge-intensive collaborative design modeling and support- Part I: Review, distributed models and framework. Comp. Ind. 57, 39–55 (2006)
5. Stokes, M.: Managing Engineering Knowledge: MOKA Methodology for Knowledge Based Engineering Applications. MOKA Consortium, London (2001)
6. Gero, J.S., Kannengiesser, U.: The situated function–behaviour–structure framework. De-sign Studies 25(4), 373–391 (2004)
7. Sudarsan, R., Fenves, S.F., Sriram, R.D., Wang, F.: Product information modeling frame-work for PLM. C.A.D. 37, 1399–1411 (2005)
8. Denkena, B., Shpitalni, M., Kowalski, P., Molcho, G., Zipori, Y.: Knowledge Management in Process Planning. CIRP Annals - Manufacturing Technology 56(1), 175–180 (2007)

9. Ming, X.G., Yan, J.Q., Wang, X.H., Li, S.N., Lu, W.F., Peng, Q.J., Ma, Y.S.: Collaborative process planning and manufacturing in product lifecycle management. Comp. Ind. 59, 154–166 (2008)
10. Hugo, J., Vliegen, W., Herman, H.: Van Mal: The Structuring of Process Knowledge: Function, Task, Properties and State. Robotics & Computer-Integrated Manufacturing 6(2), 101–107 (1989)
11. Huet, G., Fortin, C., Mcsorley, G., Toche, B.: Information Structures and Processes to Support Data Exchange between Product Development and Resource Planning Systems. In: IESM 2009, Inter. Conf. on Ind. Eng. and Syst. Mngt., Montreal, Canada, May 13-15 (2009)
12. Sly, D.: Manufacturing Process Management (MPM). Proplanner whitepaper (2004), http://www.proplanner.net/Product/Whitepapers/
13. Fortin, C., Huet, G.: Manufacturing Process Management: iterative synchronisation of engineering data with manufacturing realities. International Journal of Product Development 4(3/4), 280–295 (2007)
14. Gordon, J.L.: Creating knowledge maps by exploiting dependent relationships. Knowledge-Based Systems 13, 71–79 (2000)
15. Abramovici, M., Sieg, O.C.: Status and development trends of product lifecycle management systems. In: International Conference on Integrated Product and Process. Development – IPPD, Wroclaw, Poland, November 21-22 (2002)
16. Saaksvuori, A., Immonen, A.: PLM. Springer, Berlin (2004)
17. Jun, H., Kiritsis, D., Xirouchaki, P.: Research issues on closed-loop PLM. Computer in Industry 57 (2007)
18. Schuh, G., Rozenfeld, H., Assmus, D., Zancul, E.: Process oriented framework to support PLM implementation. Comp. Ind. 59, 210–218 (2008)

Part V

Performances

Proposal of a Performance Measurement System for Professional Non-profit Service Organizations

Michela Benedetti and Sergio Terzi

Department of Industrial Engineering, Università degli Studi di Bergamo
24045 Dalmine (BG), Italy
{michela.benedetti,sergio.terzi}@unibg.it

Abstract. The paper aims at presenting a Performance Measurement System (PMS) developed in an Italian project, performed by the authors within a Nonprofit Service Organization (NSO). Like profit organizations, nonprofit ones must measure their performances, in order to define possible improvements. The paper proposes a PMS, derived from the well known Balanced Scorecard approach, specifically dedicated to NSOs. In particular, a case study has been conducted within an Italian NSO, active in the construction sector, located in the Northern Italy, in the county of Bergamo.

Keywords: Keywords Performance Measurement, Non-profit Organization, Balanced Scorecard.

1 Introduction

The term non-profit organization generally refers to public welfare organization; however, such organizations are also referred to as non-governmental organizations, the non-statutory sector, the third sector foundation, the independent sector, the voluntary sector, the tax-free sector and the philanthropic sector, etc. The primary characteristic of a non-profit organization is that it is without commercial purpose: revenue can be used only to pay expenses incurred in its mission. Italian Non-Profit health and safety Service Organizations (NSOs) have a trade-union origin and they are constituted and governed by collective agreements with management of equality between the workers representatives and employers [1]. NSOs are designed to meet clearly shared interests. Their general purpose is to provide collective resources to their members, resources deemed important by the parties to encourage the consolidation and safety of labor and enterprise [2]. Like profit organizations, non-profit organizations must measure their performances, in order to define possible improvements in their activities. Within NSOs, service providers are even stressed in this issue, since they are in contact with a plethora of service users. Within such a context, the present paper proposes a Performance Measurement System (PMS), derived from the well known Balanced Scorecard approach, specifically dedicated to non-profit organizations. In particular, a case study has been conducted within an Italian NSOs active in the construction sector, located in the Northern Italy, in the county of Bergamo, where the proposed PMS has been tested.

B. Vallespir and T. Alix (Eds.): APMS 2009, IFIP AICT 338, pp. 483–490, 2010.

2 Performance Measurement in Non-Profit Organizations

Performance Measurement is a wide topic in the scientific and business literature and many Performance Measurement Systems have been developed in the last 20 years. Among the most relevant contributions, the following systems and models might be quoted:

- *Performance Measurement Matrix* [3]. A two-by-two matrix combines cost and non-cost perspectives with external and internal perspectives. It is a balanced model, and it is cited in the literature for its simplicity and flexibility.
- *Performance Pyramid System* [4]. This model is a pyramid built on four levels, showing the links between corporate strategy, strategic business units and operations.
- *Performance Measurement System for Service Industries* [5], also called the *Results and Determinants Framework*. It focuses on six dimensions divided into results (*Competitiveness, Financial performance*) and determinants of these results (*Quality of service, Flexibility, Resource utilization and innovation*).
- *Balanced Scorecard* (BSC, [6], [7], [8]). It aims to provide management with balanced measures based on four perspectives (*Financial, Customer, Internal processes* and *Innovation and learning*).
- *Integrated Performance Measurement System* [9]. The model underlines two main facets of the performance measurement system: integrity and deployment. It is based on four levels (*Corporate, Business units, Business processes* and *Activities*) and at each of these levels five key factors are considered (*Stakeholders, Control criteria, External measures, Improvement objectives* and *Internal measures*).
- *Performance Prism* [10]. A prism graphically represents the architecture of the model, and each face of the prism corresponds to a specific area of analysis: *Stakeholder satisfaction, Strategies, Processes, Capabilities* and *Stakeholder contribution*.
- *Organizational Performance Measurement* (OPM, [11]). This model was developed specifically for SMEs and is based on three principles: alignment, process thinking and practicability. The framework is based on two key management constructs, namely *Zone of management* and *Open systems theory*.
- *Integrated Performance Measurement for Small Firms* [12]. The model was specifically designed to be used in SMEs. It is based on seven main dimensions of measures, classified as two external dimensions (*Financial performance* and *Competitiveness*) and five internal dimensions (*Costs, Production factors, Activities, Products* and *Revenues*) connected by a causal chain.

Most of the models/systems above show a set of key features that allow to an organization to identify a set of personalized measures to evaluate own performance. These models emphasize that the measures used by an organization must provide a business balanced frame. The measures should include both financial and non-financial measures, both internal and external measures and both efficiency and effectiveness measures. Among these models, Balanced Scorecard (BSC) plays a relevant role in literature, where it is a very well known framework, adopted around the world. It has been widely used in many profit-based sectors, from industrial to service companies (e.g. [13], [14], [15], [16], [17]), thank to its easily adaptability and modularity. BSC, through the appropriate adaptations, can be extremely useful also to the management of non-profit companies, in order to identify the elements and the phenomena that affect positively and negatively their operation. Indeed, the prospects for improving management offered by BSC approach within the non-profit organizations are in some ways even more significant than in the area for profit [7].

Based on these considerations – and also considering it is one of the most popular models in literature and in practice – BSC appears the model more suitable for an application in the non-profit sector, also because of its simplicity compared to other models. Performance measurement in non-profit organizations must take into account the particular characteristics of these organizations. In fact, it is not always possible a simple transposition of the BSC model canonical form, but it requires specific adaptations, because the different purposes of the two typologies of organizations (profit and non-profit) do not allow that the classic BSC tools and criteria can be transferred tout-court from an area to another. The main changes to the original model concern the architecture of the framework, the type of analysis perspectives to be considered and their relative importance [18]:

- Mission moves to the top of the BSC, because non-profit organizations exist to serve a higher purpose and they generate value directly through the pursuit of their mission.
- Customer perspective is elevated: flowing from the mission is a view of the organization's customers, not financial stakeholders. Achieving a mission does not equate to fiscal responsibility and stewardship, instead the organization must determine whom it aims to serve and how their requirements can best be met.
- Parallel reduction of the importance attached to economic and financial perspective.
- Substantial persistence of the perspectives related to internal processes, learning and innovation.

3 Proposal of the Performance Measurement System

The proposed model is composed by key five areas. For each macro-area it is possible to identify categories that may also relate to different objectives. In turn, for each category there are several important dimensions, which would identify specific measures of performance. The generic user that applies this framework to generic non-profit organization can customize his own set of measures to be obtained, in order to effectively measure his own company. For each measure are quantified: (i) the measured value, (ii) the value on the previous survey, (iii) the average value among all values (benchmark), (iv) the best value obtained until the time of detection (best-to-date), (v) the worst value (worst-case) and (vi) the values target, i.e. the limit values, both in terms of minimum, both in terms of maximum, entered by the user. The five areas are the followings:

- *Mission area.* This is a perspective not provided as part of applications in profit businesses. The purpose of a profit organization is to make money, however non-profit organizations also need money in the form of donations to support their operations. But the organization does not prioritize money when developing its strategy or proposal, its mission should be its top priority. The mission defines this core purpose and articulates the reasons for the organization existence. The problem is, first, in defining the mission, since in the non-profit organizations is widespread the tendency to regard their mission as implicit and implied, with the effect of treating as a priority the implementation of improvement activities only with regard to efficiency.

- *Users area.* It is modulated on the basis of the customer perspective of BSC, but renamed in "users area". In this way it takes on a connotation more in line with the institutional role and highlights the feature that distinguishes non-profit companies from the profit one.
- *Internal processes area.* It is the most specific of the sector. The need to monitor internal processes is linked to the need to understand which are the activities for creating value within the organization.
- *Learning and innovation area.* It is specific for the service provided. Also for non-profit organization basic condition to achieve the desired outcomes is to develop appropriate procedures for maintaining, consolidating and developing the knowledge and skills of human resources, maintaining a good level of organizational climate and adequate information systems.
- *Suppliers area.* Only if there are particularly close relationships with suppliers, such as to fall in the strategy leading to a decisive improvement of performance in respect of users, suppliers area must be included.
- *Financial area.* In general, it is not a prospect to be eliminated completely, because even non-profit companies should be subject to the principle of cost to sustain: therefore this area becomes marginal.

Unlike the canonical BSC that does not take into account all the stakeholders of the organization or rather it prefers some over others, this model puts the different areas on the same level. For example, the classical BSC raises the learning and growth perspective of secondary importance compared to the other, while for a non-profit organization its staff is the first primary resource, essential to the sustainability and the success. In fact, users have their first contact with the company through its personnel and on the basis of that contact they express their opinions on the quality of service provided (this applies to the generic service company). Therefore, promoting the development of the employees is an essential activity. By defining the PMS, the satisfaction degree measures appear as very significant indicators of performance, as they represent an opportunity for verification about the non-profit organization ability to pursue its mission. The satisfaction degree depends on the gap between user expectations and his perceptions of benefits received. The proposed model is an adaptation of the scheme developed by Parasuraman and colleagues in 1985 [19]. A set of gaps exists regarding executive perceptions of service quality and the tasks associated with service delivery to consumers. These gaps can be major hurdles in attempting to deliver a service which consumers would perceive as being of high quality. The gaps are [19]:

- GAP 1 (*user expectation – management perception gap*): the gap between user expectations and management perceptions of those expectations will have an impact on the user's evaluation of service quality.

- GAP 2 (*management perception – service quality specification gap*): the gap between management perceptions of user expectations and the firm's service quality specifications will affect service quality from the user's viewpoint.
- GAP 3 (*service quality specifications – service delivery gap*): the gap between service quality specifications and actual service delivery will affect service quality from the user's standpoint.
- GAP 4 (*service delivery – external communications gap*): the gap between actual service delivery and external communications about the service will affect service quality from a user's standpoint.
- GAP 5 (*expected service – perceived service gap*): the quality that a user perceives in a service is a function of the magnitude and direction of the gap between expected service and perceived service.

Further three gaps (Figure 1) should be added to the five above:

- GAP 1b: differences between family expectations and management perceptions. It may be that managers are not fully aware of what characteristics of the structures and processes are able to meet the family members wishes.
- GAP 5b: deviation which is connected to the level of family members satisfaction.
- GAP 6: differences between the expectations expressed by users and family members. This difference is typically manifested in the different weight given to the various service dimensions (health, welfare, social, etc.).

3.1 Case Study

The paper concerns a case study (EA) about an Italian NSO of the construction sector in the Northern Italy. It delivers services designed to support the construction sector on issues such as safety and prevention in the workplace, providing coverage to all workers in that industry, regulating and maintaining their expectations. EA delivers services such as building professional seniority, economic integration (in case of illness, accidents and occupational diseases), integrating pension, Christmas bonus and holiday, assistance (health, insurance, support, recreational), insurance for extra-professional accidents to employees and owners, mountain and marine colonies for dependent children, training and careers guidance, notarized statement for regular contributions, promotion of initiatives for the health and safety in the workplace, prevention clothing and equipment supply, organization of courses aimed at training and information regarding the prevention legislation, medical visits and inspections.

In the territory there are two organizations of the same type in the construction industry, but they turn to two different types of building companies: the craft (EA) and the industrial enterprises. The other organization is addressed exclusively to industrial companies, while EA focuses mainly on the craft clients. The five BSC key areas have been defined as follows in detail.

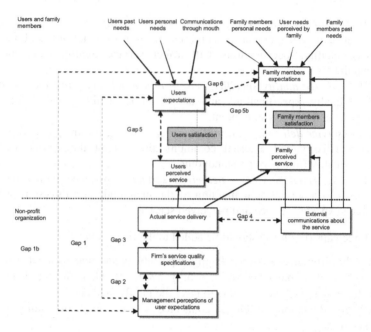

Fig. 1. Users and family members satisfaction

Within the *Mission area*, the proposed BSC can assist the NSO to transform its mission into clear goals that link all members in the organization. The mission is divided into the results to be achieved: for example, the culture of prevention. To take into account the external environment, thus overcoming one of the limits of BSC, it is possible to consider some exogenous measures, such as number of accidents at work, number of fatalities and number of registered occupational diseases. In this way, it is possible to evaluate the effectiveness of own initiatives for the health and safety in the workplace.

Within the *Users area*, there are some dimensions that are also found in the canonical BSC customer perspective (*Market share, Loyalty, Customer acquisition, Customer loss, Customer satisfaction, Image and reputation*). For example, addressing to two different types of construction companies (the industrial and the craft), EA is not prohibited by contracts to turn to the industrial ones, so the capture of industrial market shares is an indication of preference for these companies ((*Number of industrial companies registered / Number of total industrial companies*)%). Other measures may be obtained through survey. The category *User as partner* evaluate the collaboration which is created between the organization and its users to grow together, such as proposals for the improvement of services received by users themselves, or the number of projects undertaken in collaboration between institution and business.

Within the *Internal processes area*, the *Operations* category focuses on existing products and services delivery to existing users and it must be efficient, regular and timely. The existing operations tend to be repetitive, so it is possible to promptly apply scientific management techniques to control and improve the service delivery process. The *Defects and complaints management* category identifies an important aspect in assessing the internal processes quality and, especially, in the primary objective of users satisfaction. This way it is possible to assess the need for initiatives and programs to improve quality. Especially service businesses have more difficulty to assess the quality of delivered service (due to the four characteristics of intangibility, heterogeneity, inseparability and perishability identified in the service literature [19]).

In the *Learning and innovation area*, the *Human resources* category emphasizes the importance of human capital in NSOs and, in general, in business services: the staff is the true wealth of these companies. In fact, if an organization wants to grow it is not enough that it adheres to standard operating procedures set by top management. It is necessary that the ideas for improving processes and performance to the users benefit come from front line employees, who are in direct contact with internal processes and with users. The *Competitiveness* category addresses all the elements that add value compared with other companies. They may relate to innovations in Information Technology (IT): having an excellent IT system is an indispensable requirement so that employees can improve the processes. Or the elements that add value may refer to improvements in organization and management.

The *Suppliers area* depends by the external structure of the organization. For its purposes the EA has qualified staff and works with local specialized organizations skilled in prevention, hygiene and safety in the workplace. The primary services depend on outside professional and it is therefore essential to evaluate them, because the main contact with the users takes place through them: the medical visits through doctors, training with teachers and tutors, clothing with a company specialized in providing clothing and equipment work. The perceived quality depends on the manner in which these contacts take place. The dimensions are similar to those considered for the *Operations* category in the *Internal processes area*, referred to only part of process in outsourcing. The only variation is the *Price* dimension, because it is important to consider the increases or decreases in prices, so it is possible consider other suppliers if necessary.

The last area is the *Financial* one. As the economic side has never been discussed during the case study in a direct way, but only indirectly through considerations in relation to the time and cost reduction, this view is not considered. However, it might be noticed that, in general, it is not a prospect to be eliminated completely, because even NSOs should be subject to the principle of cost to sustain: it becomes a marginal area.

4 Conclusions

The model has been developed for an Italian NSO in the construction sector. It has been tested and it is currently under deployment in the company itself. In order to validate it, more adaptations are needed in other NSOs, also in other NSO contexts. Thank to its generic approach – derived by the BSC approach – it constitutes a valuable starting point for measuring performances in NSOs. In particular, the satisfaction measures are important both within and outside the company. As for the internal feedback, information from users is a trace that the management can use to reflect the strengths and weaknesses of the company and, consequently, to identify what changes should be made. As for the exterior, the voice on the user satisfaction degree is one of the major business determinants. Information systematically collected and collated in special reports can be used to document to a third the level of service provided.

References

1. Paparella, D.: La bilateralità nel sistema di relazioni industriali italiane. Working Paper Cesos (2002)
2. Lai, M.: Appunti sulla bilateralità. Diritto delle Relazioni Industriali 4 (2006)
3. Keegan, D.P., Eiler, R.G., Jones, C.R.: Are your performance measures obsolete? Management Accounting (US) 70(12) (1989)
4. Lynch, R.L., Cross, K.F.: Measure Up – The Essential Guide to Measuring Business Performance, Mandarin, London (1991)
5. Fitzgerald, L., Johnson, R., Brignall, T.J., Silvestro, R., Voss, C.: Performance Measurement in Service Businesses. The Chartered Institute of Management Accountants, London (1991)
6. Kaplan, R.S., Norton, D.P.: The Balanced Scorecard – Measures That Drive Performance. Harvard Business Review 70(1) (January/February 1992)
7. Kaplan, R.S., Norton, D.P.: Using the Balanced Scorecard as a Strategic Management System. Harvard Business Review 74(1) (January/February 1996)
8. Kaplan, R.S., Norton, D.P.: The Balanced Scorecard: Translating Strategy into Action. Harvard Business School (1996)
9. Bititci, U.S., Carrie, A.S., McDevitt, L.: Integrated performance measurement systems: a development guide. International Journal of Operations and Production Management 17 (1997)
10. Neely, A., Adams, C., Kennerley, M.: The Performance Prism: the Scorecard for Measuring and Managing Stakeholder Relationship. Prentice Hall, London (2002)
11. Chennell, A., Dransfield, S., Field, J., Fisher, N., Saunders, I., Shaw, D.: OPM: a system for organisational performance measurement. In: Proceedings of the Performance Measurement – Past, Present and Future Conference, Cambridge, July 19-21 (2000)
12. Laitinen, E.K.: A dynamic performance measurement system: evidence from small Finnish technology companies. Scandinavian Journal of Management 18 (2002)
13. Aidemark, L., Funck, E.K.: Measurement and Health Care Management. Financial Accountability & Management 25(2), 253–276 (2009)
14. Beard, D.F.: Successful Applications of the Balanced Scorecard in Higher Education. Journal of Education for Business 84(5), 275–282 (2009)
15. Impagliazzo, C., Ippolito, A., Zoccoli, P.: The Balanced Scorecard as a Strategic Management Tool: Its Application in the Regional Public Health System in Campania. Health Care Manager 28(1), 44–54 (2009)
16. Kong, E.: The development of strategic management in the non-profit context: Intellectual capital in social service non-profit organizations. International Journal of Management Reviews 10(3), 281–299 (2008)
17. Urrutia, I., Eriksen, S.D.: Application of the Balanced Scorecard in Spanish private health-care management. Measuring Business Excellence 9(4), 16–26 (2005)
18. Niven, P.: Balanced Scorecard for government and non-profit agencies. Wiley and Sons, Hoboken (2003)
19. Parasuraman, A., Zeithaml, V.A., Berry, L.L.: A Conceptual Model of Service Quality and Its Implications for Future Research. Journal of Marketing 49(4) (1985)

Total Cost of Ownership Considerations in Global Sourcing Processes

Robert Alard, Philipp Bremen, Josef Oehmen, and Christian Schneider

ETH Center for Enterprise Sciences (BWI), Department of Management, Technology, and Economics, ETH Zurich, Zurich, Switzerland
ralard@ethz.ch

Abstract. Even within the financial crisis Global Sourcing is gaining more and more importance. Although a lot of European companies have already a long experience with international supply markets, uncertainties about the consequences and the costs related to a specific international supplier selection still remain. The Total Cost of Ownership concept is an interesting approach in order to cope with this problem. In the present paper key requirements for a Total Cost of Ownership concept from an industrial perspective are described. In the following, a Total Cost of Ownership concept is presented which allows conducting detailed Total Cost of Ownership calculations structured in different key modules. These key modules base on macroeconomic and microeconomic aspects which can also be largely used independently.

Keywords: Global Supply Networks, Total Cost of Ownership, Global Total Cost of Ownership, Global Procurement, Outsourcing, Supplier Evaluation, Country Assessment.

1 Global Sourcing

Global Sourcing is gaining more and more importance. For many European companies East European and Asian supply markets are promising alternatives to local sources. The key reasons for Global Sourcing initiatives from a European perspective are a) cost reductions, b) market access considerations (e.g. access through a supplier to promising sales markets, regional knowledge), c) technological requirements (e.g. some supplier or technology cluster can only be found in some supply markets) d) the proximity to customers (e.g. to follow a key customer into these markets) or e) legal issues (e.g. need for local content, tax issues, subsidies, certificates). Nevertheless Global Sourcing is - from a procurement perspective - a challenging topic with serious pitfalls for the customer. So it is essential to adapt the procurement processes for Global Sourcing activities and implement important global aspects ex-ante. Figure 1 describes an enhanced strategic process model including relevant considerations related to international procurement initiatives.

An interesting approach within this context is the Total Cost of Ownership (TCO) model which can be defined as an estimation of all direct and indirect costs associated with a specific procurement object over its entire life cycle. An integral

B. Vallespir and T. Alix (Eds.): APMS 2009, IFIP AICT 338, pp. 491–498, 2010.

TCO approach is of big support for the Make-or-Buy decision and the supplier evaluation (ex-ante) as well for the supplier development and supplier controlling in the operative procurement (ex-post). Even if TCO is a well-known term in the scientific community and some approaches have been developed (see [2, 3, 4, 5, 6, 7, and 8]), no viable integral models are known for Global Sourcing procurement activities which are in use in daily business. An analysis conducted with 24 Swiss industrial companies in two research projects (see [9, 10]) showed that from procurement perspective no full TCO approach is available in industrial practice. In some cases calculations or estimations for specific cost blocks are used (e.g. transports costs, quality costs) with strong limitations of the scope. For example the calculations are only focused on specific procurement object groups, e.g. the internal procurement from an international subsidiary. Especially long-term implications of Global Sourcing activities are often not considered in a systematic way or even calculated. For example long transport lead times caused by container shipping from Asian suppliers to the customer's reception point (e.g. warehouse in Europe) lead to a loss of flexibility and high safety stocks for the European buyer, both factors which should be seriously considered and calculated when setting up a global supply network. A critical issue from an industrial perspective regarding the use of the existing TCO concepts seems to be the high complexity and the mostly theoretical background of existing models. Most of the industrial partners accentuate the easy-to-use, adaptive and comprehensible character of a modern TCO concept in order to fulfill their daily needs and requirements (see chapter 4).

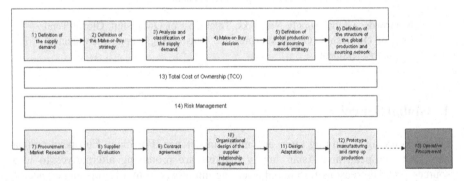

Fig. 1. Global Sourcing process and its steps (strategic procurement perspective) (adapted from [1])

2 Objectives of the TCO Concept

The objective of this paper is to describe an integral TCO concept focusing on Global Sourcing projects for the mechanical engineering industry. This concept covers amongst others relevant strategic and operative procurement processes and cost drivers in a quantitative and qualitative way and should be applicable for small- and medium-sized companies as well for mid-sized companies. The life cycle cost examination for this TCO concept is - according to complexity limitations and practical requirements - bordered to the phases from contract agreement (strategic procurement) up to goods receiving / quality control (operative procurement) at the customer's site or up to the delivery on the construction site for plant construction business (until the final customer acceptance procedure has been completed). Further aspects like for example operating costs, maintenance costs or recycling costs of the procurement object are not focus of this TCO concept – the Life Cycle Cost approach is hence limited to a procurement perspective. The described TCO concept will enable the management, the procurement and logistics specialists to conduct a holistic supplier evaluation (ex-ante) (e.g. comparing different supplier alternatives in different countries), to perform make-or-buy decisions as well as supporting the supplier development and supplier controlling (ex-post) including macroeconomic aspects. Figure 2 shows the different potential applications (and outputs) of the TCO concept.

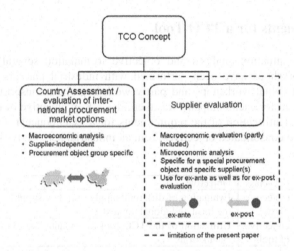

Fig. 2. TCO Concept and use of the concept in different context

Besides the supplier evaluation from a holistic perspective (ex-ante as well as ex-post) a country assessment can be performed, based on macroeconomic indicators and export statistics (see left side of figure 2). Country assessments describe the evaluation of international procurement markets for a specific procurement object group. For example it could be interesting to know which procurement markets are most promising to search for suppliers specialized on specific procurement object groups (e.g. solar equipment or printed circuit boards). The topic of the country assessment (left part of figure 2) will not be described further in this paper. A general procedure of this top-level supplier market analysis based on macroeconomic data and export statistic ratios can be found in [11].

3   Research Method

The research method used to develop the TCO concept followed the problem solving cycle of the Systems Engineering (SE) method [12]. The first phase of SE can be subdivided into situation analysis (system delimitation, strengths and weaknesses analysis, opportunities and threats analysis) and goal definition, the second phase into concept synthesis and concept analysis, and the third into evaluation, decision and implementation. Within the concept synthesis innovations are developed to address the given constraints either through creation of alternative concepts or also through deductions from the existing literature [13].

This general approach was combined with the more specific case study research method. To obtain the results, holistic multiple case studies were conducted (19 general case studies, 5 detail case studies). The detail case studies were conducted in Swiss mechanical engineering industry (three make-to-stock companies, two plant construction companies). In order to reach a broad usability of the TCO tool in the future, companies of different sizes were included in the detail case studies / analyses, e.g. two large companies and three small-to-medium sized companies.

4 Requirements for a TCO Tool

As part of the situation analysis and objective formulation several half-day and whole-time workshops have been performed with industrial partners. These workshops were individual workshops and partly workshops in a consortium group, the average time used for each company was there days. Key objective of the first workshops was the identification of the requirements for a TCO concept. Figure 3 shows an excerpt of the consolidated objectives from an industrial perspective (excerpt).

Class	Sub-class	Objective	Priority
Functionality	Objective of tool	Evaluation of different supply options / suppliers in the local and global context	Must
Functionality	Objective of tool	Utilization of the TCO tool for ex-ante and ex-post calculations	Must
Functionality	Objective of tool	Analysis of the cost structure of a supplier (RFQ)	Nice to have
Functionality	Cost elements	Structuring of the cost elements into modules (should be as independent as possible)	Must
Functionality	Cost elements	Consideration of dynamic changes of input data (e.g. currency exchange rates)	Must

Fig. 3. Example of some consolidated objectives for a TCO concept / TCO tool from an industrial perspective (excerpt)

Some of these objectives are described in the following. Generally the tool should be able to consider and evaluate different supply options / suppliers in the local and global context (e.g. comparison of an existing supplier in Europe with a new supplier in China). An important point for the TCO tool will be the inclusion of dynamic factors, e.g. the fluctuations of currency rates or transport costs. These issues can be seen as critical limits included in the TCO tool, e.g. if the exchange rate of RMB/€ reaches a certain level a specific supply situation may not be worthwhile anymore, or in the opposite sense, a supply option may be revaluated again if the currency exchanges develops in favor for the customer. A data set of macroeconomic parameters for a specific country should be accordingly provided periodically, so it is important to find a procedure to update this data set in regular time intervals (e.g. labor cost, skill base, research and developments capacity, currency rates, inflation). Specialized providers of such macroeconomic data are available, see for example [14]. One important requirement for the TCO concept / tool is the IT-support. Following the potential industrial user needs, the TCO tool should be based on standard IT tools like for example Microsoft Excel. Proprietary software tools are not requested as traceability, interdepartmental implementations (e.g. use in the procurement and logistics department), daily use as well as company-specific adaptations and changes would be complicated. Another key requirement is a top-down model for the TCO tool. It should be possible to fill in costs blocks as a whole (black box approach), but if there is a need or the request it should be possible as well to conduct a detailed calculation (opening the black box, detail data, bottom-up approach).

5 Design of the TCO Tool

According to the requirements described in chapter 4, the TCO model is designed following a top-down (black box) approach with different key modules. The key modules can be further analyzed in order to fill in base data (bottom-up approach). The key modules of the TCO tool are:

- a macroeconomic analysis module,
- a microeconomic analysis module consisting of:
  - a contract price module (purchasing price of the procurement object),
  - a strategic procurement module,
  - an operative procurement module,
  - a transport and logistics module,
  - an usage of the procurement object module,
- And a summary module.

The "macroeconomic analysis" module includes all factors and criteria relevant from a macroeconomic perspective. For the procurement decision macroeconomic criteria like oil price, tax rates, inflation, exchange rates or labor costs in a specific country can be of big importance for the customer. An oil price increase or decrease for example will have a direct influence on the transport costs, especially if the distance between the supplier location and the customer's warehouse is long. Secondary effects of an oil price increase may result in longer lead-times for container lines as container ships could reduce travel speed in order to save fuel. In most instances the data set used within this module is comparable to the country assessment module described in chapter 2. A regular update of this data set is required (e.g. every 6 months) as these macroeconomic aspects are normally not in scope of the daily business within the logistics or procurement department.

The module "contract price" (price for the procurement object based on the contract) consists of different sub-elements which are mainly well-known in industrial practice as these elements are often part of the negotiation with the supplier or during the request for quotation (RFQ) [15]. The contract price can be breached down into further elements like material costs (e.g. material weight percentage of different metals components in an alloy and their prices), production costs (e.g. costs for different production process steps like turning, milling, welding or polishing), taxes, packaging and so on. Within the TCO tool there is the option to fill in these details in order to use this information for further negotiations with the supplier or to define a contract price as a general input (e.g. contract price per procurement object = 167.80 €).

The module "strategic procurement" includes all issues related to the strategic procurement process in a holistic sense, see figure 1. These can be for example processes or costs related to the supplier audit (qualification), the supplier development (e.g. costs associated to jointly setting up a production process, know-how transfer from the customer to the supplier in order to improve the production for the required procurement objects), travel costs for integrating a specific supplier or the support for the ramp-up, contracting or specific investments.

The module "operative procurement" includes all issues related to the operative procurement process following the strategic procurement, see [16, 17]. Processes which have to be analyzed within this module are for example the order processing, order monitoring, stock receipt, product qualification and invoicing.

The module "transport / logistics" includes all issues related to the transport of the procurement object from the supplier's location to the customers reception point (e.g. to the warehouse or the construction site for the plant industry). Beside transport costs (e.g. costs for transporting a container from the supplier to the customer's reception point) legal costs, insurance costs and custom duties, certificate of inspections costs may occur. The module "transport / logistics" has a strong dependency with the macroeconomic module (e.g. oil price, taxes or custom duties). In order to limit the data input from a user's perspective, relevant data from the macroeconomic analysis module will be linked to the calculations in this module as far as faultless relationships can be established.

The module "usage of the material" includes issues related to the use of the material, but as described above operating costs, maintenance costs or recycling costs of the procurement object are not included. Especially for plant equipment manufacturers different supply options (suppliers) may require different adaptations of the material on the construction site. An example could be a module delivered from a supplier using own / different tube interfaces standards. In this case tube adaptors have to be used resulting in additional adaption costs.

The module "summary" gives an overview of the results from the modules described before. This module has a quantitative sub-module where the cost blocks are summarized. Another sub-module is qualitative, e.g. a description of risks of a specific supply option. Supply chain risks can be either gathered within each module described before (e.g. risks like earthquakes or piracy which can have an influence on the lead times) or being covered centrally in the summary module. The tool offers the flexibility to adapt this information gathering process as well as the results presentation (e.g. using a cost structure model commonly used within the company) according to needs of each individual company during the implementation process.

The TCO tool is designed in a manner which allows the single use of some modules. The modules can be considered independently, so that it is also possible to use only parts of the described model. It could be for example useful only to use the module "contract price" for the procurement department in order to analyze the cost structure of the supplier, e.g. to be used for negotiation or for discussing production process improvements with the supplier. In a similar way the module "transport / logistics" can be used in order to get detail information about the cost structure of the transport and logistics costs.

6 Conclusion and Outlook

The prototype version of the TCO model proves to be a robust general approach which can be adopted to individual company needs (e.g. through activating / turning off specific cost blocks). Existing rough estimations used to get the "total" landed costs (e.g. an addition of 20% of the contract price to cover all the additional costs) could be replaced with this integral TCO approach and results of much higher quality and reliability could be reached according to first analyses.

Even if first results are promising there is still a need to further investigate the TCO concept. Future research should focus especially on the following issues: the dependency of different cost elements and their calculation (e.g. long lead times and the extent of safety stocks) or influence of macro-economic elements to the cost elements (e.g. exact relation of the oil price and the transport costs for a specific route). Up to now we could only describe these relationships and dependencies coarsely. The TCO tool has to be further validated with more case studies (procurement objects), especially in order to analyze long-term consequences of different international supply options. Another interesting aspect will be the combination of the TCO tool with Life Cycle Assessment (LCA) methods (e.g. CO2 analysis) in order to get a holistic ecological-economical analysis of the supply options.

Acknowledgements

The authors would like to thank the Swiss Federal Innovation Promotion Agency CTI for their support through project 9864.1 PFES-ES (GlobalTCO) and the industry partners.

References

1. Alard, R., Oehmen, J., Bremen, P.: Reference Process for Global Sourcing. In: Proceedings of the 2007 IEEE IEEM, 13th IEEE International Conference on Industrial Engineering and Engineering Management, Singapore, pp. 367–371 (December 2-5, 2007)
2. Degraeve, Z., Labro, E., Roodhooft, F.: An evaluation of vendor selection models from a total cost of ownership perspective. European Journal of Operational Research 125, 34–58 (2000)
3. Ellram, L.M.: A Taxonomy of Total Cost of Ownership Models. Journal of Business Logistics 15(1), 171–191 (1994)
4. Ellram, L.M.: Total Cost of Ownership: an analysis approach for purchasing. International Journal of Physical Distribution & Logistics Management 25(8), 4–23 (1995)
5. Ellram, L.M.: Activity-Based Costing and Total Cost of Ownership: a critical linkage. Journal of Cost Management, 22–30 (winter 1995)

6. Degraeve, Z., Labro, E., Roodhooft, F.: Constructing a Total Cost of Ownership supplier selection methodology based on Activity-Based Costing and mathematical programming. Accounting and Business Research 35(1), 3–27 (2005)
7. Degraeve, Z., Roodhooft, F., Doveren, B.: The use of total cost of ownership for strategic procurement: a company-wide management information system. Journal of the Operational Research Society 56, 51–59 (2005)
8. Carr, L.P., Ittner, C.D.: Measuring the cost of ownership. Journal of Cost Management, 42–51 (fall 1992)
9. DC-SC-M: Project Design Chain – Supply Chain Management. CTI (Confederation's innovation promotion agency) project (2006-2008), http://www.dcscm.ethz.ch
10. GlobalTCO: Project Global Total Cost of Ownership. CTI (Confederation's innovation promotion agency) project (2009-2011), http://www.globaltco.ethz.ch
11. Alard, R., Paulsson, G.: Beschaffungsmarktforschung im Zeitalter der Globalisierung. Jahreshauptausgabe 2008 des Maschinenbau - Das Schweizer Industriemagazin, 44–46 (2008)
12. Haberfellner, R., Nagel, P., Becker, M.: Systems Engineering. Orell Füssli, 644 p. (2002)
13. Kaplan, R.S.: Innovation action research: Creating new management theory and practice. Journal of Management Accounting Research (10), 89–118 (1998)
14. Global-production.com: Global-production.com, Inc., business economics consultancy (2009), http://www.global-production.com
15. de Boer, L., Labro, E., Morlachi, P.: A review of methods supporting supplier selection. European Journal of Purchasing & Supply Management 7, 75–89 (2001)
16. Arnold, U.: Beschaffungsmanagement, p. 129. Schäffer-Poeschel, Stuttgart (1997)
17. Luczak, H., Eversheim, W., Rüttgers, M., Stich, V.: Industrielle Logistik, p. 181. Wissenschaftsverlag Mainz in Aachen, Aachen (2000)

Designing and Implementing a Framework for Process-Oriented Logistics-Costs Measurement in an Automotive-Supplier Group

Gregor von Cieminski, Michael Karrer, and Malte Zur

ZF Friedrichshafen AG, Ehlersstrasse 50, D-88038 Friedrichshafen
{Gregor.Cieminski,Michael.Karrer,Malte.Zur}@ZF.com

Abstract. Measurements of logistics costs are necessary for manufacturing companies to be able to evaluate the cost effects and trade-offs of logistics management decisions. This case study highlights the challenges ZF Friedrichshafen AG faced during the implementation of a process-oriented logistics-costs measurement framework. The discussion of possible solutions to these challenges leads to recommendations for research as well as industrial practice. Specifically, a greater degree of co-operation between logisticians and cost accountants seems necessary in both academia and industry in order to develop more standardized logistics-costs measurement methods.

Keywords: performance measurement, logistics costs, case study.

1 Introduction

The paper reports on an industrial case study of the design and implementation of a process-oriented logistics-costs measurement framework at ZF Friedrichshafen AG, a German automotive supplier. ZF's objective was to design and implement this framework so that it would be both, founded in theory and workable in industrial practice. The main purpose of the paper is to highlight the challenges the company faced in this process, to identify gaps in the theory and to provide companies engaged in comparable projects with practical recommendations. The paper presents basic background information about the company and the motivation behind the cost-measurement approach covered in the case study. The conceptual foundations of the approach are explained. The paper focuses on the challenges ZF faced during the implementation process and the theoretical and practical implications arising from them. The discussion of these culminates in the paper's conclusions.

2 Company and Project Background

ZF Friedrichshafen AG is a leading automotive supplier for driveline and chassis technology. In 2008, ZF's total sales amounted to € 12.5 bn and the company employed around 62,000 staff in its 125 worldwide production locations and over 40 sales and service centers. ZF encompasses 6 divisions and 5 business units

B. Vallespir and T. Alix (Eds.): APMS 2009, IFIP AICT 338, pp. 499–505, 2010.
© IFIP International Federation for Information Processing 2010

manufacturing a range of driveline and chassis components – such as transmissions, axle systems, suspension systems and steering systems – for the automotive, marine railway and aviation industries.

The company approaches its target markets as a technology leader, emphasizing the innovativeness, superior functionality and quality of its products. Increasingly, the ZF Group aims to provide its customers superior delivery performance as an integral part of its competitive strategy. The drive for improving the group's logistic performance is reflected in the 2008/2009 "Year of Logistics". This group-wide development program encompasses dedicated improvement initiatives for the ZF logistics function. In order to underline the strategic importance of the logistics function for ZF's business, it was decided to define four logistics key performance indicators (KPI's) to be reported to the executive board of the group, namely the delivery reliability of the group and of its suppliers, the inventory turnover rate and the logistics costs. Whereas for the first three KPI's standardized measurement methods and systems had already been put in place, these were missing for the logistics costs indicator [1]. Therefore ZF initiated a group-wide project to design and implement a logistics-costs measurement framework.

3 Framework Design and Implementation Approach

The project "Transparency of Logistics Costs" consists of two major phases: Firstly the design of the logistics-costs measurement framework and secondly the implementation of the framework in the various locations of the ZF Group. The work content of both phases will be briefly explained.

A team of experts from the logistics and controlling (management accounting) functions was formed in order to develop a logistics-costs measurement framework and prepare its implementation. The remit of the team was to design the framework in such a way that it would be founded in theory and workable in industrial practice. For this reason, the team decided to design a framework with a comprehensive logistics-process orientation, but also to consciously discard activity-based costing principles. The implementation of frameworks built on the latter costing method was deemed to require an excessive amount of effort.

Thus, the logistics-costs measurement framework is founded upon four main elements:

1. The ZF logistics reference process model which is based on the Supply-chain Operations Reference (SCOR) model [2]. The first hierarchical level of this model consists of the four SCOR processes Plan, Source, Make, Deliver. At the second level these processes are disaggregated into 14 so-called "sub processes" as shown in Fig. 1.a. The logistics costs are measured and reported with respect to these sub processes.
2. The ZF standardized logistics-costs components, a set of 15 aggregated types of logistics costs shown in Fig. 1.b, which complies with logistics-costs definitions provided in the relevant literature (e.g. [3]). The main function of each of the cost components is to aggregate a number of logistics costs accounts into standardized cost categories. The need to aggregate the accounts resulted from their non-standardized definition in the different locations of the ZF Group (see 3.). The

logistics costs are measured, but not officially reported, with respect to the logistics-costs components.
3. The logistics-costs accounts defined in the charts of accounts of the various divisions (locations) of the ZF Group. As stated above, these are specific to the divisions, or indeed locations, of the group.
4. "Logistically-relevant" cost centers, i.e. all cost centers that carry out logistics activities. This includes dedicated logistics cost centers as well as cost centers that carry out a limited number of logistics tasks but are not logistics cost centers as such, e.g. sourcing, production or sales cost centers.

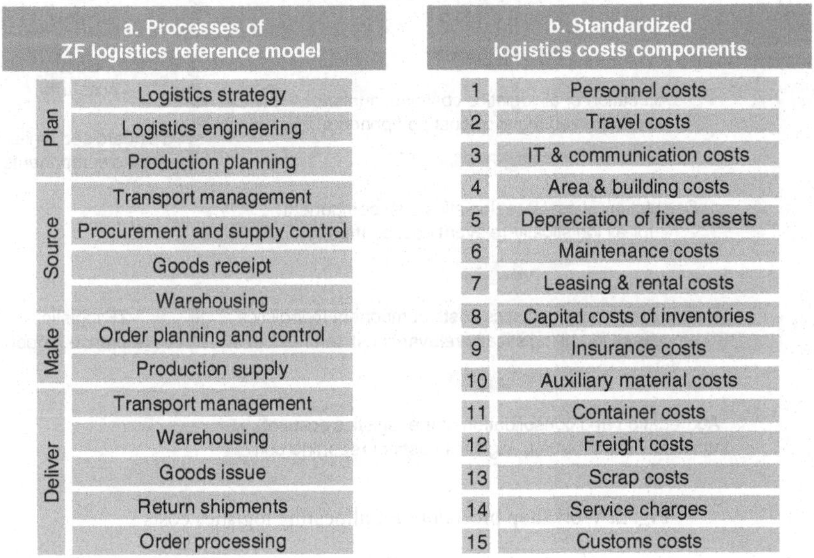

a. Processes of ZF logistics reference model		b. Standardized logistics costs components	
Plan	Logistics strategy	1	Personnel costs
Plan	Logistics engineering	2	Travel costs
Plan	Production planning	3	IT & communication costs
Source	Transport management	4	Area & building costs
Source	Procurement and supply control	5	Depreciation of fixed assets
Source	Goods receipt	6	Maintenance costs
Source	Warehousing	7	Leasing & rental costs
Make	Order planning and control	8	Capital costs of inventories
Make	Production supply	9	Insurance costs
Deliver	Transport management	10	Auxiliary material costs
Deliver	Warehousing	11	Container costs
Deliver	Goods issue	12	Freight costs
Deliver	Return shipments	13	Scrap costs
Deliver	Order processing	14	Service charges
		15	Customs costs

Fig. 1. Logistics processes and logistics-cost components as basic elements of cost-measurement framework

Within the logistics cost-measurement framework, the actual cost data calculated for the cost accounts and cost centers at the locations of the ZF Group have to be allocated to both the logistics processes and the logistics-costs components in order to be able to take the cost measurements required. For the purpose of taking initial manual measurement at the locations according to the proposed framework, a spreadsheet template was designed. This template is used as a tool for logistics-costs measurement workshops that constitute the first step of the dissemination and implementation process of the measurement framework.

The workshop procedure is shown in Fig. 2. It consists of five steps, each of which serves a specific purpose in the context of the measurement methodology. Steps 1 and 2 collect basic information from a ZF location's cost centre structure and chart of accounts. As part of step 2 the first cost allocation, namely to assign the cost accounts to the logistics cost components, is also carried out. In step 3, the costs booked into the respective accounts are accumulated in terms of the logistics-costs components so that sums for the components may be calculated for each logistically-relevant cost centre. In step 4, the sums for the logistics-costs components are further allocated to the logistics processes for these cost centers. Finally, step 5 aggregates the logistics costs of the relevant cost centers and process-based cost figures are calculated for the entire ZF location or reporting unit. Also, the logistics costs are expressed as a percentage of sales, the definition of the top-level logistics costs KPI.

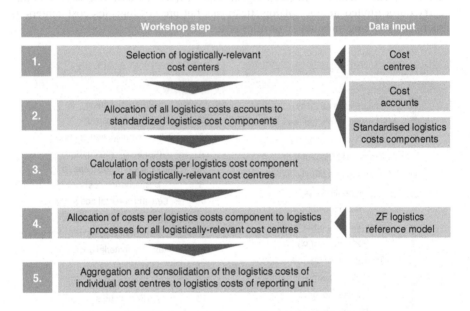

Fig. 2. Workshop procedure for allocating logistics costs

To complete the framework implementation, the results of the cost measurement workshops are transferred from the workshop spreadsheet to the so-called "logistics costs monitor", an evaluation tool that has been integrated into ZF's ERP system. Using this, the logistics-costs reports are to be produced automatically on a monthly basis.

4   Critical Evaluation of Cost Measurement Framework

The immediate benefit of the implementation of the logistics-costs measurement framework is to fulfill top management's requirement of a logistics costs KPI. ZF's aim is to measure and report around 80% of the group's logistics costs using the corporate framework by the end of 2009. This requires the implementation of the framework in around 30 of the group's major locations from different divisions and business units. Despite its "practical inaccuracies", the use of the standardized logistics-cost measurement approach enables ZF to collect cost figures for the logistics function that are comparable across the company's divisions for the first time. The cost measurements assist logistics managers in predicting the cost effects of planning and control actions as well as of logistics-process improvements. Also, the cost trade-offs across the boundaries of the logistics processes that result from pursuing a certain course of action become more readily quantifiable. In order to further enhance the utility of the logistics-costs measurement framework, the company intends to use it as a basis for a formal logistics-costs management process. By combining the measurement framework with an inter-dependency framework of the cost effects of logistics management actions, the logistics staff are provided with a clear indication of the economic viability of their management decisions.

In the design and implementation of the logistics-costs measurement framework, the authors were able to identify gaps in the theory of logistics-costs measurement. Also, the strengths and weaknesses of the ZF approach can be developed into general practical recommendations.

4.1 Implications for Academic Research

The authors' manifest objective was to develop and implement the ZF logistics-costs measurement framework in accordance with current performance measurement theory. Thus, they were able to identify apparent conceptual gaps:

1. The aggregation of collections of the logistics-costs metrics available in the literature references, such as those provided by the SCOR model [2], requires companies to develop their own metrics at higher levels of detail. In this context, more research is required for the "real" standardization of single metrics or frameworks of metrics as pointed out by von Cieminski et al. [4]. Also, judging from the cost accounting practice found in international locations of the ZF Group, there is a lack of standardization of the charts of accounts of manufacturing companies. Indeed, in a – somewhat limited – literature review, the authors were not able to identify a reference to standard charts of accounts specifically defined for the manufacturing industries.
2. Echoing findings by Bourne et al [5], only few references were identified that suggest detailed procedures for the implementation of performance measurement frameworks. Evidently, there is a need for action research projects that aim to develop such procedures which are applicable for different types of performance metrics and different types of companies.
3. As yet, there seems to be insufficient knowledge transfer between the research areas of logistics and supply chain management on the one hand and cost accounting on the other hand. The underlying principles of both areas are not readily compatible. The cost information yielded by standard cost-accounting principles, i.e. allocating costs to cost centers and cost accounts does not easily facilitate a "clear and fair" allocation of logistics costs. Conversely, process orientation is one of the overriding principles of current logistics thinking. Aspects of logistic performance as well as logistics costs are therefore normally considered with respect to logistics processes. This logistic performance measurement principle is set in contrast to the cost-centre orientation found in cost-accounting theory and practice. Thus, if the objective of a company's logistics-costs measurement system is to provide a process orientation, complicated cross-allocations between the cost-centre structure already in place and the structure of the logistics processes are required. Therefore, there is a need to define the structure of logistics cost centers in consideration of

the process view of the logistics function. Despite the abundance of publications on activity-based costing in relation to logistics, this is an aspect that is not widely covered in the literature.

4.2 Implications for Industrial Practice

On the basis of the experience of the framework implementation process, a number of general practical recommendations can be made. These relate to the design of cost-measurement frameworks as well as the implementation and use of such frameworks.

1. The ZF logistics reference model provides a relatively aggregated definition of logistics processes. Models of this type offer the advantage of being valid even for those locations of a company which are not fully structured in accordance with standardized, and detailed, process models. At the same time, process models serve to arrive at the common understanding of logistics activities that is required in order to establish standardized logistics-cost measurements across industrial groups.
2. For reasons of practicality, the logistics-costs measurement framework is implemented as a descriptive rather than prescriptive performance measurement tool. Standard definitions of the elements of the logistics-costs reports, the logistics processes and the logistics-cost components, exist. However, there is no binding definition of the mode of allocation of the cost accounts and cost centers to these standard elements that the ZF locations are obliged to use. Therefore, in the implementation process, the emphasis was placed on collecting the logistics costs as completely as possible and not necessarily as "correctly" as possible. Thus, although the approach fulfilled its purpose in terms of practical applicability, its limitations in terms of accuracy have to be consciously considered.
3. The implementation process in the different ZF locations highlighted the lack of standardization of the group's charts of accounts as well as the cost centre structures. Obviously, this has an adverse effect on the comparability of the logistics-costs reports across the ZF divisions and locations. As a consequence, two recommendations can be made:
    - Fundamentally, there is a need for standardizing the chart of accounts of the ZF Group so as to increase the comparability of the logistics-costs reports. Realistically, the standardization process requires organizational changes of such a magnitude that it would have been unrealistic in terms of effort and time-scale to combine it with the implementation of the logistics-costs measurement framework. From the particular perspective of the project, it would be of special importance to consider the requirements of the logistics function in the definition of the standard accounts. Care should be taken, to define accounts that inherently incorporate a meaningful orientation
    - The experience gained during the implementation of the framework shows that a cost-centre structure defined with regard to the logistics processes not only greatly simplifies the allocation of logistics costs. It also leads to an unambiguous allocation of costs according to the process orientation. Therefore, as much as is practically possible cost centers should be defined in such a way that they are responsible for a single logistics process
4. One of the main advantages of a process-oriented framework for logistics-costs measurement is its facility to reveal cost trade-offs across process boundaries. In

order to effectively manage logistics costs it was found to be insufficient to merely provide a transparency of the logistics costs. Additionally, staff responsible for logistics costs also have to be provided with structured action frameworks so that the right decisions may be taken on the basis of the logistics-costs measurements. For logistics and other areas of business management characterized by complex decisions contexts, this aspect can be generalized: Providing operational practitioners with performance measurements does not fully help them to take appropriate decisions. The effects of the various decision alternatives on the aspects of performance considered have to be made obvious as well.

5 Conclusions

The evaluation of a case study of the implementation of a logistics-costs measurement framework in an automotive supplier group in this paper leads to the identification of valuable future research activities in the context of logistics-cost measurement and management as well as to practical recommendations for these areas of logistics management. A general conclusion is that action research projects of performance measurement system implementations would be beneficial for improving the understanding the requirements of the implementation process itself and of the particular requirements that logistics practitioners have of performance measurement systems to help them in their day-to-day management tasks. An aspect the paper does not consider is the definition of appropriate change management approaches for the introduction of new performance measurement systems. In the opinion of the authors, this also represents an area that has to be further addressed in research and practice.

References

1. Karrer, M., Zur, M.: Logistikkostentransparenz zur Erhöhung der Supply Chain-Performance – Erfahrungen der ZF Friedrichshafen AG. In: Proceedings of Supply Chain Controlling and Performance Management Conference, Berlin (2009)
2. Supply Chain Council: Supply-Chain Operations Reference model (SCOR) Version 9.0, http://www.supply-chain.org
3. Lin, B., Collins, J., Su, R.K.: Supply chain costing: an activity-based perspective. Int. J. Physical Dist. & Logistics Mgmt. 31, 702–713 (2001)
4. Von Cieminski, G., Nyhuis, P.: Developing a Coherent Logistic Performance Measurement System for Manufacturing Companies. In: Smeds, R., et al. (eds.) Innovations in Networks: Proceedings of the IFIP WG5.7 APMS 2008 Conference. Helsinki University of Technology, Espoo (2008)
5. Bourne, M., Mills, J., Wilcox, M., Neely, A., Platts, K.: Designing, implementing and updating performance measurement systems. Int. J. Oper. Prod. Mgmt. 20, 754–771 (2000)

Analysis of Quality in Brazilian E-Commerce (B2C)

Pedro Luiz de Oliveira Costa Neto[1], José Paulo Alves Fusco[1,4],
and João Gilberto Mendes dos Reis[1,2,3]

[1] Departament of Production Engineering, Paulista University
Dr. Bacelar 1212, 04026002 São Paulo, Brasil
[2] College of Technology, Centro Estadual de Educação Tecnológica Paula Souza
Sonho Gaúcho 641, 03685000 São Paulo, Brasil
[3] Departament of Production and Logistics, Camilo Castelo Branco University
Carolina Fonseca, 584, 08230030 São Paulo, Brasil
[4] Departament of Production Engineering, São Paulo State University,
Engineer Luiz Edmundo Carrijo Coube 14-01, 17033360 São Paulo, Brasil
politeleia@uol.com.br,
jpafusco@uol.com.br,
betomendesreis@msn.com

Abstract. The business world has changed the way how people think and act on products and services. In this context, the most recent amendment of the scenarios of retail operations has been the use of technology in sales and distribution. The internet has revolutionized the way people communicate, and moreover as they purchase their goods and services. Thus, the e-commerce, specifically the relation business to customer, or simply B2C, has acted so convincingly in this change of paradigm, namely the purchases in the physical location for the virtual site. Quotes online, ease of payment, price, speed of delivery, have become real order winners of applications for companies that compete in this segment. With the focus on quality of services on e-commerce, the research examines the dimension related to the quality of services, and looks for what of these factors are winners of applications.

Keywords: Supply chain; business to customer; dimensions of quality; quality of services; order winners.

1 Introduction

The globalization process, seen in the late years, has led companies into a never ever seen or dreamt competition before, the introduction of new commercial ways, provides by information technology and communication (ITC) such, for example the advent of internet, has enabled companies with new ways to reach their clients, in this global environment, finding a great opportunity, due to growing necessity of saving time in operations. Thus, companies have started to use these technologies developed to reach their clients faster and with more practicality, which has made e-commerce possible as we know today. In this context, understanding which are consumers´ expectations is crucial to the development of the whole Supply Chain.

B. Vallespir and T. Alix (Eds.): APMS 2009, IFIP AICT 338, pp. 506–513, 2010.

To this extent, this research lies on the width analysis of quality and also how it can contribute so that the enterprise can become more competitive in the attendance of consumers´ expectations in the B2C segment keeping its procesing costs and reasonable delivery orders and also producing benefits to all stakeholders.

2 Backgrounds

2.1 Supply Chain Management

The Supply Chain (SC) can be defined as a net of independent companies or partially independent ones, which are effectively responsible for the acquisition, products and release of a certain product or service to the final costumer [1].

Analysing the general concept Supply Chain, we can amplify the idea by using the definitions of management of these processes. The Supply Chain Management (SCM) covers all the mentioned activities to the flow and merchandise transformation, from the extraction to the final consumer, as the flow of information [2]. The management of the SC is the integration of these activities through enhanced relationships in the Supply chain, having as a goal conquering sustainable competitive advantage [2].

Thus, managing effectively the SC is essential to reach sustainable competitive advantage, reduce the use of resources in the process of production and pricipally ensure the survival and profit of involved partners.

2.3 E-Business

The new information technology and communication have approached clients to enterprises and improved the access to information about accomplished transactions,

	Company	Customer
Company	**B2B** Relationship • More common. Present throughout the whole network except the last point in the supply chain **Examples of e-commerce** • EDI Networks	**B2C** Relationship • Retail Operations • Catalogues Operations and others. **Examples of e-commerce** • Web Retail Store
Customer	**C2B** Relationship • Customer "offers", the company answers **Examples of e-commerce** • Some Air Line Tickets Operators	**C2C** Relationship • Auctions Relationships, "exchange" and trading **Examples of e-commerce** • Collectors Web Sites

Fig. 1. Relationship Matrix between customer/company. Source: Adapted from [4].

which has made a real revolution. All this range of information and speed in processes have led consumers to demand only fast-delivered and reasonable-priced products whose quality fulfills or exceeds their expectations. Consumers are willing to pay for the price of a product once they believe they can get the sales value similiar or superior to their investments [3].

In this paradigm change, the e-commerce having the final consumer as a goal has become an important tool to accomplish not only internal but also foreign markets.

Nowadays the e- commerce is considered just a bone in the vast range of business known as e-business which has contributed to increase the speed of the cycles of orders and the ease of the consumers´ products purchase process. Today, we can claim that the e-business is divided into four categories, as demonstrated in Figure1. This article concentrates its focus on the second superior quadrant, in short the B2C.

2.4 Quality of Service

The highlighting of concept is a crucial element to the reaching of operations´ strategical objectives [5]. The conception of service lies on the operation mission system, in other words, the definition in which the operation systems must reach excellence [5]. The main characteristics of the service operations are the intangibility of services, the necessity of the clients´ presence or a possession of his property, the fact in general that the services are produced and consumed simultaneously. [5]

Parasuraman, Zeithaml and Berry propose ten dimensions to quality in services [6] which are summarized in Table 1.

Table 1. Dimensions of Quality of Parasuraman, Zeithaml and Berry

Dimension	Aspects
Reliability	Consistence of service and service reliability.
Sensitiveness	Promptness of employees to costumer service.
Competence	Required abilities to fulfill services.
Access	Ease of approach and contact.
Courtesy	Politeness, respect from the people in charge of contact.
Communication	Keeping clients informed by using language they are able to understand.
Credibility	It means being trusty and honest.
Security	It means being rid of danger, risk or doubt.
Comprehension	It has to do with the efforts to attend clients´neccessities.
Tangibles	Physical facilities, personnel appearance, equipment.

Rotondaro and Carvalho also present a relation of dimensions to evaluate the quality of a certain service, based upon Parasuraman, Zeithaml and Berry [7]. These dimensions include not only the ones presented by Parasuraman, Zeithaml and Berry, but also the dimensions presented in Table 2.

Table 2. Dimensions of Quality of Rotondaro and Carvalho

Dimension	Aspects
Costumer Service	Level of employees attention in contact with consumers.
Resposiveness	Willingness to help and provide fast services to customers.
Competence	Having the required ability and knowlege to accomplish provided services.
Consistency	Degree of lack of variability between specification and provided service.
Convenience	Proximity and availability at any time from delivered benefits by services.
Speed	Speed to commence and accomplish costumer service.
Flexibility	Capacity of changing the provided services to clients.

These dimensions are used as basis for a model creation to evaluate the quality of services of B2C enterprises.

3 Methodology

Two questionnaires have been elaborated for the research, base on the Table 3, created by an adaptation of Parasuranaman, Zeithaml and Barry [6], Rotondaro and Carvalho [7]. At first a questionnaire with open directed questions was sent to companies, having as a goal knowing their proceedures towards sales services, distribution and post-sale from commercialized products through sites.

In a secondary moment, the research was characterized by the data obtained from consumers, in comparison with the data obtained in the companies so that we could have an evaluation from the Quality services. The users of the Brazilian B2C replied to adapted questionnaires through "closed questions". Although the analyses of the obtained data must be done through quality manners [8]. In the present work we understand this qualification as reference to quality responses obtained through the analyses of obtained responses. This accordingly to the conception of FORZA, which claims the obtaining of individuals information or from their environment through questionnaires, interviews or other sources being exploratory, explanatory, interviews or discriptive [9].

Thus, 120 consumers have been interviewed without personal identification neccessity from purchase sites. This is explained, once in these markets clients tend to buy from various sites, accordingly to sales conditions, reliability, credibility, among other characteristics. The answers highlight five categories [10], being A (very important), B (important), C (average importance), D (fair importance) and E (irrelevant).

Table 3. Dimensions of Quality Evaluation

Dimensions	Aspects
Reliabiliy	The enterprise capacity to accomplish what has been promised.
Sensitiveness of Service	Employees capacity to attend and solve the entry sites consumers problems and solve doubts quickly.
Competence	Contact employees ability with entry site consumers.
Acess	Entry sites consumers ease to get services through telephoning.
Courtesy	Presserving clients products and being kind in the delivery.
Communication	Communicating clearly all relevant pieces of information to clients especially concerning purchasing, delivery and payment conditions.
Credibility	Companies credibility towards entry sites consumers.
Security	Security to the client ensuring his personal data are going to be preserved and also that they will not have problems concerning the purchase or payment.
Comprehension	The capacity the company has to understand and award most frequent consumers.
Tangibles	Delivery, such as vehicle and personnel appearance, expectations, besides the operational aspects of their entry sites navigation.
Speed	Time of order accompliment.
Flexibility	The capacity of allowing the client to cancel, change, return and change address as well after the order accomplishment.

4   Survey

4.1   Companies

For this survey 5 companies from the Brazilian B2C have been studied, they are now described, these answers from the applied questionnaires have enabled the demonstrated analysis in the item 5. The surveyed companies are described as mentioned below.

Enterprise 1. The first company is a subsidiary of a big department store, which has commenced its operations in the traditional retail market and later has adhered to e-commerce creating an exclusive brand in reference to its physical store, with the grownth of its business it was joined by the merge of other brands in the mentioned subsidiary. The company provides 700.00 items distributed in 30 different categories, it consists of six different stores, being 3 of varied items, such as electronics, telephonic, auto products, among others, a store that sells tickets to events, another for the selling of traveling packages and a financing one.

Enterprise 2. The second enterprise is one of the pioneers, has worked since its foundation in 1948 in the retail of food. Nowadays, the group has got 340 stores making about US$ 2,7 billions a year. It has began its operations in the eletronics business in 1995 with the launching in CD-ROM, becoming the first virtual supermarket in Brazil. Later, the group created an entry site which started having not only food products but also non- food products. In 2002 it used to offer eletronics and home appliances, besides food products. After a 30 million - dollar investment, the entry site was among the 20th most profitable companies in the group.

Enterprise 3. The third surveyed enterprise was an airline though not being a specific enterprise from the B2C, it sells its tickets through the web, having this way a client-company relationship, thus being part of the B2C. Lately it has become the third biggest airline in Brazil.

Enterprise 4. The fourth company is one of the oldest editors in Brazil, founded in 1944, it has published over 300 titles in Accounting, Economy, Business Administration, Law, Human science, Quantitive methods and Informatics located in São Paulo, it has created an entry site for the selling of its products.

Enterprise 5. The last surveyed company is the biggest producer of CD medias in Brazil, besides producing CDs and DVDs for the main music studious and record companies. Founded in 1988, for the manufacture of video-tapes, since 2005 is on the internet selling CDs and DVDs, it has gradualy increased its products portifolio in its entry site.

4.2 Customers

The final survey among clients in the B2C has been made through a non probabilistic sample, but believed as reasonably representative of the surveyed population. This has happened due to inaccessibility to all target population object- just a parto f the population is accessible, which is called demonstrated population [11]. This sample has been take adrift among accessible people to the researcher.

The users have been questioned about the importance degree of various items from each of the mentioned aspects, the aim was to get users used to about what each of these quality aspects was about.

Aiming at getting consolidated results and allow a classification, the intervieees were required to stablish from the dimensions of quality, the 3 main in the order of their preferences. Once the users have answered 36 questions. Through the application of a moderate media related to how many times each item was mentioned in first, second or third position, being applied respectively 4, 2 and 1 measures, we can then stablish the winner factors related to the quality of services B2C, shown on Table 4.

Table 4. Dimensions of Quality Responsible for Order Winner

Priority	Dimension
1st	Realibility
2nd	Security
3rd	Credibility
4th	Speed
5th	Communication

5 Analysis of Results

The B2C enterprises understand that their service reliability is crucial for their businesses and they try to optimize their services more and more. However, they tend to have little influence in the outbound logistics, outsourcing operations and trusting these outsourcing companies services, which are number one responsible in services dissatisfaction in consumers point of view.

We should notice that reliability is the main winner factor of orders after determining the price. The biggest problem of reliability delegation of outsourcing operators towards order delivery is that the bad logistics service can lead them into future order losses.

In relation to the service sensitiveness, there is no standard, varying accordingly to their activities and entry site structure in providing the service. As the sensitiveness of services, the access does not have a defined standard either, presenting great variation in the surveyed enterprises. Although, both have little impact in the winning of orders accordingly to the surveyed clients answers.

Regarding competence, these enterprises believe to be able to attend completely these requirements, which can bring about subjective self confidence, though this does not present great impact in the final consumer. Enterprises point courtesy towards their consumers necessary, though they do not control this aspect effectively in relation to the delivery carrier.

Enterprises expose information clearly on their sites, presenting their exchanging policy, price, and their products technical data, which are considered pretty relevant to their customers, who have determined communication as the fifth order winner factor. The company credibility is essential in enterprises and consumers point of view.

Consumers understand security as a key point in the process of purchasing products through e-commerce. Thus companies have been invested in security services to avoid frauds and preserve their clients personal data.

The enterprises understand their equipment and delivery services are suitable to the B2C service, despite clients are more and more demanding, look for short time delivery services, keeping prices acceptable.

Regarding flexibility, we have notice that some restrictions still exist in the segment once orders have already been accomplished-though this has not been an impacting factor such as speed, which leads to order winning.

6 Conclusions

Basing on the quality of services, we have established the quality of services in the e-commerce accordingly to Parasuraman, Zeithaml and Berry [6], Rotondaro and Carvalho [7]. Having twelve applicable quality dimensions to the B2C, we have based on a qualitative and exploratory methodology to identify which of those dimensions could be considered order winners and trace a quality profile towards these features within companies.

The results have provided us with a mapping from this market, which is in visible growth, allowing the participating enterprises to concentrate their efforts on the dimensions of their quality services which really can take them to order winning.

We do not expect this work to be conclusive about this subject, because this survey may be and will be amplified towards competitiveness and ownership, so that it can catch up with the constant changing in this segment.

Finally, the survey has aimed to explore a so far just little explored and studied segment in Production Engineering, which involves the relationship consumers versus retail service producers in the e-commerce, thus expecting to have some useful contribution to the ones interested in this subject.

References

1. Pires, S.R.I.: Gestão da Cadeia de Suprimentos: Conceitos, Estratégias, Práticas e Casos. Atlas, São Paulo (2009)
2. Handfield, R.B., Nichols, E.L.: Introduction to Supply Chain Management-Business. Prentice Hall, Upper Saddle River (1999)
3. Laudon, K.C., Laudon, J.P.: Management Information Systems: Managing the Digital Firm. Prentice Hall, Upper Saddle River (2007)
4. Slack, N., Chambers, S., Johnston, R.: Operations Management. Prentice Hall, Upper Saddle River (2007)
5. Gianese, I.G.N., Corrêa, H.L.: Administração Estratégica de Serviços. Atlas, São Paulo (1994)
6. Parasuraman, A., Zeithaml, V.A., Berry, L.L.: Delivering Service Quality: Balancing Customers Perceptions and Expectations. Free Press, New York (1990)
7. Rotondaro, R.G., Carvalho, M.M.: Qualidade em Serviços. In: Carvalho, M.M., Paladini, E.P. (eds.) Gestão da Qualidade: Teoria e Casos, pp. 331–355. Campus, São Paulo (2005)
8. Gil, A.C.: Como Elaborar Projetos de Pesquisa, 4th edn., Atlas, São Paulo (2002)
9. Forza, C.: Survey Research in Operations Management: Process Based Perspective. International Journal of Operations & Production Management 2, 152–194 (2002)
10. Alves-Mazzotti, A.J., Gwandsznajder, F.O.: Método das Ciências Naturais e Sociais: Pesquisa Quantitativa e Qualitativa. Pioneira, São Paulo (1999)
11. Costa Neto, P.L.O.: Estatística. Blucher, São Paulo (2002)

Implementing Six Sigma in Challenging Times: A Case Study

Jose Hernandez and Trevor Turner,

DMEM, University of Strathclyde, James Weir Building,
75 Montrose St, Glasgow, UK, G1 1XJ
jose.hernandez@strath.ac.uk, t.turner@strath.ac.uk

Abstract. This paper presents the findings of a two year Knowledge Transfer Partnership (KTP) project between the University of Strathclyde and a small Scottish manufacturing company. The aim of this KTP is to bring stability and continuity to the organisational processes of the business by introducing Six Sigma. The paper discusses the effects that the current economic climate has had in the business and presents the findings of a Six Sigma project implementation.

Keywords: Six Sigma, SMES, Cost of Quality (COQ), Recession.

1 Introduction

This paper presents the findings of a two year Knowledge Transfer Partnership (KTP) project between the University of Strathclyde and a small Scottish manufacturing company. KTP is a UK wide programme aimed at helping businesses become more competitive through the use of the knowledge and skills that exist within academic institutions.

This KTP project will be concluded in November of 2009 and its aim is to bring stability and continuity to the manufacturing processes of the partner company by introducing the Six Sigma approach.

Six Sigma is a recognised Quality Improvement tool aimed at reducing and controlling variation in strategically selected processes to achieve the required customer specifications.[1] The potential benefits that Six Sigma can create in terms of cost savings and improved customer satisfaction have been widely documented and proved by many organisations around the globe.[2, 3] Despite the successes from many high profile organisations the adoption of this practice by UK enterprises particularly SMEs is not widespread.

Six Sigma practitioners suggest that the introduction of Six Sigma is more challenging in SMEs in comparison to large manufacturing firms.[4] The rationale is that in SMEs employees tend to fulfil an array of functions and are therefore more likely to be distracted by external & internal business pressures. In addition, the organisational structure of some SMEs discourages the introduction of dedicated Six Sigma Black Belts to complete projects as this approach is deemed impractical and financially difficult to justify.

B. Vallespir and T. Alix (Eds.): APMS 2009, IFIP AICT 338, pp. 514–521, 2010.

As a result of the above the involvement from Senior Management to actively support and drive the introduction of Six Sigma becomes increasingly critical. This resource requirement in combination with the current economic climate has the potential of further reducing the adoption of Six Sigma by industry. Companies in their struggle to remain profitable during recession periods have taken drastic measures to reduce their internal expenditure. Regrettably in some cases this involves the disruption of fundamental quality practices as they are considered non value adding activities.[6]

Few companies have truly achieved Six Sigma levels of quality. However, in the authors' experience small process improvements have the potential to create significant benefits for a business. The introduction of Six Sigma can be a daunting experience and it will require understanding of the practice, resources and a disciplined approach from the organisation. However, the cost of not addressing quality issues properly i.e. identification and elimination of the root cause, and failing to meet the customer requirements will be far more costly in the long term.

It is important to mention that due to the sensitivity and nature of the information disclosed in this paper the company wishes to remain anonymous and will be referred to in this paper as Company B.

2   Background to the Company

Company B is a well established business that manufactures bespoke timber wood windows and doors. Over the years the company has invested in developing its brand and today the company is recognised as a provider of *bespoke high quality timber wood products*. In the past 5 years the business has developed good links with academic institutions and has participated in 2 previous KTP programs which increased the business manufacturing capacity by 25%. Even though the turnover increased considerably the profit margins were smaller than expected. The reason behind this was an increase in the business' operational costs as a result of an increase in both internal and external failures.

It is understood that the business used to capture data on defects during final inspection. However, the information gathered was not being used to remove failure modes leading to customer complaints. As a result customer complaints have increased significantly since 2007. This shows lack of understanding of the COQ model i.e. failure, appraisal and prevention. The inspection activity (appraisal) was not being used strategically to introduce process improvement actions (prevention) to reduce customer complaints and quality costs (failures).

The Company recognised that it required external support and knowledge to improve the reliability of its products and decided to embark on a third KTP project aimed at reducing the Cost of Quality (COQ). Evidence suggests that COQ can account for up to 40% of the annual Operating Cost of an organisation.[7] In the case of Company B this represents a cost of £3.2M per annum.

It was understood from the outset that change management issues would be a risk to the project. Approximately one third of employees have worked for the company for over 20 years. During that period a number of Continuous Improvement and Quality initiatives were attempted but due to external business pressures, lack of ownership and the lack of a structured implementation approach the initiatives were abandoned.

It is well known that companies that fail in their first attempt at introducing change find it increasingly difficult to reintroduce similar practices as behavioural issues and change resistance attitudes become deeply rooted.

However, it was considered advantageous that the company had previously worked on KTP projects and was therefore familiar with the conditions needed for its success.

3 Methodology

The methodology used throughout this project is Action Research. Action Research promotes action through change and follows an iterative cycle of action and reflection.[8] The change in this case is the introduction of a strategic approach to Continuous Improvement.

The researcher working on this KTP was embedded in the partner company for the duration of the project. However, he is officially a member of the academic institution. This longitudinal research approach enabled the researcher to gather consistent data from the business whilst allowing him to act exclusively in the introduction of Six Sigma into the business. Research suggests that one of the Critical Success Factors behind Six Sigma implementation is having a dedicated Black Belt to complete projects.[9]

The researcher undertaking this KTP fulfilled the function of Black Belt and was responsible for the facilitation of Six Sigma projects and training of teams in the use of reliability tools and techniques.

3.1 The Current State

The first phase of this project involved familiarising the researcher with the organisation. This enabled the researcher to discover the current state of the business. An initial examination showed that Company B interacts with its customers mainly through the sales department which is responsible for capturing product stipulations such as quantity, type, finish, etc. This allows the company to manufacture products to specification but it fails to capture the unspoken needs of the customer.

Understanding the customer requirements is one of the critical success factors for Six Sigma and therefore was a logical starting point for this project. The Company does not actively seek feedback from its customers. However, the company does capture information from clients in the form of customer complaints.

The initial examination of the organisation also highlighted fundamental flaws in the processes followed to select and undertake Continuous Improvement Projects. Not only was the selection of projects ad hoc but financial considerations such as expected benefits, resource allocation, scoping and duration were not clearly defined. As a result, on occasions projects ran for longer than expected. Some of these projects were abandoned as other projects deemed as "more important" took priority and those which were completed failed to demonstrate benefits to the business.

3.2 A Strategic Approach to Continuous Improvement

The second phase of this project involved introducing a strategic approach to project selection and problem solving. The customer complaints were analysed by means of a

Pareto diagram to illustrate how this information could be used strategically to identify areas of improvement.

Based on the findings from this analysis a number of Six Sigma Continuous Improvement projects were undertaken. The aim of these projects was to:

- Create a critical mass of individuals that would be familiar with Continuous Improvement tools and techniques and that would eventually be trained to Six Sigma Green Belt level.
- Demonstrate the importance of a strategic approach to Continuous Improvement.
- Modify attitudes and perceptions of those involved towards change.

4 The Effects of a Global Recession

In November of 2008 Company B began to witness a slowdown in its product demand as a result of the financial crisis affecting the construction & manufacturing sectors. The current situation was quite severe during the first trimester of 2009 as its product demand was reduced by 90% in comparison to previous years. This caused cashflow problems which forced the company to cut its expenditure and release a considerable number of employees. This had an impact in all on going KTP Continuous Improvement projects as resources were pulled out to fulfil other functions in the business that were perceived as more critical. During the cutback process all quality administrative salaries were terminated. As a result, all Company led Continuous Improvement initiatives and practices including quality inspection and internal audits were abandoned.

This action was necessary to allow the company to survive and continue in operation.

Despite the above the Company decided to continue with the KTP as the project had already generated benefits and was well underway. However, it was agreed that the researcher would have limited access to the resources of the Company. Unfortunately this meant that:

- All on going Continuous Improvement projects undertaken through the KTP project would be temporarily stopped.
- The already programmed but not commenced Continuous Improvement projects would have to be redefined and scoped as the researcher would have to take a more hands on approach and perform a majority of the project activities.
- The data capture would be constrained to smaller samples reducing the statistical significance of results.
- Brainstorming sessions and collaborative work would be replaced by informal conversations and shadowing.
- No more training programmes would be introduced into the business.

5 The Post-Recession Six Sigma Project

This section will present a recently commenced Six Sigma project aimed at improving the reliability of glazing beads and which commenced in April 2009.

The analysis of customer complaints previously discussed showed that *paint delaminating* is the most common failure in the company's products. The researcher shadowed the field service team during a number of customer visits aimed at dealing with delaminating failures. A close examination of failed windows highlighted that there is a relationship between poorly fitted beads and paint delaminating issues. Furthermore, it was suggested by the field service operators that poorly fitted beads have the potential to critically affect the reliability of products by causing water ingress failure.

A more in depth study of the bead manufacturing process highlighted a number of quality issues, e.g. broken beads, excess clearance and poor mitre joints. These issues are frequently identified during the final assembly process and rectified during a touch up operation after the product has been fully assembled. It is important to mention that this is a non value adding activity and as demonstrated by our customer complaints not always successful.

This highlighted the importance of identifying the true root causes behind the lack of consistency in beads and introducing a robust solution.

5.1 Data Capture

A standard definition for flawed beads was created and used to capture data on bead related failures prior to the touch up operation.

Bead quality issues were classified into 5 main failure modes. This study highlighted that 29% of our beads get damaged during the manufacturing and assembly process; 22% have poor material finish; 20% are loose or show excess clearance; 13% have poor joints; and 11% project from the sash.

Each of these failure modes had subcategories to allow for a more detailed analysis. This enabled the researcher to link the individual failures to the responsible manufacturing processes. The following Pareto diagram in Figure 1 shows the findings from this exercise.

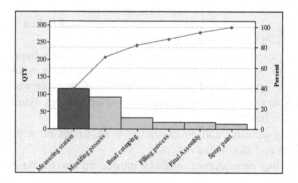

Fig. 1. Pareto of Bead Failures by Process

5.2 The Cost of Quality

Concurrently to the data capture stages the COQ for this particular failure was established. This exercise was undertaken to justify further investigation and create a cost estimate for process improvements. Members from the production and engineering team were involved in this process to achieve an accurate estimate. It was discovered that the COQ for bead failures was of approximately £68,000 per annum and is broken down as follows in Figure 2.

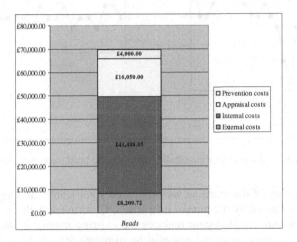

Fig. 2. Cost of Quality Model

External and internal failures represent roughly 70% of the COQ for beads and appraisal and prevention costs represent approximately 23% and 6% respectively. This is a shocking discovery if we consider that in organizations in which COQ is 40% of their running costs the breakdown is 50% for failures, 38% appraisal and 13% prevention. The current situation of the business is not healthy and it highlights the stress that the current economic situation is putting on the business.

5.3   Analysis and Solution

Due to the resource limitations previously discussed the decision was made to focus only on the most critical process affecting the reliability of beads i.e. the measuring station.

A Type 1 Gauge study was used to asses the accuracy of the measuring machine. The findings from the study highlighted that the machine was incapable of achieving repeatable measurements as significant bias from human interaction is present. As a result, beads are frequently sized incorrectly which causes dimensional fitting issues during the final assembly process such as breakages and excess clearance in beads. It was understood that the business would be against acquiring new equipment and as a result the decision was made to modify and refurbish the measuring station.

The machine was refurbished and modified during the summer shutdown to prevent interference with production. A similar repeatability analysis (See figure 3) was undertaken to observe improvements in the measuring station.

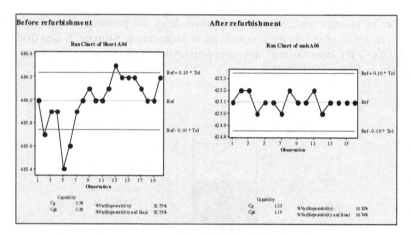

Fig. 3. Findings from repeatability study for the bead measuring station

The repeatability of the machine was improved significantly although there is still a degree of bias caused by the human interaction. Unfortunately this bias can only be eliminated if an automated system replaces the existing manual system. Regardless, the improvements made have the potential to eliminate 40% of bead related failures and consequently generate annual savings to the business of £27,200. This is without considering intangible benefits such as improved customer satisfaction and reduced manufacturing cycle times.

6 Discussion

The Action Research has revealed that Company B was unable to sustain Continuous Improvement activity during the current recession and cost cutting needed for survival of the business has led to an increase in customer complaints. This in turn has led to an increase in operating costs associated with COQ as a consequence of the reduction in resources allocated to prevention and appraisal activities. A continuation of this situation over the long term would lead to the business becoming uncompetitive as customers changed to competitor's products and high operating costs led to reduced margins. These findings confirm the difficulty that SMEs experience in allocating resources to strategic improvement programmes. Even though a structured approach was in place using a KTP programme, with a dedicated resource leading the change management process, the business imperative to cut costs to ensure survival derailed the implementation of Six Sigma.

7 Conclusion

For successful introduction of Six Sigma in Company B the cash flow of the business needs to be such that an increase in costs due to prevention and appraisal activities can be sustained over a long enough period to allow a systematic approach to Continuous Improvement to become established.

References

1. Tannock, J., Balogun, O., Hawisa, H.: A variation management system supporting six sigma. Journal of Manufacturing Technology Management 18(5), 561–575 (2007)
2. Hutchins, D.: The power of Six Sigma in practice. Measuring Business Excellence 4(2), 26–33 (2000)
3. Bendell, T.: A review and comparison of six sigma and the lean organisations. The TQM Magazine, 255–262 (2006)
4. Antony, J.: Is six sigma a management fad or fact. Assembly Automation 27(1), 17–19 (2007)
5. Raisinghani, M.S.: Six Sigma: concepts, tools and applications. Industrial Management & Data Systems 105(4), 491–505 (2005)
6. Choppin, J.: Recession or Opportunity. The TQM Magazine, 139–140 (1991)
7. Morgan, J.: The Lean Six Sigma Improvement Journey. Catalyst Consulting Limited (2006)
8. Dick, B.: Postgraduate programs using action research. The Learning Organization 9(4), 159–170 (2002)
9. Nonthaleerak, P., Hendry, L.: Exploring the six sigma phenomenon using multiple case study evidence. International Journal of Operations & Production Management 28(3), 279–303 (2008)
10. Prestwood, D., Schumann, P.: Discovering Opportunities and Threats in a Market. The Innovation Road Map (2002)

Development of Manufacture Support System Using Taguchi Methods

Ikuo Tanabe

Professor, Department of Mechanical Engineering,
Nagaoka University of Technology,
1603-1 Kamitomioka-machi, Nagaoka, Niigata, 940-2188 Japan
tanabe@mech.nagaokaut.ac.jp

Abstract. A Manufacture Support System using Taguchi Methods was developed and evaluated. This system consists of a Taguchi methods part, a CAE simulation part and a management part of productivity. The Taguchi methods part was firstly used for calculating the average and the standard deviation regarding all combinations using all parameters. The CAE part was then used for shortening the total time of evaluation. The management part of productivity was finally used to select the optimum combination of all parameters for success percentage, accuracy, manufacturing time and total cost. The spring back of warm press forming on magnesium alloy plate was investigated for evaluating this system. It is concluded from the result that (1) This method effectively predicted optimum process conditions in each priority and (2) The predicted results conformed to the results of the spring back test.

Keywords: Taguchi methods, Computer Integrated Manufacturing, CAE, Finite Element Method, Productivity, Management.

1 Introduction

Recently a developments with short-term and lower cost are strongly required for shorten products life cycle. Therefore FEM simulation is used for predicting the result of design process instead of doing experiments. On the other hand, Taguchi methods [1], [2], [3] is also used for deciding optimum process conditions. However these methods are not enough to develop a new product with high quality and accuracy.

In this study, a manufacture support system using Taguchi methods was developed and evaluated. Spring back of warm press forming on magnesium alloy plate was investigated for evaluating this system in the experiment.

2 Explanation of Manufacture Support System

Flow chart of the manufacture support system using Taguchi methods for products was shown in Fig.1. This system consists of a Taguchi methods part, a CAE simulation part and a management part of productivity.

Control and noise factors are shown in Table 1. These factors are used in the later experiment and are important factors in the Taguchi methods. Each factor has several

B. Vallespir and T. Alix (Eds.): APMS 2009, IFIP AICT 338, pp. 522–529, 2010.

levels. Control factors are equal to the design factors. Noise factors are occurred for the error of function on the product. Here, when the distribution data or many values for noise factors were used, SN ratios and sensitivity of the desired property or averages and standard deviations for all combinations of the control factors were calculated with very high accuracy. Then calculation accuracy of this system became very good. All combinations using all control factors are $4374(=6\times3^6)$ kinds for Table 1, however these combinations were compressed to 18 kinds of orthogonal table in Table 2. Influence of the nose factors was investigated regarding 2^5 times (=2: maximum and minimum vales of each noise factor, 5: number of noise factor) for each combination of the control factors. Therefore number of the CAE calculations in this case was 576times (=18 kinds$\times2^5$ times). SN ratio and Sensitivity were calculated by equations of (1) and (2).

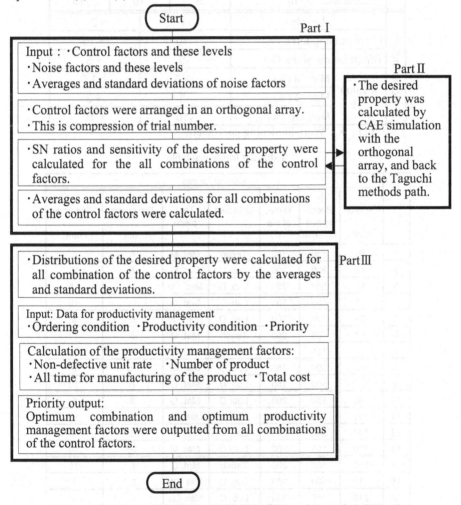

Fig. 1. Flow chart of the manufacture support system using Taguchi methods

Table 1. Control and noise factors

<table>
<tr><td rowspan="8">Control factors</td><td colspan="2">Levels</td><td>1</td><td>2</td><td>3</td><td>4</td><td>5</td><td>6</td></tr>
<tr><td colspan="2">a: Tension (MPa)</td><td>10</td><td>50</td><td>90</td><td>130</td><td>170</td><td>210</td></tr>
<tr><td colspan="2">Levels</td><td colspan="2">1</td><td colspan="2">2</td><td colspan="2">3</td></tr>
<tr><td colspan="2">b: Punch speed (mm/min)</td><td colspan="2">150</td><td colspan="2">300</td><td colspan="2">500</td></tr>
<tr><td colspan="2">c: Temperature of die (°C)</td><td colspan="2">150</td><td colspan="2">200</td><td colspan="2">250</td></tr>
<tr><td colspan="2">d: Lublicant</td><td colspan="2">Teflon</td><td colspan="2">Lub. C</td><td colspan="2">Lub. D</td></tr>
<tr><td colspan="2">e: Test piece</td><td colspan="2">Mat. M</td><td colspan="2">Mat. O</td><td colspan="2">Mat. Ob</td></tr>
<tr><td colspan="2">f : Die radious (mm)</td><td colspan="2">6</td><td colspan="2">8</td><td colspan="2">10</td></tr>
</table>

g: Clearance (mm) | 5 | 10 | 15

<table>
<tr><td rowspan="6">Noise factors</td><td colspan="2">Levels</td><td>1</td><td>2</td></tr>
<tr><td colspan="2">Blank holding force (%)</td><td>-10</td><td>+ 10</td></tr>
<tr><td colspan="2">Temperature of die (%)</td><td>-5</td><td>+ 5</td></tr>
<tr><td rowspan="3">k value ※1</td><td>Mat. M (%)</td><td>-1.5</td><td>+ 1.5</td></tr>
<tr><td>Mat. O (%)</td><td>-3</td><td>+ 3</td></tr>
<tr><td>Mat. Ob (%)</td><td>-10</td><td>+ 10</td></tr>
</table>

※1   k : Work hardening coefficient

Table 2. Orthogonal table

	a: Tension Mpa	b: Punch speed mm/min	c: Temp. of die °C	d: Lublicant	e: Test piece	f: Die radius mm	g: Clearance mm
1	10	150	150	Teflon	Mat. M	6	5
2	10	300	200	Lub. C	Mat. O	8	10
3	10	500	250	Lub. D	Mat. Ob	10	15
4	50	150	150	Lub. C	Mat. O	10	15
5	50	300	200	Lub. D	Mat. Ob	6	5
6	50	500	250	Teflon	Mat. M	8	10
7	90	150	200	Teflon	Mat. Ob	8	15
8	90	300	250	Lub. C	Mat. M	10	5
9	90	500	150	Lub. D	Mat. O	6	10
10	130	150	250	Lub. D	Mat. O	8	5
11	130	300	150	Teflon	Mat. Ob	10	10
12	130	500	200	Lub. C	Mat. M	6	15
13	170	150	200	Lub. D	Mat. M	10	10
14	170	300	250	Teflon	Mat. O	6	15
15	170	500	150	Lub. C	Mat. Ob	8	5
16	210	150	250	Lub. C	Mat. Ob	6	10
17	210	300	150	Lub. D	Mat. M	8	15
18	210	500	200	Teflon	Mat. O	10	5

$$\text{SN ratio (db)} = 10 \log (\mu^2 / \sigma^2) \qquad (1)$$

$$\text{Sensitivity (db)} = 10 \log \mu^2 \qquad (2)$$

Where μ is average of the evaluation value, and σ is standard deviation of the evaluation value in the results of CAE. The evaluation vale is the spring back in the later CAE simulation. Then most of users write the effective figure of the control factors and zealously search the combination of the control factors for little SN ratio. A product using the combination isn't influenced by noise factors.

The CAE part was then used for shortening the total time of evaluation regarding the design factors of the development. The CAE part is a sub program for the part of Taguchi methods. This simulation can calculate much behavior; those are static, dynamic and thermal behaviors, vibration, flow of a fluid, large deformation such as cutting, press forming, crash or explosion. The control factors in the Taguchi methods can directly input to the CAE simulation. With regard to the noise factors in the Taguchi methods, it also can input directly or the properties of dependence on temperature, time or boundary conditions.

At last, the average and the standard deviation regarding all combinations using all parameters are calculated by the SN ratio and Sensitivity with 18 kinds. The addition theorem in the Taguchi methods was used for calculating the results for all combinations. For example, when m is a control factor and n is the level for the factor, the SN ratio SN_{mn} and Sensitivity S_{mn} for the control factor m and the level n are calculated by the addition theorem. Moreover the SN ratio $SN_{a4 \cdot b2 \cdot c1 \cdot d3 \cdot e2 \cdot f1 \cdot g2}$ and the Sensitivity $S_{a4 \cdot b2 \cdot c1 \cdot d3 \cdot e2 \cdot f1 \cdot g2}$ for a4, b2, c1, d3, e2, f1, g2 using control factors (a, b, c, d, e, f, and g) and levels (1, 2, 3, 4, 5 and 6) were calculated by the equations (3) and (4), respectively.

$$SN_{a4 \cdot b2 \cdot c1 \cdot d3 \cdot e2 \cdot f1 \cdot g2} = SN_{a4} + SN_{b2} + SN_{c1} + SN_{d3} + SN_{e2} + SN_{f1} + SN_{g2} \\ -(7-1)SN_{ave} \qquad (3)$$

$$S_{a4 \cdot b2 \cdot c1 \cdot d3 \cdot e2 \cdot f1 \cdot g2} = S_{a4} + S_{b2} + S_{c1} + S_{d3} + S_{e2} + S_{f1} + S_{g2} \\ -(7-1)S_{ave} \qquad (4)$$

Where SN_{ave} and S_{ave} are each average of the all SN ratio and the all Sensitivity, respectively.

This method has several features; it can reduce the trial numbers in the CAE simulation, it can show the influence of the error factors and it can quickly calculate all of the results regarding all combinations of all parameters.

The management part of productivity was finally used for selecting the optimum value regarding all parameters. This part received both the average and the standard deviation for all combinations of all parameters on the Taguchi methods part, the all frequencies of occurrence are then calculated by the cumulative distribution function with the average and the standard deviation. A cumulative distribution function is shown in Fig. 2. If the tolerance η_{tol} is decided, non-defective unit rate G is calculated by the cumulative distribution function [4] such as equation (5).

$$G = f (\eta_{tol}, \mu, \sigma) \qquad (5)$$

$$N = N_{ord} / G \qquad (6)$$

$$T_m = \sum^{\text{(from 1 to final machine number)}} T_V \tag{7}$$

$$T_{all} = N \; T_m \tag{8}$$

$$C_{all} = \left[C_{mat} + C_{was} + C_{dis}(1-G) + C_{m\text{-}pri} \right] N + T_{all} \; C_m \tag{9}$$

When number N of all products is calculated by using the order entry N_{ord} and the non-defective unit rate G such as equation (6), the working time T_V for the machine tool V is calculated by each machine tool, the number of all products N, machining condition, the arrangement time and the progress of the work. The working time T_m for the product is calculated by the equation (7), total working time T_{all} is calculated by the working time T_m and number N of all products such as equation (8), and unit cost of material is C_{mat}, unit cost of consumption article is C_{was}, waste cost for inferior goods is C_{dis}, amortize cost of the used machine tools for the product is $C_{m\text{-}pri}$ and labor cost for one hour is C_m. Total production cost is calculated by the equation (9).

The order condition and the cost table are shown in Table 3. This is the data for the later evaluation on the press. Then the optimum combination of the control factor for the priority item was decided. The priority items are success percentage, accuracy, manufacturing time or total cost. At that time, the designer can select the priority in the productivity factors on the design stage.

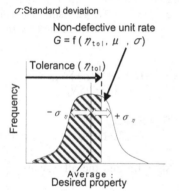

σ:Standard deviation

Non-defective unit rate

$G = f(\eta_{tol}, \mu, \sigma)$

Tolerance (η_{tol})

Fig. 2. Cumulative distribution function

Table 3. Order condition and cost table

Ordering condition	Tolerance			0.01
	Order entry (unit)			1000
	Delivery (hour)			24
Cost	Magunesium sheet	Mat.M (yen / unit)		260
		Mat.O (yen / unit)		180
		Mat.Ob (yen / unit)		180
	Lublicant	Teflon (yen / unit)		50
		Lub.D (yen / unit)		0.0531
		Lub.C (yen / unit)		0.304
	Disposal cost (yen / unit)			2.16
	Charge rate (yen / hour)			2000

3   Evaluation Using Spring Back on Press of Magnesium Alloy

CAE and an experiment using the press of magnesium alloy were performed for evaluation of this system. Experimental set-up of press with AZ31 magnesium alloy was shown in Fig.3 [5]. This evaluation was used a spring back such as Fig. 4. This value became the desired value in our system. Simulation model for the CAE was shown in Fig.5. This is a quarter model of the experimental set-up. The control factor and the noise factor in Table 1 were input data of the CAE. Data of the management for productivity was shown in Table 3. This is important data for deciding the optimum condition of the design.

Results of evaluation for this system are shown in Table 4. These results are the each priority for accuracy, total cost, manufacturing time or non-defective unit rate. The optimum combination using the control factors and its levels for each priority are also shown in Table 4. These were each best combination for the priority item. The experiment for evaluation of the calculation accuracy was performed by using the spring-back. Spring-backs in the experiment are between 0.1 and 0.5. Therefore the combinations of the control factors for 0.1 spring-back (=Best condition) for 0.5 spring back (=Worst condition) were experimented. The SN ratio and the Sensitivity for both the best and worst conditions are shown in Table 5. And gain deference between the prediction using our system and the experimental results are shown in the Table 6. The predictions using our system are equal to the results of the experiment. Therefore our system will be used for calculating the optimum conditions at the design stage.

Twice examples using this system were also shown in Table 7. These are the best condition for the cost or the time both before and after change of the test piece. When you must use the only Test piece: 3 (=Mat O_b with large dispersion of the property),

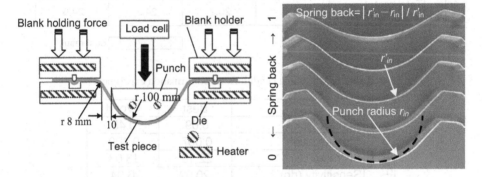

Fig. 3. Schematic view of spring-back testing mold   **Fig. 4.** Spring back

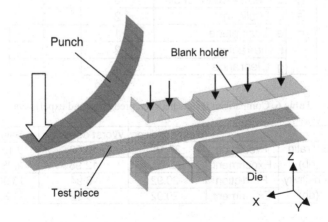

Fig. 5. Simulation model for the CAE (A quarter model)

Table 4. Result of evaluation for this system

	Priority item	Spring back η_{ave}	Total cost C_{all}	Total time T_{all}	Non defective unit rate G
Conditions	a: Tension	5	5	5	5
	b: Punch speed	2	2	3	2
	c: Temp. of die	2	2	2	2
	d: Lublication	1	3	1	1
	e: Test piece	2	2	2	2
	f: Die-radius	3	3	3	3
	g: Clearance	1	1	3	3
Results	Spring-back	0.0039	0.0091	0.0071	0.0042
	Non defective unit rate (%)	100	97	99	100
	Number of processing (unit)	1000	1029	1013	1000
	Total time (hour)	7.8	8.0	4.7	7.8
	Total cost (10000yen)	24.6	20.2	24.2	24.6

▭ Best result

Table 5. Machining conditions for confirmation experiment

			Best	Worst
Predicted results		Spring-back	0.09	0.45
		Std. deviation	0.007	0.100
		SN ratio (db)	22.18	13.03
		Sensitivity (db)	-20.92	-6.94
Conditions		a: Tension	6	2
		b: Punch speed	1	2
		c: Temperature of die	3	3
		d: Lublicant	2	1
		e: Tesit piece	1	1
		f: Die-radius	2	2
		g: Clearance	2	2

Table 6. Comparison results between prediction and experiment

		Best condition	Worst condition	Gain
SN ratio (db)	Prediction	22.18	13.03	9.15
	Experiment	22.06	12.98	9.08
Sensitivity (db)	Prediction	-20.92	-6.94	-13.98
	Experiment	-20.92	-9.12	-11.80

Table 7. Change of condition by improvement

Priority item		Total cost C_{all}		Total time T_{all}	
Improvement		Before	After	Before	After
Conditions	a: Tension	5	5	5	5
	b: Punch speed	2	2	3	2
	c: Temp. of die	2	2	2	2
	d: Lublication	3	1	1	1
	e: Test piece	3			
	f: Die-radius	3	3	3	3
	g: Clearance	1	3	3	3
Results	Spring-back	0.0145	0.0067	0.0113	0.0067
	Non defective unit rate (%)	0.02	96	36	96
	Number of processing (unit)	6087694	1045	2806	1045
	Forming time (sec/parts)	28.0	28.0	16.8	28.0
	Total time (hour)	47348.0	8.1	13.1	8.1
	Total cost (10000yen)	120548.0	25.7	67.5	25.7

you should change the conditions in Table 4. At that time, this system can swiftly calculate the optimum condition in several condition changes. Therefore this system was very useful for manufacture.

4 Conclusion

It is concluded from the result that;

(1) The manufacture support system using Taguchi methods was manufactured.
(2) The proposed method predicted optimum processing conditions effectively in each priority.
(3) The predicted results conformed to the results of the actual spring back test.

References

1. Makino, T.: Optimization of Exhaust Port using Computer Simulation. In: Proceedings of the 13th Quality Engineering Society Conference, pp. 6–9 (2005)
2. Fujikawa, S.: Optimum Parameter Design using the Taguchi methods for Finite-Element Analysis of 3D Forging Deformation. Journal of the Japan Society of Technology, for Plasticity 40(466), 1061–1065 (1999)
3. Tatebayashi, K.: Computer Aided Engineering Combined with Taguchi methods. In: Proceeding of the 2005 Annual Meeting of the Japan Society of Mechanical Engineering, vol. 8, No. 05-1, pp. 224–225 (September 2005)
4. Nagakura, S., et al.: Iwanami Physics and Chemistry Dictionary, Iwanami Shoten, p. 1234 (1988) (in Japanese)
5. Sugai, H., et al.: Prediction of Optimum Machining Condition in Press Forming Using Taguchi methods and FEM Simulation. Transactions of the JSME 72(721), 3044–3051 (2006) (in Japanese)

Integration of Requirements for Performance Indicator System Definition and Implementation Methods

Michel Ravelomanantsoa, Yves Ducq, and Bruno Vallespir

University of Bordeaux, IMS-LAPS/GRAI, UMR 5218 CNRS
351 Cours de la Libération, 33405 Talence, France
surname.name@ims-bordeaux.fr

Abstract. The topic of Performance Measurement and Management has been investigated for more than twenty five years leading to more than thirty five methods around the world, developed either by researchers or more pragmatically by practitioners, in order to define and implement indicators. Most of them are more oriented for the definition and few for the implementation. Other are simply a list of recommended PI's. Several studies have been done to compare some of these methods and to explain the reasons of PI's implementation failures. The objectives of this paper is to go deeper in detail in the comparison and in a second time to define a generic framework that could help to detect what should contain a generic method for Performance Indicator System definition and implementation and what is the knowledge that must be included in this kind of method to be more efficient.

Keywords: Performance measurement, Framework, GERAM.

1 Introduction

The topic of Performance Measurement and Management has been investigated for more than twenty five years leading to more than thirty five methods around the world, developed either by researchers or more pragmatically by practitioners, in order to define and implement indicators. Most of these methods are dedicated to the Performance Indicator (PI) definition and few of them are for the implementation. All these methods have been developed independently based on system theory, production management theory or accounting methods, according to the background of developers. Among all these methods, more or less used and well known, one can cite the famous ones or the most used or disseminated around the world as Balanced Score Card [1], the Performance Prism [2], ECOGRAI [3], IPMS [4], Medori [5] or DPMS [6].

Several studies were performed to compare methods for PMS from several points of views. For instance, [7] classifies these methods according to three categories: financial, goal centred and behavioural, concluding that each one has its own advantages to obtain a consistent PIS. In [8] seventeen definitions of what a Business Process Measurement System is, are analysed through methods available or theoretical articles. This analysis was made on the main features of a PIS, on its role in an organisation and on the process of use it. The main conclusions are that a PIS must be

B. Vallespir and T. Alix (Eds.): APMS 2009, IFIP AICT 338, pp. 530–537, 2010.
© IFIP International Federation for Information Processing 2010

multi-dimensional (financial and non-financial), must include strategic objectives, performance targets and supporting infrastructure. [9] uses systematic review to analyse few methods in order to detect why some of them are more useful to manage organisations through measure, i.e. to obtain an efficient PIS. The most important aspect is that a method for PIS must help to the definition of detailed action plans extracted from measures, to measure progress, to have a vision (a perspective as a strategic map) and to have cause and effect relationships (links between indicators).

In conclusion of these studies, it is noticeable that several recurrent points exist in each method such as a methodological approach to build the PIS, some basic concepts to define performance indicators as objectives, action means, etc. However, each of them has also some lacks in order to obtain an efficient PIS, easy to build and easy to use for decision makers. So, the conclusion is that each method, even the most famous ones, can be improved based on qualities of other ones.

So, The objective of this paper is to go further not only in the comparison of methods but also in the definition of a generic framework that could help to define what should contain a method to define and implement Performance Indicator System. The objective is not to define a new method by itself but to build the base for the future combination of methods to collect, and to manage in order to use at the best the enterprise knowledge required to build an efficient PIS.

So, in a first part, the paper will explain the difference between a method and a framework and why it is obvious to start from GERAM framework to perform this work. In a second part, a complementary analysis will be presented, highlighting what are the concepts and the components required for a method for PIS design and implementation. In a third time the paper will present GERAM framework developed by IFAP/IFIP taskforce. In a fourth time, GERAM is adapted to the domain of PIS and the base for the framework for PIS methods is presented. Then, perspectives for future works are proposed.

2   A Framework Dedicated to PIS Methods

2.1   Why and What Is a Framework

As mentioned previously, the few analyses conducted to compare PIS methods show that even if all these methods were based on theoretical or practical points of view, none are complete and none can ensure to collect the whole required knowledge to obtain an efficient PIS for a single enterprise or a supply chain. The objective of this work is to "set in order" the various existing methods. Indeed, the goal of the framework is to answer to the large diversity of objectives pursued by all PIS methodologies, and then to federate them.

A lot of experiences, led in the domain of modelling for Information Systems with Unified Modelling Language [10] or in the domain of enterprise modelling with Unified Enterprise Modelling Language[11], have shown the necessity to work at a generic level of modelling instead of the level of methods in order to obtain coherent models leading to implement efficient systems. This generic level may be constituted of meta-model (such as for UEML), frameworks, etc. This is why it was decided to develop a framework, a kind of meta-model or meta-structure which will help to define the required content of a method for PIS definition and implementation. In our point of view, a method is composed of: a set of concepts called also structural framework in [12] which must be identified in the enterprise in order to build the PIS, some formalisms to represent the PIS at work, and a structured approach, called also procedural framework in [12].

A framework is a generalised architecture composed of elements, recommended in PIS engineering and integration, and thereby sets the standard for the collection of related tools and methods. The objective is to allow any enterprise to more successfully tackle initial PIS design, implement and make it evolve during enterprise operational lifetime. This framework does not impose any particular set of tools or methods, but defines the criteria to be satisfied by any set of selected tools and methods.

The main advantage of the framework is not only to present the elements but also the links between these elements. It is clear that the final objective of this framework is also to allow, in the future, to improve each existing method and to inform the practitioners about what to add to these methods.

In order to define this kind of framework, the authors propose to follow the same approach that was used in the domain of enterprise modelling methods and which led to develop GERAM (Generalised Enterprise Reference Architecture and Methodology). GERAM was first selected for two main reasons. The first one is the genericity of the framework that can be applied for each enterprise modelling method. The second reason is the domain of enterprise modelling (EM) which is very closed to the domain of PIS in the sense that EM is the art of externalising enterprise knowledge that adds value to the enterprise (single, extended or virtual organisation). This knowledge is related to the representation of the structure, the behaviour and the organisation of the enterprise according to different points of views: functional, decisional, business, IT... This knowledge is also required to design and implement a PIS.

The interest of this approach linked to GERAM is to avoid to start from scratch when analysing the methods and to define relevant criteria for comparison being specific enough to keep only those interesting for PIS methods. The interest to work at a generic level is to have a global view on the requirements for a PIS without being polluted by a specific context or by a specific function of the enterprise which led to consider only one kind of PI or one decision level. Moreover, the modules are not defined independently in the sense that they are linked together, each one being required to go from user specifications to the implemented Performance Indicator System. For instance, concepts need an architecture to put them in coherence, the architecture need an engineering method to be implemented to define the PIS, which requires a software tool to be used and updated.

2.2 Methodology of Work

The methodology used to develop the framework is presented figure 1.

After a state of the art of existing PIS methods, as exhaustive as possible, a state of the art of existing framework was performed, and GERAM was chosen due to reasons mentioned previously. Then, the various methods were "disassembled" and compared, and commonalities were identified. These commonalities were compared with GERAM modules exposed hereafter. Then, a first version of the framework for PIS methods was elaborated.

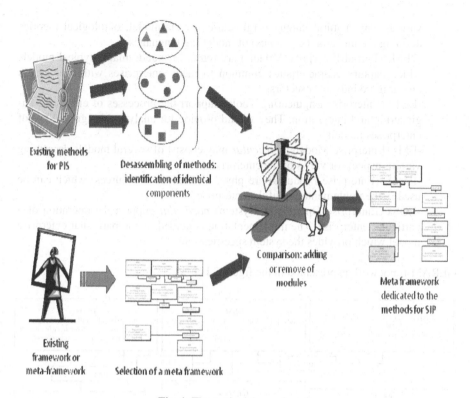

Existing methods
for PIS

Desassembling of methods:
identification of identical
components

Comparison: adding
or remove of
modules

Meta framework
dedicated to the
methods for SIP

Existing
framework or
meta-framework

Selection of a meta framework

Fig. 1. The methodology of work

3   The GERAM Framework

GERAM (Generalised Enterprise Reference Architecture and Methodology) frame-work was developed by the IFIP-IFAC Task Force on Architectures for Enterprise Integration [13]. This generalised architecture was developed from the evaluation of three existing enterprise integration architectures (CIMOSA, GRAI and PERA) and concluded that each of them had something to offer. To do so, a generalised architecture is required. It defines a tool-kit for designing and maintaining enterprises for their entire life-history and it has the potential for application to all types of enterprises. The set of components identified in GERAM is briefly described in the following:

-GERA (Generic Enterprise Reference Architecture) defines generic concepts recommended for use in enterprise engineering and integration projects. They can be categorised as: human, process and technology oriented concepts.
-EEMs (Enterprise Engineering Methodologies) describe the processes of en-terprise engineering and integration in the form of a process model or struc-tured procedure with detailed instructions.
-EMLs (Enterprise Modelling Languages) define the generic modelling con-structs adapted to the need of people creating and using enterprise models.
-GEMCs (Generic Enterprise Modelling Concepts) define and formalise the most generic concepts of enterprise modelling which may be defined in

various way: natural language (glossaries), meta-model, ontological theories defining the meaning (semantics) of modelling languages.

-PEMs (Partial Enterprise Models) are reusable, paradigmatic, typical models which capture characteristics common to many enterprises within or across one or more industrial sectors.

-EETs (Enterprise Engineering Tools) support the processes of enterprise engineering and integration. They should provide for analysis, design and use of enterprises models.

-EMs (Enterprise Models) *particular* may consist of several models describing various aspects or views of the enterprise.

-EMOs (Enterprise Modules) are physical elements (resources) which can be used in the implementation of the enterprise.

-EOSs (Enterprise Operational System) *particular* support the operation of a particular enterprise. The implementation is guided by the particular enterprise model which provides the system specifications.

GERAM framework is presented in the figure 2 below:

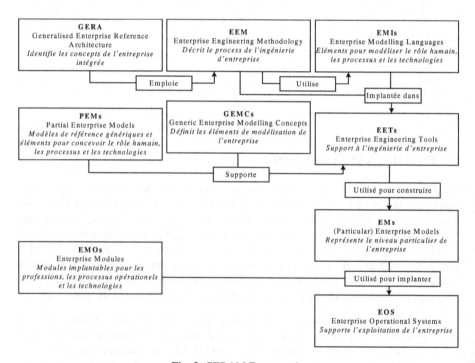

Fig. 2. GERAM Framework

GERAM can be more considered as a set of requirements than as a real practical enterprise modelling method but all the existing methods can consider GERAM to evaluate their completeness.

4 The Framework for PIS Methods

Based on the disassembling of the set of PIS methods and based on the components of GERAM, the following elements are proposed to be included. It means that, in comparison to GERAM, some components are kept because they correspond to PIS methods as for EM methods, other components were removed and then other were added to complete the framework.

GEPISA: GEneral Performance Indicator System Architecture
GEPISA is a crucial component because it aims to structure the future PIS. This contains guides and rules for designing PIS. This is closed to the structural framework as defined by [12]. GEPISA aims also to describe the way of running for the PIS. GEPISA can contain the different architecture included in the studied methods:

- architectures based on audit methods to seek areas to improve (audit led),
- architectures based on enterprise models (model led),
- architectures based on perspectives (need led).

PISEM: Performance Indicator System Engineering Method
PISEM describes the process to design and to implement PIS. It is expressed in the form of a structured procedure composed of steps as the procedural framework in [12] or the structured approach of ECOGRAI [3].

GEPISC: GEneral Performance Indicator System Concepts
GEPISC defines all required concepts to design and implemented PIS as objectives, decision variables, customer…

PPIS: Partial Performance Indicator System
PPIS concerns the use of reference PIS which enables to save time in the definition of PI's. It provides referential PIS reusable according to a specific context (bank, industry, construction …sectors). It is materialised for instance by a list of PI's as in [13]. The interest of PPIS is also to allow benchmarking as in ENAPS European Project.

PISET: Performance Indicator System Engineering Tool
PISET concerns the setting up of a technological infrastructure in order to process various aspects such as data collection, coherence, aggregation and consolidation of data, development and presentation of indicators etc…EIS, OLAP, ROLAP, datawarehouse, datamart, datamining, ETL, etc… belong to PISET. The use of decisional computing technology is essential for the implementation of PIS.

COPIS: Conceptual Performance Indicator System
COPIS consists is PI's description at the conceptual level, i.e. using description tools as specification sheets, maps… At this stage, the PIS is not concrete nor implemented.

OPIS: Operational Performance Indicator System
OPIS consists in the PIS at the operational level. In this case, the PIS is implemented and composed of customised/parameterised PISET for the particular enterprise.

It is also possible to define other modules that GERAM does not propose. For instance, based on the literature and on the practice of PIS implementation, it seems necessary to have a module dedicated to the choice and implementation of PISET. This module would aim to define the steps and tools for the parameterisation and implementation of PISET to obtain PIS at the operational level.

5 Conclusions and Perspectives

The comparison of methods led to the conclusions that each of them has advantages and points to improve, either in the definition or in the implementation of PIS. It was then necessary to determine the required elements of such methods to be efficient.

The interest of a framework is to work at a meta level of comparison and then to avoid to start from scratch when analysing the methods, to define relevant criteria for comparison but to be enough specific to keep only those interesting for PIS methods. The modules are linked together, each one being required to start from user specifications towards the implemented Performance Indicator System. In conclusion, the authors will insist on the necessity to continue the survey of existing methods to define and implement performance indicator systems and the detection of required generic modules.

References

[1]   Kaplan, R.S., Norton, D.P.: The Balanced Scorecard. Harvard Business School Press, Boston (1996)

[2]   Neely, A., Adams, C., Kennerley, M.: The performance Prism. The scorecard for measuring and managing Business Success, p. 394. Prentice Hall, Englewood Cliffs (2002)

[3]   Ducq, Y., Vallespir, B.: Definition and aggregation of a Performance Measurement System in three Aeronautical workshops using the ECOGRAI Method. International Journal of Production Planning and Control 16(2), 163–177 (2005)

[4]   Bititci, U.S., Carrie, A.S., Mcdevitt, L.: Integrated Performance Measurement System: a development guide. International Journal of Operations & Production Management 17(5-6), 522–534 (1997)

[5]   Medori, D.: The development and implementation of an integrated performance measurement framework. In: Proceedings of Performance Measurement-Theory and Practice: International Conference of European Operations Management Association, June 27-29, pp. 313–318 (1998)

[6]   Ghalayini, A.M., Noble, J.S., Crowe, T.J.: An integrated dynamic performance measurement system for improving manufacturing competitiveness. International Journal of Production Economics 48, 207–225 (1997)

[7]   Kihn, L.A.: Comparing performance measurement approaches. In: PMA Conference, Edinburgh (July 2004)

[8]   Franco, M., Maar, B., Martinez, V., Gray, D., Adams, C., Micheli, P., Bourne, M., Kennerley, M., Mason, S., Neely, A.: Towards a definition of a business performance measurement system

[9]   Franco, M., Bourne, M.: An examination of the literature relating to issues affecting how companies manage through measures. In: Proceedings of the 3rd International IFIP Workshop on Performance Measurement, Bergamo, June 19-20, 2003, PMA Conference, Edinburgh (July 2004)

[10] OMG,Object Management Group. Unified Modeling Language Specification, Version 1.5, formal/03-03-0 (2003)

[11] Supply-Chain Operations Reference-model, Overview of SCOR Version 8.0, Supply-Chain Council, Inc. (2006), http://www.supply-chain.org

[12] Berio, G.: Requirements analysis: initial core constructs and architecture, UEML Thematic Network, Contract no: IST 2001 – 34229, Work Package 3 Deliverable 3.1 (May 2003)

[13] Folan, P., Jagdev, H., Browne, J.: Providing for Inter-Organisational Performance Measurement: Challenges and Concepts. In: Proceedings of the 4th International IFIP Workshop on Performance Measurement "implementation of performance measurement systems for supply chains", Bordeaux, June 27-28 (2005)

[14] GERAM – GERAM: Generalised Enterprise Reference Architecture and Methodology, Version 1.6.1, IFIP-IFAC Task Force on Architectures for Enterprise Integration (March 1999)

Innovation Management in European Projects

Bernard Monnier[1] and Marc Zolghadri[2]

[1] Monnier Innovation Management, 40, rue Charles de Montesquieu, 92160 Antony, France
mim.innovation@ymail.com
[2] IMS – University of Bordeaux, 351, Cours de la Liberation, 33405 Talence, France
Marc.Zolghadri@ims-bordeaux.fr

Abstract. Companies need innovation to increase their market share and profit margin. Innovation is the successful product put on the market using a new idea. At the beginning of the process, it is not simple to evaluate if the novelty will be or not an innovation. It is in general after launching and selling the new product that the innovation level can be assessed. This paper addresses one main issue: "How to anticipate the innovation performance for the decision making process?". It suggests a method to measure the innovation level of a product or a service, based on MIM© (Monnier's Innovation Matrix). This tool could be used for decision making process to support marketing and corporate strategy or a collaborative research project. The added value of this method is that it allows to manage innovation projects. As far as we know, this problem has never been addressed before. The only document, which could be mentioned in this field, is the "Oslo Manual" from European Community. This document is more focused on the innovation issued by technology than services and it concerns large organisation. The MIM tool can also be used as a criterion for advanced partners selection paradigm.

Keywords: Innovation, Monnier's Innovation Matrix©, innovation process, innovation measurement.

1 Introduction

Innovation is the successful exploitation of new ideas. Creativity is the production of new ideas. Innovation is about bringing new knowledge and processes into business and/or developing new, high value-added products, processes and services. The main issue is to find a way to evaluate the level of innovation, as soon as possible in New Product Development projects.

There is no definite metrics for innovation. Measures of innovative success vary according to companies and industries. The goal of this paper is to propose a tool which can be used for measuring the innovation level of an existing product and determining the best strategy to improve its level. This point will be discussed hereafter. Authors believe that this measurement can also be used as a high-level selection driver within the advanced partners selection paradigm. The major part of the paper

B. Vallespir and T. Alix (Eds.): APMS 2009, IFIP AICT 338, pp. 538–544, 2010.
© IFIP International Federation for Information Processing 2010

will be focused on the first purpose while a short description will be provided at the end of the paper discussing this latter issue.

2 Innovation Measurement

The Monnier's Innovation Matrix© (MIM©) is a new tool aimed at measuring the level of innovation of an offer (in a general sense, a product and/or a service) or a company. The objective of this study is to suggest a new method for measuring innovation in 7 levels. These levels can be applied to most industrial companies.

The Monnier's Innovation Matrix© tool is mainly composed of a two-dimensional matrix where the "X" axis represents the market level and the "Y" axis the new idea (see Figure 1). The technical level of the products or the relevance of a new service based on this new idea will be evaluated. Several parameters are taken into consideration to assess each axis.

This matrix could be considered as a standard measure for different products or services, similar to a diagnostic framework where analysts may identify some parameters to focus on in order to improve the innovation level. This paper describes how this matrix is built and how to increase the innovation level from one situation "As Is" to another more favorable "To Be".

The performance of this measurement depends on the accuracy of information reported on the axes. The measurement methodology is based on specific **questionnaire** depending on the application domain and the company. This tool is used for evaluating innovation level of an offer as well as company's innovation capability.

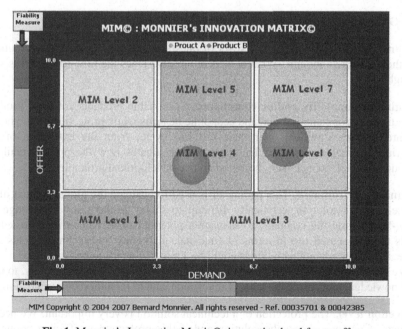

Fig. 1. Monnier's Innovation Matrix©: innovation level for an offer

3 The Assessment of Each Axis

The quality of a measure depends on the definition of the axes. The questions behind the measurement of the market are split into some parameters such as the market, the competitors, the business model defined by the organization for promoting the evaluated offer. Regarding the idea, the offer axis the parameters are: the maturity of the offer, the environment, the protection level (patents) and the respect of the main rules about sustainable development.

3.1 Market Axis: The Demand

Market. The market is evaluated in terms of volume, expected returns and growth margin. Innovation is also useful for increasing the market share, therefore the expected level of future growth has also to be considered.

The market parameter has to be modulated by the risks of this market and the reliability of the previous "quotation".

Competitors. This parameter captures the evaluation of the competitors, their number and the level of their competence. We suggest evaluating the difficulties for a new entrant to this market, as well as the level of protection against the new comers. We can also include the evaluation of a really new function or process that consists of differentiating the product from those of the competitors.

Business Model. This parameter is dedicated to the evaluation of the business model efficiency *(flexibility, ...)*.

3.2 Offer Axis

Maturity level of the offer. A first set of questions is about the technical solutions: Are they validated enough? What is their reliability? Does the time-to-market is short enough?

Sustainable capability and/or compliance. Sustainable products are those products providing environmental, social and economic benefits while protecting public health, welfare, and environment over their full life cycle, from the extraction of raw materials to final disposition. This parameter evaluates how the product could be considered in accordance with these sustainable development principles.

Technical environment. This parameter is used to evaluate the global context of the problem. Is the solution technically difficult to solve? Is there any knowledge and know-how within the company to manage a potential new problem? The risk level needs to be assessed too in terms of financial, marketing and technical fields. The respect of environmental conditions could be a risk that needs to be considered.

We also have to evaluate if there are method and tools to enhance creativity, to manage knowledge, to measure the level of innovation, and to monitor recommendations.

Protection level. The protection of a technical solution is very important. We need to evaluate if patents protect the solution and if this protection is efficient enough to avoid copyright infringement: is it easy to copy and is it easy to detect a copy of the product?

4   From Measurement to Strategy

The following stage is dedicated to decide and define a strategy. We propose a dedicated process in four steps that leads to assessment of the degree of innovation of the global supply chain:

- Situation analysis, a shared vision with partners
- Definition of a strategy for each stakeholder
- Implementation of the action plan adopted in accordance with the strategy
- Re-evaluation of the offer innovation

Analysis of the Situation

We may deduce from the MIM© referential that the best value is on the 7th level. At this level, the market is at its highest score; that means that a market has been found and the margin is more than expected. If the assessment of the current situation is not yet evaluated to the 7th level, we have to define how to reach this best value of innovation, how to move from initial position to another more favorable quadrant. All partners need to share the same vision of the current position and the expected one. In this case, the contract which is needed to join all the parties, will probably be easier to provide if everyone knows where it starts and where it will want to go, thanks to the partnering driven for innovation.

Defining a Strategy

A detailed analysis of each criterion on each axis could help to define a strategy for the move. Generally, the only movement we wish to increase is along the market axis; that means to move from the left to the right side. But sometimes, if we expect to reach a high level of market share, we also need to move up from a lower to a higher quadrant. For this reason, methods have been provided for both movements in the matrix each arrow has a cost which needs to be estimated in a strategic "action plan".

Implementation of Methods

After defining the best strategy, it is necessary to manage the implementation of the method described above.

Re-evaluation of the Modified Product/Service

During the process and obviously at the end, the product or service should be quite different from the initial one. The modification shall imply a move to a better quadrant *(see Figure 2 MIM© : a strategic tool)*. The goal of this phase is mainly to confirm that the expected position in the matrix has been reached or in the right way to reach this position at the expected time. *(otherwise, the cycle needs to be executed once more)*.

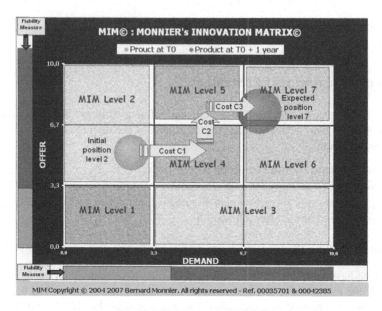

Fig. 2. MIM© : a strategic tool

5   Reliability Issues and MIM as a Selection Tool

The innovation level measurement needs to be reliable. The performance depends on the accuracy of information given for providing the innovation measurement. We need to put trust in the person or the group of people who will assess the parameters on each axis. In order to achieve it, several activities need to be carried out in order to be able to assess with a high level of confidence, all parameters of the axis. The activities are as well as in the technical field or in the marketing domain. The result of this analysis is superposed on the same graph *(see Figure 1)*. The green color indicates the level of trust *(percentage)* in the innovation measurement process.

Finally, it should be underlined that the measurement of innovation capability of the potential partners can be used a high-level selection criterion. A successful NPD project needs efficient partners. The partners capability allows to ensure projects success or on the contrary to its failure. In order to be able to use this tool for partners selection, we suggest the consideration of most probable scenarios considering major and most important potential partners. The feasibility of such project consortium is measured by auditing experts. Each scenario should show the As Is situation of the product and the effort required by the companies to reach the target, To Be. By comparing these scenarios it is then possible to choose the most relevant partners regarding the project target. In fact each scenario corresponds to a given trajectory in MIM and represents the efforts necessary to go from As Is to To Be situations by considering the partners possibilities.

6 Morgan Project: An Example of Program That Drives Our Study

Some European projects are managing innovation with MIM© methodology. As an example, the MORGaN project includes a dedicated WP for evaluating innovation. An "Innovation plan" will be provided in addition to the exploitation plan and the dissemination plan, required by all European Projects.

MORGaN project (Materials fOr Robust Gallium Nitride, www.morganproject.eu) addresses the need for a new materials basis for electronics and sensors that operate in extreme conditions, especially high temperature and high electric field. It will take advantage of the excellent physical properties of diamond and gallium nitride (GaN) based heterostructures. The association of the two materials will give rise to better materials and devices for ultimate performance in extreme environments.

This project benefits from the MIM© tool in order to manage innovation with a great number of different partners (academic institutes, SMEs, Industrial, ...) around "Open Innovation" organization. We also benefit from this use case to drive our study on supply chain management. The questionnaire is dedicated to evaluate the outcomes and the innovation capability of each partner in this project. Such information is essential for managing an innovative supply with different partners in the loop.

This method could gain to be shared by a lot of other organizations in order to improve this methodology and to share the same referential. The more it will be used, the better this tool will become. A new application in a new domain would be appreciated; this paper could be an efficient way to build more case studies.

Finally, the MIM© referential is a new process dedicated to work in "open innovation". It is dedicated to:

- Evaluate the level of innovation
- Define a strategy to improve innovation
- Decision-making process
- Action plan and continuous improvement monitoring
- Communicate

7 Conclusion

Innovation is defined as the successful development and exploitation of a new idea. It is the incentive to increase market share, higher growth rate and greater profitability. Innovation applies to new technologies, products and processes, as well as to the implementation of best practices in industry. MIM© referential could be efficient to measure innovation and to define a strategy to increase it. The action plan to improve our current position may be followed using the same tool. It could be considered as an efficient collaborative work platform, for the benefits of an open innovation project management.

The applications of innovation level measurement are not restricted to R&D or Marketing. The multiple application of the MIM© methodology is one of the reason why this framework seems to be appreciated by a lot of department within a company, for example, purchasing and supply chain management.

The following list gives some examples of different use of the MIM© methodology:

- Evaluation of innovation level for an offer (product and/or service),
- Innovation level of a supplier,
- Evaluation of the innovation capability of the main outputs of a research study,
- A strategic tool for decision making about patents,
- A tool for developing a market for a doctoral thesis,
- A framework for managing a collaborative work with multiple partners, academic, SME, industrials,

The MIM© tool could be seen as an efficient collaborative tool to be fostered in partnership contract with supplier(s). That helps to share a same view of the product or service you work on in team with innovative supplier(s). European projects are interesting cases for evaluating the process of managing a supply chain organization in order to improve innovation.

References

1. Christensen, Harper Collins edition, The Innovator's Dilemma: The Revolutionary Book That Will Change the Way You Do Business (2003)
2. Christensen, Hardcover edition, The Innovator's Solution: Creating and Sustaining Successful Growth (1997)
3. Kraljic, Harvard Business Review, pp 109-117, Purchasing must become supply management (September-October 1983)
4. Millier, Palmer, Wiley edition, Nuts, Bolts & Magnetrons: A Practical Guide for Industrial Marketers (2000)
5. Millier, Dunod, Stratégie et Marketing de l'Innovation Technologique (1997)
6. Millier, Edition d'Organisation, L'Etude des Marchés qui n'Existent pas Encore (2002)
7. Monnier, IPSERA International Conference, Archamps, France. A new tool to evaluate supplier's level of innovation (March 20-23, 2005)
8. Monnier, IPSERA International Conference, San Diego, USA. Supplier's Innovation Management by Portfolio Model (April 6-8, 2006)
9. Monnier, TRIZ Future International Conference, Florence, Italy. Application of the TRIZ method to business management activities (November 3-5, 2004)
10. Monnier, SAM International Conference, Las Vegas, USA. A New Process For Innovation Improvement (April 2-5, 2005)
11. Monnier, AMETRIZ International Conference, Puebla, Mexico. Innovation Improvement Strategy Using TRIZ (September 4-7, 2006)
12. Monnier, Josset, SAFE 2007 International Conference, Ramla Bay, Malta, Innovation Measure through the European Project SERKET (June 25-27, 2007)
13. Monnier CIGI, 8ième Congrès international de Génie Industriel, Bagnères de Bigorre, Méthode de mesure de l'Innovation (June 10-12, 2009)
14. Van Weele, Thomson edition: Purchasing and Supply Chain Management, Analysis, Planning and Practice, 3rd edn. (2002)
15. Zouggar, Zolghadri, Girard, CIGI, 8ième Congrès international de Génie Industriel, Bagnères de Bigorre, Une meilleure sélection des partenaires pour une performance optimale (June 10-12, 2009)

Understanding Process Quality in the Context of Collaborative Business Network Structures

Patrick Sitek[1], Novica Zarvić[2], Marcus Seifert[1], and Klaus-Dieter Thoben[1]

[1] BIBA Bremer Institut für Produktion und Logistik GmbH, Hochschulring 20,
28359 Bremen, Germany
{sit,sf,tho}@biba.uni-bremen.de
[2] Universität Osnabrück, Informationsmanagement und Wirtschaftsinformatik,
Katharinenstr. 3, 49069 Osnabrück, Germany
novica.zarvic@uni-osnabrueck.de

Abstract. Demanding customer requirements have led to the situation where products are realised in collaborative business networks by different cooperating companies. In an extreme case such networks exist only for one specific customer order. Such temporary and dynamic organisation forms make new demands on Quality Management (QM) approaches. Existing QM practices mostly focus on assuring and improving quality of standardised processes inside single companies or long-term relations between business partners in supply chains. This paper discusses in particular the exchange of quality-relevant information flows and processes in the different constellations of collaborative business networks that are conceivable in real life.

Keywords: Quality Management, Process Quality, Collaborative Business Network Structures, Core Competencies.

1 Introduction

Global competition, highly dynamic markets, reduced investment capability, and many other external influences exert great pressure on manufacturing companies to react, change and adapt proactively to the environment. Customers expect personalised, complex and "end-to-end" solutions made of customised products complemented by related after-sales services. A major trend is related to the fact that no individual company is able to be competitive and develop or provide alone the whole spectrum of products, as well as services around these products, to satisfy today's customer demands and needs. To face these challenges companies have to become more flexible, adaptable, in order to easily find other companies and integrate them for working in collaborative business networks. This requires not only the capability for enterprises (and SMEs in particular) to identify, model and expose their core competencies, but the capability to run their business processes in highly dynamic, short-time and often not-hierarchical business environments.

In general business networks are defined by nodes (network members) and relationships between these nodes [21]. Real life networks can be seen more or less as complex combinations of various types of bilateral relationships between those nodes.

B. Vallespir and T. Alix (Eds.): APMS 2009, IFIP AICT 338, pp. 545–552, 2010.
© IFIP International Federation for Information Processing 2010

The multitude of conceivable business network constellations makes it therefore a necessity to look in more detail at the commonalities of these constellations, in order to be able to define general valid claims with respect to the flows of quality-relevant information. The extraction of properties common to all conceivable networks contributes therefore to the body of principles relevant in QM, because it allows us to discuss process quality in the context of any conceivable cooperation form.

The paper is organised as follows: section 2 provides background information and a scientific discussion on business network forms. Section 3 discusses process quality in an inter-organisational context and brings it into relation with the previously discussed inter-organisational structures. In section 4 we discuss new directions on process quality from an inter-organisational perspective. The presented idea contributes to second the need for the further development of existing approaches to competence management in order to support QM by modeling of communication structures in business networks. Finally, section 5 concludes the paper.

2   On Collaborative Business Network Structures

2.1   Collaboration Types

Several classification approaches of inter-organisational collaboration types are conceivable. For instance, classifications of the participating business actors e.g. according to the branches they are operating in or even according to the geographical application areas can be performed. However, these examples do not consider deep enough the previously mentioned concepts by Thoben and Jagdev [21], namely nodes and edges that make up a collaboration structure.

In the field of organisation theory, Thompson [22] investigated how relationships between organisational tasks influence the structure of an organization [7] and discussed three forms of interdependencies that can arise between working units. He distinguished *sequential interdependency, pooled interdependency* and *reciprocal interdependency*. These interdependencies are building the basis for the inter-organisational system (IOS) typology that was later created by Kumar and van Dissel [9]. The nodes in their typology represent (business) systems and the edges indicate on interdependencies between the nodes. In the following we look more detailed at three IOS types, which are the value/supply chain IOS, the pooled information resource IOS, and the networked IOS. The first type, *value/supply chain IOS* supports the relationships between customers and suppliers that appear sequentially. Thus, it represents sequential interdependency between companies. This type is represented by Kumar and van Dissel as a directed graph, where the arrows between the nodes go sequence-wise from left to right. The next type, *pooled information resource IOS*, is representing an inter-organisational sharing of common IT resources. Data movement is directed towards a central entity, explaining the direction of the arrows in the graph, which in turn show the interdependence on the central node. The last type *networked IOS* "operationalises and implements reciprocal interdependencies between organizations". This type is also represented as a graph, where each node is connected with all other nodes, and the edges between the nodes have arrows in both directions.

A. Interdependency type B. IOS type	Graph-based representation	Support type and examples
A. Sequential interdependency B. Value/Supply chain IOS	 A B C D E (nodes connected in a path)	- Support of Porter's value system concept - e.g. EDI applications for IT-enabled supply chains
A. Pooled interdependency B. Pooled Information Resource IOS	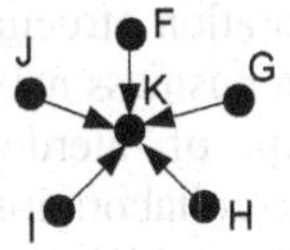 J F K G I H (star graph)	- Marketplaces, shared databases, central production points - e.g. support usage of pooled resource, support of centralized production points
A. Reciprocal interdependency B. Networked IOS	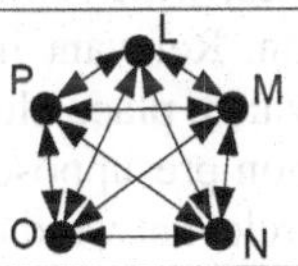 L P M O N (clique graph)	- Networks - e.g. support of n-to-n communication between all participants

Fig. 1. IOS typology (adapted from [9])

2.2 Graph-Theoretical Considerations

The three types of inter-organisational collaboration discussed in the previous subsection represent the possible collaboration structures that can appear. It is clear that we can find inter-organisational business structures that differ much from these three types, so that the question arises whether these three types suffice for explaining all the collaborative business network structures that are omnipresent in real-life. We claim that each conceivable collaborative business network structure can be decomposed into these three types, which means that each business network is either representable by one of these types or by a combination of these types. In the following we provide a graph-theoretical discussion, which proves our claim:

In Fig. 1 three IOS types are considered and represented by means of graphs. Graph-theoretically these are, in the undirected case, paths P_n, stars $K_{1,n}$ and cliques K_n. Remember that nodes and relationships between them are defining business networks as stated by Thoben and Jagdev [21]. Therefore we can consider here undirected graphs, because the pure existence of an edge suffices for representing a relationship between nodes. The reader may wonder whether the number of types discussed in this paper is not too restrictive for representing all conceivable collaboration structures. Therefore we need to consider another basic structure, which is the *bipartite graph*, where two sets of n_1, respectively n_2 nodes are considered, and edges only connect two nodes from different sets. The star $K_{1,n}$ is a special case of a bipartite graph. Now, we consider an arbitrary connected graph G, representing a collaboration structure. Suppose we have determined all cliques in G of order greater than 2. We then remove all the edges in these cliques, which gives a graph G^* without cliques of order greater than or equal to 3. G^* needs not be connected anymore. Now consider these nodes in G^* that have degree greater than 2. These are central nodes of stars. We now remove the edges of these stars to obtain a graph G^{**}. Graph G^{**} has only nodes of degree 0, 1, or 2 and therefore consists of single nodes, single edges and paths. The conclusion of this decomposition procedure is that the three types of IOS forms indeed suffice to describe any collaboration structure or communication structure in collaborative business networks respectively as will be explained in the next subsection.

2.3 Summary and Conclusions

In this section it was shown that the three discussed collaboration types suffice for representing any conceivable collaboration structure. Further, they build a suitable basis for discussing communication in business networks, because for each collaboration structure there exists another type of interdependence. For managing such an interdependence, thus for enabling the collaboration, information exchange is at least conditionally needed between the nodes, which in turn also implies the aspect of exchange of quality-relevant information. Relevant information flows, including those which affect process-quality, can only take place along the collaboration structure of a business network, because collaboration presupposes a certain degree of communication and information exchange. With relevant we mean information that contributes to the fulfillment of the end customers' requirements on the product itself. Considering only product structure logic might not suffice, because information exchange to guarantee process-quality can depend on the collaboration type.

Another asset of considering the collaborative business network structure is given by the fact that by considering the degree of a node, we can beforehand determine the number of business actors one actor will collaborate and hence communicate with, which is very helpful for developing the inter-organisational workflow as well as to determine the number of partners one company has to communicate with in a network as can be seen from Table 1.

Table 1. Bilateral vs. multilateral relations in collaborative business network structures

	Sequential					Pooled						Reciprocal				
	A	B	C	D	E	F	G	H	I	J	K	L	M	N	O	P
Bilateral	X				X	X	X	X	X	X						
Multilateral		X	X	X							X	X	X	X	X	X

In the sequential collaboration type only the first and last network members are in bilateral relation, which means that they communicate with exactly one other member, whereas all other nodes are in multilateral relation and are communicating with two other network members. In the pooled collaboration type all outer nodes are in bilateral relation to the central node, which has on the other side multilateral relation to all outer nodes. Lastly, the reciprocal collaboration type is characterized by the fact that all member nodes are standing in multilateral relation, indicating that the number of communication channels for each network member is $n-1$. Having this knowledge about communication channels enables us also to reason about the flows of quality-relevant information in a structured way.

3 Process Quality in a Networked Business Context

Robinson and Malhotra's [15] intensive literature study published in 2005 of leading journals from the field of Production and Operations Management uncovered that only few studies examine the topics of QM and collaborative enterprise networks in combination. Their study indicates the main finding that product quality is not the only aspect which leads to quality in networks, but the process quality. Therefore a smooth and synchronised linkage between processes (process integration) is critical to an efficient and operative network [16]. Already the movement in long-term networks, like supply chains, embraces process quality management initiatives. The shift from product to process orientation to achieving quality and ultimately customer satisfaction was therefore the premise of the ISO 9001 standard as revised in the year 2000 [6]. Processes in networks can be aligned to different classified collaboration levels. Following [5] there are four different levels:

(1) Level of individual network actors in a company (intra-organisational viewpoint; relations between single persons in different departments)
(2) Level of single domains in a company (intra-organisational viewpoint; relations between departments within an organisation)
(3) Level of inter-organisational relations between companies (inter-organisational viewpoint; relations between network members)
(4) Level of institutional contexts (inter-organisational viewpoint; relations between networks)

The definition of quality in this paper follows the guidelines of the Quality Management DIN EN ISO 9001:2000 fundamentals and vocabulary [6]. Thereafter, requirements to a final outcome (e.g. product, service) are communicated from the customer towards an organisation. These requirements are transferred as information into process instructions, which present the way to execute organisational processes to guarantee quality [11]. From the inter-organisational perspective (level 3+4) contributions of each actor might have an impact on the outputs of another actor in the collaborative business networks. This is also explained by the interdependencies discussed in section 2. Such an impact would also have consequences for the internal process instructions of an actor and thus the need to adapt and to diverge from the actor's standard processes. In such a case today's QM would fail due to the lack of information to adapt internal processes (level 1+2) resulting from dependencies caused by the specific constellation of actors (level 3+4) [19].

The challenge is to exchange right information with right content between right actors. Therefore an effective communication structure is indispensable between the actors on the inter-organisational level. Such a communication structure is to understand as a guideline in order to identify and coordinate the information exchange between actors. The aim should be to avoid misunderstandings and a lack of information which could affect process descriptions in a negative way. Such a coordination of information via communication structures cannot be specified in collaborative business networks in general, because the relations between actors and the issues of controlling actors also cannot be generalised and pre-defined as they are situation and case dependent.

Today's business networks manage their communication structures by using product structure logic as an indicator for the inter-organisational exchange of information. This is due to the fact that the production function provided by an actor drives the partnership and the acting in the collaborative business networks. As discussed in section 2, unfortunately a product structure logic that is following a sequential interdependency (see Fig.1) is not sufficient to represent a communication structure in business networks. While using a product structure as communication logic, business networks run the risk not to identify all dependencies between their actors and thus not to exchange all information needed between the actors (Fig. 2).

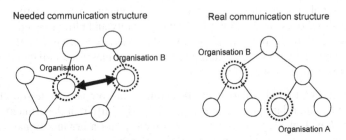

Fig. 2. Needed vs. real communication structure

Product structure logic (e.g. Bill of Material) can only reveal dependencies on the product level, not dependencies caused by the specific constellation of actors in a business network. This is due to the fact that actors contribute not only with a product, but with their core competences. As a matter of fact, for each actor's contribution these inter-organisational dependencies might have an unforeseen impact on defining and communicating the right information to other actors. Consequently they are very critical to quality aspects in satisfying the customer requirements [13].

4   Linked Competences as Model to Define Communication Structures

Core competence is a significant factor that influences the management and design of an enterprise structure [1]. Prahalad and Hamel [14] introduced the concept of core competences. They define a core competence as "an area of specialised expertise that is the result of harmonising complex streams of technology and work activity". Competence is the main concept for the definition of the competitiveness of a company [12], especially on entering environments like collaborative business networks. Molina and Bremer [12] define the constituent information elements of a competence. The information entities that describe a competence are [4]:

> • *Product/ Service:* core product/service of a company, which are attractive from the perspective of the customer and the market, and which could make a substantial contribution to the business network
> • *Processes (Business Processes):* All the core processes that are needed to offer the company's product/service to the business network
> • *Skills (Technology):* Theoretical and practical knowledge, skills and abilities that are used to develop the product/service

Each actor's unique combination of these entities constitutes its identity as competence. Completed by the business opportunity driven "task" as a part of the information entity of a competence, the competence provides a defined set of data specific to a selected consortium in a business network. Thus, the competence defines the actor's specific role in the network and unique need for information.

In business networks competences are already used to set up actors' profiles and to measure their performance prospectively [17] in order to search for and to select the right actors for a specific business opportunity [18, 4, 17]. But they are not regarded in terms of modeling communication structure. To face the challenge to model communication structures in business networks, the idea is not to follow the product structure logic but the structure of linked competences in a business network. It is well known, by linking competences of actors in business networks, that a temporary value chain will be created [2, 10]. The logic of linking competences follows the given task dependence that may be seen as the concept of division of work [20]. In a network it is not the division of work between workers but between actors which are specialised units connected in a global network. Actors' processes are ideally allocated to where they are carried out in the most effective way and contributing value to the customer's final product in an integrated global production system [8]. Actors in business networks link, change and exchange resources via processes with other actors. As a result of the task dependence between actors the information to be exchanged by transactions of one actor might affect processes and so the competence of the next actor in the value chain.

5 Summary and Conclusions

Inter-organisational relations and dependences have a much higher and yet rather unknown influence on the quality delivered by business networks to the final customer. A deeper analysis of the dependences on actor's competences in business networks might be a comprehensive approach to guarantee process quality on inter-organisational level. The main goal is to identify, out of these dependences, information that might affects processes between actors in a business network. Additional information exchanged by the help of an inter-organisational communication structure can be used as input information to adapt process instructions on intra-organisational level. Existing QM approaches would then make sure that the output contributed from each actor is conforming to the specifications of the overall business network outcome.

The analysis of dependences between competences deserves further study. The main goal at the end is to provide smart guidelines to model quickly and easily a communication structure based on competences for a specific business network from an inter-organisational perspective. As in any other scientific discipline, network organisations require the development of models to better understand the area [3]. Modelled inter-organisational communication structures could help to guarantee a successful distribution of customer's requirements through the entire value chain of a business network and thus contribute to process quality.

References

1. Binder, M., Clegg, B.T.: Enterprise management: a new frontier for organizations. International Journal of Production Economics 106(2), 406–430 (2007)
2. Camarinha-Matos, L.M., Afsarmanesh, H.: A framework for virtual organization creation in a breeding Environment. Annual Reviews in Control 31(1), 119–135 (2007)

3. Camarinha-Matos, L.M., Afsarmanesh, H.: A comprehensive modeling framework for collaborative networked organisaztions. J. for Intellect. Manufact. 18, 529–542 (2007)
4. Ermilova, E., Afsarmanesh, H.: Competency and Profiling Management in Virtual Organization Breeding Environments. In: Camarinha-Matos, L.M., Afsarmanesh, H., Ollus, M. (eds.) Network-Centric Collaboration and Supporting Frameworks. IFIP, pp. 131–142. Springer, New York (2006)
5. Gilbert, D.U.: Vertrauen in strategischen Unternehmensnetzwerken – ein strukturaktionstheoretischer Ansatz. DUV, Wiesbaden (2003)
6. ISO 9001:2000: Quality management systems - Requirements ICS: 03.120.10 (2000)
7. Jones, G.R., Bouncken, R.B.: Organisation, Theorie, Design und Wandel, 5th edn. Pearson Studium Verlag (2008)
8. Karlsson, C.: The development of industrial networks: challenges to operations management in an extraprise. Int. J. of Operat. & Production Management. 23(1), 44–61 (2003)
9. Kumar, K., van Dissel, H.: Sustainable Collaboration: Managing Conflict and Cooperation in Interorganizational Systems. MIS Quarterly 20(3), 279–300 (1996)
10. Martinez, M.T., Fouletier, P., Park, K.H., Favrel, J.: Virtual enterprise - organisation, evolution and Control. Int. J. of Product. Econom. 74(1-3), 225–238 (2001)
11. Masing, J.: Handbuch Qualität: Grundlagen und Elemente des Qualitätsmanagement: Systeme-Perspektiven. Carl Hanser Verlag, München (2007)
12. Molina, A.G., Bremer, C.F.: Information model to represent the core competences of virtual industry clusters. Technical Note (1997)
13. Petridis, K.D.: Qualität in der Informationsgesellschaft – Die Rolle der Qualität in virtuellen Unternehmen und E-Commerce-Strukturen. QZ – Qualität und Zuverlässigkeit (2001)
14. Prahalad, C.K., Hamel, G.: The core competence of the corporation. Harvard Business Review 68(3), 79–91 (1990)
15. Robinson, C.J., Malhotra, M.K.: Defining the concept of supply chain quality management and its relevance to academic and industrial practice. Int. J. Prod. Econ. 96, 315–337 (2005)
16. Romano, P., Vinelli, A.: Quality management in a supply chain perspective – Strategic and operative choices in a textile-apparel network. Int. J. Operations & Production Management 21(4), 446–460 (2001)
17. Seifert, M.: Collaboration Formation in Virtual Organisations by applying prospective Performance Measurement, Ph.D. Thesis, University of Bremen (2009)
18. Sitek, P., Graser, F., Seifert, M.: Partner profiling to support the initiation of collaborative networks. In: Pawar, K.S., Thoben, K.-D., Pallot, M. (eds.) Proc. 13th International Conference on Concurrent Enterprising of Concurrent Innovation: an emerging paradigm for Collaboration & Competitiveness in the extended enterprise, Sophia-Antipolis, pp. 213–220 (2007)
19. Sitek, P., Seifert, M., Thoben, K.-D.: On inter-organisational effects on the quality of products in collaborative networked enterprises. In: Smeds, R. (ed.) Innovations in Networks, Proc. of APMS 2008, Helsinki University of Technology, Espoo, pp. 517–528 (2008)
20. Taylor, F.W.: Principles of Scientific Management. Scientific Management - Reprint (1947)
21. Thoben, K.-D., Jagdev, H.S.: Typological Issues in Enterprise Networks. J. Production Planning and Control 12(5), 421–436 (2001)
22. Thompson, J.D.: Organizations in Action. McGraw Hill, New York (1967)

Part VI

Service

The Concept of Modularisation of Industrial Services

Fabrice Seite, Oliver Schneider, and Andreas Nobs

Center for Enterprise Sciences (BWI), ETH Zurich,
8092 Zurich, Switzerland
fseite@ethz.ch,
oschneider@ethz.ch,
anobs@ethz.ch

Abstract. The paper summarises findings from an action research project on modularisation of industrial services. Based on literature about modularisation of physical goods and literature on modularisation of services, several research gaps are highlighted and appropriate approaches discussed. Module drivers addressing modularisation benefits are transferred to services. Interdependencies among service elements are presented. Research gaps on design opportunities of modular service products are addressed and possible analogies from modularisation of physical goods are introduced.

Keywords: industrial service, service modularisation, modularity, service engineering.

1 Introduction

Industrial service is an important field of business for many industrial companies, traditionally manufacturing and selling physical goods. Services benefit their customer with added value and in return increase their turnover and profitability [1].

Customers of industrial services are themselves companies often active in different businesses or on regionally different markets. Due to the variation of their business conditions their requirements regarding services (availability, intervention times, service levels) may vary.

Spath et al. [2] emphasize the need to orientate service offerings strictly towards customer requirements. In a research project with industrial partners the interest in customizing services was found. Industrial partners saw turnover potential or possible cost benefits in offering services with for instance longer or shorter lead times. A study on logistics services by Mentzer et al. [3] shows similar results. As a result of the study it is found, that different customer segments emphasise different aspects of a logistics service. Consequently, the authors suggest logistics services to be customized to cater to customer segment desires.

Contemplating the developing need to adapt service to customer specific requirements, parallels to physical goods are imposed. An widely applied and successful concept in industry is *modularisation*. It can be seen as the best way to provide variety demanded by customers [4]. Modularisation also enables standardisation and hence the realisation of economies of scale [5]. For this reason transferring the concept of modularisation to industrial services seems to be a promising approach to cope with the current need for efficient service customisation.

B. Vallespir and T. Alix (Eds.): APMS 2009, IFIP AICT 338, pp. 555–562, 2010.
© IFIP International Federation for Information Processing 2010

1.1 Background and Objective of This Paper

The transfer of the concept of modularisation raises different challenges arising from the difference between physical products and services. In literature distinct characteristics of services compared to physical products such as intangibility, inseparability and simultaneity are being discussed. The findings address challenges in transferring modularisation concepts from goods to services due to these characteristics.

While there are certain differences between goods and services, there are also many aspects they have in common [6]. Due to the parallels, the concept of modularisation may be transferrable with adaptations to industrial services. The paper will highlight aspects of modularisation that would be of benefit to transfer to services and point out promising approaches.

Literature on modularisation of services can be found already. This paper will argue that some special requirements of services remain unaddressed leaving important gaps. Hence, there is inconsistency especially when compared to concepts from physical goods industry. In order to achieve practical applicability in terms of modular services offered to customers, further research needs to be conducted.

In summary, the objective of this paper is to highlight major gaps in the concept of modularisation of services and point out promising approaches to filling these gaps.

1.2 Methodology

The paper gives insight into a research project carried out with several industrial companies active in investment goods industry. The commercial goal of the project is to allow the participating companies to establish service variants in order to enrich their service portfolio. Different workpackages address the practical needs of the companies, from the identification of useful service variants to the estimation of cost and risk for introducing a service variant.

The presented research is based on the principles of action research [11], [12]. Ideas, approaches and concepts are developed through cycling through literature and desk research, interviews with companies, company specific consultancy and joint workshops with different companies. Through presentation of preliminary findings, industrial partners are confronted with the ideas, validate the correctness and applicability and give new stimuli for refinement of the findings.

Following the collaboration with different companies the relevance beyond the special need of one industrial project partner was identified. Thus, the characteristics and requirements of action research [13], [14] were considered.

1.3 Basic Definitions

Authors of literature on modularisation do not provide or use consistence terms and definitions. Especially concerning services, terminology needs clarification. For this reason, the main terms are introduced and defined briefly, forming a basis for further thoughts.

Modularisation is the action of decomposing a product into its elements, analysing interdependencies between the elements and integrating them into modules in order to reduce complexity [7]. Modularity allows changes within one module without requiring changes on other modules. A service can be decomposed into service elements on the basis of the service process.

Elements are the units of which a product is made or assembled. A service element comprises a service process element, required resources for the process and leads to a partial result of the overall service product.

There can be *interdependencies* between elements of a product, meaning that either an element influences another one or in turn it is being influenced itself [7]. Interdependencies exist, when a change on one aspect of an element requires a change on another element of the product. The interdependencies between elements can be different in strength. This definition of interdependence is applicable to services as well, but leads to the main challenges in service modularisation as highlighted in the findings.

Modules integrate elements with strong interdependencies among each other. Elements of different modules are meant to have little interdependencies, which gives modules a high degree of independence among each other facilitating exchangeability. A service module can integrate different service elements.

Interfaces between modules are needed in order to enable a coaction of different modules within the product. Often these interfaces are related to the interdependencies of the elements integrated into a module. For services, interfaces are usually related to the service process, where the output of one service process needs to be a compatible input for the succeeding service process.

The *product architecture* is the scheme by which the functions of a product are allocated to physical components, i.e. elements and modules [5]. It can be modular or integral. In practice, modularity in product architecture can be more or less extensive. Service architecture in industrial services is most likely modular to a certain degree, as processes describing a service are always a decomposition of required actions into parts.

A *service product* can be described through a three level model [8]. The top level is the *service result*, i.e. the result of a service operation visible to the customer. It can be specified through performance metrics (see table 1). The second level offers a perspective on the *processes* enabling the service result. The third level of the model addresses the required *resources* for performing the processes leading to the final result. Barney [9] identifies human resources, physical resources and information as three categories of resources.

Table 1. Attributes and possible performance indicators of service result

Variable Attributes of a Service Result (Performance Indicators)		
Time	**Content**	**Price**
• Reaction time	• Horizontal range	• Level of price
• Service execution time	• Vertical range	• Mode of charge
• Availability time	• Quality	

A *service variant* is a service product derived from a standard service product. Both service products offer a very similar service result, but differ in a certain aspect of their performance characteristics. This difference can be specified through one or more performance metric on the service result level [10].

Through modularisation the change on only one module of the standard service product creates a service variant. Only a small part of the service would have to be redesigned allowing economies of scale for all carry-over modules. Figure 1 shows two service variants offering different service levels perceivable by the customer on the result level.

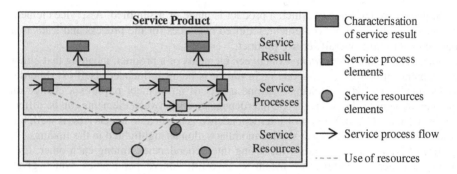

Fig. 1. Service Variants in the Service Model

2 Literature on Service Modularisation

When screening literature on service modularisation it can be found, that a few German authors have addressed the topic without tempting to offer a comprehensive transfer of the concept of modularity to industrial services.

Burr [15] discusses the opportunities and threats of modularisation of industrial services. The evaluation is founded on the resource-based view of the firm. After a short overview on the concept of modular service architecture, the effect of exploitation and exploration of resources through modularisation of services is analysed.

Hermsen [16] develops a construction kit for customized configurations of product related services based on existing service products with a high variety of service processes. His approach bases on modular service objects, i.e. service processes, which are modelled in a UML (unified modelling language) related form (meta-model). A predefined construction kit, containing all service processes currently being carried out in the company is compiled to a digital landscape of all service processes.

Corsten [17] points out that from a coordination point of view there are other interdependencies apart from the process output-input interdependence. These are evaluated qualitatively in a design structure matrix (DSM). Mathematical algorithms are used to reorder the process elements aiming at modules to be performed by one organisational unit.

Bohmann et al. [18] discuss modular service architectures on a theoretical basis and give a practical example from IT industry. After highlighting the relevance of modularisation for services the principles of modularisations are presented generically with illustrating examples. Additionally modularisation is put in relation to service engineering, supporting the development of innovative service products.

All authors contribute valuable aspects to transferring modularity to services. Nevertheless, important aspects related to the key characteristics of services remain unaddressed, leaving gaps for further research as the findings show.

3 Findings

In the findings, insights and thoughts from the research project not covered by existing literature are summarized. The findings are structured into three categories, raising challenging questions each and relating to concepts from physical goods industry that may be transferred and used to approach the questions.

3.1 Reasons for Modularisation

Ulrich [5] states that modularisation of products is not free of cost and will not necessarily result in economical benefits for a company. Therefore a clear objective related to economical benefits needs to be defined. Although Burr [15] discusses the benefits of service modularisation from a resource point of view, possible objectives or benefits remain unnamed.

This paper emphasizes the benefit of offering service variants based on a modular service architecture due to the character of the research project with industrial partners. However, other objectives may exist. In modularisation of physical goods various *module drivers* (module indicators) are named each emphasising a different reason why an element of a product should be integrated into a module [19] [20] [21] [22] [23]. Table 2 shows an overview of the module drivers in physical goods industry and possible analogue reasons for modularising industrial services.

Table 2. Module drivers for physical goods and according analogies for industrial services

Module driver for physical goods	Analogy for industrial services
• Functional interdependence	• Are functional interdependencies facilitated?
• Isolation of risk	• Can service elements with high risk of failure be isolated?
• Assembly requirements	• Are similar resources required in order to perform service?
• Sourcing capabilities	• Are capabilities of different organisational units considered?
• Standardisation potential	• Are service elements carried out often in a standardized way?
• Concentration of change	• Will service elements be replaced in the future?
• Concentration of variability	• Can the exchange of service elements create a variant?
• Geometrical independence	• --
• Facilitate maintenance	• Are service elements likely to fail concentrated for easy recovery?
• Input-Output relations	• Do service elements input-output interdependencies exist?
• Testing	• --
• Recycling	• --

3.2 Analysis of Interdependencies

Interdependencies are usually assessed through the different module drivers. Thinking of industrial services from the model perspective of Meffert & Bruhn [8], the interdependencies between service elements show a different complexity compared to physical goods. Figure 3 shows the interdependencies one service element can have to another one, affecting the way elements are bundled into modules and the way a change on one service element or module may affect the rest of the service product.

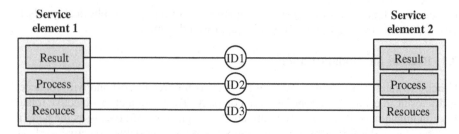

Fig. 2. Interdependencies between service elements

ID1 addresses the interdependence between the results of two service elements. Changing the lead time of element one may for instance require changes on other service elements in order to have an impact on the overall product result. The content of service element one in contrast may be effective without changing any of the other service elements in the service product. For example, reducing delivery times for a spare part would be of no use, if the technician fitting the part into the machine is not be available in a similar range of time. Still this important aspect has not been addressed. Applying quality function deployment (QFD) for unveiling these interdependencies is useful especially when the designing of service variants is relevant.

ID2 addresses the interdependencies of the processes in terms of their output-input relationship. This interdependence affects the timely order in which the processes have to be performed. These interdependencies can be clarified in a service blueprint [24] or in a time-based design structure matrix (DSM) [25]. The DSM then allows a reordering of the process elements in order to avoid interdependencies between the service elements. For example can loops in different processes be identified, rated and possibly reduced.

ID 3 addresses the interdependencies there are between resources of different service elements. There are two possible interdependencies: First, the compatibility of resources and second the capacity interdependence. The compatibility interdependence addresses for instance language skills of workers or technical restrictions of used equipment that need to match resources applied in another service element. The capacity interdependence is of relevance when different service elements require identical resources. This interdependence may affect attributes on the service result level and hence is very important for the creation of service variants.

3.3 Design Opportunities

A service variant is created through exchanging one service module through another. These changes can be achieved through changes within a module or element on the process level or on the resource level [10]. But through change of the process or resources, the interdependence to other modules of the service product may be affected, as discussed above. Identifying possible generic changes on a service module for different attributes on the service result level can be elaborated and rated by their impact on other modules through the given types of interrelations.

In modularisation of physical products Baldwin & Clark [7] argue, that all possible design changes are realised basically by six simple modular design operators. An analogy for industrial services highlighting design opportunities and giving insight into their impact on interdependencies would be of help for practical application of the concept.

Ulrich [5] as well as Ulrich & Tung [26] characterise different types of modularity in respect to the criterion of how the final product is built and about the nature of the interface. The different types of modularity like component swapping, combinatorial [27], fabricate-to-fit, bus, sectional or slot modularity all offer different potential in respect to the different module drivers. An analogy for industrial service would clarify design opportunities in terms of guidelines on how to achieve a specific goal through modularisation of services.

4 Conclusion and Outlook

In the present paper an overview on the topic of service modularisation was given from a perspective of enabling the efficient creation of service variants. A comparison between literature on modularisation of physical products and literature on service modularisation highlighted aspects relevant to practical application and not covered by research to date. Literature on modularisation of physical goods does not address specific requirements of industrial service in terms of their process and resource re-lated character. An adaptation of existing concepts on modularisation of physical products would be required.

Literature on modularisation of industrial services already addresses different as-pects of the topic. But still there are interesting and challenging questions remaining as the findings summarise.

Finally, the future theoretical findings are to be brought to practical application. Procedure models as developed in the community of service engineering are an ap-propriate mean to achieve practical acceptance and use.

References

1. Koudal, P.: The Service Revolution in Global manufacturing Industries. Deloitte Research. 2 (2006)
2. Spath, D., Zahn, E.: Kundenorientierte Dienstleistungsentwicklung in deutschen Unternehmen. Springer. Stuttgart (2003)
3. Mentzer, J., Flint, D., Hult, T.: Logistics Service Quality as a Segment-Customized Proc-ess. J. of Marketing. 65, 82--104 (2001)
4. McCutcheon, D.M., Raturi, A.S., Meredith, J.R.: The customization responsiveness squeeze. Sloan Management Review. Vol. 35. Iss. 2. 89--99 (1994)
5. Ulrich, K.T.: The Role of Product Architecture in the Manufacturing Firm. Research Pol-icy, Vol. 24. 419--440 (1995)
6. Morris, B., Robert J.: Dealing with Inherent Variability: The Difference between Manufac-turing and Service? IJ of Production Management, Vol. 7, Iss. 4. 13--22 (1987)
7. Baldwin, C.Y., Clark, K.B.: Design Rules: The Power of Modularity, Volume 1. Cam-bridge, MA: MIT Press (2000)

8. Meffert H., Bruhn, M.: Dienstleistungsmarketing: Grundlagen, Konzepte, Methoden. Gabler, Wiesbaden (1995)
9. Barney, J. 1991. Firm Resources and Sustained Competitive Advantage. In: J of Management; Vol. 17. Iss. 1. 99--121 (1991)
10. Seite, F., Nobs, A., Minkus, A.: Flexibility of Resources in Global After-Sales Service Networks. Proceedings of the 5th International Symposium on Management, Engineering and Informatics (MEI 2009), Orlando, 132--137 (2009)
11. Eden, C., Huxham, C.. Action Research for Management Research. British J of Management, Vol. 7, Iss. 1, 75--86 (1996)
12. McKay J., Marshall, P.:The dual imperatives of action research. Information Technology & People, Vol. 14, Iss.1. 46--59 (2001)
13. Susman, G.I., Evered, R.D.. An Assessment of the Scientific Merits of Action Research. Administrative Science Quarterly, Vol. 23, 582--603 (1978)
14. Baskerville, R.: Distinguishing Action Research From Participative Case Studies. Journal of Systems and Information Technology. Vol. 1. Iss. 1. 25--45 (1997)
15. Burr, W.: Chancen und Risiken der Modularisierung von Dienstleistungen aus betriebswirtschaftlicher Sicht. In: Herrmann, T., Kleinbeck, U., Krcmar, H.: Konzepte fur das Service Engineering. 17--44. Physica, Heidelberg (2005)
16. Hermsen, Martin: Ein Modell zur kundenindividuellen Konfiguration produktnaher Dienstleistungen : Ein Ansatz auf Basis modularer Dienstleistungsobjekte. Aachen : Shaker, 2000. Bochum, Univ., Diss., (2000)
17. Corsten, H., Dresch, K., Gossinger, R.: Gestaltung modularer Dienstleistungsproduktion. In: Bruhn, M., Strauss, B.: Wertschopfungsprozesse bei Dienstleistungen. 96--117. Gabler, Wiesbaden (2007)
18. Bohmann, T., Krcmar, H.: Modular Servicearchitekturen, In: Bullinger, H.J., Scheer, A.-W (eds.): Service Engineering. Entwicklung und Gestaltung innovativer Dienstleistungen, 2. Aufl., Berlin, pp377-401, (2006)
19. Blackenfelt, M.: Managing Complexity by Product Modularisation: Balancing the Aspects of Technology and Business during the Design Process. Stockholm, Royal Institute of Technology, Dept. of Machine Design, Diss (2001)
20. Ericsson, A., Erixon, G.: Controlling Design Variants: Modular Product Plattforms. Dearborn, MI: Society of Manufacturing Engineers (1999)
21. Goepfert, J.: Modulare Produktentwicklung: Zur gemeinsamen Gestaltung von Technik und Organisation, Dissertation, Dt. Univ.-Verlag; Wiesbaden (1998)
22. Koeppen, B.: Modularisierung komplexer Produkte anhand technischer und betriebswirtschaftlicher Komponentenkopplungen, Shaker, Aachen, Diss (2008)
23. Wildemann, H.: Produkte & Services entwickeln und managen, Strategien, Konzepte, Methoden; 1.Auflage, TCW Transfer-Centrum GmbH & Co. KG, München. (2008)
24. Shostack, L.: How to design a service. In: European J of Marketing. Vol.16. Iss.1. p.49 (1982)
25. Browning T.: Applying the design structure matrix to system decomposition and integration problems: a review and new directions. IEEE Trans Eng Management. Vol. 48. Iss. 3. 292—306 (2001)
26. Ulrich, K.T., Tung, K.,.. Fundamentals of Product Modularity. Working Paper WP3335-91-MSA. MIT Sloan School of Management. Cambridge, MA (1991)
27. Salvador, F., Forza C., Rungtusanatham, M.: Modularity, product variety, production volume, and component sourcing: Theorizing beyond generic prescriptions," J. of Operations Management.,Vol. 20. 549--575 (2002)

A Multi-dimensional Service Chain Ecosystem Model

Frédérique Biennier, Régis Aubry, and Youakim Badr

INSA-Lyon, LIESP, INSA de Lyon Bat Blaise Pascal
F-69621 Villeurbanne, France
{frederique.biennier,regis.aubry,youakim.badr}@insa-lyon.fr

Abstract. The globalised and moving economical environment leads enterprises to develop networked strategies. Such collaborative networks are by now often based on trusted and well known communities and require IT support agility and interoperability. The European Union promotes solutions to support and favor innovative business networks on the basis of an internet of services: these FP6 and FP7 projects results provide a consistent environment (including design, methods and developments related to Enterprise Service Bus (ESB) technology) to support technologically Business Service oriented organizations and the large-scale reinforcement of collaborative business and networked organization strategies. Nevertheless these works are mostly focused on an IT vision without taking into account business constraints. To overcome this limit, we propose a multi-dimensional service-chain ecosystem model, paying attention on service functional and non-functional properties description to support an efficient and consistent business service selection and composition process so that large-scale service based collaborative organization can emerge.

Keywords: Business Services, Modeling, Service Ecosystem, Process Maturity.

1 Introduction

Currently, the market is undergoing structural changes from mass customisation to increased interest in product and service management. Conversely, industries are shifting from labour-intensive jobs to the outsourcing of production in low-labour cost countries. Competition in overcrowded and existing industries is also moving to uncontested market spaces that make competition irrelevant. Such an economical context will favour in the coming years the emergence of an ecosystem of services. According to the Blue Ocean Strategy [5], demand is created rather than fought over. Services can allow firms to appropriate uncontested marketplace that creates and captures new demand while aligning the whole system of a firm's activities in pursuit of differentiation and low-cost. According to this strategy, product-service systems are built dynamically to anticipate consumer demand and will support new business opportunities and innovation.

In the most general sense, an ecosystem of services is a complex system of services, consisting of services and the relationships between them. This perceived assemblage of interrelated services comprises a unified whole to facilitate the flow of resources such as knowledge, competences and added-value. The integration of services when selling a product-service association increases the need for inter-firm

B. Vallespir and T. Alix (Eds.): APMS 2009, IFIP AICT 338, pp. 563–570, 2010.

collaborations and leads to the organization of industrial activities according to dynamic added-value networks instead of Porter's traditional value chain model [10].

In order to improve the enactment of an ecosystem of services, various services must identified by partners and published so that more complex services chain can be built, leading to a service chain organisation. Nevertheless, such collaborative organizations are limited as they require each partner to develop a consistent collaboration strategy. To overcome this drawback and provide extended business service communities, we propose to develop a service publication strategy requiring convenient selection and composition processes so that large scale service-oriented communities can emerge.

After describing globally the context associated to both product-service systems and the technological solutions, we propose our multi-dimensional service ecosystem model before setting the principles of a consistent Industrial-service bus.

2   Context

To fit the renewed globalised economical environment, enterprises, and mostly SMEs, have to develop new networked and collaborative strategies, focusing on their core business. The increased call for massively customised products also networked value creation (instead of the classical value chain vision). These collaborative organisations increase the call for interoperability at the technological, business and decisional levels.

o   Focusing on the technological level, the FP6 and FP7 work programs have launched different project based on the Internet and service technology. Reference Architectures defined by IT professionals or administrative organisations such as TOGAF, FEAF, MODAF… promotes multi-layered architectures so that different tiers are used to decouple the data storage, the business rule implementation and the user interface. Coupled to SOA organisation and standards, these architectures increase the global interoperability level.

o   At a conceptual layer, interoperability stakes are mostly related to business semantics (business data as well as business rules).

o   At an organisational layer, [3] proposes a consistent decisional framework, paying attention to responsibility areas identification

The interoperability framework proposed by the ATHENA project [2] includes different dimensions (enterprise level, interoperability barriers…). This multi-dimensional framework can be used to identify a first interoperability taxonomy but it lacks of taking into account industrial strategies. This last point involves paying attention to the value-chain identified by the client, leading to a product service strategy to fit the best the customer needs. Product-service systems have been pointed out since the beginning of the 2000s [6]. Different organisation can be identified [11]:

o   Product oriented Product-service systems: the physical product is owned by the consumer and services (mostly delivery services) are attached to the product itself

o   Use-oriented product Service System configuration: the consumer only
    buys the right to use the physical product
o   Result-oriented Product-service system: the product is substituted by a
    service which is bought by the consumer. In this case, the physical prod-
    uct can not be easily identified.

These different models lead to a product-service taxonomy based on the product identification and ownership but they lack of taking into account the global product service supply-chain organisation. To overcome these limits, a global product-service-
chain organisation taxonomy is required.

3   Multi-dimensional Service Ecosystem Model

We define a service ecosystem recursively either as a service-chain ecosystem which
links a set of service ecosystems, or as a simple, stand-alone service. Services are
mostly associated with "intangible assets" which require precise specifications so that
the consumer can "recognise" the asset he or she receives in addition to adapted management strategy. Consequently, the traditional supply chain, manufacturing chain
management and value models must be adapted [4] to take into account the intangible
characteristics and various delivery channels. Delivery channels are direct when the
consumer receives the service asset, and indirect when the consumer benefits from the
service. When intangible service assets are concerned, services can either be delivered
virtually through the internet; or when the service can be associated with a tangible
asset, logistics are required to deliver the real asset.

3.1   Multi-view Model Organisation

Based on these constraints, we propose to analyse and model the service eco-system
according to three different points of view:

o   **Internal view:** this includes different facets:
    o   **Product-Service competencies:** This describes what the product and
        or service can be used for. As proposed in the Shostack model [7],
        these "competencies" can be related either to intangible and tangible
        assets in a product-service logic. The service competencies are related
        to a business-area ontology and pays attention on the production re-
        sources (machines, materials…), the produced product and / or service
    o   **Service production system:** this part is devoted to "non functional
        properties" description. It includes the service production process de-
        scription, the production management strategy based on the Silvestro
        matrix [8], as well as monitoring and management information (in-
        cluding both key performance indicator collection and consolidation
        and process maturity control based on the CMMI for services classi-
        fication [9].
    o   **IT facet:** This last facet includes service data description (in order to
        improve mediation processes), process description (based on BPMN)
        and security requirements.

o   **Service Chain view:** this view is related to the role a service can play in service chain assembly and represents the public aspect of the service model. It uses the service interface such as the service's competencies to select the convenient service to set an adapted service ecosystem. In this view, emphasis is placed on how global synergy can create added value for the global chain assembly. This model is described according to three dimensions taken with respect to the service internal view: the intangible/tangible axis, the production organisation strategy and process maturity. By such, service chain profiles can be set up and used in order to build a consistent service chain and support a trusted management organisation.

o   **Environmental view:** this last view describes the service chain selection policy in terms of goals, service chain roles, strategic selection criteria, management criteria and environmental impact. The environmental view is related to the value perceived by consumers or other service providers. It can be associated to the prices the consumer pays for the different service chain components. In order to capture the client value-added point of view, we propose to use two elements, namely   intangible/tangible characteristics and the direct/indirect delivery channel to describe the service asset. A third element is based on Maslow's pyramid of needs so that the service consumer goal can be described more precisely.

Gathering these different views leads us to build a global, multi-dimensional value-added model. The perception of this model's taxonomy, regardless of its complexity, depends on best practices and pre-defined patterns. As a result, ecosystem evolution can be captured and adapt itself in a large, heterogeneous socio-economical and organisational context.

These collaborative and opened organizations make a heavy use of ICT, calling for information system agility and interoperability. Nevertheless, the underlying business-area oriented IT organization does not take into account the business process organization and can hardly support efficient traceability features as each business area is supported by an independent software environment and leads to inefficient information exchange, process organization and supervision..

Of course B2B and e-business tools (as e-market places for example) can be used to support web-based interactions between enterprises. Nevertheless, these web-economy oriented collaborative frameworks are devoted to commercial relationships and do not integrate any industrial constraints nor business related knowledge. This can lead to inconsistent industrial collaborative organization, decreasing the global efficiency and increasing waste rate due to non value-added activities. To overcome these limits, we propose to add an industrial service layer on the traditional ESB organization so that industrial constraints can be taken into account.

3.2   Industrial Service Bus Organisation

To support the Service Ecosystem model, an adapted environment, paying attention on the Business and industrial semantics, is required. The Industrial Service Bus we propose couples a Semantic Enterprise Service Bus organisation (based on the ESB PETALS and its semantic SEMEUSE extension) and a Registry and Governance toolset to a dedicated industrial-service management level (see fig. 1).

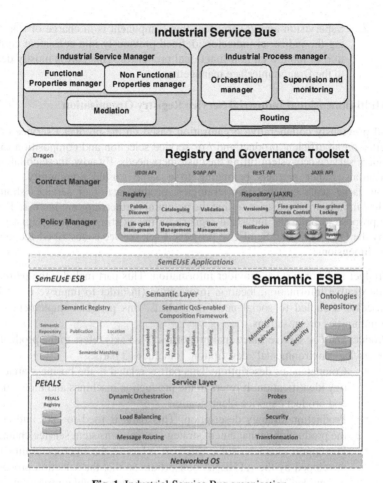

Fig. 1. Industrial Service Bus organisation

This Industrial service layer integrates different components:

o   The Industrial Service manager includes 2 sub-parts
  o   Selection and composition: this module is the interface with the industrial service registry. It allows the organisation of the functional properties (based on the business area ontology) and of the non functional properties (based on the production, security and Industrial Quality of Service ontologies)
  o   Mediation: this block relies on a common ontology linking the different business areas concepts so that an efficient semantic and syntactic mediation can be set.
o   The Industrial Process manager includes also 2 main components:
  o   Choregraphy and orchestration: This component is in charge of the service combination so that a collaborative process can be built. It includes a high-level BPEL description turned into a concrete BPEL model transferred to the semantic ESB middleware

o   Supervision and governance: this component is in charge of transforming the industrial indicators defined previously in a consistent composition of monitored non-functional properties. This part is mostly devoted to the Dragon interface management

3.3   Multi-dimensional Industrial Service Registry Organisation

As said previously collaborative organisation based on the product / service ecosystem relies on an efficient product and / or service selection and composition to set a convenient service ecosystem fitting the customers needs. By now, these collaborative organisations gather partners belonging to a same trusted community. In order to allow large scale collaborative strategies, product and / or services should be published in industrial registries so that the potential partnerships are increased.

We propose to build the industrial registry on the existing semantic registry managed by the DRAGON and SemEUse projects. Each service is described according to 3 main dimensions:

o   Product and / or service provider information: This part includes the partner administrative information, location information (in order to improve the delivery process). Coupled to social network toolsets, this part can implement trusted communities organisations.

o   Product and / or service functional properties: This axis refers to the product and / or service "environmental" description. It includes 3 parts:

- Competencies description: This part is related to the business area ontology identification. It refers to the production machines and tools, material and product / service identification

- Production strategy description: This parts is used to take into account the production management strategy (to set consistent service chain),

- IT support characteristics: this part refers to the interoperability model developed by the ATHENA consortium so that the selection process can be "guided" to select partners supporting interoperable infrastructures.

o   Product and / or service non functional properties: This part includes:

- Security requirements: This part allows different security strategies depending on the trust level the product/service provider has on the current environment. These annotations refers to the perceived risks and are used Quality of Protection Agreements

- Quality requirements: This part is based on the CMMI classification. First defined in the software development context, the Capability Maturity Model Integration has been fruitfully adapted to other production contexts including service environment [9]. We use the different classification strategies as basic ontology entries so that the global quality can be evaluate. It includes 4 main classes: risk management (referring to contextual information to identify success / failure factors), requirement development (to identify the customisation parameters) configuration management (if the product / service can be tuned according to given patterns), Organizational Process Definition (referring to the way the production process is integrated in the global service chain). Each of these classes is evaluated according to 4 points of view: the ecosystem management strategy, the global, production process management, support functions and / or associated services and engineering activities (if required)

- Industrial Quality of service requirements: This Industrial Quality of Service ontology is organised according to x topics: mean cost, production delay, reporting facilities and the adaptation level. This last part is coupled to the supervision and governance module. This module orchestrates probes services to set continuous monitoring. As proposed in [1] each dimension is associated to a reference model (based on ontologies) used to support the service semantic description as WSDL annotations (see fig. 2). By this way both functional and static non functional properties can be used to select the product / service candidates to establish the ecosystem fitting the best the customers needs. Quality requirements and Industrial Quality of Service requirements are gathered to set manufacturing Service Level agreements so that the contractual part can also be generated "on the fly".

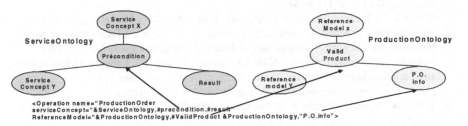

Fig. 2. Semantic annotation using YASA4WSDL

4   Conclusion

Due to increased customization in a globalized economy and to the development of "Service Oriented Products," enterprises have to adapt their organizational and business strategy, enhancing their own agility, reducing waste or non value-added activity and focusing on their core-business. Setting collaborative processes between enterprises and especially among SMEs is a promising approach to industrial competitiveness and is expected to generate substantial savings, expand market positions or develop new opportunities for the participants. To develop large-scale collaborative organization, we propose a product / service ecosystem taxonomy so that the different components of the ecosystem can be identified and selected. This leads us to define an "industrial service bus" layer. Based on a semantic ESB, this project is currently under development.

Acknowledgments. This work is partly supported by the Rhone-Alpes Area council via the Cluster GOSPI Sim-SyProd project and by the ANR organisation via the SemEUse project under ANR 20707TechLog018 grant.

References

1. Chabeb, Y., Tata, S.: Yet Another Semantic Annotation for WSDL. In: IADIS International Conference WWW/Internet 2008, pp. 437–441 (2008)
2. Daclin, N., Chen, D., Vallespir, B.: Decisional Interoperability: Concepts And Formalisation. In: Proceedings of Network-Centric Collaboration and Supporting Frameworks, PRO-VE 2006. IFIP, vol. 224, pp. 297–304. Springer, Heidelberg (2006)
3. Daclin, N., Chapurlat, V.: Evaluation de l'interopérabilité organisationnelles et manageriale des systèmes industriels: Le projet CARIONER, http://www.supdeco-montpellier.com/fileadmin/cerom/docs_telechargement/MTO_2008/Daclin_Chapurlat_MTO_2008.pdf
4. Ellram, L.M., Tate, W.L., Billington, C.: Services Supply Management: The Next Frontier for Improved Organisational Performance. California Management Review 49(4), 44–66 (2007)
5. Kim, W.C., Mauborgne, R.: Blue Ocean Strategy. Harvard Business Review, 76-84 (October 2004)
6. Mont, O.: Product-service systems: panacea or myth? PhD Dissertation. Lund University (reference IIIEE2004.1) (2004)
7. Shostack, L.: Breaking Free from Product Marketing. Journal of Marketing 41 (1977)
8. Silvestro, R., Fitzgerald, L., Johnston, R., Voss, C.: Towards a Classification of Service Processes. International Journal of Service Industry Management 3(3), 62–75 (1992)
9. Software Engineering Institute: CMMI for Services, version 1.2. Carnegie Mellon University Technical Report (February 2009), http://www.sei.cmu.edu/publications/documents/09.reports/09tr001.html
10. Tekes, S.: Value Networks in Construction 2003-2007. Sara Technology Programme, http://www.tekes.fi/english/programmes/sara
11. Yang, X., Moore, P., Pu, J.S., Wong, C.B.: A practical methodology for realizing product service systems for consumer products. Computers & Industrial Engineering 56, 224–235 (2009)

Hypergraph of Services for Business Interconnectivity and Collaboration

Alida Esper, Youakim Badr, and Frédérique Biennier

INSA-Lyon, LIESP, F-69621, Villeurbanne, France
{alida.esper,youakim.badr,frederique.biennier}@insa-lyon.fr

Abstract. Due to the impacts of structural market evolution (globalization, sustainable growth, mass customization, product-service development...) enterprise are more and more focusing on their core business, developing outsourcing and collaborative strategies to support value-added customized product-service for the customers. This involves developing agile and interoperable information system. To achieve this goal, Service Oriented Architecture has been introduced to support systems interconnection by mean of service composition. Nevertheless, this approach do not integrate service contextual configuration so that different services must be defined according to the context, leading to un-consistent systems. To overcome this limit, we propose a Model Driven Engineering approach to support contextual service refinement. Thanks to an hypergraph organization of the different partial models, services can be contextually instantiated and contextual information can be either inherited from the global model or propagated through the service chain.

Keywords: SOA, Interoperability, dynamic context, service modeling, graph, collaboration.

1 Introduction

The need for increased customization and service-oriented products has forced firms to adapt their organizational strategy. While focusing on their core business competencies, outsourcing and collaborative strategies are developed making an heavy use of ICT. Unfortunately, enterprise information systems consist in several support systems devoted to different business areas (ERP for the management part, CRM for customer management, MES at a workshop level...), exhibiting poor interconnection and agility abilities.

To overcome these limits, the Service-Oriented Architectural style (SOA) [1] has bee introduced. Thanks to standardized component interface definition and publication, processes can be built by service selection and composition mean [2] to provide a basic technologically interoperable IT support.

Despite these intrinsic openness, SOA infrastructures are mostly designed to support intra-enterprise processes as they use only mono-contextual business processes without taking into account actor preferences, underlying resources, service delivery channels or business agreements.

B. Vallespir and T. Alix (Eds.): APMS 2009, IFIP AICT 338, pp. 571–578, 2010.

As far as collaborative processes are concerned, a multi-contextual service environment is required, paying attention on information mediation, access rights management, business rules adaptation and user preferences. For example, different actors (final client, transportation firms, hotels or travel agencies) may use the same flight booking service but each of these actors will execute it in a given context, requiring different information, billing policies...

Our solution is based on a model-driven architecture: services are associated to contextualized models organized in an hypergraph so that model selection and service instantiation is achieved dynamically depending on the context: services properties and contextual parameters are either propagated among the service chain or inherited from higher levels models, taking advantage of the object-oriented paradigms [3].

After stating the context and current works, (section 2), we propose our solution globally before describing more precisely the propagation and inheritance mechanisms.

2 Business Collaboration

The growth of the internet appears as a driving force for enterprises to develop direct collaborations with their "professional" partners and customers. Several companies have already moved their operations onto the Web to collaborate with each other, where collaboration between enterprises means the interconnection and coordination of their business processes.

Corporate processes interconnection has been studied for several years. The old-fashion EDI standards ([4], [5], [6]) have been worthy introduced to support inter-organizational application-to-application transfer of business documents (e.g., purchase orders, invoices, shipping notices). As this approach is associated to interchange contracts, it is well suited for formal and administrative exchanges but it involves complex support systems and lacks of agility. More recently, Web Services have been introduced to support technological interoperability and seem to be the most popular implementation of the service oriented architecture. Web services are defined as a "business function made available via the Internet by a service provider, and accessible by clients that could be human users or software applications" [7] and are associated to a set of standards so that technological interoperability requirements can be fulfilled: WSDL (Web Services Description Language) [8] is an XML-based language for describing operational features of Web services, UDDI (Universal Description, Discovery, and Integration) [9] is used to support service publishing and discovery features, SOAP (Simple Object Access Protocol) [10] also messaging abilities between services....

Organising collaboration process involves taking into account the way tasks and activities are organised and coordinated as well as defining the actors involvement (role played...). Workflow process models provided by the Workflow Management Coalition (WfMC) and the Workflow Management Systems (WfMSs) provide convenient frameworks. Based on a predefined activities organisation and on a centralised organisation, they lack of agility. As far as distributed systems are concerned, another strategy consists in focusing on messaging flows. Both of these approaches have bee taken in the web-service environment. On one hand, WSFL [11][12] is based on a flow model, specifying data exchanges as the execution sequence between component services. As WSFL exposes a WSDL interface, recursive composition is allowed. On the other hand, XLANG[13][12] supports a behavioural description of Web services. It also provides features to combine those services to build multi-party business processes and to support message exchange among services. Lastly, BPEL4WS [14][12] combines both WSFL and XLANG features for defining business processes, consisting in different activities. BPEL4WS defines a collection of primitive activities (such as invoking a Web service operation.) that can be combined into more complex primitives. It includes the ability to: (1) define an ordered sequence of activities (sequence); (2) have branching using the now common "case-statement" approach (switch); (3) define a loop (while); (4) execute one of several alternative paths (pick); and (5) indicate that a collection of steps should be executed in parallel (flow).

Nevertheless, these works do not provide multi-contextual execution support. Moreover, they lack taking into account environmental requirements (as security or other non functional requirements for example). To overcome these limits, service description, selection, composition and orchestration must be enriched to take into account environmental and contextual descriptions.

3 Contextual Collaborative Process Organisation

To support collaborative process enactment, we propose to enrich the traditional service architecture to manage multi-context service execution. Our solution is based on the Model Driven Engineering approach to generate dynamically contextual services. Each process is defined by a set of views, related to enterprise policies such as security issues, management strategy and mediation constraints. These models are gathered in the Enterprise Meta-Model Architecture (EMMA), providing classes used to generate the convenient contextual service, linking the core-process services to technological services supporting security or mediation functions (Figure 1).

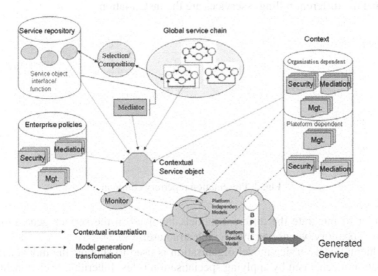

Fig. 1. Principle of the Dynamic Service Generation

The Enterprise Meta-Model architecture we propose gathers different kinds of models:

Conceptual service models: these models are associated to generic conceptual activities (ordering, billing,...). They are used to set generic classes description, focusing on common functional properties (namely data and operations) and can be defined recursively as a combination of other generic conceptual models.

E-services models are instances from the previous models. They can inherit functional properties from the class they belong to so that the interface benefits from a global consistency.

Preferences oriented models are used to store in a similar way actors preferences and contextual policies. Generic models are used to define classes so that models that will be applied during the generation process will be instantiated according to the context.

Each enterprise publishes its conceptual and real models in its own service repository. Then, the services that can be used in inter-enterprise collaborative processes are also published in a common repository as well as pre-defined collaborative processes (Figure 2)

This approach allows to organise a service-chain according to the following steps:

Conceptual services are selected depending on the activities involved in a generic workflow

Actors preferences and contextual information is used to identify both e-services and contextual non-functional models

The convenient models are extracted from the repositories and are used to "instantiate" the global service chain. This is achieved thanks to a service mediator in charge of selecting and generating the convenient service depending on the context. For example, while buying a train ticket, different billing services can be instantiated ("internal billing service" for a ticket bought at the station, on-line e-card billing for Internet based transactions or phone-card based billing...). This leads to a hierarchical organisation of the billing activities in a tree where the conceptual "billing service" is a root and the different billing e-services are the instantiation.

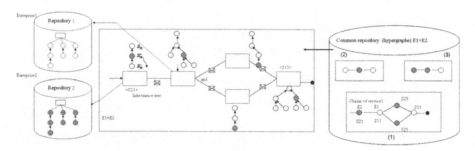

Fig. 2. Presentation repertory common

In order to integrate the different models involved in the service generation in a common repository, we use an hypergraph structure:

The hierarchical service model organisation is used to support the model / service instantiation mechanism by applying specialisation rules. Inheritance relationships are used to support consistent interface definition.

Different "horizontal relationships are introduced":

- o   Equivalence relationships are used to link models from different enterprises offering the same "conceptual service". By this way, context-dependant partnership selection can be improved by developing "service substitution" mechanisms
- o   Context relationships are used to combine different kinds of models (for example security policies coupled with conceptual services) so that context application can be simplified
- o   Service-chain relationships are used to store well-identified service chain so that already defined service chains can be reused more efficiently.

Due to this hypergraph organisation, classical inheritance mechanisms can not be implemented directly. Consequently, we'll detail in the next section the inheritance mechanism.

4 Service Refinement and Constraint Propagation

The inheritance relationship favors reusing abilities between class and subclass, allowing the transmission of properties (attributes and methods) from a super class to its subclasses. Subclasses may re-define an attribute or change a method by "overloading".

As far as functional properties are concerned, the inheritance mechanism allows the transfer of properties (attributes and methods) of the object which are in the super class to the objects that are subclasses. In our case when the service S_2 (object o_2) inherits of service S_1 (object o_1) we can keep the parameters or we can add another parameter, for example if we have both service (consult account) and (consult account in another country) the inheritance between S_2 and S_1 impose to take into account a new parameter (country) (Figure 3).

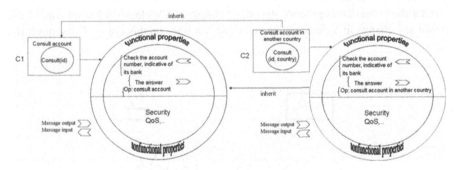

Fig. 3. Contextual inheritance

Taking into account non-functional properties can provide additional information on the service. These attributes include security, reliability, messaging facilities, response time, availability, accessibility... [15] defines the Quality of Service as "quality is expressed referring to observable parameters, relating to non-functional property", ,including runtime quality and business quality [16]. By developing a late-binding process, quality of service parameters (including both business oriented parameters (price, delay, performance level) and technical parameters (execution delay, security requirements, resources required...) can be worthy used to select (and then instantiate) the best service to fit the contextual user's needs.

To interconnect the different services in a consistent service chain, we define the following inheritance algebra:

Each conceptual model is associated to a tree h_c. The classes (associated to the different e-service models) c_i are gathered in a set $c= \{c_i\}$. Hierarchical links between classes $(_{ci}a_{cj}=(c_i,c_j)$ from c_i à c_j) are gathered in a set $a=\{_{ci}a_c\}$. We call $(A_{ip}, p=1,2, ...n,)$ the set of the attributes of the class c_i. Each class c_i inherits the attributes from the preceding classes in the hierarchy (Figure 4).

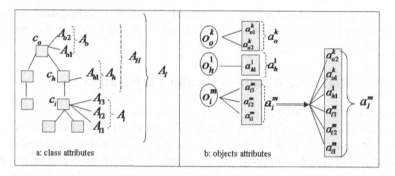

a: class attributes   b: objects attributes

Fig. 4. Class and object attributes organisation in the hypergraph structure

We call o_i^m an object of the class c_i, $o_i=\{ o_i^m \}$ is the set of objects of class c_i, $o_i^m \in o_i$. We call a_{ip}^m the attributes of the object o_i^m. Instantiating the object o_i^m involves merging the attributes from the preceding classes (from set a) leading to a_i^m of the attributes of this object o_i^m.

After the instantiation process, the object is linked to le classes it has inherited from so that any change in a class will be achieved "on line" on this object. Consequyently,

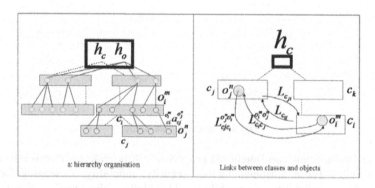

a: hierarchy organisation   Links between classes and objects

Fig. 5. Object integration in the hypergraph organization

we establish an arc $^{o_i^m}_{ci}a^{o_j^n}_{cj}$ with the condition that the vertice o_j^n has the same set a_i^m

comme the o_i^m, O={ o_i^m }, $^{o_i^m}_{ci}a^{o_j^n}_{cj}$ =(o_i^m, o_j^n),a= $^{o_i^m}_{ci}a^{o_j^n}_{cj}$ $\in o^2$,h_o=<o,a>,

"Horizontal" relationships between nodes from different hierarchies are organised in a "preceding list" so that predecessors can be found automatically and "horizontal inheritance" mechanism can be processes in a similar way (Figure 5).

5 Conclusion and Further Works

In this paper, we presented an approach that allows dynamic enactment for inter-firms collaboratice process. Thanks to an hypergraph repository organisation, service composition can be achieved contextually. Inheritance mechanisms are used to provide a consistent support as objects are generated according to the context and inherits the attributes of both conceptual models (seen as super-class) and of preceding objects in the service chain.

Next steps will focus on business transaction orchestration in order to improve late-binding facilities.

References

[1] Thomas, E.: Service-Oriented Architecture: Concepts, Technology, and Design. Prentice Hall, Englewood Cliffs (2005)
[2] Kuppuraju, S., Kumar, A., Kumari, G.P.: Case Study to Verify the Interoperability of a Service Oriented Architecture Stack. In: IEEE International Conference on Services Computing (2007)
[3] Esper, A., Sliman, L., Badr, Y., Biennier, F.: Towards Secured and Interoperable Business Services. In: Enterprise Interoperability, vol. III, pp. 301–312 (2008)
[4] X12EDI (Electronic Data Interchange), http://www.x12.org/
[5] Huemer, C., Quirchmayr, G., Tjoa, A.M.: A Meta Message Approach for Electronic Data Interchange (EDI). In: Tjoa, A.M. (ed.) DEXA 1997. LNCS, vol. 1308, pp. 377–386. Springer, Heidelberg (1997)
[6] EDIFACT, http://www.edifact.fr/ (last visited, 2009)
[7] Casati, F., Shan, M.: Models and Languages for Describing and Discovering E-services. In: Proceedings of the ACM SIGMOD International Conference on Management of Data, p. 626. ACM, Santa Barbara (2001)
[8] W3C: Web Services Description Language (WSDL) (2003),
http://www.w3.org/TR/wsdl
[9] W3C: Universal Description, Discovery, and Integration (UDDI) (2003),
http://www.uddi.org
[10] W3C: Simple Object Access Protocol (SOAP) (2003),
http://www.w3.org/TR/soap
[11] IBM : Web Services Flow Language (WSFL) (2003),
http://xml.coverpages.org/wsfl.html
[12] Peltz, C.: Web Services Orchestration and Choreography. Computer 36, 46–52 (2003)
[13] Thatte, S.: XLANG: Web Services for Business Process Design, Microsoft (2001),
http://xml.coverpages.org/XLANG-C-200106.html

[14] Business Process Execution Language for Web Services,
     http://msdn.microsoft.com/en-us/library/aa479358.aspx
[15] Ludwig, H.: Web Services QoS: External SLAs and Internal Policies or How Do We De-
     liver What We Promise? In: Proceedings Fourth International Conference on Web Infor-
     mation Systems Engineering Workshops, pp. 115–120 (2003)
[16] Yu, Q., Liu, X., Bouguettaya, A., Medjahed, B.: Deploying and Managing Web Services:
     Issues, Solutions, and Directions. The VLDB Journal 17, 537–572 (2008)

Lean First, Then Automate: An Integrated Model for Process Improvement in Pure Service-Providing Companies

Thomas Bortolotti[1,*], Pietro Romano[2], and Bernardo Nicoletti[3]

[1] Department of Electrical, Managerial and Mechanical Engineering, via delle Scienze 208,
33100 Udine, Italy
thomas.bortolotti@unibg.it
[2] Department of Electrical, Managerial and Mechanical Engineering, via delle Scienze 208,
33100 Udine, Italy
pietro.romano@uniud.it
[3] Via Leon Pancaldo 26, 00147 Roma, Italy
bnicoletti@hotmail.com

Abstract. Born in manufacturing environment, only recently Lean Management has been implemented in service context. However, in literature we didn't find a strong empirical evidence to clarify how Lean Management can be applied in a pure-service context, such as banking/financial services, where there is an intensive use of automation and Information Technology Systems. This work aims to define a methodology to streamline and automate processes and reduce waste in the pure service-providing companies. To achieve the study aims we conducted three case studies. Based on the empirical investigation, a framework was developed. We found out that the automation of a process not streamlined can generate problems that can slow down the flow and increase errors. A process must be mapped to highlight waste. Only when the new process is streamlined it can be automated. In doing so the new process will automate only value-added activities recognized by the customers.

Keywords: Lean Management, Multiple Case Study, Lean Service.

1 Introduction

Lean Management is recognized as one of the most effective methodologies to improve business processes. Lean Management aims to satisfy customers in terms of product and service quality and to reduce simultaneously the lead times [1] and [2]. These objectives are achieved through the use of methods and tools, which allow to eliminate waste, reduce process time and simplify operations [3]. In the past, Lean Management has been applied in the production of physical goods, the context in which it was born and has evolved. Also for this reason, Lean Management focuses mainly on the flow of materials, on the layout design and on the study of production

---

* Corresponding author.

B. Vallespir and T. Alix (Eds.): APMS 2009, IFIP AICT 338, pp. 579–586, 2010.
© IFIP International Federation for Information Processing 2010

and distribution timing, but it omits the study of the automation flow and the interactions between Information Systems and manual activities. The introduction of Jidoka systems in the physical flow of materials (automated systems for detection of abnormal conditions) is the only element of automation provided by Lean Management [4]. In Lean optics, automation has to be avoided because it increases the rigidity and complexity. The automation of information flow is not examined, on the contrary, Lean Management tends to reduce the automation forms to manage the information, such as MRP systems, through the introduction of manual systems, such as kanban cards and the Heijunka boxes [4].

Both in literature and in practice we found that the main problem is the excessive separation between improvements of manual activities and automated activities, between optimization and automation, between "factory" and Information Systems. This problem is even more evident if we focus on pure service sector such as banking and financial services, where the processes are essentially driven by automation and Information Systems [5]. The main question that we pose is: "How can introduce Lean principles in the pure-service context, where the typical production elements are missing and information management prevails?" The lack of an effective response to this question generates a serious problem encountered at managerial level: a problem of sequence. Because it is not clear when streamline and when automate the processes, you could automate errors and waste.

The research presented in this paper aims to develop a model called "Lean first, then Automate", a useful model to streamline and automate processes in the pure-service context. The scientific method adopted is the multiple case study. We analyzed three organizations involved in banking / financial sector that have adopted a methodology for process reengineering using Lean principles and automation and digitization techniques. Comparative analysis of these case studies made it possible to give a valid answer to the main question highlighted. The final model shows clearly the sequence of activities that should be done to integrate the methods of automation and digitization in the activities of process streamlining, in order to obtain competitive advantages, especially for pure service companies in which there isn't the "factory". In order to avoid the automation of errors and waste, the research suggests to (1) map the manual and automated activities, (2) highlight and delete every non value added activity for the final customer, (3) redesign the new process made lean (lean first), and only at the end (4) automate and digitize (then automate).

The automation is like a magnifying glass that reveals, accelerates and exalts the improvements, such as the errors. While the automation of an incorrect process helps to wrong faster, it is equally true that the automation of a streamlined process accelerates the achievement of the objectives and amplify the competitive advantages.

2   Literature Review

2.1   Quality-Efficiency Trade-Off in Service Management

The quality in the service context is a strategic element because it allows to gain competitive advantages, reduce costs and increase market share and profits [6] and [7]. Service processes are fundamentally different than manufacturing processes. The factors that differentiate services from manufacturing are: the active participation of the customer into the delivery process, the place of delivery and the place of use of the service are often the same, the service intangibility and the impossibility of service storing [8]. It is also proved that service processes are not as efficient as manufacturing processes [9]. This implies that, following a much debated topic by researchers and practitioners, there is the need to transfer in the world of services the practices commonly adopted in the manufacturing context [10], despite the substantial differences described above. The first author in support of this argumentation was Levitt, who has argued that the delivery of services should be designed and managed following the approach of the manufacturing process line [11]. Subsequently, other authors have confirmed the possible application of the methodologies for process improvement developed in the manufacturing sector, in order to solve performance problems related to inefficiency, poor quality and low productivity [12]. One of the most effective methodologies to conduce and execute projects for process improvement in the manufacturing sector is Lean Management.

2.2 Lean Management: Recent Developments

Back in the 50's, Eiji Toyoda and Taiichi Ohno joined craftsmen's knowledge and abilities with typical mass production assembly lines, defining the Toyota Production System (TPS), from which Lean Production was created. The "Lean Production" term was coined by James Womack, Daniel Jones and Daniel Roos in "The Machine that Changed the World" [3]. The main objective of Lean Production is the elimination of waste (Muda in Japanese). "Muda" were defined as every human activity which doesn't provide any added value for the customer [13]. He identified seven different sources of waste: overproduction, defects, transportation, waiting, inventory, motion and processing. Lean Production is therefore defined as a systematic waste removal from every value stream part, by every organization member. "Value stream" can be defined as the whole set of activities to obtain a finished product from raw materials [1]. Lean Production implementation provides several benefits, among which: cost reduction, productivity increase, quality improvement, lead time reduction, supplies reduction, flexibility and customer satisfaction improvement. Five main principles were set by [3], in order to achieve a lean business model: value, value stream, flow, pull and perfection. In the late 90's, the concept of the value stream has evolved and has been extended beyond individual company boundaries, starting with customer needs until raw materials [14]. This is the link between Lean Production and Supply Chain Management. Lean Production is not confined within the company, since the mid 90's Lean Production has been applied to various activities: product development, relations with suppliers and customers, distribution, thus becoming a general methodology, called Lean Management. Lean Management has been applied in the service context through recent "Lean Service" studies, among which the most important are: [2], [15] and [16]. However, these studies focused on process streamlining of services associated with products (e.g. Taco Bell, Tesco, etc.), services in support of production (administration of a manufacturing organization) or services in healthcare. Almost none of these studies focused on the application of lean principles to streamline pure services, such as banking and financial services [5].

2.3 Automation and Lean Management

Sugimori et al. argued that the use of the information and communication systems for production planning introduces unnecessary costs, overproduction and uncertainty [17]. This theory contrasted with the trends of the 70's and 80's, when the interest on MRP systems, numerical control machines and production lines fully-automated was huge. The highly automated companies were less vulnerable to the typical problems of manual work. However, there were examples of over-investment in automation and digitization that have worsened the flexibility and the ability to respond to the demand changes (e.g. General Motors in the'80s; CIM) [18]. Lean Management focuses on flexible and "intelligent" automation and "low cost" technologies. MRP is replaced by Just-In-Time techniques such as Kanban and Heijunka boxes, much more simple and controllable, the numerical control machines and production lines fully-automated are replaced by cells with less automation. However, it is not clear how the principles, techniques, tools and approach of Lean Management can be applied in the pure-service context, where there is an intensive use of Information and Communication Technology and automation to process the huge quantity of information, representing the flow of the delivery process [19].

3   Methodology

To address the research questions we have chosen the exploratory multiple case study research design. Exploratory case studies are particularly suitable if researcher intends to extend the applicability of a theory in a new context [20], the purpose of this specific research. We decided to analyze several case studies, given the limited generalizability of a single case results [21]. After the review of literature, we selected organizations operating in pure service context which extensively automated information flows and adopted a methodology to streamline their delivery processes. We used the method of retrospective analysis, for this reason we chose examples of Best Practice in order to analyze the critical factors of success [20]. We selected three organizations operating in banking and financial sector, two of them were Italian banking groups (cases 1 and 2) and one Asian (case 3). However, firstly, we study an installation service organization in order to do a pilot and test the data gathering procedures [22]. For each Best Practice case, we selected the experts to be interviewed to gather empirical data. The managers interviewed were chosen for their role and their skills in relation to the topic investigated [20]. The interview was the main instrument used for the data-gathering [20]. The data collected through interviews were integrated with additional sources, such as analysis of company archives, records and direct observations [20], [21] and [22].

The collection of information relating to the same phenomenon through different methods and tools (e.g. interviews, archives, observations), allowed us to execute the data triangulation [20]. The interpretation of data, mostly qualitative, generated a description of the three case studies. Cause - effect evidence, supported by the qualitative data triangulation, ensured the internal validity [21]. The results of this analysis are three models that define the sequence of operations implemented to streamline and automate the delivery processes. The three models have been interpreted through the literature in order to highlight the strengths and weaknesses.

Afterwards, we carried out the comparative analysis of the case studies to find similarities and differences between the three models, and extrapolate the results in response to the research question: the final model "Lean first, then Automate". Comparative analysis, following the dictates of Ehsenhardt and Yin, was characterized by an iterative process of systematic comparison of the three case study with the literature references in order to integrate empirical evidence with the scientific basis, ensuring the external validity of results and, consequently, their generalizability [21] and [22]. Finally, to increase the research robustness, the "Lean first, then Automate" model was tested in two additional cases outside the banking and financial sector. The two organizations studied operate in the installation and testing services context. The positive results of both tests increased the external validity and generalizability of empirical evidences.

4 Results: The "Lean First, Then Automate" Model

4.1 Define and Measure

The "Lean first, then Automate" model begins with the "Define and Measure" phase. "Lean first, then automate" projects must be supported by the company and assigned to a project team of people from all functions involved. Firstly, the project team has to "listen" the voice of the customer (VOC) to focus on what is really important for the success. It is necessary to detail the customers needs to understand what are the metrics that should be measured, monitored and improved. Generally the most important metrics are cycle time and inventories. After that, the project team has to map the "As-Is" process. The process mapping involves both the manual and the automated flows. Specifically, the project team has to observe the sequence of manual operations and the layout, to understand how the physical flow is regulated, and the applications, systems and automated sequences, to understand how the automated flow is regulated. Mapped the process, the project team measures the metrics and identify the critical points related to the "As-Is" process.

The analysis of case 1 revealed a point of weakness: the method adopted for the measurement, the interview, caused loss of time and poor accuracy of the data gathering. The analysis of case 2 was rather an example of Best Practice: processes are measured extracting data from the Information Systems, which provides a fast and accurate measurement. This example shows how the involvement of the Information and Communication Technology in the "Lean first, then automate" projects would accelerate and optimize the measurement phase.

4.2 Analyze and Process Design

Ended the "Define and Measure" phase, the project team has to note every waste present in the "As-Is" process and redesign the sequence of activities eliminating all sources of waste and variability. The process was redesigned through: the elimination of non value added and not necessary activities; the redesign of operations that produce waiting times, unproductiveness, batches, queues, stocks; the outsourcing or centralization of activities with low value added but necessary; the simplification, standardization, optimization and automation of some manual activities; the reduction of excessive and not controlled automation (first lean, ...).

Case 3 is an example of Best Practice: The "As-Is" process of data cross-checking was managed as follows: printouts were printed, operators controlled manually matching data, and analyzed the exceptions detected. The "As-Is" analysis found waste of material and time in the print activity, a low value added activity in data control, while the analysis of the exceptions was considered a high value activity. The "To-Be" process was redesigned with an introduction of an automated tool: data streams are defined parametrically, the new tool automatically checks the data and highlights the exceptions, and operators can focus on the only high value-added activity: the exceptions analysis.

4.3 Architecture Design

The "To-Be" process describes the sequence of activities that will form the future delivery process. These activities may be part of the manual flow or automation flow. The tasks of the Architecture Design phase are to plan in minute detail the technical and functional characteristics of each activity, component and service that are part of the two flows, to design any interface between automated and manual activities, and to regulate the process flow to make it continuous and connected with the final customer.

4.4 Build, Test and Deploy

During the "Build, Test and Deploy" phase the "To-Be" process is implemented and tested. The new physical structure, new software and new interfaces are developed, following the functional and technical specifications designed in the previous phase of "Architecture Design". Every part is then tested individually to verify the correctness of development. Verified the correctness of the development, a pilot is launched. Following the design process and architecture, the process is implemented and simulated on a small scale, in order to verify the real functions, and in case of disease, appropriate changes are made. Verified the correctness of the new process, it can be introduced within the delivery system (... then Automate).

4.5 Control

The model "Lean first, then Automate" ends with the "Control" phase. The process must be constantly monitored measuring the reference metrics. A process not monitored could degrade and cause huge losses due to a possible customer satisfaction decrease. At the start of the "Control" phase, when the process becomes effective, any changes after installation and the plan for decommissioning of parallel processes no longer active must be made.

5 Conclusions

The three case studies are examples of a quality and efficiency improving methodology, Lean Management, transferred from the manufacturing to the pure-service context, in banking and financial sectors. Starting from this statement, and with a focus on the "Lean first, then Automate" model, the result of this exploratory research, it is possible to assume two propositions, that will be the starting point for a subsequent study on a larger sample of companies:

Proposition 1: unlike the manufacturing context, where Lean Management requires a reduction of automation and digitization, in the pure-service context automation and digitization are desirable.

Proposition 2: In the pure-service context, automate and/or digitize a process not streamlined is counterproductive.

Corollary to proposition 2: in the pure-service context, it is convenient to take the sequence of implementation that provides firstly an accurate streamlining of the process by the elimination of any source of waste and then automates and/or digitizes (lean first, then automate).

The final model responds to the lack in literature of a consistent methodology that manages and integrates the classical activities of streamlining a delivery process with the activities of automation and digitization. In addition to the academic contribution, the study allows to solve the managerial problem of sequence shown previously in this study. The model provides a logical sequence to the activities of streamlining and automating processes: first streamline, and only after, automate the value-added activities recognized by the final customer, avoiding to enter in the information system and in the automation flows any waste that could be the cause of delivery process delays or blocks. The main research limitation of this study is associated with the number of companies studied. The study used a selection of large enterprises, an other possible future research should be the adaptation of the framework in the context of Small and Medium Enterprises (SMEs). In conclusion, the framework developed provides a logical sequence to reengineer service-providing processes, as a matter of fact, we suggest "Lean first, than Automate". To be more precise: lean the process first, then automate value-added activities.

References

1. Womack, J.P., Jones, D.T.: Lean Thinking: Banish Waste and Create Wealth in your Corporation. Simon and Schuster, New York (1996)
2. Atkinson, P.: Creating and implementing lean strategies. Management Services 48(2), 18–33 (2004)
3. Womack, J.P., Jones, D.T., Roos, D.: The Machine That Changed The World. Rawson Associates, New York (1990)
4. Monden, Y.: Toyota production system: practical approach to production management. Engineering & Management Press, Norcross (1983)
5. Piercy, N., Rich, N.: Lean transformation in the pure service environment: the case of the call service centre. International Journal of Operations & Production Management 29(1), 54–76 (2009)
6. Thompson, P., DeSouza, G., Gale, B.T.: Strategic management of service quality. Quality Progress, 20–52 (June 1985)
7. Zeithaml, V.A., Berry, L.L., Parasuraman, A.: Communication and control processes in the delivery of service quality. Journal of Marketing 52, 35–48 (1988)

8. Fitzsimmons, J.A., Fitzsimmons, M.J.: Service Management for Competitive Advantage. McGraw-Hill, Inc., New York (1994)
9. Lovelock, C., Gummesson, E.: Whither services marketing? In search of a new paradigm and fresh perspectives. Journal of Service Research 7(1), 20–41 (2004)
10. Bowen, D.E., Youngdahl, W.E.: "Lean" service: in defense of a production-line approach. International Journal of Service Industry Management 9(3), 207–225 (1998)
11. Levitt, T.: Production-line approach to service. Harvard Business Review 50(5), 20–31 (1972)
12. Hayes, R.H., Wheelwright, S.C.: Link manufacturing process and product life cycles. Harvard Business Review 57(1), 133–140 (1979)
13. Ohno, T.: The Toyota Production System. Productivity Press, Cambridge (1988)
14. Hines, P., Rich, N.: The seven value stream mapping tools. International Journal of Operations & Production Management 17(1), 46–64 (1997)
15. Abdi, F., Shavarini, S., Hoseini, S.: Glean lean: how to use lean approach in services industries? Journal of Services Research, special issue 6, 191–206 (2006)
16. May, M.: Lean thinking for knowledge work. Quality Progress 38(6), 33–40 (2005)
17. Sugimori, Y., Kusunoki, F., Cho, F., Uchikawa, S.: Toyota production system and kanban system: materialization of just-in-time and respect for human systems. International Journal of Production Research 15(6), 553–564 (1977)
18. Bowen, D.E., Youngdahl, W.E.: "Lean" service: in defense of a production-line approach. International Journal of Service Industry Management 9(3), 207–225 (1998)
19. Uday, M.A., Chon, G.: Applying lean manufacturing principles to information intensive services. International Journal of Services Technology and Management 5(5-6), 488–506 (2004)
20. Voss, C., Tsikriktsis, N., Frohlich, M.: Case research in operations management. International Journal of Operations & Production Management 22(2), 195–219 (2002)
21. Yin, R.K.: The Case Study Crisis: Some Answers. Administrative Science Quarterly 26(1), 58–65 (1981)
22. Eisenhardt, K.M.: Building Theories from Case Study Research. The Academy of Management Review 14(4), 532–550 (1989)

Implementing Lean into a Servicing Environment

Ross Ritchie and Jannis Angelis

Warwick Business School, University of Warwick, Coventry, CV4 7AL, UK
r.a.ritchie@warwick.ac.uk
jannis.angelis@wbs.ac.uk

Abstract. The study provides a description of what Lean means in a service context, focused on the energy sector. The study covered a range of operational processes, including TQM, Six Sigma and freestanding benchmarking and Kaizen initiatives. A divide between managers actively implementing Lean and those that are not is clear in both survey results and interviews; this divide is driven wider by the misunderstanding of what is actually being implemented, sometimes inappropriately assigned as Lean. Moreover, only a core of Lean manufacturing attributes are carried through into services: waste removal, responding to customer demand and increased breadth of communications in the firm. The study also finds that Lean is consistently confused with Six Sigma, but that this does not negatively impact the Lean implementation.

Keywords: Lean, services, implementation.

1 Introduction

This study was borne through interest in 'Lean servicing', and whether its implementation is consistently adopted across distributed teams. The study analyses the fashionable process of Lean; both for its development to servicing, and how the different aspects of this approach may be understood. Servicing in the UK has become increasingly important as now a quarter of imports and about 40% of exports are defined as services [11].

Haywood-Farmer and Nollet [7] define service largely in terms of output: 'intangibility', 'heterogeneity', 'perishability' and 'customer participation in the production process. Other definitions expand this with ever increasing complexity, whilst the service/goods mix causes further strain; especially where the supply of physical artifacts and application of perishable skills are supplied within the same process. We supplement the definition with the requirement that value originates from the original process and the knowledge employed and not from the supply of the physical artifact (Herzenburg et al., 1998). We complete this definition by adding the use of 'variability' and 'inseparability' attributes [10]. Hence, service is where output is clearly exhibiting both intangibility and perishability, majority of processes exhibit output variability and process inseparability at the point of supply; and output is the point at which the value of process is added. The study investigates three questions:

RQ1: Are Lean servicing and Lean Production comparable techniques?
RQ2: Is employee response to Lean servicing derived from specific and defined Lean techniques or from the activity of undertaking a change program?
RQ3: Is implementation of Lean servicing consistent across role types?

B. Vallespir and T. Alix (Eds.): APMS 2009, IFIP AICT 338, pp. 587–594, 2010.
© IFIP International Federation for Information Processing 2010

2 Literature Review

Lean has been characterized as customer-focused, knowledge-driven, eliminating waste, creating value, dynamic and continuous. The ongoing evolution of term 'Lean' is stimulus to practitioners as well as academics to question and in many parts disagree with the basic concept definition. With developments of a concept into Lean servicing, we observe concept stretching, where individual researchers try to enrich a concept making it less precise. [14]. Lean is case in point; where the 'concept' has undergone a thirty year evolution, and the focus of much academic redefinition. [8]. Because of this continual addition, reclassification and embellishment we see the original definition become supplemented and amended, so that no one paper can claim to have the current definitive description of the concept.

When applied to industry the term 'Lean' has a multitude of meanings. In production the main attributes are high levels of intra-department communication, focus on error reduction and the use of continuous improvement programs, operations responsive to customer demand, a focus on waste removal, and the development of the supplier role. In addition, Lean attributes in services add emphasis on customer communication, flexible yet standardized processes, quality consistency and investments in workforce training.

Table. 1. Operational attributes

Approach	Key characteristics
Total Quality Management (TQM)	Benchmarking
	Inter-department communications
	Intra-department communications
	Customer communication
	Detailed process analysis
	Consistency of quality
	Error reduction
	Continual improvement
	Empowerment
	Training
	Supplier role
Six Sigma	Detailed process analysis
	Failure analysis
	Consistency of quality
	Error reduction
	Respond to customer demand
	Waste removal
Benchmarking	Benchmarking
	Inter-department communications
	Intra-department communications
	Detailed process analysis
	Continual improvement
	Wholesale process redesign
Kaizen	Inter-department communication
	Continual improvement
	Process standardisation
	Innovation
	Waste removal

In operations management, differences between many strategic programs are not readily apparent. TQM, JIT, Lean manufacturing, and continuous improvement may even share concepts. [14]. Many authors of operational improvement techniques would argue that these are not techniques, rather states of mind, cultures or strategic initiatives. [2].

The job-types used to segment the organization are used as reasonable generalizations of behavior, culture and background; looking at their roles and responsibilities and the context and environment they live and work within. They are classified in terms of the decision making responsibility afforded to them. A bespoke model incorporating characteristics from Murdick *et al.* (1990) and Herzenburg *et al.* (1998), identify 'skill type' through classification of the type and investment for a role. Further separated into high-discretion and low-discretion types, the "freedom or authority to make judgment and act as one sees fit". Finally high-discretion roles are split into high or low levels of autonomy, the ability "to direct and control the policy and affairs".

3   Case Study

3.1   Case Background

The studied firm - 'Energie' is a 'vertically integrated Pan-European Power and Gas' company. The study focused on the UK market unit of this organisation containing six separate Business Units (BU). The dynamics between BUs is critical, as the proliferation of Lean has been part politics and part local design. In 2004 Energie's Lean journey began. After nearly 10 years of stable management, the leadership team of one of the BUs was changed. Brought about by a visible failure in industry league tables and increasing complaints. The old management team had led a very involved management style, with high levels of access and detailed control of the operational processes. Backlogs had started to build up, teams were working at unsustainable levels to try and recover the position. This became a vicious circle with directors needing to become increasingly involved in every operational issue, as the middle management lost faith in their own ability to recover the situation. A new Director of Service was appointed and subsequently became the epitome of Lean; he himself had completed an identical 'intervention' in two preceding organisations.

A number of key activities took place. A 'commercial' consultancy was brought in to make a three month assessment of areas most likely to benefit from Lean implementation. All remaining operational managers were sent on a two week Lean appreciation course. Finally a systematic PR campaign was started at senior management level spanning the entire Market Unit to explain the benefits of Lean. By 2005, the industry league table positions were recovered, morale within the teams was noticeably improved, and the business was generally more stable. The processes of rolling out Lean now became a company-wide challenge rather than one restricted to just the operational core of one BU.

From initial rollout there was nearly 15% of the EUK workforce under Lean management in 2007. The first spread of Lean was politically driven within the UK Board and influenced through observation of industry improvements being made. The desire for Lean was taken and passed into this second BU. However, the approach taken was somewhat different as the consultancy and approach to management change was not adopted. The third BU to adopt a Lean methodology was influenced through one of the many seminars and distribution of a text book [12] given out to all senior managers in EUK.

3.2   Research Method

The study is based on a combination of semi-structured interviews and surveys of managers and employees at a service organization operating in the energy sector. A total of fifteen senior managers were interviewed and surveyed, and 98 employee surveys collected. For comparisons, the study covered a range of operational processes, including TQM, Six Sigma and freestanding benchmarking and Kaizen initiatives.

Participants were provided with a wide set of attributes by which to describe their jobs and environment, allowing them to select attributes against understanding of their operation. Information about the individual was measured education level, sex and time in company. The target was to have a maximum of one question per attribute, which on a timed run was expected to meet tough criteria set by many of the operational managers. Interviewees were asked to rate priority objectives from 1 (unimportant) to 4 (very important) detailing whether certain 'operational priority' objectives were important first to their customer, and secondly as a reflected priority in their operation. The final section asked respondents whether they thought they were using a Lean approach, and for those that were, what the outcome had been in terms of perceived performance.

3.3   Case Results

Lean operation A: The first operation has a wide range of texts and training manuals for implementing and maintaining a Lean approach. The key attributes consisted of:

➢   Workforce engagement, in stark contrast to the previous operational approach of command and control, where it was felt that there was little dialogue between staff and management.
➢   An increased attention to customer communications, leading to better service alignment and response to customer demand.
➢   A focus on making failure analysis a routine and normal activity. Specifying activities and processes to adopt continual error reduction.
➢   Creation of pre-emptive poka-yoke processes, with focus on systems and customer data.
➢   Increased empowerment with the expectation that first line call handlers can rectify 90% of issues on first contact.
➢   Multi-skilling of the organisation with greater training and increased functional flexibility.
➢   Investment in simplifying processes and waste removal designed during previous acquisitions and mergers.
➢   Remove waste from the system. There was no description of waste provided, leaving the staff challenging and thinking whether anything could be construed as waste.

Lean operation B: in the second operation communication between staff and managers was more selective. Guiding principles chosen in the second operation were:

➢ Detailed process analysis
➢ Respond to customer demand
➢ Consistency in quality
➢ Workforce empowerment
➢ Waste removal and error reduction
➢ Customer communications
➢ Workforce engagement
➢ Enjoying the journey

Management Result Summary:

1. Formal Lean attributes are identified by both Lean and Non-Lean managers respectively, with local Lean variants better identified by Lean managers
2. Six Sigma attributes are identified by managers as Lean attributes, due to conscious incorporation within local variants.
3. High levels of alignment exist between operational priority and customer priority for both Lean and Non-Lean managers
4. Team and manager alignment, is far more prevalent in Lean adopters.

Team Result Summary:

1. Job-types with greater autonomy have increased consensus as to their adopted attributes
2. Lean teams have a higher propensity to reflect on their inadequacies in relation to the customer.
3. Operational priority alignment is much lower in Lean teams, demonstrating awareness of deficiencies.

3.4 Operational Impact

The study indicates that Lean in Energie is consistently confused with the Six Sigma concept. Illustrated in Burton and Boeder's [2] analogy of where Lean, TQM and Six Sigma boundaries reside, explain that the approaches are complementary rather than exclusive of each other. A Lean operation has a high level of consistency of attribute selection across both job-types and teams, but this is no different to non-Lean adopters. We conclude that a Lean implementation does not increase uncertainty or confusion in the adopting teams; but it also does not provide greater clarity to the role.

Where the adoption of 'Lean' comes into its own, is in its ability to educate workers of their deficiencies, the comparison between where they are and where they should be. [4]. We observed that teams subjected to 'Lean interventions' were most aware of their shortfall, in respect to customer requirements. The process of undertaking an 'intervention' could be more important because of the thought process it causes the organisation to go through.

The study identified differences apparent between job-families, which should be central to an organisation's consideration as to whether to make investment in a Lean Intervention. Looking into how this manifests in different roles, we challenge whether it is the 'words' or the underlying 'ambition' of the change that has the greatest impact. We see positive affiliation to Lean definitions within the lower discretion job types. The more prescriptive nature of a Lean intervention engenders specific characteristics and culture; and has resonance with these lower discretion groups. The ability for low autonomy groups to understand and interpret the subtlety of the intervention, is vital to the ongoing success and consistency in application of the approach. [3].

So why did not Energie call this a Six Sigma intervention? The more rigid and codified requirement (i.e. black belt certification) in order to classify an organisation as Six Sigma compliant may well have had an impact. A reason why Lean is such a desirable approach for an organisation to adopt is that it allows flexibility under the basic premise that it is set to remove 'waste' [1], and this perception of waste is still largely left to the organisation to define.

3.5 What Is Lean Servicing?

There is no clarity in the term 'Lean', perhaps because application pre-empted concept definition [14]. Finding a clear and unambiguous definition of Lean Manufacturing in itself is not straight forward. This paper proposes the following generic objective of Lean Manufacturing: "An organization-wide and systematic investment towards removing all forms of waste in the provision of service to generate increased value in the process, through providing management frameworks, communication protocols and organisational culture"

We propose that the Lean servicing definition is not clear cut, partially because a standardised service environment is a rare thing indeed. Even if the service industry was highly standardised, the complex processes and multiple paths a customer can lead through a service organisation are not. It is hence unsurprising that Lean production processes can be carried across to Lean services with only minor modification. The concept and ambition of Lean is portable across both production and services. However, the way in which Lean is expressed and understood does change as it migrates into a service environment. We see aspects that have been refined to express the subtlety required for services i.e. process flexibility and consistency of quality [5], attributes that become less relevant and those that are so inherent in the description that the literature does not feel the need to express them (i.e. error reduction and continual improvement). Only core Lean production attributes are carried through to service descriptions: waste removal, responding to customer demand and increased breadth of communications in the firm.

Case studies A and B show that as Lean servicing becomes further developed and applied to specific situations only the core attributes of: 1) systematic waste removal; 2) responding to customer demand; 3) customer communications, are carried through from the initial service definition. These are themselves greatly supplemented by the environment and role specific attributes. Paradoxically many senior managers, who were not actively adopting Lean, did so because they thought the application to be inflexible, and by signing up to the process they would be handicapped by rigorous tool and principle adherence.

Lean servicing for the purposes of industry is a generic description for a series of activities, tools and culture that at its heart is targeted with adding value while removing waste [9]. The blinkered application of such rigid description is damaging to proliferation and uptake by managers. Rather, it should be appreciated for the framework it provides; a definition that builds upon the formal conceptual definition, through development of tools and principles whilst allowing room for tailoring appropriately to its environment, bringing with it all the subtly that change initiatives require to be successful.

4 Discussion and Conclusions

Lean intervention is a process that generates change [4]. A Lean organisation is one that is continually assessing itself to improve value. It is unlikely that all organisations find their competitive position through adoption of Lean, and it is unlikely that Lean and its many spin-offs will be the definitive and last operational programme. The nature of operations requires that an organisation will continue to explore process improvement that differentiates their operation from the rest. So as adoption of Lean principles becomes an entry level requirement, the best operations will continue to develop their mindset to improvement and maintain their lead on the pack.

We could refer to Lean as a 'brand of change'. This infers no negative connotations; the simplicity and flexibility of Lean should be its biggest selling point. In our case study we see that the 'marketing of the change' combined with an initiative that stands up under the loose description of common sense has a significant impact. Sometimes the articulation of the goal by Lean implementers has become so fervent, that it starts to be considered a mantra, "almost religious" in its following. But this religious following can be at the expense of continual check and balance to see whether it is still appropriate; and it is these challenges that organisations such as Energie will have to face.

The evolution of Lean is most noticeable as it bridged the link between production and servicing environments. Lean servicing as a specific concept continues to evolve, and because of this there is no 'formal conceptual definition' that we can rely on as agreed by all academic and consulting stakeholders. But this in its own right makes Lean servicing a commercially attractive prospect, the ability to modify the concept to best suit the environment, perhaps in multiple ways within the same firm, means that this should be applicable in all but the most unusual circumstances. The overriding ambition of Lean is to remove waste and increase value, and there would be few managers or firms that would not support this aim.

So is Lean just another management fad? Maybe, but perhaps primarily in the term being used and the narrow description of what Lean is understood to mean; we can already see concepts such as 'Agile-Lean', 'Lean Six Sigma' being commonly used. Tischler [13] argues there is nothing fundamentally radical about Lean. It is not operationally perverse, which requires a high level of faith or convincing to see the benefit. With senior management interviews we noted several occasions where Lean was referenced as 'common sense'.

This study reveals that Lean makes some job types more aware of their deficiencies and self-critical of their approach. In some cases it increased alignment between workers and management, the use of consistent terms, the shared knowledge of a common goal. These are consistent with other studies indicating that Lean is a vehicle for change rather than a very specific set of attributes that in themselves are revolutionary. [4]. For instance, as stated by Fujimoto [6]: "the Toyota-style system has been neither purely original nor totally imitative, it is essentially a hybrid...". Nonetheless, there is something inherently positive about Lean servicing. Rather than a random collection of activities, there is a logical and emotional strength in the proposition that has resonance with teams, and in particular low discretion roles showing not just a surface appreciation but a more considered awareness of what Lean is trying to achieve.

As whether performance improvement comes from the adoption of Lean or how you choose to implement it, the results indicate that Lean servicing encourages worthwhile generic objectives to be adopted by an operation. Lean provides an appropriate framework not dissimilar to what many consider as 'common sense practice', but crucially it is the approach to implementation that makes or breaks the investment. Hence, this study reveals that the perception and emotion that Lean brings with it, as a change program, significantly assists the rollout effort, in itself the organisation feels that it has improved before it has even commenced the journey.

References

1. Boyer, K.: An assessment of managerial commitment to Lean production. International Journal of Operations and Production Management 16(9), 48–59 (1996)
2. Burton, T. and Boeder, S., The Lean Extended Enterprise, Ross, US (2003)
3. Conti, R., Angelis, J., Cooper, C., Faragher, B., Gill, C.: Lean production implementation and worker job stress. International Journal of Operations and Production Management 26, 1013–1038 (2006)
4. Drew, J., McCallum, B., Roggenhoffer, S.: Journey to Lean. Palgrave, Oxford (2004)
5. Ehrlich, B.: Service with a smile. Industrial Engineer, 40–44 (August 2006)
6. Fujimoto, T.: The Evolution of a Manufacturing System at Toyota. Oxford University Press, Oxford (1999)
7. Haywood-Farmer, J., Nollet, J.: Services Plus Effective Service Management, Morin, Quebec (1991)
8. Hines, P., Holweg, M., Rich, N.: Learning to evolve. International Journal of Operations and Production Management 24(10), 994–1011 (2004)
9. Katayama, H., Bennett, D.: Agility, adaptability and Leanness. International Journal of Production Economics, 60-61, 43–51 (1999)
10. Korczynski, M.: Human Resource Management in Service Work. Palgrave, Hampshire (2002)
11. National Statistics (2008), National Statistics Online
    http://www.statistics.gov.uk
12. Seddon, J.: Freedom from Command and Control. Moreton Press (2005)
13. Tischler, L.: Bringing Lean to the office. Quality Progress 39(7), 32–38 (2006)
14. Wacker, J.: A theory of formal conceptual definitions. Journal of Operations Management 23(4), 629–650 (2004)

Health Care Provider Processes Analysis

Lukasz Kawczynski and Marco Taisch

Department of Management, Economics and Industrial Engineering,
Politecnico di Milano,
Piazza L. da Vinci, 32 I-20133 Milano, Italy
{lukasz.kawczynski,marco.taisch}@polimi.it

Abstract. In every society there is a need for an efficient health care system. This is a case study paper that summarizes process analysis performed at a US provider clinic. This paper provides an analysis of factors (arrival accuracy and no shows) influencing main processes within the clinic. The numerical relations between influencing factors and key processes are exhibited. Moreover, the abilities of a health care provider to deal with variations of arrival time are exhibited. The predicted probabilities for arrival accuracy and no shows are discussed. The paper provides an interesting statistical approach to analyze operations of a health care provider, which can be beneficial for stakeholders of the clinic.

Keywords: Health care, Process analysis, Arrival time, No shows.

1 Introduction

Health care is an important aspect of every society. Recently, the subject itself is getting more attention as it is in need for change in many countries. Improvements have to be made in order to make it more efficient and patient driven. This is a case study paper describing part of the research conducted at a US nationwide health care provider, specializing in children care. This paper is part of larger research. Based on the study of outpatient clinic, the research aims to propose value definition and value chain model, which will be supported by simulation. This paper is analyzing flow of the patients through the clinic, aiming to show dependencies and relations between key processes, and how they are influenced by arrival times of patients. As a consequence, the ability of providers to deal with various scenarios are analyzed and the factors that could help predicting no shows and late arrival pointed.

2 Literature Review

Many authors were studying health care with focus on various aspects for inpatient and outpatient environment. The inpatient settings have received so far more attention in the literature than outpatient.

[10] analyzed length of stay (LoS) of patient in a hospital taking into consideration various data like: admission time, destination, discharge time, etc. The authors

B. Vallespir and T. Alix (Eds.): APMS 2009, IFIP AICT 338, pp. 595–602, 2010.
© IFIP International Federation for Information Processing 2010

described and discussed couple of data models that could be used in connection with particular data warehouse environment. A transaction based model was proposed for facilitating LoS analysis and a snapshot-based for admissions, discharges and bed occupancy. [4] developed quality management model, which identifies problems, suggests solutions, develops a framework for implementation, and helps evaluate performance of inpatient health care services. [9] used industrial management principles to improve quality and efficiency of inpatient urgent care. Authors looked at urgent surgeries as an industrial process. General process analysis tools and process reengineering were used to develop the process. Process was described and measured to identify the bottlenecks. The care process was developed on the basis of the Deming cycle or the Plan-Do-Check-Act (PDCA) cycle. After implementation of suggested improvements authors found significant decrease in waiting times, rise in efficiency, and decrease of overtime hours. [2] proposed a flexible framework for modeling and simulation of inpatient health care. Authors offered a methodology which accommodates three types of view on health care system: process, resource, and organization. With a case study the use of the model is illustrated. [8] described a generalized net model of patient flows. The model aims to help improve management of the diagnostic consultative centers, through optimization of the use of resources. [6] proposed research a use of data mining and visualization techniques for decision support in planning and regional level management of Slovenian public health-care. They took attempt to identify areas which are atypical in terms of accessibility and availability. The authors contribute to theory by developing visualization methods that can be used to facilitate knowledge management and decision making processes. [3] presented a stochastic model of an individual patient's experience during a visit to a doctor's office. Authors apply semi Markov processes within outpatient clinic settings in order to model patient flow. The paper uses logical framework analysis (LFA), a matrix approach to project planning for managing quality. After applying in studied case, authors found improvements in quality performance of hospital. [1] were researching patient volume forecasting methods in walk-in outpatient clinics. On a large set of data they compared implementation of two forecasting models – autoregressive and growth curve of means. [5] described application of the discrete event simulation model to support analysis which led to improvement of outpatient procedure center processes Authors showed a bottleneck and as a result a need for additional resources. After reorganization of processes authors are examining 4 scenarios of different hedging strategies. The waiting times, efficiency, and utilization of an operation room are compared. Authors concluded with proposing an optimal design, i.e. being able to serve an assumed number of patients and at the same time minimizing waiting times and maximizing utilization. [7] concentrated on solving scheduling problems in ambulatory outpatient environment where patients are scheduled a few days in advance. With multi agent simulation researchers brought waiting times to constant level (little variation). Authors haven't been able to report significant decrease in waiting times.

Researchers have directed a lot of attention so far to the inpatient processes analysis. The outpatient clinic processes have received significantly less attention in the literature.

3 Methodology

The methodology of this research could be divided into two parts. First part is responsible for picturing the processes and gathering the data. The process mapping activities were conducted in order to understand what processes are in the clinic. The data were gathered from the systems supporting every day operation of health care provider (patient management system).

The second part is data analysis aiming to show dependencies and relations between variables describing process performance. The analysis is divided into three stages. In the first one we want to show how arrival times are influencing operation. Regression models are built in STATA and relevant dependent variables screened. In the second step, we want to show the model for predicting time to appointment variable and no-shows. The regression models are constructed for each variable aiming to estimate prediction for early arrival for patients and prediction of no shows. In the final part, we want to determine how likely a clinic is able to cope with late arrivals and what are the consequences. The Markov chains are employed to study delayed arrivals and operational performance.

4 Health Care Provider Description

The health care provider taking part in this research is specialized in children care. The provider is operating through the chain of clinics all over east and south US. The studied clinic has 13 sub-clinics representing different specialties. The provider operates from 8 AM to 4 PM, Monday through Friday. The clinic serves on average 93 patients daily, which makes it a medium size health care provider.

5 Processes at Health Care Provider

The mapping activities revealed seven main groups of the processes, which are: pre-registration, scheduling, eligibility verification (for insured patients), check-in, pre-examination, medical examination, and billing. In this paper we are focusing on the processes within clinic (check-in, pre-examination, and medical examination). These processes are describing patient flow from arrival at the facility to check out.

The check-in process is including several sub processes. After patient arrival at the clinic, the sign in sub-process is performed during which patient information is verified and the system updated. This sub-process is followed by check-in, during which the final insurance verification is performed and co-pay (if any) collected. Patient is issued a buzz pager and is proceeding to a central waiting area.

The pre-examination process starts when patient's record is checked for any missing data. Afterwards, patient is called (via buzz pager) to pre-examination room. The reason for the visit is confirmed, appropriate vitals gathered and entered into the system.

The medical examination is started with a verification of allergies, medical reconciliation, medical and social history. Afterwards, the physical examination is performed. Doctor provides a diagnosis and updates patient record, entering any additional tests (if needed). After the visit is completed the nurse checks out patient.

6 Data description

The system data count for 15000+ records. During quality screening of system dataset we removed records that did not contain a complete data or contained an obvious error. After verification we received 4600+ valid records. This data set is used for analyzing processes and arrival times. The dataset included variables as described in Table 1.

Table 1. Variables' means, standard deviations, and distributions

Variable	Sample mean (minutes)	Standard deviation (minutes)	Distribution
Appointment time	11,9 (hours)	144,6	Beta
Time to appointment	-22,8	31,2	Normal
Arrival time	11,48 (hours)	141,6	Beta
Check in time	6,6	7,2	Exponential
Waiting time	25,2	24,6	Weibull
Vitals time	23,4	22,8	Gamma
Medical examination and check out (including waiting time for provider)	58,8	52,8	Erlang

For analysis of no shows we used full dataset of 15000+ records, which describes an 8 month period of operation. More than 6500 records are no shows. Taking this into consideration no-shows seem to be an important problem in every day operation.

7 Clinic Performance Influencing Factors

We aim to determine what is influencing patient flow through the clinic by establishing links between variables describing main operational performance. The analysis is started with building statistical models in STATA linking medical examination length (the time that patient spends with a doctor including check out time and waiting time in exam room) and waiting time in lobby with other variables.

The linear regression model that is using medical examination time as a dependent variable showed with a p-value of zero that the variables that have influence are the ones that are describing late arrival of patient to the appointment and the time needed to gather vitals. Based on beta coefficients the most influence has a delay of arrival time. The regular coefficients indicate that for every 12 minutes of delay in patient arrival there is an hour increase in medical examination time (while other variables are hold constant). Naturally, this time is mostly consumed by waiting time, not the physical examination performed by a care provider. The variable describing time to gather the vitals suggest that there is negative correlation with medical examination (-0,175). The longer time needed to gather the vitals the shorter medical examination time.

The Poisson regression model that is using waiting time as a dependent variable with a p-value of zero indicated that the variables influencing a waiting time are the ones that describe late arrival and the length of check in process. Every 10 minutes of late arrival is causing more than 12 minutes of additional waiting time in provider's lobby area (while other variables are hold constant). Moreover, the model suggests that every additional 5 minutes needed for check in would result in more than 2,5 minutes of additional waiting time (while other variables are hold constant).

The above statistical analysis is pointing out the dependencies between key processes performance and arrival times of patients.

8 Prediction of Arrival Time and No Shows

In order to analyze the probabilities of particular arrival times we created an additional binominal variable which classifies all the patients that arrived at least 5 minutes before an appointment as 1 (early arrival) and the rest as 0 (late arrival). The logistic regression model was built in STATA. The model indicated with a p-value of zero that there are two variables significant: appointment time and day of the week. Based on model, predicted probabilities suggested that patients that are having appointments early in the morning on Mondays on average are 7% less likely to arrive on time than patients having the same appointment on Friday. The difference is reduced to 4% for late afternoon appointments respectively. The probability of patient arriving at least 5 minutes before a scheduled appointment time is lower for first appointment in the morning (between 0,6 and 0,67 depending on a day of the week) than for the last one of the day (between 0,83 and 0,87 depending on a day of the week). Predicted probabilities of early arrival for a different appointment times are exhibited in Figure 1.

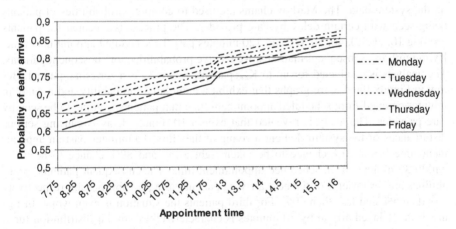

Fig. 1. Probability of early arrival as a function of appointment time

Moreover, within studied data period there is improvement in the patient early arrival time. During 8 months the early arrival probability increased by 0,1.

In case of variable describing no shows, logistic regression was used. The variable has binominal values only. The model with a p-value zero suggest that variable describing day of the week and variable describing type of patient (new or returning) are significant only. The statistical model suggested based on predicted probabilities values that the probability of no show for a new patient is close to 0,46, while for returning one only 0,37. Taking into consideration the day of the week, there is higher chance of no show on Monday (0,43) than on Friday (0,4), and its constantly decreasing through the week.

9 Process Implications of Late Arrivals

The Markov chains are employed in order to determine how the clinic is able to deal with late arrivals and what the consequences are. The first step is the calculation of the matrix describing delays in arrival time and the difference between scheduled time and the actual time when patient was seen by care provider. In order to provide visibility, both variables are converted into interval variables. The implemented interval is 10 minutes, and the data is rounded down toward zero. The difference between arrival time and scheduled appointment time is taking into consideration only records that are having positive value, which means that patient had arrived late or in the best case right on time. Both variables have been limited by upper bound of 180 minutes, which is reasonable boundary for practical analysis. We built a 19 x 19 matrix where on one horizontal axis is an interval variable describing how long after scheduled appointment time patients arrive, while on vertical axis there is an interval variable which describes how many minutes after scheduled appointment time patient was seen by care provider. The matrix computes probabilities for each possible state based on the system data. The Markov chains are used to compute probabilities of patients being seen with certain delay by care provider. The process is repeated for patients arriving 10, 20, 30, 40, 50, 60, and 120 minutes past the scheduled appointment time. By multiplying subsequent matrixes, we receive probabilities for subsequent patients. The analysis is conducted for up to K_{n+5} patient, where K_n is a zero time patient. Below in Figure 2 and 3 are graphs that exhibit a cumulative probability and a delay in minutes counted from scheduled appointment time that patients is going to be seen by care provider. The analysis revealed that even a 10 minute delay is causing serious disturbances of the system. Patient arriving at the clinic 10 minutes past an appointment time has a 20% chance to be taken right away and 80% chance to be taken within 30 minutes from scheduled appointment time. The subsequent patients' probabilities are far lower. For the next arriving patient these probabilities are respectively less then 5% and less then 40%. For third patients the situation is even worst. In figure 3, the delayed arrival by 30 minutes is characterized by similar distribution function than the first case. Patient has less then 9% chance to be taken right away, and around 80% chance to be taken within 50 minutes from the scheduled appointment. In case of patients arriving after delayed one, they have less then 1% and 22% of chance respectively. Both graphs (for 10 and 30 minutes delay) are looking alike, and so are the plots for other delays' values. The difference might be notice in the angle of the rise. In case of relatively small delays this angle is pretty high, which means that clinic is likely to cope with this situation, while in case of large delays the angle becomes lower.

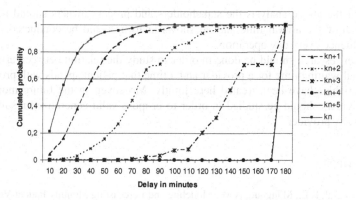

Fig. 2. Cumulative probability as a function of delay of patient being seen by care provider for patient arriving 10 minutes after an appointment time

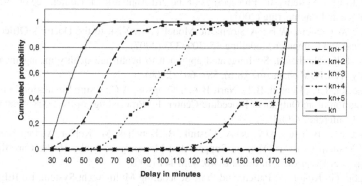

Fig. 3. Cumulative probability as a function of delay of patient being seen by care provider for patient arriving 30 minutes after an appointment time

10 Conclusion and Further Research

Health care is an important and at the same time difficult sector to manage. Many of the processes are sensitive and not all of them are manageable. The above analysis reveled how much the medical examination time and waiting times depends on patient accurate arrival. The analysis showed as well how the clinic is coping with late patients' arrivals. Based on above analysis, health care provider should implement tools encouraging patients to accurate arrival. Provider should emphasize to the patient while scheduling the appointment, how important is his/her arrival on time. It should be clear for patient that his/her on time arrival will minimize total time spent in the clinic. Moreover, provider should analyze the influence of various medical visit windows (the time in the system for one patient) on system sensitivity to late arrivals. This gap at studied case is established individually by each care provider, who is guided more by common sense than by hard data.

Out of the above analysis the stakeholders and process owners should benefit by learning how the arrival time and no shows analysis could be conducted, and how they influence every day operation.

Further research should be done in order to study the relation between arrival time and actual waiting time for a provider and a time that patient spends with provider, as these variables have been treated here jointly. Moreover, in the future more health care providers should be studied in order to propose valid generalized results, applicable to any provider.

References

1. Abdel-Aal, R.E., Mangoud, A.M.: Modeling and Forecasting Monthly Patient Volume at a Primary Health Care Clinic Using Univariate Time-Series Analysis. Computer Methods and Programs in Biomedicine 56, 235–247 (1998)
2. Augusto, V., Xie, X., Grimaud, F.: A Framework for the Modeling and Simulation of Health Care Systems. In: Proceedings of the 3rd Annual IEEE Conference on Automation Science and Engineering (2007)
3. Cote, M.J., Stein, W.E.: A Stochastic Model For a Visit to the Doctor's Office. Mathematical and Computer Modelling 45, 309–323 (2007)
4. Dey, P.K., Hariharan, S.: Integrated approach to healthcare quality management: a case study. The TQM Magazine 18(6), 583–605 (2006)
5. Huschka, T.R., Denton, B.T., Narr, B.J., Thompson, A.C.: Using Simulation in the Implementation of an Outpatient Procedure Center. In: Proceedings of the 2008 Winter Simulation Conference (2008)
6. Lavrac, N., Bohanec, M., Pur, A., Cestnik, B., Debeljak, M., Kobler, Andrej: Data Mining and Visualization for Decision Support and Modeling of Public Health-Care Resources. Journal of Biomedical Informatics 40, 438–447 (2007)
7. Stiglic, G., Kokol, P.: Patient and Staff Scheduling Multi-Agent System. In: IEEE 3rd International Conference on Computational Cybernetics - Proceedings, vol. 2005, pp. 25–28 (2005)
8. Tasseva, V., Peneva, D., Atanassov, K., El-Darzi, E., Chountas, P., Vasilakis, C.: Generalized Net Model for Outpatient Care in Bulgaria. In: Twentieth IEEE International Symposium on Computer-Based Medical Systems, CBMS 2007 (2007), 0-7695-2905-4/07
9. Torkki, P.M., Alho, A.I., Peltokorpi, A.V., Torkki, M.I., Kallio, P.E.: Managing urgent surgery as a process: Case study of a trauma center. International Journal of Technology Assessment in Health Care 2, 255–260 (2006)
10. Vasilakis, C., El-Darzi, E., Chountas, P.: An OLAP-Enabled Software Environment for Modeling Patient Flow. In: 3rd International IEEE Conference Intelligent Systems (September 2006)

Networked Service Innovation Process in the Production of a New Urban Area

Erja Väyrynen and Riitta Smeds

Helsinki University of Technology TKK, Enterprise Simulation Laboratory SimLab,
P.O. Box 9220, FI-02015 TKK, Finland
erja.vayrynen@tkk.fi, riitta.smeds@tkk.fi

Abstract. When a newly completed urban area does not conform to the visions, this brings disappointment for the residents and losses for the service providers in the area. In order to specify process innovations required in urban development, we conceptualise new urban areas as service innovations, and compare urban development to new service development. We conclude that developing urban areas as a process of customer-oriented service development and production is likely to lead to the satisfaction of all stakeholders.

1 Introduction

New urban areas require heavy investments and involve a large number of actors during the long process from visions to implementation. However, the users find the completed built environment often unsatisfactory. The residents may complain about construction defects or about missing services, and the service providers may find their location quite unsuitable for attracting clients. The developers may be in trouble with unsold flats. Our assumption is that this kind of situation calls for innovative new solutions, not only for the end-product, i.e. the built environment, but even more importantly, for the process that produces this output. In this paper, we raise the following question: *What kind of process innovations could be used to mediate innovative ideas throughout the urban development process, from visioning to use?*

In our earlier study, we have conceptualised new urban areas in a novel way as service innovations: as physical, social, environmental, economic, technological, aesthetic, etc. configurations that support the customers (i.e. residents and other users of the area) in their daily living and enable their manifold activities [1]. We applied the theories of process management and new service development (NSD), and considered the users of a new area as customers that continuously co-develop this service. We assumed that a successful design and timing of customer involvement enhance the quality of a service innovation and help manage the complex user expectations, and thus increase customer satisfaction. We concluded that process innovations would be needed to promote this kind of networked co-development. We continue in this paper by comparing urban development to NSD and by analysing the result from the customer perspective. Our final aim is to develop a new model of urban development, considered as a networked service development process.

B. Vallespir and T. Alix (Eds.): APMS 2009, IFIP AICT 338, pp. 603–610, 2010.

2 Background

The process of urban development, from visioning and goal setting to implementation and use, is commonly modelled as presented in Fig. 1.

Fig. 1. The process of urban development

When we remodel this conventional process by emphasising the amount of new ideas and alternatives under consideration in each stage of the process and by showing the main actors, we are able to discern some problematic points in the conventional urban development process (Fig. 2).

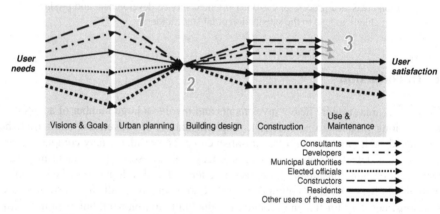

Fig. 2. Conventional process of urban development with main actors

The points of concern are the following (ref. numbering in Fig. 2): 1. Visions do not steer implementation, 2. Discontinuity in the information transfer, 3. Lack of interest in the phase of use and maintenance

We have studied the urban development process through in-depth case studies of four innovative housing areas: Suurpelto, "the Garden city of information age" (Case 1), Viikki, "the Ecological city" (Case 2), Vuores, "the Small town in the midst of nature" (Case 3), and Nupuri, "Individual design for a coherent community" (Case 4). In these case studies, we found certain innovative practices that had been developed to mitigate the above mentioned process deficiencies. We interpreted these empirical findings through a theoretical framework and defined three new generic principles of urban development:

   A. Vision guides the process from planning to implementation
   B. Continuous learning and interaction act as a support for innovation
   C. Commitment of all actors to quality leads to user satisfaction.

To develop a new model of urban development as a networked service innovation process, these principles are now further analysed and tested based on the theories of new service development.

3 Theoretical Scope

Services differ from physical products, which brings particular features also to their development efforts. Several studies show, nevertheless, that many of the concepts originating from the new product development (NPD) literature are also applicable to service companies. Customer-oriented NPD requires collecting knowledge about the customers' needs in a systematic way and designing products based on this knowledge; the same applies to services.

Grönroos [2] points out that services are processes by nature. They are produced and consumed at least partly simultaneously, and the customer participates in the production of the service. The simultaneity of production and consumption, and the customer's participation, make it even more important to involve customers in the development efforts than in the case of physical products.

Innovations in services can be related to changes in various dimensions: in the service concept, in the client interface, in the delivery system, in technological options etc. [3]. Most innovations would involve a combination of changes in several dimensions. New service ideas may emerge already in the planning of service objectives and strategy [4].

Valkeapää et al. [5] have studied how to enhance customer orientation in NSD in a strategic alliance. They present a new framework illustrating the prerequisites of a customer-oriented NSD process in alliance context (Fig. 3). They point out that collaborative service processes have potential for service innovations, and therefore their development should be encouraged.

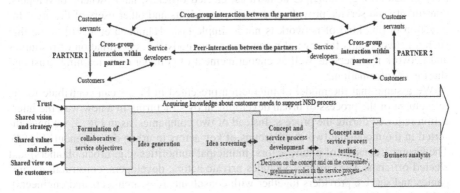

Fig. 3. The model of a customer-oriented NSD process in a strategic alliance, with the model of interaction [5]

According to the conclusions of Valkeapää et al. [5], joint service processes in alliance context easily become complex, which highlights the importance of a carefully planned and collaborative development. In their framework, Valkeapää et al. have modelled a NSD process in a case study of a strategic alliance of two partner companies. The case alliance consisted of an insurance organization (Partner 1, in Fig. 3) and a group of banks (Partner 2). The model also includes various methods for identification of customer needs in each stage of the service development process.

Based on their case study, Valkeapää et al. [5] confirm that factors such as shared vision, values, and rules were important prerequisites for the NSD in the case alliance. Another important prerequisite for the development of the new collaborative service was a *shared view on the customers,* which also contributed to trust between the partners. The study [5] further highlights the significance of interaction between different parties in the collaborative NSD process. A collaborative NSD process should support *peer-interaction* between the personnel of the strategic partners. This peer-interaction between the partners is crucial in order to build common vocabulary and consensus about the collaborative service.

A special emphasis should also be put to the *interaction with customers* through the service process, in order to discover customer needs. In the case studied by Valkeapää et al., the phases of concept and service process development and testing included interaction between the service developers, the customer servants, and the representatives of customers. This *cross-group interaction* should take place *within* one company but also *between* the partners [5].

In this paper, we compare the model of interaction and the process model ([5], Fig. 3) analytically with the development process of a new urban area. The similarities identified in this comparison are tested in our four cases, to develop hypotheses for an innovative service-oriented urban development and production process.

4   NSD in the Context of Urban Planning: Model of Interaction

In a process of urban development, the network of actors consists of a challenging variety of actors: e.g. municipal authorities, elected officials, land owners, developers, consultants and service providers, as well as residents and other users of the area. Interaction in this kind of network is not a simple task. Hänninen et al. [6] argue that such a network calls for several management methods: e.g. coordination of resources and network members, as well as encouragement of collaboration, learning, trust and sharing of information.

We assume that the model of interaction presented in Fig. 3 can contribute to the refinement of the process of urban development by structuring in a new way the interaction required during the process. Instead of two companies, as in Fig. 3, we have inserted in the model the two main groups of key actors in urban development (Fig. 4). The Group 1 consists of public actors: municipal authorities (e.g. urban planners) and elected officials. The Group 2 includes private actors: developers, construction companies and service providers together with consultants (e.g. architects and engineers). Following the model of Valkeapää et al., these groups should practise interaction both within the group and between the groups. In addition, they should regularly interact with their customers, i.e. the future residents or other users of the new urban area, and also create a shared view of their customers.

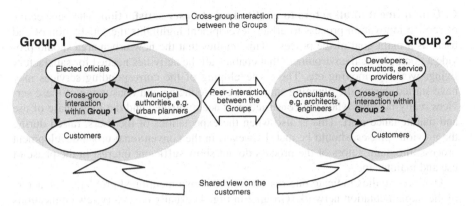

Fig. 4. Interaction between the key groups in urban development (modified from [5])

The three new principles, suggested earlier in Chapter 2, are now analysed through the model of interaction presented in Fig. 4.

A. Vision guides the process from planning to implementation. Visions are usually created within Group 1, and they are implemented by Group 2. Our case studies indicate that *cross-group interaction between the groups* is essential for a successful implementation of visions, and that this interaction should be carried on already from the early phases of the process. The case studies 2 and 3 also reveal the importance of deriving measurable criteria from the vision in order to enhance innovation. The use of criteria increases the understanding of the common goals, and also serves as a practical tool during the follow-up of the implementation.

The end users of the future area or their representatives were not involved in the visioning process in any of the cases studied. Compared to a NSD process, this implies that a significant potential for innovation is usually being lost.

B. Continuous learning and interaction act as a support for innovation. The discontinuity in the information transfer, illustrated as No. 2 in Fig. 2, occurs at the same time when the main responsibility of the process moves on from Group 1 to Group 2. In all the cases studied, new practices were created to urge developers and constructors to examine carefully the information produced in the visions and plans for the area. In addition to cross-group interaction, this necessitates *peer-interaction* between the groups.

In one of the cases, residents were included in the interaction through an innovative web based on-line participation method, the Planning Forum (Case 4). This enabled *cross-group interaction within* Group 1, which is generally neglected. (Residents' statutory participation in the urban planning process does not comply here with the definition of interaction.) In the Planning Forum, a special content management system enables maintaining the material related to the planning projects, including conversation and comments, for years. All users have access to the stored content. This offers a new opportunity to exploit the potential for innovations, as referred to in the NSD process. In addition to *interaction with customers*, the Planning Forum also provides a possibility for Group 1 and Group 2 to create a *shared view on the customers*.

C. Commitment of all actors to quality leads to user satisfaction. The perspective of service innovation process to urban development highlights the satisfaction of end users as a main goal of the process. This implies that the new urban area should provide a good physical environment that enables all the activities needed for satisfactory living, working, moving etc. The co-developing of the corresponding services may have started during the planning stage, but co-producing and consuming of these services really take off when the construction is accomplished and the long phase of use and maintenance start. This is also when the expectations of the users, raised during the previous phases, should be met. However, in the conventional urban development process, the main actors of the process do not show sufficient interest in the phase of use and maintenance.

Our case studies indicate one reason for the above mentioned problem. The actors of the implementation network (Group 2 in Fig. 4) usually have very few connections to the early stages of the process, and thus have difficulties to be committed to quality targets that have been set by quite another group of actors (Group 1). We assume that a *shared view on the customers* is the prerequisite for both groups to understand the importance of creating and maintaining customer satisfaction after the completion of a new area. In one the cases, residents could act as co-producers by using a special tool for selection of optional elements to shape their future environment (Case 4). This method can increase *cross-group interaction within* Group 2 and enhance the commitment of all its actors to quality.

Table 1 summarises the different modes of interaction typically related to each of the new principles for the innovative development of new urban areas.

Table 1. Modes of interaction typical to each new principle (shaded cells)

Modes of interaction	Three new principles for urban development		
	A	B	C
Cross-group interaction between the Groups			
Cross-group interaction within the Group			
Peer- interaction between the Groups			
Interaction with customers and shared view on the customers			

5   NSD in the Context of Urban Planning: Process Model

Two features of the NSD process are of particular interest to the urban development process: Firstly, the importance of developing and testing the service concept already in the early phases of the collaborative NSD process, along with the service process; And secondly, acquiring knowledge about customer needs throughout the NSD process to support service innovation.

The conventional process for urban planning (cf. Fig. 2) is aimed at achieving a document called the local detailed plan, and the processes of building design and construction are aimed at achieving the physical environment consisting of buildings, streets and parks. None of these processes is given the task of considering the service concept, not to mention the service process, of a new urban area.

The areas chosen for our case studies were all innovative areas with a strong vision. Some of these visions were developed further in a systematic way, resulting in a service concept followed by some kind of a service process. The case that was the most organised in this procedure, also reached its targets very well (Case 2).

When striving to develop new services that match customers' needs, most attention should be paid to customer input in the idea generation stage of the development process [4]. Furthermore, Jong and Vermeulen [3] advise that the creation of a climate supportive for innovation requires concentrating on both people-related and structural factors in the NSD process. Customer involvement is often claimed to be time-consuming. Related to time saving, Alam and Perry [4] remind that the stages of idea screening, concept development, concept testing, and business analysis can be carried out in parallel.

Customer needs are seldom studied systematically in the course of an urban development process. Contrary to common suppositions, appropriate techniques can be found for studying customer needs in all process phases. In two of our cases, the future residents were involved in the planning process (Case 1 and Case 4). The methods included e.g. a participative social process simulation method, as well as net based surveys and discussion forums. The impact of this involvement is not yet discernible, because the case areas are still under planning, but the feedback from the other actors in the process has been positive.

6 Conclusions and Discussion

This study reveals the following possibilities for process innovations in the urban development process:

1. Customer orientation: It is of particular importance that the two interacting groups, public and private, create a shared view about the customers. The methods of acquiring knowledge about customer needs and the timing of customer interaction have to be adjusted to the different stages of the process.

2. From idea generation to service concept: The interaction between the public and private groups should create a climate supportive for innovation. Customers should be involved in the idea generation, and attention should be paid to the formulation of the service concept as a substantial part of the planning process.

3. Duration of the process: Instead of being organised in a sequential way, as usual, the development process may contain overlapping and parallel stages, which can shorten the lead time of the process. In the case of urban development where the life-cycle of the output is exceptionally long, we suggest, however, that the speed of the process should not be prioritised in the same way as in NSD.

Developing an urban area as a customer-oriented service development and production process is likely to lead to the satisfaction of all stakeholders. According to our new urban development process model, customer needs should be identified at an early stage, and a shared view on the customers should be maintained during the long process of planning and implementation of a new area. Developers and construction companies should be involved in a collaborative innovation process together with their public counterparts as well as with the customers, which can bring innovation to the construction business that is usually considered quite reluctant to new ideas. Other service providers that aim to operate in the new urban area should get access to the planning process, which helps them adjust their service offerings to the needs of the future inhabitants and to the physical premises earlier than usual.

The development and production of an urban area as a networked service innovation between the public and private actors and the customers, is a novel approach, both theoretically and in practice. The results raise important hypotheses about the characteristics of urban development processes, to be further tested in multiple case studies. We hypothesise that with a collaborative, service-oriented urban development and production process, a more efficient use of public resources and a higher quality of the built environment will be achieved for the end-users than with conventional processes. The construction companies as well as the service providers will gain the possibility to develop synergistic innovations in this process.

Acknowledgements. The research reported in this paper has been conducted in the OPUS research project at the Enterprise Simulation Laboratory SimLab, Department of Computer Science and Engineering, Helsinki University of Technology TKK. The authors are grateful to the multidisciplinary OPUS research team for their creative research effort. The research is financially supported by the Finnish Funding Agency for Technology and Innovation Tekes, with municipalities and companies, which is gratefully acknowledged.

References

1. Väyrynen, E., Smeds, R.: Urban Planning as a Networked Development Process of Service Innovation. In: Smeds, R. (ed.) Proceedings of the APMS 2008 International Conference on Innovations in Networks, pp. 591–601. Helsinki University of Technology TKK, Finland (2008)
2. Grönroos, C.: Adopting a service logic for marketing. Marketing Theory 6(3), 317–333 (2006)
3. De Jong, J.P.J., Vermeulen, P.A.M.: Organizing successful new service development: a literature review. Management decision 41(9), 844–858 (2003)
4. Alam, I., Perry, C.: A customer-oriented new service development process. Journal of Services Marketing 16(6), 515–534 (2002)
5. Valkeapää, E., Södergård, R., Jaatinen, M., Smeds, R.: New Service Development Process in a Strategic Alliance. In: Proceedings of the 13th International Product Development Management Conference, Milan, pp. 1487–1501. EIASM and Politecnico di Milano (2006)
6. Hänninen, K., Huhta, E., Väyrynen, E.: Management of Change in Complex Networks. In: Smeds, R. (ed.) Proceedings of the APMS 2008 International Conference on Innovations in Networks, pp. 293–302. Helsinki University of Technology TKK, Finland (2008)

Health Care Provider Value Chain

Lukasz Kawczynski and Marco Taisch

Department of Management, Economics and Industrial Engineering,
Politecnico di Milano,
Piazza L. da Vinci, 32 I-20133 Milano, Italy
{lukasz.kawczynski,marco.taisch}@polimi.it

Abstract. In every society there is a need for an efficient health care system. This paper aims to propose a value definition and a value chain model within the health care. In order to define value patients and experts were surveyed. The proposed definition offers a complex way of looking at the value within the health care sector. The proposal of the value chain model is anticipated with a value stream mapping activities and experts interviews. Proposed model offers consistent way of looking at the value chain from health care provider perspective.

Keywords: Health care, Value Chain Model, Value Definition.

1 Introduction

In nowadays of a high competitive market, companies compete by creating more efficiently a greater value for customers. The way to create a value for a customer is through an efficient, well organized value chain, and an understanding of the mechanism supporting value creation process. Recently health care has been having a lot of problems in many countries and at the same time is a strategic sector for every economy. This paper is part of larger research and is providing a summary of the value chain and value investigation performed so far. The research aims to investigate US healthcare value chain with a focus on operational perspective. The ultimate goal is to offer value definition within health care, health care provider value chain, and support it with a simulation model. The paper offers a consistent value chain model and a complex value definition. Good quality value chain model with a focus on health care provider perspective has not yet been proposed in the literature. Proposed definition is enhancing current understanding of value within health care.

2 Literature Review

There are three streams that should be reviewed under this section: the value chain within the health care, value definition, and as a linked, subject patient satisfaction mechanism. Many authors were defining and discussing concepts of value. Mostly the concept of value was discussed based on manufacturing environment, although some of the authors took an attempt to focus on services. [8] defined value as a utility combination of price and non-price benefits offered to the consumer. The author admitted

B. Vallespir and T. Alix (Eds.): APMS 2009, IFIP AICT 338, pp. 611–618, 2010.
© IFIP International Federation for Information Processing 2010

as well that a value is a relative measure that each consumer determines by comparison of product with similar market offerings. [10] defined value as a result of products or service's ability to meet a customer's priorities. As an alternative, [5] offered a value equation concept one of the few authors who took an attempt to define a value within health care was [12]. Authors defined value as benefits and costs for patients and the internal activities or processes necessary to produce benefits for the patient. [9] focused strictly on patient value as a health outcome achieved per dollar of cost compared to peers.

The direct consequence of value perceived is a satisfaction. The commonly used indicator that utilizes customer expectations, customer satisfactions, and customer loyalty intentions is Customer Satisfaction Index (CSI), [4]. The CSI is a structural model based on the assumptions that customer satisfaction is caused by some factors such as perceived quality (PQ), perceived value (PV), expectations of customers, and image of a firm. One way of measuring PQ is SERVQUAL a framework introduced by [6]. SERVQUAL is the most prominent and widely used model for measuring service quality. [3] proposed alternative tool to SERVQUAL dedicated for healthcare. [11] developed and empirically tested a model to examine the major factors affecting patients' satisfaction that depict and estimate the relationships between service quality, patient's emotions, expectations, and involvement.

Each company, whether representing a manufacturing or service sector, satisfies customer and delivers a value to the customer through the value chain. The concept of the value chain was first introduced in the literature by [7]. The value chain was defined as an entire production chain from input of raw materials to the output of final products consumed by end user. [2] proposed concept dedicated for health care – named continuum. Under this concept there is neither a beginning nor an end – all the stages and activities are continuously performed. [1] offered in his book a general model of value chain dedicated for health care. The model is consisting of five different parties (payers, fiscal intermediaries, providers, purchasers, and producers).

Many authors were taking an attempt to provide value chains for different industry sectors. Manufacturing industry was the most studied . Few value chains with different perspectives were proposed for health care.

3   Methodology

The current paper is divided into two parts. The first part aims to propose a value definition based on patients' surveys and interviews with experts, while the second part aims to propose a consistent value chain model based on process mapping activities.

In order to understand the value mechanism we ran patient satisfaction survey. On selected days, before the medical appointment, patients were asked to complete a survey and returned it in the enclosed envelope. Three hundred and thirty valid responses were received. The survey tool was divided into five subsections (access to care, experience during the visit, opinions about care provider, personal issues, and overall assessment). Each group was containing questions regarding the satisfaction / perceived value within particular area of health care provider activity. With 42 questions, on a five point Likert scale (very poor, poor, fair, good, and very good) patients were asked to express their opinion. Additionally, patients were asked to answer three supportive questions. First question was asking if this was the patients first visit at this particular clinic, while the second and third were asking about the waiting time before the patient was called to the exam room and time spent in the exam room. This tool allowed us to survey for patient satisfaction and consequently for the value perception. Moreover, to enhance value understanding we conducted interviews with experts. We interviewed appropriate process owners. The interviews were not structured and are rather having an open form and are aiming to exhibit how each process creates a value (if any) and how this value can be better created for patient.

The second part aims to propose a value chain model. The analysis started with drawing value stream map for the clinic. Both process owners and shop floor workers were interviewed. The final value stream map was evaluated by process owners (supervisors and managers of particular sections). The value stream map provides us with information on the processes that are involved in value creation mechanism for the patient. Based on the map we divided processes into logical groups, in order to be able to accommodate them within the value chain model. The value stream map with the support of the interviews with the experts provides a base for proposing a value chain model.

4   Health Care Provider Description

The health care provider taking part in this research is specialized in children care. The provider is operating through the chain of clinics all over east and south US. The studied clinic has 13 sub-clinics representing different specialties. The provider operates from 8 AM to 4 PM, Monday through Friday. The clinic serves on average 93 patients daily, which makes it a medium size health care provider.

5   Patient Value

The patient value analysis started with the survey of patients. Within the survey 28 % of respondents were new patients. 48 % of patients were waiting between 0 and 5 minutes after scheduled appointment time to be called to the pre-examination room. Respectively, 27 % were waiting 6 to 10 minutes, 10 % - 11 to 15 minutes, 10% - 16 to 30 minutes, and 4 % were waiting more than 31 minutes. In the exam room 63 % of patients were waiting less than 5 minutes for care provider, while 18 % were waiting between 6 and 10 minutes. Remaining 20 % of patients were waiting more than 11 minutes. In order to provide statistical analysis we have assigned to each of the points on Likert scale a value from 0 (Very poor) through 50 (fair) to 100 (very good). This converts responses into five values interval variable. The questions were assigned to five groups in order to be analyzed. The clinics overall facility rating mean was found to be 90.7. The subsections scores are exhibited in statistic summary in Table 1.

Table 1. Survey groups summary.

Questionnaire group	Mean	Standard deviation
Overall facility rating	90,7	10,8
Registration	91,5	11,8
Facility	89,2	14,5
Treatment	91,9	11,7
Personal	91,5	11,3
Overall assessment	94,0	10,8

The first step was the correlation analysis. There was significant correlation found between overall respondent satisfaction and particular questions within the subsections. This suggests that certain factors are more important than others in the satisfaction (value) mechanism. The 22 out of 43 questions with the highest correlation coefficients are exhibited in Table 2.

Table 2. Top correlation coefficients questions

No.	Question	Correlation coefficient	No.	Question	Correlation coefficient
1	Courtesy of person that scheduled appointment	0,79	12	Helpfulness of registration person	0,71
2	Overall rating of care	0,76	13	Concern for privacy	0,71
3	Precautions for safety	0,76	14	Degree of safety and sec.	0,71
4	Staff concern for worries	0,75	15	Ease of moving around	0,70
5	Team work of staff	0,75	16	Ease of registration	0,70
6	Staff concern for comfort	0,75	17	Ease of scheduling	0,70
7	Comfort of waiting area	0,74	18	Effort of staff to introduce themselves	0,70
8	Concern for child's comfort	0,73	19	Courtesy of medical staff	0,69
9	Sensitivity to your needs	0,73	20	Cleanliness of facility	0,68
10	Friendliness of staff	0,72	21	Skills of staff	0,68
11	Response to concerns	0,72	22	Explanation given	0,68

The highest correlation coefficient was found between the overall satisfaction and a courtesy of personnel scheduling the appointment (0,79). The second highest correlation coefficient was found to be overall rating of care. This question describes how the medical side of the appointment is assessed by a patient. Within top ten questions with the highest coefficients we might notice that most of them are the questions concerning staff behavior (courtesy, friendliness, concern). Out of the top ten questions the only ones that are not addressing staff behavior are questions 2, 3, and 7. This confirms that the very important aspect within patient quality (and consequently shaping perceived value and patient satisfaction) is human interaction factor. This seems to put in doubt the definition of value within a health care proposed by [9], as it assumes that the important factors are medical benefits and cost. This definition abandoned completely the way how the medical benefits are delivered (human factor). The correlation table reveals as well importance of process and facility related factors.

Among others are degree of safety and security felt, ease of finding your way around, ease of the registration process, ease of scheduling appointment, cleanliness of facility, and waiting times. Most of these factors could be assign as well as a group that explains the way the service was delivered, while waiting times are related to the cost of obtaining a medical service.

The interviews with the experts included five interviews with supervisors and middle level managers. The interviews were having an open form, with questions regarding how patients perceived value, how patients' satisfaction is achieved, and what processes are involved in the value creation process. Four out of five respondents were highlighting an importance of medical outcomes in the satisfaction (perceived value) mechanism. The medical outcomes were pointed to have two meanings. Medical outcomes defined as an improvement of medical status (recovery) and change in the patient's awareness about sickness. Interviewee were pointing out that usually the first aspect is not fully in control of the health care provider, as it takes time, might be influenced by other providers and physically happens outside the clinic. The interviewees were stretching the importance of perceived value as a direct indicator of patient satisfaction and loyalty. Moreover, the cost of the medical appointment, especially for self paying patients and partly for insured patients (co-pay), was mentioned as secondary factor influencing patient perceived value and consequently satisfaction.

Additionally, according to American Customer Satisfaction Index framework the important factor influencing a customer satisfaction and perceived value are the expectations. Based on the patients and experts surveys ran within studied case and investigation of ACSI we took an attempt to formulate a value definition within the health care as *a relation of medical recovery progress or acknowledge of medical state, under the way the product and / or service was delivered, to the expectations, time, and overall costs associated with obtaining medical products and / or services received.* The proposed definition offers a complex way of looking at the value within the health care and at the same time enhances quality of proposed definitions within literature. For the first time the proposed definition takes into consideration medical acknowledgements as a factor that brings value, expectations, time, and overall costs associating with obtaining the medical product or service. Additionally, the definition points out that the care provider can influence the value perceived by the patient by the way products or services were delivered.

6 Value Stream Mapping

For the purpose of value chain analysis we ran a value stream mapping. The value stream mapping revealed a process that has a few variations. The variations are caused among others by sickness type, payer type (self paid, insured, and underinsured patient) or whether it is a new patient or returning one. The whole value stream flow is centralized around a patient management system (PMS), which keeps patients' medical history file, stores referrals, and provides appointment scheduled. The main processes brining a value that were identified are:

1. Pre-registration - gathers data from the guardian (medical history, reason for a visit, insurance data). The insurance is verified and data documented in the PMS.
2. Scheduling - provides patient with a suitable opening.

3.   Check-in - provides final verification of the data in the PMS (names spellings, addresses, and contact information), verifies insurance and let processes downstream know that the patient arrived in the clinic (through PMS).
4.   Pre-examination – verifies patients medical record and gathers basic vitals (weight, height, temperature and in some cases blood pressure).
5.   Medical exam - based on medical history file (located in PMS), additional tests, labs (if required), and physical exam provides diagnosis.
6.   Check-out - closes in the system the patients' medical appointment.

Each of the processes of the value stream has its own laws, regulations, and institutions external interaction. The process and personnel executing the process has to comply with various regulations and laws (for instance HIPAA).

The value stream map has a couple of interactions with external entities that are being part of the value creation process. These units are not part of the clinic itself, but are involved in value generation process: payors (for instance insurance companies), referring physicians (if any), external laboratories (when needed), and external health care provider (for additional consultations if needed).

6 Value Chain Model

The value stream analysis is a base for development of a value chain model. The model provided by Porter in 1985 was used as a framework. The main processes bringing value from the patient point of view are pre-registration, scheduling, check-in, pre-examination, and medical examination. It is essential to notice that for an insured patient, billing does not bring itself a value, although could be classified as a value adding process. Patient is not involved in billing processes and in fact is not even aware how this process is working. However, the important issue for a patient is the fact that the care provider is accepting the insurance policy, which is verified during pre-registration, and later on during check in. In order to be able to accept insurance policy, the care provider has to have a contract with the payor. This reasoning led to the conclusion that sales and contracting is an important part of the value creation process. The process itself is executed before actual interaction of the clinic with the patient begins. Moreover, as pointed out by experts during value definition phase, the health problems are requiring supervision over the recovery process. It is executed by follow up appointments and makes the recovery and follow up from the patients' point of view, a process that brings a value. The first moment, when the value might be created for a patient, starts actually before sales and contracting. The marketing and patient education done by health care provider brings a value for a patient. Through this processes patients are gaining knowledge about available treatments, sicknesses, threats, new diseases, preventive actions, and health care providers available on the market. Some of the value creating processes might be performed partly or totally outside clinic boundaries. The service delivery itself might be done partly outside boundaries of health care provider by referring patient to external laboratories. The same situation might occur with follow up and recovery. The patient might decide to be seen by a different care provider that is not part of the clinic that the medical treatment was started in. Interestingly, marketing and education processes might also be influenced by the activities of companies not depending on health care provider. For instance, education efforts done by competitors, trying to create patient awareness of crone diseases might bring a patient to a totally different health care provider than the one that was running the advertising campaign.

For proposing a value chain model we used Porter's model as a frame. The generic support activity categories do not require modifications for health care, as they are the same as Porter's (infrastructure, human resource management, development and innovation, and procurement). The primary activities are going to be changing depending on the payor type. In case of insured patients (the most common case), the primary activities are going to be: marketing & patient education, sales & contracting, pre-registration, scheduling, service delivery, and recovery and follow-up. Some of the primary activities will be influenced by the forces being located outside provider's boundaries as exhibited in Figure 1. For the simplicity of the drawing we accumulated check in, pre-examination, medical examination, and check out into service delivery block.

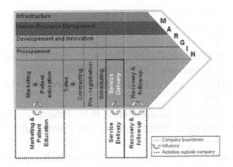

Fig. 1. Proposed value chain model (insured patients).

In case of the uninsured patients, the value chain model is going to differ than the one in Figure 1. The modifications will be a consequence of presence of different payors. The sales and contracting activities are not going to be a part of the primary activities.

For underinsured patients – the patients that are not able to afford medical bills or insurance, the value chain model is going to differ than the one for uninsured patients. The financial counseling activity with financial aid assistance will be an additional primary process bringing value. The three models of value chain are offering consistent way of looking at the value creation process from the health care provider perspective.

10 Conclusion and Further Research

The proposed definition of value within health care provides a new innovative way of looking at and analyzing a value (and consequently satisfaction) mechanism. The definition offers an incremental improvement comparing to the definitions dedicated for health care available in the literature, by considering additional factors.

The value chain model provides differentiation that is dependent on payor type. The proposed model highlights phenomena of value creation outside boundaries of the health care provider, which is a new aspect that has not been yet proposed. These processes are very important from the patient perspective, since they are going to be associated in patients mind with main health care provider. In the past this issue has not been well discussed in the literature for health care.

This research has certain limitations that should be studied in the future with more details. The expectation, as an aspect influencing patient value perception should be researched more deeply by conducting a mutual survey of patient expectations and patient satisfaction. This would precisely picture how the medical experience (perceived quality) is shaping the satisfaction (and perceived value) and how the satisfaction is shaped by the expectations. Conclusively, although the models were internally validated, the research should be enhanced on other health care providers in order to ensure external validity.

References

1. Burns, L.R.: The health care value chain: producers, purchasers and providers. Jossey-Bass A Wiley Company, San Francisco (2002) ISBN: 0-7879-6021-7
2. Deffenbaugh, J.L.: Health-care Continuum. Health Manpower Management 20(3), 37–39 (1994), ISSN: 0955-2065
3. Duggirala, M., Rajendran, C., Anantharaman, R.N.: Patient-perceived dimensions of total quality service in healthcare. Benchmarking: An International Journal 15(5), 560–583 (2008)
4. Fornell, C.: A national satisfaction barometer: the Swedish experience. Journal of Marketing 56, 6–21 (1992)
5. Heskett, J.L., Sasser, W.E., Schlesinger, L.A.: The service profit chain: How leading companies link profit and growth to loyalty, satisfaction and value. The Free Press, New York (1997)
6. Parasuraman, A., Zeithaml, V.A., Berry, L.L.: SERVQUAL: a multiple-item scale for measuring consumer perceptions of service quality. Journal of Retailing 64(1), 12–40 (1988)
7. Porter, M.E.: Competitive advantage: Creating and sustaining superior performance. The Free Press, New York (1985)
8. Porter, M.E.: What is strategy? Harvard Business Review (November/December 1996)
9. Porter, M.E., Teisberg-Olmsted, E.: Redefining health care – Creating value-based competition on result. Harvard Business School Press, Boston (2006), ISBN13: 978-1-591139-778-6
10. Slywotzky, A.J., Morrison, D.J.: The Profit Zone. Wiley, New York (1997)
11. Vinagre, M.H., Neves, J.: The influence of service quality and patients' emotions on satisfaction. International Journal of Health Care Quality Assurance 21(1), 87–103 (2008)
12. Walters, D., Jones, P.: Value and value chains in healthcare: a quality management perspective. The TQM Magazine 13(5), 319–335 (2001), ISSN: 0954-478X

Contribution to the Definition and Modeling of Service and Service Activities

Mounir Badja, Wael Touzi, and Thècle Alix

IMS, University of Bordeaux, CNRS, 351 Cours de la Libération,
33405 Talence Cedex, France
Tel.: +33 (5) 4000 6532; Fax: +33 (5) 4000 66 44
{Mounir.Badja,Wael.Touzi,Thécle.Alix}@ims-bordeaux.fr

Abstract. For a long time, it was highlighted that the service is intangible or immaterial; these characteristics are mainly used to distinguish the service, making it incomparable with good. The set of proposed definitions and characteristics that led to debates between specialists in economics for several years and gave place to a variety of visions and approaches are still not consensual and science engineers challenge. Goal of this paper is to present, on the one hand, the existing literature proposed by economists concerning services (definitions and specificities) and, on the other, arguments proposed by science engineers that challenge them. That study allows us to propose a generic definition of what a service is and a preliminary model of a service activity.

Keywords: Service characteristics, Service modeling, Process modeling.

1 Introduction

Services have been recently powerful engines of economic growth in many economies with such sign that today, a developed economy, would be a "tertiarized" economy [1]. Economists, Marketers, Human Resource Managers have studied the service economy, service marketing and service relation for a long time [2], [3], [4]. All have proposed definitions, associated different characteristics and defined specific tools for management.

Now that services represent a way to innovate in any sector of activity and since they have spread, particularly in the manufacturing area to differentiate from competitors and offer advantages, it becomes obvious to increase service efficiency and to cross disciplinary efforts to enrich services research [5]:

- Academics belonging to the manufacturing community are interested in investigating this sector and propose methods and tools to help modeling and controlling firms that are redeployed in product-service systems.

- Industrialists, for their concern, aims at developing coherent tools to manage efficiently service offers and service innovations that are synonyms of profitability and customers' loyalty.

Defined by these latest in a rather negative sense and considered as residual, dependent on manufacturing, technologically backward and not very innovative for a long time, services activities and services in general receive now a better echo. Studies led concern service delivery systems analysis, service operation management,

B. Vallespir and T. Alix (Eds.): APMS 2009, IFIP AICT 338, pp. 619–626, 2010.
© IFIP International Federation for Information Processing 2010

business process modeling, service quality evaluation and performance measurement, service value, service engineering, etc. and meet the studies already performed.

All these investigations that are necessary to deliver high value to the customer and to reach firms' objectives in terms of profitability and durability rest on the understanding of what a service is conceptually and on the analysis of the differences and similarities between products and services to help manufacturers understand what is specific to service delivery and what might be adapted. On the basis of a literature review presented in the following part and, on a qualitative survey presented in the third part of this paper, a definition and modeling principles are proposed in the fourth part before concluding.

2 Definitions and Characteristics of Services in the Literature Review

2.1 Service Definitions

A general consensus exists regarding the definition and execution of industrial production activities; it is less certain for the questions related to services, service activities and service execution. This is mainly due to the structural change of the service sector and to the historical tradition to consider services as a homogenous residual of a more "productive" manufacturing. Indeed, service is a complex and subjective matter, which allows individual interpretation and perception.

Nevertheless, it is useful to present some literature definitions to structure our approach and to better define the different characteristics of services that will be used thereafter for the model. The ones that are proposed here are the most cited in the literature:

- *"A service may be defined as a change in the condition of a person, or of a good belonging to some economic unit, which is brought about as the result of the activity of some other economic unit, with the prior agreement of the former person or economic unit"* [6].

- *"Service is a transformation of existence mode and/or dispositions of the person himself, of his body and his mind. While goods modify the existence conditions, services modify the existence modes, where goods are only supports"* [7].

- *"A service is an act (or a succession of acts) of duration and localization defined, achieved thanks to human and/or material means, implemented for the benefit of an individual or collective customer, according to processes, codified procedures and behaviors"* [8].

These definitions have in common the notion of activity or process, the notion of time and the concept of interaction between a supplier and a customer. They all gather characteristics that led to the definition of specific tools and methods of analysis and management.

2.2 Characteristics of Services

Researchers started to enumerate distinctive characteristics of services in order to distinguish them from goods [9] [10] [11]:

- A service is not owned, but there is a restricted access.
- Services have intangible results.

- Customers are involved in the service production process.
- Other persons than the customer can be involved in the service process.
- Quality in service is difficult to control while increasing productivity.
- Quality in service is difficult to apprehend.
- Service cannot be stored.
- Service delivery delay is crucial.
- Service delivery integrates physical and electronic way.

Based on these assertions, four characteristics named IHIP characteristics (i.e. Intangibility, Heterogeneity, Inseparability and Perishability characteristics) have merged to exemplify a service.

As related by the management literature, there are also some key characteristics that are common of all service activities. The main features of the service activity stems from the specific role played by the customer source of other attributes such as a co-production with the firm contact personnel and an uncertainty concerning the service outcome link to the conditions of the interpersonal exchange [6].

3 Qualitative Survey

A new community coming from the engineering science is investigating the service domain. In order to cross the points of view and enrich our understanding on services, a survey was carried out by the way of several interviews of engineers. Performed in facing each other, they focused on three main themes: an individual definition of services and associated characteristics, an analysis of the link existing between a product and a service and finally a comparison of the key elements to manage to produce a product and a service or more specifically a comparison between the model of production of a product and the "servuction" model.

3.1 Presentation of the Qualitative Survey

About eleven engineers were questioned during the survey carried out by two persons in the following way: a document presenting the results of the literature review was performed and sent to the interviewed persons by e-mail. Appointments were taken and conversations on the above-mentioned themes were recorded.

3.2 Processing and Analysis of Interviews

During the interviews, each interviewee expressed his own opinion on a service definition. Gathering and analysing these definitions, we have noted some key elements:

- The service is an answer to a need,
- The human factor impacts the production of the service,
- The service process impacts its outputs as well as all the elements which play a role during its execution,
- An ontology of service might be defined because of the multiplicity of terms used and underlying concepts.

Concerning the characteristic of inseparability and perishability, there was a total convergence of views. Interviewees were also in agreement with the fact that a service is produced at the same time it is consumed. Concerning the intangibility and heterogeneity characteristics, the points of view diverge.

Indeed, regarding the intangible nature of service (in the sense of impalpable), 80% of respondents supports this hypothesis but affirm that the value and effect of service is tangible and that the service should be supported by substantial resources.

Regarding the heterogeneity of services, opinions are more divided. 20% think that service is homogenous and 30% of respondents have a shared view on the subject. Note that, here, heterogeneity is defined by the fact that "... *a same service has a different result according to the person who provides it, the customer who receives it and the moment when this exchange is done*" [12]. This difference in opinion stems from the fact that some think that service is heterogeneous with a generic base, and also depend from a deference between customer view (perceived service) and supplier view (delivered service).

Regarding the characteristic of storability, although opinions are divided, the majority thinks that service is non-storable due to the impossibility of their storage (the service being an interaction between customer and provider). Some others think that a service is storable and affirm that it can be viewed as a sort of pass for press.

For perishability, the concept of time could be a common discriminator between a product and a service as a service might meet a need during a limited time (e.g. transport).

The observed divergences and the interviewee responses depend narrowly on their initial service definitions and their research topic. The gathering of definition and points of views allow us to propose our definition of services taking account of the duality between goods and services.

4   Service Definition Proposition

The definition proposal is not an aim in itself, but is an essential step without which we cannot claim to seriously work on service. Based on the previous literature review and the results of the survey interpretations, we propose to define the service *as the execution or the instantiation of an activity generating, an artifact and/or a state change of the artifact or the input agent, consuming entities (capacity to serve) grouped in resources, inputs and controls; attempting to satisfy customer needs.*

To make explicit the proposed definition, it is necessary to define the meaning of each term that is used and illustrate the definition using some conceptual diagrams.

We define the service as an execution activity, without taking account of the activity output nature (material/immaterial) and without distinguish the service provider from the service customer (self-service/customer-provider). From an operational and modeling point of view the execution activity can be seen as the instantiation of an activity done by affecting a value to the activity, resources, inputs, controls and outputs.

4.1   Service Meta-model

We assume that the service consumes and produces entities classified as artifacts or agents (Fig.1). "*An artifact may be defined as an object that has been intentionally made or produced for a certain purpose*" [13][14]. The artifact intentionality is a fundamental element [15], thus natural entity become artifact by attributing an intentionality (a pebble used like a paperweight is an artifact). We distinguish physical and no physical artifacts [16], where the firsts are the only ones having direct spatial dimensions and functions, these functions provide no physical artifacts. An agent is an entity having the capacity to accomplish actions using some competency and to provide no physical artifacts [16].

These entities take part in a service as an inputs, outputs, resources and controls. The entity serve capacity depends on its capability to provide no physical artifacts (broken car has no transport serve capacity), the entity with low serve capacity needs to consume a service to increase this capacity and be able to participate in the supported service (broken car needs mechanical repair service to be able to perform transport).

According to serve capacity possible values, we can define several entity states; the transition between two entity states can be induced by consuming service or by participating to service providing. The serve capacity evolution of service participating entities depends on the entity nature (a software developer increases his competency and developing serve capacity when he participates to development service) (a knife deceases its cutting serve capacity when it's used in a service).

If we assume that in our view the entity is not all the time participating in service, then the transition between two entity states can also be induced by other factors such as events or the time.

The service consumption responds to entity need, artifact need is different from agent need. The artifact need is closely linked to its serve capacities and needs services to be able to provide other services. An artifact with no functions will certainly disappear. The agent need for its concern includes two views: the first one is similar to the artifact need i.e. where the agent consumes services to provide other ones (a machine operator needs to consume formation service to provide a service on a specific machine). The second view is to consider the intrinsic human needs, which "... *arrange themselves in hierarchies of pre-potency...*" where "... *the appearance of one need usually rests on the prior satisfaction of another ...*" [17].

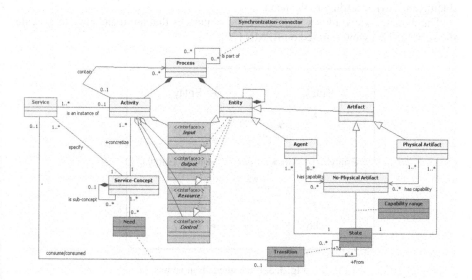

Fig. 1. Proposed service meta-model

4.2 Service Modeling

We gather considered concepts using UML class diagram (Fig. 1) [18] within which three class groups coexist, representing three views: (i) the functional view (Service, Activity, Entity, Process and Service-Concept), (ii) the interaction view (Service, State, Transition, Need and Entity) and (iii) the dynamic view (Activity, Entity, Process and Synchronization-connector).

The functional view allows to model the service, its inputs, its outputs and its activity using a mix of IDEF0, IEM [19] languages and integrating UML instantiation notion (Fig. 2). The activity represents a proposed response for the service-concept gathering customer needs, and the service an instantiation of this response.

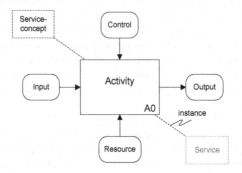

Fig. 2. Service functional view

Based on the UML state machine diagrams [18], the interaction view allows modeling the entities states and the transitions between them (fig. 3). The service here consumes serve capacities (and/or entities) inducing entity state change (and/or producing entities) according to the need.

The dynamic view allows to describe the sequences that are mandatory to execute the service. This view is based on BPMN [20].

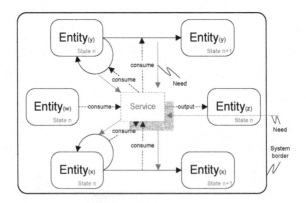

Fig. 3. Service interaction view

4.3 The Definition Proposal and the IHIP

After having proposed a definition and a modeling of the service, we check the IHIP characteristics and there link with the proposed point of view. The service defined as an execution activity is:

- Intangible; the execution being an order of actions, it is immaterial but can act on physical or no physical entities.
- Heterogeneous; the service being an activity instantiation each instance is different, with a common base (activity description).
- Inseparable; the execution gathers the provider and the customer during the execution duration (self-service/customer-provider).
- Perishable; the execution taking a finite time, the service only exists during its execution.

5 Conclusion

In the current economic context, the problem of service becomes a key issue. This article points both the contributions of the economic literature and the recent developments in service theory. We have proposed a definition and a service model that takes into account the service nature and characteristics and the links service/resources, which are considered as serve capability container. This view of service allows a better action on service.

Various questions suggest new fields of investigation, and future pathways of research to the evaluation of performance in services, study the quality of services, the definition of a production typology for material product and/or immaterial product, the formalization of public services, and new typology of services.

References

1. Edvardson, B., Gustafsson, A., Roos, I.: Service portraits in service research: a critical review. International journal of service industry management 16(1), 107–121 (2005)
2. Berry, L.L.: Relationship marketing of services – growing interest, emerging perspectives. Journal of the Academy of Marketing Science 23(4), 236–245 (1995)
3. Fisk, R.P., Grove, S.J., John, J.: Services Marketing Self-Portraits: Introspections, Reflections, and Glimpses from the Experts. American Marketing Association, Chicago (2000)
4. Zeithaml, V.A., Berry, L.L., Parasuraman, A.: The behavioral consequences of service quality. Journal of Marketing 60, 31–46 (1996)
5. Wild, P.J., Clarkson, P.J., McFarlane, D.C.: A framework for Cross Disciplinary Efforts in Services Research. In: CIRP IPS2 Conference, Cranfield, UK, April 1-2 (2009)
6. Hill, T.P.: On Goods and Services. Review of Income and Wealth, series 23(4) (1977)
7. Zarifian, P.: Evénement et sens donné au travail",In, coordonné par Gilles Jeannot et Pierre Veltz, "Le travail, entre l'entreprise et la cite, éditions de l'Aube, pp. 109–124 (2001)
8. Dumoulin, C., Flipo, J.P., et al.: Entreprise de service: 7 facteurs clés de success, les editions d'organisation, p. 211 (1991)
9. Lovelock, C., Wirtz, J., Lapert, D.: Marketing des services, p. 620. Pearson Education, London (2004)

10. Touzi, W., Alix, T., Vallespir, B.: An investigation into service and product characteristics to expand innovation. In: ERIMA 2008 Conference, Porto, Portugal, November 6-7 (2008)
11. Alix, T., Vallespir, B.: Gathering production Process of services and goods: towards the mixed enterprise. In: APMS 2006, IFIP. lean business systems and beyond, vol. 257, pp. 317–325 (2006)
12. Eiglier, P., Langeard, E.: Servuction: Le Marketing des Services. McGraw-Hill, Paris (1987)
13. Baker, L.R.: The Ontology of Artifacts. Philosophical Explorations. An International Journal for the Philosophy of Mind and Action 7, 1741-5918, 99–111 (2004)
14. Hilpinen, R.: Artifact: Stanford Encyclopedia of Philosophy, http://plato.stanford.edu/entries/artifact/
15. Vieu, L., Borgo, S., Masolo, C.: Artefacts and Roles: Modelling Strategies in a Multiplicative Ontology. In: Proceedings of the Fifth International Conference, FOIS, pp. 121–134. Saarbrücken, Germany (2008)
16. Kassel, G.: Vers une ontologie formelle des artefacts.: 20es Journées Francophones en Ingénierie des Connaissances, Tunisie (2009)
17. Maslow, A.H.: A Theory of Human Motivation. Psychological Rev., 370–396 (1943)
18. Fowler, M.: UML Distilled: A Brief Guide to the Standard Object Modeling Language, 3rd edn. Addison Wesley, Reading (2003)
19. Spur, G., Mertins, K., Jochem, R.: Integrated Enterprise Modelling, Berlin, Wien, Zürich Berlin (1996)
20. OMG: Business Process Modeling Notation (BPMN), Version 1.0, OMG Final Adopted Specification. Object Management Group (2006)

A Structured Comparison of the Service Offer and the Service Supply Chain of Manufacturers Competing in the Capital Goods and Durable Consumer Goods Industries

Donatella Corti and Alberto Portioli-Staudacher

Politecnico di Milano
Department of Management, Economics and Industrial Engineering,
P.za Leonardo daVinci, 32 - 20133 Milano, Italy
donatella.corti@polimi.it, alberto.portioli@polimi.it

Abstract. The increasing importance of the service offer for manufacturing companies has lead to the development of different service chains and service package in different industries. The main aim of this paper is to provide a structured comparison of the service offer and configuration in the capital goods and durable consumer goods industries. Even though the paper is mainly of a conceptual nature, the discussion is based on empirical findings collected. Main trends of the service provision within the corresponding supply chains are also highlighted and some guidelines for the service development are introduced.

Keywords: after-sales services, capital goods, durable consumer goods, after-sales supply chain.

1 Introduction

Since it is more and more difficult to differentiate products on the basis of technological superiority only and margins associated to the product sell are decreasing, services have become a possible source of competitive advantage (Wise and Baumgartner, 1999; Goffin, 1999; Cohen et al., 2006; Gebauer, 2008). The strategic consideration of services in manufacturing sectors is quite a recent phenomenon and the relevance of services in this context is expected to increase further in the next years, nonetheless the adoption of a service orientation is not a trivial task (Mathieu, 2001; Oliva and Kallenberg, 2003) and the literature focused on the servitised supply chains is still scarce; much empirical research in this area is thus called for (see for example Johnson and Mena, 2008).

The increasing importance of the service offer is common to many manufacturing sectors, yet service needs have evolved over the last years following different paths depending on the product's features (e.g. value and volume of products sold, degree of customization, etc.) and the type of customer (industrial or consumer).

The aim of this paper is twofold. On the one hand, a structured comparison of the service offer and configuration in the capital goods and durable consumer goods

B. Vallespir and T. Alix (Eds.): APMS 2009, IFIP AICT 338, pp. 627–635, 2010.
© IFIP International Federation for Information Processing 2010

industries is carried out in order to indentify drivers that lead to different configuration choices. Secondly, main trends of the service provision within the corresponding supply chains are highlighted and some guidelines for the service development are introduced.

Even though the paper is mainly of a conceptual nature, the discussion is based on empirical findings gathered by authors in different sectorial analysis carried out in the Italian market. In particular, the main reference for this paper is an empirical research that involved 21 companies operating in the consumer electronics (11 companies) and in the capital goods (10 companies) markets. The sampled companies have been selected in such a way all the main roles of the supply chain have been investigated. For both industries, at least one actor with the following roles has been analyzed: spare parts producer, OEM, wholesaler, dealer and assistance center. Data have been collected by means of face-to-face interviews based in a structured questionnaire different for each role.

2 Capital Goods and Durable Consumer Goods: Main Differences

It is a basic assumption of this paper that different requirements in terms of service management can be traced back to differences in terms of product use and nature of the supplier-customer relationship. The reason why it has been decided to focus also on the customer type is due to the central role the customer has in the service offering of any industry. In fact, it has been stated in several research (see for example Oliva and Kallenberg, 2003; Gebauer et al., 2008) that the offer of services by a manufacturing company requires the adoption of a customer oriented perspective according to which strategic decisions are made starting from the understanding of customer needs and requirements. As a consequence, not only the type of product, but also the type of customer, should drive the development of a service strategy that could strengthen the competitive position.

Part of the reasoning that is being presented in this paper could have a wider application and could be extended to the business-to-business (B2B) and business-to-consumer (B2C) markets. Nonetheless, due to the source of empirical data the discussion is based on, the reference industries are capital goods (for the B2B world) and the durable consumer electronics goods (for the B2C world). More specifically, in this paper capital goods are those machines and equipments that becomes part of the production process of the customer (textile machines, woodworking machines, machines tools, etc.).

2.1 Differences in Terms of Product Characteristic

Table 1 summarizes for each category of products the main features that have an influence on the after-sales requirements as are also introduced, for example, by Armistead and Clark (1992) and Legnani et al. (2009).

Table 1. Comparison of the features of the product and its use in the capital goods industry vs the consumer electronics industry

Characteristic	Consumer electronics goods	Capital goods
Lifecycle	Short	Long
Degree of customization	Usually very low	Medium- high
Frequency of contacts with supplier during the lifecycle	Very low	Medium-high
Level of customer's product expertise	Usually fairly low	Usually fairly high
Cost of ownership	Low-medium	High
No. of customers/ installed base	Usually high	Usually low
Level of response time	High/fixed	Low/variable
Replace costs/repair costs	Low	High
Cost of failure	Relatively low	Relatively high

2.2 Differences in Terms of After-Sales Network Configuration

The sale and the after-sales networks in the two analyzed industries often differ from each other. In this context it is of interest a detailed analysis of the after-sales channel. In most cases the after-sales channel is not the same as the sale channel: different actors are involved and also the responsibilities are different.

The most evident difference between the B2B and a B2C network is the "width" of the channel: where the network has to be as widespread as possible to reach the high number of customers in the B2C channel, in the B2B context a few highly specialized actors form the after-sales channel. The customer proximity is an essential element that influences the customer satisfaction for consumer goods, while an industrial customer is mainly interested in having the problem fixed as soon as possible. The limited number of customers is another reason that does not make economically feasible to set up of a widespread assistance network for industrial products. The number of intermediaries is limited for the capital goods market not only because the number of customers is low, but also because the level of expertise needed to carry our assistance activities is fairly high and only the supplier has the knowledge to fix problems. At this regard, it has also to be remembered that industrial goods are often customized and it is not possible to identify standard procedures that could be transferred to operators along the after-sales network as it is the case for some consumer products.

Figure 1 shows a generalized configuration of an after-sales network for servicing consumer products. It is referred to the Italian market, since for consumer goods the after-sales network is different depending on the market (like it is the sale channel). The interface for the customer is merely the producer and this means that customer satisfaction is heavily dependent upon intermediaries that most of the time are not owned by the producer (this is not only the case of consumer electronics, but also home appliances and automotive sectors). When a problem arise with the use of a consumer product, the end user can decide either to contact the dealer where the product was bought or one assistance center.

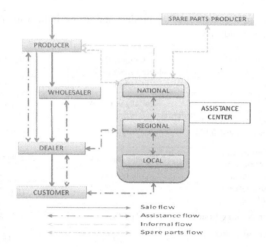

Fig. 1. Consumer electronics after-sales supply chain

The typical configuration of the after-sales supply chain for industrial goods is shown in Figure 2. The producer is the focal point who deals direclty with most of the other actors involved, including the customer. Unlike for the consumer goods after-sales chain, in this case the network could cover an internationl area since in many cases customers are spread all over the world, whilst the production could be in a single country. The distance between the customer and the manufacturer along with the limited number of specilized technicians who are able to carry out assistance activities, make it necessary for the producer to rely on local parterns for servicing local markets. The most common solution is the establishment of a local representative office that coordinates both the sales and the after-sales activities. Another reason why the direct contact between the supplier and the customer is relevant in this context, is the importance of the pre-sale services. The higher the level of customization

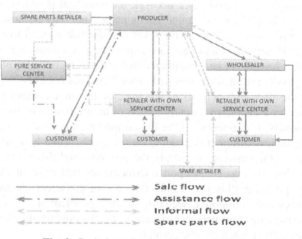

Fig. 2. Capital goods after-sales supply chain

Table 2. After-sales supply chain: criticalities of different roles in the consumer goods and capital goods industries

	MARKET	
PRODUCER	**Consumer electronics**	**Capital goods**
Interaction with customer	Indirect	Direct/Indirect
Services portfolio	Traditional	Wider
Specific features	Large companies externalize the execution of operative	
	processes, while they maintain the control on the network	
WHOLESALER	**Consumer electronics**	**Capital goods**
Interaction with customer	Indirect	Direct
Services portfolio	Traditional	Value added services
Specific features	Full intermediary role	Innovative role
SERVICE CENTERS	**Consumer electronics**	**Capital goods**
Interaction with customer	Direct/Indirect	Direct
Services portfolio	Specialized	Wide
Specific features	Focus on capillarity	Focus on customer closeness
	Multi-brand	Multi-brand/Mono-brand
	Hierarchical organization	Informal interrelationships
RESELLERS	**Consumer electronics**	**Capital goods**
Interaction with customer	Direct	Direct
Services portfolio	No intervention	Intervention
Specific features	After-sale intermediary	Assistance on all products
	Assistance on own sold	Informal interrelationships
	products	
	Bind to trade channel	
SPARE PARTS SUPPLIER	**Consumer electronics**	**Capital goods**
Interaction with customer	Absent	Direct/Indirect
Services portfolio	Absent	Wide
Specific features	Spare parts provisioning to	Active role within the supply
	service centers	chain

of the product, the higher the need of interaction between the two parties to identify the most suitable solution for the user or to devleop an ad hoc soluton.

Even though the type of actors is similar in the two channels, there are differences in terms of nature of links, relationships and flows among the nodes of the network.

On the one hand, the B2C chain features a more hierarchical organization of the flow management that is dependent upon decisions made by the producer even though there is not direct link between the customer and the producer. On the other hand, the B2B channel is often characterised by more flexible links among different actors.

The main differences in term of roles of the same actors in the two channels are summarized in Table 2.

Another difference is the nature of the logistics flow. In the B2C market the more relevant flow is the one of substitutive products, whilst the spare parts flow is being reduced over time due to the fast rate of new product introduction. Assistance center thus tend to minimize the spare parts stock and, in case of need, the order is placed directly to the OEM or to a spare part producer. On the contrary, in the B2B market, the spare part flow is the main one due to the product nature. The spare parts management is less critical then in the B2C channel for two reasons: the longer life cycle of components (lower risk of obsolescence) and the higher inventory turn-over index.

The focus of the improvement interventions in the logistics are thus different in the two markets: optimization of the spare parts management in the B2B market due to the high level of customization and the long life cycle; optimization of the substitutive product flow in the B2C market where the degree of customization is low and the life cycle is short.

2.3 Differences in Terms of Value Added Services

Empirical findings show that there is a difference between what is considered to be a value added service in the two markets even though in both cases new services are of an immaterial nature (traditional services like maintenance, spare part provision are given for granted in all markets). In the B2C context (for example for the consumer electronics) technical advice, training courses, home support, software upgrade and on-line monitoring are value added service. Guarantee extension, remote assistance, customization of training and maintenance and retrofitting are among the most valued services in the B2B market. Some services that are standard for one customer type becomes value added in the other market and vice-versa.

The comparison of these findings lead to the identification of two main drivers that influence the development of additional services. They are:

- the degree of innovation embedded in the service meaning its technological content and the level of the service novelty for the particular market sector;
- the degree of service customization in terms of a company's ability to tailor the service to the customer's needs.

Companies operating in the B2B market develop the service area by customizing their value added services in order to follow the customer's requests, whereas the trend in the B2C channel is to increase the level of innovation included in the service that is standard.

3 Discussion

One of the main objective of the after-sales service provision is to make customers loyal. At this regard, there is a big difference between the two chains. In the B2B market, the supplier-customer relationship is more developed: product support is essential for the product use (maintenance, spare parts,...) and during the product life cycle the need for the user to contact the supplier is frequent. The direct contact with the customer and the necessity of contacts (alternative service supplier are not common) makes it easier for the supplier to establish a long-term relationship with the customer and, as a consequence, there will be a strong motivation for the user to stay with the same supplier for the next purchase.

On the contrary, in the consumer electronics market, the short life cycle of products and the presence of different substitutive products, lead the producer to find different ways to retain customers. A good marketing strategy is one of the available tool to reach a high number of potential customers, even though there is not the possibility to have a face-to-face relationship with them. The low value of the replace costs/repair costs ratio could prevent the customer to ask any assistance. As a consequence, it is not enough to have an excellent technical assistance, a set of innovative and additional services are needed to attract new customers and to retain the old ones.

In the capital goods market, to best tailor the service offer to the specific user, the supplier should have a deep knowledge of the operations of the customer and the effect the product-service package will have on the customer's process and performance. The different use of the product in the consumer electronics market makes this point less critical this point: the product is purchased to satisfy a personal need and there is no need for the supplier to enter the whole process use that, however, less complex.

Even though the main differences in terms of service offer and service channel configuration are dependent upon the product nature and the type of the customer, it could be interesting to identify possible guidelines to further develop the service offer trying to transfer some approaches from one market to the other.

Two main considerations can be drawn at this regard:

- Value added services: in order to fully exploit the potentialities of the service offer to improve the competitive advantage the two channels can learn something looking at the best practices in the other market. In particular, in the B2B market, an higher level of embedded technology should improve the service offer. Not only remote assistance tools are needed, but also the internet channel could be further exploited (online catalogues, online training are still scarce in this context). On the other hand, the B2C market could benefit by the introduction of an higher level of customization of service. In this case, what can be customized is the time within each intervention has to be satisfied. Considering that customers are sensible to service time and cost variation, it would be interesting to offer the same service at a different cost depending on the time the customer is willing to wait for having the problem fixed.

- Configuration of the after-sales supply chain. Starting from the capital goods market, one of the main problem is the presence of independent actors (like pure serviced center or retailers with their own service center) who can attract users at the end of the guarantee period, thus reducing the service business for the original manufacturer. As a consequence, this situation could lead to a loss of brand visibility for the producer. A possible solution could be the creation of a more widespread owned assistance network or the development of formal partnership agreements with the already existing independent service provider and retailers. The first solution is feasible only for the biggest companies whose installed base is higher (thus volume becomes a relevant parameter), while the second one can be attained by small companies as well. Always looking at the consumer electronics market, it would be useful to strengthen the service marketing. In most cases, the service is not advertised at all by the company making thus it difficult for customers to appreciate a diversified service offer.

The rigidity of the after-sales network in the consumer electronics market makes it more difficult to change the configuration of the channel. The existence of different actors in the capital goods channels could be a possible source of inspiration to widen the business of the assistance centers and the dealers which need to find a way to remain profitable in the future. For example, the dealers could be provided with an owned assistance center authorized for the sold products or the assistance center could increase the business by starting selling products.

Of course, a careful analysis would be need to analyze the cost/benefit trade-off associated to these possible development and further empirical analysis is needed to test their feasibility.

4   Conclusion

Findings show how the service offer should be organized and managed depending on the company's position in the market in order to fully exploit the potential contribution of services to the overall performance. The different configuration and level of complexity of the after-sales supply chain is also taken into consideration in order to identify how responsibilities and risks are shared among the actors in the network and how these relationships are evolving over time.

Furthermore, the cross-industry analysis is used to identify possible practices that can be transferred from one sector to another one or from one channel to the other.

This paper is a contribution to the service literature that is still fragmented and lacks of a structured comparison that can help in better understanding the key differences affecting companies service performances.

In order to improve the validity of the findings a wider empirical analysis should be needed. The conceptual framework that is derived could be easily extended to some industries like the one of home appliances that share some features with the consumer electronics. For a more generalized discussion that could be applied to the B2B and B2C markets more empirical research is needed, in particular focused on those products, like the copy machines, that can be sold in the two channels. Finally, the proposed discussion could be used as a starting point to identify specific topics that can be analyzed in depth by means of specific research project.

References

1. Armistead, C., Clark, G.: A Framework for Formulating After-sales Support Strategy. International Journal of Operation & Production Management 11, 111–124 (1992)
2. Cohen, M.A., Agrawal, N., Agrawal, V.: Winning in the Aftermarket. Harvard Business Review 84(5), 129–138 (2006)
3. Gebauer, H.: Identifying service strategies in product manufacturing companies by exploring environment – strategy configurations. Industrial Marketing Management 37, 278–291 (2008)
4. Gebauer, H., Krempl, R., Fleisch, E., And Friedli, T.: Introduction of product-related services. Managing Service Quality 18(4), 387–404 (2008)
5. Goffin, K.: Customer support - A cross-industry study of distribution channels and strategies. International Journal of Physical Distribution and Logistics Management 29(6), 374–397 (2009)

6. Johnson, M., Mena, C.: Supply chain management for servitised products: a multi-industry case study. International Journal of Production Economics 114, 27–39 (2008)
7. Legnani, E., Cavalieri, S., Ierace, S.: A framework for the configuration of the after-slaes service processes. Production Planning and Control 20(2), 113–124 (2009)
8. Mathieu, V.: Service strategies within the manufacturing sector: benefits, costs and partnership. International Journal of Service Industry Management 12(5), 451–475 (2001)
9. Oliva, R., Kallenberg, R.: Managing the transition from products to services. International Journal of Service Industry Management 14(2), 160–172 (2003)
10. Wise, R., Baumgartner, P.: Go downstream - the new profit imperative in manufacturing. Harvard Business Review 77(5), 133–141 (2003)

Business Process Management Systems – Enabling Continuous Improvement in Industrial Services

Heikki Hirvensalo, Jan Holmström, and Timo Ala-Risku

Aalto University School of Science and Technology, Department of Industrial Engineering and
Management, POB 15500, Otaniementie 17, Espoo, FI-00076 Aalto, Finland
{Jan.Holmstrom,Timo Ala-Risku,LNCS}@tkk.fi

Abstract. The paper aims to analyze the opportunities that modern business
process management systems (BPMS) provide in improving industrial service
processes. A case study identifies improvement opportunities in the order-to-
cash process in two service lines of a large industrial service provider.
Implementing a business process management system in the studied case
context potentially enhances service process quality and significantly speeds up
the order-to-cash process. The practical implication is that providers of
industrial services should consider BPMS as a potential means to improve
profitability through a faster order-to-cash process.

Keywords: Industrial services, order-to-cash, BPM.

1 Introduction

The aim of this paper is to analyze opportunities that modern Business Process
Management Systems (BPMS) provide for managing industrial service business
processes. Good results have been achieved with BPMS implementations, especially
in back office dominated service industries like for instance banking and insurance
[1,2]. However, applying it in industrial services is largely unexplored. In the last few
years BPMS have improved to a level that potentially facilitates smooth process
modifications, coordination and tracking of geographically dispersed process
instances as well as monitoring process progress and analyzing process performance.
The research problem is that BPMS could perhaps be exploited in managing complex
and fast changing industrial service processes, but this proposition has not been tested
in practice, nor have results been document and presented in academic literature.

2 Literature Review

Process management is a structured approach to design, execute and analyze a
company's business processes for improved performance [3]. Its adaption has become
common in the past few decades as business leaders realized that the traditional
function based management structure easily leads to sub optimization in which the
cost of coordinating the whole company is above the cost savings gained from
different functional areas [4]. Hence, the idea of process management is to strengthen

B. Vallespir and T. Alix (Eds.): APMS 2009, IFIP AICT 338, pp. 636–643, 2010.
© IFIP International Federation for Information Processing 2010

the company by getting rid of fragmented functional management and focusing on work and information flows that cut across different functions and eventually deliver value for customers [5]. The objective is to integrate processes from end-to-end.

Industrial services are services, offered by manufacturing companies to organizational customers. They require competences, information, equipment and tools to create value for the customer [6], [7], [8]. It has been noted that transaction-oriented traditional ERPs, designed for stable businesses processes, have problems in supporting complex industrial services business processes [9], [10], [11]. Service oriented firms need to compete through use of knowledge to gain agility in altering processes quickly based on customer needs as well as to provide adequate visibility and control of ongoing processes [12]. Therefore a management mechanism that supports fast and flexible, but still controlled business process management is needed [13].

The development of business process management systems relates closely to Workflow Management (WfM), i.e. the automation of a business process, in whole or part, during which documents, information or tasks are passed from one participant to another for action, according to a set of procedural rules [14]. A critical milestone was the foundation of Workflow management coalition (WfMC) in 1993, when companies, who realized the need, started the development of standards in order to enable different workflow products, i.e. contemporary IT systems, and applications to communicate and work together [15]. The key development step was the separation of the management and execution function of a workflow. This enabled dynamic re-designing or adjustment of business processes separated from the execution environment. In other words, the entire business process could be revised and modified on the fly without disturbing the process components or the cases in progress. [16], [17], [18]

Over time system vendors started to talk about business process management systems (BPMS) instead of WfMS, e.g. [13], [19]. The reason was that workflow management referred too much to re-design and automated coordination and execution of intra-organizational business processes. The main ancillary feature in a BPMS compared to the earlier WFMS is the capability to analyze potential targets for development of cross-organizational business processes using detailed level operational process data. Current BPMS are generally web-enabled, meaning that parts of processes can be exchanged as web-services, in which the service provider accounts for fulfilling a certain process and providing required information for the service recipient. BPMS are also capable of maintaining larger repositories of hierarchical processes, managing quick process modifications as well as handling flexibly special cases, providing a potential mechanism for managing cross-organizational service business processes. [20], [21], [22], [23]

The generally stated benefits achieved by implementing a BPMS businesses processes include enhanced process efficiency and control through automated workflow coordination, improved process quality and customer service, increased agility and responsiveness through ability to modify process models flexibly, better process visibility and overall process understanding, consistent means for monitoring, analyzing and redesigning business processes, smooth integration of BPMS with legacy and new systems. [2], [4], [13], [15], [17], [20], [24, [25, [26, [27]

3 Methodology and Research Process

The empirical research was carried out as a qualitative case study in co-operation with a large, manufacturing company that increasingly is in the industrial service business. The case-company had faced serious problems in managing service deliveries with a highly networked service supply chain, which had become evident by very slow capital turnover. To improve its order-to-cash process management, the company started a pilot project in which it implemented a workflow management system to manage the order-to-cash process. The purpose of the case study was to examine the challenges faced by the case-company in managing its order-to-cash process in service business and to evaluate the potential of a more advanced BPMS to achieve improvement.

Data collection on existing challenges in the order-to-cash process and potential impacts of introducing BPMS was gathered with open interviews. A questionnaire form was used as a guideline, but the interviewees were able to bring out issues they considered important. The focus was kept on the current order-to-cash processes in two different service lines, i.e. installation and maintenance services, covering commonly faced problems and development needs. Each session lasted about one and half hours and they were held mostly face to face, though in some cases telephone interviews were held due to long distances. All interviews were recorded and notes were taken during each session. Afterwards the interviews were replayed to ensure that all relevant points were noted. The notes summarizing the interviews were sent back to the interviewees so that they could make corrections and additions if needed. This way the risk of misunderstanding in data collection was decreased. In addition to the interviews, internal company documents and workshops served as an important source of information.

4 Case study - Service Order-to-Cash Process Development in a Industrial Services Providing Company

The case study focused on the order-to-cash process of two separate service business lines, i.e. installation and maintenance. Installation delivers service solutions ranging from pure equipment and software implementation to turnkey solutions that include planning of equipment and services, site acquisition, construction works, equipment deliveries, installing, integrating and commissioning.

Regardless of scope, the installation service process is a phased, small scale construction project which is executed up to thousands of times depending on the size of the customer project. The scale and content of the service offering depends on the customer, but the case company is typically responsible for coordinating the whole process, i.e. synchronizing the service supply chain including several different parties, e.g. customer, customer's partners, own material and service suppliers. Maintenance services is an ongoing process including reactive and proactive services responsible for keeping the installed base operating and ensuring the agreed service level specified with the customer. Maintenance service deliveries also involve people, parts and equipment from a networked service supply chain constituting of internal and external parties. In many cases a solution offered to a customer includes services from both service business lines in which case the service responsibility is transferred gradually from installation to maintenance.

The structure of the order-to-cash process depends on the customer case. In turnkey solutions the order-to-cash process starts already in the tendering phase, as the case company participates in network planning and suggests a suitable service package per individual site (Figure 1). The customer may accept or modify the suggested product and service modules, before actual ordering. Several iteration rounds may occur. In more simple installation cases the customer simply orders predefined services.

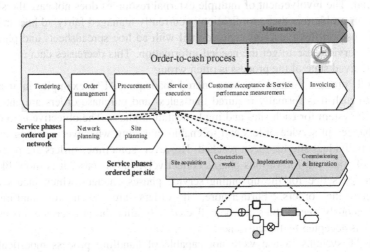

Fig. 1. Order-to-cash process structure depends on the service solution content. Some services are ordered per network and others per site. Installation order-to-cash is transaction based whereas Maintenance order to cash is triggered periodically.

The invoicing in installation services is always transaction based, though billing milestones differ subject to project and customer. Thus the order-to-cash process performance is strongly tied up with service supply chain performance and the service process flow across different functions. The more efficient and higher quality the service process, the smoother the execution of the order-to-cash process and the faster the revenues are collected. In maintenance, invoicing is made periodically. The order-to-cash process is initiated at the time when the service contract is made and triggered according to an agreed billing plan throughout the validity of the contract. Timely contract updates, good tracking of changes in the installed base and delivered services is required to be able to ensure cost efficient service deliveries and cash flow.

4.1 Challenges in the Existing Service Order-to-Cash Process

Challenges in the studied order-to-cash process management and execution relate to end-to-end process understanding and visibility, information sharing, coordination and control, flexibility as well as IT infrastructure. The net business impact is seen as slow capital turnover and high operating costs.

First, the overall understanding of the cross-functional order-to-crash process is considered inadequate. In an example project the network planners had a wrong picture of the possibilities to make changes in the service configurations during the order-to-cash process. They did not understand the overall process and how their actions affected upcoming process steps [28]. Although process flowcharts and written instructions were available, having them in Corporate Intranet is not enough to ensure sufficient understanding and motivation to follow the process.

Another major challenge is coordination and communication between front- and back-end. The involvement of multiple external resources does not ease the situation. The main problem is that coordination is currently managed fairly ad hoc and people have to use, in-flexible IT-systems, e-mail with ad hoc spreadsheets and phone calls in each service case to get the needed information. This decreases data accuracy and the perceived state of the process is often wrong.

Third, process control was considered inadequate. For example, in installation order-to-cash it is formally required that sales- and purchase orders are entered into the ERP system for each site- and implementation phase. The objective is to decrease late changes in service orders and to enable invoicing whenever a billing milestone for an individual site has been reached. However, sometimes orders are placed for a group of sites and for various phases collectively. In this case, it is more likely that the service scope for the upcoming service phases changes which incurs costs of reversing the orders. Furthermore, if orders are taken for multiple sites simultaneously, receivables can be collected only after the last service process at the last site is accepted by the customer.

The IT systems in use were not capable of handling process modifications of individual order-to-cash process instances. The missing flexibility encourages people to work ad hoc, which again complicates monitoring and management of the order-to-cash process as a whole. In milestone based invoicing, the problem with inflexibility results in costs related to reversed transactions, delayed service deliveries and accumulated workload. In periodical billing unexpected process changes create costs related to excess capacity or alternatively costs related to not hitting the agreed service level.

Finally, a challenge faced by the case company relates to process tracking and performance measurement. The case company lacks detailed and accurate tracking of order-to-cash process data, which could be systematically analyzed to support decision making at all organizational levels. For instance information to answer the following questions was found lacking: What service offerings were ordered by the customer and sold by the company?; What services and equipment were planned to be delivered and on what schedule?; What services and equipment were actually delivered, where and by whom?; How long did each activity last and what did it cost?

All in all, difficulty in service process re-design, poor process coordination as well as inadequate monitoring and analysis capabilities currently hinders a continuous service order-to-cash process development, as illustrated by figure 2.

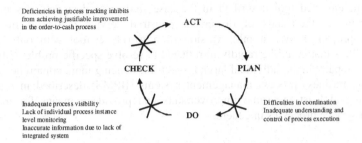

Deficiencies in process tracking inhibits
from achieving justifiable improvement
in the order-to-cash process

ACT

CHECK   PLAN

Inadequate process visibility
Lack of individual process instance
level monitoring
Inaccurate information due to lack of
integrated system

DO

Difficulties in coordination
Inadequate understanding and
control of process execution

Fig. 2. Order Continuous order-to-cash process improvement in installation and maintenance was hindered due to the lack of feedback between process planning, execution, monitoring and analysis

4.2 Overcoming the Challenges with the Support of BPMS

The challenges described above were tackled successfully in a large network project in the case company. The project comprised the installation service of over 20 000 sites. An improvement initiative was launched aiming to improve the order-to-cash cycle during the project. A key enabler was the adaption of a primitive WfMS called Flexible Order Management tool (FOM). FOM provided customers a web-interface to make service requests per site, which triggered each time the initiation of a new order-to-cash process instance. It automatically coordinated the work of geographically dispersed resources, requested for approvals when needed, informed about pending tasks for different resources in different locations, and at the same time collected important data about each individual process instance for monitoring and analysis purposes. Process status could be updated by simply clicking visually presented process steps online. Some service steps were recognized automatically, since the installed equipment and parts can communicate over a wireless network. The workflow included remote monitoring of what new parts or software was installed at specific sites. The relevant data for the remote monitoring process was collected in an installed base data warehouse and translated by FOM to produce reports on the order-to-cash status and performance of installation work. FOM also cross-checked ordered, installed and invoiced services automatically from other relevant systems and ensured communication related to invoicing with the customer's financial system.

Although a rather simple workflow-tool, it provided a controllable and traceable process for customer interaction: no uncontrolled order changes could take place and reliable measures on delivery lead times could be provided. The tool provided needed flexibility to adjust the order-to-cash process for individual service sites but also provided the desired level of control in execution. It also introduced clear process milestones and brought the real-time status of each individual order-to-cash process instance visible via web for responsible people. This improved process understanding and facilitated the monitoring and management of the whole service supply chain in a cost efficient way. The improvement in process quality, efficiency and responsiveness achieved was a 45% reduction in receivables cycle time, over 90% reduction in number of inaccurately filled orders and over 75% reduction in the service delivery cycle time. (for more details see [28])

The implemented tool described in the case study was designed to support the management of thousands of dispersed industrial service deliveries in a huge customer project. It was a pilot version of a workflow tool with only selected functionalities that could be rapidly introduced to resolve specific problems faced by the case company in an individual large project. Introducing more comprehensive and up to date business process management systems (BPMS) described in this paper could bring at least the same improvements and provide a means for managing industrial service processes in general.

5 Conclusions

The study shows how high variability and the requirement for responsiveness in industrial services is a challenge for the order-to-cash process management. Customer inputs might change during the service process execution, which means that changes must be managed in a controlled manner. Service processes involve typically geographically dispersed stationary as well as mobile, internal and external, human and application resources that need to be coordinated efficiently. Flexibility and agility are needed to modify and improve processes quickly to meet changing circumstances. In addition, there must be a way to trace and monitor individual service process instances and to analyze the impact of any changes on process performance. Without adequate instance level monitoring it is hard to achieve improvement in a business environment, where customer requirements and service processes change.

BPMS provide a mechanism for tracking service process instances individually and using this information first to analyze business process performance efficiently on different organizational levels but also to flexibly re-engineer and adopt processes to meet the changing service business environment. That is, they ensure feedback between enacting, monitoring, analyzing and redesigning industrial service processes facilitating continuous improvement.

References

1. Agostini, A., De Michelis, G., Grasso, M.A., Patriarca, S.: Reengineering a business process with an innovative workflow management system: a case study. In: Proceedings of the conference on Organizational computing systems. ACM, New York (1993)
2. Küng, P., Hagen, C.: The fruits of Business Process Management: an experience report from a Swiss bank. Business Process Management Journal 13(4), 477–487 (2007)
3. Hammer, M.: Process management and future of Six Sigma. MIT Sloan Management Review (2002)
4. Becker, J., Kugeler, M., Rosemann, M.: Process management: a guide for the design of business processes. Springer, Berlin (2003)
5. Hammer, M., Stanton, S.: How process enterprises really work. Harvard Business Review 77(6), 108 (1999)
6. Vargo, S.L., Lusch, R.F.: The Four Service Marketing Myths: Remnants of a Goods-Based, Manufacturing Model. Journal of Service Research 6(4), 324 (2004)

7. Auramo, J., Ala-Risku, T.: Challenges for going downstream. International Journal of Logistics: Research & Applications 8(4), 333–345 (2005)
8. Sampson, S.E., Froehle, G.M.: Foundations and Implications of a Proposed Unified Services Theory. Production & Operations Management 15(2), 329–343 (2006)
9. Akkermans, H., Bogerd, P., Yücesan, E., van Wassenhove, L.: The impact of ERP on supply chain management: Exploratory findings from a European Delphi study. European Journal of Operations Research 146, 284–301 (2003)
10. Brax, S.: A manufacturer becoming service provider - challenges and a paradox. Managing Service Quality 15(2), 142–155 (2005)
11. Cohen, M.A., Agrawal, N., Agrawal, V.: Achieving Breakthrough Service Delivery Through Dynamic Asset Deployment Strategies. Interfaces 36(3), 259 (2006)
12. Poirier, C.C.: Business process management applied: creating the value managed enterprise. J. Ross Pub., Boca Raton (2005)
13. BPM Focus: An introduction to Business Process Management (BPM), BPM Focus (2008)
14. Workflow Management Coalition: The Workflow Management Coalition Specification: terminology and glossary, Workflow Management Coalition, UK (1999)
15. Workflow Management Coalition, http://www.wfmc.org
16. Hollingsworth, D.: Workflow Management Coalition: The Workflow Reference Model edn, WfMC, UK (1995),
    http://www.wfmc.org/standards/referencemodel.htm
17. Wade, V., Lewis, D., Malbon, C., et al.: Approaches to integrating telecoms management systems. In: Delgado, J., Mullery, A., Start, K. (eds.) IS&N 2000. LNCS, vol. 1774, pp. 315–332. Springer, Heidelberg (2000)
18. Leymann, F., Roller, D., Schmidt, M.-T.: Web services and business process management. IBM systems journal 41(2), 198 (2002)
19. Hill, J.B.: Magic Quadrant for Business Process Management Suites 2007, Gartner (2007)
20. Aalst, W.v.d., van Hee, K.: Workflow management: models, methods, and systems. MIT Press, Cambridge (2002)
21. Weske, M., Aalst, W.v.d., Verbeek, H.M.V.: Advances in business process management. Data & Knowledge Engineering 50(1), 1–8 (2004)
22. Nickerson, J.V.: Logical channels: using web services for cross organizational workflow. Business Process Management Journal 11(3), 224–235 (2005)
23. Swenson, K.D.: Workflow and web service standards. Business Process Management Journal 11(3), 218–223 (2005)
24. Hong, D.W., Hong, C.S.: A flow-through workflow control scheme for BGP/MPLS VPN service provision. In: Freire, M.M., Chemouil, P., Lorenz, P., Gravey, A. (eds.) ECUMN 2004. LNCS, vol. 3262, pp. 397–406. Springer, Heidelberg (2004)
25. Liu, J., Zhang, S., Hu, J.: A case study of an inter-enterprise workflow-supported supply chain management system. Information & Management 42(3), 441–454 (2005)
26. Rouibah, K., Caskey, K.: A workflow system for the management of inter-company collaborative engineering processes. Journal of Engineering Design 14(3), 273–293 (2003)
27. Tarantilis, C.D., Kiranoudis, C.T., Theodorakopoulos, N.D.: A Web-based ERP system for business services and supply chain management: Application to real-world process scheduling. European Journal of Operational Research 187(3), 1310 (2008)
28. Ala-Risku, T., Collin, J.: Project supply chain management and integrated IT - a case from telecom industry. In: 19th Annual Conference of the Nordic Logistics Research Network (NOFOMA), Reykjavik, Iceland, June 7-8 (2007)

A Framework for Product-Service Design for Manufacturing Firms

Thècle Alix and Bruno Vallespir

IMS, University of Bordeaux / CNRS, 351 Cours de la Libération,
33405 Talence Cedex, France
{thecle.alix,bruno.vallespir}@ims-bordeaux.fr

Abstract. Manufacturers propose services around the products they deliver to increase their competitiveness and reach objectives of profitability satisfying specific customer needs. Loyalty can be obtained under the condition that isolated offerings are replaced by integrated value adding solution composed of a product and of one or more product-service. The design of such solution requires to take account of four narrowly overlapping dimensions: the product, the product-service, the process and the organization. A challenge is to propose a model to support the firm core competence widening taking account of all the dimensions together, analyzing how they are interlinked and how they allow to design the coherent value adding solution. In this paper the two first stages of a methodology for new product-service development for manufacturing firms are presented that take account of firm's environment, core competence, processes as well as the benefits expected by service delivery and the service value.

Keywords: Product-service systems, service value, service engineering.

1 Introduction

Service activities have become since few years a current way to differentiate from competitors and make customers loyal. Manufacturers propose services around the main product they deliver and customer loyalty can be obtained under the condition that isolated offerings are replaced by integrated value adding solution composed of the product and associated product-service [1]. Consequently they must be thought and designed together before being sold as an integrated offer.

Even if currently the way of doing of industrialists is far from a co-design product-service system concept [2], a survey performed during the summer 2008 [3] has shown that most of the services proposed by big manufacturing companies are dedicated to the core product and that they are developed accordingly. For the most part, they are completely integrated in the product offer (for 75% of them) and performed by the manufacturing company (for 95%). Underlying objective of profitability can be reached under the condition that firms manage all the changes that are necessary to deliver a service, as well as the transition allowing to reach the stable condition of product-service high value solution provider.

Changes to control can be split in: (i) Strategic changes due to the necessity to define common organization, management and control principles, (ii) Marketing

B. Vallespir and T. Alix (Eds.): APMS 2009, IFIP AICT 338, pp. 644–651, 2010.

changes as the analysis and understanding of the customers requirement to provide the good service (high value) is crucial, (iii) Commercial changes to determine the differentiation potential regarding competitors to valorize the offer and make it worth in the eyes of the customer, (iv) Economical changes as the product functionalities centric discourse had to be changed in an integrated value centric one to convince the customer and (v) Cultural modifications of firm employee's skills and focus that must be less technical and back office and more commercial and front office. The design and delivery of an integrated solution requires to take account of four narrowly overlapping dimensions related to: (i) the product (object that corresponds to the firm core competence, initial object of the selling), (ii) the product-service (service supplied in addition to the product and increasing its value for the customers), (iii) the processes (used to create the product and/or the product-service) and the organization (the context in which the process unfold is launched); while managing the value, risks and knowledge inherent to new development (Fig.1).

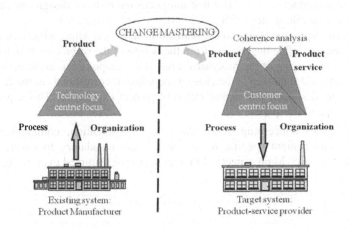

Fig. 1. From manufacturing business to product-service solution providers business.

Service research is wide and integrates different communities who have already responds to some problematic [4], [5], [6], [7] but as Wild *et al.* mentioned it *"each discipline involved in service research appears to have their own dogma and mythology, and all too often end up with minimal interaction with relevant areas"* [8]. A cross disciplinary approach could be useful to combine the points of views, analysis methodologies and tools to properly cover all the aspects of service delivery and to help characterize the stable condition abovementioned.

The challenge is then to propose a method to support firm core competence widening taking all the dimensions and changes into account, analyzing how they are linked and how they allow to design the coherent value adding solution using the most appropriate methodologies and tools whatever the discipline is concerned. To reach this objective, we propose to analyze new product-service development using a project management centric view as it encompasses the firm's environment, core competence, process, organization as well as benefits, risks and value.

2 Product-Service Design as a Project of New development

Based on the previous hypothesis, we assume that the project of product-service development can be split as any project of product design in four main steps (Fig.2.):

- The first common step consists in a starting sequence and allows to analyze customer expectations and to explore the positioning of the firm. This is a sort of strategic analysis based among other things on the study of environmental factors and criteria allowing to determine the strengths, weaknesses, opportunities and threat of the new development and to choose between several different ones. This step is discussed in section 3.

- The second step is a definition sequence that allows to precise the specifications of the product-service to deliver and its value for both the customer and the manufacturer. Based on a functional analysis and a value engineering approach, value results can be gathered in a matrix that can be used as a strategic tool to analyze the relevance of a product-service offer that integrates the costs of design and delivery as well as the mercantile strategy. This step is developed in section 4.

- The third step corresponds to the realization sequence whose objective is, in that particular case, to define the process from the design of the service to its delivery. The definition and modeling of the processes is out of the scope of this contribution.

- The fourth and final step is the closing sequence. It corresponds to the real service delivery to the customer and capitalization of project experience. This aspect is also out of the scope of this paper.

Support activities concerning delay, cost, risk, organization, communication and knowledge management specific to the project are mandatory to ensure the new development success. Main aspects of their concern are skimmed over in Fig.2.

	Project sequences			
	Starting sequence	Definition sequence	Realization sequence	Closing sequence
Operational activities	Requirement analysis Firm positioning	Specification of the service Value analysis	Definition of the process from design to delivery	Service delivery Project experience capitalization
Delay	First planning	Master Planning	Control Planning	Review Planning
Cost	Resource evaluation	Cost estimation	Expenses control	Cost control improvement
Risk	Risk analysis	Risk scenario	Hazard management	Risk control improvement
Communication	Informative communication	Definition of the communication system	Conflict management	Communication control improvement
Knowledge	Data management	Information management	Knowledge management	Knowledge control improvement
Organization	Project actor identification	Project structuring	Project control	Organization improvement

Fig. 2. Sequences and activities of a project of new product-service development

This project must also come within the scope of the firm and be coherent with the core product development, existing process and organization. This implies that all the data related to these 3 items have to be compiled with data coming from the operational and support activities as sort of control.

3 Starting Sequence

As outlined in section 2, the starting sequence proceeds to a strategic analysis that consists in a diagnosis and strategic segmentation [9]. The diagnosis can be performed using the SWOT matrix.

3.1 The SWOT Matrix to Diagnose and Position the Firm

The SWOT analysis (Strengths, Weaknesses, Opportunities and Threats analysis) is a tool for auditing an organization and its environment. It can help managers to determine if their objective -in term of new development for example- is attainable or not by the identification of internal and external key factors useful to achieve them. The SWOT analysis gathers key pieces of information in two main categories:

- Internal factors cover strengths and weaknesses internal to the organization that are helpful or harmful to achieve the objective. Usually, they include the 4P's of mix marketing (Product, Price, Place, Promotion); as well as personnel, finance, manufacturing capabilities, etc. The customer's requirements in term of service associated to the product are taken into account by the way of the mix marketing study that will reveal the components of the value for the customers. Note that in that case the first P stands for product-service.

- External factors concern opportunities and threats that are helpful or harmful external conditions to achieve the objective. They include macroeconomic matters, technological change, legislation, and socio-cultural changes, as well as changes in the marketplace or competitive position.

All these factors gathered in a matrix permit to define the risks and benefits of a new product development strategy. If the objective is attainable, the SWOTs can be used as inputs to the creative generation of possible further strategies.

3.2 List of Internal Factors: Strengths and Weaknesses

The identification of strengths and weaknesses can be done regarding inside the firm and analyzing its culture and main economic functions in term of organization, product and process and their interrelations. Then, taking account of the changes mentioned in section 1, internal factors may stem from:

- Firm culture and organization: enterprise identity, brand image, organisation structure mode; industry specialization; project experience, membership, sales office;

- Marketing and commercial ins and outs aspects: market share, Product-service / Price / Place / Promotion coherence;

- Human resources ins and outs: skills; motivation, involvement, project team, project manager, top management commitment, contact personnel training, contact personnel quality, sales team;
- Financial ins and outs: results, benefits, possibilities of investment and investors;
- Technical ins and out as a product-service can be material or not and/or technologically complex in particular if it uses TIC. Then factors coming from design (technological innovation potential, R&D opportunities) and production (Capacity/load ratio; Delay; Partners relationship; Resource competencies, stock level Production, service definition, process definition identified procedures) are relevant to analyze product-service development.

The Justification of Each Factor and Sub Factor Is Given in [14]

3.3 List of External Factors: Opportunities and Threats

External factors stem from the study of the micro-, macro- and meso-environment of the firm. The Macro-environment picture can be obtained by the way of a PEST analysis (Political (and legal), Economic, Social, Technological). The PEST factors can be used to assess the market for a business or organisational unit strategic plan [10]. The micro-environment can be studied by analysing the firm' strength and weakness regarding the five strengths of its sector of activity: the relationship with its customers, with its suppliers, the competitor's pressure, the threat of new competitors and the substitute products [11]. The Meso-environment focuses on person that could influence the economical relations in a market. The list of external factors and sub factors of interest is detailed in [10].

3.4 Definite List of Factors

The factors abovementioned can be gathered by aggregation and according to their relevance in the following set: Project team, Manufacturing resources, Technological potentiality, Operations/ process, Partners relationship, Brand image, Cost base, Cash flow, Sales team, Distribution, Political environment, Economic outlook, Cultural changes, Technical context, Customers position, Suppliers position, Competitors position, Substitute, Product to integrate [14].

Note that we do not mention if an internal factor is a strength or a weakness as there is a continuum between both; id. for the threats and opportunities. The project team leader will first have to determine the consequences of a factor: whether it is a benefit (strength or opportunity) or a risk (weakness or threat). Subsequently, the relevance of each internal factor as well as the probability of occurring of each external factor will be defined. Finally the impact of each factor on the organisation could be discussed and results plotted in a chart (see © Copyright MarketWare International 2001-2004). A visual representation of the risks and benefits of a new product-service development could be obtained and compared to other ones. The position of the firm will result from the comparison that takes parameters relative to the product, organisation and processes into account by the way of the factors.

4 Definition Sequence

The definition sequence consists, once the development direction is chosen, in defining the solution that will be profitable for both new manufacturer and customers; to determine its position in the portfolio of the firm and its legitimacy to be proposed and enhance firm competitiveness and profitability.

This second stage rests on the use of the value analysis methodology and compares the value of the offer for the manufacturer taking account of its expected benefits and the value of the same offer for the customers defined by the way of expected quality criteria. All these developments are based on the assumption that the value can be defined by the ratio between the performance of some functions and their cost [12].

Currently two functions are defined: (i) "basic function" which correspond to anything that makes the product work or sell and (ii) "secondary functions" or "supporting functions" that describe the manner in which the basic function(s) are implemented.

4.1 Product-Service Value Analysis: From the Manufacturer Point of View

We assume that the functions which participate to the definition of the value for the provider focus on the expected benefits of a product-service proposal. Based on [13] and a literature review in the management area, benefits usually mentioned concern: (i) the construction of a customer loyalty by the building of dependency relationships between a consumer and a provider that can lead toward profitability, (ii) the search for differentiation that allows retaining and attracting consumers, (iii) the increase and stabilizing of firms' turnover due to the possibility to generate regular income and to have cash flow disposal, (iv) the corporate image reinforcement linked to technological advanced, product quality... (v) the occupation of an existing or new market to participate to market share division, (vi) the possibility to create alliance with service providers and to share risks, (vii) the possibility to increase the quickness of a design or production process using product-service based on information and communication technologies, (viii) the possibility to shorten sales delay or negotiation phase using financial services and (ix) the search for a product-service system that is designed to have a lower environmental impact than traditional business models [14].

Each benefit can be defined as expected performances that stem from a strategy and have priorities one to the other. Quantifiable criteria can be associated to each one whose level also stem from the strategy. The level really measured, that reflect the performance of the function, compared to the global cost of the service allows to determine the value of the service for the firm.

Costs to take into account can be divided in direct and indirect costs. Regarding product-service characteristics, several costs can be addressed that depends (i) on its degree of tangibility, (ii) on the degree of interaction that is necessary between the firm contact personnel and the customer to deliver it and, (iii) on the degree of standardization of the product-service delivery process. They can encompass component costs, cost of labor, and overheads.

The description of the functions from the manufacturer point of view and the consciousness of the product-service costs allow to build a value analysis matrix [14].

4.2 Product-Service Value Analysis: From the Customer Point of View

According to [15], customers challenge the overall value of an offer to its complete cost. The overall value refers to the different advantages obtained, supported by the firm brand image. Advantages may gather both benefits expected on technical functionalities and subjective criteria as lots of studies have shown that customers are waiting for something from the exchange with the firm. [16] has proposed a list of criteria and dimensions allowing to evaluate the quality of a standard service These criteria can be associated to implicit functions whose fulfillment can lead to customer loyalty and value increase.

Then, the list of functions of a product-service expected by customers consists in: (i) the product-service raison d'être: help choosing, acquiring or using the main product [1], (ii) secondary functions linked to its interactions with the contact personnel, users and means necessary to realize it, the partners, environmental and legislative constraints and the realization constraints as mentioned previously and, (iii) the implicit functions coming from quality criteria discharged from the functions that refers to the delivery process: to obtain a tangible service.

The value determined by the firm from the customer point of view will be determined by putting in opposite the previous list of function and the distribution of the above mentioned costs via another value analysis matrix.

4.3 Synthesis

Using aggregation operator, it is possible to deduce the whole value of the product-service proposed by a manufacturing firm. This one can have two positions: high or low and can be analyzed regarding two dimensions: the customer dimension and the firm dimension Fig.3.

		Firm value	
		High	Low
Customer value	High	The product service is profitable for the firm and satisfies customers. It might accompany the product	To make the customer loyal, firm may propose the service but found solution to increase its value by decreasing its price if it is worth in the eye of the consumer or adding others services located in the high/high value.
	Low	This position is synonymous of customer loyalty if the customer participates or if the cost of the offer is not too important. Otherwise, he won't be interested by this list of sales point.	The abandon of the product-service or not will depend on the cash that is necessary to provide it or on the delivering difficulties

Fig. 3. Value matrix

The value analysis of each product-service coherent with the firm position from the two points of view will provide a synthetic view of the equilibrium of the global offer. To ensure firm global profitability, the portfolio of product-services has to be shared out between all categories (High/low).

5 Conclusion

We have proposed in this contribution the two first steps of a methodology in four steps to support manufacturing firm core competence widening by the furniture of product-service taking account of the changes that are necessary to become a "service" as well as the product, the organization and its process. The first step developed here provides keys to choose an orientation for product-service new development. The second step allows to analyze the relevance of a product-service offering based on its value analysis. Further works include the definition of tools to help characterize the two last steps as well as a refinement of the two first one.

References

1. Furer, O.: Le rôle stratégique des services autour des produits. In: Revue Française de Gestion, mars-avril-mai, pp. 98–108 (1997)
2. Baines, T.S., et al.: State-of-the-art in product-service systems. In: Proceedings of the Institution of Mechanical Engineers. Part B. Journal of engineering manufacture, vol. 221(10), pp. 1543–1552. Mechanical Engineering Publications, London (2007)
3. Alix, T., Touzy, W., Vallespir, B.: Product-service value analysis: two complementary points of view. In: Proc of the 13th IFAC Symposium on Information Control Problems in Manufacturing (2009)
4. Berry, L.L.: Relationship marketing of services – growing interest, emerging perspectives. Journal of the Academy of Marketing Science 23(4), 236–245 (1995)
5. Fisk, R.P., Grove, S.J., John, J.: Services Marketing Self-Portraits: Introspections, Reflections, and Glimpses from the Experts. American Marketing Association, Chicago (2000)
6. Lovelock, C., Wirtz, J., Lapert, D.: Marketing des services. Pearson Education, London (2004)
7. Zeithaml, V.A., Berry, L.L., Parasuraman, A.: The behavioral consequences of service quality. Journal of Marketing 60, 31–46 (1996)
8. Wild, P.J., Clarkson, P.J., Mc Farlane, D.C.: A framework for Cross Disciplinary Efforts in Services Research. In: Proc of CIRP IPS2 Conference, pp. 145–152. Cranfield Univeristy Press, United Kingdom (2009)
9. Alix, T., Vallespir, B.: New product development: material versus immaterial. In: Proc of Extended Product and Process Analysis aNd Design EXPPAND workshop (2009)
10. Armstrong, M.: A handbook of Human Resource Management Practice, 10th edn. Kogan Page, London (2006)
11. Porter, M.E.: The Competitive Advantage: Creating and Sustaining Superior Performance. Free Press, N.Y (1985)
12. Goyhenetche, M.: Le marketing de la valeur, Créer de la valeur pour le client. INSEP (1999)
13. Baglin, G., Malleret, V.: Le developpement d'offres de services dans les PMI. Cahier de recherché du groupe HEC (2005)
14. Alix, T., Ducq, Y., Vallespir, B.: Product-service value analysis: two complementary points of view. In: Proc of CIRP IPS2 Conference, pp. 157–164. Cranfield Univeristy Press, United Kingdom (2009)
15. Hermel, L., Louyat, G.: La qualité de service. AFNOR, France (2005)
16. Zeithmal, A., Parasuraman, A., Berry, L.: Delivering quality service. The free Press, New York (1991)

Lean Implementation in Service Companies

Alberto Portioli-Staudacher

Politecnico di Milano
Department of Management, Economics and Industrial Engineering,
P.za Leonardo daVinci, 32 - 20133 Milano, Italy
alberto.portioli@polimi.it

Abstract. Service companies have been implementing Lean only in recent years. In this research three third party logistic companies and seven companies of the financial sector have been thoroughly interviewed and showed a few interesting aspects on the way they implemented Lean. They are implementing Lean in high volume low variety processes and focus on back office activities, which are most similar to manufacturing. Focus on flow, releasing real pull systems and attention to pacing the flow are the aspects that have been less developed and considered not applicable –or not worth applying- in services.

Keywords: lean services, service operations, banking, insurances, lean implementations.

1 Introduction

Focusing on the service sector has an outstanding importance, because of its increasing relevance on GDP of western economies: in the European Union, the percentage of employees in services was near 49% in 1971 and it became 68% in the late 1990s. In these nations the service sector contributes three times more to the GDP than the industry sector (Wolfl, 2005).

Nonetheless, referring to the labour productivity increase, it is evident services are lagging behind industry, especially in Europe. Increasing the productivity of the tertiary could give an impulse to the development of this sector and to the growth of the economy. Services represent the future source of growth for developed nations and it is in their best interest to understand the underlying causes of the low productivity growth (Druker, 1991). Despite operations is the area where most service people work -and the area where labour productivity increase can have the larger impact- there are still very few research works on service operations.

Adopting manufacturing proven management techniques, such as Lean Thinking, that had already helped the manufacturing sector improving its performances, service industries could improve their efficiency too. These would allow them to have more efficient and productive operations, and deliver better and more competitive services (Roach, 1998). However, Lean methodology can not be implemented in the same way in every situation: it needs to be tailored to the particular characteristics of each sector (Ahlstrom, 2004; Jones e Womack, 2005).

B. Vallespir and T. Alix (Eds.): APMS 2009, IFIP AICT 338, pp. 652–659, 2010.

The purpose of this paper is to investigate different contexts of application of the Lean methodology in the tertiary, in order to understand the differences in implementing Lean in services compared with manufacturing, and what are the typical ways of adopting it.

Which are the guidelines they follow, the objectives, the tools they use and the areas in which they preferably adopt the approach.

2 Lean Implementation in Services

Fist of all we started by interviewing about 600 service companies on the phone, to understand whether they were adopting Lean or, at least, implementing any Lean technique.

Out of the 600 companies contacted, less than 2% claimed they were adopting any Lean technique. Financial services (Banking and Insurances) are the ones where Lean is more known, and where an increasing number of companies are implementing Lean.

Healthcare organisations are starting to learn something about Lean, but implementations are rare; in tourism, rental, hotels and restaurants none of the companies contacted were implementing Lean.

Because Lean implementation in services has just started, it is important to understand how to make it successful. What to start from, and what possible similarities and differences there are from manufacturing. Therefore we decided to deepen the knowledge through structured interview in the few service companies that were implementing Lean. 10 companies agreed to participate to the research: 3 pertaining to third party logistics and 7 from the financial sector (banks and insurance companies).

Our research questions were the following:

1. What areas/processes are the first one to implement Lean?
2. What aspects of Lean are implemented? What others are more difficult to implement or left for the future?

2.1 Processes

Ahlstrom (2004) investigated four services:

- Street maintenance;
- Train maintenance;
- A School;
- A Hospital.

Ahlstrom identifies 7 aspect that characterise Lean: waste elimination, zero defects, pull rather than push, multifunctional teams, decentralised responsibilities, information flow, continuous improvement.

Ahlstrom conclusions are that Lean is applicable in all 4 services, but he highlights differences in term of relevance of different aspects of Lean and difficulties for implementation.

Many other authors also agree that Lean principles are valid for both manufacturing and service companies but we believe that for a successful implementation it is important not to focus only on the differences among industries, but, most of all, on differences among processes (value streams in the Lean terminology). In fact, within the same industry there are companies competing on the base of very different processes, and different use of resources. For example, if we compare large Law Firms in Canada and in Italy, the offer of services is quite similar in range and variety, so it could seem that they should have a similar service delivery system. But if we take a closer look, we see that in Canada companies are structured with a more rigid allocation of resources to the different type of service offering, with a kind of sub systems with resources dedicated to a subset of services. Therefore each sub system has a narrower set of services to deliver. This means that if we take a look at this deeper level, resources in Canada handle a much lower variety and higher volumes than in the Italian Law Firms. The processes have quite a different structure.

In general, within a company there are low volume high variety processes, and high volume low variety processes. The management of these two types of processes is quite different.

In manufacturing, Lean started in the automotive industry and then spread to white goods and electronic appliances, i.e. to large volume production. Starting point for implementation is in virtually all cases the internal production process, from raw material to finished products. Then implementation spreads to the external production process, going upstream to suppliers and downstream to distributors. Implementing Lean to administrative processes and new product development it is usually the last stage (Portioli and Tantardini 2007). Therefore we expect a similar trend in Services also, where we expect that companies start from high volume processes.

Moreover services have large differences from manufacturing, and most operations management books start the chapter on service operations with a list of key element differentiation services from products: they are intangible, perishable, etc. But in our opinion the most important single difference in Operations between services and manufacturing is the presence of the customer in the service delivery system.

The interaction with the customer brings an element that is totally new to manufacturing operations.

Therefore we expect that service companies start implementing Lean on processes that are high volume low variety, and focused on back office, where there is not the new element of the customer presence.

Table 1 presents the results of the research, showing the characteristics of the processes involved in the Lean transformation for all companies analysed. Certain companies changed more than one process, but all processes showed the same characteristics, therefore they have been grouped in one single column for each company.

All companies interviewed but one implemented Lean in high volume processes. Company B implemented Lean in process with a medium low volume compared with the other companies, but it is still one of the processes with the highest volume among the ones within the company.

Table 1. Characteristics of the processes affected by the Lean implementation

Process characteristics		Company									
		Warehousing and Shipping			Financial services						
		H	I	L	A	C	B	E	F	D	G
Volume	High	√	√	√	√	√		√	√	√	√
	Low						√				
Variety	High						√				
	Low	√	√	√	√	√		√	√	√	√
Process focus	Front Office						√				
	Back Office	√	√	√	√	√	√	√	√	√	√
Operators' discretion	High						√				
	Low	√	√	√	√	√		√	√	√	√
Customisation	High						√				
	Low	√	√	√	√	√		√	√	√	√

Similarly, variety in those processes is low, except for company B where the process shows a higher variety.

The difference is due to the fact that B is a corporate bank, while the others are retail banks and insurances. Therefore overall volume of transactions in B is much smaller.

All companies have selected back office processes for implementing lean, with the only exception of B that worked also on a process mainly focused on back office but that has also a part in front office.

The processes under consideration involve operators with a low degree of discretion, B presents operators with a higher degree of discretion compared with the other companies, but most of the operators involved in B do not have a higher degree of discretion than the average in the company

The processes involved allow a low degree of customisation for all companies, except for B.

The results presented in Table 1 confirm that service companies start implementing lean in processes with higher volume and lower variety. This is mainly due to the following reasons:

- Changing a high volume process usually affects a larger portion of the business, therefore with one intervention there is a benefit on a significant portion of the output.
- It is easier to find a sponsor when the benefits expected are large (due to large volume)
- Low variety makes it easier to understand the process and to make changes

In particular, variety is a critical aspect in services: all employee think that all customer requests are different from one another, and have to be addressed specifically. "Every customer has specific needs and specific situations, and we have to satisfy it. Out job is not like producing iron pieces!"

This is true if we passively ask the customers to tell us what they want and then try to satisfy it; but not all differences have the same relevance. In many cases, most differences have no real value for the customer, and can be easily eliminated by a better customer management. But in order to achieve this it is important to make the employee understand on the one hand that customers can be directed, and in many cases they like to be directed by someone who knows their needs and how to satisfy them. On the other hand, the huge impact that a reduction in variety and variability has on productivity. This leads to lower costs -lower prices for the customers- and shorter response time. The front office should handle all the variety from the customer, and funnel it into the few standard alternatives that the service provider has designed. In the back office there should not be other than standard requests. If there are customers with really exceptional needs, they should be directed to a different process that addresses high variety low volume, non standard customers. Or they should be rejected.

In other words, front office has to manage variety and variability, because it is due to the customer. A new element compared with manufacturing. On the contrary, back office should reduce variety and variability, as in manufacturing.

Almost all lean implementation considered, addressed back office processes only, and processes where little or no customisation were allowed.

2.2 Lean Elements

The second research question is related with what Lean aspects are implemented, and how.

In order to understand this, we defined nine elements: seven are based on the one defined by Ahlstrom, even though in certain cases with a deeper meaning, two have been added.

For each element we also defined a level of implementation, so to highlight how far the company has gone in adopting it in line with the Lean approach.

For example, as for *pull rather than push*, most service companies start from a customer order, therefore the company as a whole is acting on a pull base, but this does not mean that pull is preserved along the delivery system (through the value stream). Let's consider the mortgage granting process: all starts with a request from the customer, it is pulled by the customer, but this does not mean that there is pull between each stage. Usually, each stage is asked to process the requests as fast as possible: result is that there is a large variation in the response time to the customer. An analysis of the different mortgage requests at a bank highlighted an average response time of 15 days, but certain customer got the answer in 5 days and others took as long as 30. The first reaction was to think that response time was linked to the amount requested, but a segmentation with different amounts requested gave no evidence in this direction. The answer is that there was no pull in place between stages and each stage processed requests so to optimise its own performances, with no view on overall. End to end, process.

A better pull solution is to set a service level at each stage –say 90% of requests processed within 3 days- so to avoid that requests remain at a single stage for too long.

The full pull solution is a sequential pull, with FIFO line between stages. Each stage processes the requests in the same order that they have arrived from the upstream stage and the queue at each stage has a maximum number of request that it can hold: when the queue is full the stage upstream cannot process any more request till the stage downstream does pick up a request from the queue, and frees up a place. This reduces dramatically variations in response time and sets up a clear system that highlights any problem as soon as it arises. If the maximum is reached it is a signal that there in an unbalance between the two stages. Similarly when the queue is empty.

Zero defects has as a basic level the recording of defects and targets on their maximum levels, and as an advanced level a system that systematically analyses defects to find the root cause in order to solve it, and set ups pokayoke devices to prevent errors from happening.

Pace. Basic element is to use the takt time to have a target for the daily, or weekly, output. The target level is to have a system that gives the operators a sense of the pace, help them to keep up with it and triggers an alert when pace is not met: not for blaming anybody, but for spotting improvement opportunities.

Flow is a key aspect for lean, and we analysed which company exploited it till the level of having the flow as the central point for the allocation of resources, the organisation, and even the layout. A basic level is to identify a flow of the service required and have an overall view and understanding, from beginning to end. Many companies did this in conjunction with the process mapping activity required by quality certification. But the target level is to dedicate resources to the flow, to manage the flow as a whole, to review the layout to support the flow. IT systems and procedure design is also considered in this direction, looking for systems that are designed to support the flow, not the single stage.

Finally, continuous improvement is at a basic level the tension to improve results, but the target level is to have the operators to proactively, and on a continuative base, present, select, implement improvements.

Table 2 shows the results of the research on Lean elements: third party logistics is ahead of financial services on almost all items, despite these companies did not start before the others. The key point seems to be the presence of a physical item, with simple operations (no transformation and little assembly, if any). Storing and moving something are operations that have been performed massively by manufacturing companies and addressed by Lean researchers and practitioners, unlike operations in banks and insurance companies, where activities are mostly related to information processing.

There are differences in the degree of implementation in the different companies but there are some common elements:

- Waste elimination is pursued in all companies, but what is missing is to have this attitude disseminated among all operators, making waste elimination a continuous process in all the company;
- Multifunctional teams are common practice but they are used on a project base rather than a continuative base

- Continuous improvement is intended more as spreading practices to the other part of the company/group performing the same process, or to other similar processes rather than setting up a system that continuously improve a process.

The dominant culture in the companies interviewed is to set up a multifunctional team, give it a process and a target, achieve results (new practice), and spread to other part of the company. Rather than setting up a system based on operators, that continuously reduce waste, find improvement opportunities and realise them.

Table 2. Degree of implementation of key elements of Lean on a 0-4 scale

Process characteristics	Company									
	Warehousing and Shipping			Financial services						
	H	I	L	A	C	B	E	F	D	G
Waste elimination	4	4	4	4	4	2	2	2	2	2
Zero defects	2	4	0	2	2	2	2	2	2	0
Multi functional teams	2	4	2	4	2	2	2	2	2	2
Decentr. responsibilities	0	4	2	0	4	2	2	2	2	2
Information flow	4	4	2	0	2	2	2	2	2	2
Continuous improvement	2	4	2	0	2	2	2	2	2	0
Pull	2	2	2	2	2	3	1	1	1	2
Pace	0	3	3	2	3	2	1	2	1	1
Flow	3	3	2	2	3	2	1	2	2	2

Pull, Pace and Flow are at an intermediate level of development, but companies are not striving to improve them very much. The dominant feeling is that in services it is not possible –or it is not worth- develop them further.

Therefore, there are no FIFO line with limited capacity between stages, takt time is used only to set target output per day or week, and flow is not affecting layout, nor organisation, nor IT system design and development.

3 Conclusions

Services are different from manufacturing and Lean implementation has just started. This research identified two key elements in Lean implementation: the need to address the issue at a single process level, highlighting the fact that service companies start from high volume, low variety processes, which are focused on the back office. This to avoid the criticality customer interaction, which is not present in manufacturing operations and has therefore not been addressed before.

Nine key elements of Lean have been defined and their degree of implementation investigated. Results shows that third party logistic companies, that process a physical product, are more advanced in Lean implementation than banks and insurance companies (financial services). These latter types of companies are lagging behind manufacturing in particular in implementing a sequential pull system between stages, in putting the flow at the center of operation's organisation, layout and IT systems, and in considering Pace as a key tool for highlighting deviations and therefore improvement opportunities.

The feeling emerged from the people interviewed is that these elements are not possible to implement, or not key, in services.

Improvement achieved so far are so interesting that they are focusing on spreading the new practices to other part of the company/group, rather than seeking to achieve further improvements in the process already tackled through Lean.

Finally, the improvement approach is still based on the idea of improvement projects with a multifunctional project team, a start and an end, rather than working for setting up a system, based on operators, that continuously seek opportunities to improve, find solutions and implement them.

References

1. Ahlstrom, P.: Lean service Operation: translating lean production principles to service operations. International Journal of Services Technology and Management 5(5/6), 545–564 (2004)
2. Drucker, P.F.: The new productivity challenge. Harvard Business Review 69(6), 69–79 (1991)
3. Portioli, A., Tantardini, M.: Lean production implementation: a survey in Italy. In: International conference on Industrial engineering and Industrial Management, Madrid, September 5-7 (2007)
4. Roach, S.S.: In Search of Productivity. Harvard Business Review, 158 (September-October 1998)
5. Wölfl, A.: The service Economy in OECD Countries. STI Working Paper Series, 2005/3. OECD (2005)
6. Womack, J.P., Jones, D.: Lean Consumption. Harvard Business Review (2005)

Exploring the Causal Relationships of KPIs in after Sales Service Systems

Elena Legnani and Sergio Cavalieri

CELS – Research Center on Logistics and After-Sales Service
University of Bergamo, Department of Industrial Engineering
Viale Marconi, 5 – 24044 Dalmine, Italy
(elena.legnani,sergio.cavalieri)@unibg.it

Abstract. A plethora of research and industrial contributions emphasizes the economic and strategic role of services in adding further value to a product throughout its lifelong journey with the customer. However, there is still a limited comprehension of the dynamics underlying After-Sales (AS) processes along the whole service network - which usually encompasses a manufacturer, spare parts wholesalers/retailers and technical assistance centres - till the final user. AS can be no more considered as a mere corporate function, but rather as a series of interconnected activities involving more independent organizations, each one having different objectives and perspectives to be properly aligned. Starting from previous contributions of the same authors on this research topic, aim of the paper is to examine AS as a complex system of interlinked processes, to elaborate a proposal of the main Key Performance Indicators (KPIs) which can take into account the various perspectives of the different actors involved, and, as a main result, to explore the most relevant causal relationships among these KPIs.

Keywords: After-Sales Service System, Product-Services, Performance Measurement System, Systems Thinking, System Dynamics.

1 Introduction

Given the high market pressure, the increased competition in several industries and the reduced margins on undifferentiated products, the search for new business opportunity is emphasizing the strategic and economic role of service activities as powerful add-ons to the mere delivery of a manufactured product. The provision of services can be both an effective commercial tool during the transactional phase of product sale and a means of enduring a durable relation with the customer. In the long term, this strategy can ensure to a manufacturer and its service network stable and long-lasting cash flows and empower the degree of retention and loyalty of the client. However, despite the potential advantages, this transition from a pure manufacturer to a product-service provider is not immediate and, if not properly managed, it could have some negative side-effects [10], [18].

Provision of services require the adoption of specific forms of organizational principles, structures and processes, which could constitute a major managerial challenge for a manufacturer [9]. In addition, what is usually neglected in the industrial practice

B. Vallespir and T. Alix (Eds.): APMS 2009, IFIP AICT 338, pp. 660–668, 2010.
© IFIP International Federation for Information Processing 2010

is the involvement of the whole downstream service network which acts as the real front-end with the final user. As a service manager of an important multinational company operating in the consumer electronics industry stated, *"we do not have any direct interaction with our customers, since when they need to buy our products they go to large multi-branded retailing chains; when they have specific claims, they call at our contact centres, which we have outsourced to an external partner; when they need repair or refurbishment activities they go to our technical assistance centres, which in most cases are still run in a "mom-and-pap" way"*. Hence, AS service cannot be considered as a mere ancillary function within a manufacturing company but it needs to be re-interpreted as a more complex system which encompasses a series of primary and supporting processes and involves independent organisations with very often conflicting objectives and behaviours. Thus it is essential to: i) be able to develop a Performance Measurement System (PMS) which incentives all the different actors and aligns their perspectives through a common set of measurable KPIs and ii) explore and understand the beneath interrelationships among these KPIs.

Regarding the scientific literature, contributions deal essentially with descriptive models which identify and depict the main elements that constitute the service system. However, they do not capture the underneath interrelations and its intrinsic dynamic nature. Moreover, the main works propose linear models which cover just local aspects related to the service management [11], [7] without providing a whole picture of the AS system and without embracing different perspectives and effects.

An appealing challenge is to define a model which highlights the causal relationships existing among some key indicators and explore the effect that they exert on the management of the main processes and on the enhancement of the overall company performance. The analysis proposed in this paper aims at emphasizing the causal-loop relationships existing within the main KPIs of the AS system, taking into account: i) the *customer perspective*, in terms of customer perceived value and repurchasing attitudes; ii) the *service network* operational results; iii) the *company perspective*, in terms of profitability and investment strategies.

The paper is organized as follows: §2 explains the meaning of modelling a global system considering overall structures, patterns and feedback loops, and it gives some insights about the adopted methodologies, namely *Systems Thinking* and *System Dynamics*; §3 reports the causal relationships among the KPIs for each of the three identified perspectives and the main literature contributions used to build, strengthen and reinforce the elements and the relations pinpointed. §4 shows the developed model which embraces together all the three perspectives while §5 draws some conclusions and further developments of the work.

2 Systems Thinking and System Dynamics

The term *System* is used for many purposes ranging over economic, political and ecological issues. A system consists of distinguishable elements which are linked to each other in a certain structure. The nature of the relations can be flows of material, information as well as cause and effect loops [6]. Systems are generally open as they interact with elements of the environment and are related each other through a hierarchical architecture. Moreover, every system is active and changes its status over time: in fact, without the recognition of time, systems would be static and not realistic. According to [16], many advocate the development of *Systems Thinking* as the ability to see the world as a complex system where everything is connected to everything else. It is argued that if people had a holistic worldview, they would act in consonance with the long-term best interests of the system as a whole, identify high leverage points and avoid policy resistance. An action of one element causes effects on other elements altering the state of the system and, therefore, leading to further actions to restore the balance. These interactions or feedbacks are usually the main reasons for the complex behaviour of a system.

Modelling complex structures such as AS service systems requires a powerful tool or method which helps to understand complexity, to design better operating polices and to guide change in systems: *System Dynamics* is a method used to represent, analyse and explain the dynamics of complex systems along the time. The main goal of System Dynamics is to understand, through the use of qualitative and quantitative models, how the system behaviour is produced and to exploit this understanding to predict the consequences over time of policy changes to the system [12]. In the field of Supply Chain Management there are several applications of System Dynamics – [1], [16] report the main uses – while contributions that explore the main causal relations of KPIs are still quite few.

Referring to the specific case of this paper, Systems Thinking is adopted as the approach to foster the understanding of the logic underlying performance generation and to identify the factors that may trigger off effective changes in the AS service system. System Dynamics will be exploited in further contributions to make simulation and what-if analyses on the developed Systems Thinking logic model.

3   AS Service Perspectives and Related Causal Relationships

As outlined in §1, an AS service system can be depicted as powered by three actors: the customer, the manufacturing company and the service network. The strong interaction among them is the key for managing the AS activities and achieving high performance results.

The *customer* is the main trigger for the AS business: his/her satisfaction and, hopefully, loyalty have a significant influence on the company profitability. Moreover, his/her continuous involvement is the fundamental basis for developing new services and co-creating value.

The *company* has the goal of being competitive, growing and achieving loyalty from its customers through the Product-Services offered. The company does not act alone but it operates within a *service network,* where different actors (e.g. spare parts wholesalers, retailers and technical assistance centres) play to guarantee a reliable, responsive and flexible service to the customers.

These powerful and intense interactions generate results that the company aims at measuring through some KPIs. A PMS for analysing the main AS KPIs has been proposed by the same authors in a previous paper presented at APMS Conference 2008 [8]. After an in-depth literature review and a validation with an industrial case study, the proposed PMS provides an integrated and multi-levelled set of measures for the AS area. It classifies metrics considering both strategic and operational perspectives. Indicators have been arranged in a hierarchical structure according to the following construction:

- *performance attributes* (reliability - RL, responsiveness - RS, agility - AG, assets - AM, costs – CO and growth - GR), which are groupings for metrics used to explain company strategies and to analyse and evaluate them against others with competing approaches;
- *level 1 metrics*, which are strategic indicators (Key Performance Indicators - KPIs) used to monitor the overall performance of the company and its service network;
- *level 2* and *level 3 metrics*, respectively tactical and operational indicators, which serve as diagnostic measures to identify critical processes and variations in performance against the plan.

For the sake of clarity, the main *level 1 metrics (KPIs)* have been reported and associated to the proper performance attributes in Table 1.

Table 1. Performance attributes and associated Level 1 metrics (KPIs) for AS

LEVEL 1 METRICS (KPIs)	PERFORMANCE ATTRIBUTES					
	RL	RS	AG	CO	AM	GR
Perfect Assist Completion	X					
Assist Cycle Time		X				
Assist Agility			X			
Assist-Warranty-Spare Parts Costs				X		
Return on Assist Assets					X	
Assist Operating Income						X
Customer Loyalty						X

Goal of this section is to explore and highlight the causal relationships existing among the main AS KPIs according to the three different players' perspectives. To support the model building, a literature analysis has been reckoned to be essential: the main contributions have helped to make and reinforce the identified relations. In literature there are few contributions that deal with service and, more specifically, with AS service as an overall system. Some contributions can be found in [3], [6] and [5]. However, it turns out that most of the analyses reported regard just a portion of the entire system with a local perspective on few specific aspects.

3.1 The Customer Perspective

The *customer perspective* is the underlying rationale that derives the customer repurchasing attitude based on his/her needs and wants. *Customer loyalty* is the metric explored in this loop. The service management literature discusses the links between customer satisfaction, customer loyalty and profitability. This theory argues that:

- customer satisfaction is the result of a customer perception of the value received in a transaction or relationship relative to the value expected from transactions or relationships with competing vendors [19]. In accordance with [13], [7], customer value is a balance between perceived benefits and perceived costs and sacrifices.

- loyalty behaviours, including relationship continuance and recommendation, such as positive word of mouth or advertising, result from customer belief that the amount of value received from one supplier is greater than that available from other suppliers. Loyalty, measured in the form of customer retention, creates increased profits to the company through enhanced revenues, reduced costs to acquire customers, lower customer-price sensitivity, and decreased costs to serve customers familiar with a firm service delivery system.

Other proponents who believe that customer satisfaction influences customer loyalty, which in turn affects the profitability of a company are [5], [11] and [14].

Figure 1 shows the main elements which make the customer perceived value and the relations to customer satisfaction (measured through *Recruitment rate*) and loyalty. Moreover, from the graph it turns out that the demand of product-services is generated by the repeated business of loyal customers together with the assist requests coming from new customers.

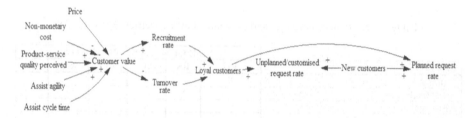

Fig. 1. The customer perspective

3.2   The Service Network Perspective

The *service network perspective* is related to operational results that the service network can achieve through its ability in satisfying both planned and unplanned/customised pending requests. This area depicts the relations existing among:

- reliability (RL), measured by the combinations of *perfect assist completion* of planned and unplanned/customised requests;
- responsiveness (RS), measured through the *assist cycle time*;
- agility (AG), measured through *assist agility*.

The performance and operational outcomes strongly depend on the interrelations among all the actors of the service network and on the effectiveness of their coordination. Some interesting contributions that helped to build the loop can be found in [6], [4] and [16]. The main relations are shown in Figure 2.

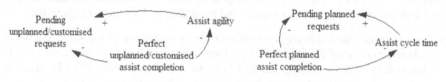

Fig. 2. The service network perspective

3.3 The Company Perspective

The *company perspective* is more related to the financial performance results which justify the costs and investments carried out on the AS unit. It aims at identifying the relations among:

- costs (CO), measured through the *assist-warranty-spare parts costs*;
- growth (GR), measured in terms of *assist operating income*;
- asset management (AM) investment strategies, measured in terms of *return on assist assets*.

This diagram starts with the generation of AS revenue, that is the key to profitability and company growth [7]. According to [15], it is important that a company understands the way a service system can be improved over time through investments in order to achieve high efficiency, effectiveness and sustainability. Literature contributions that have been analysed to build this loop are [2] and [17]. The main relations are shown in Figure 3.

Fig. 3. The company perspective

4 The Developed Model

From the analysis reported in §3, it comes out that the main scientific works describe locally or partially the AS service system elements and relations. According to the three main identified actors, the customer perspective can count on numerous contributions since this is a topic widely covered and argued by the marketing literature. Few works dealing with the operations management field, instead, have been found covering the company and the service network perspectives: this may be due to the fact that AS is still a relatively new topic not yet completely exploited. Examples of complete service or AS service system modelling are also quite scant. The model displayed in Figure 4 aims at describing the whole AS system and at capturing the interactions among the KPIs reported in Table 1. It has been conceived according to a Systems Thinking logic and is based on the following hypothesis:

- it represents the behaviour of the AS service system as an independent business unit which strongly interacts with a downstream service network;
- it refers to services supporting the product (Product-Services), where the service focus is on basic services such as documentation, installation, help desk, repairs, upgrades, reconstruction and recycling.

The model highlights the interlinked relations which make up the AS system and how the three perspectives are related each other. Referring to the dotted lines in Figure 4, starting from the customer perspective, the perceived *Customer value* is derived from some *non-monetary costs*, the *perceived quality of product-services*, the service network operational results - in terms of responsiveness (*Assist cycle time*), flexibility (*Assist agility*) and indirectly reliability (*Perfect planned and unplanned/customised assist completion*) – and the *price* set up by the company. Moreover, the customer purchasing requests of loyal customers (measured in terms of *Planned and Unplanned/customised request rate*) have an impact both on the service network, which needs to be organised to satisfy the demand (*Pending planned and unplanned/customised requests*), and the company costs (*Assist, warranty, spare parts costs*). Regarding the company perspective, as just mentioned, operational costs depend on the number of customer requests (*Planned and unplanned/customised requests*); revenues are influenced by the number of reliable assistance interventions performed by the service network (*Perfect planned and unplanned/customised assist completion*). The company, furthermore, if it is profitable, can make strategic investments to improve its tangible and intangible assets (*Quality of investments*) and consequently the relations with its service network.

In conclusion, as also Figure 4 shows, AS system and its dynamics cannot be depicted through a linear representation: there are lots of interlinked relations and feedback loops that need to be considered and explored.

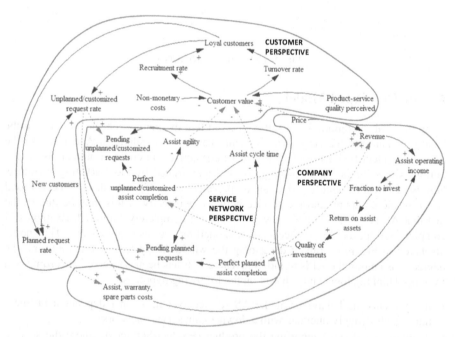

Fig. 4. Relationships within the AS service system and its performance results

5 Conclusions and Further Developments

Although in the past and present years a considerable amount of literature has dealt with the topic of service modelling, most of these contributions are about descriptive models which depict scenarios in a static and linear form without any evaluation analysis of the underneath dynamics. In this paper, the causal-loop relationships existing among AS performance KPIs and their connections with the three main identified actors, have been explored and supported by a literature analysis. The proposed model has been carried out through a Systems Thinking approach in order to identify the key logic relations; it is based on some assumptions and actually it is strongly theoretically based. Further work will imply a more massive use of System Dynamics methodology and, in particular, it will regard the identification of causal diagrams showing stock and flow structures, the definition of mathematical and logic equations, simulation runnings and what-if analyses. To make a quantitative examination, data will be collected through a survey conducted within the ASAP Service Management Forum network (http://www.asapsmf.org/), an Italian forum finalized to the promotion of cultural and scientific activities in the AS area, with specific know-how in the automotive, domestic appliances, machinery and digital systems industries. Final goal will be to identify the main prior relations among the KPIs for some specific industries and, consequently, find out the beneath related AS processes to enhance.

References

1. Angerhofer, B.J., Angelides, M.C.: System dynamics modelling in supply chain management: research review. In: Proc. of the 2000 Winter Simulation Conference, pp. 342–351 (2000)
2. Camerinelli, E., Cantu, A.: Linking supply chain measures with financial performance: a framework.Technical Report, Supply Chain Council Research (2006)
3. Crespo, M.A., Blanchar, C.: A decision support system for evaluating operations investments in high-technology business. Decision Support Systems 41, 472–487 (2006)
4. Gaiardelli, P., Saccani, N., Songini, L.: Performance measurement systems in the after-sales service: an integrated framework. International Journal Business Performance Management 9(2), 145–171 (2007)
5. Heskjett, J., Jones, T., Loveman, G., Sasser, W., Schlesinger, L.: Putting the service-profit chain at work. Harvard Business Review (March-April 1994)
6. InCoCo's 2007, EU-funded project (2007), http://www.incoco.net/
7. Kingman-Brundage, J., George, W.R., Bowen, D.E.: "Service logic": achieving service system integration. International Journal of Service Industry Management 6(4), 20 (1995)
8. Legnani, E., Cavalieri, S.: Measuring the performance of after-sales service processes. A hierarchical approach. In: Proc. of APMS 2008, International Conference on Innovations in network, Espoo, Finland, pp. 359–368 (2008)
9. Oliva, R., Kallenberg, R.: Managing the transition from products to services. International Journal of Service Industry Management 14(2), 160–172 (2003)
10. Potts, G.W.: Exploiting your product's service life cycle. Harvard Business Review 66(5), 32–35 (1988)
11. Rust, R.T., Metters, R.: Mathematical models of service. European Journal of Operational Research 91, 427–439 (1996)
12. Santos, S.P., Belton, V., Howick, S.: Adding value to performance measurement by using system dynamics and multicriteria analysis. International Journal of Operations & Production Management 22(11), 1246–1272 (2002)
13. Sawhney, M., Balasubramanian, S., Krishnan, V.V.: Creating growth with services. MIT Sloan Management Review (2004)

14. Schneider, B., Bowen, D.E.: Winning the service game. Harvard Business School Press, Boston (1995)
15. Spohrer, J., Maglio, P.P., Bailey, J., Gruhl, D.: Steps toward a science of service systems. Computer 40(1), 71–77 (2007)
16. Sterman, J.: Business dynamics: system thinking and modelling for a complex world. McGraw-Hill, New York (2000)
17. Supply Chain Council (SCC): Supply Chain Operations Reference model (SCOR), version 9.0 (2008), http://www.supply-chain.org
18. Wise, R., Baumgartner, P.: Go downstream - the new profit imperative in manufacturing. Harvard Business Review 77, 133–141 (1999)
19. Zeithaml, V.A., Parasuraman, A., Berry, L.L.: Delivering quality service: balancing customer perceptions and expectations. Free Press, New York (1990)

Author Index